SPEECHES AND WRITINGS
OF
DADABHAI NAOROJI

SPEECHES AND WRITINGS
OF
DADABHAI NAOROJI

BY
DADABHAI NAOROJI

GYAN

Published by

Gyan Publishing House
5, Ansari Road
Daryaganj, New Delhi-110002
Phone: 011-47034999, 9811692060
E-mail: books@gyanbooks.com

Distribution Network
gyanbooks.com
India, USA, Canada, UK, Australia, France

ISBN: 978-81-212-8258-1 (PB)
First Published, 1893

2nd Impression 2023

Printed at: Gyan Press, Delhi.

SPEECHES AND WRITINGS OF DADABHAI NAOROJI
Author: DADABHAI NAOROJI

SPEECHES AND WRITINGS

OF

DADABHAI NAOROJI

SECOND EDITION

Price Rs. Three

G. A. NATESAN & CO.
Madras

PUBLISHERS' NOTE

This is the first attempt to bring under one cover an exhaustive and comprehensive collection of the speeches and writings of the venerable Indian patriot, Dadabhai Naoroji. The first part is a collection of his speeches and includes the addresses that he delivered before the Indian National Congress on the three occasions that he presided over that assembly; all the speeches that he delivered in the House of Commons and a selection of the speeches that he delivered from time to time in England and India. The second part includes all his statements to the Welby Commission, a number of papers relating to the admission of Indians to the Services and many other vital questions of Indian administration. The Appendix contains, among others, the full text of his evidence before the Welby Commission, his statement to the Indian Currency Committee of 1898, his replies to the questions put to him by the Public Service Commission, and his statement to the Select Committee on East Indian Finance. Dadabhai was in the active service of his Motherland for over sixty years and during this long period he was steadily and strenuously working for the good of his countrymen; it is hoped that his writings and speeches which are now presented in a handy volume will be welcomed by thousands of his admiring countrymen.

CONTENTS

PART I: SPEECHES

PART II: WRITINGS

APPENDICES

FAITH IN BRITISH FAIR PLAY AND JUSTICE

Our fate and our future are in our own hands. If we are true to ourselves and to our country and make all the necessary sacrifices for our elevation and amelioration, I, for one, have not the shadow of a doubt that in dealing with such justice-loving, fair-minded people as the British, we may rest fully assured that we shall not work in vain. It is this conviction which has supported me against all difficulties. I have never faltered in my faith in the British character and have always believed that the time will come when the sentiments of the British Nation and our Gracious Sovereign proclaimed to us in our Great Charter of the Proclamation of 1858 will be realised, (applause), viz., "In their prosperity will be our strength, in their contentment our best reward." And let us join in the prayer that followed this hopeful declaration of our Sovereign : " May the God of all-power grant to us and to those in authority under us strength to carry out these our wishes for the good of our people— From the Presidential Address to the Lahore Congress, 1893.

DADABHAI'S EXHORTATION

My last prayer and exhortation to the Congress and to all my countrymen is—Go on united and earnest, in concord and harmony, with moderation, with loyalty to the British Rule and patriotism towards our country, and success is sure to attend our efforts for our just demands, and the day, I hope, is not distant when the world will see the noblest spectacle of a great nation like the British holding out the hand of true fellow-citizenship and of justice to the vast mass of humanity of this great and ancient land of India with benefits and blessings to the human race (loud and prolonged cheering).—From the Presidential Address to the Lahore Congress, 1893.

SPEECHES OF DADABHAI NAOROJI.

Second Congress—Calcutta—1886.

PRESIDENTIAL ADDRESS.

INTRODUCTION.

I need not tell you how sincerely thankful I am to you for placing me in this position of honour. I at first thought that I was to be elevated to this proud position as a return for what might be considered as a compliment paid by us to Bengal, when Mr. Bonnerjee was elected President of the first Congress last year at Bombay. I can assure you, however, that that election was no mere compliment to Bengal, but arose out of the simple fact that we regarded Mr. Bonnerjee as a gentleman eminently qualified to take the place of President, and we installed him in that position, in all sincerity, as the proper man in the proper place. I now see, however, that this election of my humble self is not intended as a return of compliment, but that, as both proposer and seconder have said, you have been kind enough to select me, because I am supposed to be really qualified to undertake the task. I hope it may prove so and that I may be found really worthy of all the kind things said of me; but whether this be so, or not, when such kind things are said by those who occupy such high positions amongst us, I must say I feel exceedingly proud and am very grateful to all for the honour thus done me. (*Loud cheering.*)

Your late Chairman has heartily welcomed all the delegates who come from different parts of India, and with the same heartiness I return to him and all our Bengal friends, on my own behalf and on that of all the delegates from other Provinces, the most sincere thanks for the cordial manner in which we have been received. From what has been done already and from what is in store for us during our short stay here, I have no doubt we shall carry away with us many and most pleasant reminiscences of our visit to Calcutta. (*Cheers.*)

You will pardon me, and I beg your indulgence when I say that, when I was asked only two days ago to become your President and to give an inaugural address, it was with no small trepidation that I agreed to undertake the task; and I hope that you will extend to me all that indulgence which my shortcomings may need. (*Loud cheers.*)

IMPORTANCE OF THE CONGRESS.

The assemblage of such a Congress is *an event of the utmost importance in Indian History.* I ask whether in the most glorious days of Hindu rule, in the days of Rajahs like the great Vikram, you could imagine the possibility of a meeting of this kind, whether even Hindus of all different provinces of the kingdom could have collected and spoken as one nation. Coming down to the later Empire of our friends, the Mahomedans, who probably ruled over a larger territory at one time than any Hindu monarch, would it have been, even in the days of the great Akbar himself, possible for a meeting like this to assemble composed of all classes and communities, all speaking one language, and all having uniform and high aspirations of their own.

ADVANTAGES OF BRITISH RULE.

Well, then, what is it for which we are now met on this occasion? We have assembled to consider questions upon which depend our future, whether glorious or inglorious. It is our good fortune that we are under a rule which makes it possible for us to meet in this manner. (*Cheers.*)

It is under the civilizing rule of the Queen and people of England that we meet here together, hindered by none, and are freely allowed to speak our minds without the least fear and without the least hesitation. Such a thing is possible under British rule and British rule only. (*Loud Cheers.*) Then I put the *question* plainly: Is this Congress a nursery for sedition and rebellion against the British Government (*cries of "No, no"*); or is it another stone in the foundation of the stability of that government? (*Cries of "Yes, yes."*) There could be but one answer, and that you have already given, because we are thoroughly sensible of the numberless blessings conferred upon us, of which the very existence of this Congress is a proof in a nutshell. (*Cheers.*) Were it not for these blessings of British rule, I could not have come here, as I have done, without the least hesitation and without the least fear that my children might be robbed and killed in my absence; nor could you have come from every corner of the land, having performed, within a few days, journeys, which in former days would have occupied as many months. (*Cheers.*) These simple facts bring home to all of us at once some of those great and numberless blessings which British rule has conferred upon us. But there remain even greater blessings for which we have to be grateful. It is to British rule that we owe the education we possess; the people of England were sincere in the declarations made more than half a century ago that India was a sacred charge entrusted to their care by Providence, and that they were bound to administer it for the good of India, to the glory of their own name, and the satisfaction of God. (*Prolonged cheering.*) When we have to acknowledge so many bless ings as flowing from British rule,—and I could descant on them for hours, because it would simply be recounting to you the history of the British Empire in India—is it possible that an assembly like this, every one of whose members is fully impressed with the knowledge of these blessings,* could meet for any purpose inimical to that rule to which we owe so much? (*Cheers.*)

RELATION BETWEEN OURSELVES AND OUR RULERS.

The thing is absurd. Let us speak out like men and proclaim that we are loyal to the backbone (*cheers*); that we understand the benefits English rule has conferred upon us; that we thoroughly appreciate the education that has been given to us, the new light which has been poured upon us, turning us from darkness into light and teaching us the new lesson that kings are made for the people, not peoples for their kings; and this new lesson we have learned amidst the darkness of Asiatic despotism only by the light of free English civilization. (*Loud cheers.*) But the question is, do the Government believe us? Do they believe that we are really loyal to them; that we do truly appreciate and rely on British rule; that we veritably desire its permanent continuance; that our reason is satisfied and our sentimental feelings gratified as well as our self-interest? It would be a great gratification to us if we could see, in the inauguration of a great movement like this Congress, that what we do really mean and desire is thoroughly and truly so understood by our rulers. I have the good fortune to be able to place before you testimony which cannot be questioned, from which you will see that some at least of the most distinguished of our rulers do believe that what we say is sincere; and that we do *not* want to subvert British rule; that our outspoken utterances are as much for their good as for our good. They do believe, as Lord Ripon said, that what is good for India is good for England. I will give you first the testimony as regards the educated classes which was given 25 years ago by Sir Bartle Frere. He possessed an intimate knowledge of the people of this country, and with regard to the educated portion of them, he gave this testimony. He said, 'And now wherever I go I find the best exponents of the policy of the English Government, and the most able co-adjutors in adjusting that policy to the peculiarities of the natives of India, among the ranks of the educated natives.' This much at least is testimony to our sincerity, and strongly corroborates our assertion that we, the educated classes, have become the true interpreters and mediators between the masses of our countrymen and our rulers. I shall now place before you the declaration of the Government of India itself, that they have confidence in the loyalty of the whole people, and do appreciate the sentiments of the educated classes in particular. I will read their very words. They say in a despatch addressed to the Secretary of State (8th June, 1880), 'But the people of India accept British rule without any need for appeal to arms, because we keep the peace and do justice, because we have done and are doing much material good to the country and the people, and because there is not inside or outside India any power that can adequately occupy our place.' Then they distinctly understand that we do believe the British power to be the only power that can, under existing circumstances, really keep the peace and advance our future progress. This is testimony as to the feeling of the whole people. But of the educated classes, this despatch says, 'To the minds of at least the educated among the people of India—and the number is rapidly increasing—any idea of the subversion of British power is abhorrent, from the consciousness that it must result in the wildest anarchy and confusion.' (*Loud cheers.*)

We can, therefore, proceed with the utmost serenity and with every confidence that our rulers do understand us ; that they do understand our motives and give credit to our expressions of loyalty, and we need not in the least care for any impeachment of disloyalty or any charge of harbouring wild ideas of subverting the British power that may be put forth by ignorant, irresponsible or ill-disposed individuals or cliques. (*Loud cheers.*) We can, therefore, quietly, calmly and, with entire confidence in our rulers, speak as freely as we please, but of course in that spirit of fairness and moderation, which becomes wise and honest men, and in the tone which every gentleman, every reasonable being, would adopt when urging his rulers to make him some concession. (*Hear, hear.*) Now although, as I have said, the British Government have done much, very much for us, there is still a great deal more to be done if their noble work is to be fitly completed. They say this themselves ; they show a desire to do what more may be required, and it is for us to ask for whatsoever, after due deliberation, we think that we ought to have. (*Cheers.*)

THE JUBILEE OF OUR QUEEN-EMPRESS.

Therefore, having said thus much and having cleared the ground so that we may proceed freely and in all confidence with the work of our Congress, I must at once come to the matter with which I should have commenced, had I not purposely postponed it, until I had explained the relations between ourselves and our rulers ; and that is the most happy and auspicious occasion which the comming year is to bring us, *viz.*, the Jubilee of our good Queen-Empress's reign. (*Loud cheers.*) I am exceedingly glad that the Congress has thought it right to select this, as the subject of the initial resolution, and in this to express, in humble but hearty terms, their congratulations to our Gracious Empress. (*Cheers.*) There is even more reason for us to congratulate ourselves on having for half a century enjoyed the rule of a Sovereign, graced with every virtue, and truly worthy to reign over that vast Empire on which the sun never sets. (*Loud cheers.*) That she may live long, honoured and beloved, to continue for yet many years that beneficial and enlightened rule with which she has so long reigned, must be the heart-felt prayer of every soul in India. (*Prolonged cheering.*)

And here you must pardon me if I digress a moment from those subjects which this Congress proposes to discuss to one of those which we do not consider to fall within the legitimate sphere of its deliberations.

CONGRESS AND SOCIAL REFORM.

It has been asserted that this Congress ought to take up questions of social reform (*cheers and cries of "Yes, yes"*) and our failure to do this has been urged as a reproach against us. Certainly no member of this National Congress is more alive to the necessity of social reforms than I am ; but, gentlemen, for everything there are proper times, proper circumstances, proper parties and proper places (*cheers*) ; we are met together as a political body to represent to our rulers our political aspirations, not to discuss social reforms, and if you blame us for ignoring these, you should equally blame the House of Commons for not discussing the abstruser problems on mathematics or metaphysics. But, besides this, there are here Hindus of every caste, amongst whom, even in the same province, customs and social arrangements differ widely,—there are Mahomedans and Christians of various denominations, Parsees, Sikhs, Brahmos and what not—men indeed of each and all of those numerous classes which constitute in the aggregate the people of India. (*Loud cheers.*) How can this gathering of *all* classes discuss the social reforms needed in each individual class? What do any of us know of the internal home life, of the customs, traditions, feelings, prejudices of any class but our own? How could a gathering, a cosmopolitan gathering like this, discuss to any purpose the reforms needed in any one class? Only the members of that class can effectively deal with the reforms therein needed. A National Congress must confine itself to questions in which the entire nation has a direct participation, and it must leave the adjustment of social reforms and other class questions to class Congresses. But it does not follow that because this national, political body does not presume to discuss social reforms, the delegates here present are not just as deeply, nay in many cases far more deeply, interested in these questions than in those political questions we do discuss, or that those several communities whom those delegates represent are not doing their utmost to solve those complicated problems on which hinge the practical introduction of those reforms. Any man who has eyes and ears open must know what struggles towards higher and better things are going on in every community, and it could not be otherwise with the noble education we are receiving. Once you begin to think about your own actions, your duties and responsibilities to yourself, your neighbours and your nation, you cannot avoid looking round and observing much that is wrong amongst you; and we know, as a fact, that each community is now doing its best according to its lights, and the progress that it has made in education. I need not, I think, particularise. The Mahomedans know what is being done by persons of their community to pus on the education their brethren so much need; the Hindus are everywhere doing what they *can* to reform those social institutions which they think require improvement. There is not one single community here represented of which the best and ablest men do not feel that much has to be done to improve the social, moral, religious status of their brethren, and in which, as a fact, they are not striving to effect, gradually, those needful improvements; but these are essentially matters too delicate for a stranger's handling—matters which must be left to the guidance of those who alone fully understand them in all their bearings, and which are wholly unsuited to discussion in an assemblage like this in which all classes are intermingled. (*Loud cheers.*)

TRUST IN ENGLAND.

I shall now refer briefly to the work of the former Congress. Since it met last year, about this time, some progress, I am glad to say, has been made, and that is an encouragement and a proof that, if we do really ask what is right and reasonable, we may be sure that, sooner or later, the British Government will actually give what we ask for. We should, therefore, persevere having confidence in the conscience of England and resting assured that the English nation will grudge no sacrifice to prove the sincerity of their desire to do whatever is just and right. (*Cheers.*)

ROYAL COMMISSION.

Our first request at the last Congress was for the constitution of a Royal Commission. Unfortunately, the authorities in England have not seen their way to grant a Royal Commission. They say it will upset the authorities here; that it will interfere with the prestige and control of the Government here. I think that this is a very poor compliment to our rulers on this side. If I understand a man like Lord Dufferin, of such vast experience in administration, knowing, as he does, what is to rule an Empire, it would be impossible for him to be daunted and frigntened by a Commission making enquiries here. I think this argument a very poor one, and we must once more say that to the inhabitants of India a Parliamentary Committee taking evidence in England alone can never be satisfactory, for the simple reason that what the Committee will learn by the ear will never enable them to understand what they ought to see with their eyes, if they are to realize what the evidence of the witnesses really means. Still, however, it is so far satisfactory that, notwithstanding the change of government and the vicissitudes which this poor Parliamentary Committee has undergone, it is the intention of Parliament that under any and all circumstances a Committee shall be appointed. At the same time, this Committee *in future* ties the hands of the authorities here to a large extent and prevents us from saying all we do really want.

LEGISLATIVE COUNCILS FOR N.-W. PROVINCES AND PUNJAB.

Another resolution on which we must report some progress was to the effect that the N.-W. Provinces and the Punjab ought also to have Legislative Councils of their own. We know that the Government has just given a Legislative Council to the N.-W. Provinces, and we hope that this progress may extend further and satisfy our wishes as to other provinces also.

THE PUBLIC SERVICE COMMISSION.

The fourth resolution had regard to the Service question. In this matter, we really seem to have made some distinct progress. The Public Service Commission is now sitting, and if one thing more than another can prove that the Government is sincere in its desire to do something for us, the appointment of such a Commission is that thing. You perhaps remember the words which our noble Viceroy used at Poona. He said :

> However, I will say that, from first to last, I have been a strong advocate for the appointment of a Committee or Commission of this sort, and that when succeeding Governments in England changed, I have on each occasion warmly impressed upon the Secretary of State the necessity of persevering in the nomination of a Commission. I am happy to think that, in response to my earnest representations on the subject, Her Majesty's present Ministers have determined to take action. I consequently, do not really see what more during the short period I have been amongst you, the Government of India could have done for that most important and burning question, which was perpetually agitating your mind and was being put forward by the natives, as an alleged injustice done to the educated native classes of this country, in not allowing them adequate employment in the Public Service. I do not think you can point out to me any other question which so occupied public attention or was nearer to the hearts of your people. Now the door to inquiry has been opened, and it only remains for you, by the force of logic of your representations and of the evidence you may be able to submit, to make good your case; if you succeed in doing so, all I can say is, that nobody will be better pleased than myself. In regard to other matters, which have been equally prominent in your newspapers and your addresses, and which have been so constantly discussed by your associations, I have also done my best to secure for you an ample investigation.

LORD DUFFERIN AND THE PUBLIC SERVICE COMMISSION.

There we have his own words as to his intentions and the efforts he made to get this Commission. This should convince us of his good faith and sympathy with us. When I think of Lord Dufferin, not only as our present Viceroy, but bearing in mind all we know of him in his past career, I should hesitate to believe that he could be a man devoid of the deepest sympathy with any people struggling to advance and improve their political condition. Some of you may remember one or two extracts, which I gave in my Holbern Town Hall speech from Lord Dufferin's letters to the *Times*, and I cannot conceive that a person of such warm sympathies could fail to sympathise with us. But I may say this much that, feeling as I naturally do some interest about the views and intentions of our Viceroys and Governors, I had the opportunity of getting some information from friends on whom I can rely and who are in a position to know the truth; and I am able to say in the words of one of these friends that 'the Viceroy's instincts are eminently liberal, and he regards with neither jealousy nor alarm the desire of the educated classes to be allowed a larger share in the administration of their own affairs. Indeed, he considers it very creditable to them that they should do so.' As Viceroy, he has to consider all sides of a question from the ruler's point of view, and to act as he thinks safe and proper. But we may be sure that we have his deep and very genuine sympathy, and we may fairly claim and expect much good at his hands.

HOME AUTHORITIES AND PUBLIC SERVICE COMMISSION.

But yet further I would enquire whether the intentions of the Secretary of State for India and of the other home authorities are equally favourable to our claims. The resolution on its very face tells us what the intention of the Secretary of State is. It says, 'In regard to its object, the Commission would, broadly speaking, be required to devise a scheme which may reasonably be hoped to possess the necessary elements of finality, and to do full justice to the claims of natives of India to a higher and more extensive employment in the Public Service.'

There we have the highest authority making a declaration that the desires to do full justice to the claims of the natives of India. Now, our only reply is that we are thankful for the enquiry, and we hope that we may be able to satisfy all, that what we ask is both reasonable and right.

INTENTION OF OUR RULERS.

As another proof of the intentions of our British rulers, as far back as 53 years ago, when the natives of India did not themselves fully understand their rights, the statesmen of England, of their own free will, decided what the policy of England ought to be towards India. Long and important was the debate; the question was discussed from all points of view; the danger of giving political power to the people, the insufficiency of their capacity and other considerations were all fully weighed, and the conclusion was come to, in unmistakable and unambiguous terms, that the policy of British rule should be a policy of justice (*cheers*), the policy of the advancement of one-sixth of the human race (*cheers*); India was to be regarded as a trust placed by God in their hands, and in the due discharge of that trust, they resolved that they would follow the 'plain path of duty,' as Mr. Macaulay called it; on that occasion he said, virtually, that he would rather see the people of India free and able to govern themselves than that they would remain the bondsmen of Great Britain and the obsequious toadies of British officials. (*Cheers.*) This was the essence of the policy of 1833, and in the Act of that year it was laid down, 'That no native of the said territories, nor any natural-born subject of His Majesty resident therein, shall, by reason only of his religion, place of birth, descent, colour or any of them, be disabled from holding any place, office or employment under the said Company.' (*Prolonged cheering.*)

We do not, we could not, ask for more than this; and all we have to press upon the Commission and Government is that they should now honestly grant us in practice here what Great Britain freely conceded to us 50 years ago, when we ourselves were too little enlightened even to ask for it. (*Loud cheers.*)

ROYAL PROCLAMATION.

We next passed through a time of trouble, and the British arms were triumphant. When they had completely surmounted all their difficulties and completely vanquished all their adversaries, the English nation came forward, animated by the same high and noble resolves, as before, and gave us that glorious Proclamation, which we should for ever prize and reverence as our Magna Charta, greater even than the Charter of 1833. I need not repeat that glorious Proclamation now, for it is engraven on all your hearts (*loud cheers*); but it constitutes such a grand and glorious charter of our liberties that I think every child, as it begins to gather intelligence and to lisp its mother-tongue, ought to be made to commit it to memory. (*Cheers.*) In that Proclamation, we have again a confirmation of the policy of 1833 and something more. In it are embodied the germs of all that we aim at now, of all that we can desire hereafter. (*Cheers.*) We have only to go before the Government and the Commission now sitting and repeat it, and say that all we want is only what has already been granted to us in set terms by that Proclamation, and that all we now ask for is that the great and generous concessions therein made to us in words shall actually be made ours by deeds. (*Loud cheers.*) I will not, however, enter into further details, for it is a subject on which I should be led into speaking for hours, and even then I should fail to convey to you an adequate idea of all that is in my heart. I have said enough to show our rulers that our case is complete and has been made out by themselves. (*Cheers.*) It is enough for me, therefore, to stop at this point.

ENLARGEMENT OF LEGISLATIVE COUNCILS.

Another resolution is the improvement and enlargement of the Legislative Councils, and the introduction into them of an elective element, but that is one on which my predecessor in the chair has so ably descanted, that I do not think I should take up more of your time with it. I need only say that in this matter we hope to make a further advance, and shall try to place before our rulers what we consider a possible scheme for the introduction of an elective element into the Legislative Councils. I need not say that if this representation is introduced, the greatest benefit will be conferred upon the Government itself, because at present whatever Acts they pass that do not quite please us, we, whether rightly or wrongly, grumble and grumble against the Government, and the Government only. It is true that we have some of our own people in Councils. But we have no right to demand any explanation, even from them; they are not our representatives, and the Government cannot relieve themselves from any dissatisfaction we may feel against any law we don't like. If our own representatives make a mistake and get a law passed, which we do not want, the Government, at any rate, will escape the greater portion of the consequent unpopularity. They will say—here are your own repeesentatives; we believed that they represented your wishes, and we passed the law. On the other hand, with all the intelligence, all the superior knowledge of the English officials, let them come as angels from heaven, it is impossible for them to enter into the feelings of the people, and feel as they feel, and enter into their minds. (*Cheers.*) It is not any disparagement of them, but in the nature of things it cannot be otherwise. If you have, therefore, your representatives to represent your feelings, you will then have an opportunity of getting something which is congenial and satisfactory to yourself; and what will be satisfactory to you must also be satisfactory to and good for the Government itself. (*Cheers.*)

REPRESENTATION IN PARLIAMENT.

This brings me also to the point of representation in Parliament. All the most fundamental questions on which hinge the entire form and character of the administration here are decided by Parliament. No matter what it is, Legislative Councils or the Services,—nothing can be reformed until Parliament moves and enacts modifications of the existing Acts. Not one single genuine Indian voice is there in Parliament to tell at least what the native view is on any question. This was most forcibly urged upon me by English gentlemen, who are in Parliament themselves; they said they always felt it to be a great defect in Parliament, that it did not contain one single genuine representative of the people of India.

POVERTY OF INDIA.

One of the questions which will be placed before this Congress and will be discussed by them, is the deep sympathy which this Congress feels for the poverty of the people. It is often understood and thought that, when we struggle for admission into the Services, it is simply to gratify the aspirations of the few educated. But if you examine this question thoroughly, you will find that this matter of the Public Services will go far to settle the problem of the poverty of the Indian people. One thing I congratulate myself upon. I don't trouble you with any testimony about the poverty of India. You have the testimony of Sir Evelyn Baring given only a couple of years ago, who told us in plain terms that the people of India were extremely poor, and also of the present Finance

Minister who repeats those words. But amongst the several causes, which are at the bottom of our sufferings, this one and that the most important cause, is beginning to be realized by our rulers, and that is a step of the most hopeful and promising kind. In the discussion about the currency, the Secretary of State for India, in a letter to the Treasury of the 26th January 1886, makes certain remarks which show that our rulers now begin to understand and to try to grapple with the problem; and are not ostrich-like, shutting their eyes to it. I was laughed at when I first mooted the question of the poverty of India, and assigned as one of its causes the employment of an expensive foreign agency. But now the highest authority emphasizes this view. The Secretary of State, in the letter just referred to, said :—

> The position of India in relation to taxation and the sources of the public revenues is very peculiar, not merely from the habits of the people and their strong aversion to change, which is more specially exhibited towards new forms of taxation, but likewise from the character of the government, which is in the hands of foreigners, who hold all the principal administrative offices, and form so large a part of the Army. The impatience of new taxation which would have to be borne, wholly as a consequence of the foreign rule imposed on the country and virtually to meet additions to charges arising outside of the country would constitute a political danger, the real magnitude of which, it is to be feared, is not at all appreciated by persons who have no knowledge of, or concern in, the Government of India, but which those responsible for that government have long regarded as of the most serious order.

We may be sure that the public conscience of England will ask why the natives of India, after a hundred years of British rule, are so poor; and as John Bull, in a cartoon in *Punch*, is represented as doing, will wonder that India is a beggar when he thought she had a mint of money.

INDIA'S FABULOUS WEALTH.

Unfortunately, this idea of India's wealth is utterly delusive, and if a proper system of representation in the

2

Councils be conceded, our representatives will then be able to make clear to these Councils and to our rulers those causes which are operating to undermine our wealth and prosperity, and guide the Government to the proper remedies for the greatest of all evils—the poverty of the masses. All the benefits we have derived from British rule, all the noble projects of our British rulers, will go for nothing if after all the country is to continue sinking deeper and deeper into the abyss of destitution. At one time, I was denounced as a pessimist; but now that we have it on the authority of our rulers themselves that we are *very* poor, it has become the right, as well as the duty, of this Congress to set forth its convictions, both as to this widespread destitution and the primary steps needful for its alleviation. Nothing is more dear to the heart of England—and I speak from actual knowledge—than India's welfare; and if we only speak out loud enough, and persistently enough, to reach that busy heart, we shall not speak in vain. (*Prolonged cheering.*)

CONCLUSION.

There will be several other questions brought before the Congress at their committe meetings during the next three days, and I am sure from the names of the delegates, as far as I am informed, that they will prosecute their deliberations with all possible moderation. I am sure that they will fully appreciate the benefits of the rule under which they live, while the fact that our rulers are willing to do whatever we can show them to be necessary for our welfare, should be enough to encourage all in the work. I do not know that I need now detain you with any further remarks. You have now some idea of what progress has been made in respect of the matters which were discussed last year. I hope we may congratulate ourselves next year that we have made further progress in attaining the objects alike of the past year's resolutions and those we may this year pass. I, for one, am hopeful that, if we are only true to ourselves, if we only do justice to ourselves, and the noble education which has been given to us by our rulers and speak freely, with the freedom of speech which has been granted to us, we may fairly expect our Government to listen to us and to grant us our reasonable demands. (*Loud cheers.*)

I will conclude this short address by repeating my sincere thanks to all of you for having placed me in this honourable position and by again returning thanks to our Bengal brethren on behalf of all the delegetes whom they have so cordially welcomed here.

Ninth Congress—Lahore—1893.

PRESIDENTIAL ADDRESS.

INTRODUCTION.

Ladies and Gentlemen,—I need not say how deeply I feel the honour you have done me by electing me a second time to preside over your deliberations. I thank you sincerely for this honour. In the performance of the onerous duties of this high position, I shall need your great indulgence and support, and I have no doubt that I shall receive them. (*Applause.*)

I am much pleased that I have the privilege of presiding at the very first Congress held in Punjab, as I had at Calcutta in 1886. I have taken, as you may be aware, some interest in the material condition of Punjab. In my first letter to the Secretary of State for India, in 1880, on the material condition of India, I took Punjab for my illustration, and worked out in detail its total annual income and the absolute wants of its common labourer. As to the loyalty of the Punjabis—Hindus, Sikhs, or Muhammadans—it has proved true through the most fiery ordeal on a most trying and critical occasion. (*Applause.*)

The occasion of this Session of the Congress in Punjab has been a most happy coincidence. On Punjab rests a double responsibility, one external and one internal. If ever that hated threatened invasion of the Russians comes on, Punjab will have to bear the first brunt of the battle, and contented under British rule, as I hope India will be, Punjab will fight to her last man in loyalty and patriotism—loyalty to the British Power, and patriotism to protect the hearths and homes of her beloved country of India. (*Loud applause.*)

PUNJAB'S RESPONSIBILITY IN SAFEGUARDING THE EMPIRE.

The internal responsibility which at present rests upon the Punjabis and other warrior races of India is this. I have always understood and believed that manliness was associated with love of justice, generosity and intellect. So our British tutors have always taught us and have always claimed for themselves such character. And I cannot understand how any one could or should deny to you and other manly races of India the same characteristics of human nature. But yet we are gravely told that on the contrary the manliness of these races of India is associated with meanness, unpatriotic selfishness, and inferiority of intellect, and that therefore like the dog in the manger, you and the other warrior races will be mean enough to oppose the resolution about Simultaneous Examinations, and unpatriotic and selfish enough to prevent the general progress of all India. (*Shame.*)

Can offence and insult to a people, and that people admitted to be a manly people, go any further? Look at the numbers of Punjabis studying in England. Now this happy coincidence of this meeting in Punjab: you, considering every son of India as an Indian and a compatriot, have invited me—not a Punjabi, not a Muhammadan, nor a Sikh—from a distance of thousands of miles to enjoy the honour of presiding over this Congress, and with this gathering from all parts of India as the guests of the Punjabis, you conclusively once for all and for ever, set the matter at rest that the Punjabis with all other Indians do earnestly desire the Simultaneous Examinations as the only method in which justice can be done to all the people of India, as this Congress has repeatedly resolved. And moreover, Punjab has the credit of holding the very first public meeting in favour of the Resolution passed by the

House of Commons for Simultaneous Examinations. (*Cheers.*)

When I use the words English or British, I mean all the peoples of the United Kingdom.

DEATH OF JUSTICE TELANG.

It is our melancholy duty to record the loss of one of our greatest patriots, Justice Kasinath Trimbak Telang. It is a heavy loss to India; you all know what a high place he held in our estimation for his great ability, learning, eloquence, sound judgment, wise counsel and leadership. I have known him and worked with him for many years, and I have not known any one more earnest and devoted to the cause of our country's welfare. He was one of the most active founders of this Congress, and was its first hard-working Secretary in Bombay. From the very first he had taken a warm interest and active part in our work, and even after he became a Judge, his sound advice was always at our disposal.

RECENT HIGHER APPOINTMENTS TO INDIANS.

I am glad Mr. Mahadev Govind Ranade is appointed in his place. (*Cheers.*) It does much credit, indeed, to Lord Harris for the selection, and I am sure Mr. Ranade will prove himself worthy of the post. I have known him long, and his ability and learning are well-known. (*Applause.*) His sound judgment and earnest work in various ways have done valuable services to the cause of India. (*Applause.*)

I am also much pleased that an Indian, Mr. Pramada Charan Bannerji, succeeds Mr. Justice Mahmud at Allahabad. (*Cheers.*)

I feel thankful to the Local Governments and the Indian Government for such appointments, and to Lord Kimberley for his sanction of them among which I may include also the decision about the Sanskrit Chair at Madras. (*Applause.*) I feel the more thankful to Lord Kimberley, for I am afraid, and I hope I may be wrong, that there has been a tendency of not only not loyally carrying out the rule about situations of Rs. 200 and upwards to be given to Indians, but that even such posts as have been already given to them are being snatched away from their hands. Lord Kimberley's firmness in not allowing this is, therefore, so much the more worthy of praise and our thankfulness.

Lord Kimberley also took prompt action to prevent the retrograde step in connection with the Jury system in Bengal for which Mr. Paul and other friends interested themselves in Parliament; and also to prevent the retrograde interference with the Chairmanship of Municipalities at the instance of our British Committee in London. I do hope that in the same spirit Lord Kimberley will consider our representations about the extension of the Jury system.

A MESSAGE FROM CENTRAL FINSBURY.

Before proceeding further, let me perform the gratifying task of communicating to you a message of sympathy and goodwill which I have brought for you from Central Finsbury. (*Loud applause and three cheers for the electors of Central Finsbury.*) On learning that I had accepted your invitation to preside, the Council of the Central Finsbury United Liberal and Radical Association passed a Resolution, which I have now the pleasure of placing before you, signed by Mr. Joseph Walton, the Chairman, and forwarded to me by the Honorary Secretary, Mr. R. M. H. Griffith, one of my best friends and supporters.

The Central Finsbury United Liberal and Radical Association, in view of Mr. Naoroji's visit to India at the end of November next, have passed the following Resolution :—

"1. That the General Council of the Central Finsbury United Liberal and Radical Association desire to record their high appreciation of the admirable and most exemplary manner in which Mr. Dadabhai Naoroji has performed his duties as representative of this constituency in the House of Commons and learning that he is, in the course of a few months, to visit India to preside over the Ninth Session of the Indian National Congress, request him to communicate to that body an expression of their full sympathy alike with all the efforts of that Congress for the welfare of India, and with the Resolution which has been recently passed by the House of Commons (in the adoption of which Mr. Dadabhai Naoroji has been so largely instrumental) in favour of holding Simultaneous Examinations in India and in Britain of candidates for all the Indian Civil Services, and further express the earnest hope that full effect will, as speedily as possible, be given by the Government to this measure of justice which has been already too long delayed, *(Applause.)*

"2. That a copy of this Resolution be forwarded to Mr. Dadabhai Naoroji.

"(Signed) JOSEPH WALTON,
Chairman of Meeting."

The Resolution has been sent to Mr. Naoroji with an accompanying letter, which says:—

"Central Finsbury United Liberal and Radical Association,
20, St. John Street Road, Clerkenwell,
London, E.C.

"DEAR SIR,—I have been directed to forward to you the enclosed copy of Resolution passed at the last meeting of the Council of this Association.

"Joining in the hope of my colleagues that the result of our efforts may be of material and lasting good and wishing you a fruitful journey, with a speedy return to us, the constituents you so worthily represent in Parliament.

"I am, yours faithfully,
"R. M. H. GRIFFITHS,
Honorary Secretary.

"The Honourable DADABHAI NAOROJI, M.P.,
House of Commons, Westminster,
August 1893."

ANGLO-INDIAN VIEWS ON THE EDUCATED NATIVES.

The fact is, and it stands to reason, that the thinking portion and the educated, whether in English or in their own learning, of all classes and creeds, in their common nationality as Indians, are naturally becoming the leaders of the people. Those Indians, specially, who have received a good English education, have the double advantage of knowing their own countrymen as well as understanding and appreciating the merits of British men and British rule, with the result, as Sir Bartle Frere has well put it: "And now wherever I go I find the best exponents of the policy of the English Government, and the most able co-adjutors in adjusting that policy to the peculiarities of the natives of India, among the ranks of the educated natives." (*Applause.*)

Or as the Government of India has said, "To the minds of at least the educated among the people of India —and the number is rapidly increasing—any idea of the subversion of the British power is abhorrent." (*Hear hear.*) Government of India's despatch, dated 8th June 1880, to Secretary of State for India.

And as Lord Dufferin, as Viceroy of India, has said in his Jubilee Speech, "We are surrounded on all sides by native gentlemen of great attainments and intelligence, from whose hearty, loyal and honest co-operation we may hope to derive the greatest benefit." (*Applause*)

It would be the height of unwisdom, after themselves creating this great new force, "which is rapidly increasing" as "the best exponents and co-adjutors," as "abhorring the subversion of the British power," and from whose "hearty, loyal and honest co-operation the greatest benefit can arise," that the ruling authorities should drive this force into opposition instead of drawing it to their own side by taking it into confidence and thereby strengthening their own foundation. This Congress represents the Aristocracy of intellect and the new political life, created by themselves, which is at present deeply grateful to its Creator. Common sense tells you—have it with you, instead of against you.

SIMULTANEOUS EXAMINATIONS IN ENGLAND AND INDIA.

With regard to your other most important Resolution, to hold examinations simultaneously both in India and England for all the Civil Services, it would not have become a practical fact by the Resolution of the House of Commons of 2nd June last, had it not been to a large extent for your persevering but constitutional demand for it made with moderation during all the years of your existence. (*Applause.*) I am glad that in the last Budget debate the Under-Secretary of State for India has given us this assurance :—

"It may be in the recollection of the House that, in my official capacity, it was my duty earlier in the Session to oppose a Resolution in favour of Simultaneous Examinations, but the House of Commons thought differently from the Government. That once done, I need hardly say that there is no disposition on the part of the Secretary of State for India or myself to attempt to thwart or defeat the effect of the vote of the House of Commons on that Resolution." (*Hear, hear and applause.*) *Debates Vol. XVII*, 1893, *p.* 1835.

We all cannot but feel thankful to the Secretary of State, Lord Kimberley and the Under-Secretary of State, Mr. George Russell, for this satisfactory assurance.

I may just remark here in passing that I am not able to understand why the higher Civil and Educational Medical Services are handed over to Military Medical Officers, instead of there being a separate Civil Medical Service, dealt with by Simultaneous Examinations in India and England, as we expect to have for the other Civil Services. I also may ask why some higher Civil Engineering posts are given to Military Engineers.

BRITISH INTEREST IN INDIAN AFFAIRS.

One thing more I may say. Your efforts have succeeded not only in creating an interest in Indian affairs, but also a desire among the people of the United Kingdom to promote our true welfare. (*Hear, hear.*) Had you achieved in the course of the past eight years only this much and no more, you would have amply justified your existence. (*Cheers.*) You have proved two things—that you are moderate and reasonable in what you ask, and that the British people are willing to grant what is shown to be reasonable.

It is not necessary for me to enlarge upon the subject of your justification further than this, that all the Resolutions you have formulated have more or less advanced; that they are receiving attentive consideration is testified by the continuous discussions that have been going on in the Press and on the Platform both here and in England. In England itself many a cause, great or small, has to agitate long before making an impression. What struggles have there been in Parliament itself and out of Parliament for the Corn Laws, Slavery Laws, Factory Laws, Parliamentary Reforms, and many others, in short, in every important Legislation? We must keep courage, persevere, and "never say die." (*Loud applause.*)

RECEPTION TO DADABHAI NAOROJI IN PARLIAMENT.

One more result, though not the least, of your labours, I shall briefly touch upon. The effect which your labours produced on the minds of the people of the United Kingdom has helped largely an Indian to find his way into the Great Imperial Parliament, and in confirmation of this, I need not go further than remind you of the generous action of Central Finsbury and the words of the Resolution of the Council of its United Liberal and

Radical Association which I have already placed before you. (*Applause.*)

As you are all aware, though it was long my wish, my friend the Hon. Mr. Lal Mohan Ghose made the first attempt, and twice contested Deptford, with no little chances of success, but adverse circumstances proved too strong for him. We owe a debt of gratitude to Deptford, and also to Holborn, which gave me the first lift, and in my contest there, though a forlorn hope, the Liberal electors exerted their utmost, and gave me a very satisfactory poll. (*Cheers.*)

My mind also turns to those good friends of India—Bright, Fawcett, Bradlaugh and others, (*applause*)—who pioneered for us, prepared for the coming of this result, and helped us when we were helpless.

This naturally would make you desire and lead me to say a few words about the character of the reception given to the Indian Member in the House of Commons. It was everything that could be desired. (*Cheers.*) The welcome was general from all sides, as the interest in Indian affairs has been much increasing, and there is a desire to do justice to India. (*Renewed cheering.*) Mr. Gladstone on two occasions not only expressed his satisfaction to me at finding an Indian in the House, but expressed also a strong wish to see several more.

The attendance on Indian questions has been good, and what is still better, the interest in the Indian debates has been earnest, and with a desire to understand and judge rightly. India has, indeed, fared well this Session, notwithstanding its other unprecedentedly heavy work.

PARLIAMENTARY INTEREST IN INDIAN QUESTIONS.

Thankful as we are to many Members of all sides, I am bound to express our special thanks to the Irish,

Labour and Radical Members. (*Loud cheers.*) I heard from Mr. Davitt, two days before my departure, "Don't forget to tell your colleagues at the Congress that every one of Ireland's Home Rule Members in Parliament is at your back in the cause of the Indian People." (*Prolonged cheering.*) All our friends who had been working for us before are not only as zealous and staunch as ever, but more active and earnest. I cannot do better than to record in this place with thankfulness the names of all those Members from all parties who voted for the Resolution of 2nd June last in favour of Simultaneous Examinations in England and India for all the Indian Civil Services.*

As the ballot fell to Mr. Herbert Paul, (*three Cheers for Mr. Paul*) he, as you are aware, moved the Resolution, and you know also how well and ably he advocated the cause, and has ever since kept up a watchful interest in and eye on it. I may mention here that I had sent a whip or notice to every Member of the House of Commons for this debate.

Motion made, and Question proposed, "That Mr. Speaker do now leave the Chair":

Amendment proposed, to leave out from the word "That" to the end of the Question, in order to add the words "all open Competitive Examinations heretofore held in England alone for appointments to the Civil Services of India shall henceforth be held simultaneously both in India and England, such Examinations in both countries being identical in their nature, and all who compete being finally classified in one list according to merit.—(*Mr. Paul.*)

---

* The names are omitted.

Question put, "That the words proposed to be left out stand part of the Question":—

The House divided; Ayes 76, Noes 84.

I may say here a few words about the progress we are making in our Parliamentary position. By the exertions of Sir William Wedderburn, (*applause*), Mr. Caine, (*applause*), and other friends, an Indian Parliamentary Committee has been formed, of which Sir William Wedderburn is the Chairman and Mr. Herbert Roberts is the Secretary. (*Applause.*) The Committee is not yet fully formed. It will, we hope, be a larger General Committee of our supporters with a small Executive Committee, like other similar Committees that exist in the House for other causes. I give the names of the Members now fully enrolled in this Committee:—Mr. Jacob Bright, Mr. Caine, Mr. John E. Ellis, Dr. W. A. Hunter, Mr. Illingworth, Sir Wilfred Lawson, Mr. Walter B. McLaren, Mr. Swift MacNeill, Mr. Dadabhai Naoroji, Mr. H. Paul, Sir Joseph Pease, Mr. T. H. Roberts, Mr. R. T. Reid, Mr. Samuel Smith, Mr. C. E. Schwann, Mr. Eugene Wason, Mr. Webb, Sir W. Wedderburn.

Besides these, there are a large number of Members (exclusive of the 70 or 80 Irish Members already referred to) whom we count as supporters, and hope to see fully enrolled Members on our Indian Parliamentary Committee before long.

On the eve of my departure, the Committee invited me to a private dinner at the House, and gave me a hearty Godspeed and wishes of success, with an expression of their earnest desire to see justice done to India. (*Applause.*)

Before leaving this subject of Parliament, let me offer to Mr. George Russell, the Under-Secretary of State for India, my sincere thanks for his sympathetic and cordial treatment of me in all I had to do with him, and for his personal good feeling and kindness towards me. (*Applause.*)

FUTURE OF THE CONGRESS.

With all that has been done by the Congress, we have only begun our work. We have yet much and very much more work to do till that political, moral and material condition is attained by us which will raise us really to the level of our British fellow-citizens in prosperity and political elevation, and thereby consolidate the British power on the imperishable foundation of justice, mutual benefit and the contentment and loyalty of the people.

The reason why I have dwelt upon our past life is that it shows that our future is promising and hopeful, that our faith in the instinctive love of justice and fair play of the people of the United Kingdom is not misplaced, and that if we are true to ourselves and learn from the British character the self-sacrifice and perseverance which the British so largely possess, we need never despair of obtaining every justice and reform which we may reasonably claim as our birthright as British citizens. (*Cheers.*)

What then is to be our future work ? We have yet to surmount much prejudice, prepossessions, and misapprehension of our true, material and political condition. But our course is clear and straight before us. On the one hand, we need not despair or quarrel with those who are against us ; we should, on the other hand, go on steadily, perseveringly and moderately with the representation of our grievances and just rights.

REFORM OF LEGISLATIVE COUNCILS.

In connection with the question of our Legislative Councils we have yet very much work before us. Not only are the present rules unsatisfactory even for the fulfilment of the present Act itself as interpreted in the House by Mr. Gladstone, not only have we yet to obtain the full "living representation" of the people of India in these Councils, but also much further extension of their present extremely restricted powers which render the Councils almost a mere name. By the Act of 1861 (19), without the permission of the Governor-General, no member can introduce any measure (which virtually amounts to exclusion) about matters affecting the public debt or public revenues or for imposing any charge on such revenue, or the discipline and maintenance of any part of Her Majesty's Military or Naval forces. This means that, as far as the spending of our money is concerned, the Legislative Council is simply as if it did not exist at all. (*Cries of "Shame, shame."*) No motion can be made by any member unless such motion be for leave to introduce some measure or have reference to some measure actually introduced thereunto. Thus, there is no opportunity of calling any Department or Government to account for their acts. (Section 52.) All things which shall be done by the Secretary of State shall have the same force and validity as if this Act (1861) had not been passed. Here is full arbitrary power. By the Act (1892, Section 52), no member shall have power to submit or propose any resolution or to divide the Council in respect of any such financial discussion, or the answer to any question asked under the authority of this Act or the rules made under this Act. Such is the poor character of the extent of concession made to discuss finances or to put questions. Rules made under this Act (1892) shall not be subject to alteration or amendment at meetings for the purpose of making Laws and Regulations. Also (Act 1861,

Section 22) the Secretary of State for India can by an Act of Parliament raise any money in the United Kingdom for the Government of India, and thus pile up any amount of burden on the Indian taxpayer, without his having a word to say upon it. We are to all intents and purposes under an arbitrary rule, and are just only about at the threshold of a true Legislative Council.

INDIAN BUDGET DEBATE.

Amongst the most important work of the Councils is the Budget. What is the condition of the Budget debate both here and in England? The House of Commons devotes week after week for supply of the English Budget, when every item of expenditure is discussed or may be altered; and not only that, but the conduct of the department during the year is brought under review, which becomes an important check to any arbitrary, unjust or illegal action. But what is the Indian Budget debate or procedure? Here the Financial Statement is made by the Finance Minister. Then a week or so after, a few speeches are made to no practical effect, no practical motion or resolution, and the whole thing is over. (*Shame.*) Somewhat similar is the fate of the Indian Budget in the House of Commons, with the advantage of proposing any amendments and, at least, of having one amendment with practical effect of a division, or vote. But there is also the important advantage of bringing in any Indian measure or motion in the course of the Session in accordance with the rules and orders of the House like any other measure or motion. I felt thankful that at the last Budget debate, though there was the usual additional agony of the last day of the Session, yet there was not also the agony of scanty attendance, thanks to the increasing interest in the House in Indian matters and to the friends of India. (*Applause.*)

In both places no practical check on any waste, extravagant or unnecessary expenditure. I am not at present discussing the merits of such Councils and restriction of powers, but that such matters will require your attention and consideration, that even in this one matter of Legislative Councils you have yet to secure Mr. Gladstone's "real living representative voice of the people" being heard upon every detail of the Government of British India. (*Hear, hear.*)

INDIAN REPRESENTATION IN PARLIAMENT.

There is, however, another important matter—I mean the direct representation from India in the Imperial Parliament. (*Applause.*) As all our Imperial questions and relations between India and the United Kingdom, all amendments of Parliamentary Acts already passed and existing, or all important Acts that may be and can be only passed hereafter in Parliament, and all our ultimate appeals can be settled in Parliament alone, it is of extreme importance that there should be some reasonable direct representation from India in the House of Commons and the representatives may be Indians or Europeans as long as they are the choice directly of Indian Constituencies, just as you have delegates to this Congress of Indians or Europeans.

Central Finsbury has been generous to us; other constituencies may also extend to us such generous consideration and help, but it is not fair that we should be left to depend upon the generosity of English Constituencies. (*Hear, hear.*) Under present circumstances we have a right to have direct representation. I hope the time is not very distant when we may successfully appeal to Parliament to grant us the true status of British political citizenship. (*Cheers.*) I do not overlook that several matters will have to be considered, and I am not at present placing before you a cut-and-dry scheme. My only object is to draw your attention to this vital subject.

POVERTY OF INDIA.

But the greatest question before you, the question of all questions, is the poverty of India. (*Hear, hear.*) This will be, I am much afraid, the great future trouble both of the Indian people and of the British Rulers. It is the rock ahead. In this matter we are labouring under one great disadvantage. This poverty we attribute to the system, and not to the officials who administer that system. (*Hear, hear and applause.*) But unfortunately for us, for themselves and the British people, the officials (with clear-sighted exceptions of course) make the matter personal, and do not consider impartially and with calmness of judgment this all-important subject. The present Duke of Devonshire has well put this state of the official mind, which is peculiarly applicable in connection with this subject. He said, "The Anglo-Indian, whatever may be his merits, and no doubt they are just, is not a person who is distinguished by an exceptionally calm judgment."—*Speech, H. of C.*, 23*rd August*, 1883.

Mr. Gladstone also lately, in the Opium debate, remarked :—"That it was a sad thing to say, but unquestionably it happens not infrequently in human affairs, that those who from their situation ought to know the most and the best, yet from prejudice and prepossessions knew the least and the worst." (*Hear, hear.*)

This has been our misfortune with officials. But there have been and are some thoughtful officials who know the truth, like Lord Lawrence and others in the past, and in the present times like the latest Finance Ministers, Lord Cromer, Sir Auckland Colvin and Sir David Barbour, who have perceived and stated the terrible truth that British India is extremely poor. Among other officials several have testified to the sad fact, in "Confidential Reports," which Government do not publish—and this after a hundred years of the work of these officials under the present unnatural system. The system being unnatural, were the officials the very angels themselves, or as many Gladstones, they cannot prevent the evils of the system and cannot do much good. When Mr. Bayley and I moved for a Royal Commission of Inquiry, it was said that I had not produced evidence of poverty, it was not so; but it is difficult to make those see who would not see. (*Laughter and applause.*) To every member of the House I had previously sent my papers of all necessary evidence on the annual income and absolute wants of the people of India. I do not know whether any of those who opposed us had taken the trouble to read this, and it was unfair to expect that in making out a *prima facie* case for our motion, I should reiterate, with the unnecessary waste of some hours of the precious time of the House, all the evidence already in their hands.

POVERTY OF INDIA AND OFFICIAL STATISTICS.

You remember my papers on the Poverty of India, and I have asked for Returns to bring up information to date, so that a fair comparison of the present with the past may enable the House to come to a correct judgment. I am sorry the Government of India refuses to make a return of a Note prepared so late as 1881 by Sir David Barbour, upon which the then Finance Minister (Lord Cromer) based his statement in his speech in 1882 about the extreme poverty of the mass of the people. I do not see why the Government of India should refuse. The Note, I am told, is an important document. Government for its own sake should be ready to give it. In 1880, the present Duke of Devonshire, then Secretary of State for India, readily gave me some statistics and information prepared by Mr. F. Danvers, though I did not know of their existence. This enabled me to point out some errors and to explain some points which had been misunderstood. Such information is extremely necessary, not merely for the sake of the exceedingly poor masses of the people, but for the very stability of the British power itself.

The question of the Poverty of India should be fully raised, grappled with and settled. The Government ought to deal boldly and broadly with it. Let there be a return in detail, correctly calculated, made every year of the *total* annual income of *all* British India, per head of population, and of the requirements of a labourer to live in working health, and not as a starved beast of burden. Unless such complete and accurate information is given every year in detail, it is idle and useless to make mere unfounded assertions that India is prospering.

It must also be remembered that Lord Cromer's annual average of not more than Rs. 27 per head is for the whole population, including the rich and all classes, and not what the great mass of the population can or do actually get. Out of the total annual income of British India, all that portion must be deducted which belongs to European Planters, Manufacturers, and Mine-owners, and not to the people of British India, excepting the poor wages they receive, to grudge to give away their own country's wealth, to the benefit of a foreign people. Another portion is enjoyed in and carried out from the country on a far larger share per head by many who are not the children of the soil—official and non-official.

Then the upper and middle classes of the Indians themselves receive much more than their average share. The great mass of the poor people, therefore, have a much lower average than even the wretched "not more than Rs. 27" per head.

You know that I had calculated the average of the income as being Rs. 20 per head per annum, and when Lord Cromer's statement of Rs. 27 appeared, I requested him to give me his calculations but he refused. However, Rs. 20 or "not more than Rs. 27"—how wretched is the condition of a country of such income, after a hundred years of the most costly administration, and can such a thing last? (*Cries of "No, no".*)

It is remarkable that there is no phase of the Indian problem which clear-headed and fair-minded Anglo-Indians have not already seen and indicated. More than a hundred years ago, in 1787, Sir John Shore wrote these remarkable, far-seeing, and prophetic words :—

> Whatever allowance we may make for the increased industry of the subjects of the State, owing to the enhanced demand for the produce of it (supposing the demand to be enhanced), there is reason to conclude that the benefits are more than counter-balanced by evils inseparable from the system of a remote foreign dominion.—*Parl. Ret.* 377 *of* 1812.

And these words of prophecy are true to the present day. I pass over what has been said by other European officials at different times during the hundred years. I come to 1886, and here is a curious and complete response after a hundred years by the Secretary of State for India. In a despatch (26th January, 1886) to the Treasury, he makes a significant admission about the consequences of the character of the Government of the foreign rule of Britain. He says :—

> The position of India in relation to taxation and the sources of the public revenues is very peculiar, not merely from the habits

of the people and their strong aversion to change which is more specially exhibited to new forms of taxation, but likewise from the character of the Government, which is in the hands of foreigners, who hold all the principal administrative offices and form so large a part of the Army. The imposition of new taxation which would have to be borne wholly as a consequence of the foreign rule imposed on the country and virtually to meet additions to charges arising outside of the country would constitute a political danger, the real magnitude of which, it is to be feared, is not at all appreciated by persons who have no knowledge of or concern in the Government of India, but which those responsible for that Government have long regarded as of the most serious order.

What a strange confirmation, fulfilment and explanation of the very reason of the prophecy of a hundred years ago, and admission now that because the character of the present Government is such that "*it is in the hands of the foreigners who hold all the principal administrative offices and form so large a part of the army*," the consequence of it is a "*political danger*," the real magnitude of which is "*of the most serious order.*"

Need I, after this declaration even, despair that some of our Anglo-Indian friends would not take a lesson from the Secretary of State and understand the evil of the system under which India is suffering? Have I ever said anything clearer or stronger than this despatch has done? It gives my whole fear of the future perils to the people of India and political danger to the British power in a nutshell. This shows that some of our Anglo-Indian authorities have not been, nor are, so dull and blind as not to have seen before or see now the whole peril of the position, and the unnatural and suicidal system of administration.

Yes, figures are quoted by some of what they call "increase of trade," "balance of trade in favour of India," "increase of industry," "hoarding of treasure in British India," etc., etc., ; but our misfortune is that these people, with bias and prejudices and prepossessions, and apparently having not very clear ideas of the principles, processes, and details of commercial and banking operations and transactions, and of the perturbations of what Sir John Shore called "the evils of a distant foreign dominion," are not able to understand and read aright these facts and figures of the commercial and economic conditions of British India. These people do not realise or seem to understand that what are called "the trade returns of British India" are misleading, and are not the trade returns of British India. A good portion of both the imports and exports of both merchandise and treasure belong to the Native States and to countries beyond the borders, and not to British India. A separate return must be made of the imports and exports of the non-British territories, so that a correct account of the true trade of British India may be given by itself—and then there should be some statement of the exports which are not trade exports at all, but only political and private European remittances; and then only will it be seen how wretched this British Indian true trade is, and how fallacious and misleading the present returns are. A return is made every year called "The Material and Moral Progress of India." But that part regarding "Material Progress" to which I am confining my observations is very imperfect and misleading. As I have already said, nothing short of a return every year of the average annual income per head of population of British India, and of the absolute necessaries of life for a healthy labourer, in detailed calculation, can give any correct idea of the progress or otherwise of the material condition of the people of British India. I ask for "detailed calculation" in the returns, because some of the officials seem to have rather vague notions of the Arithmetic of Averages, and though the foundation figures may be correct, they bring out results far from truth. I have pointed out this with instances in my papers. I have communicated with the Secretary of State for India, and he has communicated with the Governments in India. But I do not know how far this correction has been attended to by those who calculate averages.

TRADE BETWEEN ENGLAND AND INDIA.

What is grievous is that the present unnatural system, as predicted by Sir John Shore, is destructive to us, with a partial benefit to the United Kingdom with our curse upon it. But were a natural system to prevail, the commercial and industrial benefits aided by perfect free-trade that exists between India and the United Kingdom will be to both countries of an extent of which we can at present form no conception.

But here is an inexhaustible market of 221,000,000 of their own civilized fellow-citizens with some 66,000,000 more of the people of the Native States, and what a great trade would arise with such an enormous market, and the United Kingdom would not for a long time hear anything about her "unemployed." It is only some people of the United Kingdom of the higher classes that at present draw all the benefit from India. The great mass of the people do not derive that benefit from the connection with India which they ought to get with benefit to both countries. On the other hand, it is with the Native States that there is some comparatively decent trade. With British India, as compared with its population, the trade of the United Kingdom is wretched indeed after a century of a very costly administration paid for by the poverty-stricken ryots.

Truly as Macaulay said emphatically:

> To trade with civilised man is infinitely more profitable than to govern savages; that would indeed be a doting wisdom, which, in order that India might remain a dependency, would make it a useless and costly dependency, which would keep a hundred millions (now really 221,000,000) of men from being our customers in order that they might continue to be our slaves.

Should this doting wisdom continue?

It is impossible for me to explain in this address all the misapprehensions. I have already explained my views as fully as possible in my papers. These views were at first ridiculed and pooh-poohed till the highest financial authorities, the latest Finance Ministers themselves, admitted the extreme poverty of India. Lord Cromer summed up the situation in these remarkable words in 1882: "It has been calculated that the average income per head of population in India is not more than Rs. 27 a year." "In England the average income per year per head of population was £33; in France it was £23; in Turkey which was the poorest country in Europe, it was £4 a head." Comment is unnecessary. Let us and the Government not live in a fool's paradise, or time may bring disasters to both when it is too late to stop them. This poverty is the greatest danger both to us and the rulers. In what shapes and varieties of forms the disease of poverty may attack the body-politic, and bring out and aggravate other evils, it is difficult to tell or foresee, but that there is danger of "most serious order," as the Secretary of State declares, nobody can deny.

INDIAN LOYALTY

Were the people of British India allowed to enjoy the fruits of their own labour and resources, and were fair relations established between the British and Indian peoples, with India contented and prosperous, Britain may defey half-a-dozen Russias. (*Loud cheers.*) Indians will then fight to the last man and to the last rupee for their share, as patriots and not as mercenaries. The rulers will have only to stamp their foot, and millions will spring up to defend the British power and their own hearths and homes. (*Renewed cheering.*)

We, the Congress, are only desirous of supporting Government, and having this important matter of poverty grappled with and settled, we are anxious to prevent "the political danger" of the "most serious order," declared to exist by the Secretary of State himself. We desire that the British connection should endure for a long time to come for the sake of our material and political elevation among the civilised nations of the world. It is no pleasure or profit to us to complain unnecessarily or wantonly about this poverty.

Were we enemies of British rule, our best course would be, not to cry out, but remain silent, and let the mischief take its course till it ends in disaster as it must. But we do not want that disaster, and we therefore cry out, both for our own sake, and for the sake of the rulers. This evil of poverty must be boldly faced and remedied.

This is the question to which we shall have to devote our best energies. We have, no doubt, to contend against many difficulties, but they must be surmounted for everybody's sake.

COSTLY ARMY AND CIVIL SERVICES.

The next subject to which I desire to draw your attention is this. We have a large costly European Army and European Civil Services. It is not to be supposed that in these remarks I accept the necessity for them. I take at present the situation as it is. I now submit to the calm consideration of the British people and Government these questions. Is all this European service entirely for the sole benefit of India? Has the United Kingdom no interest or benefit in it? Does not the greatness of, and the greatest benefit to, the United Kingdom arise from its connection with India? Should not the cost of such greatness and great benefits be shared by the United Kingdom in proportion to its means and benefits? Are not these European services especially imposed upon us on the clearly admitted and declared ground of maintaining the British power? Let us see what our rulers themselves say.

BRITISH VIEWS ON THE COSTLY INDIAN ADMINISTRATION.

Lord Beaconsfield said:—

> **We had to decide what was the best step to counteract the efforts Russia was then making, for though war had not been declared, her movements had commenced in Central Asia, and the struggle has commenced which was to decide for ever which power should possess the great gates of India, and that the real question at issue was whether England should possess the gates of her own great empire in India and whether the time had not arrived when we could no longer delay that the problem should be solved and in a manner as it has been solved by Her Majesty's Government.—**
> (*Hansard, Vol*, 250. *p*. 1094, 25*th February* 1880.)

Again he says:—

> **We resolved that the time has come when this country should acquire the complete command and possession of the gates of the Indian Empire. Let me at least believe that the Peers of England are still determined to uphold not only the empire but the honour of this country.**

Can any words be more emphatic to show the vast and most vital stakes, honour and interests of the United Kingdom?

Lord Kimberley, the Secretary of State for India, tells us:—

> **We are resolutely determined to maintain our supremacy over our Indian Empire . . . . that among other things, he says, that supremacy rests upon the mainteuance of our European Civil Service, that we rest also upon the magnificent European Force which we maintain in that country.—"*Times*," 13*th June*, 1893. *Mansion House Dinner to Lord Roberts.***

This again is another emphatic declaration of the vast stakes and interests of the United Kingdom for which the European Services are maintained entirely at our expense.

I shall give one more authority only.

See what a man like Lord Roberts, the symbol of physical force admits. He says to the London Chamber of Commerce :—

> I rejoce to learn that you recognise how indissolubly the prosperity of the United Kingdom is bound up with the retention of that vast Eastern Empire.—("*Times*," 25 *May*, 1893. *Dinner by the London Chamber of Commerce.*)

And again he says at Glasgow :

> That the retention of our Eastern Empire is essential to the greatness and prosperity of the United Kingdom.—("*Times*," *29th July*, 1893.)

Now, I ask again, that with all such deep, vast and great interests, and the greatness and prosperity of the United Kingdom, essentially depending on the Eastern Empire, and indissolubly bound up with it, is it reasonable, is it just and fair, is it British that all the cost of such greatness, glory, and prosperity of the United Kingdom should be entirely, to the last farthing thrown upon the wretched Indians, as if the only relations existing between the United Kingdom and India were not of mutual benefit, but of mere masters and slaves as Macaulay pointed out to be deprecated. (*Applause and cries of* "*No, no.*")

As for the Navy, the *Times* regards and it is generally admitted that the very existence of Britain itself depends upon the command of the sea. The *Times* says :—

> They will never forgive the Minister or the Ministry that leaves them weaker at sea than any possible combination of France and another power.

By a telegram I read at Aden, I found Mr. Gladstone "re-affirmed the necessity of British supremacy."

For any war vessels that may be stationed in India for the protection of the interests of both, the expenditure may be fairly shared.

IRELAND AND INDIA CONTRASTED *re*: FINANCIAL ADJUSTMENT.

In the Bill for the better government of Ireland there are provisions by which Ireland is required to pay a certain share of the Imperial expenditure according to its means, and when necessary to pay a similar share of any extraordinary expenditure, Ireland having all its resources at its own command. Now see how vastly different is our position. Not only will Ireland have all her internal services, Irish or under Irish rules causing no foreign drain from her, but she will also, as she has always enjoyed, continue to enjoy her share in all the gain and glory of the British Empire. Irishmen can be Viceroys, Governors, and have any of the appointments in the military or civil services of the Empire, with the additional advantage of a large number of Members in Parliament. The Indians, on the other hand, have not only no such share at all in the gains and glory of the British Empire but are excluded even from the services of their own country, with the consequences of an exhausting foreign drain, of the deplorable evils foretold by Sir John Shore and subjected to the imposition of every farthing of the expenditure. Nor has India any votes in Parliament. And we have now the additional misfortune that the British Cabinet, since the transfer to the Crown, is no longer the independent tribunal to judge between us and the Indian authorities, and this adds heavily to our difficulties for obtaining justice and redress, except so far as the sense of justice of the non-official members of the Parliament helps us.

INDIAN MILITARY EXPENDITURE.

There is a strange general misapprehension among the people of the United Kingdom. They do not seem to know that they have not spent a single shilling either in the formation of the British Indian Empire or in its maintenance and that as far as I know, every farthing is taken from the Indians, with the only exception in my knowledge that Mr. Gladstone with his sense of justice allowed £5,000,000 towards the last Afghan War, which, without having any voice in it, cost India £21,000,000. (*Loud cries of "Shame."*) I cannot blame the people of the United Kingdom generally for this mistake, when even well-informed papers give utterances to this most unfortunate fallacy. As, for instance, a paper like the *Statist*, in the extract which my friend Mr. Dinshaw E. Wacha gave you last year, says: "Whatever may happen, we must defend India to our last shilling and our last man," while the fact is that they have not spent even their first shilling or any shilling at all (*laughter*), but on the contrary derived benefits in various ways from India of millions on millions every year. (" *Shame.* ") Nor have the fighters in creating and maintaining the British Indian Empire been only the British soldier to " the last man. " Indian soldiers have done the main work, and if India can be made prosperous and contented as it can be by true statesmanship, the Indian soldier will be ready to fight to " the last man " to defend British power. (*Loud cheers.*)

Britain, in fact, cannot send to India "to its last man." The very idea is absurd ; on the contrary she can draw from India for her European purpose an inexhaustible strength.

Again, the *Statist* says :—" We are at this moment spending large sums of money in preparing against a

Russian attack." Not a farthing of the British money!! Every farthing of these "large sums," which are crushing us, is "imposed" upon the people of British India. Such misleading statements are often made in the English Press to our great injury. ("*Shame*.")

I repeat, then, that we must submit to the just consideration of the British people and Parliament whether it is just and right that they should not pay a fair share according to their stakes and means, towards all such expenditure as is incurred for the benefit of both India and the United Kingdom, such expenditure, and the respective share of each, being settled on a peace footing, any extraordinary expenditure against any foreign invasion being also further fairly shared.

Before closing this subject, I may just remark that while leaving necessarily the highest offices of power and control, such as Viceroys and Governors to Europeans, I regard the enormous European Services as a great political and imperial weakness, in critical political times to the British power, as well as the cause, as the present Duke of Devonshire pointed out, of the insufficiency of an efficient administration of the country; and also the main cause of the evils foretold by Sir John Shore, and admitted by the Secretary of State for India, after a hundred years, as a political danger of "a most serious order;" and of the poverty of India.

THE BURDEN OF THE INDIAN TAXPAYER.

I would not say much upon the next subject, as you have had only lately the highest testimonies of two Viceroys and three Secretaries of State for India—of Lord Northbrook and Lord Ripon, and of the Duke of Argyll, Lord Cross, and Lord Kimberley. You remember the debate raised by Lord Northbrook in the House of

Lords a few months ago that the Home Military Charges were unfair and unjust, and all the authorities I have named endorsed the complaint. But even the heads of the Indian authorities are so much in terror of the Treasury that Lord Kimberley said :—" The India Office has no particular desire that the question should be re-opened and discussed anew, for bitter experience has taught the department that the re-opening of a question of this kind generally results in the imposition of additional charges." Is this one other disadvantage of the transfer to the Crown? Lord Kimberley hit the nail on the head why India was so unfairly treated (and the same may be applied to such other treatment of India by the Indian authorities themselves) when he said :—" The reasons why proposals that must throw fresh burdens on the Government of India are so frequently made in the House of Commons is that those who make them know that their own pockets will not suffer in the desire to make things agreeable and comfortable. (*Laughter.*) The taxpayers of the country exercise no check upon such proposals, and the consequence is that charges are sometimes imposed upon the Government of India which that Government thinks unjust and unnecessary." It must be borne in mind that charges " imposed on the Government of India " means the suffering party is the poor taxpayer of India.

The Duke of Argyll characterises these charges as "unjust and illegal tribute to England." But mark the words of Lord Cross :—" I am certain that in the course of a few years the Indian people will force us to do them justice." This is just the feature " to be forced to do justice " which I always deplore. We desire that all necessary reforms and acts of justice should be spontaneous on the part of Britain, in good grace in and good time as gifts claiming our gratitude, and not to wait till "forced," with loss of grace from the giver and the loss of gratitude from the receiver. (*Hear, hear.*)

I offer my thanks to Lord Northbrook and other Lords for that debate, though yet barren of any result. But we may fairly hope that such debate must sooner or later produce good results. It is like a good seed sown and will fructify.

Here are some smaller items: The cost of the India Office Building of about half-a-million, of the Royal Engineering College of £134,000, and of other buildings is all cast on India. The cost of the Colonial Office Building, £100,000, is paid from the British Exchequer. The India Office Establishment, etc., about £230,000 a year, is all imposed on India, while the £41,000 of the Colonial Office and £168,000 for Colonial Services are paid from the British Exchequer. The public debt of India (excluding Railway and Productive Works) is incurred in creating and preserving the British power, but all our cries to give us at least the benefit of a British guarantee have been in vain, with the curious suicidal effort of showing to the world that the British Government itself has no confidence in the stability of its own power in India. (*Hear, hear.*)

In 1870, Mr. Gladstone declared India to be "too much burdened," when the Annual Expenditure was £39,000,000; what expression can be used now when, with an extremely poor income, the burden now is nearly 75 per cent. heavier, or Rs. 68,000,000 this year.

SEPARATION OF EXECUTIVE AND JUDICIAL FUNCTIONS.

Passing on to the other subjects, I hope the separation of Executive and Judicial functions will receive attention as its necessity has been recognised. We have to persevere for this as well as for other parts of our programme, bearing in mind one great difficulty we have to contend with. Unfortunately the Indian authorities, when they determine to do or not to do a thing under the notion of preserving prestige and strength, as if any false prestige can be a strength, disregard even Resolutions or Acts of Parliament itself, and resort to every device to carry their own point of view. (*Loud cries of "Shame."*) We cannot expect Parliament to watch Indian affairs from day to day, and therein lies the impunity and immunity of the Indian administration.

I shall refer to only two instances, first, the case of the misleadingly called "The Statutory Service," and what in reality was created out of, and as a part and parcel of, the Covenanted Civil Service. I can speak with some authority, for I was the very proposer of the Memorial of the East India Association to Sir Stafford Northcote which resulted in the Clause of the Act of 1870. But the Indian authorities would not have it. They moved heaven and earth to thwart it; it is a long and a sad story for the good name of Britain, and they never rested till they made the Statute a dead letter, though it still stands on the Statute Book of the Imperial Parliament. ("*Shame.*") However, I hear with pleasure, and I hope it is true, that a disposition has arisen, for which I understand Lord Kimberley is to be thanked, to redress this glaring and unfortunate wrong—unfortunate for British prestige, for British honour and British good faith, and I do hope that the Government would do this redress ungrudgingly, with good grace, completeness and generosity. This instance illustrates another unfortunate phase of the Administration.

INDIAN FOREST SERVICE.

The Forest Department is recruited by examinations in England and by selection in India. Such selection is not based upon a Resolution or Act of Parliament, but upon the will of the authorities and consisting of Europeans. The Government of India in Resolution No. 18 F, of 29th July 1891, have described them as untrained and uncovenanted officers, who have been unconditionally appointed in past years, and yet they are ordered in the regular Indian Forest Service; while those Native Civilians, created and backed by an Act of Parliament, as distinctly belonging to the Covenanted Civil Service, are excluded from that Civil Service to which the Act distinctly appointed them. Can such difference of treatment of Europeans and Indians preserve British prestige for honour and justice, and would it increase or diminish the existing attachment of the Indians to British rule?

THE STATE REGULATION OF VICE.

The second instance was the practical disregard of the Resolution of the House of Commons about the State regulation of vice. But in this case there were vigilant watchers like Mrs. Butler, Mr. Stansfeld, M. P., Mr. Stuart, M.P., and others, and they did not allow the Resolution to become a dead letter. In this case also I am glad to find that the Indian authorities now mean to give loyal effect to the Resolution, and well may they do so for the sake of the British good name, fame, and prestige, for morality of every kind upon which mainly British strength and influence rest.

THE CURRENCY QUESTION.

On the Currency Question I need not dwell much. My views are not unknown to you. Now that the Sherman Law is repealed by the United States, we may hope to see a settled condition in time. No amount of currency, jugglery or devices in this country could have any influence (except that of creating troubles in the country itself, as has happened) on the loss in the remittances to England for Home Charges which must be paid in gold, and will fluctuate with the rise or fall of gold in the United Kingdom. As if this crushing loss was not enough for the wretched taxpayers, further burdens were laid to make things agreeable and comfortable with other people's money, as Lord Kimberley would say, of high exchange to the European officials, and the further most unwarranted payment of £138,000 to the banks, with whose transactions in profits or loss the taxpayer has no connection whatever. ("*Shame, shame.*") Some strange precedents are made in this matter to silence opposition and to support banks at the expense of the taxpayers, which will lead to serious troubles in the future. Should not the millowners and other concerns also claim compensation for the dislocation of their industry or transactions by the currency action of the Government, as Government itself admits to have caused such dislocation? Would the British Exchequer have paid any such money to the British banks? Such a thing would never have been thought of. The utmost that is done in any crisis is allowing the Bank of England to issue more notes under strong restrictions. Had the banks made profits instead of loss, would they have handed them to the taxpayer? Then it would have been called the reward of shrewdness, foresight, enterprise, etc., etc.

The whole currency troubles from which India is suffering, and which are so peculiar to India and so deplorable to the Indian taxpayer, and from which no other silver-using country suffers, is one of the best illustrations and object-lessons, and proof of the soundness of Sir John Shore's prophecy about the evil consequences of the present unnatural system of a remote foreign dominion, or as the Secretary of State called the danger of "a most serious order."

The currency muddle will necessitate new taxation. The usual easy and unchecked resource of putting off the evil day by borrowing is already resorted to, and in the spirit of keeping things agreeable and comfortable to those who have votes in Parliament, there is danger of increase in the salt tax. I do hope that Government will have some moral courage and some mercy upon the wretched taxpayer, and reduce even the salt tax by re-imposing the cotton duties. Not that by this means India will be saved a pie from the addition of burdens, but that a little better able shoulders will have to bear them, or, as Lord Salisbury once coolly put it, that as India must be bled, the lancet should be directed to the parts where there was at least sufficient blood, not to those which are already feeble from the want of it.

THE GOVERNMENT AND THE NATIVE STATES.

Another subject of our future work to which I need only touch now is the relations of the Government with the Native States. There is much unnecessary irritation and dissatisfaction where there ought to be the pleasantest harmony with much greater devoted loyalty than what even now really exists. And it is also a great mistake for a foreign power not to draw the military capacity and spirit of the country to their own side by giving it a fair career and interest in their own service. Make the military races feel it to their advantage and interest to be loyal to the British rule instead of keeping them alienated from the Government.

FELLOW FEELING AND COMMON NATIONALITY.

I need not say more upon our future work, as various Resolutions of importance will be placed before you for your consideration, and I am sure you will deliberate with that moderation and fairness for which you have already distinguished yourselves and acquired just credit, and for which I offer you my hearty congratulations. You recognise, I have no doubt, that at every turn you have yet serious questions to grapple with and much work to do.

Any one who has watched my public career must have seen that my main underlying principle and the desire of my heart is to promote, as far as I can, good fellow-feeling among all my countrymen. (*Loud applause.*) And I have no doubt that all the educated and thinking men and all true friends of our own country will continue to do all that lies in their power to bring about stronger and stronger friendly ties of common nationality, fellow-feeling and due deference to each other's views and feelings amongst the whole people of our country.

GOVERNMENT AND LAWLESSNESS.

Government must be firm and just in case of any unfortunate differences; as far as Government are concerned their duty is clearly to put down with a strong hand any lawlessness or disturbance of the peace, no matter who the parties concerned may be. They can only stand, as they ought, on the only sure and right foundation of even-handed justice to all, and cannot allow any one to take the law into his own hands; the only wise policy is to adhere to their declared policy of strict neutrality and equal protection and justice to all creeds. (*Hear, hear.*)

I was much pleased to read in the papers that cordial conferences had been held between Muhammadans and

Hindus in various places to device means to prevent any deplorable occurrences happening in the future.

HARMONY AND UNION BETWEEN DIFFERENT RACES.

Looking back to the past as my own personal experience of my life, and as far back as I know of earlier days, at least on my side of India, I feel a congratulation that all associations and societies of members of all creeds have worked together in harmony and union, without any consideration of class or creed in all matters concerning our common national public and political interests. No doubt, latterly, even in such common matters, differences of views have arisen and will arise, but such differences of views, when genuine, are healthy, just as is the case in the United Kingdom itself with its two political parties. (*Hear, hear.*)

What makes me still more gratified and look forward hopefully in the future is that our Congress has not only worked so far in the union and concord of all classes and creeds, but has taken care to provide that such harmony should continue in the future. As early as in the Congress at Allahabad of 1888, you passed this Resolution (XIII):—

> That no subject shall be passed for discussion by the Subjects Committee, or allowed to be discussed at any Congress by the President thereof, to the introduction of which the Hindu or Muhammadan delegates as a body object unanimously or nearly unanimously; and that if, after the discussion of any subject which has been admitted for discussion, it shall appear that all the Hindu or all the Muhammadan delegates as a body are unanimously or nearly unanimously opposed to the Resolution which it is proposed to pass thereon, such Resolution shall be dropped; provided that this rule shall refer only to subjects in regard to which the Congress has not already definitely pronounced an opinion.

As I have already said, the highest wish of my heart is that all the people of India should regard and treat each other as fellow-countrymen, with fellow-feeling for the good of all. (*Applause.*)

We may, I am convinced, rest fully assured that whatever political or national benefit we may acquire will in one or other way benefit all classes, (*Hear, hear.*) the benefit of each taking various forms. The interests of us all are the same. We are all in the same boat. We must sink or swim together. Government cannot but treat us all alike. It is unreasonable for us to expect from them, and unjust and unwise for them to show, any undue favour to any particular class or community. The only solid foundation for them is justice and impartiality, and the only just demand from us also can only be justice and impartiality. (*Loud applause.*)

If the country is prosperous, then if one gets scope in one walk of life, another will have in another walk of life. As our Indian saying goes: "If there is water in the well it will come to the cistern." If we have the well of prosperity we shall be able to draw each our share from it. But if the well is dry we must all go without any at all.

FOUNDATIONS OF BRITISH POWER IN INDIA.

A word for the basis upon which the strength of British power stands. Britain can hold India, or any one country can hold another, by moral force only. You can build up an empire by arms or ephemeral brute physical force, but you can preserve it by the eternal moral forces only. Brute force will, some time or other, break down; righteousness alone is everlasting. (*Cheers.*) Well and truly has Lord Ripon said "that the British power and influence rests upon the conviction of our good faith more than upon the valour of our soldiers or the reputation of our arms." (*Applause.*) Mr. Gladstone says:

> It is the predominance of that moral force for which I heartily pray in the deliberations of this House and the conduct of our whole public policy, for I am convinced that upon that predominance depends that which should be the first object of all our

desires, as it is of all our daily official prayers, namely, that union of heart and sentiment which constitutes the truest basis of strength at home, and therefore both of strength and good fame throughout the civilised world.—Debates, 9th August, 1892. p. 1892. *(Applause.)*

And here is a remarkable instance cited by Mr. Gladstone of a people of a different race becoming attached even to the much despised Turkish rule. How much more will the people of India, if contented and prosperous, become attached to the rule of such a people as the British? Referring to Lebanon, Mr. Gladstone said :—

> Owing to the wise efforts of Lord Dufferin and others about thirty years ago, local management was established since which the province has become contented and attached to the Turkish Empire.

Lord Roberts, the apostle of British strong arm to maintain British power, and though much imbued with many of the prejudices against the progress of the Indians, as a true soldier, admits without hesitation what he considers as the only solid foundation upon which British strength must for ever rest. He says :

> But however efficient and well-equipped the army of India may be, were it indeed absolute perfection and were its numbers considerably more than they are at present, our greatest strength must ever rest on the firm base of a united and contented India.

Truer and more statesmanlike words could not be uttered. Permit me to give one more extract. Mr. Gladstone, referring to Irish Home Rule, said :

> There can be no nobler spectacle than that which we think is now drawing upon us, the spectacle of a nation deliberately set on the removal of injustice, deliberately determined to break, not through terror and not in haste, but under the sole influence of duty and honour, determined to break with whatever remains still existing of an evil tradition, and determined in that way at once to pay a debt of justice and to consult by a bold, wise, and good act its own interests and its own honour.

Am I at all unreasonable in hoping that such noble statesmanship, honour, and good faith of the British people will, in fullness of time, also extend to India similar justice? I shall hope as long as I live.

INDIAN NATIONALITY.

Let us always remember that we are all children of our mother country. Indeed, I have never worked in any other spirit than that I am an Indian, (*cheers.*) and owe duty to my country and all my countrymen. Whether I am a Hindu, a Muhammadan, a Parsi, a Christian, or of any other creed, I am above all an Indian. Our country is India; our nationality is Indian. (*Loud cheers.*)

The question for us, especially a body like this, who have received the blessings of education, is: How are we to perform our duty to our country? Certainly no one requires to be taught that no great cause or object can ever be accomplished without great sacrifices—personal and pecuniary. We can never succeed with the British people by mere declamations. We must show that we believe in the justice of our cause by our earnestness and self-sacrifice. (*Hear, hear.*)

LEARN TO MAKE SACRIFICES.

I desire now to impress upon my countrymen with all the earnestness I am capable of to prepare themselves for sacrifices. We observe every day what sacrifices the British people make for attaining any object, great or small and how persistently they stick to it; and among the lessons which we are learning from them let us learn this particular one, with the double advantage and effect of showing that Indians have public spirit and love of their country, and also proving that they are earnest in what they are asking. (*Applause.*)

ORGANISED EFFORTS.

Our work for the amelioration of our country and for obtaining all the rights and benefits of British citizenship will go on increasing, and it is absolutely necessary that our organization, both here and in the United Kingdom, should be much improved and made complete. Without good organization no important work can be successfully done; and that means much pecuniary and personal sacrifice. We must remember the Congress meets once a year. The General Secretaries and the Standing Committees have to carry out the details and inform the circles of the work and resolutions of the Congress.

CONGRESS WORK IN LONDON.

But the most important and national work formulated by the Congress has to be done with watchfulness, day after day, in London by your British Committee. (*Cheers.*) And, further, by your Resolution XII, of the seventh Session, you "urged them (the Committee) to widen henceforth the sphere of their usefulness by interesting themselves not only in those questions dealt with by the Congress, but in all Indian matters submitted to them and properly vouched for in which any principle accepted by the Congress is involved." (*Renewed cheering.*)

Fancy what this means. Why, it is another India Office! You have put all India's every-day work upon the shoulders of the Committee. It becomes exceedingly necessary for efficient and good work to have some paid person or persons to devote time to study the merits of all the representations which pour in with every mail, or by telegrams, before any action can be taken on them. It is in the United Kingdom that all our great fights are to be fought, all our national and imperial questions are to be settled, and it is to our British Committee in London that we have to look for the performance of all this responsible and arduous work, with the unfortunate feature that we have to contend against many adverse influences, prepossessions and misunderstandings. We have to make the British people unlearn a good deal.

On the other hand, we have this hopeful feature also that we have not only many British friends, but also Anglo-Indians, who, in the true spirit of justice and of the gratitude to the country to which they owe their past career and future provision, appreciate the duty they owe to India, and are desirous to help us, and to preserve the British Empire by the only certain means of justice, the honour and righteousness of the British people, and by the contentment and prosperity of India.

You know well how much we owe to the present English members of our Committee, Sir William Wedderburn, *(Three cheers for Sir William Wedderburn.)* Mr. Hume, Mr. Reynolds, Mr. Adam, Mr. Schwann, M.P., and Mr. McLaren, M.P., If we want all such help at the fountain head of power without which we cannot do much good, we must take care to supply them always, promptly and accurately, all necessary sinews of war. (*Hear, hear.*)

CONGRESS ORGAN "INDIA."

Then there is the journal "INDIA," without which our work will not be half as efficient as with it. It is an absolute necessity as an instrument and part of the organization. Every possible effort must be made to give it the widest circulation possible both hear and in the United Kingdom. I wish it could be made weekly instead of monthly.

With proper effort ten-thousand copies should be easily disposed of here as a beginning, and we must do this.

DADABAHI'S ELECTION TO THE BRITISH PARLIAMENT.

This is the first opportunity I have of meeting you after the Congress of 1886, over which I had the honour to preside at Calcutta. Let me now thank you personally for your constant remembrance of me, for your unceasing encouragement, and for your two most kind and gratifying resolutions passed at the last two sessions as representatives of every class and creed, and almost wholly consisting of Hindu and Muhammadan delegates, and each delegate being elected by and representative of the whole mixed community of the place he represents, on the basis of common interest and nationality. . . .

I need not say how right earnestly Central Finsbury listened to your appeal and fulfilled your hope, for which we owe them our most unstinted thanks, and to all those who helped in or out of Central Finsbury. (*Cheers.*)

I may hear once more express my hearty thanks to many ladies and gentlemen who worked hard for my election. After I was elected, you passed the second Resolution (XIV.) in the last Session. I may point here to the significant incident that in that Congress there was, I think, only one Parsi delegate and he even not the delegate of Parsis, but of all classes of the people.

DADABHI RETURNS THANKS TO ALL INDIANS.

Let me also now take this opportunity, on Indian soil, to tender my most heartfelt thanks for the telegrams, letters, and addresses of congratulation which I received from all parts and classes of India—literally I may say from the prince to the peasant, from members of all creeds, from Hindus, Muhammadans, Christians, Parsis, from Ceylon, from the High Priest of Buddhists, and Buddhists, and other residents from the Cape, British Guiana, Australia, and in short from every part of the British Empire where there were Indian residents. Ladies and Gentlemen, put aside my personality and let me join in your rejoicings as an Indian in the great event in Indian annals of an

Indian finding his way in the Imperial Parliament. (*Loud and prolonged cheering*).

And lastly, beginning from the distant Western Gate of India, where the Indian residents of Aden, of all creeds, gave me a most hearty reception; then the great portal of India, the dear old City of my birth, gave me a most magnificent welcome with its never-ceasing kindness towards me, Poona doing her best to vie with Bombay, and through the Punjab so splendidly; and this series of welcome now ending in your extraordinary one which I am utterly unable to describe. Is there any reward more grand and more gratifying than the esteem, the joy with my joy, the sorrow with my sorrow, and above all the "unshaken confidence" of my fellow-countrymen and country-women of our grand, old, beloved country?

I may refer to an incident which, as it is satisfactory, is also very significant of the real desire of the British people to do justice to India. The congratulations on my election from all parts of the United Kingdom also were as hearty and warm as we could desire, and expressing satisfaction that an Indian would be able to voice the wants and aspirations of India in the House of Commons.

LONDON CONGRESS.

I can assure the Congress that, as I hope and wish, if you will pay an early visit to the United Kingdom and hold a Session there, you will obtain a kind and warm reception from its peoples. And you will, by such direct and personal appeal to the British Nation, accomplish a vast amount of good. (*Hear, hear.*)

FAITH IN BRITISH FAIR-PLAY AND JUSTICE.

Our fate and our future are in our own hands. If we are true to ourselves and to our country and make all the necessary sacrifices for our elevation and amelioration, I, for one have not the shadow of a doubt that in dealing with such justice-loving, fair-minded people as the British we may rest fully assured that we shall not work in vain. It is this conviction which has supported me against all difficulties. I have never faltered in my faith in the British character and have always believed that the time will come when the sentiments of the British Nation and our Gracious Sovereign proclaimed to us in our Great Charter of the Proclamation of 1858 will be realised, (*Applause.*) *viz.*, "In their prosperity will be our strength, in their contentment our best reward." And let us join in the prayer that followed this hopeful declaration of our Sovereign: "May the God of all power grant to us and to those in authority under us strength to carry out these our wishes for the good of our people."

DADABHAI'S EXHORTATION.

My last prayer and exhortation to the Congress and to all my countrymen is—Go on united and earnest, in concord and harmony, with moderation, with loyalty to the British rule and patriotism towards our country, and success is sure to attend our efforts for our just demands, and the day I hope is not distant when the World will see the noblest spectacle of a great nation like the British holding out the hand of true fellow-citizenship and of justice to the vast mass of humanity of this great and ancient land of India with benefits and blessings to the human race. (*Loud and prolonged cheering.*)

Twenty-Second Congress—Calcutta—1906.

—:o:—

PRESIDENTIAL ADDRESS.

INTRODUCTION.

Raja Peari Mohun Mukerjee, Dr. Rashbehari Ghose, and my friends,—I thank you from the bottom of my heart for proposing me to be the President of the Indian National Congress on this occasion. You may rest assured that I feel from the bottom of my heart the honour that you have done me and in my humble way I would fulfil the important duty you have called me to perform. I cannot undertake at present to read my whole address though I expected I would be able to do so. I would ask my friend Mr. Gokhale to read it for me. I would just make the beginning and say that I thank you most sincerely for honouring me for the third time by electing me to the Presidentship of the Indian National Congress. I hope I shall have your co-operation, help and support. I am obliged to express my deep sorrow at the losses which the country has sustained by the deaths of Mr. W. C. Bonnerjee, Mr. Anand Mohan Bose, Mr. Budruddin Tyabji and Mr. M. Veeraraghava Chariar.

Mr. Gokhale then read the following Presidential Address at the request of Mr. Dadabhai Naoroji :—

PRESIDENT'S ADDRESS.

"Good government could never be a substitute for government by the people themselves."—*Sir Henry Campbell-Bannerman, Stirling,* 23-11-1905.

"But this I do say that political principles are after all the root of our national greatness, strength and hope."
—*Mr. John Morley, King's Hall, Holborn*, 4-6-1901.

"But if you meddle wrongly with economic things, gentlemen, be very sure you are then going to the very life, to the heart, to the core of your national existence."—*Free-Trade Hall, Manchester*, 19-10-1903.

Ladies and Gentlemen,—I thank you most sincerely for honouring me for the third time with the Presidentship of the Indian National Congress. I hope I shall have your cordial help and support.

I may here express my deep sorrow at the loss India has suffered in the deaths of Mr. W. C. Bonnerjee, Justice Budruddin Tyabji, Mr. Anand Mohan Bose and Mr. Veeraraghava Chariar.

I offer my sincere thanks to the "Parliament Branch of the United Irish League," the Breakfast Meeting, the North Lambeth Liberal and Radical Club and the National Democratic League for their enthusiastic and cordial god-speed to me.

This is the first Congress after its having come of age. It is time that we should carefully consider what the position of the Indians is at present and what their future should be.

In considering this important matter I do not intend to repeat my lamentations over the past. I want only to look to the future.

The work of the Congress consists of two parts:—

First and most important is the question of the policy and principles of the system of government under which India ought to be governed in the future.

Second is to watch the operation of the administration as it now exists, to propose from time to time any reforms and changes that may be deemed necessary to be made in the various departments, till the present system of government is radically altered and based upon right principles and policy in the accomplishment of the first part mentioned above.

I desire to devote my address mainly to the first part of the work of the Congress, *viz.*, the policy and principles which ought to govern India in future.

What position do the Indians hold in the British Empire? Are they British citizens or not is my first question? I say we are British citizens and are entitled to and claim all British citizen's rights.

I shall first lay before you my reasons for claiming that we are British citizens.

REASON I, THE BIRTHRIGHT.

The acknowledgment of this birthright was declared on the very first occasion when England obtained the very first territorial and sovereign possession in India. The British statesmen of the day at once acted upon the fundamental basis of the British constitution and character that any one who came howsoever and wheresoever, under the British flag, was a free British citizen "as if born and living in England."

The fundamental basis in the words of the present Prime Minister is :—

> Freedom is the very breath of our life . . . . We stand for liberty, our policy is the policy of freedom.

In the words of Mr. Morley :—

> Yes, gentlemen, the sacred word "free" which represents as Englishmen have always thought until to-day the noblest aspiration that can animate the breast of man.

This birthright to be "free" or to have freedom is our right from the very beginning of our connection with England when we came under the British flag.

When Bombay was acquired as the very first territorial possession, the Government of the day in the very first grant of territorial rights to the East India Company declared thus:

Extract from the "Grant to the First East India Company of the Island of Bombay, dated 24th March 1669.":—

And it is declared that all persons being His Majesty's subjects inhabiting within the said Island and their children and their posterity born within the limits thereof shall be deemed free denizens and natural subjects "as if living and born in England."

And further all the terms of the first grant are extended in it to all future British territorial acquisitions. Thus is the claim of Indians to be "free" and to all the rights of British natural subjects "as if living and born in England" are distinctly acknowledged and declared from the very first political connection with England.

Having given the declaration made some two and a half centuries back in the 17th century that the moment we Indians came under the British flag we were "free" citizens, I next give you what two of the prominent statesmen of this the 20th century have said. When the Boers were defeated and subjugated, and came under the British flag, the present Prime Minister said on the 14th June 1901:—

These people with whom we are dealing are not only going to be our fellow-citizens; they are our fellow-citizens already.

Sir William Harcourt at the same time said:—

This is the way in which you propose to deal with your fellow-citizens.

Thus the moment a people came under the British flag they are "free" and British "fellow-citizens." We Indians have been free British citizens as our birthright, "as if born and living in England" from the first moment we came under the British Flag.

The Boer War cost Britain more than two hundred millions and 20,000 dead, and 20,000 wounded. India, on the other hand, has enriched Britain instead of costing anything—and yet this is a strange contrast. The Boers have already obtained self-government in a few years after conquest, while India has not yet received self-government though it is more than 200 years from the commencement of the political connection.

All honour and glory to the British instincts and principles and to the British statesmen of the 17th century. The Liberals of the present day and the Liberal Government have every right to be proud of those "old principles" and now that a happy and blessed revival of those sacred old principles has taken place, the present Government ought fairly to be expected to act upon those old principles, and to acknowledge and give effect to the birthright of Indians "as if living and born in England." England is bound to do this. Our British rights are beyond all question. Every British Indian subject has franchise in England as a matter of course, and even to become a Member of Parliament. Nobody in England dreams of objecting to it. Once in my case, from party motives, an objection was suggested to entering my name on the register as an elector, and the revising barrister at once brushed aside the objection, for that as an Indian, I was a British citizen.

REASON II, PLEDGED RIGHTS.

The grant to the first East India Company cited in Reason 1, is both a declaration of the rights of Indians as British citizens as well as a pledge of those rights by that declaration.

Queen Victoria, in her letter to Lord Derby asking him to write the Proclamation himself, said :—

> And point out the privileges which the Indians will receive in being placed on an equality with the subjects of the British Crown and prosperity flowing in the train of civilization.

Thereupon the Proclamation then declared and pledged unreservedly and most solemnly calling God to witness and bless :—

> We hold ourselves bound to the Natives of our Indian Territories by the same obligations of duty which bind us to our other subjects, and these obligations by the blessing of Almighty God we shall faithfully and conscientiously fulfil.

Can there be a more sacred and solemn pledge before God and man?

On the occasion of the Proclamation of the Queen as Empress of India, she sent a telegram to Lord Lytton which he read in the open Durbar consisting of both Princes and Peoples. In this telegram the Queen Empress said :—

> That from the highest to the humblest all may feel that under our rule, the great principles of liberty, equity and justice are secured to them, and that to promote their happiness, to add to their prosperity and advance their welfare are ever present aims and objects of our Empire.

And it is clear that this object of promoting our happiness, etc., etc., can only be attained by our enjoyment of the principles of liberty, equity and justice, *i. e.*, we must have the British liberty of governing ourselves.

On the occasion of the Jubilee of 1887, the Queen-Empress again pledged and emphasised the pledges of the Proclamation thus :—

> Allusion is made to the Proclamation issued on the occasion of my assumption of the direct government of India, as the Charter of the liberties of the Princes and Peoples of India. It has always been and will be continued to be my earnest desire that the principles of that Proclamation should be unswervingly maintained.

We are now asking nothing more or less than the liberties of our Charter,—our rights of British citizenship.

The present King-Emperor has pledged :—

> I shall endeavour to follow the great example of the first Queen-Empress to work for the general well-being of my Indian subjects of all ranks.

Again, the King-Emperor in his speech, on 19th February, 1906, said :—

> It is my earnest hope that in these Colonies as elsewhere *throughout my dominions* (the italics are mine) the grant of free institutions will be followed by an increasing prosperity and loyalty to the Empire.

And the Prime Minister clinches the whole, that :—

> Good government could never be a substitute for government by the people themselves.

How much less is then an economically evil government and constitutionally an unconstitutional despotic government, a substitute for self-government,—and how much absolutely necessary it is to produce "increasing prosperity and loyalty to the Empire," by "the grant of free institutions."

With the solemn pledges I have mentioned above, we have every right to claim an honourable fulfilment of all our British pledged rights. And so we claim all British rights as our birthright and as our solemnly pledged rights. Britain's duty, humanity, honour, instincts and traditions for freedom, solemn pledges, conscience, righteousness, and civilization demand the satisfaction to us of our British rights.

REASON III, REPARATION.

All our sufferings and evils of the past centuries demand before God and man a reparation, which we may fairly expect from the present revival of the old noble British instincts of liberty and self-government. I do not enter into our past sufferings as I have already said at the outset.

REASON IV, CONSCIENCE.

The British people would not allow themselves to be subjected for a single day to such an unnatural system of government as the one which has been imposed upon India for nearly a century and a half. Sir H. Campbell-Bannerman has made a happy quotation from Mr. Bright :—

> I remember John Bright quoting in the House of Commons on one occasion two lines of a poet with reference to political matters :—
>
> There is on Earth a yet diviner thing,
> Veiled though it be, than Parliament or King.

Then Sir Henry asks :—

> What is that diviner thing ? It is the human conscience inspiring human opinion and human sympathy.

I ask them to extend that human conscience, "the diviner thing," to India in the words of Mr. Morley :—

> It will be a bad day indeed if we have one conscience for the Mother Country and another conscience for all that vast territory over which your eye does not extend.

And now the next question is : What are the British rights which we have a right to "claim ?"

This is not the occasion to enter into any details or argument. I keep to broad lines.

(1) Just as the administration of the United Kingdom in all services, departments and details is in the hands of the people themselves of that country, so should we in India claim that the administration in all services, departments and details should be in the hands of the people themselves of India.

This is not only a matter of right and matter of the aspirations of the educated—important enough as these matters are—but it is far more an absolute necessity as the only remedy for the great inevitable economic evil which Sir John Shore pointed out a hundred and twenty years ago, and which is the fundamental cause of the present drain and poverty. The remedy is absolutely necessary for the material, moral, intellectual, political, social, industrial and every possible progress and welfare of the people of India.

(2) As in the United Kingdom and the Colonies all taxation and legislation and the power of spending the taxes are in the hands of the representatives of the people of those countries, so should also be the rights of the people of India.

(3) All financial relations between England and India must be just and on a footing of equality, *i.e.*, whatever money India may find towards expenditure in any department—Civil or Military or Naval—to the extent of that share should Indians share in all the benefits of that expenditure in salaries, pensions, emoluments, materials, etc., as a partner in the Empire, as she is always declared to be. We do not ask any favours. We want only justice. Instead of going into any further divisions or details of our rights as British citizens, the whole matter can be compromised in one word—"Self-Government" or *Swaraj* like that of the United Kingdom or the Colonies.

Mr. Morley says very truly and emphatically (Banquet, King's Hall, Holborn, 4th June 1901) :—

> But this I do say that political principles are after all the root of our national greatness, strength and hope.

So, for India also, there can be no national greatness, strength and hope except by the right political principles of self-government.

Now the next important question is, whether it is practicable to grant these rights of self-government at once or when and in what way? Nobody would, I think, say that the whole present machinery can be suddenly broken up at once and the rights which I have defined of self-government can be at once introduced.

RIGHT NO. I, EMPOYMENT IN THE PUBLIC SERVICES.

The right of placing all administration in every department in the hands of the people of India. Has the time arrived to do anything loyally, faithfully and systematically as a beginning at once, so that it may automatically develop into the full realisation of the right of self-government?

I say,—yes. Not only has the time fully arrived but had arrived long past, to make this beginning. The statesmen of nearly three-quarters of a century ago not only considered the point of making a beginning, not merely made a pious declaration, but they actually passed an Act of Parliament for the purpose. Had that Act been honourably and faithfully fulfilled by the Government from that time to this, both England and India would have been in the position, not of bewailing the present poverty, wretchedness and dissatisfaction of the Indian people, but of rejoicing in the prosperity of India and of still greater prosperity of England herself.

In the thirties of the last century, England achieved the highest glory of civilization by its emancipation of the body and soul of man—by abolishing slavery and by freedom of conscience to enjoy all the rights of British citizenship. During these glorious days of English history, the statesmen of the time did not forget their duty to the people of India. They specially and openly considered the question of self-government of India, not only in connection with Britain, but even with the result of entire independence from Britain. When the Act of 1833 was passed

Macaulay made that memorable speech about the duty of Britain towards India, of which Britain shall for ever be proud. I cannot quote that whole speech here. Every word of it is worth study and consideration from the statesmen of the day. I shall give only a few extracts. He first said :

> "I must say that, to the last day of my life, I shall be proud of having been one of those who assisted in the framing of the Bill which contains that Clause" . . . "It would be on the most selfish view of the case far better for us that the people of India were well governed and independent of us than ill-governed and subject to us." . . . "We shall never consent to administer the *pousta* (a preparation of opium) to a whole community—to stupify and paralyse a great people, whom God has committed to our charge, for the wretched purpose of rendering them more amenable to our control." . . "We are free, we are civilized, to little purpose, if we grudge to any portion of the human race an equal measure of freedom and civilization." . ." I have no fears. The path of duty is plain before us and it is also the path of wisdom, of national prosperity, of national, honour." . . . "To have found a great people sunk in the lowest depths of slavery and superstition, to have so ruled them as to have made them desirous and capable of all the privileges of citizens, would, indeed, be a title to glory all our own."

Such was the glorious spirit in and auspices under which was enacted in Macaulay's words "that wise, that benevolent, that noble clause" :—

> That no native of the said territory, nor any natural born subject of His Majesty, resident therein, shall by reason only of his religion, place of birth, descent, colour or any of them, be disabled from holding any place, office or employment under the said company.

I would not repeat here what I have often stated about this clause. Sufficient to say that simultaneous examinations in India have been declared authoritatively as the only honourable fulfilment of the clause.

Here is, then, the beginning that can be made at once not as a new thing but as one fully considered and settled by Act of Parliament 73 years ago. The power is ready in the hands of the Secretary of State for India to be put into execution at once without the necessity of any reference to Parliament or any authority.

And, in connection with this step, I would earnestly urge upon the Secretary of State to retrace the pernicious step which has lately been taken in India of abolishing competition for the services to which admission is made directly in India. In England, competition is the basis of all first admissions in all the services, and the same must be the basis in India as the fairest and most in accordance with justice.

This beginning will be the key, the most effective remedy for the chief economic and basic evil of the present system.

Mr. Morley has truly said :—

> But if you meddle wrongly with economic things, Gentlemen, be very sure you are then going to the very life, to the heart, to the core of your national existence.

And so the economic muddle of the existing policy is going to the life, to the heart, to the core of our national existence. A three-fold wrong is inflicted upon us, *i.e.*, of depriving us of wealth, work and wisdom, of everything, in short, worth living for. And this beginning will begin to strike at the root of the muddle. The reform of the alteration of the services from European to Indian is the keynote of the whole.

On the score of efficiency also foreign service can never be efficient or sufficient. Sir William Hunter has said :—

> If we are to govern the Indian people efficiently and cheaply, we must govern by means of themselves.

The Duke of Devonshire, as Indian Secretary, has said (23rd August 1883) :

> There can in my opinion be very little doubt that India is insufficiently governed.

In the very nature of things it cannot be otherwise.

After the simultaneous examinations are carried on for some years, it will be time to transfer the examinations altogether to India to complete the accomplishment of the rights (No. 1) of self-government without any disturbance in the smooth working of the administration.

Co-ordinately with this important beginning for Right (No. 1) it is urgent to expedite this object that education must be most vigorously disseminated among the people—free and compulsory primary education, and free higher education of every kind. The Indian people will hail with the greatest satisfaction any amount of expenditure for the purpose of education. It was free education that I had at the expense of the people that made me and others of my fellow-students and subsequent fellow-workers to give their best to the service of the people for the promotion of their welfare.

Education on the one hand, and actual training in administration on the other hand, will bring the accomplishment of self-government far more speedily than many imagine.

Heavy expenditure should be no excuse. In fact, if financial justice, to which I shall refer hereafter, is done in the relations between England and India, there will be ample provision even from the poor revenues of India—and with every addition of Indians in place of Europeans, the resources of India for all necessary purposes will go on increasing.

RIGHT NO. II, REPRESENTATION.

In England itself Parliamentary Government existed for some hundreds of years before even the rich and middle classes and the mass of the people had any voice or vote in it.

Macaulay pointed out in 1831 that the people living in the magnificent palaces surrounding Regent's Park and in other such places were unrepresented. It is only so late as 1832 that the middle classes obtained their vote, and it is only so late as 1885 that most of the mass of the people obtained their franchise. Women have no vote. Adult franchise is yet in struggle.

It is no use telling us, therefore, that a good beginning cannot be made now in India for what Mr. Gladstone called "living representation." The only thing needed is the willingness of the Government. The statesmen at the helm of the present Government are quite competent and able to make a good beginning—such a systematic beginning as that it may naturally in no long time develop itself into full legislatures of self-government like those of the self-governing colonies. I need not go into any details here of the scope and possibilities of representation. The educated and thinking classes in India who have attended English schools and colleges are not the only people to be reckoned with. There is a large body who now are informed of the events of the world and of all British institutions by the vernacular press and literature in their own language.

The peasants of Russia are fit for and obtained the Duma from the greatest autocrat in the world, and the leading statesman, the Prime Minister of the free British Empire, proclaimed to the world, "the Duma is dead, long live the Duma!" Surely the fellow-citizens of that statesman and the free citizens of that Empire by birthright and pledged rights are far more entitled to self-government, a constitutional representative system, than the peasants of Russia. I do not despair. It is futile to tell me that we must wait till all the people are ready. The British people did not so wait for their Parliament. We are not allowed to be fit for 150 years. We can never be fit till we actually undertake the work and the responsibility. While China in the East and Persia in the West of Asia are awakening and Japan has already awakened, and Russia is struggling for emancipation—and all of them despotisms—can the free citizens of the British Indian Empire continue to remain subject to despotism—the people who were among the first civilizers of the world? Modern world owes no little gratitude to these early civilizers of the human race. Are the descendants of the earliest civilizers to remain, in the present times of spreading emancipation, under the barbarous system of despotism, unworthy of British instincts, principles and civilization?

RIGHT NO. III, JUST FINANCIAL RELATIONS.

This right requires no delay or training. If the British Government wills to do what is just and right, this justice towards self-government can be done at once.

First of all take the European Army expenditure. The Government of India in its despatch of 25th March 1890, says :—

> Millions of money have been spent on increasing the Army in India, on armaments, and on fortifications to provide for the security of India, not against domestic enemies or to prevent the invasions of the warlike peoples of adjoining countries, but to maintain the supremacy of British Power in the East.

Again, the Government of India says :—

> It would be much nearer the truth to affirm that the Imperial Government keeps in India and quarters upon the revenues of that country as large a portion of its army as it thinks can possibly be required to maintain its dominion there, that it habitually treats that portion of its army as a reserve force available for imperial purposes ; that it has uniformly detached European regiments

from the garrison of India to take part in imperial wars whenever it has been found necessary or convenient to do so; and more than this that it has drawn not less freely upon the native army of India towards the maintenance of which it contributes nothing to aid it in contests outside of India with which the Indian Government has had little or no concern.

Such is the testimony of the Government of India that the European Army is for Imperial purposes.

Now I give the view taken in the India Office itself.

Sir James Peile was a member of the Council of the Secretary of State for India, and represented the Indian Secretary on the Royal Commission (Welby's) on Indian expenditure. Sir James Peile, in a motion, after pointing out that the military policy which regulated Indian military expenditure was not exclusively Indian, urged that :—

It is worthy of consideration how far it is equitable to charge on a dependency the whole military cost of that policy, when that dependency happens to be the only part of the Empire which has a land frontier adjacent to the territory of a great European power.

Here then these extracts of the Government of India and the India Office show that the European Army expenditure is entirely for British imperial purposes, and yet with flagrant injustice the burden is thrown by the Treasury upon the helpless Indian people.

In the same way all the Government expenditure in England which entirely goes to the benefit of the people in England, and which is for British purposes, is imposed on the Indian people while the Colonies do not pay any portion for similar expenditure in England. This expenditure should in common justice not be imposed on India. It is unjust. Here then, if we are relieved of burdens which ought not in common justice to be imposed upon us, our revenues, poor as they are at present, will supply ample means for education and many other reforms and improvements which are needed by us. This question is simply a matter of financial justice. I have put it on a clear just principle and on that principle India can be quite ready to find the money and its own men for all her own needs—Military, Naval, Civil or any other. For imperial expenditure we must have our share in the services in proportion to our contribution.

These just financial relations can be established at once. They require no delay or preparation. It only needs the determination and will of the British Government to do justice. Lastly, as to self-government. If the British people and statesmen make up their mind to do their duty towards the Indian people, they have every ability and statesmanship to devise means to accord self-government within no distant time. If there is the will and the conscience, there is the way.

Now I come to the most crucial question—particularly crucial to myself personally.

I have been for some time past repeatedly asked whether I really have, after more than half a century of my own personal experience, such confidence in the honour and good faith of British statesmen and Government as to expect that our just claims to self-government as British citizens will be willingly and gracefully accorded to us with every honest effort in their power, leaving alone and forgetting the past.

Ladies and gentlemen, I shall give you a full and free answer.

In 1853, when I made my first little speech at the inauguration of the Bombay Association, in perfect innocence of heart influenced by my English education into great admiration for the character, instincts and struggles for liberty of the British people, I expressed my faith and confidence in the British Rulers in a short speech from which I give a short extract :—

When we see that our Government is often ready to assist us in everything calculated to benefit us, we had better than merely complain and grumble, point out in a becoming manner what our real wants are.

And I also said :

If an association like this be always in readiness to ascertain by strict enquiries the probable good or bad effects of any proposed measure and, whenever necessary, to memorialise Government on behalf of the people with respect to them, our kind Government will not refuse to listen to such memorials.

Such was my faith. It was this faith of the educated of the time that made Sir Bartle Frere make the remark which Mr. Fawcett quoted, *viz.*, that he had been much struck with the fact that the ablest exponents of English policy and our best coadjutors in adapting that policy to the wants of the various nations occupying Indian soil were to be found among the natives who had received a high-class English education. And now, owing to the non-fulfilment of solemn pledges, what a change has taken place in the mind of the educated !

Since my early efforts, I must say that I have felt so many disappointments as would be sufficient to break any heart and lead one to despair and even, I am afraid, to rebel.

My disappointments have not been of the ordinary kind but far worse and keener. Ordinarily a person fights—and if he fails he is disappointed. But I fought and won on several occasions, but the executive did not let us have the fruit of those victories—disappointments quite enough, as I have said, to break one's heart. For instance, the "Statutory" Civil Service, Simultaneous Examinations, Lord Lawrence Scholarships, Royal Commission, etc. I am thankful that the repayment from the Treasury of some unjust charges has been carried out, though the Indian Secretary's salary is not yet transferred to the Treasury as it was hoped.

But I have not despaired. Not only that I have not despaired, but at this moment, you may think it strange, I stand before you with hopefulness. I have not despaired for one reason—and I am hopeful for another reason.

I have not despaired under the influence of the good English word which has been the rule of my life. That word is "Persevere." In any movement, great or small, you must persevere to the end. You cannot stop at any stage, disappointments notwithstanding, or you lose all you have gained and find it far more difficult afterwards even to begin again. As we proceed, we may adopt such means as may be suitable at every stage, but persevere we must to *the end*. If our cause is good and just, as it is, we are sure to triumph in the end. So I have not despaired.

Now to the reason of my hopefulness which I feel at this moment after all my disappointments. And this also under the influence of one word "Revival"—the present "revival" of the true old spirit and instinct of liberty and free British institutions in the hearts of the leading statesmen of the day. I shall now place before you the declarations of some of the leading statesmen of the day and then you will judge that my faith and hope are well-founded, whether they will be justified or not by future events.

Here, I give you a few of those declarations. But I give an Appendix A of some of these declarations out of many.

SIR H. CAMPBELL-BANNERMAN.

We believe in self-government. We treat it not as an odious necessity, not as a foolish theory to which unfortunately the British Empire is committed. We treat it as a blessing and a healing, a sobering and a strengthening influence.—Bradford 15-5-1901.

I remain as firm a believer as ever I was in the virtue of self-government.—Ayr, 29-10-1902.

But here is another—Self-government and popular control—and we believe in that principle.

MR. JOHN MORLEY.

Yes, gentlemen, the sacred word 'free' which represented, as Englishmen have always thought until to-day, the noblest aspirations that can animate the breast of man.—Palmerston Club, 9-6-1900.

In his view the root of good government was not to be found in bureaucracy or pedantocracy. They must seek to rouse up the free and spontaneous elements lying deep in the hearts and minds of the people of the country.—Arbroath, 23-10-1903.

The study of the present revival of the spirit, instincts and traditions of Liberty and Liberalism among the Liberal statesmen of the day has produced in my heart full expectation that the end of the evil system, and the dawn of a righteous and liberal policy of freedom and self-government are at hand for India. I trust that I am justified in my expectations and hopefulness.

Ladies and gentlemen, we have all the powerful moral forces of justice, righteousness and honour of Britain, but our birthright and pledged rights and the absolute necessity and humanity of ending quickly all the sufferings of the masses of the people, from poverty, famine, plague, destitution and degradation, etc. On our side if we use those moral forces, which are very effective on a people like the British people, we must, we are bound to, win. What is wanted for us is to learn the lesson from Englishmen themselves—to agitate most largely and most perseveringly by petitions, demonstrations and meetings, all quite peacefully but enthusiastically conducted. Let us not throw away our rights and moral forces which are so overwhelming on our side. I shall say something again on this subject.

With such very hopeful and promising views and declarations of some of the leaders of the present Government, we have also coming to our side more and more Parliament, Press and Platform. We have some 200 Members in the Indian Parliamentary Committee. The Labour Members, the Irish Nationalist Members, and the Radicals are sympathetic with us. We have several Liberal papers such as "The Daily News," "The Tribune," "The Morning Leader," "The Manchester Guardian," "The Star," "The Daily Chronicle," "Justice," "Investors' Review," "Reynolds," "New Age," and several others taking a juster view of India's rights and needs. We must make "India" a powerful organ. We have all sections of the Labour or Democratic Party, the British Nationalist Party, the Radicals and Liberals generally taking larger interest in Indian matters. The large section of the British people, to whom conscience and righteousness are above every possible worldly thing, are also awakening to a sense of their duty to the vast population of India in their dire distress and poverty, with all its dreadful consequences. When I was in Parliament and the only Indian, I had the support of the Irish, Radical and Labour Members. I never felt helpless and alone, and I succeeded in several of my efforts. We must have many Indian Members in Parliament till we get self-government. Under such favourable circumstances let us not fail to make the most of our opportunity for our political emancipation. Let us, it is true, at the same time do, what is in our power, to advance our social and industrial progress. But for our political emancipation, it will be a great folly and misfortune for us to miss this good fortune when it has at last come to us, though I fully admit we had enough of disappointments to make us lose heart and confidence.

I base my hope upon the "revival" of the old British love of liberty and self-government, of honour for pledges, of our right of fellow British citizenship. Within the short life, that may yet be vouchsafed to me, I hope to see a loyal, honest, honourable and conscientious adoption of the policy for self-government for India—and a beginning made at once towards that end.

I have not expressed to you my hopes and reasons for such hopes for ourselves. But as the Moral Law, the greatest force of the Universe, has it,—in our good will be England's own greatest good. Bright has wisely said :—

> The good of England must come through the channels of the good of India. . . . In order that England may become rich, India itself must become rich.

Mr. Morley has rightly said :—

> No, gentlemen, every single right thing that is done by the Legislature, however moderate be its area, every single right thing is sure to lead to the doing of a great number of unforeseen right things.—Dundee, 9-12-1889.

If India is allowed to be prosperous by self-government, as the Colonies have become prosperous by self-government, what a vista of glory and benefits open up for the citizens of the British Empire, and for mankind, as an example and proof of the supremacy of the moral law and true civilization!

While we put the duty of leading us on to self-government on the heads of the present British statesmen, we have also the duty upon ourselves to do all we can to support those statesmen by, on the one hand, preparing our Indian people for the right understanding, exercise and enjoyment of self-government and, on the other hand, of convincing the British people that we justly claim and must have all British rights. I put before the Congress my suggestions for their consideration. To put the matter in right form, we should send our "Petition of Rights" to His Majesty the King-Emperor, to the House of Commons and to the House of Lords. By the British Bill of Rights of 1689—by the 5th Clause—"the subjects have the right to present petitions to the Sovereign."

The next thing I suggest for your consideration is that the well-to-do Indians should raise a large fund of patriotism. With this fund we should organise a body of able men and good speakers, to go to all the nooks and corners of India and inform the people in their own languages of our British rights and how to exercise and enjoy them. Also to send to England another body of able speakers, and to provide means to go throughout the country and by large meetings to convince the British people that we justly claim and must have all British rights of self-government. By doing that I am sure that the British conscience will triumph and the British people will support the present statesmen in their work of giving India responsible self-government in the shortest possible period. We must have a great agitation in England, as well as here. The struggle against the Corn Laws cost, I think, two millions, and there was a great agitation. Let us learn to help ourselves in the same way.

I have said at the beginning that the duties of this Congress are twofold. And of the two, the claim to a change of the present policy leading to self-government is the chief and most important work.

The second part of the work is the vigilant watch over the inevitable and unnecessary defects of the present machinery of the Administration as it exists and as long as it exists. And as the fundamental principles of the present Administration are unsound, there are inherent evils and others are naturally ever arising from them. These the Congress has to watch and adopt means to remedy them, as far as possible, till self-government is attained, though it is only when self-government is attained that India will be free from its present evils and consequent sufferings. This part of the work, the Congress has been doing very largely during all the past twenty-one years, and the Subjects-Committee will place before you various resolutions necessary for the improvement of the existing administration, as far as such unnatural and uneconomic administration can be improved. I would not have troubled you more but that I should like to say a few words upon some topics connected with the second part of the work of the Congress—Bengal Partition and *Swadeshi* movement.

In the Bengal Partition, the Bengalees have a just and great grievance. It is a bad blunder for England. I do not despair, but that this blunder, I hope, may yet be rectified. This subject is being so well threshed out by the Bengalees themselves that I need not say anything more about it. But in connection with it we hear a great deal about agitators and agitation. Agitation is the life and soul of the whole political, social and industrial history of England. It is by agitation the English have accomplished their most glorious achievements, their prosperity, their liberties and, in short, their first place among the nations of the world.

The whole life of England, every day, is all agitation. You do not open your paper in the morning but read from beginning to end it is all agitation—Congresses and Conferences—Meetings and Resolutions—without end, for a thousand and one movements, local and national. From the Prime Minister to the humblest politician, his occupation is agitation for everything he wants to accomplish. The whole Parliament, Press and Platform is simply all agitation. Agitation is the civilised, peaceful weapon of moral force, and infinitely preferable to brute physical force when possible. The subject is very tempting. But I shall not say more than that the Indian journalists are mere Matriculates while the Anglo-Indian journalists are Masters of Arts in the University of British Agitators. The former are only the pupils of the latter, and the Anglo-Indian journalists ought to feel proud that their pupils are doing credit to them. Perhaps a few words from an English statesman will be more sedative and satisfactory.

Macaulay has said in one of his speeches :—

> I hold that we have owed to agitation a long series of beneficent reforms which would have been effected in no other way . . . . . the truth is that agitation is inseparable from popular government . . . . . Would the slave-trade ever have been abolished without agitation? Would slavery ever have been abolished without agitation?

For every movement in England—hundreds, local and national—the chief weapons are agitation by meetings, demonstrations and petitions to Parliament. These petitions are not any begging for any favours any more than that the conventional "Your obedient servant" in letters makes a man an obedient servant. It is the conventional way of approaching higher authorities. The petitions are claims for rights or for justice or for reforms,—to influence and put pressure on Parliament by showing how the public regard any particular matter. The fact that we have more or less failed hitherto, is not because we have petitioned too much but that we have petitioned too little. One of the factors that carries weight in Parliament is the evidence that the people interested in any question are really in earnest. Only the other day Mr. Asquith urged as one of his reasons against women's franchise, that he did not see sufficient evidence to show that the majority of the women themselves were earnest to acquire the franchise. We have not petitioned or agitated enough at all in our demands. In every important matter we must petition Parliament with hundreds and thousands of petitions—with hundreds of thousands of signatures from all parts of India. Taking one present instance in England, the Church party has held till the beginning of October last 1,400 meetings known and many more unknown against the Education Bill and petitioned with three-quarters of a million signatures and many demonstrations. Since then they have been possibly more and more active. Agitate, agitate over the whole length and breadth of India in every nook and corner—peacefully of course—if we really mean to get justice from John Bull. Satisfy him that we are in earnest. The Bengalees, I am glad, have learnt the lesson and have led the march. All India must learn the lesson—of sacrifice of money and of earnest personal work.

Agitate; agitate means inform. Inform, inform the Indian people what their rights are, and why and how they should obtain them, and inform the British people of the rights of the Indian people and why they should grant them. If we do not speak, they say we are satisfied. If we speak, we become agitators! The Indian people are properly asked to act constitutionally while the Government remains unconstitutional and despotic.

Next about the "settled fact." Every Bill defeated in Parliament is a "settled fact." Is it not? And the next year it makes its appearance again. The Education Act of 1902 was a settled fact. An act of Parliament, was it not? And now within a short time what a turmoil is it in? And what an agitation and excitement has been going on about it and is still in prospect? It may lead to a clash between the two Houses of Parliament. There is nothing as an eternal "settled fact." Times change, circumstances are misunderstood or changed, better light and understanding or new forces come into play, and what is settled to-day may become obsolete to-morrow.

The organizations which I suggest, and which I may call a band of political missionaries in all the Provinces, will serve many purposes at once—to inform the people of their rights as British citizens, to prepare them to claim those rights by petitions and when the rights are obtained to exercise and enjoy them.

"Swadeshi" is not a thing of to-day. It has existed in Bombay as far as I know for many years past. I am a free-trader, I am a member, and in the Executive Committee of the Cobden Club for 20 years, and yet I say that "Swadeshi" is a forced necessity for India in its unnatural economic muddle. As long as the economic condition remains unnatural and impoverishing, by the necessity of supplying every year some Rs. 20,00,00,000 for the salary, pensions, etc., of the children of a foreign country at the expense and impoverishment of the children of India, to talk of applying economic laws to the condition of India is adding insult to injury. I have said so much about this over and over again that I would not say more about it here—I refer to my book. I ask any Englishman whether Englishmen would submit to this unnatural economic muddle of India for a single day in England, leave alone 150 years? No, never. No, Ladies and Gentlemen, England will never submit to it. It is, what I have already quoted in Mr. Morley's words, it is "the meddling wrongly with economic things that is going to the very life, to the very heart, to the very core of our national existence."

Among the duties which I have said are incumbent

upon the Indians, there is one, which, though I mention last, is not the least. I mean a thorough political union among the Indian people of all creeds and classes. I make an appeal to all—call it mendicant if you like—I am not ashamed of being a mendicant in any good cause and under necessity for any good cause. I appeal to the Indian people for this, because it is in their own hands only just as I appeal to the British people for things that are entirely in their hands. In this appeal for a thorough union for political purposes among all the people I make a particular one to my friends, the Mahomedans. They are a manly people. They have been rulers both in and out of India. They are rulers this day both in and out of India. They have the highest Indian Prince ruling over the largest State, *viz.*, H. H. the Nizam. Among other Mahomedan Princes they have Junagad, Radhanpur, Bhopal and others.

Notwithstanding their backward education, they have the pride of having had in all India the first Indian Barrister in Mr. Budrudin Tyabji and the first Solicitor in Mr. Kamrudin Tyabji, two Mahomedan brothers.* What a large share of Bombay commerce is in the hands of Maho-

* As regards the first Indian Barrister and the first Indian Attorney, it appears that Mr. Dadabhai Naoroji was wrongly informed. Of course, any community would be proud of two such distinguished members as were the Tyabji brothers, both of whom met with great success and attained the highest positions in their respective professions, but they were not the first Indians to adopt those professions. Mr. Budrudin Tyabji was called to the Bar on the 30th April, 1867, and there were at least two or three Indian Barristers before him. Mr. M. Ghose was called on the 6th June 1866, and Mr. G. M. Tagore, who is believed to be the first Indian Barrister, was called to the Bar on the 11th June, 1862, and long before that, Babu Baney Madhub Banerjee became an Attorney of the Calcutta High Court, and he was believed to have been the first Indian Attorney, whereas Mr. Kamrudin Tyabji was a contemporary of his other brother.

medans is well known. Their chief purpose and effort at present must be to spread education among themselves. In this matter among their best friends have been Sir Syed Ahmed and Justice Tyabji in doing their utmost to promote education among them. Once they bring themselves in education in a line with the Hindus, they have nothing to fear. They have in them the capacity, energy and intellect, to hold their own and to get their due share in all the walks of life—of which the State Services are but a small part. State Services are not everything.

Whatever voice I can have, I wish Government would give every possible help to promote education among the Mahomedans. Once self-government is attained, then will there be prosperity enough for all, but not till then. The thorough union, therefore, of all the people for their emancipation is an absolute necessity.

All the people in their political position are in one boat. They must sink or swim together. Without this union, all efforts will be vain. There is the common saying—but also the best commonsense—" United we stand—divided we fall."

There is one other circumstance I may mention here. If I am right, I am under the impression that the bulk of the Bengalee Mahomedans were Hindus by race and blood only a few generations ago. They have the tie of blood and kinship. Even now a great mass of the Bengalee Mahomedans are not to be easily distinguished from their Hindu brothers. In many places they join together in their social joys and sorrows. They cannot divest themselves from the natural affinity of common blood. On the Bombay side, the Hindus and Mahomedans of Gujarat all speak the same language, Gujarati, and are of the same stock, and all the Hindus and Mahomedans of Maharashtric

Annan—all speak the same language, Marathi and are of the same stock—and so I think it is all over India, excepting in North India where there are the descendants o the original Mahomedan invaders, but they are now also the people of India.

Sir Syed Ahmed was a nationalist to the backbone. I will mention an incident that happened to myself with him. On his first visit to England, we happened to meet together in the house of Sir C. Wingfield. He and his friends were waiting, and I was shown into the same room. One of his friends recognising me introduced me to him. As soon as he heard my name, he at once held me in strong embrace and expressed himself very much pleased. In various ways, I knew that his heart was in the welfare of all India as one nation. He was a large and liberal-minded patriot. When I read his life some time ago, I was inspired with respect and admiration for him. As I cannot find my copy of his life, I take the opportunity of repeating some of his utterances which Sir Henry Cotton has given in *India* of 12th October last:

Mahomedans and Hindus were, he said, the two eyes of India. Injure the one and you injure the other. We should try to become one in heart and soul and act in unison; if united, we can support each other, if not, the effect of one against the other will tend to the destruction and downfall of both.

He appreciated when he found worth and freely expressed it. He said:—

I assure you that the Bengalees are the only people in our country whom we can properly be proud of, and it is only due to them that knowledge, liberty and patriotism have progressed in our country. I can truly say that they are really the head and crown of all the communities of Hindustan. In the word "nation" I include both Hindus and Mahomedans, because that is the only meaning which I can attach to it.

Such was the wise and patriotic counsel of that great man, and our Mahomedan friends will, I hope, take it to heart. I repeat once more that our emancipation depends upon the thorough union of all the people of India without any obstruction.

I have often read about the question of a constitution for the Congress. I think the gentlemen who raise this question would be the proper persons to prepare one like a Bill in the House of Commons in all its details. The Congress then can consider it and deal with it as the majority may decide.

Let every one of us do the best he can, do all in harmony for the common object of self-government.

Lastly, the question of social reforms and industrial progress—each of them needs its own earnest body of workers. Each requires for it separate, devoted attention. All the three great purposes—Political, Social and Industrial—must be set working side by side. The progress in each will have its influence on the others. But, as Mr. Morley truly and with deep insight says:—"Political principles are, after all, the root of our national greatness, strength and hope," and his other important utterance which I repeat with this one sums up the whole position of the Indian problem. He says: "The meddling wrongly with economic things, that is going to the very life, to the very heart, to the very core of our national existence."

This meddling wrongly with economic things is the whole evil from which India suffers—and the only remedy for it is—"Political principles are, after all, the root of our national greatness, strength and hope." And these political principles are summed up in self-government. Self-government is the only and chief remedy. In self-government lies our hope, strength and greatness.

I recommend to your serious notice the treatment of British Indians in South Africa.

Well, ladies and gentlemen, I have finished my task. I do not know what good fortune may be in store for me during the short period that may be left to me, and if I can leave a word of affection and devotion for my country and countrymen, I say, be united, persevere and achieve self-government, so that the millions now perishing by poverty, famine and plague, and the scores of millions that are starving on scanty subsistence may be saved, and India may once more occupy her proud position of yore among the greatest and civilized nations of the world.

APPENDIX TO CALCUTTA CONGRESS PRESIDENTIAL ADDRESS.

Here I confine myself to some of the declarations as to the duty of Liberalism and the absolute necessity of self-government for progress and prosperity.

DECLARATIONS OF THE RIGHT HON'BLE SIR HENRY CAMPBELL-BANNERMAN.

The British power cannot there and elsewhere rest securely unless it rests upon the willing consent of a sympathetic and contented people.

[*Oxford, 2-3-1901.*]

It is only by the consent of the governed that the British Nation can govern.

[*Plymouth, 19-11-1901.*]

We Liberals are accustomed to freedom of thought and action. Freedom is the breath of our life. . . It possesses in two of its most sacred dogmas, the only solution of the chief problems which confront our country in Imperial Policy and in regard to our domestic needs. . . It is the universal doctrine of government by assent—government with the consent of the governed. . . . Why there is but one cardinal condition again of Liberal principle—that of direct popular control by those concerned. Now these are two of the beacons by which Liberal policy should be guided.

[*National Liberal Club, 5-3-1902.*]

6a

Good government could never be a substitute for government by the people themselves.

[*Stirling, 23-11-1905*]

Ladies and gentlemen, so much for peace, so much for economy—two cardinal Liberal principles. But here is another—self-government and popular control: and we believe in that principle, not only on grounds of justice and on the grounds of effective administration, but on this other ground—that it exercises a wholesome influence on the character of the people who enjoy the privilege.

[*Albert Hall, 21-12-1905.*]

Sir, in all these subjects on which I have been touching, what is the aim to be kept in view, what is the star which we ought to keep our eyes upon to see that we are moving in the right direction? It is that we should promote the welfare and happiness and interests not of any particular class or section of the community but of the nation at large. That is the work of true patriotism, these are the foundations upon which a solid empire may be built.

[*Albert Hall, 15-12-1905.*]

DECLARATIONS OF THE RIGHT HON'BLE JOHN MORLEY.

Imperialism by all means, if it means mercy, if it means humanity, if it means justice, but if it means your own demoralization, if it means lowering your own standard of civilization and humanity, then in the name of all you hold precious beware of it and resist it.

[*Sydney, 25-5-1899.*]

When he [Mr. Gladstone] died, Lord Salisbury said of him that he was a great Christian. Yes, and I would add that he was not a Christian for nothing. I think he must often have used to himself the language of Wordsworth, "Earth is sick and heaven is weary of the swollen words that States and Kingdoms utter when they talk of truth and justice." He, at all events, in face of all the demands of practical politics, did his best to bring those considerations of truth and justice into the minds and hearts of his countrymen. . . . But I do say that Mr. Gladstone, when he saw the nations going on a wrong path, saw high in the heavens the flash of the uplifted sword and the gleam of the arm of the Avenging Angel.

[*Manchester—Unveiling of Statue, 10-10-1901.*]

It is this policy of passing measures for Ireland without reference to the Irish themselves that is responsible for most of the mischief and mis-government from which Ireland has so long suffered. . . . From observation of Irish Government, from experience of Irish Government, from responsibility of Irish Government, I say to you, gentlemen, face to face, it is a bad government, it is a government which no nation, no set of people can be expected to endure in peace, and it is a government which we in our conscience ought to do our very best, when the time comes, when opportunity presents itself to put right as we have put so many other evils in our own system of government right.

[*Manchester, 12-3-1902.*]

With how much more force do these words apply to India!

We are going to have I suppose—well we may have a proposal to suspend the constitution of the Cape Colony. Just picture the scene in the House of Commons. The motion is made to protest against the suspension of Parliamentary Institution in the Cape Colony. We then all get up and we all make eloquent, passionate, argumentative speeches in favour of the right of the Colonies to govern themselves. The next day Mr. Redmond makes a motion in favour of giving self-government in one shape or another to Ireland. We then all pick out a new set of arguments. What was on Monday unanswerable on Tuesday becomes not worth mentioning. What was on Monday a sacred principle of self-government becomes on Tuesday mere moonshine and clap-trap. That is a comedy in which I at least do not propose to take part. The Boers are to have self-government in order to make them loyal. The Irish are not to have it because they are disloyal.

[*Edinburgh, 7-6-1902.*]

What a true picture of the way in which India is treated!

We are citizens, common citizens of a grand country; we are the heirs of a noble tradition; we believe that human progress can only be won by human effort—and that effort, I hope, all of us in our different degrees, ages and situations will pursue with determination with unselfishness and with a resolute directness and simplicity that must in the end win a crowning victory.

[*National Liberal Federation, Annual Meeting, 13-5-1901.*]

He was for liberty wherever they could get it.

* * * * *

Appointment of a Royal Commission.

[*The following speech was delivered by Mr. Dadabhai Naoroji at the First Congress held in Bombay, 1885*].

I had no thought of speaking on this Resolution,* but I see I must say something. There is a notion running under some remarks, that if a Conservative Government appoints a Committee, it will not be a good one. I do not think there is any good reason for that assumption. The Conservatives are not so bad that they will never do a good thing, nor are the Liberals so good that they never did a bad thing. In fact we owe good to both, and we have nothing to do with them yet as parties. We are thankful to either party that does us good. The Proclamation is the gift of a Conservative Government. I have some experience of a Parliamentary Committee and that Committee, a Liberal one; and yet under the Chairmanship of a gentleman like Mr. Ayrton, you cannot be sure of a fair hearing. On the other hand, a fair-minded Chairman and similar members, be they Conservatives or Liberals, would make a good Committee, and give a fair inquiry. Much depends upon the Secretary of State for India. If he is a fair-minded person and not biassed in any particular way, you will have a fair Committee. If we are asking

* *Resolution.*—That this Congress earnestly recommends that the promised inquiry into the working of the Indian Administration here and in England should be entrusted to a Royal Commission, the people of India being adequately represented thereon, and evidence taken both in India and in England.

for a Parliamentary Committee, we need not be afraid of asking one from a Conservative Government. A Secretary of State like Sir Stafford Northcote (Lord Iddesleigh) will give a fair one, and we should not assume that the present Secretary will not give a good one. We should only desire that Anglo-Indians may not be put in it, or only a few such in whom Natives have confidence. In such an inquiry Anglo-Indian officials are on their trial, and they should not be allowed to sit in judgment upon themselves.

From the remarks already made, there appears to be an undecidedness, whether to ask for a Committee, or for a Royal Commission. And there seems also a notion underneath, that if we were not satisfied with the one we could ask for the other. Now we must bear in mind that it is not an easy thing to get a Parliamentary Committee or a Royal Commission, and that you cannot have either whenever you like. Do not suppose that if we have a Committee or a Commission and if we say we are dissatisfied with its results, we would at once get another for the asking. We must make up our minds definitely as to what we want and what would be the best thing for us. You should not leave it open whether there should be a Committee or Commission. Whichever you want, say it out once for all. In dealing with Englishmen, make up your minds deliberately, speak clearly, and work perseveringly. Then and then only can you hope to be listened to, and get your wishes. You must not show that you do not know your own mind. Therefore, know your own mind, and say clearly whether you desire a Parliamentary Committee, or a Royal Commission. It is evidently the desire here, that a full and impartial enquiry by fair and high-minded

English statesmen, with an adequate number of Natives on the enquiring body, should be carried on in India itself. If so, then we must remember that a Parliamentary Committee can consist only of members of Parliament, and can sit in the Parliament House only. For our purpose to lay bare the actual conditions of India, an inquiry *in* India, in all departments and in the whole condition of India—material and moral—is absolutely necessary. No enquiry in England, and that with the evidence of Anglo-Indians chiefly—who themselves are on trial, and who would not naturally condemn their own doings and work—can ever bring out the truth about India's true condition and wants and necessary reforms. We, then irresistibly come to one conclusion, that an enquiry in India itself is absolutely necessary, and that such an enquiry can be conducted by a Royal Commission. Only let us clearly say our mind that we ask for a Royal Commission. Do not let there be any doubt about what we do really want. If I am right in interpreting your desire, then I say let there be no vague general resolution, but say clearly and distinctly that we require a Royal Commission.

Reform of Legislative Council.*

[*The following speech was delivered by Mr. Dadabhai Naoroji at the First Congress held in Bombay 1885*].

I am glad my friends, the Hon'ble Mr. Telang and the Hon'ble Mr. S. Iyer, have relieved me of much trouble, as they have anticipated a deal of what I had to say, which I need not repeat.

We asked for representation in the Legislative Councils of India. It is not for us to teach the English people how necessary representation is for good government. We have learnt the lesson from them, and knowing from them how great a blessing it is to those nations who enjoy it, and how utterly un-English it is for the English nation to withhold it from us, we can, with confidence and trust, ask them to give us this. I do not want to complain of the past. It is past and gone. It cannot be said now that the time is not come to give representation. Thanks to our rulers themselves, we have now sufficiently advanced to know

* *Resolution.*—That this Congress considers the reform and expansion of the Supreme and existing Legislative Councils, by the admission of a considerable proportion of elected members (and the creation of similar Councils for the North West Provinces and Oudh, and also for the Punjab) essential; and holds that all Budgets should be referred to those Councils for consideration, their members being moreover empowered to interpellate the Executive in regard to all branches of the administration; and that a Standing Committee of the House of Commons should be constituted to receive and consider any formal protests that may be recorded by majorities of such Councils against the exercise by the Executive of the powers, which would be vested in it, of overruling the decisions of such majorities.

the value of representation and to understand the necessity that representation must go with taxation, that the taxed must have a voice in the taxation that is imposed on them. We are British subjects, and I say we can demand what we are entitled to and expect still at British hands their greatest and most noble institution and heritage. It is our inheritance also and we should not be kept out of it. Why, if we are to be denied Britain's best institutions, what good is it to India to be under the British sway? It will be simply another Asiatic despotism. What makes us proud to be British subjects, what attaches us to this foreign rule with deeper loyalty than even our own past Native rule, is the fact that Britain is the parent of free and representative government, and, that we, as her subjects and children, are entitled to inherit the great blessing of freedom and representation. We claim the inheritance. If not, we are not the British subjects which the Proclamation proclaims us to be—equal in rights and privileges with the rest of Her Majesty's subjects. We are only British drudges or slaves. Let us persevere. Britain would never *be* a slave and could not, in her very nature and instinct, *make* a slave. Her greatest glory is freedom and representation, and, as her subjects, we shall have these blessed gifts.

Coming to the immediate and practical part of our demand, I may say that it will be to Government itself a great advantage and relief—advantage, inasmuch as it will have the help of those who know the true wants of the Natives, and in whom the Natives have confidence, and relief so far that the responsibility of legislation will not be upon the head of Government only, but upon that of the representatives of the people also.

And the people will have to blame themselves if they fail to send the right sort of men to represent themselves. I think Government has now reason rather to thank than repel us for demanding this boon which, if granted, will, on the one hand, make government easier and more effective, and, on the other, attach the people to British rule more deeply than before.

Our first reform should be to have the power to tax ourselves. With that and another reform for which I shall move hereafter, India will advance in material and moral prosperity, and bless and benefit England. The proposal about the right of interpellation is very important,—as important and useful to Government itself as to the people. The very fact that questions will be put in the Council, will prevent in a measure that evil which at present is beyond Government's reach to redress. Government will be relieved of the odium and inconvenience which it at present suffers from misunderstanding and want of opportunities of giving explanation. The British Parliament and public, and the British Government in all its departments, benefit largely by this power of putting questions in Parliament, and the same will be the result here. There will be, in the circumstances of India, one essential difference between the British Parliament and the Indian Legislative Councils. In Parliament, the Government, if defeated, resigns, and the opposition comes into power. That cannot be done in India. Whether defeated or not, Government will remain in power. Moreover, the Secretary of State for India will have the power to veto, and no harm can happen. If the Government, either Provincial or Supreme, disregard the vote against it, and if the Secretary of State support the disregarding

Government, there will be, as a last remedy, the Standing Committee of Parliament as the ultimate appellate body to decide on the point of disagreement; and thus Parliament will truly, and not merely nominally as at present, become the final controlling authority.

We are British subjects and subjects of the same gracious sovereign who has pledged her royal word that we are to her as all her other subjects, and we have a right to all British institutions. If we are true to ourselves, and perseveringly ask what we desire, the British people are the very people on earth who will give what is right and just. From what has already been done in the past we have ample reason to indulge in this belief. Let us for the future equally rely on that character and instinct of the British. *They* have taught us our wants and they will supply them.

After some discussion, Mr. Dadabhai Naoroji said :—
Before the Hon'ble Mr. Telang replies, I may ask to be allowed to say a few words. I may just explain what an important thing this Standing Committee will be. During the East India Company's time, Parliament was entirely independent of it. Parliament was then truly an effective appellate body. It took up Indian questions quite freely and judged fairly, without the circumstance of parties ever interfering with its deliberations. If there was a complaint against the Company, Parliament was free to sit in judgment on it. What is the position since the transfer of the government to the Crown? The Secretary of State for India is the Parliament. Every question in which he is concerned becomes a Cabinet question. His majority is at his back. This majority has no concern in Indian matters further than to back the Government, *i.e.* the Secretary of State for India.

All appeals, therefore, to Parliament against the Secretary of State become a mere farce. M. Ps are utterly discouraged from their inability to do anything. And the Secretary of State becomes the true Great Moghul of India—a despotic monarch. His will is his law. Nor can the people of India influence him, as their voice is not represented in Parliament. Thus, that tribunal can scarcely exercise any effectual check over his despotism. The present legislative machinery, from the Local councils upwards, is simply a device to legalise despotism and give it the false mask of constitutionalism. The tax-payers have no voice in the imposition of the taxes they pay, and Parliament has not the ability to prevent the levy of unfair or oppressive taxation. The ultimate controlling authority seems helpless to control anything. Now if we have complete representative legislation here, and if we have a Standing Committee in Parliament, we shall have both the voice of the taxed on the one side and effectual control of Parliament on the other. Such a Standing Committee will naturally be independent of all parties. Its decision will be no defeat of Government. It will be simply a final decision on the point of difference that may have arisen between the representatives of the people in India on the one hand, and the Government on the other, on any particular question. India will thus have an effectual parliamentary control.

It is said we should propose something as a substitute for the present India office Council. The Resolution now before the Congress makes this unnecessary. The Council, when it was established, was considered to be protective of Indian interests. It has not proved so. When it suits the Secretary of State, he screens himself behind that Council. When it does not suit him, he flings the Council aside. We have no means of knowing what good at all is done by the Council. Its irresponsibility and its secrecy are fatal objections to its continuance. Such a thing in the Government of an Empire of 200 millions of people and under the British is an utter and inexplicable anachronism. Moreover, the majority of the Council consists of Anglo-Indians. These, sitting in judgment on their own hand-work, naturally regard it as perfect. Having left India years ago, they fail to realise the rapid changes that are taking place here in our circumstances, lose touch with us and offer resistance to all progress. Times are now changed. The natives, I may say, have come of age. They can represent directly their wishes and views to the Government here, and to the Secretary of State. They do not require the aid of this Council at the India Office for their so-called representation or protection.

I may here remark, that the chief work of this the first National Congress of India is to enunciate clearly and boldly our highest and ultimate wishes. Whether we get them or not immediately, let our rulers know what our highest aspirations are. And if we are true to ourselves, the work of each delegate present here will be to make the part of India where he happens to live devote itself earnestly to carrying out the objects resolved upon at this Congress with all due deliberation. If, then, we lay down clearly that we desire to have the actual Government of India transferred from England to India under the simple controlling power of the Secretary of State, and of Parliament, through its Standing Committee, and that we further desire that taxation and legislation shall be imposed here by representative Councils, we say what we are aiming at.

And under such an arrangement no Council to advise the Secretary of State is necessary. Neither is a Council needed to attend to the appellate executive work. There is a permanent Under-Secretary of State who will be able to keep up continuity of knowledge and transact all current business. There are, besides, Secretaries at the head of the different departments as experts. I do not deny that at times the India Office Council has done good service. But this was owing to the personality and sympathy of individual men like Sir E. Perry. The constitution of the body as a body is objectionable and anomalous. When the whole power of imposing taxation and legislation is transferred here, the work of the Secretary of State will be largely diminished. It will only be confined to general supervision of important matters. Whatever comes before him for disposal will be set forth by the Government from here fully and fairly in all its bearings. No Council will be needed to aid him in forming his judgment. Thus no substitute is required for the India Office Council. It is enough for us to formulate the scheme, now submitted for your consideration, as one which India needs and desires, *viz.*, representative Legislative Councils in India, with full financial control and interpellatory powers. And we shall not need to trouble much the authorities in England.

Simultaneous Examinations in England and India.

The Hon'ble Mr. Dadabhai Naoroji, in moving the fourth Resolution,* said :—The Resolution which I am proposing does not in any way involve the question whether the distinction between the covenanted and uncovenanted services should be abolished or not. That is a separate question altogether, and in fact, if my Resolution is adopted that question will become unnecessary or very subordinate. The Resolution which I propose to you is of the utmost possible importance to India. It is the most important key to our material and moral advancement. All our other political reforms will benefit us but very little indeed if this reform of all reforms is not made. It is the question of poverty or prosperity. It is the question of life and death to India. It is the question of questions. Fortunately, it is not necessary for me on this occasion to go into all its merits, as I hope

*" That in the opinion of this Congress the Competitive Examinations now held in England, for first appointments in various Civil departments of the public service, should henceforth, in accordance with the views of the India Office Committee of 1860, 'be held simultaneously, one in England and one in India, both being as far as praticable identical in their nature, and those who compete in both countries being finally classified in one list according to merit,' and that the successful candidates in India should be sent to England for further study, and subjected there to such further examinations as may seem needful. Further, that all other first appointments (excluding peonships and the like) should be filled by competitive examinations held in India, under conditions calculated to secure such intellectual, moral and physical qualifications as may be decided by Government to be necessary. Lastly, that the maximum age of candidates for entrance into the Covenanted Civil Service be raised to not less than 23 years."

you are all already well aware of my views and their reasons, or it would have been very difficult for me to lay before you all I should have had to say without speaking for hours. There is an additional good fortune for me that what I want to propose was already proposed a quarter of a century ago by no less an authority than a Committee of the India Office itself. The report of this Committee gives the whole matter in a nutshell from the point of the view of justice, right, expediency and honest fulfilment of promises. And the reasons given by it for the Covenanted Civil Service apply equally to all the other services in the civil department. I do not refer to the military service in this Resolution, as that is a matter requiring special consideration and treatment. To make my remarks as brief as possible, as we are much pressed for time, I shall first at once read to you the extract from the report of the Committee consisting of Sir J. P. Willoughby, Mr. Mangles, Mr. Arbuthnot, Mr. Macnaughten, and Sir Erskine Perry.

The report, dated 20th January, 1860, says :—

"2. We are, in the first place, unanimously of opinion that it is not only just but expedient that the Natives of India shall be employed in the administration of India to as large an extent as possible, consistently with the maintenance of British supremacy, and have considered whether any increased facilities can be given in this direction.

"3. It is true that, even at present, no positive disqualification exists. By Act 3 and 4, Wm. 4, C. 85, S. 87, it is enacted "that no Native of the said territories, nor any natural born subject of His Majesty resident therein, shall, by reason only of his religion, place of birth, descent, colour or any of them, be disabled from holding any place, office or employment under the said Company." It is obvious therefore that when the competitive system was adopted it could not have been intended to exclude Natives of India from the Civil Service of India.

"4. Practically, however, they are excluded. The law declares them eligible, but the difficulties opposed to a Native leaving India, and residing in England for a time, are so great that as a general rule, it is almost impossible for a Native successfully to compete at the periodical examination held in England. Were this inequality removed, we should no longer be exposed to the charge of keeping promise to the ear and breaking it to the hope.

"5. Two modes have been suggested by which the object in view might be attained. The first is by allotting a certain portion of the total number of appointments declared in each year to be competed for in India by Natives and by other natural-born subjects of Her Majesty's residents in India. The second is, to hold simultaneously two examinations, one in England and one in India, both being, as far as practicable identical in their nature, and those who compete in both countries being finally classified in one list according to merit by the Civil Service Commissioners. The Committee have no hesitation in giving the preference to the second scheme, as being the fairest, and the most in accordance with the principles of a general competition for a common object."

Now according to strict right and justice the examination for services in India ought to take place in India alone. The people of Australia, Canada and the Cape do not go to England for their services. Why should Indians be compelled to go to England to compete for the services, unless it be England's despotic will. But I am content to propose the Resolution according to the views of the Committee for simultaneous examinations, both in England and in India, and reasons that apply to the Civil Service apply equally well to the other services in the Civil Department, *viz.*, Engineering, Medical, Telegraph, Forest, and so on.

I may here remind you that in addition to the Act of 1833 referred to by the Committee, we have the solemn promises contained in the Proclamation of our gracious Sovereign. The fact is told to us in unmistakable language :—

"We hold ourselves bound to the Natives of our Indian territories by the same obligations of duty which bind us to all our other subjects; and those obligations, by the blessing of Almighty God, we shall faithfully and conscientiously fulfil."

And then they declared her gracious promise specifically on this very part of the services :—

"And it is our furthar will that, so far as may be, our subjects of whatever race or creed be freely and impartially admitted to offices in our service, the duties of which they may be qualified, by their education, ability and integrity, duly to discharge."

This gracious proclamation and the promises contained therein were made known in 1858. And the India Office Committee showed, in 1860, in what way these promises could be fulfilled, so as to relieve the English nation from "the charge of keeping promise to the ear and breaking it to the hope." With the Act of Parliament of 1833, the solemn promises of 1858, of our Sovereign before God and man, and the declaration by the India Office of the mode of fulfilling those promises in 1860, it is hardly necessary for me to say more. Our case for the Resolution proposed by me is complete. As a matter of justice, solemn promises and even expediency, I would have ended my speech here, but my object in proposing this Resolution rests upon a far higher and a most important consideration. The question of the extreme poverty of India is now no more a controversial point. Viceroys and Finance Ministers have admitted it. The last official declaration by Sir E. Baring is complete and unequivocal. In his budget speech of 18th March, 1882, he said :—

"It has been calculated that the average income per head of population in India is not more than Rs. 27 a year; and though I am not prepared to pledge myself to the absolute accuracy of a calculation of this sort, it is sufficiently accurate to justify the conclusion that the taxpaying community is exceedingly poor. To derive any very large increase of revenue from so poor a population as this is obviously impossible, and, if it were possible, would be unjustifiable."

Again, in the discussion on the budget, after repeating the above statement regarding the income of Rs. 27 per head per annum, he said :—

"But he thought it was quite sufficient to show the extreme poverty of the mass of the people. In England the average income per head of population was £33 per head; in France it was £23; in Turkey, which was the poorest country in Europe, it was £4 per head. He would ask Honorable members to think how Rs. 27 per annum was to support a person, and then he would ask whether a few annas was nothing to such poor people."

With this emphatic and clear opinion before you, I need not say more. The question is what is the cause of this poverty? I have shown in my papers on the poverty of India, and in my correspondence with the Secretary of State for India, that the sole cause of this extreme poverty and wretchedness of the mass of the people is the inordinate employment of foreign agency in the government of the country and the consequent material loss to and drain from the country. I request those who have not already seen these papers to read them, for it is utterly impossible for me to go through the whole argument here. It will be, therefore, now clear to you that the employment of Native agency is not merely a matter of justice and expediency, according to the views of the India Office Committee, but a most absolute necessity for the poor, suffering, and starving millions of India. It is a question of life and death to the country. The present English rule is no doubt the greatest blessing India has ever had, but this one evil of it nullifies completely all the good it has achieved. Remove but this one evil, and India will be blessed in every way and will be a blessing to England also in every way. The commerce between England and India will increase so that England will then be able to benefit herself ten times more by India's prosperity than what she does now. There will be none of the constant struggle that is at present to be witnessed between the rulers and the ruled—the one screwing out more and more taxes, like squeezing a squeezed orange—inflicting suffering and distress, and the other always crying itself hoarse about its inability to provide them owing to extreme poverty. By the removal of the evil—India will be able not merely to supply a revenue of £70,000,000, but £170,000,000, with ease and comfort. England takes over 50 shillings a head for her revenue, why may not India under the same rule be able to take even 20 a head ? Indians would easily pay £200,000,000. I should stop now. I hope you will see that this Resolution is of the greatest possible importance to India, and I implore every one of you present here to-day to strain every nerve and work perseveringly in your respective localites to attain this object. With regard to the second part of the Resolution, the uncovenanted services, the same reasoning and necessity apply. A fair system of competition, testing all necessary qualifications—mental, moral and physical—will be the most suitable mode of supplying the services with the best and most eligible servants, and relieve Government of all the pressure of back door and private influences, and jobbery.

The subject of the age of candidates for the Civil Service examination needs no lengthened remarks from me. It has been only lately thrashed out, and it has been established beyond all doubt that the higher age will give you a superior class of men, whether English or Native. I conclude, therefore, with the earnest exhortation that you will all apply yourselves vigorously to free poor India from the great evil of the drain on her resources.

If the British will once understand our true condition, their conscientious desire to rule India for India's and humanity's good, will never allow the evil to continue any longer. Lastly, I hope and trust that our rulers will receive our representations in their proper spirit. We sincerely believe that the good we propose for ourselves is also a good for them. Whatever good they will do to us cannot but in the very nature of things be good to them also. The better we are in material and moral prosperity, the more grateful, attached and loyal we shall be, the worse we are the less our gratitude and loyalty shall naturally be. The more prosperous we are, the larger shall be their custom; the worse we are, the condition will be the reverse. The question of our prosperity is as much the question of the prosperity of England and her workingmen. England's trade would be enriched by £250,000,000, if with our prosperity each unit of the Indian population is ever able to buy from England goods worth only £1 per annum. What is wanted is the fructification in our own pocket of our annual produce. I repeat that it is my hope and trust that our rulers may receive our prayers in their right spirit and do us all the good in their power, for it will rebound to their good name, honour and everlasting glory. Let us have the Royal Proclamation fulfilled in its true spirit and integrity and both England and India will be benefited and blessed.

With these observations I beg to propose the Fourth Resolution.

The Hon'ble Mr. Dadabhai Naoroji, in reply to the discussion, said :—I am glad I have not much to reply to. The appreciation of the importance of the Resolution is clear. My remarks will be more as explanations of a few matters. I had much to do with the passing of the clause for granting to us the Statutory Civil Service. It is an important concession, and we have to be very grateful for it. I need not here go into its history. The statesmen in England who gave us this were sincere and explicit in the matter. Whatever complaint we have, it is with the authorities here. First of all, after the clause was passed, the Government of India entirely ignored it and did nothing to give it effect for 6 years! It was only when pressure was applied to it from England, into the details of which this is not the time or place for me to enter, that the necessary rules were at last prepared and published. These rules have been so drafted that they may be carried out in a way to bring discredit on the Service. And whether this is done intentionally or not, whether the subsequent objectionable action upon it was also intentional or not, I cannot say. But the most important element in the carrying out of this clause was partially or wholly ignored, and that has been the real cause of its so-called failure,—I mean educational competence, ascertained either by suitable competition, or proved ability, was an absolutely indispensable condition for admitting candidates to this service. It is just this essential condition that has been several times ignored or forgotten. Let therefore your efforts be devoted strenuously not against the clause itself, but against the objectionable mode in which the nominations are made. The Bengal Government has moved in a satisfactory direction, and its example should be followed by all the Governments. It will be the height of folly on our part to wish the abolition of this Statutory Civil Service—excepting only when simultaneous examinations are held in England and

India giving a fair field to all, as proposed in the present Resolution. In this fair competition, Eurasians, or domiciled Englishmen, in fact all subjects of Her Imperial Majesty, will have equal justice. I understand that the Eurasians and domiciled Anglo-Indians come under the definition of what is called "Statutory Natives." It is only right that those whose country is India should be considered as Natives, and should enjoy all the rights and privileges of Natives. United action between the Natives and Eurasians and domiciled Anglo-Indians will be good for all. What is objectionable is, that Eurasians and domiciled Anglo-Indians blow hot and cold at the same time. At one moment they claim to be Natives, and at another they spurn the Natives and claim to be Englishmen! Common sense must tell them that this is an absurd position to take up and must ultimately do them more harm than good. I desired that there should be cordial union between all whose country is, or who make their country, India. One of the speakers remarked that the employment of Natives will be economical. This is a point which I am afraid is not clearly understood. The fact is that the employment of a Native is not only economy, but *complete gain* to the whole extent of his salary. When a European is employed, he displaces a Native whom nature intended to fill the place. The Native coming in his place is natural. Every pie he eats is therefore a gain to the country, and every pie he saves is so much saved to the country for the use of all its children. Every pie paid to a foreigner is a *complete material loss* to the country. Every pie paid to a Native is a *complete material saving* to the country. In fact, as I have already endeavoured to impress upon you as earnestly as possible, it is the whole question of the poverty or prosperity of the country. We should of course pay a reasonable price for English rule, so that we may have the highest power of control and supervision in English hands, but beyond that is simply to ruin India and not such a benefit to England as she would otherwise have, were India a prosperous country. Our friend there expressed some doubt about the necessity of going to England. I say without the least hesitation that the candidate himself as well as the service will be vastly benefited by a visit to England. The atmosphere of freedom and high civilization which he will breathe will make him an altered man—in character, in intelligence, in experience, in self-respect and in appreciation of due respect for others. In short, he will largely increase his fitness and command more respect in his responsible service. I mean, of course, in the Resolution that the expenses of such visits to England by the candidates who have successfully passed the different examinations for the different services in India, should be paid from the public revenue. It may be made clear in the Resolution, by adding "at the public expense."

I conclude with my most anxious and earnest exhortation to this Congress, and to every individual member of it, that they should perseveringly strain every nerve to secure the all-important object of this Resolution as early as possible. Once this foreign drain, this "bleeding to death," is stopped, India will be capable, by reason of its land, labour and its vast resources to become as prosperous as England, with benefit to England also and to mankind, and with eternal glory to the English name and nation.

SPEECHES IN THE HOUSE OF COMMONS

Maiden Speech.

[*On the 9th August, 1892, Mr. Naoroji made his maiden speech in the House of Commons, during the debate on the address to the Queen*].

It may be considered rather rash and unwise on my part to stand before this House so immediately after my admission here : and my only excuse is that I am under a certain necessity to do so. My election for an English constituency is a unique event. For the first time during more than a century of settled British rule, an Indian is admitted into the House as a member for an English constituency. That, as I have said, is a unique event in the history of India, and, I may also venture to say, in the history of the British Empire. I desire to say a few words in analysis of this great and wonderful phenomenon. The spirit of the British rule, the instinct of British justice and generosity, from the very commencement, when they seriously took the matter of Indian policy into their hands, about the beginning of this century, decided that India was to be governed on the lines of British freedom and justice. Steps were taken without any hesitation to introduce Western education, civilisation, and political institutions in that country; and the result was that, aided by a noble and grand language in which the youth of that country began to be educated, a great movement of political life—I may say new life—was infused into that country which had been decaying for centuries. The British rulers of the country endowed it with all their own most important privileges. A few days ago, Sir, you demanded from the Throne the privileges which belong to the people, including freedom of speech, for which they fought and shed their blood. That freedom of speech you have given to us, and it enables Indians to stand before you and represent in clear and open language any desire they have felt. By conferring those privileges you have prepared for this final result of an Indian standing before you in this House, becoming a member of the great Imperial Parliament of the British Empire, and being able to express his views openly and fearlessly before you. The glory and credit of this great event—by which India is thrilled from one end to the other—of the new life, the joy, the ecstacy of India at the present moment, are all your own; it is the spirit of British institutions and the love of justice and freedom in British instincts which has produced this extraordinary result, and I stand here in the name of India to thank the British people that they have made it at all possible for an Indian to occupy this position, and to speak freely in the English language of any grievance which India may be suffering under, with the conviction that though he stands alone, with only one vote, whenever he is able to bring forward any aspiration and is supported by just and proper reasons, he will find a large number of other members from both sides of the House ready to support him and give him the justice he asks. This is the conviction which permeates the whole thinking and educated classes of India. It is that conviction that enables us to work on, day after day, without dismay, for the removal of a grievance. The question now being discussed before the

House will come up from time to time in practical shape and I shall then be able to express my humble views upon them as a representative of the English constituency of Central Finsbury. I do not intend to enter into them now. Central Finsbury has earned the everlasting gratitude of the millions of India, and has made itself famous in the History of the British Empire, by electing an Indian to represent it. Its name will never be forgotten by India. This event has strengthened the British power and the loyalty and attachment of India to it ten times more than the sending out of one hundred thousand European soldiers would have done. The moral force to which the Right Hon'ble Gentleman, the member for Midlothian (Mr. W. E. Gladstone), referred is the golden link by which India is held by the British power. So long as India is satisfied with the justice and honour of Britain, so long will her Indian Empire last, and I have not the least doubt that, though our progress may be slow and we may at times meet with disappointments, if we persevere, whatever justice we ask in reason we shall get. I thank you, Sir, for allowing me to say these few words and the House for so indulgently listening to me, and I hope that the connection between England and India—which forms five-sixths of the British Empire—may continue long with benefit to both countries. There will be certain Indian questions, principally of administration, which I shall have to lay before the House, and I am quite sure that when they are brought forward they will be fairly considered, and if reasonable, amended to our satisfaction.

AN INQUIRY INTO THE CONDITION OF INDIA.

AMENDMENT FOR A FULL AND INDEPENDENT PARLIAMENTARY ENQUIRY.

August 14th, 1894.

Mr. Naoroji (Finsbury, Central) said he undertook now to second this Resolution, and before going into the subject of the different parts of which it consisted he would say a few preliminary words. The Government of India distinctly admitted and knew very well that the educated people of India were thoroughly loyal. The Hon'ble Member for Kingston (Sir R. Temple) had stated that the state of the country and of the people often invited or demanded criticism on the part of the Natives. It was in every way desirable that their sentiments and opinions should be made known to the ruling classes, and such outspoken frankness should never be mistaken for disloyalty or disaffection. Nothing was nearer to his (Mr. Naoroji's) mind than to make the fullest acknowledgment of all the good that had been done by the connexion of the British people with India. They had no complaint against the British people and Parliament. They had from them everything they could desire. It was against the system adopted by the British Indian authorities in the last century and maintained up till now, though much modified, that they protested. The first point in the Motion was the condition of the people of India. In order to understand fully the present condition of the people of India, it was necessary to have a sort of sketch of the past, and he would give it as briefly as possible. In the last century the Administration was everything that should not be desired. He would give a few extracts from letters of the Court of Directors and the Bengal Government. In one of the letters the Directors said (8th of February, 1764) :—

"Your deliberations on the inland trade have laid open to us a scene of most cruel oppression; the poor of the country, who used always ,to deal in salt, beetlenut, and tobacco, are now deprived of their daily bread by the trade of the Europeans."

Lord Clive wrote (17th of April, 1765) :—

"The confusion we behold, what does it arise from?—rapacity and luxury, the unwarrantable desire of many to acquire in an instant what only a few can or ought to possess."

Another letter of Lord Clive to the Court of Directors said (30th of September, 1765) :—

"It is no wonder that the lust of riches should readily embrace the proffered means of its gratification or that the instruments of your power should avail themselves of their authority and proceed even to extortion in those cases where simple corruption could not keep pace with their rapacity. Examples of this sort set by superiors could not fail of being followed in a proportionate degree by inferiors; the evil was contagious, and spread among the civil and military down to the writer, the ensign, and the free merchant."

He would read one more extract from a letter of the Court of Directors (17th of May, 1766) :—

"We must add that we think the vast fortunes acquired in the inland trade have been obtained by a scene of the most tyrannic and oppressive conduct that ever was known in any age or country."

Macaulay had summed up :—

"A war of Bengalees against Englishmen was like a war of sheep against wolves, of men against demons. . . . . The business of a servant of the Company was simply to wring out of the Natives a hundred or two hundred thousand pounds as speedily as possible."

Such was the character of the Government and the

Administration in the last century; when all this was disclosed by the Committee of 1772, of course, change was made, and a change for the better. He would now give the opinion of Anglo-Indian and English statesmen, and the House would observe that he did not say a single word as to what the Indians themselves said. He put his case before the House in the words of Anglo-Indian and English statesmen alone; some of them had expressed great indignation with usual British feeling against wrong-doing, others had expressed themselves much more moderately. Sir John Shore was the first person who gave a clear prophetic forecast of the character of this system and its effects as early as 1787. He then said (Ret. 377 of 1812):—

"Whatever allowance we may make for the increased industry of the subjects of the State, owing to the enhanced demand for the produce of it (supposing the demand to be enhanced), there is reason to conclude that the benefits are more than counterbalanced by evils inseparable from the system of a remote foreign dominion."

The words were true to the present day. In 1790 Lord Cornwallis said, in a Minute, that the heavy drain of wealth by the Company, with the addition of remittances of private fortunes, was severely felt in the languor thrown upon the cultivation and commerce of the country. In 1823 Sir Thomas Munro pointed out that were Britain subjugated by a foreign Power, and the people excluded from the government of their country, all their knowledge and all their literature, sacred and profane, would not save them from becoming in a generation or two to a low-minded, deceitful, dishonest race. Ludlow, in his *British India*, said:—

"As respects the general condition of the country, let us first recollect what Sir Thomas Munro wrote years ago, 'that even if we could be secured against every internal commotion and could retain the country quietly in subjection, he doubted much if the condition of the people would be better than under the Nativ Princes': that the inhabitants of the British Provinces were 'certainly the most abject race in India'; that the consequences of the conquest of India by the British arms would be, in place of raising, to debase the whole people."

Macaulay, in introducing the clause of our equality with all British subjects, our first Charter of our emancipation in the Bill of 1833, said in his famous and statesmanlike speech :—

"That would, indeed be a doting wisdom which, in order that India may remain a dependency . . . . which would keep a hundred millions of men from being our customers in order that they might continue to be our salves."

And to illustrate the character of the existing system, he said :

"It was, as Bernier tells us, the practice of the miserable tyrants whom he found in India when they dreaded the capacity and spirit of some distinguished subject, and yet could not venture to murder him, to administer to him a daily dose of the pousta, a preparation of opium, the effect of which was in a few months to destroy all the bodily and mental powers of the wretch who was drugged with it, and to turn him into a helpless idiot. This detestable artifice, more horrible than assassination itself, was worthy of those who employed it. It is no model for the English nation. We shall never consent to administer the pousta to a whole community—to stupify and paralyse a great people whom God has committed to our charge—for the wretched purpose of rendering them more amenable to our control."

In a speech (19th of February, 1844) he said :—

"Of all forms of tyranny I believe that the worst is that of a nation over a nation."

Lord Lansdowne, in introducing the same clause of the Bill of 1833 into the House of Lords, pointed out that he should be taking a very narrow view of this question, and one utterly inadequate to the great importance of the subject, which involved in it the happiness or misery of 100,000,000 of human beings, were he not to call the attention of their Lordships to the bearing which this question, and to the influence which this arrangement must exercise upon the future destinies of that vast mass of people. With such high sense of statesmanship and responsibility did Lord Lansdowne of 1833 break our chains. The Indian authorities, however, never allowed those broken chains to fall from our body, and the grandson—the Lord Lansdowne of 1893—now rivetted back those chains upon us. Look upon this picture and upon that! And the Indians were now just the same British slaves, instead of British subjects, as they were before their emancipation in 1833. Mr. Montgomery Martin, after examining the records of a survey of the condition of the people of some Provinces of Bengal or Behar, which had been made for nine years from 1807-16, concluded :—

"It is impossible to avoid remarking two facts as peculiarly striking: First, the richness of the country surveyed; and, second, the poverty of its inhabitants."

He gave the reason for these striking facts. He said:—

"The annual drain of £3,000,000 on British India has amounted in 30 years at 12 per cent. (the usual Indian rate) compound interest to the enormous sum of £723,900,000 sterling. So constant and accumulating a drain, even in England, would soon impoverish her. How severe, then, must be its effects in India where the wage of a labourer is from *2d*. to *3d*. a day."

The drain at present was seven times, if not ten times, as much. Mr. Frederick Shore, of the Bengal Civil Service, said, in 1837 :—

"But the halcyon-days of India are over. She has been drained of a large proportion of the wealth she once pessessed, and her energies have been cramped by a sordid system of misrule to which the interests of millions have been sacrificed for the benefit of the few. The fundamental principle of the English had been to make the whole Indian nation subservient in every possible way to the interests and benefits of themselves."

And he summarised thus :—

"The summary was that the British Indian government had been practically one of the most extortionate and oppressive that ever existed in India. Some acknowledged this and observed that it was the unavoidable result of foreign yoke. That this was correct regarding a Government conducted on the priniciples which had hitherto actuated us was too lamentably true, but, had the welfare of the people been our object, a very different course would have been adopted, and very different results would have followed. For again and again I repeat that there was nothing in the circumstance itself of our being foreigners of different colour and faith that should occasion the people to hate us. We might thank ourselves for having made their feelings towards us what they were. Had we acted on a more liberal plan we should have fixed our authority on a much more solid foundation."

After giving some more similar authorities, Sir R. Temple and others, the Hon'ble Gentleman proceeded: Mr. Bright, speaking in the House of Commons in 1858, said :—

"We must in future have India governed, not for a handful of Englishmen, not for that Civil Service whose praises are so constantly sounded in this House. You may govern India, if you like, for the good of England, but the good of England must come through the channels of the good of India. There are but two modes of gaining anything by our connexion with India—the one is by plundering the people of India, and the other by trading with them. I prefer to do it by trading with them. But in order that England may become rich by trading with India, India itself must become rich.

Sir George Wingate, with his intimate acquaintance with the condition of the people of India, as the introducer of the Bombay land survey system, pointed out, with reference to the economic effects upon the condition of India, that taxes spent in the country from which they were raised were totally different in their effect from taxes raised in one country and spent in another. In the former case the taxes collected from the population were again returned to the industrial classes; but the case was wholly different when taxes were not spent in the country from which they were raised, as they constituted an absolute loss and extinction of the whole amount withdrawn from the taxed country; and he said, further, that such was the nature of the tribute the British had so long exacted from India—and that with this explanation some faint conception may be formed of the cruel, crushing effect of the tribute upon India—that this tribute, whether weighed in the scales of Justice or viewed in the light of the British interests, would be found to be at variance with humanity, with common sense, and with the received maxim of economical science. Mr. Fawcett quoted Lord Metcalf (5th May, 1868), that the bane of the British-Indian system was, that the advantages were reaped by one class and the work was done by another. This havoc was going on increasing up to the present day. Lord Salisbury, in a Minute [Ret. c. 3086-1 of 1881], pointed out that the injury was exaggerated in the case of India, where so much of the revenue was exported without a direct equivalent—that as India must be bled, the lancet should be directed to the parts where the blood was congested or at least sufficient, not to the rural districts which were already feeble from the want of blood. This bleeding of India must cease. Lord Hartington, the Duke of Devonshire, declared (23rd August, 1883) that India was insufficiently governed, and that if it was to be better governed, that could only be done by the employment of the best and most intelligent of the Natives in the Service and he further advised that it was not wise to drive the people to think that their only hope lay in getting rid of their English rulers. Lastly, with regard to the present condition of India, and even serious danger to British power, a remarkable confirmation was given, after a hundred years, to Sir John Shore's prophecy of 1787, by the Secretary of State for India in 1886. A letter of the India Office to the Treasury said (Ret. c. 4868 of 1886):—

"The position of India in relation to taxation and the source of the public revenue is very peculiar, not merely from the habits of the people and their strong aversion to change, which is more specially exhibited to new forms of taxation, but likewise from the character of the Government, which is in the hands of foreigners, who hold the principal administrative offices and form so large a party of the Army. The impatience of the new taxation which will have to be borne wholly as a consequence of the foreign rule imposed on the country and virtually to meet additions to charges arising outside of the country, would constitute a political danger the real magnitude of which, it is to be feared, is not at all appreciated by persons who have no knowledge of or concern in the government of India, but which those responsible for that government have long regarded as of the most serious order."

To sum up—as to the material condition of India—the main features in the last century were gross corruption and oppression by the Europeans; in the present century, high salaries and the heavy weight of European services—their economic condition. Therefore, there was no such thing as finance of India. No financier ever could make a real healthy finance of India, unless he could make two and two equal to six. The most essential condition was wanting. Taxes must be administered by and disbursed to those who paid. That did not exist. From the taxes raised every year a large portion was eaten up and carried away from the country by others than the people of British India. The finances of that country were simply inexplicable, and could not be carried out; if the extracts he had read meant anything, they meant that the present evil system of a foreign domination was destroying them, and was fraught with political danger of the most serious order to British power itself. It had been clearly pointed out that India was extremely poor. What advantage had been derived by India during the past 100 years under the administration of the most highly-praised and most highly-paid officials in the world? If there was any condemnation of the existing system, it was in the result that the country was poorer than any country in the world. He could adduce a number of facts and figures of the practial effect of the present system of administration, but there was not the time now. The very fact of the wail of the Finance Ministers of this decade was a complete condemnation. He was quite sure that the Right Hon'ble Gentleman, the Secretary of State for India, was truly desirous to know the truth, but he could not know that clearly unless certain information was placed before the House. He would suggest, if the Right Hon'ble Gentleman allowed a certain number of Returns which would give the regular production of the country year by year, and the absolute necessaries of a common labourer to live in working health. In connexion with the trade test there was one fallacy which he must explain. They were told in Statistical Returns that India had an enormous trade of nearly £196,000,000, imports and exports together. If he sent goods worth £100 out of this country to some other country, he expected there was £100 of it returned to him with some addition of profit. That was the natural condition of every trade. In the Colonies and in European countries there was an excess of imports over exports. In the United Kingdom for the past 10 years—1883 to 1892—the excess had been 32 per cent., in Norway it was 42 per cent., Sweden 24 per cent., Denmark 40 per cent., Holland 22 per cent., France 20 per cent., Switzerland 28 per cent., Spain 9 per cent., Belgium 7 per cent., and so on. Any one with common sense would, of course, admit that if a quantity of goods worth a certain amount of money were sent out, an additional profit was expected in return ; if not, there could not be any commerce ; but a man who only received in return 90 of the 100 sent out would soon go into the Bankruptcy Court. Taking India's profits to be only 10 per cent. instead of 32 per cent., like those of the United Kingdom, and after making all deductions for remittances for interest on public works loans, India had received back Rs. 170,000,000 worth of imports less than what she exported annually. On the average of 10 years (1883 to 1892) their excesses of exports every year, with compound interst, would amount to enormous sums lost by her. Could any country in the world, England not excepted, stand such a drain without destruction? They were often told they ought to be thankful, and they were thankful, for the loans made to them for public works; but if they were left to themselves to enjoy what they produced with a reasonable price for British rule, if they had to develop their own resources, they would not require any such loans with the interest to be paid on them, which added to the drain on the country. Those loans were only a fraction of what was taken away from the country. India had lost thousands of millions in principal and interest, and was asked to be thankful for the loan of a couple of hundreds of millions. The bulk of the British Indian subjects were like hewers of wood and drawers of water to the British and foreign capitalists. The seeming prosperity of British India was entirely owing to the amount of foreign capital. In Bombay alone, which was considered to be a rich place, there were at least £10,000,000 of capital circulating belonging to foreign Europeans and Indians from Native States. If all such foreign capital were separated there would be very little wealth in British India. He could not go further into these figures, because he must have an occasion on which he could go more fully into them. If only the Right Hon'ble Gentleman, the Secretary of State for India, would give them the Returns which were necessary to understand more correctly and completely the real condition of India, they would all be the better for it. There was another thing that was very serious. The whole misfortune at the bottom, which made the people of British India the poorest in the world, was the pressure to be forced to pay, roughly speaking, 200,000,000 rupees annually for European foreign services. Till this evil of foreign domination, foretold by Sir John Shore, was reduced to reasonable dimensions, there was no hope, and no true and healthy finance for India. This canker was destructive to India and suicidal to the British. The British people would not stand a single day the evil if the Front Benches here—all the principal military and civil posts and a large portion of the army—were to be occupied by some foreigners on even the plea of giving service. When an English official had acquired experience in the service of twenty or thirty years, all that was entirely lost to India when he left the country, and it was a most serious loss, although he did not blame him for leaving the shore. They were left at a certain low level. They could not rise; they could not develop their capacity for higher government, because they had no opportunity; the result was, of course, that their faculties must be stunted. Lastly, every European displaced an Indian who should fill that post. In short, the evil of the foreign rule involved the triple loss of wealth, wisdom, and work. No wonder at India's material and moral poverty! The next point was the wants of the Indians. He did not think it would require very long discussion to ascertain their wants. They could be summed up in a few words. They wanted British honour, good faith, righteousness, and justice. They should then get everything that was good for themselves, and it would benefit the rulers themselves, but unfortunately that had not been their fortune. Here they had an admission of the manner in which their best interests were treated. Lord Lytton, in a confidential Minute, said :—

> No sooner was the Act passed than the Government began to devise means for practically evading the fulfilment of it...... We all know that these claims and expectations never can or will be fulfilled. We have had to choose between prohibiting them and cheating them, and we have chosen the least straightforward course.

He would not believe that the Sovereign and the Parliament who gave these pledges of justice and honour intended to cheat. It was the Indian Executive who had abused their trust. That Act of 1833 was a dead letter up to the present day. Lord Lytton said :—

> Since I am writing confidentially, I do not hesitate to say that both the Governments of England and of India appear to me up to the present moment unable to answer satisfactorily the charge of having taken every means in their power of breaking to the heart the words of promise they had uttered to the ear.

What they wanted was that what Lord Salisbury called "bleeding" should have an end. That would restore them to prosperity, and England might derive ten times more benefit by trading with a prosperous people than she was doing now. They were destroying the bird that could give them ten golden eggs with a blessing upon them. The Hon'ble Member for Kingstone, in his "India in 1880," said:—

Many Native statemen have been produced of whom the Indian nation may justly be proud, and among whom may be mentioned Salar Jung of Hyderabad, Dinkar Rao of Gwalior, Madhao Rao of Baroda. Kirparam of Jammu, Pundit Manphal of Alwar, Faiz Ali Khan of Kotah, Madhao Rao Barvi of Kolaphur, and Purnia of Mysore.

Mountstuart Elphinstone said before the Committee of 1833:—

The first object, therefore is, to break down the separation between the classes and raise the Natives by education and public trust to a level with their present rulers.

He addressed the Conservative Party. It was this Party who had given the just Proclamation of 1858—their greater Charter—in these words:—

We hold ourselves bound to the Natives of our Indian territories by the same obligations of duty which bind us to all our other subjects, and those obligations, by the blessing of Almighty God, we shall faithfully and conscientiously fulfil.

It was again the Conservative Party that, on the assumption of the Imperial title by our Sovereign, proclaimed again the equality of the Natives, whatever their race or creed, with their English fellow-subjects, and that their claim was founded on the highest justice. At the Jubilee, under the Conservative Government again, the Empress of India gave to her Indian subjects the gracious assurance and pledge that—

It had always been and always will be her earnest desire to maintain unswervingly the principles laid down in the Proclamation published on her assumption of the direct control of the Government of India.

He (Mr. Naoroji) earnestly appealed to this Party not to give the lie to these noble assurances, and not to show to the world that it was all hypocrisy and national bad faith. The Indians would still continue to put their faith in the English people, and ask again and again to have justice done. He appealed to the Right Hon'ble Gentleman, the Secretary of State for India, and to the Government, and the Liberal Party who gave them their first emancipation. They felt deeply grateful for the promises made, but would ask that these words be now converted into loyal, faithful deeds, as Englishmen for their honour are bound to do. Some weeks ago the Right Hon'ble Gentleman, the member for Midlothian, wrote a letter to Sir John Cowan in which he stated that the past sixty years had been years of emancipation. Many emancipations had taken place in these years; the Irish, the Jews, the slaves, all received emancipation in that wave of humanity which passed over this country, and which made this country the most brilliant and civilised of the countries of the world. In those days of emancipation, and in the very year in which the Right Hon'ble Gentleman began his political career, the people of India also had their emancipation at the hands of the Liberal Party. It was the Liberal Party that passed the Act of 1833 and made the magnificent promises explained both by Macaulay and Lansdowne. He would ask the Right Hon'ble Gentleman, the member for Midlothian, to say whether, after the Liberal Party having given this emancipation at the commencement of his political career, he would at the end of it, while giving emancipation to 3,000,000 of Irishmen, only further enslave the 300,000,000 of India? The decision relating to the simultaneous examinations meant rivetting back upon them every chain broken by the act of emancipation. The Right Hon'ble Gentleman in 1893, in connexion with the Irish question, after alluding to the arguments of fear and force, said :—

"I hope we shall never again have occasion to fall back upon that miserable argument. It is better to do justice for terror than not to do it at all; but we are in a condition neither of terror nor apprehension; but in a calm and thankful state. We ask the House to accept this Bill, and I make that appeal on the grounds of honour and of duty."

Might he, then, appeal in these days when every educated man in India was thoroughly loyal, when there was loyalty in every class of the people of India and ask: Was it not time for England to do justice to India on the same grounds of "honour and duty"? The Right Hon'ble Member also said :—

There can be no more melancholy, and in the last result no more degrading spectacle upon earth than the spectacle of oppression, or of wrong in whatever form, inflicted by the deliberate act of a nation upon another nation, especially by the deliberate act of such a country as Great Britain upon such a country as Ireland.

This applied to India with a force ten times greater. And he appealed for the nobler spectacle of which the Right Hon'ble Gentleman subsequently spoke. He said :—

But, on the other hand, there can be no nobler spectacle than that which we think is now dawning upon us, the spectacle of a nation deliberately set on the removal of injustice, deliberately determined to break—not through terror, not in haste, but under the sole influence of duty and honour—determined to break with whatever remains still existing of an evil tradition, and determined in that way at once to pay a debt of justice, and to consult by a bold, wise, and good act, its own interests and its own honour.

These noble words applied with tenfold necessity to Britain's duty to India. It would be in the interest of England to remove the injustice under which India suffered more than it would be in the interest even of India itself. He would repeat the prayer to the Right

Hon'ble Gentleman, the member for Midlothian, that he would not allow his glorious career to end with the enthralment of 300,000,000 of the human race whose destinies are entrusted to this great country, and from which they expect nothing but justice and righteousness. The Right Hon'ble Gentleman, the Secretary of State for India, the other day made a memorable speech at Wolverhampton. Among other things, he uttered these noble words:—

> "New and pressing problems were coming up with which the Liberal Party would have to deal. These problems were the moral and material conditions of the people, for both went very much together. They were the problems that the statesmen of the future would have to solve. Mr. Bright once said that the true glory of a nation was not in ships and colonies and commerce, but in the happiness of its homes, and that no Government and no Party deserved the confidence of the British electorate which did not give a foremost place in its legislation and administration to those measures which would promote the comfort, health, prosperity, well-being, and the well-doing of the masses of the people."

He would appeal to the Right Hon'ble Gentleman, the Secretary for India, that in that spirit he should study the Indian problem. Here in England they had to deal with only 38,000,000 of people, and if the Right Hon'ble Gentleman would once understand the Indian problem and do them the justice for which they had been waiting for sixty years, he would be one of the greatest benefactors of the human race. He appealed also to the present Prime Minister with confidence, because he had had an opportunity of knowing that the Prime Minister thoroughly understood the Indian problem. Few Englishmen so clearly understood that problem or the effect of the drain on the resources of India. He saw clearly also how far India was to be made a blessing to itself and to England. Would he begin his promising career as Prime Minister by enslaving 300,000,000 of British subjects? He appealed to him to consider. He could assure the Right Hon'ble Gentleman, the Secretary of State for India, that the feeling in India among the educated classes was nearing despair. It was a very bad seed that was being sown in connexion with this matter if some scheme was not adopted, with reasonable modifications, to give some effect to the Resolution for simultaneous examinations as was promised a few months ago. The Under-Secretary for India assured them in the last Indian Budget Debate that neither he nor the Secretary of State for India had any disposition of thwarting or defeating that Resolution. Indians then felt assured on the point, and their joy was great. But what must be their despair and disappointment when such statements are put before the House of Commons and the country as were to be found in this dark Blue Book. It was enough to break anybody's heart. It would have broken his but for the strong faith he had in the justice of the British people and the one bright ray to be found even in that Return itself, which had strengthened him to continue his appeal as long as he should live. That ray has come from the Madras Government. They had pointed out that they felt bound to do something. They also pointed out the difficulties in the way, but these difficulties were not insurmountable. About the want of true living representation of the people he would not now say anything. Every Englishman understood its importance. The next point in the Motion was the ability to bear existing burdens. Indians were often told by men in authority that India was the lightest taxed country in the world. The United Kingdom paid £2 10*s*. per head for the purposes of the State. They paid only 5*s* or 6*d*. per head, and, therefore, the conclusion was drawn that the Indians were the most lightly-taxed people on earth. But if these gentlemen would only take the trouble of looking a little deeper they would see how the matter stood. England paid £2 10*s*. per head, from an income of something like £35 per head, and their capacity, therefore, to pay £2 10*s*. was sufficiently large. Then, again, this £2 10*s*. returned to them—every farthing of it—in some form or another. The proportion they paid to the State in the shape of Revenues was, therefore, something like only 7 or 8 per cent. India paid 5*s*. or 6*s*. out of their wretched incomes of £2, or 20 rupees, as he calculated, or 27 rupees, as calculated by Lord Cromer. But even taking the latter figure, it would not make any great difference. The three rupees was far more burdensome compared with the wretched capacity of the people of India to bear taxation than the £2 10*s*. which England paid. At the rate of production of Rs. 20 per head India paid 14 per cent. of her income for purposes of revenue—nearly twice as heavy as the incidence of the United Kingdom. Even at the rate of production of Rs. 27 per head the Indian burden was 11 per cent. Then, again take the test of the Income Tax. In the United Kingdom 1*d*. in the Income Tax gave some £2,500,000; but in India, with ten times the population, 1*d*. only gave about Rs. 300,000, with an exemption of only Rs. 50 instead of £150 as in this country. In the last 100 years the wealth of England had increased by leaps and bounds, while India, governed by the same Englishmen, was the same poor nation that it was all through the century that had elapsed, and India at the present moment was the most extremely poor country in the world, and would be poor to the end of the chapter if the present system of foreign domination continued. He did not say that the Natives should attain to the highest positions of control and power. Let there be Europeans in the highest positions, such as the Viceroy, the Governors, the Commander-in-Chief of the Forces, and the higher military officers, and such others as might be reasonably considered to be required to hold the controlling powers. The controlling power of Englishmen in India was wanted as much for the benefit of India as for the benefit of England. The next point in the Motion was, what were the sources of Indian Revenue? The chief sources of the Revenue were just what was mainly obtained from the cultivators of the soil. Here in this country the landlords—the wealthiest people—paid from land only 2 or 3 per cent., of the Revenues, but in India land was made to contribute something like Rs. 27,000,000 of the total Revenue of about Rs. 67,000,000. Then the Salt Tax, the most cruel Revenue imposed in any civilised country, provided Rs. 8,600,000, and that with the opium formed the bulk of the Revenue of India, which was drawn from the wretchedness of the people and by poisoning the Chinese. It mattered not what the State received was called—tax, rent, revenue, or by any other name they liked—the simple fact of the matter was, that out of a certain annual national production the State took a certain portion. Now it would not also matter much about the portion taken by the State if that portion, as in this country, returned to the people themselves, from whom it was raised. But the misfortune and the evil was that much of this portion did not return to the people, and that the whole system of Revenue and the economic condition of the people became unnatural and oppressive, with danger to the rulers. In this country the people drank nearly £4 per head, while in India they could not produce altogether more than half that amount per head. Was the system under which such a wretched condition prevailed not a matter for careful consideration? So long as the system went on so long must the people go on living wretched lives. There was a constant draining away of India's resources, and she could never, therefore, be a prosperous country. Not only that, but in time India must perish, and with it might perish the British Empire. If India was prosperous, England would be prosperous ten times more than she was at present by reason of the trade she could carry on with India. England at present exported some £300,000,000 worth of British produce yet to India she hardly exported produce to the value of 2*s*. 6*d*. per head. If India were prosperous enough to buy even £1 worth per head of English goods she would be able to send to India as much as she now sent to the whole world. Would it not, then, be a far greater benefit to England if India were prosperous than to keep her as she was? The next point in the Motion was the reduction of expenditure. The very first thing should be to cancel that immoral and cruel "compensation" without any legal claim even. That was not the occasion to discuss its selfishness and utter disregard of the wretchedness of the millions of the people. But as if this injustice were not enough, other bad features were added to it, if my information be correct. The compensation was only for remittances to this country. But instead of this, every European and Eurasian, whether he had to make any family remittances or not, was to have a certain addition to his salary. That was not all. The iniquity of making race distinctions was again adopted in this also; Europeans and Eurasians, whether remittances had to be made or not, were to receive compensation: but an Indian who had actually to make remittances for the education of his sons, could have no consideration. But he (Mr. Naoroji) deprecated the whole thing altogether—to take from the wretched to give to the better-off. This compensation should be cancelled as the first step in reduction. As the Chancellor of the Exchequer said the other day in his splendid speech at his magnificent ovation by the Liberal Members, in speaking of the land-owners, the burden was always shifted on to other shoulders, and always on those least able to pay. This was exactly the principle of Anglo-Indian authorities. If it was really intended to retrench with regard to expenditure in India why not begin with the salary list? The Viceroy surely could get his bread and butter with £20,000 a year instead of £25,000. The Governors could surely have bread and cheese for £6,000 or £8,000 instead of £10,000, and so on down till the end of the salary list was reached at Rs. 200 a month. This would afford a much-needed relief, because India could not really afford to pay. Sir William Hunter had rightly said that if we were to govern the Indian people efficiently and cheaply we must govern them by means of themselves, and pay for the administration at the market rates of Native labour; that the good work of security and law had assumed such dimensions under the Queen's government of India that it could no longer be carried on or even supervised by imported labour from England, except at a cost which India could sustain, and he had prophesied that 40 years hereafter they would have had an Indian Ireland multiplied fifty-fold on their hands. The Service must charge from that which was dear, and at the same time unsatisfactory, to one which would require less money and which would at the same time be fruitful to the people themselves. Next, three Secretaries of State and two Viceroys the other day in the House of Lords condemned in the strongest terms the charge that was made by the War Office for troops in India. But it seemed that one Secretary for India (Lord Kimberley) trembled to approach the War Minister, because each new discussion resulted in additional charges and additional burdens. He also truly said that the authorities here, not having to pay from their own pockets, readily made proposals of charges which were unjust and unnecessary, to make things agreeable. The consequence was that charges were imposed which were unjust and cruel. In fact, whatever could have the name of India attached to it, India was forced to pay for it. That was not the justice which he expected from the English. With reference to these military charges, the burden now thrown upon India on account of British troops was excessive, and he thought every impartial judgment would assent to that proposition, considering the relative material wealth of the two countries and their joint obligations and benefits. All that they could do was to appeal to the British Government for an impartial consideration of the relative financial capacity of the two countries, and for a generous consideration to be shown by the wealthiest nation in the world to a dependency so comparatively poor and so little advanced as India. He believed that if any Committee were appointed to enquire, with the honest purpose of finding out to make India prosperous and at the same time to confer as much if not more benefit to England, they could very easily find out the way, and would be able to suggest what should be done. Now, with regard to the financial relations between India and England, it was declared over and over again that this European Army and all European servants were for the special purpose of maintaining the power of the British Empire. Were they, therefore, not for some benefit to England? Were they only for the service of India, for their benefit and for their protection? Was it right that they did avowedly use machinery more for their own purposes than for the purposes of India, and yet make India pay altogether? Was it right, if India's prosperity was, as Lord Roberts said, so indissolubly bound up with their own, and if the greatness and prosperity of the United Kingdom depended upon the retention of India, that they should pay nothing for it, and that they should extract from it every farthing they possibly could? They appealed to their sense of justice in this matter. They were not asking for this as any favour of concession. They based their appeal on the ground of simple justice. Here was a machinery by which both England and India benefited: and it was only common justice that both should share the cost of it. If this expenditure on the European Army and the European Civil Services, which was really the cause of their misery, was for the benefit of both, it was only right that they, as honourable men, should take a share. Their prayer was for an impartial and comprehensive enquiry so that the whole matter might be gone into, and that the question of principles and policy which, after all, was one for their statesmen to decide, should be properly dealt with. They knew that during the rule of the East India Company an enquiry was made every 20 years into the affairs of India. This was no reflection upon the Government; it was simply to see that the East India Company did their duty. There was such an enquiry in 1853, and he thought it was time, after 40 years had elapsed since the assumption of British rule by the Queen, that there should be some regular, independent enquiry like that which used to take place in former days, so that the people and Parliament of this country might see that the Indian authorities were doing their duty. The result of the irresponsibility of the present British Administration was that the expenditure went on unchecked. He admitted fully that expenditure must go on increasing if India was to progress in her civilisation; but if they allowed her to prosper, India would be able not only to pay her £60,000,000 out of the £300,000,000 of population, but she would be able to pay twice, three times, and four times as much. It was not that they did not want to expend as much as was necessary. Their simple complaint was that the present system did not allow India to become prosperous, and so enable her to supply the necessary revenue. As to the character of the enquiry, it should be full and impartial. The Right Hon'ble Member for Midlothian said on one occasion not long ago, when the question of the Opium Trade was under discussion in that House:—

> I must make the admission that I do not think that in this matter we ought to be guided exclusively, perhaps even principally by those who may consider themselves experts. It is a very sad thing to say, but unquestionably it happens not infrequently in human affairs that those who might from their position, know the most and the best, yet, from their prejudices and prepossessions, know the least and the worst.

I certainly for my part do not propose to abide finally and decisively by official opinion.

And the Right Hon'ble Gentleman went on to say that what the House wanted, in his opinion, was "independent but responsible opinion," in order to enable him to proceed safely to a decision on the subject which was to be considered. He was asking by this Resolution nothing more than what the Right Hon'ble Gentleman, the member for Midlothian, had said was actually necessary for the Opium Commission. How much more necessary it was when they meant to overhaul and examine all the various departments of administration, and the affairs of 300,000,000 of people all in a state of transition in civilisation—complicated especially by this evil of foreign rule! What was wanted was an independent enquiry by which the rulers and the ruled might come to some fair and honourable understanding with each other which would keep them together in good faith and good heart. He could only repeat the appeal he had made, in the words of the Queen herself, when her Majesty in her great Indian Proclamation said :—

In their prosperity will be our strength, in their contentment our security, and in their gratitude our best reward!

And then she prayed :—

And may the God of all power grant to us and to those in authority under us strength to carry out these our wishes for the good of our people!

He said Amen to that. He appealed once more to the House and to the British people to look into the whole problem of Indian relations with England. There was no reason whatever why there should not be a thorough good understanding between the two countries, a thorough good-will on the part of Britain, and a thorough loyalty on the part of India, with blessings to both, if the principles and policy laid down from time to time by the British people and by the British Parliament were loyally, faithfully, and worthily, as the English character ought to lead them to expect, observed by the Government of the country.

Amendment proposed to leave out from the word "That," to the end of the Question, in order to add the words—

In the opinion of this House, a full and independent Parliamentary enquiry should take place into the condition and wants of the Indian people, and their ability to bear their existing financial burdens; the nature of the revenue system and the possibility of reductions in the expenditure; also the financial relations between India and the United Kingdom, and generally the system of Government in India.—(*Mr. S. Smith.*)

ENGLAND AND INDIA.

AMENDMENT TO THE ADDRESS.

February 12th, 1895.

Mr. Naoroji (Finsbury, Central) moved an Amendment to add the following to the Address :—

And we humbly pray that Your Majesty will be graciously pleased to direct Your Majesty's Ministers to so adjust the financial relations between the United Kingdom and British India, with regard to all the expenditure incurred in the employment of Europeans in the British-Indian Services, Civil and Military, in this Country and in India, that some fair and adequate portion of such expenditure should be borne by the British Exchequer in proportion to the pecuniary and political benefits accruing to the United Kingdom from Your Gracious Majesty's sway over India ; and that the British Treasury should sustain a fair and equitable portion of all expenditure incurred on all military and political operations beyond the boundaries of India in which both Indian and British interests are jointly concerned.

Having expressed his regret that generally it was not the practice to mention India and to indicate any concern for its interests in the Queen's Speech, he said he was ready to acknowledge with gratitude the advantage which had ensued to the people of India from British rule. He had no desire to minimise those benefits : at the same time he did not appeal to that House or to the British nation for any form of charity to India, however poverty-stricken she is. He based the claims of India, on grounds of justice alone. The question was not at all one of a Party character and therefore he addressed what he had to say to the English people as a whole. He was often supposed to complain about the European officials personally. It was not so. It was the system which made the officials what they were, that he complained about. They were the creatures of circumstances. They could only move in the one-sided groove in which they were placed by the evil system. Further, his remarks applied to British India and not to the Native States. It had been sometimes said that he resorted to agitation in bringing forward the claims of India, but on that point he would only quote a few words from Macaulay, who said in one of his speeches :—

> I hold that we have owed to agitation a long series of beneficent reforms which could have been effected in no other way. . . . The truth is that agitation is inseparable from popular Government. . . . Would the slave trade ever have been abolished without an agitation? Would slavery ever have been abolished without agitation?

He would add that their slavery would not be abolished without agitation and it was well that it should be abolished by peaceful agitation, rather than by revolution caused by despair. He next proposed to consider the respective benefits to Britain and India from their connexion. From the annual production of India the Government took about 700,000,000 rupees for the expenditure of the State. The first result of this cost was law and order, the greatest blessing that any rule could confer, and Indians fully appreciated this benefit of safety from violence to life, limb, and property. Admitting this benefit to India, was it not equally or even more vitally beneficial to the British in India, and more particularly to the British rule itself? Did not the very existence of every European resident in India depend upon the law and order, and so also of the British power itself? The Hindus (and the Mahomedans also, the bulk of whom are Hindus by race) were, by their nature, in their very blood, by the inheritance of social and religious institutions of some thousands of years, peaceful and law-abiding. Their division into the four great divisions was the foundation of their peaceful nature. One class was devoted to learning. Peace was an absolute necessity to them. The fighting and ruling and protecting business was left to the small second class. The third and the largest class—the industrial, the agricultural, the trading, and others—depended upon peace and order for their work, and the fourth serving class were submissive and law-abiding. The virtue of law-abiding was a peculiarly and religiously binding duty upon the Hindus, and to it does Britain owe much of its present peaceful rule over India. It will be Britain's own fault if this character is changed. It was sometimes said that England conquered India with the sword, and would hold it by the sword; but he did not believe this was the sentiment of the British people generally. He could not better emphasise this than in the words of their present great Indian General Lord Roberts had said that :—

> However efficient and well-equipped the Army of India might be—were it indeed absolute perfection, and were its numbers considerably more than at present—our greatest strength must ever rest on the firm base of a united and contented people.

That was the spirit in which he spoke. At present India shared far less benefits than justice demanded. Hundreds of millions of rupees were drawn from, and taken out of, the country for the payment of European officials of all kinds, without any material equivalent being received for it; capital was thus withdrawn, and the Natives prevented from accumulating it; and under the existing system a large part of the resources and industries of the country was thrown into the hands of

British and other capitalists. The 300,000,000 or so of rupees which the India Office draws every year at present is so much British benefit in a variety of ways. British India was indeed British India, and not India's India. He next examined the material or pecuniary benefit derived by Britain and India. Out of about 700,000,000 rupees raised annually from the annual production of the country, nearly 200,000,000 rupees were appropriated in pay, pensions, and allowances to Europeans in this country and in India. This compulsorily obtained benefit to Britain crippled the resources of British Indians, who could never make any capital and must drag on a poverty-stricken life. Hundreds and thousands of millions of wealth passed in principal and interest thereon from India to Britain. Thousands of Europeans found a career and livelihood in India, to the exclusion of the children of the soil, who thus lost both their bread and their brains thereby. Not only that. This crippled condition naturally threw nearly all the requirements of India more or less into British hands, which, under the patronage and protection of the British officials, monopolised nearly everything. British India was, next to officials, more or less for British professionals, traders, capitalists, planters, shipowners, railway holders, and so on, the bulk of the Indians having only to serve for poor income or wages that they earned. In a way a great mass of the Indians were worse off than the slaves of the Southern States. The slaves being property were taken care of by their masters. Indians may die off by millions by want and it is nobody's concern. The slaves worked on their masters' land and resources, and the masters took the profits. Indians have to work on their own land and resources, and hand the profits to the foreign masters. He offered a simple test. Supposing that by some vicissitudes of fortune, which he hoped and prayed would never occur, Britain was conquered by a foreign people. This was no impossible assumption in this world. When Cæsar landed in this country no one could have dreamt that the savages he met here would in time be the masters of the greatest Empire in the world, and that the same Rome and Italy, then the masters of the world, would in turn become a geographical name only. Well, suppose this House was cleared of Englishmen and filled with foreigners, or perhaps shut up altogether, all power and plans in their hands, eating and carrying away much of the wealth of this country year after year, in short, Britain reduced to the present condition and system of government of India, would the Britons submit to it a single day if they could help it? So law-abiding as they are, will not all their law-abiding vanish? No! The Briton will not submit; as he says, "Britons will never be slaves," and may they sing so for ever. Now, he asked whether, though they would never be slaves, was it their mission to make others slaves? No; the British people's instincts are averse to that. Their mission is and ought to be to raise others to their own level. And it was that faith in the instinctive love of justice in the British heart and conscience that keeps the Indian so loyal and hopeful. There was no doubt an immense material benefit to England accruing from the administration of India, but there was no corresponding benefit to the Indian people under the present evil system. For the sake of argument merely, he would assume that the material benefit was equal to the inhabitants of India as well as to the British people, and even on that assumption he contended that the British people were bound for the benefit they derived to take their share of the cost of producing that benifit. The position had been correctly described by Lord Salisbury, who said :—

> The injury is exaggerated in the case of India, where so much of the Revenue is exported without a direct equivalent. As India must be bled, the lancet should be directed to the parts where the blood is congested, or at least sufficient, not to those already feeble for the want of it.

That was correct as far as the present British system in India was concerned, and "India must be bled." The result of this was that their Finance Ministers were obliged to lament and complain, year after year, of the extreme poverty of India, which did not enable them to bring its finances into a properly sound condition. The subject of the poverty of India embraced many aspects in its cause and effects. But this was not the occasion on which such a vast subject could be dealt with adequately. It was the natural and inevitable results of the evil of foreign dominion as it exists in the present system, as predicted by Sir John Shore, above a hundred years ago. In order to give an idea of the position of India as compared with that of England he would point only to one aspect. The Secretary of State for India in his speech last year, on going into Committee on the Indian Budget, made a very important statement. He said :—

> Now as to the Revenue, I think the figures are very instructive. Whereas in England the taxation is £2 11*s*. 8*d*. per head, in Scotland, £2 8*s*. 1*d*. per head, and in Ireland, £1 12*s*. 5*d*. per head, the Budget which I shall present to-morrow will show that the taxation per head in India is something like 2*s*. 6*d*., or one-twentieth the taxation of the United Kingdom, and one-thirteenth that of Ireland.

The Member for Flintshire (Mr. S. Smith) then

asked, "Does he exculde the Land Revenue?" and the Right Hon'ble Gentleman replied :—

> Yes. So far as the taxation of India is concerned, taking the rupee at 1*s*. 1*d*., it is 2*s*. 6*d*. per head.

The exclusion of Land Revenue was unfair, but this was not the time to discuss that point fully. The Land Revenue did not rain from heaven. It formed part and parcel of the annual wealth from which the State Revenue is taken in a variety of different names—call it tax, rent, excise, duty, stamps, income-tax, and so on. It simply meant that so much was taken from the annual production for the purposes of Government. The figures taken by the Right Hon'ble Gentleman for the English taxation is also the gross Revenue, and similarly must this Indian Revenue be taken, except Railway and Navigation Revenue. That statement of the Right Hon'ble Gentleman, if it meant anything, meant that the incidence of taxation in India was exceedingly light compared with the incidence of taxation in England. It was the usual official fiction that the incidence of taxation in India was small as compared with that of this country. But when they considered the incidence of taxation they must consider not simply the amount paid in such taxation, but what it was compared with the capacity of the person who paid it. An elephant might with ease carry a great weight, whilst a quarter ounce or a grain of wheat might be sufficient to crush an ant. Taking the capacity of the two countries, the annual product or income of England was admitted to be something like £35 per head. If there was a taxation of £2 10*s*. as compared with that it was easy to see that the incidence or heaviness was only about 7 per cent., of the annual wealth. If, on the other hand, they took the production of India at the high official estimate of 27 rupees per head—though he maintained it was only 20 rupees—even then the percentage, or incidence of taxation, was about 10 or 11 per cent., or at 20 rupees the incidence was nearly 14 per cent., *i.e.*, nearly double what it was in England. To say, therefore, that India was lightly taxed was altogether a fiction. The fact was, as he stated, that the pressure of taxation in India, according to its means of paying, was nearly double that of wealthy England, and far more oppressive, as exacted from poverty. That was not all. The case for India was worse, and that was the fundamental evil of the present system. In the United Kingdom, if about £100,000,000 are raised as revenue, every farthing returns to the people themselves. But in British India, out of about Rs. 700,000,000 about Rs. 200,000,000 are paid to foreigners—besides all the other British benefits obtained from the wretched produce of Rs. 20 per head. Even an ocean if it lost some water every day which never returned to it, would be dried up in time. Under similar conditions wealthy England even would be soon reduced to poverty. He hoped it would be felt by Hon'ble Members that India, in that condition, could derive very little benefit from British administration. He spoke in agony, not in indignation, both for the sake of the land of his career and for the land of his birth, and he said that if a system of righteousness were introduced into India instead of the present evil system, both England and India would be blessed, the profit and benefit to England itself would be ten times greater than it now was, and the Indian people would then regard their government by this country as a blessing, instead of being inclined to condemn it. England, with India contented, justly treated, and prosperous, may defy half-a-dozen Russias, and may drive back Russia to the very gates of St. Petersburg. The Indian will then fight as a patriot for his own hearth and home. Punjab alone will be able to provide a powerful army. Assuming again, for purpose of argument, that their benefit in India was equal to the British benefit, then he said that the British must share the cost of the expenditure which produced these results, and for which both partners profited equally. But in his amendment he did not ask that even half of the whole cost should be borne by the British people, but only for that part of the expenditure which was incurred on Europeans, and that entirely for the sake of British rule. If it was not for the necessity of maintaining British rule there would be no need to drain India in the manner in which it was now drained by the crushing European Services. Lord Roberts, speaking in London, May, 1893, said :—

> I rejoice to learn that you recognise how indissolubly the prosperity of the United Kingdom is bound up with the retention of that vast Eastern Empire.

But if the interests of England and India were indissolubly bound up, it was only just and proper that both should pay for the cost of the benefits they derived in equal and proper proportions. Lord Kimberley, in a speech at the Mansion House, in 1893, said :—

> We are resolutely determined to maintain our supremacy over our Indian Empire..........that (among other things) supremacy rests upon the maintenance of our European Civil Service......We rest also upon our magnificent European force which we maintain in that country.

The European Civil Services and European residents he contended, were the weakest part in the maintenance of their rule in India. Whenever any unfortunate trouble did arise, as in 1857, the European Civil Service, and Europeans generally, were in their greatest difficulty. They must be saved, they were in the midst of the greatest danger, and in such circumstances they became their greatest weakness. The loyal Indians saved many lives. To suppose that their Civil Service, or the British people, could have any other safety than that which arose from the satisfaction of India, was to deceive themselves. Whatever might be the strength of their military force, their true security in the maintenance, of their rule in India depended entirely on the satisfaction of the people. Brute force may make an empire, but brute force would not maintain it ; it was moral force and justice and righteousness alone that would maintain it. If he asked that the whole expenditure incurred on Europeans should be defrayed from the British Treasury he should not be far wrong, but, for the sake of argument, he was prepared to admit that the benefit derived from the employment of Europeans was shared equally by Europeans and Natives. He therefore asked that at least half of the expenditure incurred on Europeans here and in India should be paid from the British Exchequer. Indians were sometimes threatened that if they raised the question of financial relations, something would have to be said about the navy. Apart from a fair share for the vessels stationed in India, why should England ask India to defray any other portion of the cost of the navy? The very sense of justice had probably prevented any such demand being made. The fame, gain and glory of the navy was all England's own. There was not a single Indian employed in the navy. It was said the navy was necessary to protect the Indian commerce. There was not a single ship sailing from or to India which belonged to India. The whole of the shipping was British, and not only that, but the whole cargo while floating was entirely at the risk of British money. There was not an ounce exported from India on which British money did not lie through Indian banks. In the same way, when goods were exported from England, British money was upon them. The whole floating shipping and goods were first British risk. Lastly, there is every inch of the British navy required for the protection of these blessed islands. Every Budget, from either Party, emphasises this fact, that the first line of defence for the protection of the United Kingdom alone, demands a navy equal to that of any two European Powers. He had asked for several returns from the Secretary of State. If the Right Hon'ble Gentleman would give those returns, the House would be able to judge of the real material condition of India; until those returns were presented they would not be in a position to understand exactly the real condition of India under the present system. He would pass over all the small injustices, in charging every possible thing to India, which they would not dare to do with the Colonies. India Office buildings, Engineering College buildings, charge for recruiting, while the soldiers form part and parcel of the army here; the system of short service occasioning transport expenses, and so on, and so on. While attending the meeting upon the Armenian atrocities, he could not help admiring the noble efforts that the English always made for the protection of the suffering and oppressed. It is one of the noblest traits in the English character. Might he appeal to the same British people, who were easily moved to generosity and compassion when there was open violence, to consider the cause why in India hundreds of thousands of people were frequently carried away through famine and drought, and that millions constantly lived on starvation fare? Why was it that after a hundred years of administration by the most highly paid officials, the people of India were not able to pay one-twentieth part of the taxation which the United Kingdom paid, or even one-thirteenth which poor Ireland paid? Were the English satisfied with such a result? Is it creditable to them? While England's wealth had increased, India's had decreased. The value of the whole production of India was not £2 per head per annum, or, taking into account the present rate of exchange, it was only 20*s*. The people here spent about £4 per head in drink alone, while India's whole production is only a pound or two per head. Such should not be the result of a system which was expected to be beneficent. He appealed to the people of this country to ask and consider this question. If there were famine here food would be poured in from the whole world. Why not so in India? Why the wretched result that the bulk of the people had no means to pay for food? Britain has saved India from personal violence. Would it not also save millions from want and ravages of famine owing to their extreme poverty caused by the evil which Sir J. Shore predicted. The late Mr. Bright told his Manchester friends that there were two ways of benefiting themselves, the one was by plunder, and the other was by trade, and he preferred the latter mode. At present, England's trade with India was a miserable thing. The British produce sent to all India was about worth 2*s*. per head per annum. If, however, India were prosperous, and able to buy, England would have no need to complain of duties and the want of markets. In India there was a market of 300 millions of civilised people. If the wants of those people were provided for, with complete free trade in her own hands and control, England would be able to eliminate altogether the word "unemployed" from her dictionary: in fact, she would not be able to supply all that India would want. The other day the Chancellor of the Exchequer said that where injustice and wrong prevailed, as it did prevail in Armenia, a Liberal Government was called upon to obtain the co-operation of European powers in order to repress the wrong. Might he appeal to the Right Hon'ble Gentleman to give an earnest and generous consideration to India? The Right Hon'ble Gentleman, the member for Midlothian made a very grand speech on his birthday upon the Armenian question. He appealed to that Right Hon'ble Gentleman, and to all those of the same mind, to consider and find out the fundamental causes which make the destitution of forty or fifty millions—a figure of official admission—and destruction of hundreds of thousand by famine, possible, though British India's resources are admitted on all sides to be vast. In the present amendment his object was to have that justice of a fair share in expenditure to be taken by Britain in proportion to her benefits. He asked for no subsidy, but only for common justice. By a certain amount of expenditure they derived certain benefits; they were partners, therefore let them share equally the benefits and the costs. His amendment also had reference to expenditure outside the boundaries of India. He maintained that if England undertook operations in Burmah, Afghanistan, and in other places beyond the borders of India for the protection of British rule, she was bound by justice to defray at least half the cost. The benefit of these operations was for both Britain and India. The principle was admitted in the case of the last Afghan war, which was certainly not a very necessary war, but the Liberal Government defrayed a portion of the expenditure. That India should be required to pay the cost of all the small wars and aggressions beyond her boundaries, or political subsidies, was not worthy of the British people, when these were all as much or more necessary, for their own benefit and rule as for the benefit of India. He hoped he was not appealing to deaf ears. He knew that when any appeal was made on the basis of justice, righteousness, and honour, the English people responded to it, and with perfect faith in the English character he believed his appeal would not be in vain. The short of the whole matter was, whether the people of British India were British citizens or British helots. If the former, as he firmly believed to be the desire of the British people, then let them have their birthright of British rights as well as British responsibilities. Let them be treated with justice, that the costs of the benefits to both should be shared by both. The unseemly squabble that was now taking place on the question of Import Duties between the Lancashire manufacturers on the one hand and the British Indian Government on the other illustrated the helpless condition of the people of India. This was the real position. The Indian Government arbitrarily imposed a burden of a million or so a year on the ill-fed Indians as a heartless compensation to the well-fed officials, and have gone on adding to expenditure upon Europeans. They want money, and they adopt Lord Salisbury's advice to bleed where there is blood left, and also by means of Import Duties tax the subjects of the Native States. The Lancashire gentlemen object and want to apply the lancet to other parts that would not interfere with their interests—and thus the quarrel between them. However that is decided, the Indians are to be bled. He did not complain of the selfishness of the Lancashire people. By all means be selfish, but be intelligently selfish. Remember what Mr. Bright said—Your good can only come through India's good. Help India to be prosperous, and you will help your prosperity. Macaulay truly said:—

> It would be a doting wisdom which would keep a hundred millions (now more than two hundred millions) of men from being our customers in order that they might continue to be our slaves.

They had no voice as to the expenditure of a single farthing in the administration of Indian affairs. The British Indian Government could do what they liked. There was, of course, an Indian Council; but when a Budget was proposed it had to be accepted. The representatives of the Council could make a few speeches, but there the matter ended. The people of India now turned to the people of Great Britain, and, relying on the justice of their claim, asked that they should contribute their fair share in proportion to any benefits which this country might derive from the possession of India.

INDIA AND LANCASHIRE.

February 21st, 1895.

Sir Henry James, a Conservative Member moved the adjournment of the House "in order to call attention to a matter of definite and urgent public importance—the effect of the imposition of duties on cotton goods imported into India." The motion was warmly debated, and ultimately lost, the Government as a body opposing Sir Henry James. Mr. Dadabhai made the following speech on the occasion :—

At this late hour I shall not occupy the House very long, but I will ask Hon'ble Gentlemen opposite : Does England spend a single farthing in connection with India ? Hon'ble Gentlemen say they are maintaining the Empire. It is something extraordinary ! For the two hundred years they have been connected with India they have not spent a single farthing either on the acquisition or the maintenance of the Empire. However, I will not go into that large question. (*Hear, hear.*) Did I wish to see the Empire in India endangered, were I a rebel at heart, I should welcome this motion with the greatest delight. The great danger to the Empire is to adopt methods of irritation, which if continued will assuredly bring about disintegration. (*Hear, hear.*) I appeal to the Unionists to vote against this motion or they will drive the first nail in the coffin of British rule in India. You may, as Lord Roberts has told you, have a stronger and larger army in India

24—11

than you have at present; you may have that army to perfection itself; but your stability rests entirely upon the satisfaction of the people. (*Hear, hear*). I heard with great satisfaction Hon'ble Members on both sides of the House recognise this important fact, that after all, the whole safety of the British rule depends upon the satisfaction of the people, and the justice that may be done towards them. Remember whatever you are, you are still like a step-mother—children may submit to any amount of oppression from their own mother, and will be affectionate towards her, but from their step-mother they will always demand the strictest justice. (*Hear, hear.*) You must remember that you as an alien people have to rule over a large number of people in the Indian Empire, and if you do not consult their feelings, you will make a very great mistake. I am quite sure that I appeal not in vain to the Unionists, and can I appeal to the Home Rulers? (*Hear, hear.*) If they mean Home Rule, they mean that it must be entirely on the integrity of the Empire. (*Hear, hear.*) I have never known a motion brought before this House which was more separatist than the one before it now. (*Hear, hear.*) I can count upon the votes of Home Rulers. The passing of this motion would be the passing of a motion of disunion. Perhaps you may not feel the effect for some time but I impress upon this great assembly—that though a revolution may not take place to-morrow, it is the accumulation of many years, of many disappointments, many inattentions, that at last produces a revolution. Do not forget 1857. I, for one, desire from the bottom of my heart that the British rule and connection with India may last for a very long time. (*Hear, hear.*) They are dealing with many millions of people, and I desire and hope that India to-morrow will not receive a telegram saying that this motion has been passed. The feeling of injustice is very strong there. India has its agitators. What were the occupiers of the Treasury Bench? Did they not go up and down the country endeavouring to educate the people and to disseminate their own opinions? And so does the Opposition and every member. It is by peaceful agitation alone that British India is to be preserved. This is not the first occasion that our Lancashire friends have tried to force the hands of the Government to do certain things adverse to India. They began in 1700. But I am not going on this grave occasion to enter into any petty quarrel with them. (*Hear, hear.*) This I will say, British India is too poor to buy Manchester goods. People talked of the enormous Manchester trade. There was no such enormous trade, unless 15*s.* 6*d.* per head per annum was an enormous trade. I appeal to all parties not to let this motion pass. (*Hear, hear.*) I appeal to you not to let a telegram go forth to India, saying that it has been passed. It will have a very bad effect there. You have your remedy in the assurance of the Secretary of India, that if you can point out how to remove the alleged protective character of these duties, he will do it. You are bound to be satisfied with that assurance. I again earnestly hope that the motion will not be allowed to pass. (*Hear, hear.*)

MISCELLANEOUS SPEECHES AND ADDRESSES.

RETIREMENT OF LORD RIPON.

The following speech was delivered before the public meeting of the native inhabitants of Bombay in honour of Lord Ripon, on his retirement from the Viceroyalty, convened by the Sheriff in the Town Hall, on Saturday, the 29th November, 1884. The Hon'ble Sir Jamsetjee Jeejeebhoy, Bart, C.S.I., in the Chair.

Mr. Dadabhai Naoroji, who was received with loud and prolonged cheers, in supporting the Resolution, * said :—Mr. Chairman and Gentlemen,—All India from one end to the other proclaims the righteousness and good deeds of Lord Ripon. There are not many persons among the thousands that have assembled here, or among the hundreds of thousands of this city or among the millions of this Presidency, who have not his great services by heart. (*Cheers.*) It will be useless for me to waste any time in a reiteration of them. I shall touch upon what strikes me as the brightest stars in the whole galaxy of his deeds. The greatest questions of the Indian problem to my mind at present are, our material and moral loss,

---

* That this meeting, representing the various native communities of Western India, desires to place on record the deep sense of gratitude entertained by them for the eminent services to India rendered by the Marquis of Ripon during his administration as Viceroy of India.

and our political education for self-government. For the former, the first great achievement of the Ripon Government is a courageous and candid acknowledgment that the material and educational condition of India is that of extreme poverty. After this bold and righteous recognition, England will feel bound to remedy this great evil. (*Cheers.*) Lord Ripon's Government has, however, not remained satisfied with their acknowledgment, but has laid the foundation of the remedy by resolving that Indian energy, Indian resources, and Indian agency must be developed in every way and in all departments with broad and equal justice to all. For the second—our political education—nothing can be a more conclusive proof of the success of his measures in that direction than the sight of the great and national political upheaving in the ovation that is now being poured upon him throughout the length and breadth of India. And we ourselves are here to-day as the proof of the success of our political education. (*Cheers.*) We are to propose a memorial to Lord Ripon. But what will hundred such memorials be to the great monuments he has himself raised to himself? As self-government, and self-administration and education advanced, for which all he has raised great new landmarks, his memory shall exist at every moment of India's life, and they will be the everlasting monuments, before which all our memorials will sink into utter insignificance. It was asked in St. Paul where Wren's monument was. This, St. Paul itself, was his monument, was the reply. What is Ripon's monument? It will be answered India itself—a self-governing and prosperous nation and loyal to the British throne. Canning was Pandy Canning, he is now the Canning the Just of the British historian. The native historian with admiration and gratitude, and the English historian, with pride and pleasure, will point to Ripon, as Ripon the Righteous, the maker and benefactor of a nation of hundreds of millions. (*Loud cheers.*) But by far the greatest service that Ripon has done, is to England and Englishmen. He has raised the name and glory of England and the Englishmen, and rivetted India's loyalty to the British rule. Deep and unshakeable as my faith is in the English character for fairness and desire to do good to India, I must confess during my humble efforts in Indian politics, I was sometimes driven to despair, and to doubt my faith. But Ripon has completely restored it to its full intensity, that England's conscience is right and England *will* do its duty and perform its great mission in India, when she has such sons, so pure of heart and high in statemanship. (*Cheers.*) I pray that our Sovereign give us always Viceroys like Ripon. The good deeds of Ripon are sung all over the land by all from the prince to peasant. I am informed that addresses will flow from the poor agriculturists when Lord Ripon arrives here, and I have the pleasure of reading to you a letter to me from a prince. This is what H. H. the Thakore Saheb Bhagvatsinghjee of Gondal says :—" I am happy to note that a movement is being set on foot in Bombay to perpetuate the memory of the retiring Viceroy, Lord Ripon. He has stronghold on the loyalty and affection of our people, with whose vital interests he has identified himself. So the movement of which you are a promoter has my best sympathies. As a slight tribute of my admiration for the noble Lord Ripon, I beg to subscribe Rs. 3,000 to the Ripon Memorial Fund." (*Cheers.*) For the sentiments of His Highness the

Jam Saheb Vibhajee of a Jamnaggur, you can judge best when I tell you that he with his Kuvar Jasvatsinghjee has subscribed Rs. 10,000 to the Ripon Memorial. The Thakore Sahebs of Rajakote and Katosan have also subscribed. My friend Mr. Hurkissondas has just this moment received a telegram from H. H. The Thakore Saheb of Limree, the Hon'ble Jesvatsinghjee, subscribing Rs. 5,000 to the Ripon Memorial. A deputation from the great meeting of Sholapore, which was presided over by Mr. Satyendranath Tajore, has attended here. Also another deputation from Khandesh. Well, gentlemen, these two months will be an epoch and a bright page in Indian history, and we shall be for ever proud that we had the good fortune to have had a share in honouring the great name of Ripon. (*Loud and prolonged cheers.*)

THE FAWCETT MEMORIAL MEETING.

The following speech was delivered before the public meetings of the inhabitants of Bombay, held in the Town Hall, on the 2nd September, 1885, convened by the Bombay Presidency Association for the purpose of taking steps to raise a memorial to the late Professor Fawcett. His Excellency Lord Reay, Governor of Bombay, in the Chair.

Mr. Dadabhai Naoroji, who was greeted with loud and prolonged cheers, said:—Your Excellency, Ladies and Gentlemen,—I beg to propose that a committee be formed to take necessary steps for collecting funds for the memorial, and for deciding what form the memorial should take, Mr. P. M. Mehta, the Hon'ble Mr. K. T. Telang, Messrs. D. E. Wacha, R. M. Sayani, and Vandrawandas Purshotumdas acting as honorary secretaries to the fund. I take this proposition in hand with more grief than delight. I knew Professor Fawcett personally, and I know what loss we have suffered. There is a great deal that is always made public and appreciated by the public as far as it is known, but there is a great deal more that is done by good men which never sees the light of publication, and which consequently is never appreciated. I give my personal experience of the worth of this great man, which will show you that whereas in a public way he has done a great deal of good, he has also privately and behind the scenes been proved as useful a friend of India as ever any man has been. To give my own personal reminiscences of one or two incidents, I can tell you that when I appeared before the Finance Committee in England in 1873, I had perhaps the rashness of writing a letter beforehand of what I wanted to give my evidence upon. What I said there, somehow or other, did not suit Mr. Ayrton, the chairman of the committee, and he hindered and hampered me in every way. Before I went to the committee I saw Mr. Fawcett, who was always sympathising with us, and I laid before him the notes which I wanted to submit to the committee. He considered them very carefully and told me that that was the very thing that ought to be brought to the committee. But, strange to say, that when I went before the committee Mr. Ayrton chose to decide that that was just the thing that was not to be brought before the committee. On the first day I was hardly able to give evidence of what I wanted to say. But the next day, when it came to Mr. Fawcett's turn to examine me, in a series of judicious and pointed questions, he brought out all that I had to say in a brief and clear manner. You will see from this that although such little incidents scarcely become public, they are in themselves not without their value. He did, in fact, an invaluable service in enabling a native of India to say all that he wanted to say, whether it was right or wrong. Here is an instance of the justice and fearlessness with which he wanted to treat this country. (*Cheers.*) Fancy a noble commanding figure standing on the floor of the House of Commons respectfully listened to by the whole House, pleading the cause of hundreds of millions of people whom he had not seen, pleading as effectively as any of India's own sons could ever do (*cheers*), holding like unto the blind deity of justice the scales in his hands even between friends and foes in small matters and in great. (*Loud cheers.*) That is the blind man we have assembled to-day to honour. You can easily perceive how many a time, as I saw him pleading our cause, I felt a sort of awe and veneration as for a superior being. (*Cheers.*) In his speeches he never stooped to catch a momentary applause, but he always spoke in sober language words of wisdom—words that sprang from his inner conviction—that in their turn carried conviction to every one around him. (*Cheers.*) We are told that where good men stand the ground becomes holy. Here his influence and his words reach and permeate the whole atmosphere, and whoever breathes the atmosphere catches something of that goodness and that sincerity towards nature and God. He was one of those men who not only in the senate stood firm and bold and dealt out even justice to friend and foe alike, but on the stumping platform too he was the same considerate man, who never uttered a word to sink into the vulgar crowd, but always tried to raise them to a level higher and better than they were before he spoke. He himself, we know, had grappled the subject of Indian problems with perfect clearness and in all their details. He learned from Anglo-Indians, but he subsequently became the teacher of all Anglo-Indians. He told them that the time was coming when the policy of the British administration should be entirely changed, that the way in which British India was governed was not the way in which it was fit to be governed by a nation of Englishmen. He understood and always declared that he belonged to a nation to whom India was confided in the providence of God for their care and help. He felt himself to be one of that nation, and he felt the instinct of Englishmen to do that only which was just and right, and to receive the glory derived from the advancement of civilization and by the raising of mankind instead of trampling them down under foot. He felt that duty as an Englishman, and he earnestly and devotedly performed that duty as far as one man of ability and earnestness could ever do. (*Cheers.*) We are now threatened with a permanent addition to the expenditure of some two millions. Do those statesmen who make such a proposal at all think of what they are about? Fawcett's voice from the grave now rises once again, and we are reminded of his words in connection with the Licence Tax. He said that if such an odious and unjust tax had been imposed, it was because no better one could be substituted in its place, and he further stated that when the time came for them to impose another tax, the Government would be reduced to great straits, and they would have to impose a tax as must end in disaster and serious peril. (*Cheers.*) The statesmen who are now thinking of imposing the additional burden of expenditure must bear in mind the words of this great man, ponder over them, and carefully consider how far they can impose further burdens on the extremely poor people of India. (*Cheers.*) When I say the people are extremely poor, the words are mot mine, but those of Mr. Fawcett and many other eminent statesmen. I do not want to detain the audience any longer, but I will only say the man is dead, but his words will remain; and I only hope that he will inspire others to follow in his footsteps and to earn the blessings of hundreds of millions of the people of this country. (*Loud and prolonged cheers.*)

INDIA'S INTEREST IN THE GENERAL ELECTION. (1886.)

The following speech was delivered before a meeting of the members of the Bombay Presidency Association, held in the rooms of the Association on Tuesday evening, the 29th September, 1885. Mr. (now Sir) Dinsha Maneckji Petit in the Chair.

The Hon'ble Mr. Dadabhai Naoroji proposed :—"That the following candidates, on account of their services and opinions publicly expressed by them on Indian questions, are deserving of the support of the Indian people :—The Right Hon'ble Mr. John Bright, the Marquis of Hartington, Mr. J. Slagg, Sir J. Phear, Mr. L. Ghose, Mr. W. Digby, Mr. W. S. Blunt, Mr. S. Key, Mr. S. Laing, Captain Verney, and Mr. W. C. Plowden. That the views regarding Indian questions publicly expressed by the following candidates cannot be accepted as representing Indian interests ;—Sir Richard Temple, Mr. J. M. Maclean, Mr. A. S. Ayrton, Sir Lewis Pelly, and Sir Roper Lethbridge." He said :—I speak to the motion which is placed in my hands with a deep sense of its importance. Hitherto it has been said, and it will be so generally, that the English people can mostly derive their information about India from Anglo-Indians, official and non-official, but chiefly from the former. But there are Anglo-Indians and Anglo-Indians. Some, but their number is small, have used their eyes rightly, have looked beyond the narrow circle of their own office, have sympathised with the natives, and tried to understand them and to find out their true wants and aspirations. Unfortunately the large number of Anglo-Indians do not take such wide views, or such interest in the natives as would enable them to judge rightly of the actual condition of India. Now, when we consider of what extreme importance it is to us that the people of England should have correct information of our condition and wants; how almost entirely we have to depend upon the people and Parliament of England to make those great reforms which alone can remove the serious evils from which we are suffering, it is no ordinary necessity for us that we should take some steps, by which we may inform the great British public, on which sources of information they could rely with any confidence. As I have said, the number of those who have the necessary true experience and interest in the natives is very small. It is extremely necessary that such should be pointed out by us. We also find that several Englishmen visiting India, as impartial observers, without any bias or prejudices, have often formed a more correct estimate of the position and necessities of India than many an Anglo-Indian of the so-called experience of twenty or thirty years. Even some who have not been here at all, form fair and just estimates. It is not always that we can approach the British people in a way so as to secure the general attention of the whole nation at the same time. The present occasion of the new elections is one of those rare occasions in which we can appeal to the whole nation, and especially in a way most useful for our purpose. It is in Parliament that our chief battles have to be fought. The election of its members, especially those who profess to speak on Indian matters, requires our earnest attention, and we should point out clearly to the electors, which of those candidates, who make India a plank in their credentials, have our confidence. We do not at all intend to influence the electors in any way in matters of their choice of the representatives that suit them best for their local politics. What we desire to impress upon them is, that so far as the important element of the deliberations on Indian questions is concerned, we desire to name those candidates who are deserving of our confidence and support, and on whom we can rely as would fairly and righteously represent our real wants and just rights before Parliament. It is with this object that I ask you to adopt the Resolution before you. The first name in our Resolution is the bright name of the Right Hon'ble Mr. John Bright. Now, I do not certainly presume that I can say anything, or that our association can do anything that can in the least add to the high position Mr. Bright occupies. What I say, therefore, is not with any view that we give any support to him, but as an expression of our esteem and admiration, and of our gratitude for the warm and righteous interest he has evinced on our behalf. I would not certainly take up your time in telling you what he is and what he has done. His fame and name are familiar to the wide world. I may simply refer to a few matters concerning ourselves. Our great charter is the gracious Proclamation of the Queen. That proclamation is the very test by which we test friends or foes; and it is Mr. Bright, who first proposed and urged the duty and necessity of issuing such a proclamation, at a time when the heads of many were bewildered and lost, in his speech on the India Bill in 1858. I should not tarry long on the tempting subject, for, if

I went on quoting from Mr. Bright's speeches, to show what he has done more than a quarter of a century ago, asking for us what we have been only latterly beginning to give utterance to, I might detain you for hours. I must, however, give you a few short extracts, showing both the earnestness and the intense sense of justice of the man. "The people of India," he said, "have the hightest and strongest claims upon you—claims which you cannot forget—claims which if you do not act upon, you may rely upon it that, if there be a judgment for nations—as I believe there is, as for individuals—our children in no distant generation must pay the penalty which we have purchased by neglecting our duty to the populations of India." In his speech of 1853, on the occasion of the renewal of the E. I. Company's charter, referring to the miserable condition of the masses of India, he said :—"I must say that it is my belief that if a country be found possessing a most fertile soil and capable of bearing every variety of production, and that notwithstanding, the people are in a state of extreme destitution and suffering, the chances are that there is some fundamental error in the government of that country." When, may I ask, will our rulers see this "fundamental error?" I have purposely confined myself to his older utterances so far, that we may fully appreciate the righteous advocacy at a time when our own voice was feeble and hardly heard at all. You will allow me to make one reference to his later words, and you will see how he is yet the same man and the same friend of India. In his "Public Letters," in a letter written by him last year to a gentleman at Calcutta, he says :—"It is to me a great mystery that England should be in the position she now is in relation to India. I hope it may be within the ordering of Providence that ultimately good may arise from it. I am convinced that this can only come from the most just Government which we are able to confer upon your countless millions, and it will always be a duty and a pleasure to me to help forward any measure that may tend to the well-being of your people." The Marquis of Hartington also occupies a position to which we can hardly add anything. But as we have during his State Secretaryship of India observed his disposition towards a due appreciation and fulfilment of the noble principles of the Proclamation, and his emphatically identifying himself with the righteous Ripon policy at a time of crucial trial—during the excitement of the Ilbert Bill—we cannot but take this opportunity of expressing our thanks and our confidence in him. To assure you the more fully of this duty upon us, you will permit me to read a few words on this very topic from his speech of 23rd August, 1883. After pointing out the insufficiency of the administration, and the inability of India to afford more for it, he said:—"If the country is to be better governed, that can only be done by the employment of the best and most intelligent of the natives in the service. There is a further reason, in my opinion, why this policy should be adopted, and that is, that it is not wise to educate the people of India, to introduce among them, your civilization and your progress and your literature, and at the same time to tell them, they shall never have any chance of taking any part or share in the administration of the affairs of their country except by their getting rid, in the first instance, of their European rulers." I cannot refrain myself from expressing my deep regret that we are not able to include in our present list a name that stands pre-eminently high as one of our best friends—I mean Mr. Fawcett. But I trust you will allow me to give a few short extracts, as a warning and a voice from the grave, of one who had the welfare of the poor and dumb millions at heart. Though he is dead his spirit may guide our other friends, and our rulers. I give these extracts as specially bearing on the present disastrous move of imposing a permanent additional annual burden of some two to three crores of rupees upon us, and on the whole Indian problem. With reference to the Afghan policy he said in 1879:—"It cannot be too strongly insisted upon that in the existing financial condition of India, no peril can be more serious than the adoption of a policy, which, if it should lead to a large additional expenditure, would sooner or later necessitate an increase of taxation. . . The additional taxation which must be the inevitable accompaniment of increased expenditure will bring upon India the gravest perils." Again—"The question, however, as to the exact proportion in which the cost of pursuing a forward policy in Afghanistan should be borne by England and India respectively will have again to be considered anew, now that it has become necessary to renew hostilities in Afghanistan." These words apply with equal force today when we are threatened with a large unnecessary additional burden. On the subject of the whole Indian problem, he said:—"Although there is much in the present financial condition of India to cause the most serious apprehension, yet there is one circumstance connected with it which may fairly be regarded as a most hopeful omen for the future. Until quite lately, India was looked upon as an extremely wealthy country, and there was no project, however costly, that India was not supposed to be rich enough to pay for. Now, however, juster ideas of the resources of the country and of the condition of the people prevail. The recurrence of famines. . . . have at length led the English public to take firm hold of the fact that India is an extremely poor country, and that the great mass of her people are in such a state of impoverishment that the Government will have to contend with exceptional difficulties if it becomes necessery to procure increased revenue by additional taxation." "Without an hour's delay the fact should be recognized that India is not in a position to pay for various services at their present rate of remuneration. A most important saving might be effected by more largely employing natives in positions which are now filled by highly paid Europeans, and from such a change political as well as financial advantages would result." "The entire system in which the Government of India is conducted must be changed. The illusion is only just beginning to pass away that India is an extremely wealthy country." "The financial condition of India is one of such extreme peril that economy is not only desirable but is a matter of imperative necessity." "No misfortune which could happen to India could be greater than having to make her people bear the burden of increased taxation." "In order to restore the finances of India and prevent them drifting into hopeless embarrassment, it is absolutely essential that the policy of 'rigid economy in every branch of the public service' which has been recently announced by the Government should be carried out with promptitude and thoroughness." This policy was announced by the Conservative Government and now all this is forgotten and the Conservative Government are proposing to burden us with additional expenditure of two or three millions, or may be more! We cannot too strongly protest against this. In all the extracts I have read you will perceive the kind of policy which our friends have urged, and this test, or as I may shortly call, the Royal Proclamation Policy, is the principal one by which we may discriminate friends from those who either from ignorance or narrow-minded selfishness advocate a different policy. Judging by this test, I may say that all the other names in the first part of the Resolution are fairly entitled to our confidence and to an appeal from us to the constituencies to return them to Parliament as far as our interests are concerned. Their writings show that they have a good grasp of our position and wants. I may refer to Mr. Slagg's views and efforts to abolish the India Council. Nothing can be more absurd than that in the nineteenth century and in England itself, the first home of public and free discussion upon all public matters, there should exist a body to deliberate secretly upon the destinies of a sixth of the human race! It is an utter anachronism. Mr. Slagg's laudable and persistent efforts to get an inquiry into the Government of India promises to be successful. Messrs. Slagg, Digby, Keay, Blunt, and Verney's, writings show that they understand us and have done us good service. About Mr. Lal Mohun Ghose I need not say more than that he is the only one through whom the Indians will now have a chance of speaking for themselves. I have every hope that he will do justice to himself, and fulfil the expectations which India has rested on him by honest and hard work for the welfare of his country.

We must feel very thankful to the electors of Greenwich for giving him such welcome and sympathy as they have done. They have shown remarkable liberality, vindicated the English spirit of justice and philanthropy, have held out a hand to us of equal citizenship, and nobly confirmed the sincerity of the Royal Proclamation, by their action as a part of the English nation. Mr. Laing has, I am afraid, some incorrect notions about the balance of the trade of India, but we know that he understands India well and will continue to be useful in promoting our welfare. Sir John Phear and Mr. Plowden are known to us for their sympathies with us. Sir John Phear's book "The Aryan Village," shows much sympathetic study of the country and its institutions, and he proved our friend at the time of the Ilbert Bill. He said:—"We have a higher duty to India than to consult the prejudices of this kind of a few thousands of our own countrymen, who are there to-day, but may be gone to-morrow. We have to govern that vast empire in the interest of the millions who constitute the indigenous population of the country." Mr. Plowden says, with reference to Lord Ripon's policy:—"I know it to be just, I know it also to be honest and earnest, I believe it to be sound and thoroughly practical." I next come to our second list. As I have already said, we do not ask the constituencies not to return them if they are suitable to them on other grounds. We only ask that whatever weight the electors may give to their other qualifications, they would not take them as fair exponents or trustworthy interpreters of India's wants and just wishes, and as favouring us by electing them. With regard to Sir R. Temple I need say nothing more than that he endeavours to produce the wrong and mischievous impression upon the minds of the English people that India is prosperous and increasing in prosperity, in the teeth of the early and latest testimony of eminent men and in the teeth of facts. Mr. Fawcett told that the illusion was passing away, while Sir Richard keeps it up! I do not advert to some of his acts in India, such as the strange contrast of 2 lbs. rations in Bengal and the disastrous 1 lb. ration famine policy here, probably to please higher authorities—his high-handedness, his treatment of the local funds, etc., etc. I confine myself to an utterance or two of his after leaving India. It is strange that a quarter of a century ago Mr. Richard Temple was able to take and express a remarkably intelligent view of the Indian problem. In connection with the Punjab he expounded the causes of Punjab's poverty and revival in his report of 1859 in these significant and clear words:—"In former reports it was explained how the circumstance of so much money going out of the Punjab contributed to depress the agriculturist. The native regular army was Hindustani, to them was a large share of the Punjab revenue disbursed, of which a part only they spent on the spot and a part was remitted to their homes. Thus it was that year after year, lakhs and lakhs were drained from the Punjab, and enriched Oudh. But within the last year the native army being Punjabee, all such sums have been paid to them, and have been spent at home. Again, many thousands of Punjabee soldiers are serving abroad. These men not only remit their savings, but also have sent quantities of prize property and plunder, the spoils of Hindustan, to their native villages. The effect of all this is already perceptible in an increase of agricultural capital, a freer circulation of money and a fresh impetus to cultivation." Now, gentlemen, am I not justified in saying that it is strange that what Mr. Richard Temple of twenty-five years past saw so intelligently, about Punjab, Sir Richard Temple of the present day does not or would not see about India, whence, not merely "lakhs and lakhs" but hundreds and hundreds of lakhs—thirty hundred or so lakhs are drained to England. He cannot, it appears, now grasp the problem of India as he did that of the Punjab. I cannot undertake to explain this phenomenon. What may be the reason or object? He alone can explain. As he is presently doing mischief by posing as a friend, I can only say "save us from such a friend." We cannot but speak out, however unwillingly, that Sir Richard Temple is not a safe and correct guide for the people of England for India's wants and wishes. While Bright in '53, Lawrence in '64 and '73, Fawcett in '79, the *London Punch's* grand cartoom of *Disillusion* in '79 portraying the wretched Indian woman and children, with the shorn pagoda tree over their heads, begging alms of John Bull, Hunter in '80, Baring in '82, deplore the impoverishment of the masses of India, Sir Richard in a fine phrenzy talks in '85 "of their homes becoming happier, their acres broader, their harvest richer." "India is prospering, there is no lack of subsistence, no shrinkage of occupation, no discontent with the wages at home, and in consequence no searching for wages abroad." And yet some light-hearted people coolly talk of sending him as a Viceroy here! No greater misfortune could befall India! About Mr. Maclean I need not say much as you are all well aware, that he has been throughout his whole career in India a thorough partisan and an avowed and determined anti-native, with a few rare intervals of fairness. He can never be a fair and trustworthy interpreter of our views and wishes. He off-handedly says in his letter in the *Bombay Gazette* of 9th June last: "Mr. Slagg recited the usual rubbish about the deplorable poverty and overtaxation of the Indian people." So you see, gentlemen, who Mr. Maclean is. He is a great man before whom the views of such persons as Bright, Fawcett, Lawrence, the *Punch*, and Baring are all mere rubbish! Mr. Ayrton's whole policy can be summed up in a few words—treat natives gently, but give them no posts of power or responsibility, have no legislative councils with non-official element, and if you have, put no natives in them. He says:—"The power of governing must remain, as it had hitherto been, solely and exclusively in the hands of British subjects going out of this country." "Why were we to teach the natives, what they had failed in discovering for themselves, that they would one day be a great nation." This un-English narrow-mindedness and purblindness is the worst thing that can happen to England and India both, and according to it all that the best and highest English statesmen, and even our Sovereign have promised and said about high duty, justice, policy, etc., must become so many empty words, hollow promises, and all sham and delusion. My personal relations with Sir L. Pelly at Baroda were, as you know, friendly, but the reason of his name appearing in this list is that he was an instrument of Lord Lytton's Afghan policy, and that as far as his views may have coincided with the Lytton policy, he cannot fairly represent our views against that policy. About Sir Roper Lethbridge I was under the impression that when he was Press Commissioner, he was regarded as one sympathising with the natives. But when the day of the crucial trial came, the Ilbert Bill and the Ripon policy, it was then found out that his views were anything but what would be just, fair and sympathising towards the natives of India. In addition to the names I have mentioned I am required to mention Sir James Fergusson, and I cannot but agree to do so though with some reluctance. I have personally much respect for him, and I do not forget that he has done some good. In the matter of the native princes he enunciated a correct principle some eighteen years ago when he was Under-Secretary of State for India. Presiding at a meeting of the East India Association, 1867, he said :—"It is earnestly to be hoped that the princes of India look upon the engagements of the British Queen as irrevocable," and I believe he consistently carried out this principle when here with the princes of this Presidency. We cannot also forget that when acting upon his own instincts he did good in matters of education and social intercourse, and nominated to the Legislative Council our friends the Hon'ble Mr. Budroodeen and the Hon'ble Mr. Telang as representatives of the educated class, retaining also the Hon'ble Mr. Mundlik. You can easily conceive then my reluctance to speak against him, notwithstanding some mistakes and failures in his administration as Governor under official misguidance. But when I see that after his arrival in England he has made statements so incorrect and mischievous in results, in some matters most vital to India, it is incumbent upon us to say that he does not know the true state of India. Fancy, gentlemen, my regret and surprise when I read these words from the latest Governor of Bombay:—"At the present time her (India's) people were not heavily taxed, and it was a great mistake to suppose that they were." This is a matter of easy ascertainment, and the heaviness of taxation is repeated by acknowledged eminent men. Here are a few figures which will tell their own tale. The income of the United Kingdom may be roughly taken at £1,200,000,000 and its gross revenue about £87,000,000, giving a proportion of about 7½ per cent. of the income. Of British India the income is hardly £400,000,000 and its gross revenue about £70,000,000 giving 17½ per cent. of the income, and yet Sir James tells the English people that the people of India are not heavily taxed, through paying out of this wretched income, a gross revenue of more than double the proportion of what the people of the enormously rich England pay for their gross revenue. Contrast with Sir James's statement the picture which Mr. Fawcett gives in his paper in the *Nineteenth Century*, of October, 1879:—"If a comparison is made between the financial resources of England and India, it will be found almost impossible to convey an adequate idea of the poverty of the latter country * * and consequently it is found that taxation in India has *reached almost its extreme limits*." Again he says: "It is particularly worthy of remark that the Viceroy and Secretary of State now unreservedly accept the conclusion that the *limit of taxation has been reached in India*, and that it has consequently become imperatively necessary that expenditure should be reduced." (The italics are mine.) Now, gentlemen, mark this particularly. When in 1879 the Conservative Viceroy and Secretary of State had, as Mr. Fawcett says, unreservedly accepted that the limit of taxation had been reached in India, the gross revenue was only £65,000,000 while the budgetted revenue of the present year is already £72,000,000, and we are now threatened by the same Government with an addition of £2,000,000 or £3,000,000 more permanently. This is terrible. Change the entire system as Mr. Fawcett says, substitute for the present destructive foreign agency, the constructive and conservative native agency, except for the higher posts of power, and you can have a hundred millions or two hundred millions with ease for purposes of government or taxation. This is the difference between Fawcett and Fergusson. Both are gentlemen, but the former speaks from careful hard study, the latter without it. Mischievous as such statements generally are, they are still more so when delivered before a Manchester audience, who unfortunately yet do not understand their own true interests, and the interests of the English workmen. They do not understand yet that their greatest interest is in increasing the ability of the Indians to buy their manufactures. That if India were able to buy a pound worth of their cotton manufactures per head per annum, that would give them a trade of £250,000,000 a year instead of the present poor imports into India of £25,000,000 of cotton yarn and manufactures from all foreign countries of the world. Sir James, I think, has made another statement that all offices in India are occupied by the natives except the highest. I am not able to put my hand just now upon the place where I read it. But if my impression be correct, I would not waste words and your time to animadvert upon such an extraordinary incorrect statement, so utterly contrary to notorious facts. Why, it is the head and front, the very soul of all our evils and grievances that the statement is not the fact or reality as it ought to be. This is the very thing which will put an end to all our troubles, and remedy all our evils of poverty and otherwise. Let Sir James bring it about, and he will be our greatest benefactor and England's best friend. In concluding, I may lay down a test for our appeal to the electors, that whichever candidates are not in accord with the Royal Proclamation, and with the lines of the Ripon policy, they are those whom we ask to be not regarded as trustworthy and fair interpreters of our views and wishes. The Resolution has Mr. Blunt's name in the first list and Mr. Aryton's in the second. This will show that we are not actuated by a spirit of partisanship. Whoever are our real friends, be they Liberal or Conservative, we call them our friends. Differences of opinion in some details will no doubt occur between us and our friends, but we are desirous to support them, because the broad and important lines of policy, which India needs, such as those of the Proclamation and the Ripon policy, and the broad and important facts of our true condition, are well understood and adopted by those friends for their guidance in their work for the welfare of India. (*Applause*).

INDIA AND THE OPIUM QUESTION

The following speech was delivered before a Conference which took place at the offices of the Society for the Suppression of the Opium Trade, Broadway Chambers, Westminster, on Monday afternoon, October 15th, 1886, to have a frank interchange of opinion with the Hon'ble Mr. Dadabhai Naoroji, M. L. C., and other Indian gentlemen on the subject of the Opium Trade with special reference to its Indian aspect :—

Mr. Dadabhai Naoroji said,—I have listened to the remarks of the gentlemen with very great interest, for the simple reason that I am almost of the same opinion. The best proof that I can give to you not only of my own mere sentiments, but of my actual conduct in respect to opium, is that when I joined a mercantile firm in 1855, it was one of my conditions, that I should have nothing whatever to do with opium. That is as far back as 1855. In 1880, in my correspondence with the Secretary of State on the condition of India, one of the paragraphs in my letter with regard to the opium trade is this; and I think that this will give you at once an idea of my opinion :—

"There is the opium trade. What a spectacle it is to the world! In England, no statesman dares to propose that opium may be allowed to be sold in public-houses at the corners of every street, in the same way as beer or spirits. On the contrary, Parliament, as representing the whole nation, distinctly enacts that 'opium and all preparations of opium or of poppies,' as 'poison,' be sold by certified chemists only, and 'every box, bottle, vessel, wrapper, or cover in which such poison is contained, be distinctly labelled with the name of the article, and the word "poison," and with the name and address of the seller of the poison. And yet, at the other end of the world, this Christian, highly civilized, and humane England forces a 'heathen' and 'barbarous' Power to take this 'poison,' and tempts a vast human race to use it, and to degenerate and demoralize themselves with this 'poison!' And why? Because India cannot fill up the remorseless drain; so China must be dragged in to make it up, even though it be by being 'poisoned.' It is wonderful how England reconciles this to her conscience. This opium trade is a sin on England's head, and a curse on India for her share in being the instrument. This may sound strange as coming from any natives of India, as it is generally represented as if it was India that benefited by the opium trade. The fact simply is that, as Mr. Duff said, India is nearly ground down to dust, and the opium trade of China fills up England's drain. India derives not a particle of benefit. All India's profits of trade, and several millions from her very produce (scanty as it is, and becoming more and more so), and with these all the profit of opium go the same way of the drain—to England. Only India shares the curse of the Chinese race. Had this cursed opium trade not existed, India's miseries would have much sooner come to the surface and relief and redress would have come to her long ago; but this trade has prolonged the agonies of India."

In this I have only just explained to you what I feel on the matter personally. With regard to the whole of the important question, which must be looked at in a practical point of view, I must leave sentiment aside. I must, at the same time, say this that opinion of mine that the opium revenue must be abolished is a personal one. I do not put it before you as the opinion of all India. I state it on my own responsibility. There is a great fear that if the opium revenue were to cease, the people of India would be utterly unable to fill up the gap in the revenue. They feel aghast at the very suggestion of it, and they go so far as to say that the opium revenue cannot be dispensed with. I just tell you what is held there, so that you may understand both sides of the question thoroughly. Therefore you have not the complete sympathy of the natives of India in this matter, and you will find, perhaps, several members of the Indian press expressing their opinion that they could not dispense with the opium revenue. In fact, Mr. Grant Duff, in answer to some representation from your Society, or somebody interested in the abolition of the opium trade, has asked, in 1870, whether they wished to grind an already poor population to the dust. So that he showed that even with the help of the opium revenue India was just on the verge of being ground down to the dust. This, then, is the condition in which India is situated. The question is how to practically deal with it. Before you can deal with any such subject it is necessary for you to take into consideration the whole Indian problem—What has been the condition of India, and what is the condition of India, and why has it been so? Mr. Dadabhai then cited official authorities from the commencement of the present century up to the present day, including that of the late and present Finance Ministers, that British India had been all along "extremely poor." He pointed out the exceedingly low income of India, *viz.*, only Rs. 20 per head per annum, as compared with that of any tolerably well self-governed country: that a progressive and civilizing government ought to have increased revenue; but India was utterly unable to yield such increasing revenue. He explained how, comparatively with its income, the pressure of taxation upon the subjects of British India was doubly heavier than that of England; that of England being about 8 per cent. of its income, and of British India about 15 per cent. of its income; that England paid from its plenty, and India from its exceedingly poor income, so that the effect on British Indian subjects was simply crushing. He pointed out that while the trade with British India was generally supposed to be very large, it was in reality very small and wretched indeed. He illustrated this by some statistics, showing that the exports of British produce to India was only about £30,000,000., of which a portion went to the Native States of India and to part of Asia, through the northern border, leaving hardly a rupee a head worth for the subjects of British India. This certainly could not be a satisfactory result of a hundred years of British rule, with everything under British control. A quarter of a century ago, he said, Mr. Bright had used these remarkable words: "I must say that it is my belief that if a country be found possessing a most fertile soil, and capable of bearing every variety of production, and that notwithstanding, the people are in a state of extreme destitution and suffering, the chances are that there is some fundamental error in the government of that country." Mr. Dadabhai urged that the Society should find out this fundamental error, and unless they did that, and made

India prosperous they could not expect to gain their benevolent object of getting rid of the opium revenue except by causing India to be ground down to dust by increased taxation in other shapes. This of course the Society did not mean; thus they ought to go to the root of the evil. India was quite capable of giving 200 instead of 70 millions of revenue, if they were allowed to keep what they produced, and to develop freely in their material condition; and in such a condition India would be quite able to dispense with the curse of the opium revenue. Mr. Dadabhai then proceeded to point out what he regarded as the cause of the poverty of British India. He cited several authorities upon the subject, and showed it was simply the employment of a foreign agency that caused a large drain to the country, disabling it from saving any capital at all, and rendering it weaker and weaker every day, forcing it to resort to loans for its wants, and becoming worse and worse in its economic condition. He explained at some length the process and effect of this fundamental evil, and how even what was called the "development" of the resources of India was actually thereby turned into the result of the "deprivation" of the resources of India. In pointing out a practicable remedy for all the evils, he said he did not mean that a sudden revolution should be made; the remedy which had been pointed out by a Committee of the India Office in 1860 would be the best thing to do, to meet all the requirements of the case. After alluding to the Act of 1833 and the great Proclamation of 1858, a faithful fulfilment of which would be the fulfilment of all India's desires and wants, he said that the Committee of the India Office to which he had referred had recommended that simultaneous examinations should be held in India and

England, and the list be made up according to merit; and he added to this scheme, that the successful candidates of the first examination should be made to come over to England and finish their studies for two years with the successful candidates of England. This was the Resolution of the National Indian Congress which met last Christmas in Bombay. It was also necessary that some scope should be given to the military races to attach them to the British Rule. If this fairplay and justice were given to the natives in all the higher Civil Services and if some fair competition system were adopted for all the uncovenanted and subordinate services, India would have fairplay, and free development of herself, would become prosperous, would be able to give as much revenue as a progressive and a civilizing administration should want, and then only would the philanthropic object of the Society be fully achieved. Otherwise, if India continued as wretched as she was at present there was no chance of the object being attained except by great distress to the Indians themselves and grave political dangers to the British rulers, or the whole may end in some great disaster. Mr. Dadabhai was glad that British statesmen were becoming alive to this state of affairs, and the highest Indian authority, the Secretary of State, fully shared his appreciation of the position, when he wrote to the Treasury on the 26th of January last; "The position of India in relation to taxation and the sources of the public revenue, is very peculiar, not merely......but likewise from the character of the government, which is in the hands of foreigners, who hold all the principal administrative offices, and from so large a part of the army. The imposition of new taxation which would have to be borne wholly as a consequence of the foreign rule imposed on the country, and virtually to meet additions to charges arising outside of the country, would constitute a political danger, the real magnitude of which, it is to be feared, is not at all appreciated by persons who have no knowledge of, or concern in the government of India, but which those responsible for that government have long regarded as of the most serious order."

ADDRESS TO THE ELECTORS OF HOLBORN.

[*Address to the Electors of Holborn Division delivered on the* 27*th June*, 1886, *during the general election of that year in support of his candidature as the Liberal Candidate for the Holborn Division of Finsbury.*]

I really do not know how I can thank you from the bottom of my heart, for the permission you have given me to stand before you as a candidate for your borough. I appreciate the honour most highly. I will not take more of your time on this point, because you may believe me when I say that I thank you from the bottom of my heart. It is really and truly so. (*Cheers*). Standing as I do here, to represent the 250,000,000 of your fellow-subjects in India, of course I know thoroughly well my duty ; for I am returned by you, my first duty will be to consult completely and fully the interest of my constituents. I do not want at present to plead the cause of India. I am glad that that cause has been ably and eloquently pleaded by our worthy Chairman, by Mr. Wilfrid Blunt, and by Mr. Bryce. But the time must come, if I am returned, to lay before you the condition of India—what little we want from you, and with little we are always satisfied. For the present, therefore, I would come to the burning question of the day—the Irish Home Rule. (*Loud cheers.*)

"CONSISTENT WITH JUSTICE."

The question now before you is whether Ireland shall have its Home Rule or not. ("Yes, yes.") The details are a different question altogether. I will therefore confine myself to those particular points which affect the principle of Home Rule. The first thing I will say is something about Mr. Gladstone himself. (*Loud cheers.*) Grand Old Man he is—*renewed cheers*)—and not only all England, but all India says so. (*Vociferous cheers.*) He has been much twitted that he is inconsistent with himself—that he has said something some time ago and something different now. But those that can understand the man can understand how very often a great man may appear inconsistent when in reality he is consistent with truth, justice, right, and has the courage of his convictions. Mr. Gladstone thought something at one time, but as circumstances changed, and new light came, and new power was wielded by the Irish people, he saw that this change of circumstances required a reconsideration of the whole question. He came to the conclusion that the only remedy for this discord between two sisters was to let the younger sister have her own household. (*Cheers.*) When he saw that he had the courage of his conviction, the moral courage to come forward before the world and say, "I see that this is the remedy: let the English nation adopt it." And I have no doubt that they will adopt it.

"INCOMPATIBLE WITH TYRANNY."

I have lived in this country actually for twenty years, and my entire connection in business with England has been thirty years, and I say that if there is one thing more certain than another that I have learned, it is that the English nation is incompatible with tyranny. It will at times be proud and imperious, and will even carry a wrong to a long extent; but the time will come when it will be disgusted with its own tyranny and its own wrong. (*Cheers.*) When once an Englishman sees his mistake he has the moral courage to rectify it. (*Cheers.*) Mr. Gladstone, then, has represented your highest and most generous instincts, and I have no doubt that the response from the country, sooner or later, must come to the height of his argument and of his sentiment. The greatest argument against Home Rule is that it will disintegrate the Empire. Now, it has been a surprise to me how this word Empire has been so extraordinarily used and abused.

THE NONSENSE OF DISINTEGRATION.

What is the British Empire? Is it simply Great Britain and Ireland? Why it exists over the whole surface of the world—east, west, north, south—and the sun never sets upon it. Is that Empire to be broken down, even though Ireland be entirely separated? Do you mean to say that the British Empire hangs only upon the thread of the Irish will? (*Laughter.*) Has England conquered the British Empire simply because Ireland did it? What nonsense it is to say that such an Empire could be disintegrated, even if unhappily Ireland were separated! Do the Colonies hold you in affection because Ireland is with you? Is the Indian Empire submissive to you because you depend upon Ireland? Such a thing would be the highest humiliation for the English people to say. (*Cheers.*) The next question is, Will Ireland separate? ("No.") Well, we may say that because we wish it should not; but we must consider it carefully. Let us suppose that the Irish are something like human beings. (*Laughter and cheers.*) Let us suppose them to be guided by the ordinary motives of humanity. I put it to you fairly whether Ireland will separate or not. I say she will not.

HOME RULE—HOME LIFE.

What will Ireland be after it has this Home Rule? It will simply have its own household, just as a son who has come of age wishes to have a home in which his wife may be supreme. Ireland simply asks its own household independence, and that does not in the least mean that the Empire is disadvantaged. The Imperial concern is in no way concerned in it. Just as I and my partner being in business, I leave the management of the concern to him. I have confidence in him. I know he would not deprive me of a single farthing; but as a partner in the firm I am not compelled to live with him, nor to submit myself to him for food and clothing, and the necessaries of life. You do not mean to say that, because Ireland has a separate household, therefore she will also be separated from the Imperial firm, and that they would have no connection with each other? The British Empire still remains, to be shared by them.

THE ANALOGY OF THE COLONIES.

Take the Colonies. They have their own self-government, as Ireland asks, but there the position of the Colonies ends. Ireland, with this Parliament granted to it, will be in a far higher position than the Colonies are. Ireland will be a part of the ruling power of the British Empire. She and England will be partners as rulers of the British Empire, which the Colonies are not. And if the Irish separate, what are they? An insignificant country. If they should remain separate, and England and America, or England and France should go to war, they would be crushed. There is a saying among the Indians that when two elephants fight the trees are uprooted. (*Laughter.*) What could Ireland do? It would not be her interest to sever herself from England, and to lose the honour of a share in the most glorious Empire that ever existed on the face of the earth. (*Loud cheers.*) Do you then for a moment suppose that Ireland will throw itself down from the high pedestal on which it at present stands? It supplies the British Empire with some of its best statesmen and warriors. (*Cheers.*) Is this the country so blind to its own interests that it will not understand that by leaving England it throws itself to the bottom of the sea? With England it is the ruler of mankind. I say therefore that Ireland will never separate from you. (*Cheers.*) Home Rule will bring peace and prosperity to them, and they will have a higher share in the British Empire. (*Cheers.*) Depend upon it, gentlemen, if I live ten years more—I hope I shall live—if this Bill is passed, that every one of you, and every one of the present opponents of Home Rule will congratulate himself that he did, or allowed to be done, this justice to Ireland. (*Cheers.*)

A PEOPLE "VALIANT, GENEROUS, AND TENDER."

There is one more point which is important to be dealt with. I am only confining myself to the principle of Home Rule. Another objection taken to the Bill is that the Irish are a bad lot—(*laughter*)—that they are poor, wretched, ungrateful, and so forth. ("Who said so?") Some people say so. ("Salisbury," and *cheers* and *hisses.*) We shall see what one says whom you have entrusted with the rulership of two hundred and fifty millions of people—I allude to Lord Dufferin, himself an Irishman. (*Cheers.*) What does he say? How does he describe Ireland? I may shoot the two birds at once by referring to his discription of the country as well as of the people. He says that Ireland is a lovely and fertile land, caressed by a clement atmosphere, held in the embrace of the sea. With a coast filled with the noblest harbours of the world and "inhabited by a race valiant, generous, and tender, gifted beyond measure with the power of physical endurance, and graced with the liveliest intelligence." It is not necessary for me to say any more about a people of that character. I think it is a slander on humanity and human nature to say that any people, and more especially the Irish, are not open to the feelings of gratitude, to the feelings of kindness. If there is anything for which the Irish are distinguished—I say this not merely from my study of your country, but from my experience of some Irish people—that if ever I have found a warm-hearted people in the world, I have found the Irish (*Loud cheers.*)

A PEOPLE "ACCESSIBLE TO JUSTICE."

But I will bring before you the testimony of another great man, whom, though he is at present at variance with us on this question of a separate Parliament, we always respect. It is a name highly respected by the natives of India, and, I know, by the Liberals of this country. I mean John Bright. (*Hisses and cheers.*) What does he say? "If there be a people on the face of the earth whose hearts are accessible to justice, it is the Irish people." (*Cheers.*) Now, I am endeavouring to take all the important points brought forward against this

Home Rule. Mr. Gladstone proposes that they should give a certain proportion of money to the Imperial Exchequer. Their opponents say, "Oh, they will promise all sorts of things." Now, I want this to be carefully considered. The basis of the most powerful of human motives is self-interest. It is to the interest of Ireland never to separate from England.

NOT TRIBUTE, BUT PARTNERSHIP.

I will now show you that this, which is called a tribute and a degradation, is nothing of the kind. Ireland would feel it its duty to pay this. It is not tribute in any sense of the word. Ireland is a partner in the Imperial firm. Ireland shares both the glory and the profit of the British Rule. Its children will be employed as fully in the administration and the conduct of the Empire as any Englishman will be. Ireland, in giving only something like £1 in £15 to the Exchequer will more than amply benefit. It is a partnership, and they are bound to supply their capital just as much as the senior partner is bound to supply his. They will get the full benefit of it. Tribute is a thing for which you get no return in material benefit, and to call this tribute is an abuse of words. I have pointed out that those great bugbears, the separation, the tribute, and the bad character of the Irish are pure myths. The Irish are a people that are believed by many an Englishman to be as high in intellect and in morality as any on the face of the earth. If they are bad now, it is your own doing. (*Cheers.*) You first debase them, and then give them a bad name, and then want to hang them. No, the time has come when you do understand the happy inspiration which Mr. Gladstone has conceived.

HOME RULE:—THE GOLDEN RULE.

You do know now that Ireland must be treated as you treat yourselves. You say that Irishmen must be under the same laws as Englishmen, and must have the same rights. Very good. The opponents say yes, and therefore they must submit to the laws which the British Parliament makes. I put to them one simple question. Will Englishmen for a single day submit to laws made for them by those who are not Englishmen? What is the proudest chapter in British history? That of the Stuarts. You did not tolerate the laws of your own Sovereign, because you thought they were not your laws. (*Cheers*). You waged civil war, regardless of consequences, and fought and struggled till you established the principle that the English will be their own sovereign, and your own sons your own legislators and guides. You did not submit to a ruler, though he was your own countryman. Our opponents forget that they are not giving the same rights to the Irish people. They are oblivious of this right, and say Ireland must be governed by laws that we make for her. They do not understand that what is our own, however bad it is, is dearer to us than what is given to us by another, however high and good he may be. (*Cheers*). No one race of people can ever legislate satisfactorily for another race. Then they object that the Saxon race is far superior to the Celtic, and that the Saxon must govern the whole, though in the next breath they admit that the one cannot understand the other. (*Laughter*). A grand patriarch said to his people thousands of years ago, "Here is good, here is evil; make your choice: choose the good, and reject the evil." A grand patriarch of to-day—the Grand Old Man—(*loud cheers*)—tells you,

"Here is the good, here is the evil; choose the good, reject the evil." And I do not say I hope and trust, but I am sure, that the English nation, sooner or later, will come to that conclusion—will choose the good, and will reject the evil.

A WORD ABOUT INDIA.

I only want now to say one word about my own country. (*Loud cheers*). I feel that my task has been so much lessened by previous speakers, that I will not trouble you much upon this point. I appeal to you for the sake of the two hundred and fifty millions of India. I have a right to do so, because I know that India regards me—at least, so it is said—as a fair representative. I want to appeal to you in their name that, whether you send me or another to Parliament, you at once make up your minds that India ought to have some representation—(*cheers*)—in your British Parliament. I cannot place my case better than in the words of an illustrious English lady, whose name for patriotism, philanthropy, and self-sacrifice is the highest amongst your race—Miss Florence Nightingale. (*Loud cheers*). She writes to me in these words :—

MISS FLORENCE NIGHTINGALE TO THE ELECTORS OF HOLBORN.

"London, June 23, 1886.—My dear Sir,—My warmest good wishes are yours in the approaching election for Holborn, and this not only for your sake, but yet more for that of India and of England. So important is it that the millions of India should in the British Parliament here be represented by one who, like yourself, has devoted his life to them in such a high fashion—to the difficult and delicate task of unravelling and explaining what stands at the bottom of India's poverty, what are India's rights and what is the right for India: rights so compatible with, indeed so dependent on loyalty to the British Crown; rights which we are all seeking after for those great multitudes, developing, not every day like foliage in May, but slowly and surely. The last five or eight years have made a difference in India's cultivated classes which has astonished statesmen—in education, the seeds of which were so sedulously sown by the British Government—in power, of returning to the management of their own local affairs, which they had from time immemorial; that is, in the powers and responsibilities of local self-government, their right use of which would be equally advantageous to the Government of India and to India (notwithstanding some blunders); and a noble because careful beginning has been made in giving them this power. Therefore do I hail you and yearn after your return to this Parliament, to continue the work you have so well begun in enlightening England and India on Indian affairs. I wish I could attend your first public meeting, to which you kindly invite me to-morrw; but alas for me, who for so many years have been unable from illness to do anything out of my rooms.—Your most ardent well wisher, Florence Nightingale." (*Loud cheers*).

INDIA'S APPEAL.

Well, gentlemen in the words of this illustrious lady, I appeal not only to you, the constituents of Holborn, but to the whole English nation, on the behalf of 250 millions of your fellow subjects—a sixth part of the human race, and the largest portion of the British Empire, before whom you are but as a drop in the ocean; we appeal to you to do us justice, and to allow us a representative in your British Parliament. (*Loud and prolonged cheers, the audience rising in great enthusiasm*).

THE INDIAN CIVIL SERVICE

The following speech was delivered before a meeting of the East India Association, at which Mr. A. K. Connell read a paper on " The Indian Civil Service, " July, 1887. Mr. John Bright in the Chair.

Mr. Dadabhai Naoroji said :—Mr. Chairman, Ladies and Gentlemen,—My first impulse was not to send up my card at all, but after attending this meeting and hearing the paper that has been put before us, it is necessary that I should not put myself in a false position, and as I disagree with a portion of this paper, it became necessary that I should make that disagreement known. The third part of the paper is the part that is objectionable ; and it seems to me it is a lame and impotent conclusion of an able and well-considered beginning. For me to undertake to reply to all the many fallacies that that third part contains, will be utterly out of the question in the ten minutes allotted to me ; but I have one consolation in that respect—that my views are generally known, that they are embodied to a great extent in the journals of this Association ; that I also direct the attention of Mr. Connell and others to two papers that I submitted to the Public Service Commission, and that I hope there are two other papers that are likely to appear in the *Contemporary Review* in the months of August and September. These have anticipated, and will, I trust directly and indirectly answer most of the fallacies of Mr. Connell's paper. I would, therefore, not attempt the impossible task of replying to the whole of this paper, but I will make a few remarks of a different character altogether bearing upon the vital question before us. This question of the services is not simply a question of the aspirations of a few educated men; it is the question of life and death to the whole of British India. It is our good fortune that we have in the chair to-day the gentleman who put a very pertinent question, going to the root of the whole evil, as far back as a third of a century ago. Mr. Bright put the question in the year 1853. He said: "I must say that it is my belief that if a country be found possessing a most fertile soil and capable of bearing every variety of production, and that notwithstanding the people are in a state of extreme destitution and suffering, the chances are that there is some fundamental error in the Government of that country." Gentlemen, as long as you do not give a full and fair answer to that question of the great statesman—that statement made a third of a century ago—you will never be able to grasp this great and important question of the services. It is not, as I have already said, a question of the mere aspiration of a few educated men. Talking about this destitution, it is a circumstance which has been dwelt upon in the beginning of the century by Sir John Shaw. Lord Lawrence in his time said that the mass of the people were living on scanty subsistence. To the latest day the last Finance Minister, Sir Evelyn Baring, testified to the extreme poverty of the people, and so does the present Finance Minister. The fact is that after you have hundred years of the most highly-paid and the most highly-praised administration in that country, it is the poorest country in the world. How can you account for that? Grasp the question fully, and then only will you be able to see what vast interest this question of the services means. Then I come to the pledges that have been given. Here are open honourable pledges. The statesmen of 1833 laid down distinctly, in the face of the important consideration—whether India should be allowed ever to be lost to Britain. They weighed every circumstance, and they came to the deliberate conclusion which was embodied in the Act that they passed. But then you had not the experience of that fear of the risk of losing India. Twenty-five years afterwards you actually experienced that very risk; you actually had a mutiny against you, and what was your conduct then? Even after that experience, you rose above yourself; you kept up your justice and generosity and magnanimity, and in the name of the Queen, and by the mouth of the Queen, you issued a Proclamation, which if you "conscientiously" fulfil will be your highest glory, and your truest fame and reward. Gentlemen, take the bull by the horns. Do not try to shrink this question. If you are afraid of losing India, and if you are to be actuated by the inglorious fear of that risk, let that be stated at once. Tell us at once, "We will keep you under our heels, we will not allow you to rise or to prosper at any time." Then we shall know our fate. But with your English manliness—and if there is anything more characteristic of you than anything else, it is your manliness—speak out honestly and not hypocritically, what you intend to do. Do you really mean to fulfil the pledges given before the world, and in the name of God, with the sanction of God and asking God to aid you, in the execution of that pledge—do you mean to stick to that pledge or to get out of it? Whatever it be, like honest Englishmen, speak out openly and plainly. "We will do this" or "We will not do this." But do not expose yourselves to the charges—which I am not making, but your own members of the India Council have made—of "keeping the promise to the ear, and breaking it to the hope." Looking at the time I cannot now enter into all the different and important considerations that this paper raises, but I simply ask you again this question, whether like honest Englishmen such as you are, in a manly way, you say the thing and do it. If you mean to fulfil these pledges honestly, do so; if you do not mean to fulfil them honestly, say so, and at least preserve your character for honesty and manliness. Mr. Connell had, in the first part of his paper, laid down as emphatically as he could the principles upon which the English nation is bound to act, and in the third part of the paper he has done his utmost to discredit the whole thing, and to say how not to do it. But he forgets one thing: that the pledge you have given, you have never given a fair trial to: if you only give a fair trial to that pledge, you will find that it will not only redound to your glory for ever, but also result in great benefits to yourself; but if India is to be for a long time under your rule with blessing, and not with a curse, it is the fulfilment of that pledge which will secure that result. Ah! gentlemen, no eternal or permanent results can ever follow from dodging and palevering. Eternal results can follow only from eternal principles. Your rule of India is based not on sixty thousand bayonets or a hundred thousand bayonets. But it is based upon the confidence, the intense faith like the one that I hold, in the justice, the conscience, and the honor of the British nation. As long as I have that faith in me, I shall continue to urge and plead before statesmen like Mr. Bright, and before the English nation. Fulfil your pledge honestly before God, because it is upon those eternal principles only that you can expect to continue your rule with benefit to yourself and benefit to us. The reply to your (President's) question, Sir, about the fundamental error is then this. A foreign rule can never be but a curse to any nation on the face of the earth, except so far as it approaches a native rule, be the foreigners angels themselves. If this principle is not fairly borne in mind, and if honest efforts are not made to fulfil your pledges, it is utterly useless for us to plead, or to expect any good result, or to expect that India will ever rise in material and moral prosperity. I do not mean to say a word against the general *personnel* of these services, as they are at the present time—they are doing what they can in the false groove in which they are placed; to them there is every honour due for the ability and integrity with which most of them have carried on their work; but what I say is this. This system must be changed. The administration must become native under the supreme control of the English nation. Then you have one element in India, which is peculiarly favourable to the permanance of your rule, if the people are satisfied that you give them the justice that you promise. It is upon the rock of justice alone that your rule stands. If they are satisfied, the result will be this. It is a case peculiar to India: there are Mahomedans and Hindus; if both are satisfied, both will take care that your supremacy must remain over them; but if they are both dissatisfied, and there is any paltering with justice and sincerity they will join together against you. Under these circumstances you have everything in your favour; in fact, the divine law is that if you only follow the divine law, then only can you produce divine results. Do good, no matter what the result is. If you trifle with those eternal and divine laws, the result must be disastrous. I must stop as the time is up.

GREAT RECEPTION MEETING IN BOMBAY.

[*The following speech was delivered before the public meeting of the inhabitants of Bombay called by the Bombay Presidency Association at the Framjee Cowasjee Institute, on Sunday, the 13th February, 1887, to pass a vote of thanks to the Hon'ble Mr. Dadabhai Naoroji and Mr. Lal Mohun Ghose for their exertions on behalf of India at the Parliamentary elections of 1886 in England. Mr. (now Sir) Dinshaw M. Petit in the Chair*].

The Hon'ble Mr. Dadabhai Naoroji (amidst long and immense cheering), said :—Mr. Chairman, Ladies and Gentlemen,—I feel extremely obliged by the very kind reception you have given to my friend Mr. Ghose and myself, and for the confidence you have reposed in us. Such hearty acknowledgments of my humble services and of my friend's arduous exertion cannot but encourage us largely in our future work. (*Cheers*). As natives of India we are bound to do whatever lies within our power and opportunities. In undertaking the work of trying to get a seat in Parliament, the first question that naturally arose was whether it would be of any good to India and whether an Indian member would be listened to. The first thing therefore, I did on arriving in England was to consult many English friends, several of whom are eminent statesmen of the day and members of Parliament. I was almost universally advised that I should not hesitate to try to carry out my intentions, that it was extremely desirable that there should be at least one or two Indians in Parliament to enable members to learn the native view of questions from natives themselves. (*Cheers*). That if I could by any possibility work way into the House, I would certainly be doing a great service not only to India but to a large extent to England also. (*Cheers*). Several fundamental important questions of policy can be fought out and decided in Parliament alone as they depend upon Acts of Parliament, and Parliament is the ultimate appeal in every important question in which Government and the native public may differ. To get direct representation from India was not at present possible. An indirect representation through the liberality and aid of some British constituency was the only door open to us. I undertook to contest Holborn under many disadvantages. I was just occupied in making acquaintances and feeling my way. I had no time to find out and make the acquaintance of any constituency; I was quite unknown to the political world, when of a sudden the Resolution came in upon me. The Liberal leaders very properly advised me that I should not lose this opportunity of contesting some seat, no matter however forlorn a hope it might be as the best means of making myself known to the English constituencies, and of securing a better chance and choice for the next opportunity. That I could not expect to get in at a rush, which even an Englishman was rarely able to do except under particularly favourable circumstances. I took the advice and selected Holborn out of three offers I have received. I thus not only got experience of an English contest, but it also satisfied me as to what prospects an Indian had of receiving fair and even generous treatment at the hands of English electors.

The elections clearly showed me that a suitable Indian candidate has as good a chance as any Englishman, or even some advantage over an Englishman, for there is a general and genuine desire among English electors to give to India any help in their power. (*Cheers*). I had only nine days of work from my first meeting at the Holborn Town Hall, and sometimes I had to attend two or three meetings on the same day. The meetings were as enthusiastic and cordial in reception as one's heart could desire. Now, the incident I refer to is this. Of canvassing I was able to do but very little. Some liberal electors, who were opposed to Irish Home Rule, intended to vote for the conservative candidate, but to evince their sympathy with India, they promised me to abstain from voting altogether. Unknown as I was to the Holborn electors, the exceedingly enthusiastic and generous treatment they gave me,—and nearly two thousand of them recorded their votes in my favour—must be quite enough to satisfy any that the English public desire to help us to have our own voice in the House of Commons. (*Cheers*). Letters and personal congratulations I received from many for what they called my "plucky contest." Lord Ripon—(*cheers*).—wrote to me not to be discouraged, as my want of success was shared by so many other liberals as to deprive it of personal character; that it was the circumstances of the moment, as it turned out, that worked specially against me, and he trusted I would be successful on a future occasion. Now, it was quite true that owing to the deep split among the Liberals in the Home Rule question, it was estimated by some that I had lost nearly a thousand votes by the abstention of Liberal voters. In short, with my whole experience at Holborn, of both the manner and events of the contest, I am more than ever confirmed in my opinion that India may fairly expect from the English public just and generous treatment. (*Cheers*). I have no doubt that my friend Mr. Ghose—(*cheers*)—with his larger electioneering experience of two arduous contests, will be able to tell you of similar conviction and future hopefulness. There is one great advantage achieved by these contests, which in itself is an ample return for all the trouble—I mean the increasing and earnest interest that has been aroused in the English public about Indian matters. From everywhere you begin to receive expressions of desire to know the truth about India, and invitations come to you to address on Indian subjects. The moral effect of these contests is important and invaluable. (*Hear, hear*). A letter I received from an English friend on the eve of my departure for India this time fairly represents the general English feeling I have met with. Nothing would give him, he says, greater satisfaction than to see me sitting in the House of Commons—(*cheers*)—where I would arouse in the English representatives a keen sense of England's responsibilities, and show them how to fulfil them. (*Cheers*). For the sake of England and of India alike, he earnestly hoped that I might be a pioneer of this sacred work. My presence in the House of Commons was to his mind more important than that of any Englishman whom he knew—(*cheers*)—though that seemed saying a good deal. With these few remarks I once more return to you my most hearty thanks for the reception you have given us, and it would be an important credential as well as an encouragement in our further efforts. (*Loud cheers*).

INDIAN FAMINE RELIEF FUND MEETING.

[*Mr. Dadabhai Naoroji addressed a meeting held on Sunday, July 1st, 1900, at the United Methodist Free Church, Markhouse Road, Walthamstow, in aid of the Indian Famine Relief Fund. Mr. Peter Troughton occupied the Chair.*

The Chairman, in opening the proceedings, said that Indian famine was a subject of very great interest to all Englishmen, and he was sure they would all gladly welcome some authentic information on the subject. He would therefore ask Mr. Dadabhai Naoroji to start his speech right away. (Applause)].

Mr. Dadabhai Naoroji, who was received with cheers, said :—

Mr. Chairman, I feel exceedingly pleased at having to address so large a meeting of English ladies and gentlemen. I assure you it is a great consolation to me that English people are willing to hear what Indians have to say. I will make bold to speak fully and heartily, in order that you may know the truth. I will take as a text the following true words: "As India must be bled." These words were delivered by a Secretary of State for India, Lord Salisbury himself. I don't mention them as any complaint against Lord Salisbury. On the contrary, I give him credit for saying the truth. I want to impress upon you what these important words mean. Let us clearly understand what is meant by bleeding a nation. It is perfectly true that when government is carried on people must pay taxes. But there is a great difference between taxing a people and bleeding a people. You in England pay something like fifty shillings, or more now, of taxes per head per annum. We in India pay only three to four shillings per head per annum. From this you may conclude that we must be the most lightly-taxed people in the world. That is not the case, however; our burden is nearly twice as heavy as yours. The taxes you pay in this country go from the hands of the taxpayers into the hands of the Government, from which they flow back into the country again in various shapes, fertilising trade and returning to the people themselves. There is no diminution of your wealth; your taxes simply change hands. Whatever you give out you must get back. Any deficit means so much loss of strength. Supposing you pay a hundred million pounds every year, and the Government uses that money in such a way that part only returns to you, the other part going out of the country. In that case you are being bled, part of your life is going away. Suppose out of the hundred million pounds only eighty million pounds return to you in the shape of salaries, commerce, or manufactures. You will have lost twenty million pounds. Next year you will be so much the weaker; and so on each year. This is the difference between taxing people and bleeding people. Suppose a body of Frenchmen were your rulers, and that out of the hundred million pounds of taxes they took ten to twenty million pounds each year; you would then be said to be bleeding. The nation would then be losing a portion of its life. How is India bled? I supposed your own case with Frenchmen as your rulers. We Indians are governed by you. You manage our expenditure and our taxes in such a way that while we pay a hundred million pounds of taxation this hundred million never returns to us intact. Only about eighty million returns to us. There is a continual bleeding of about twenty millions annually from the revenues. Ever since you obtained territorial jurisdiction and power in India, in the middle of the last century, Englishmen and other Europeans that went to India have treated that country in the most oppressive way. I will quote a few words of the Court of Directors at the time to show this. "The vast fortunes acquired in the inland trade have been obtained by the most oppressive conduct that ever was known in any country or age." The most oppressive means were adopted in order to bring away from the country enormous quantities of wealth. How was the Indian Empire obtained by you? It has been generally said that you have won it by the sword, and that you will keep it by the sword. The people who say this do not know what they are talking about. They also forget that you may lose "it by force." You have not won the Indian Empire by the sword. During these hundred and fifty years you have carried on wars by which this great Empire has been built up; it has cost hundreds of millions of money. Have you paid a single farthing of it? You have made the Indians pay every farthing. You have formed this great British Empire at our expense, and you will hear what reward we have received from you. The European army in India at any time was comparatively insignificant. In the time of the Indian Mutiny you had only forty thousand troops there. It was the two hundred thousand Indian troops that shed their blood and fought your battles and that gave you this magnificent Empire. It is at India's cost and blood that this Empire has been formed and maintained up to the present day. It is in consequence of the tremendous cost of these wars and because of the millions on millions you draw from us year by year that India is so completely exhausted and bled. It is no wonder that the time has come when India is bleeding to death. You have brought India to this condition by the constant drain upon the wealth of that country. I ask anyone of you whether it is possible for any nation on the face of the earth to live under these conditions. Take your own nation. If you were subjected to such a process of exhaustion for years, you would come down yourselves to the condition in which India now finds herself. How then is this drain made? You impose upon us an immense European military and civil service, you draw from us a heavy taxation. But in the disbursement and the disposal of that taxation we have not the slightest voice. I ask anyone here to stand up and say that he would be satisfied if, having to pay a heavy taxation, he had no voice in the government of the country. We have not the slightest voice. The Indian Government are the masters of all our resources, and they may do what they like with them. We have simply to submit and be bled. I hope I have made it quite clear to you, that the words of Lord Salisbury which I have quoted are most significant; that the words are true and most appropriate when applied to India. It is the principle on which the system of British government has been carried on during these 150 years

What has been the consequence? I shall again quote from Lord Salisbury. He says: "That as India must be bled the lancet should be directed to the parts where the blood is congested, or at least sufficient, not to those parts already feeble from the want of it." Lord Salisbury declared that the agricultural population, the largest portion of the population of India, was feeble from the want of blood. This was said twenty-five year ago; and that blood has been more and more drawn upon during the past quarter of a century. The result is that they have been bled to death; and why? A large proportion of our resources and wealth is clean carried away never to return to us. That is the process of bleeding. Lord Salisbury himself says: "So much of the revenue is exported without a direct equivalent." I ask any one of you whether there is any great mystery in these dire famines and plagues? No other country, exhausted as India has been, exhausted by an evil system of Government, would have stood it half the time. It is extraordinary that the loyalty of the Indians who are bled by you is still so great. The reason of it is that among the Hindus it is one of their most cherished and religious duties that they should give obedience and loyalty to the powers that govern them. And they have been loyal to that sentiment, and you have derived the benefit of it. It is a true and genuine loyalty. But do not expect that that loyalty cannot fail, that it will continue in the same condition in which it is at the present time. It is for the British to rouse themselves and to open their minds, and to think whether they are doing their duty in India. The theory maintained by statesmen is that India is governed for the benefit of India. They say that they do not derive any benefit from the taxation

But this is erroneous. The reality is that India, up to the present day, has been governed so as to bring about the impoverishment of the people. I ask you whether this is to continue. Is it necessary that, for your benefit, we must be destroyed? Is it a natural consequence, is it a necessary consequence? Not at all. If it were British Rule and not un-British Rule which governed us England whould be benefited ten times more than it is. (*Cheers*). You could benefit yourselves a great deal more than you are doing if your Executive Goverment did not persist in their evil system, by which you derive some benefit, but by which we are destroyed. I say let the British public thoroughly understand this question, that by destroying us you will ultimately destroy yourselves. Mr. Bright knew this, and this is an extract from one of his speeches. He said, or to the effect: By all means seek your own benefit and your own good in connection with India; but you cannot derive any good except by doing good to India. If you do good to India you will do good to yourselves. He said there were two ways of doing good to yourselves, either by plunder or by trade. And he said he would prefer trade. Now, I will explain how it would benefit you. At the present time you are exporting to the whole world something like three hundred millions worth of your produce a year. Here is a country under your control with a population of three hundered millions of human souls, not savages of Africa. Here is India, with a perfectly free trade entirely under your control, and what do you send out to her? Only eighteen pence per year per head. If you could send goods to the extent of £1 per head per annum India would be a market for your whole commerce. If such were the case you would draw immense wealth from India besides benefiting the people. I say that if the British public do not rouse themselves the blood of every man that dies there will lie on their head. You may prosper for a time, but a time must come when you must suffer the retribution that comes from this evil system of government. What I quoted to you from Lord Salisbury explains the real condition of India. It is not the first time that English statesmen have declared this as absolutely as Lord Salisbury has done. During the whole century Englishmen and statesmen of conscience and thought have time after time declared the same thing, that India is being exhausted and drained, and that India must ultimately die. Our misery is owing to this exhaustion. You are drawing year by year thirty millions of our wealth from us in various ways. The Government of India's resources simply mean that the Government is despotic and that it can put any tax it chooses on the people. Is it too much to ask that when we are reduced by famine and plague you should pay for these dire calamities? You are bound in justice and in common duty to humanity to pay the cost of those dire calamities with which we are afflicted. I will conclude with Lord Salisbury's other true words: "Injustice will bring down the mighties to ruin." (*Great applause.*)

THE CONDITION OF INDIA.

[*Mr. Dadabhai Naoroji delivered the following address on the "Condition of India" at Toynbee Hall, Commercial Street, Whitechapel, E., on Thursday night, January* 31, 1901. *Mr. R. B. S. Tanner was in the Chair.*]

Mr. Dadabhai Naoraji, who was cordially received, said :—Mr. Chairman and Gentlemen, I feel very much obliged for having been invited to address this audience. Our subject is "India," but so large a subject cannot be dealt with in more than a passing manner in the time at our disposal. I will, however, try to put before you, in as brief a form as possible, some idea of the relations which exist between England and India. I think my best plan would be to try and strike a sort of balance between the good and evil influences of England in India, and let you understand really what your duty is towards India. One thing has been over and over again admitted —and was last admitted by Lord Curzon when he went out—that India is the pivot of the British Empire. If India is lost to the British Empire the sun of the British Empire will be set. The question is whether the responsibility devolving upon you on account of this is realised by you. Beginning at the benefits which India has received, we are grateful for a good many things. In earlier days there was infanticide, but English character, English civilisation and English humanity caused an end to be put to this, and also to the practice of burning widows with their dead husbands. By means of this you have earned the blessing of many thousands of those who have escaped death. Then there were gangs of people whose whole business it was to rob other people; you put down those gangs and are, therefore, entitled to our gratitude. If there is one thing more than another for which Indians are grateful it is for the education you gave them, which enabled them to understand their position. Then naturally follow your other institutions—namely, free speech and a free Press. You have heard of the Indian National Congress; at this Congress Indians from one end of India to the other meet together to discuss their political condition, to communicate with each other, and become, as it were, a united nation. This National Congress is naturally the outcome of the education and free speech which British rulers have given us; the result is that you have created a factor by means of this education which has, up to this time, strengthened your power immensely in India. Before you gave them education Indians never understood what sort of people you really were; they knew you were foreigners, and the treatment that they had received at your hands led them to hate you, and if they had remained of the same mind you would not have remained in India. This factor of education having come into play Indians aspired to become British citizens, and, in order to do so, they became your loyal and staunch supporters. The Congress has for its object to make you understand your deficiencies in government, the redress of which would make India a blessing to you, and make England a blessing to us, which it is not, unfortunately, at present. I now come to what you consider the highest claim you have upon our gratitude, and that is, you have given us security of life and property. But your government in

India instead of securing our life and property is actually producing a result the exact reverse. And this is what you have to understand clearly. The difficulty of Indians in addressing you is this, that we have to make you unlearn a great deal of nonsense which has been put into your heads by the misleading statements of the Anglo-Indian press. The way you secure life and property is by protecting it from open violence by anybody else, taking care that you yourselves should take away that property. (*Laughter.*) The security of life, were it not a tragic subject, would be a very funny one. Look at the millions that are suffering day by day, year after year, even in years of good harvest. Seven-eighths or nine-tenths of the people do not know what it is to have a full meal in a day. (*Hear, hear.*) And it is only when famine comes that your eyes are opened, and you begin to sympathise with us, and wonder how these famines come about. It is the Englishmen that go out to India that are in a sense the cause of these miseries. They go to India to benefit themselves. They are not the proper people to give the reasons for our misery. The greatest blessing that we thought had been bestowed upon us by Britain was contained in the Act of 1833 to which we cling even in the face of every violation of that blessing. So long as we have the hope that that blessing will become a reality some day we shall be most desirous of keeping up the connection with England. That greatest blessing is the best indication of your higher civilisation of to-day. The English have been in advance in the civilisation of humanity. The policy distinctly laid down in 1833 was that the Indians were to be treated alike with the English, without distinction of race or creed. (*Hear, hear.*) You may well be proud of that Act, but it was never carried out. Then the Mutiny took place, and you were the cause of it. After the Mutiny was put down you again emphatically laid down that the Indian people were to be treated exactly like the British people, and there was to be no difference whatever in the employment of Indians and of Englishmen in the service of the Crown. These two documents have been confirmed twice since, once on the occasion of the Queen assuming the title of Empress, and again on the occasion of the Jubilee. These are the documents—our charter—the hope and anchor upon which we depend and for which you can claim the greatest credit. The proclamation has been made before the world, praying God to bless it, and praying that our servants, the Executive to whom you trust the government, should carry out the wishes of the Sovereign, that is to say, of the people. As far as the policy laid down by the British people was concerned it is as good as we can ever desire. This promise, pledged by you in the most solemn manner possible, has been a dead letter ever since. The result is the destruction of our own interests, and it will be the suicide of yours. The violation of those promises has produced these results to us: First of all, the "bleeding" which is carried on means impoverishment to us—the poorest people on the face of the earth—with all the dire, calamitous consequences of famines, pestilences and destruction. It is but the result of what you claim as the best thing that you have conferred upon us—security of life and property—starvation, as I have told you, from one year's end to another year's end of seven-eighths of the population of the country, and something worse, in addition to the "bleeding" that is carried on by the officials of a system of government. To you, to England, the violation of these great pledges carries with it a certain amount of pecuniary benefit, and that is the only thing the Executive ever think of. But you must remember that the first consequence of such government is dishonour to your name. You inflict injustice upon us in a manner most dishonourable and discreditable to yourselves; by this mode of government you are losing a great material benefit which you would otherwise obtain. I will try to explain to you these points in as brief a manner as possible; but especially I would beg leave to draw attention to the great loss to the mass of the people of this country, which would otherwise have accrued to them. The best way I can put this before you is by giving you a comparison between two parts of the British Empire. Australia is at present before all of us. The Australian Commonwealth was formed on the first day of the first year of this century. The Australians have been increasing in prosperity by leaps and bounds. At the same time India, under this same rule, under the administration of men who are described and praised as the highest, the most cultivated, and the most capable administrators of the present time—and also the most highly paid—is suffering from the direst famines and is the poorest country in the world. Let us consider Australia first. While in 1891 the population of Australia was four millions, the population of British India was two hundred and twenty-one millions, and of all India two hundred and eighty-seven millions. Now these four millions of Australians are paying a revenue for the government of their country amounting to nearly £8 per head per annum. They can give this and are prosperous, and will go on increasing in prosperity, with a great future before them. What is India capable of doing? India can give at present, under great pressure, scarcely eight shillings per head per annum. You know that Australia has "protection" against you, and notwithstanding the "door" being shut against you, you are able to send to Australia British and Irish products, the result of your labour, to the extent of £25,500,000; that is to say, something like seven pounds' worth per head per annum. You do not send to India more than £30,000,000 altogether. That is to say, while you are sending something like seven pounds per head per annum to Australia, you do not send half-a-crown's worth of your British and Irish produce per head per annum to India. Ask yourselves this question. What is the result? Why should you not derive good substantial profits from a commercial connexion with India? The reason is simple. The people are so impoverished that they cannot buy your goods. Had your Government been such as to allow India to become prosperous, and to be able to buy your goods, let alone at the rate of seven, six, or five pounds per head—if India was allowed to enjoy its own resources and to buy from you one or two pounds' worth of your produce, what do you think you would send to India? Why, if you sent one pound's worth of produce per head to India, you would send as much there as you now send to the whole world. You have to deal with a people who belong as it were to the same race, who possess the same intelligence and same civilisation, and who can enjoy your good things as much as the Australians or anybody else. And if you could send one pound's worth to them per head you need not go and massacre savages in order to get new markets (*Laughter.*)

The mass of the people here do not understand what a great benefit there is for them in their connexion with India, if they would only do their duty, and compel their servants, the Executive, to fulfil the solemn pledges that the British nation has given to India. What I say, therefore, to you is that one of the consequences of the present system of government is an immense loss to yourselves. As it is at present, you are gaining a certain amount of benefit. You are "bleeding" the people, and drawing from their country something like thirty or forty millions a year. Ask yourselves, would you submit to such a state of things in this country for a single week? And yet you allow a system of government which has produced this disastrous result to continue. You cannot obtain a farthing from Australia unless they choose to give it to you. In the last century you pressed the people of Bengal to such an extent that Macaulay said that the English were demons as compared with the Indians as men, that the English were wolves as compared with the Indians as sheep. Hundreds of millions of India's wealth have been spent to form your British Indian Empire. Not only that but you have taken away from India all these years millions of its wealth. The result is obvious. You have become one of the richest countries in the world, and you have to thank India for it. And we have become the poorest country in the world. We are obliged to pay each year a vast amount of wealth which you need for the salaries of, and the giving of benefits to, your military and civil servants. Not once, not twice, not ten times, and the affliction is not over—but always. What was something like three millions at the beginning of the century has increased now to a tax of thirty or forty millions. You would prosper by trading with us if you would only leave us alone instead of plundering us. Your plundering will be disastrous. If yoú would allow us to prosper so that we might be able to purchase one or two pounds' worth of your produce per head, there would be no idle working classes in this country. It is a matter of the utmost importance for the working classes of England. If the connexion between England and India is to be a blessing to both, then consider what your duty and responsibility is as citizens of this great Empire. (*Applause.*)

THE CAUSE AND CURE OF FAMINE.

[*The following speech was delivered by Mr. Dadabhai Naoroji at the pulpit of the Free Church, Croydon, on Sunday the* 31*st April*, 1901.]

Mr. Naoroji, after expressing his gratitude for being invited to speak, and alluding to the sanctity of the place, said :—You have lately heard the result of the Census in India, and what an awful result it is. When you are told that something like 30 millions of people that ought to have been in India are not there, does it not disclose an awful state of things, sufficiently alarming to make one think and ponder over it ? Our close connexion, the many ties that bind us, must make you ask the question : Why is it that after 150 years of British Rule, carried on by an administration whose efficiency has been lauded up to the skies, but whose expensiveness has been grinding down the people to the dust, the result of that British Rule should be such as we see at the beginning of the twentieth century ? The cause is not far to seek. We believed that under a nation which was renowned for its justice, honour and philanthropy, we would be better off than was possible under an Asiatic despotism. But our hopes had been rudely dispelled. Unfortunately, from the very earliest times, the action of Britain in India had been based upon greed. I would not dwell longer on this part of the subject at present, as it would not redound to the credit of the British name. I would first rather say a few words on some of the great benefits that the British Rule has conferred on us.

Fortunately, or unfortunately, all the benefit that we have derived from the British connexion is from a study of the British character. The institutions which you have taken with you and introduced into our country would have borne golden fruits, and we should have reaped all the benefits as you have been doing here ; but to our misfortune we have been denied every bit of this good result. The system of government that has been adopted in that country is the root of all our misfortune and makes completely nugatory your best efforts to further some of our highest welfare. Among the benefits of the British Rule, if there is one thing more than another for which Indians are grateful, it is the education you have been giving them. It has enabled me to come here and to make known to you what my countrymen want me to tell you. It has laid the foundation of that structure which would one day be known to the world as united India. It has wiped off the first dividing line that kept Indians apart from one another. Formerly there was not a common language, no common vehicle of thought. The Bombay man did not understand a Bengal man, and a Punjabee was as unintelligible to a Madrasee as if he belonged to another country. But now English was the common language. All Indians now understand one another and freely interchange their ideas and views as to whether their common country has one hope, one fear, one aim, one future.

You have, I dare say, heard of the Indian National Congress. At this Congress Indians from one end of the country to the other meet together to discuss their political condition, to communicate with each other and become as it were a united nation. The Indian National Congress is the recognized exponent of educated India. If India had been heterogeneous before, the Congress is the proof that it is advancing rapidly towards homogeneity. It was the education that you are giving us that first demolished the dividing line that separated us from one another and is now welding us together into a nation. The Indians now stand up to tell you where your rule has been defective. It is our duty to tell you so, for the welfare of us both depends upon a clearer and truer knowledge of that fact.

The Civil Service of India which constitutes the Civil portion of the administrative machinery, and to which belong men of eminent talents and character, is anything but a blessing to us. The very abilities of these men, as I will show you later on, are in the way of the progress and prosperity of the people. It is a most melancholy fact that after 150 years of connexion, after being governed by men of such ability and integrity, the evil system of government that has been imposed on us should nullify your best efforts for our well-being and bring your great possession to bankruptcy and ruin.

I may warn you that I am not saying anything about the Native States. I only want to speak about British India, namely, that part of India which is under your direct control. During the middle of the eighteenth century when the English had the revenue administration under the Native rulers of the day, from the very commencement of the connexion between England and India the system of Government adopted had been one of greed and injustice. Those who went there went with the sole object of making fortunes, and so long as they accomplished that they cared little what occurred to the people. The hard words with which I have characterised the early British Rule are not mine. They were the words of the honourable Englishmen and Anglo-Indians who, for years, had been crying in the wilderness against the system under which India was ruled. In the last century the Court of Directors themselves and the Governor-General of the day wrote despatches in which they described acts of the grossest corruption and oppression, and abominations of every kind which were inflicted upon the poor Indian. Such cruelty towards the governed, and such corruption on the part of the Governor, as recorded in one of their minutes of those days, have been unknown in any country or at any age.

These enormities gradually led to a careful consideration of the question of the policy which should guide the British in India. And it was then also that draining away of the wealth of India into England began, which has not only not ceased, but has increased with increasing years, wiping off millions at a time, with an ever-increasing frequency. The drought was not the real cause of the famine in these days, for if the people had no food in one place and they had money, they could buy what they wanted from elsewhere. This question of famines was for that reason becoming one of the burning questions of India and England, and it would grow one day into the biggest domestic question of the time and would be the paramount question of the great British Empire. With India England must stand or fall. I would give you my authority for the statement. It was Lord Curzon—the nobleman who was now ruling India as Viceroy for England—Lord Curzon had said: "If we lose our Colonies it does not matter, but if we lose India the sun of the British Empire will be for ever set." No truer words were ever uttered. Without India England would be a third or fourth rate power. And this gradual deterioration of the country, now almost bordering on destruction, was noticed very soon after the British took India. There was a survey made of the country for nine years, from 1807 to 1816. The reports lay buried in the archives of the India House for a long time till they were unearthed by Mr. Montgomery Martin, who, in the course of a review of the reports, says, "It is impossible to avoid remarking two facts as peculiarly striking, first, the richness of the country surveyed; and second, the poverty of its inhabitants." Against this continuous drain which has now all but deprived India of its life-blood he raised his warning voice in the early years of the last century. He said: "The annual drain of three millions on British India has amounted in 30 years at 12 per cent. (the usual Indian rate) compound interest to the enormous sum of 723 millions. So constant and accumulating a drain even in England would soon impoverish her. How severe then must be its effect on India, where the wages of a labourer are from two pence to three pence a day!"

The drain which at the beginning of the century was three millions now amounts to over 30 millions a year. Mahmood Ghuzni, who invaded and plundered India 18 times, as historians say, could not make his whole booty so heavy as you take away in a single year; and, what is more, the wound on India inflicted by him came to an end after the 18th stroke, while your strokes and the bleeding from them never end. Whether we live or die, 30 millions' worth of produce must be annually carried away from this country with the regularity of the seasons. Heavy as the fine was which Germany inflicted upon France in the last Franco-German war, once the money was counted down France was set at liberty to recoup herself. But in our case the bleeding never ceases. How was India treated even in the last famine? Eighty-five millions of people were affected by the famine directly, and many more were indirectly affected by it. Yet they were being called upon to find two hundred millions of rupees yearly to pay the salaries, pensions, etc., of the European officials, military or civil, before they could have for their own enjoyment a single farthing of their own produce. And if they only took the trouble to make the calculation it would be discovered that India had had to pay thousands of millions for this purpose already. Was it to be wondered at then that India was falling and that the famines were becoming worse each time they recurred? The fact was that now-a-days the slighest touch of drought necessarily caused a famine, because the resources of the country had been so seriously exhausted. It was only when a famine took place that any interest was excited in this country in India. As a matter of fact there was a chronic state of famine in India of which the people of this country knew nothing. And even in years of average prosperity and average crops scores of millions of Indians had to live on starvation diet, and did not know what it was to have a full meal from year's end to year's end. It was only when a crisis like the present one was developed that the Government was forced to intervene, and to try to save the lives of the dying people by taxing these very people. The condition of India was an impoverished condition of the worst possible character, and one could hardly realise the poverty and misery in which scores of millions of Indians lived. But if England were placed under a similar system of government, would its condition be any better? No! even England, wealthy as she is, could not long stand the crushing tribute of a foreign yoke which, because we are a conquered nation, we are forced to pay. Suppose the French took this country, filled up all the higher posts, both civil and military, with their own people, brought French capital to develop our industries, carried away with them all the profit of their investments, leaving to the natives of this country nothing more than the wages given to mere manual labourers; suppose that, in addition to that, you had to pay a tribute (in deed though not in name) of 30 millions sterling every year to France; why, even you, wealthy as you are, would be soon reduced to the wretchedness of our want and woe, to be periodically decimated by plague and famine and disease as we are. Now, put yourselves in our place and judge whether we are British subjects or British helots. Our misfortune is that our Anglo-Indian rulers do not understand our position. Even Lord Curzon, our Viceroy, said the other day, in the course of his speech at the Kolar Gold Fields, that we ought to be very grateful to the British people for developing these mining industries. But these millions of the Kolar Gold Fields belong to the British capitalist, who is simply exploiting our land and wealth, our share being that of the hewer of wood and drawer of water.

How was the Indian Empire obtained by you? It

has been generally said that you have won it by the sword, and that you will keep it by the sword. You have not won the Indian Empire by the sword. During these hundred and fifty years you have carried on wars by which this great Empire has been built up; it has cost hundreds of millions of money. Have you paid a single farthing of it? You have made the Indians pay every farthing. You have formed this great British Empire at our expense, and you hear what reward we have received from you. The European army in India at any time was comparatively insignificant. In the time of the Indian Mutiny you had only forty thousand troops there. It was the two hundred thousand Indian troops that shed their blood and fought your battles and that gave you this magnificent Empire. It is at India's cost and blood that this Empire has been formed and maintained up to the present day. It is in consequence of the tremendous cost of these wars and because of the millions on millions you draw from us year by year that India is so completely exhausted and bled. It is no wonder that the time has come when India is bleeding to death. You have brought India to this condition by the constant drain upon the wealth of that country. I ask anyone of you whether it is possible for any nation on the face of the earth to live under these conditions.

Do not believe me as gospel. Study for yourself; study whether what I have stated is right, and, then, whether the result is logical. And the result, as revealed by the last census, is that thirty millions of human beings are not where they ought to have been. But in spite of such a gloomy outlook I do not despair. I believe in the inherent notions of justice and humanity of the British people. It is that faith which has hitherto sustained me in my lifelong work. In the name of justice and humanity then, I ask you why we to-day, instead of being prosperous as you are, are the poorest and most miserable people on the surface of the earth. Like India, Australia is a part of the British Empire, and, unlike it, prosperous. Why is it that one part of the Empire should be so prosperous and the other dwindle down and decay? Our lot is worse even than that of the slaves in America, in old days, for the masters had an interest in keeping them alive, if only they had a money value. But if an Indian died, or if a million died, there was another or there were a million others ready to take his or their places and to be the slaves of the British officials in their turn. Who was responsible for all this? You reply, "What more can we do? We have declared that India shall be governed upon righteous lines." Yes, but your servants have not obeyed your instructions, and theirs was the responsibility, and upon their heads was the blood of the millions who were starving year by year.

The principle and policy that you laid down for the government of India is contained in the Act of 1833, which we reckon as our Magna Charta. There is one clause in it which admits us to full equality with you in the government of our country. Referring to this clause, one of the men who were responsible for passing this Act, Lord Macaulay, said :—" I allude to that wise, that beneficent, that noble clause which enacts that no Native of our Indian Empire shall by reason of his colour, his descent, or his religion, be incapable of holding office." This generous promise which held out hopes of equal employment to all, which did away with distinctions of creed and colour, has remained to this day a dead letter. This promise was repeated over and over again. Nothing could be plainer, nothing more solemn, than the Queen's Proclamation of 1858, when the Crown took the country from the hands of the East India Company, and from which Proclamation I will read to you only three clauses :—

"We hold ourselves bound to the Natives of our Indian territories by the same obligations of duty which bind us to all our other subjects, and those obligations, by the blessing of Almighty God, we shall faithfully and conscientiously fulfil."

"And it is our further will that, so far as may be, our subjects, of whatever race or creed, be freely and impartially admitted to offices in our service, the duties of which they may be qualified by their education, ability, and integrity, duly to discharge."

"In their prosperity will be our strength, in their contentment our security, and in their gratitude our best reward. And may the God of all power grant to us, and to those in authority under us, strength to carry out these our wishes for the good of our people."

But all these promises and pledges have remained a dead letter to this day. The violation of the promise of the Act of 1833 is the first step, the keeping to this day inoperative the pledges contained in the Proclamation of 1858 is the second step, towards unrighteousness. Indians are kept out from their share of the administration of their own affairs just as much to-day as before the passing of that Act. Some of the most eminent Statesmen here have drawn your attention to your wrong doing. Mr. Bright pointed out the gross and rank injustice of not holding simultaneous examinations both in India and England ; and in this connexion the late Lord Derby, when Lord Stanley, once asked in the

House of Commons, how they would like to send out their children to India for two or three years to qualify themselves for, and pass, examination there for employment here. The highly expensive Military and Civil Service which is foisted on our poor land we can neither afford to keep nor do we need. If the country ever rebelled, the hardly thirty thousand civilians dotted amongst a hostile horde of about three hundred millions would be the first to suffer. The safest policy and the truest statesmanship was voiced in our Sovereign's Proclamation when she said, "in their contentment will be our security." While you here lay down in plain and unmistakable language the charter that would raise us and endow us with the power, privilege and freedom of British citizens, your servants in India make that charter a dead letter, deny to us those powers and privileges and freedom which you have empowered them to give to us, and we are made to feel that we are not British subjects, but British helots. Here, under reasonable conditions, almost every man has a vote; there two hundred and fifty millions of us have not one. Our Legislative Council is a farce, worse than a farce. It was generally believed that this Council gave to the Indian people something like what they in England enjoyed in the way of representative government, and that by those means the people of India had some voice in their own government. This was simply a romance. The reality was that the Legislative Council was constituted in such a way as to give to the Government a complete and positive majority. The three or four Indians who had seats upon it might say what they liked, but what the Government of India declared was to become law did invariably become the law of the country. In this Council the majority, instead of being given by the people, was managed and manipulated by the Government itself. But matters were even worse than this. The expenditure of the revenues was one of the most important points in the political condition of any country, but in India there was no such thing as a Legislative Budget. The representative members had no right to propose any Resolution or go to any division upon any item concerned in the Budget, which was passed simply and solely according to the despotic will of a despotic Government. The natives of India had not the slightest voice in the expenditure of the Indian revenues, and the idea that they had was the first delusion on the part of the voters of England of which they cannot be disabused too soon.

But this most solemn farce of preaching and proclaiming the most righteous Government for us, and at the same time not restraining your servants from practising what is exactly the contrary, is not confined to our Legislative Council. The right of our own men to take part in the government of their country as soon as by their character and education they should give evidence of their fitness to do so, has been repeatedly granted by the British public and Parliament, but it has as often been defiantly denied to us by your disobedient servants in India. One of the means by which this boon could be given us was by holding examinations for the Indian Civil Service simultaneously in India and in England. But this privilege, though recommended for the last time by a Resolution of the House of Commons so recently as 1893, is yet denied to us. As early as 1860 a Commission made up of five Members of the Council of the Secretary of State was appointed to consider this question of simultaneous examinations, and this is what they said :—

> Practically the Indians are excluded. The law declares them eligible, but the difficulties opposed to a Native leaving India and residing in England for a time are so great, that, as a general rule, it is almost impossible for a Native successfully to compete at the periodical examinations held in England. Weré this inequality removed, we should no longer be exposed to the charge of keeping promise to the ear and breaking it to the hope.

I will give only one more opinion of a former Governor-General, the representative of his Sovereign in India. Lord Lytton, referring to this same question of holding simultaneous examinations, said in a confidential minute :—

> The Act of Parliament is so undefined, and indefinite obligations on the part of the Government of India towards its Native subjects are so obviously dangerous, that no sooner was the Act passed than the Government began to devise means for practically evading the fulfilment of it. Under the terms of the Act, which are studied and laid to heart by that increasing class of educated Natives whose development the Government encourages without being able to satisfy the aspirations of its existing members, every such Native, if once admitted to Government employment in posts previously reserved to the Covenanted Service, is entitled to expect and claim appointment in the fair course of promotion to the highest post in that Service. We all know that these claims and expectations never can or will be fulfilled. We have had to choose between prohibiting them and cheating them; and we have chosen the least straightforward course. The application to Natives of the competitive examination system as conducted in England and the recent reduction in the age at which candidates can compete, are all so many deliberate and transparent subterfuges for stultifying the Act, and reducing it to a dead letter. Since I am writing confidentially, I do not hesitate to say that both the Governments of England and India appear to me up to the present moment unable to answer satisfactorily the charge of having taken every means in their power of breaking to the heart the words of promise they had uttered to the ear.

Even on comparatively lower grounds than that of justice and truth you ought to revise and reform the Government of India. You are a commercial people.

What you gain by trading with us, if I go into figures, that alone will tell you how poor we are. Australia, with about six millions of people, buys about 25 millions worth of articles off you per year; while we, with a population fifty times over again, hardly manage to buy even thirty millions. You sell to us per head of population only eighteen pence per year; if we were rich enough (and to make us rich or poor entirely rests with you) to buy only one pound per head per year, you could have sold to us alone 300 millions worth of goods, which is your annual trade with the whole of the world. The subject of a Native Prince in India is richer than a British subject and buys more of your goods. You launch into expensive wars in South Africa and elsewhere to create a market, while here in your own Empire you have a market ready on hand, the largest, the most civilised, the most thickly peopled portion of that Empire.

I now must conclude. I hope this cruel farce, the present system of Government which is at the root of all our evil and suffering, should for your sakes, for the sake of justice and humanity, be radically changed. The educated classes at home are throwing in their whole weight on the side of the continuance of our connexion. This connexion is a blessing to us if you would only see that it be made, as you intended your servants to make it, a blessing to us; ponder over it, think what is your duty, and perfom that duty.

BRITISH DEMOCRACY AND INDIA.

[*A meeting was held at the North Lambeth Liberal Club on Thursday evening, July* 4, 1901, *at which Mr. Dadabhai Naoroji delivered the following address on "British Democracy and India." The chair was taken at nine o'clock by Colonel Ford.*]

Mr. Naoroji, who was cordially received, said :— Mr. Chairman, Ladies, and Gentlemen, I feel very great pleasure in being permitted to address you to-night. I propose at the outset to explain to you what the condition of India is in order that you may the better understand the relations which exist between that country and England. In the first place, I will tell you what has been repeatedly laid down as the policy to be pursued towards India. In 1833, this policy was definitely decided and embodied in an Act of Parliament, and it was a policy of justice and righteousness. It provided that no Native of India, nor any natural-born subject of His Majesty resident therein, should by reason only of his religion, place of birth, descent, or any of them, be disabled from holding any place, office, or employment under the Company. That is to say, that all British subjects in India should be treated alike, and merit alone should be the qualification for employment. The Indian people asked nothing more than the fulfilment of this policy, but from that day to this no such policy has been pursued towards India. A similar declaration of policy was made in the most solemn manner after the Mutiny. The Queen's Proclamation addressed to India at that time in 1858, stated as follows :—

> "We hold ourselves bound to the Natives of our Indian territories by the same obligations of duty which bind us to all our other subjects, and those obligations, by the blessing of Almighty God, we shall faithfully and conscientiously fulfil. . . . And it is our further will that, so far as may be, our subjects, of whatever race or creed, be freely and impartially admitted to offices in our service, the duties of which they may be qualified, by their education, ability, and integrity, duty to discharge. . . . . . When, by the blessing of Providence, internal tranquility shall be restored, it is our earnest desire to stimulate the peaceful industry of India, to promote works of public utility and improvement, and to administer the government for the benefit of all our subjects, resident therein. In their prosperity will be our strength, in their contentment our security, and in their gratitude our best reward. And may the God of all power grant to us and to those in authority under us strength to carry out these our wishes for the good of our people."

Such was the solemn pledge that was made to India. But where is the fulfilment? The same distinction of race and creed exists in India now as ever existed. That pledge so solemnly made half a century ago has never been carried out. One would have thought that their sense of honour would have prompted the Executive to fulfil this pledge, but such has not been the case. These pledges and declarations of policy have been to us dead letters. (*Shame.*) This then is the first thing you have to know. What has been the result of the system of government administered in India? The result has been to bring the country to a state of poverty and misery unknown elsewhere throughout the world. This result has been accomplished by the constant draining of India's wealth, for, let it be known that we have to produce every year something like twenty million pounds by our labour and our produce and hand this over to the English before we can utilise a single farthing's worthy ourselves. This draining has been going on for years and years with ever-increasing severity. We are made to pay all the expenditure in connexion with the India Office, and every farthing that is required to keep up the Indian Army, even though this latter is supported for England's own use in order to maintain her position in the East and elsewhere. If you want to maintain your position in the East, by all means do so, but do it at your own expense. (*Hear, hear.*) Why should India be charged for it? Even if you pay half of the cost of your Indian Army we shall be satisfied and pay the other half ourselves. Every farthing of the cost of the wars by which your British-Indian Empire was formed has been paid by us, and not only was this the case, but that Empire, be it remembered, was secured to you by Indian blood. It was Indian soldiers who shed their blood in the formation of the Indian Empire, and the reward that we get is that we are treated as the helots of the British people. India is the richest country in the world in mineral and other wealth, but owing to the constant drain you have put upon our resources, you have brought our people to a state of exhaustion and poverty. At the beginning of last century the drain on Indian produce amounted to about five million pounds per annum; now, it has increased to something like thirty million pounds. Each year thirty millions sterling are exacted from India without any return in any material shape. (*Shame.*) Of this tremendous sum, however, part goes back to India, but not, mark you, for the benefit of the Indian people. It goes back under the name of British capital, and is used by British capitalists to extract from the Indian soil its wealth of minerals which wealth goes to enrich the English alone. And thus India is bled, and has been bled ever since the middle of the eighteenth century. India produces food enough for all her needs and to spare. How is it then that so many of her people die for want of it? The reason is simple. So exhausted are the people, and so heavily has the continued bleeding told upon their resources that they are too poor to purchase food, and, therefore, there is chronic famine in good years and in bad years. Do not think that famines only occur when you in England hear of them. You only hear of the very severest of them. One hundred and fifty millions of your fellow-subjects do not know what it is to have one full meal a day. What would be the position of England if she were left to feed on her own resources? She does not produce a quarter of the food required to feed her people. It is only because England is a rich country, thanks largely to India, and can, therefore, buy the produce of other countries that her people are kept from starving. Compare this with the condition of India. She produces more than she requires, and yet through their poverty her people are unable to buy food, and famine is the consequence as soon as a drought occurs. And now we come to the main point of my lecture. On whose shoulders does the responsibility for the present miserable condition of things in India rest? It rests on the shoulders of the British democracy, and I will tell you how. One elector in England has more voice in the government of his country than the whole of the Indian people have in the government of their country. In the Supreme Legislative Council in India there are only four or five Indians, and what power can so few have in that assembly? The Government appoint their own Executive Council, and it takes care that the few Indian members of the Legislative Council have no real voice in the management of their own country. A Tax Bill comes before the Council, and these Indian members have not the slightest power to vote, make a motion, or suggest an amendment. If they do not vote for it the Government turn round and say, "look at these Indians; do they think the Government can be carried on without taxation? They are not fit to govern." The fact is the Tax Bill is brought into the Council only to receive its formal sanction. No chance is given for discussion or amendment. These few Indians have to join with the other members of the Council in taxing their countrymen, without any voice in the expenditure of that taxation. Their power in fact is nil. Economically and politically India is in the worst possible position. The British public are responsible for the burdens under which India is groaning. The democracy is in power in this country, and it should understand something of our suffering, because it has suffered itself. We appeal to you to exercise your power in making your Government carry out its solemn pledges, if you succeeded in doing this, the result would be that the Empire would be strengthened and benefit would be experienced by yourselves as well as by India. India does not want to sever her connexion with England, but rather to strengthen that connexion. I wish to point out that unless the British democracy exercise their power in bringing to India a better state of things, the whole responsibility for our suffering will lie at their door. I therefore appeal to you to do your duty and relieve us from the deplorable miseries from which we are suffering. (*Cheers*).

INDIA UNDER BRITISH RULE.

[*The following speech was delivered by Mr. Dadabhai Naoroji at the annual dinner of the London Indian Society, 22nd. March,* 1902].

I can hardly express in adequate terms what I feel at the generous manner in which my health has been proposed and the cordial reception which you have given to the toast. I feel it very deeply. (*Hear, hear*). Talking of my views towards British Rule I wish to say that they have been largely misunderstood. The pith of the whole thing is that not only have the British people derived great advantage from India but that the profit would have been more than ten times as great had that rule been conducted on the lines of policy laid down by Act of Parliament. It is a pity as much for England herself as for us that that policy has not been carried out, and that the matter has been allowed to drift in the old selfish way in which the Government was inaugurated in earlier times. When I complain, I am told sometimes very forcibly, that the connexion of Britain with India is beneficial to India herself, I admit that it might be, and it is because of that that I urged over and over again that the connexion should be put upon a righteous basis—a basis of justice and liberality. It has been proved by the fact of the coming into existence of a body like the Indian National Congress that the British connexion might be made more beneficial, and I believe that if you fail to direct the force of that movement into proper channels the result will be most disastrous, for it must ultimately come into collision with British Rule. It does not require any great depth of consideration to see that. It has been repeatedly admitted by every statesman of consequence that the welfare of India depends upon the contentment of the people, and that that contentment cannot exist unless the people feel that British Rule is doing them good, is raising their political status, and is making them prosperous. (*Hear, hear*). The fact is quite the reverse, and it is no use denying that the system which has existed in India is one which has been most foolish; it has neither increased Indian prosperity nor raised her political status. If only you could make her truly imperial and unitedly in favour of British Rule I defy a dozen Russias to touch India or to do the slightest harm to the Empire. (*Cheers*). Mr. Caine has expressed regret that Indian troops were not sent to South Africa. It is quite true you cannot expect to maintain a great Empire unless you use all its imperial resources, and among those imperial resources there are none so important and so valuable as the resources of India in physical strength and in military genius and capability. There you will find that, by a simple stamp of the foot on the ground, you can summon millions of men ready to fight for the British Empire. We only want to be treated as part and parcel of the Empire, and we ask you not to maintain the relationship of master over helot. We want you to base your policy on the lines already laid down by Act of Parliament, proclaimed by the late Queen, and acknowledged by the present Emperor, as the best and truest policy towards

India for the sake of both countries. Unless that is done the future is not very hopeful. As far as I am concerned I have ever expressed my faith in the British conscience. As far back as 1853, when the first political movement was started in India, and when associations were formed in Bombay, Calcutta, and Madras in order to petition Parliament with regard to improvements necessary to be made in the Company's Charter, I expressed my sincere faith in the British people, and said I was convinced that if they would only get true information and make themselves acquainted with the realities of India they would fulfil their duty towarde her. That faith, after all the vicissitudes and disappointments which have marked the last half century, I still hold. If we only do our best to make the British people understand what their duty is, I venture to prophesy that England will have an Empire the like of which has never before existed, an Empire of which any nation may well be proud. (*Cheers.*) After all, India is the British Empire. The colonies are simply so many sons who have set up establishments of their own, but who retain their affection for the mother country, but India is an Empire which, if properly cultivated, will have a wondrous success. All we want is that there shall be a true, loyal, and real attachment between the people of the two countries. I am glad to see you young men around me. I and the older men who have worked in this movement are passing away. We began the work, we had to grope in darkness, but we leave you a great legacy, we leave you the advantages of the labours of the hundreds of us during the last 50 years, and if you only study the problem thoroughly, if you spread over the United Kingdom the true merits and defects of British Rule you will be doing a great work both for your own country and for England. I rejoice at having had something to do in that direction. I have stuck to my own view that it would be good for India if British Rule continues. But it must not be the British Rule which has obtained in the past; it must be a rule under which you treat us as brothers, and not as helots. (*Loud cheers.*)

THE INDIAN NATIONAL CONGRESS.

[*The following speech was delivered by Mr. Dadabhai Naoroji at a remarkable gathering at Westminster Palace Hotel which assembled in November* 1904, *in order to give a send off to Sir Henry Cotton on the eve of his departure to India to preside at the Twentieth Indian National Congress at Bombay.*]

The Chairman : I have now to propose the toast of the evening to our good guests Sir Henry Cotton and Sir William Wedderburn. (*Cheers*). I may first take the opportunity of expressing on behalf of the Indians here our deep regret at the death of Mr. Digby and of Lord Northbrook. I need not say much about them. There are three Viceroys who have left their names impressed on the minds of the Indian people with characteristic epithets. Those three are Mayo, "the good," Northbrook, "the just," and Ripon, "the righteous." (*Cheers.*) Two have passed away, but we hope the third may live long enough to see the realisation of his desires for the promotion of the happiness of the people of India. (*Hear, hear.*) We are met together to honour our two friends—Sir Henry Cotton and Sir William Wedderburn. The question naturally arises : Why is it that we Indians ask English gentlemen to go out to India—to preside at the Indian National Congress, and to help it? Have we in our ranks no men capable of doing the work? Cannot we help ourselves?

Those questions are natural, and they require an answer. Again it may be asked, what is it that the Indians want, and by what means do they desire to accomplish their end? I do not propose to describe what India wants in my own words, or in the words of any Indian. I propose, instead, to give you a few sentences from the writings of an Anglo-Indian whose father and grandfather have been in the service for over 60 years, who himself has been over 35 years in the service, and whose son is now in it. I refer to our guest Sir Henry Cotton. (*Cheers.*) He is as patriotic as any Englishman can be. He is proud of the service to which he belongs, and in his official capacity he has carefully weighed the position of the Indians at the present time. I will read you a few sentences from his lately-published book, "New India," and they will give you an idea of what India wants. He says: "There can be no doubt that English rule in its present form cannot continue. The leaders of the National movement assume, and assume rightly, that the connexion between India and England will not be snapped . . . . . It is a sublimer function of Imperial dominion to unite the varying races under our sway into one Empire 'broadbased upon the people's will' . . . to afford scope to their political aspirations, and to devote ourselves to the peaceful organisation of their political federation and autonomous independence as the only basis of our ultimate relationship between the two countries." Again, taking another point, Sir Henry Cotton writes on the drain of taxes from India to England: "Taking these (all drain from India to England in various shapes) into consideration, it is a moderate computation that the annual drafts from India to Great Britain amount to a total of thirty millions. . . . . It can never be to the advantage of the people of India to remit annually these enormous sums to a foreign country. . . . . Lord Curzon has very forcibly said, in a speech delivered by him in November, 1902, at Jaipore : 'there is no spectacle which finds less favour in my eyes, or which I have done more to discourage, than that of a cluster of Europeans settling down upon a Native State and sucking from it the moisture which ought to give sustenance to its own people'." He adds : "Lord Curzon has lost sight of the fact that what is true of the Native States is true of the whole of India. . . . . The keynote of administrative reform is the gradual substitution of Indian for European official agency. This is the one end towards which the educated Indians are concentrating their efforts. The concession of this demand is the only way by which we can make any pretence of statisfying even the most moderate of their legitimate aspirations. It is the first and most pressing duty the Government is called on to discharge. It is necessary as an economic measure. But it is necessary also on higher grounds than those of economy. . . . The experiment of a 'firm and resolute government' in Ireland has been tried in vain, and the adoption of a similar policy in India is inevitably destined to fail." Next, Sir Henry gives an extract from the celebrated speech of Lord Macaulay in 1833:—"It may be that the public mind of India may expand under our system till it has outgrown our system ; that by good government we may educate our subjects into a capacity for better government—that having become instructed in European knowledge, they may in some future age demand European institutions. Whether such a day will ever come.

I know not. But never will I attempt to avert or retard it. Whenever it comes it will be the proudest day in English history." Next there is an extract from Mountstuart Elphinstone, in 1850 :—" But we are now doing our best to raise them in all mental qualities to a level with ourselves, and to instil into them the liberal opinions in government and policy which have long prevailed in this country and it is vain to endeavour to rule them on principles only suited to a slavish and ignorant population." On this Sir Henry Cotton remarks : " The experience of more than half a century since they were written merely confirms their truth." And after these I propose to give only one other extract, and to read just one sentence from Burke, who says : " Magnanimity in politics is not seldom the truest wisdom, and a great Empire and little minds go ill together. We ought to elevate our minds to the greatness of that trust to which the order of Providence has called us." Now, these extracts which I have read to you explain what Indians ask for. Their wishes are embodied in the language of an Anglo-Indian, but I accept them as a very fair expression of our views. (*Cheers.*) The question is : How is this to be accomplished ? There are only two ways of doing it—either by peaceful organisation or by revolution. It must be done either by the Government itself or by some revolution on the part of the people. It may be asked what do our present reformers want, and which of these two policies they desire to adopt. I will give a direct answer to that. (*Hear, hear.*) In the year 1853, as far as I know the first attempt was made by Indian politicians or by Indians to form a political organisation and to express in words their wishes and demands. That was the period of the renewal of the East India Company's Charter, and three associations were then formed: one in Bombay, another in Calcutta, which is still in existence, and a third in Madras. The fundamental principle on which they based their whole action was contained in the words used by Sir Henry Cotton—that the connexion between England and India will not snap. That was the foundation of their action in 1853, when they made their first attempt at political organisation. As I have said, the British India Association at Calcutta is still in existence; that in Bombay was succeeded by the Bombay Presidency Association, and that in Madras by the Madras Mahajana Sabha. All along they have gone on the same principle, that the connexion between England and India will continue. In the evolution of time, as we know, the Indian National Congress came into existence, twenty year ago, and I may say that it is the best product of the most beneficial influence of the connexion between England and India. This unique phenomenon of different races and different peoples in a large continent containing an area equal to Europe (Russia excluded), and embracing quite as many different nationalities, coming together to consider proposals for the amelioration of the condition of the people of India and giving expression to their views and aspirations in the noble English language, is a product of which the British people may well be proud. The next Congress will be the twentieth, and, I repeat, that from the very beginning the principle acted upon has been a continuance of the policy adopted by the earlier Associations to which I have referred—the continuance of the connexion between England and India. Then the question is: How are we going to carry out that policy? The only way in which the desired change can be brought about is, in our opinion, by a peaceful organisation, as Sir Henry Cotton has described it: it must be effected by the Government itself. (*Cheers.*) Why is it that the Indian National Congress and we Indians here have solicited Sir Henry Cotton and Sir William Wedderburn to go out to India to assist at the twentieth Congress? The answer is simply this: that if these reforms are to be carried out at all, they are entirely in the hands of the English people. The Indians may cry aloud as much as they like, but they have no power whatever to bring about those reforms—the power is entirely in the hands of the English people and of the English Government, and our ideas and hopes can meet with no success unless we get men like Sir Henry Cotton and Sir William Wedderburn and others to help us to prove to the Indian people that they need not yet despair, for the British conscience is not altogether lost yet—(*hear, hear*)—and, on the other hand, to persuade the British people to do that which is right and just. We Indian people believe in one thing, and that is that although John Bull is a little thick-headed, once we can penetrate through his head into his brain that a certain thing is right and proper to be done, you may be quite sure that it will be done. (*Cheers.*) The necessity, therefore, of English help is very great—(*hear, hear*)—and we want English gentlemen to go out to India, not in their twos and fours, but in their hundreds, in order to make the acquaintance of Indians, to know their character, to learn their aspirations, and to help them to secure a system of self-government worthy of a civilised people like the British. (*Cheers.*) On this occasion we Indians have invited a number of English gentlemen to come and sympathise with us in giving a good send-off to our two guests, and it is a most gratifying fact that there has been so cordial a response to our invitation, and that we have here gentlemen like Mr. Courtney, Mr. Lough, Mr. Frederic Harrison, and others. We cannot in the face of this, but hope that good days are coming, and we should never despair. Mr. Courtney was a member of Royal Commission of which I was also a member. We agreed, and we disagreed. But what was his line of action all through? He displayed a spirit of fairness in the consideration of every question which came before the Commission. (*Hear, hear*). Mr. Lough has long been helping us, and when I was a member of the House of Commons I always found him a staunch and good friend of India in the House, while outside he has always accepted our invitations to help us wherever possible. Mr. Frederic Harrison has also been a great source of strength to our cause. I am sorry Mr. Hyndman is not here. He has been for twenty-six years a steady friend of the amelioration of the condition of India, and we hope that after the next General Election we may have his valuable support in the House of Commons. I appeal to every Englishman, for his own patriotism and for the good of his own country, as well as ours, if he wishes the British Empire to be preserved, to exert himself to persuade the British people that the right course to be adopted towards India is one worthy of British civilisation—worthy of those great days in the thirties—the days of emancipation, of the abolition of slavery, and of the amelioration of many forms of human suffering. It was in the year 1833 that we got our great Charter—the Charter confirmed by the Proclamation of 1858. We ask for nothing more than the fulfilment of the pledges contained in that Charter. Those are our demands as put forward by Sir Henry Cotton, and I can only say that they constitute a reversion to the policy of 1833—a policy embodied in promises which, had they been fulfilled in their entirety, would have resulted in their meeting that day being of an entirely different nature—they would have been proclaiming their gratitude, instead of pleading to the English to reverse their policy and introduce one worthy of their name and civilisation. (*Cheers.*). As Macaulay had declared: "It was to no purpose if they were free men and if they grudged the same freedom to other people." (*Hear, hear.*) I therefore appeal to every Englishman, for the sake of his own patriotism, as well as for the cause of humanity—for all reasons good and beneficent—to reverse their policy towards India and to adopt one worthy of the British name. I was one of those who started the Bombay Association in 1853, and from that time until now I have always been a worker in the cause. (*Cheers.*) My principle has been from the beginning based on the necessity of the continuance of the connexion between England and India. I hope I may hold that view to the end of my life. I am bound, however, to mention one fact, and I will do so without comment. Leaving aside the general system of Government, which we condemn, there have been during the past six or seven years repressive, restrictive, and reactionary methods adopted, and there has been, further, a persistence in the injustice of imposing upon India the burden of expenditure incurred for purely Imperial purposes. What I want to point out is that the rising generation of Indians may not be able to exercise that patience which we of the passing and past generations have shown. A spirit of discontent and dissatisfaction is at present widely spread among the Indians in India, and I wish our rulers to take note of that fact and to consider what it means. An Empire like that of India cannot be governed by little minds. The rulers must expand their ideas, and we sincerely hope that they will take note of this unfortunate circumstance and will adopt measures to undo the mischief. (*Cheers.*) In the name of my Indian friends I thank the guests who have accepted our invitation, and I now call upon Sir Henry Cotton to respond to the toast.

ENGLAND'S PLEDGES TO INDIA.

[*The following speech was delivered by Mr. Dadabhai Naoroji in* 1904, *at the Wesley Hall, Clapham Park.*]

Mr. Dadabhai Naoroji, candidate for North Lambeth, addressed a meeting under the auspices of the J. P. Health Lodge of the Sons of Temperance, at the Wesley Hall, Clapham Park, on "British Rule in India: Promises and Performances." There was, considering the unpleasant character of the weather, an excellent attendance, and the audience followed with marked interest Mr. Naoroji's eloquent pleading for his oppressed countrymen, while they also appreciatively watched the magic lantern views which vividly presented varied aspects of Indian manners, customs, and architecture. The views were graphically explained by Mr. J. C. Mukerji, and the lantern was manipulated by Mr. W. Hanmer Owen. The chair was occupied by Mr. Mason, who, in briefly introducing Mr. Naoroji as the Grand Old Man of India, explained that although the Sons of Temperance formed a friendly society, the members were always glad to keep themselves in touch with the topics of the day, and hence their invitation to Mr. Naoroji to address them.

Mr. Naoroji, who was loudly cheered, said that in order to understand throughly the subject he was announced to lecture upon, and in order to realise the full significance of British promises and performances in

India, it was necessary he should narrate a few of the historical facts which led to the promises being given. British Rule in India at its inception was one marked by greed, oppression, and tyranny of every kind—so much so that even the Court of Directors of the East India Company were horrified at what was going on. That was the first fact to be borne in mind. The second was that subsequent to the rise of the British Empire in India all war expenditure incurred in connexion with India, and by means of which the Empire had been built up, had been paid out of Indian resources entirely, and the bloodshed which was the necessary accompaniment of war was mainly Indian. In the late Transvaal war Great Britain lost thousands of her sons and spent nearly 250 millions sterling, and the people of this country consequently had brought forcibly home to them what war meant, but in India, while the British claimed all the glory and reaped all the benefits, the burdens of war were borne by the Natives. India had, in fact, cost Great Britain nothing in money and very little in blood. But its wealth had thereby been exhausted; it had become impoverished, and it had further been subjected to a system of government under which every Indian interest was sacrificed for the benefit of the English people. The system of corruption and oppression continued until at last the British Government was shamed by it. Anglo-Indians of high position in the service had again and again denounced the system in the most scathing terms, but it would suffice for his present purpose to remind them that Edmund Burke pointed out how every position worth having under the Government was filled by Europeans, to the absolute exclusion of Natives. The result was that there was a constant and most exhausting drain of Indian wealth. Even in those days it was estimated that the official remittances to England amounted to three millions sterling, and the capacity of the people's produce went on diminishing, until it was now only about £2 per head, as compared with £40 per head in Great Britain. This country, too, enjoyed the benefit of its wealth circulating at home, while India laboured under the disadvantage that what it produced was sent to England, and it got nothing in return. She was, in fact, deprived of wealth without mercy year after year, and, in addition to the official remittances home, to which he had already referred, the servants of the Government sent home, privately, an almost equal sum, which they themselves obtained from the Natives on their own account. In the early part of last century there was a Government enquiry every 20 years into the administration of the East India Company, and these at last proved so effective that the statesmen of the day began to realise the responsibilities and duty of England to India, and to seriously discuss what should be Great Britain's policy. It was in 1833 that they got the first pledge, and in that year a clause was inserted in the Charter of the East India Company providing that in the service of the Government there should be no distinction raised of race, creed, or colour, but that ability should be the sole qualification for employment by the State. That was the first promise, made to the people of India in the name of the people of the United Kingdom, and it was embodied in an Act of Parliament. Had it been faithfully and loyally carried out, the existing state of affairs in India would have been vastly different and it would not have been necessary for him to go about the country complaining of the dishonour and disgrace of England, and of the enormity of the evils of British Rule. The first promise was made in 1833, the period at which the British were rising to their highest glory in civilisation, an era of emancipation of all kinds, from the abolition of slavery onwards. Macaulay himself declared that he would be proud to the end of his life of having taken part in preparing that clause of the Charter, and clearly the policy of the statesmen of that day was to extend to India the freedom' and liberty which England enjoyed. But 20 years passed, and not the slightest effect was given to the clause : it remained a dead letter, as if it had never been enacted, and the policy of greed and oppression continued to obtain in the Government of India. In 1853, the East India Company's Charter was again revised, and in those days Mr. John Bright and Lord Stanley (afterwards Lord Derby) urged strongly that the service should be open to all and not reserved exclusively for Europeans—for the nominees and friends of the Directors of the Company. They contended, too, for the holding of simultaneous examinations in India and England, but it was without avail. Then came the Mutiny of 1857, and after that had been suppressed, the statesmen of Great Britain were again forced to consider what should be the policy of this country in India. The administration of India was taken over from the Company, and the Proclamation which was issued was drawn up by Lord Derby, at the special request of Queen Victoria, in terms of generosity, benevolence, and religious toleration, such as might well be used by a woman sovereign speaking to hundreds of millions of people the direct government of whom she was assuming after a bloody civil war. Nothing could have been more satisfactory than the promise embodied in that Proclamation, and the Indian people heartily blessed the name of Queen Victoria for the sympathy she always evinced towards her Indian subjects. This Proclamation constituted the second pledge—it was a promise to extend British institutions to India, to, in fact, give them self-government, it reaffirmed the promise of the Charter of 1833, and it declared that her Majesty held herself bound to the Natives of her Indian territories by the same obligations of duty as bound her to all her other subjects. Indians were, in fact, to become true British subjects, with all the rights and privileges of British subjects, and the government of the country was to be administered for the benefit of all the people resident therein; for, concluded the Proclamation, "in her prosperity will be our strength, in her contentment our security, and in her gratitude our best reward." This had well been called "India's Greater Charter." It was everything they desired. But, unfortunately, it, too, had remained a dead letter up to the present time, and to the great and bitter disappointment of the people of India the promises therein contained had not been faithfully and honorably fulfilled. In defiance of the Proclamation, every obstacle had been placed in the way of Natives obtaining admission to posts under the Government, the efforts of men like Mr. John Bright, Lord Derby, and Mr. Fawcett to secure the holding of simultaneous examinations in England and India had been frustrated. In 1870, no doubt, an effort was made by Sir Stafford Northcote, and later on by the Duke of Argyll, to give effect to the promise of admission of Natives to the service, but it was defeated by the action of the Indian Government. A Native service was established, but it was made entirely distinct from the European service—a distinction which was never intended—and it was so arranged that it was bound to prove a failure. Appointments to it were made by nomination, not by examination; back-door jobbery took the place of the claims of ability, and naturally, at the end of ten years, the service was abandoned because it had never answered. In 1877, on the proclamation of Queen Victoria as Empress of India, Lord Lytton issued another Proclamation in the name of Queen Victoria reiterating the promises contained in her former Proclamation, but again the pledge was violated. At the Jubilee in 1887 there was a renewal of the promise, again to be followed by its being utterly ignored; while, later on, a Resolution of the British House of Commons in favour of the holding of simultaneous examinations in India and England was carried by Mr. Herbert Paul, in spite of the opposition of the Government, and that too had been ignored. Thus, they had a long series of solemn promises made to the ear but absolutely violated in spirit and in letter, to the great dishonour and disgrace of Great Britain. Eminent statesmen and officials had frequently admitted the breaking of these pledges. A Committee appointed by the then Secretary for India unanimously reported in 1860 that the British Government had been guilty of making promises to the ear and breaking them to the hope; and that the only way in which justice could be done to Indians was by holding simultaneous examinations in England and India, of the same standard and on the same footing, instead of forcing Indians to go to London at an expense of thousands of pounds in order to secure admission to the Government service. In 1870, the Duke of Argyll declared: "We have not fulfilled our duty or the promises and engagements we have made"; later, Lord Lytton made the confession that deliberate and transparent subterfuges had been resorted to in order to reduce the promise of the Charter of 1833 to a dead letter; and that the Governments of England and of India were not in a position to answer satisfactorily the charge that they had taken every means in their power to break to the heart the promises they had made to the ear. The Duke of Devonshire, in 1883, asserted that if India was to be better governed it was to be done only by the employment of the best and most intelligent of the Natives in the service; while, finally, the late Lord Salisbury described the promises and their non-fulfilment as "political hypocrisy." That was a nice description indeed of the character of the British Rule in India; it was an admission that the conduct of the British Government in India had been disgraceful. But let them not forget that the promises were made by the British Sovereign, the British Parliament, and British people, of their own free will, while the disgrace for their non-fulfilment attached solely to the British Government, which by its refusal to act had sullied the honour of the British people. Two of the greatest offenders in this respect had been Lord George Hamilton and Lord Curzon, both of whom had very unpatriotically introduced most reactionary measures, and had pursued a mischievous policy which had resulted in the gravest injury to the Indian Empire and the British people. Lord George Hamilton, whose object surely should have been to make the people attached to British Rule, had openly declared that it never would be popular with them; while Lord Curzon had done his very utmost to make it unpopular. He was going back to that country for a second term of office as Viceroy but the suggestion that the people would welcome his reappearance was falsified by the authoritative expression of the best Native opinion, and his continuance in the office of Viceroy could only be productive of serious injury, both to England and to India. What had been the result of the non-fulfilment of this long series of promises? The system of greed and oppression still obtained in the Government of India; the country was being selfishly exploited for the sole benefit of Englishmen; it was slowly but surely being drained of its wealth, for no country in the world could possibly withstand a drain of from 30 to 40 millions sterling annually, such as India was now subjected to; its power of production was diminishing, and its people were dying of hunger by the million. The responsibility for all this rested upon British rule. What was the remedy? Not the mischievous, reactionary policy now being pursued by Lord Curzon, but the taking of steps to transform and revolutionise in a peaceful manner the present evil and disastrous system of government, so as to enable the people themselves to take their full and proper share in the administration of the affairs of their country. Lord Curzon had described India as the pivot of the British Empire. India could not be content with the present state of affairs, and he earnestly appealed to the people of Great Britain themselves to compel the Government to redeem the promises so often made, and to secure for India real self-government, subject, of course, to the paramountcy of Great Britain. (*Cheers.*)

THE LEGACY OF LORD CURZON'S REGIME.

[*A great meeting of Indians resident in the United Kingdom was held in May* 1905, *at the Caxton Hall, Westminster, to protest against Lord Curzon's aspersions upon the Indian People and their sacred writings, and against the reactionary legislation that has characterised his administration. Mr. Dadabhai Naoroji presided and made the following speech*] :—

We are met together to-day for a very important purpose. A unique event has happened, showing significantly a sign of the times. We have had in India a great uprise, and in the chief towns there have been held monster meetings of Indians, denouncing and protesting against the sayings and doings of the highest authority there, making a protest in clear, unmistakable terms against the policy under which India is ruled. It is, indeed, a unique event. I, at any rate, do not remember anything similar having ever taken place in the history of British India. The Indians have very unanimously, very earnestly, and very emphatically declared that the system of rule they are now under should not continue to be. (*Loud cheers.*) Let us consider what that means. More than 50 years ago—I will not go back to an earlier period of our history—Mountstuart Elphinstone said :—

> It is in vain to endeavour to rule them (the Indians) on principles only suited to a slavish and ignorant population.

And 40 years after—in the last 10 or 12 years—we find, not only a continuance of the same old system, but we find it brought to bear on the people with even more energy and more vigour. (*"Shame."*) Some 11 years ago Sir Henry Fowler distinctly and decidedly showed us that India was to be governed on the principles condemned by Elphinstone, for, by his conduct in refusing to give effect to the Resolution regarding simultaneous examinations, passed in 1893, he proved that it was intended to continue the same evil system under which the country had been governed so long. Then followed Lord George Hamilton as Secretary of State, and what did he tell the whole world? He said :—

> Our rule shall never be popular. Our rule can never be popular.

These were his own words, in one of his early speeches, and he has taken very good care that his prophecy shall be fulfilled. But his doings were not so serious as Lord Curzon's, although he managed to go quietly on issuing regulation after regulation with the object of depriving Indians as far as possible of an opportunity of making any further progress. But then comes Lord Curzon, and he out-Herods them all. In the first Resolution you have enumerated a number of his measures —and not a complete list, for there are some more of them—which he passed with the declared and clear intention of continuing to govern India only on principles suitable to slavish and ignorant populations. Here, then, we have a clear and distinct issue. Our rulers—the officials—tell us we shall have no chance of ever becoming a self-governing country—that they will not give us an opportunity of preparing ourselves for it. Undoubtedly, the character of the whole of the measures passed within the last 10 years points towards such an intention, and to the retraction of the generous mode which was adopted on some occasions in the time of Lord Ripon. Now, the Indian people have, for the first time, risen up and declared that this thing shall not be. (*Loud cheers.*) Here is a clear issue between the rulers and the people: They are come face to face. The rulers say: "We shall rule, not only as foreign invaders, with the result of draining the country of its wealth, and killing millions by famine, plague, and starving scores of millions by poverty and destitution." While the ruled are saying for the first time, "That shall not be." I regard the day on which the first Calcutta meeting was held as a red-letter day in the annals of India. (*Cheers.*) I am thankful that I have lived to see the birthday of the freedom of the Indian people. (*Renewed cheers.*) The question now naturally arises, what will be the consequences of this open declaration of war—as you may call it—between the rulers and the people? I will not give you my own opinions or my own views. Anglo-Indian officials have told us that persistence in the present evil system of government will lead to certain consequences. Sir John Malcolm, a well-known Governor of Bombay, who had a very distinguished career as a political agent and as an official, after describing the system that obtained in the government of India, prophesied what would be the necessary consequences, and said :—

"The moral evil to us does not stand alone. It carries with it its Nemesis: the seeds of the destruction of the Empire itself."

Again, Sir Thomas Munro said :—

It would be more desirable that we should be expelled from the country altogether, than that the result of our system of government should be such an abasement of a whole people.

Mr. Bright spoke on many occasions, always denouncing the existing system of government. He always regarded it as an evil and a disgraceful system, and, after describing the system, he wound up with these words :—

> You may rely upon it that if there be a judgment of nations—as I believe there is—as for individuals, our children, in no distant generations, must pay the penalty which we have purchased by neglecting our duty to the populations of India. ......I say a Government like that has some fatal defect which at some distant time, must bring disaster and humiliation to the Government and to the people on whose behalf it rules.

Sir William Hunter, you know, was a very distinguished official, and while he spoke as favourably as he possibly could of the existing system, he did not fail to point out the evil part of it, and he summed up one of his lectures in these words :—

> We should have had an Indian Ireland multiplied 50-fold on our hands.

Again, Lord Cromer—(*cheers*)—said :—

> Changes should be taking place in the thoughts, the desires, and the aims of the intelligent and educated men of the country, which no wise and cautious Government can afford to disregard, and to which they must gradually adapt their system of administration, if they do not wish to see it shattered by forces which they have themselves called into being, but which they have failed to guide and control.

Then, Lord Harington, when Secretary for India, pointed out that the exclusion of Indians from the government of their own country could not be a wise procedure on the part of the British people, as the only consequence could be to

> make the Indians desirous of getting rid, in the first instance, of their European rulers.

I have read to you only these four or five opinions of men of position—of high position in the Government, and of official Anglo-Indians—opinions to the effect that if the present evil system is to continue the result will be to bring disaster to the British Empire—that, in fact, the British Empire in India will vanish. That is the position in which we are at the present time, under an evil system of rule. Either that evil system must cease or it must produce disastrous results to the British Empire itself. (*Cheers.*) The issue before us is clear. Is India to be governed on principles of slavery or is she to be governed so as to fit herself as early as possible to govern herself?

* * * * *

Anyone who reads the items enumerated in the first Resolution will see that Lord Curzon has set himself most vigorously and most earnestly to the task of securing that Indians shall be treated as slaves, and that their country shall remain the property of England, to be exploited and plundered at her will. ("*Shame.*") That is the task to which Lord Curzon has set himself with a vigour worthy of a better cause. Now, that being the case, there is a duty on the Indians themselves. (*Cheers.*) They have now broken the ice; they have declared that they will not be governed as slaves; and now let them show a spirit of determination, for, I have very little doubt that, if the British public were once satisfied that India is determined to have self-government, it will be conceded. I may not live to see that blessed day, but I do not despair of that result being achieved. (*Cheers.*) The issue which has now been raised between the Governors and the governed cannot be put aside. The Indian people have as one body and in a most extraordinary way, risen for the first time to declare their determination to put an end to the present evil system of rule. (*Cheers.*) Now, I come to the first part of the first Resolution—the aspersions and attacks Lord Curzon has thought proper to make—in, I am afraid, a little spirit of peevishness—against the character and religion of the East. I do not need, however, to enter into any refutation of what he has said, for the simple reason that, as far as I am concerned, I performed that task 39 years ago, when Mr. Crawford, the President of the Ethnological Society, wrote a paper full of the very same ignorant and superficial charges. I replied to that, and I find that the *Oriental Review* of Bombay has reprinted my reply for the present occasion. (*Cheers.*) There are one or two other aspects of the matter I should like to dwell upon. It is very strange Anglo-Indian officials should throw stones in this matter. Let us have some enquiry about the manner in which the British Government have behaved towards India. Again, I will not give you my own views or ideas. I will give you those of Englishmen themselves— of men of the very highest authority. A Committee was formed in the year 1860, of five members of no less a body than the Council of the Secretary of State, in order to enquire what the Government of the day should do with regard to the Act of 1833, by which all disqualification of race and creed was abolished. This Committee of five men—all high Anglo-Indian officials, who had done much work in India, and whose names were all well known, gave a very decided opinion that the British Government had exposed itself to the charge of "having made promises to the ear and broken them to the hope." This was in 1860. In 1869, the Duke of Argyll clearly acknowledged what had been the conduct of the British Government towards the Indian people in these words :—

> I must say that we have not fulfilled our duty or the promises and engagements which we have made.

That does not look very like sincerity and righteousness on the part of the British Government. (*Cheers.*) Then comes Lord Lytton. Something like 18 years after the Committee had given their opinion—an opinion of which we knew nothing because the report was pigeonholed—Lord Lytton, in a private despatch to the Secretary of State, used these words :—

> No sooner was the Act (1833) passed, than the Government began to devise means for practically evading the fulfilment of it . . . . all so many deliberate and transparent subterfuges for stultifying the Act, and reducing it to a dead letter. . . . . I do not hesitate to say that both the Government of England and of India appear to me, up to the present moment, unable to answer satisfactorily the charge of having taken every means in their power of breaking to the heart the words of promise they had uttered to the ear.

Lastly, no less a personage than Lord Salisbury summed up the whole thing in two words. He declared that the conduct of the British Government to the Indian people was "political hypocrisy." It does not, then, lie very well in the mouth of Anglo-Indian officials to talk of lapses of Indian character and morality. (*Cheers.*) They forgot that they themselves had a very large beam in their own eyes when they were pointing to a little mote which they fancied was in the eyes of others. (*Renewed cheering.*) They ought to remember that they are living in glass houses, and should not throw stones. The next aspect of Lord Curzon's charges on which I wish to speak is this: He does not seem to realise the responsibility of the position in which he has been placed. He is there representing the Sovereign of the Empire—as Viceroy or Second King—the head of a great people, 300 millions in number, who had possessed civilisation for thousands of years, and at a time when his forefathers were wandering in the forests here. (*Cheers and laughter.*) He had a special mission. His duty as Viceroy is to attract as much as possible and to attach the good feeling of the Indian people to the rule of the British Sovereign. What does he do? By his acts he deals a deadly blow to British Rule, and then, by a peculiarly ignorant and petulant speech, he creates almost a revolution in the whole of the Empire. It is really very strange that he should do so. But I am not surprised at what he has done, and I will give you the reason why. But, first, I will certainly mention one circumstance in his favour and to his credit. As we all know, he made a very firm stand against any brutal treatment of the Indian people by Europeans, and, in so doing, caused dissatisfaction to his own countrymen. In that he really did a service, not only to Indians, but to the whole British Empire. (*Cheers.*) That one act of his shall not be forgotten by Indians, for it showed his sense of the justice he as a Viceroy should exercise. (*Renewed cheering.*) But by all the acts and measures mentioned in the first resolution he has tried to Russianise the Indian Administration, and with that narrow statesmanship with which he has all along associated himself, he has forgotten that while Russianising the Indian Administration, he is Russianising also the people of India, who live at a distance of 6,000 miles from the centre of the Empire, and who, consequently, are in a very different position from the Russians themselves, who are struggling against their own Government in their own country. (*Hear, hear.*) It is remarkable that

Lord Curzon, when he was first appointed Viceroy, said that India was the pivot of the British Empire, that if the Colonies left the British Empire it would not matter much, whereas the loss of India would be the setting of the sun of the Empire. What does he do? How does he strengthen that pivot? One would think he would put more strength, more satisfaction, and more prosperity under the pivot, but, instead of that, he has managed to deposit under it as much dynamite as he possibly can—dynamite in the form of public dissatisfaction, which, even in his own time, has produced the inevitable explosion. Surely, that is a remarkable way of strengthening the connexion between the British and the Indian peoples. But, as he had said, he was not surprised at the Viceregal career of Lord Curzon: he was only disappointed and grieved that the fears he entertained when Lord Curzon was appointed had been fulfilled. It had been a great disappointment to him, because he had hoped against hope for something better. The announcement of his appointment was made in August, 1898, and in the following September he wrote to a friend in these terms:—

> I am hoping against hope about Mr. Curzon, for this reason. Lord Salisbury was at one time not a little wild. When he came to the India Office he seemed to have realised his responsibility, and proved a good Secretary of State, as things go —at least, an honestly outspoken one. Will Curzon show this capacity? That is to be seen.

My disappointment is that he did not show this capacity, and did not realise the responsibility of his position—he did not know how to govern the Indian Empire. I will not take up more of your time. The crisis has come; the people and the rulers are face to face. The people have for 150 years suffered patiently, and, strange to say, their patience has been made a taunt as well as viewed as a credit to them. Often I have been taunted with the fact that 300 millions of Indians allow themselves to be governed like slaves by a handful of people. And then it is stated to their credit that they are a law-abiding, civilised, and long-suffering people. But the spell is broken. (*Cheers.*) The old days have passed, and the Indian of to-day looks at the whole position in quite a different light. New India is becoming restless, and it is desirable that the Government should at once realise it. I hope that the next Government we have will reconsider the whole position, and will see and understand the changes that have taken place in the condition, knowledge, and intelligence of the Indian people. (*Cheers.*) I hope that steps will be taken more in conformity with the changes that have taken place, and that things will not be allowed to go on in their present evil way, to the detriment of the Empire itself as well as the suffering of the people. (*Loud cheers.*)

PART II.

Dadabhai Naoroji's Writings

I.—ADMINISTRATION AND MANAGEMENT OF INDIAN EXPENDITURE. *

DEAR LORD WELBY,—I beg to place before you and other Members of the Commission a few notes about the scope and importance of its work.

The Reference consists of two parts. The first is: "To enquire into the Administration and Management of the Military and Civil Expenditure incurred under the authority of the Secretary of State for India in Council, or of the Government of India."

This enquiry requires to ascertain whether the present system of the Administration and Management of Expenditure, both here and in India, secures sufficiency and efficiency of services, and all other satisfactory results, at an economical and affordable cost; whether there is any peculiar inherent defect, or what Mr. Bright called "fundamental error" † in this system; and the necessity or otherwise of every expenditure.

I shall deal with these items as briefly as possible, simply as suggestively and not exhaustively:—

"SUFFICIENCY."—The Duke of Devonshire (then, 1883, Lord Hartington) as Secretary of State for India

---

* Submitted by Mr. Naoroji to the Welby Commission, October 1895.

† Speech in House of Commons, 3/6/1853.

has said * : "There can in my opinion be very little doubt that India is insufficiently governed."

Sir William Hunter has said † : "The constant demand for improvement in the general executive will require an increasing amount of administrative labour."

"EFFICIENCY".—It stands to reason that when a country is "insufficiently governed," it cannot be efficiently governed, however competent each servant, high and low, may be. The Duke of Devonshire assumes as much in the words, "if the country is to be better governed." So does Sir William Hunter: "If we are to govern the Indian people efficiently and cheaply." These words will be found in the fuller extracts given further on.

"ECONOMICAL AND AFFORDABLE COST."—The Duke of Devonshire has said ‡ : "The Government of India cannot afford to spend more than they do on the administration of the country, and if the country is to be better governed, that can only be done by the employment of the best and most intelligent of the Natives in the Service."

Sir William Hunter, after referring to the good work done by the Company, of the external and internal protection, has said § : "But the good work thus commenced has assumed such dimensions under the Queen's Government of India that it can no longer be carried on, or even supervised by imported labour from England except at a cost which India cannot sustain," . . . . "forty years hereafter we should have had an Indian

* Ib., 23/8/83.
† "England's Work in India," p. 131, 1880.
‡ House of Commons, 23/8/1883.
§ "England's Work in India," p. 130.

Ireland multiplied fifty-fold on our hands. The condition of things in India compels the Government to enter on these problems. Their solution and the constant demand for improvement in the general executive, will require an increasing amount of administrative labour. India cannot afford to pay for that labour at the English rates, which are the highest in the world for official service. But she can afford to pay for it at her own Native rates, which are perhaps the lowest in the world for such employment." "You cannot work with imported labour as cheaply as you can with Native labour, and I regard the more extended employment of the Natives not only as an act of justice but as a financial necessity." "The appointment of a few Natives annually to the Covenanted Civil Service will not solve the problem. . . . . If we are to govern the Indian people efficiently and cheaply, we must govern them by means of themselves, and pay for the Administration at the market rates of Native labour." *

"ANY INHERENT DEFECT."—Mr. Bright said† :—"I must say that it is my belief that if a country be found possessing a most fertile soil capable of bearing every variety of production, and that notwithstanding the people are in a state of extreme destitution and suffering, the chances are there is some fundamental error in the government of that country."

I take an instance: Suppose a European servant draws a salary of Rs. 1,000 a month. He uses a portion of this for all his wants, of comfort, living, etc., etc. All this consumption by him is at the deprivation of an Indian who would and could, under right and natural

* "England's Work in India," pp. 118-19.
† House of Commons, 3/6/1853.

circumstances, occupy that position and enjoy that provision. This is the first partial loss to India, as, at least, the services enjoyed by the Europeans are rendered by Indians as they would have rendered to any Indian occupying the position. But whatever the European sends to England for his various wants, and whatever savings and pension he ultimately, on his retirement, carries away with him, is a complete drain out of the country, crippling her whole material condition and her capacity to meet all her wants—a dead loss of wealth together with the loss of work and wisdom—*i.e.*, the accumulated experience of his service. Besides, all State expenditure in this country is a dead loss to India.

This peculiar inherent evil or fundamental error in the present British Indian administration and management of expenditure and its consequences have been foretold more than a hundred years ago by Sir John Shore (1787):

"Whatever allowance we make for the increased industry of the subjects of the State, owing to the enhanced demand for the produce of it (supposing the demand to be enhanced), there is reason to conclude that the benefits are more than counterbalanced by evils inseparable from the system of a remote foreign dominion." *

And it is significantly remarkable that the same inherent evil in the present system of administration and management of expenditure has been, after nearly a hundred years, confirmed by a Secretary of State for India. Lord Randolph Churchill has said in a letter to the Treasury (1886) †:

"The position of India in relation to taxation and the sources of public revenue is very peculiar, not merely from the habits of the people and their strong aversion to change, which

* Parliamentary Return 377 of 1812. Minute, para. 132.
† Par. Return [C. 4868], 1886.

is more specially exhibited to new forms of taxation, but likewise from the character of the government, which is in the hands of foreigners who hold all the principle administrative offices and form so large a part of the Army. The impatience of the new taxation which will have to be borne wholly as a consequence of the foreign rule imposed on the country, and virtually to meet additions to charges arising outside of the country, would constitute a political danger the real magnitude of which it is to be feared is not at all appreciated by persons who have no knowledge of our concern in the Government of India, but which those responsible for that government have long regarded as of the most serious order."

Lord Salisbury, as Secretary of State for India, put the same inherent evil in this manner: "The injury is exaggerated in the case of India, where so much of the revenue is exported without a direct equivalent." And he indicates the character of the present system of the administration and management of expenditure as being that "India must be bled."* I need not say more upon this aspect of the inherent evil of the present system of expenditure.

"THE NECESSITY OR OTHERWISE" of any expenditure is a necessary preliminary for its proper administration and management, so as to secure all I have indicated above. You incidentally instanced at the last meeting that all expenditure for the collection of revenue will have to be considered—and so, in fact, every expenditure in both countries will have its administration, management and necessity, to be considered.

The second part of the Reference is "The apportionment of charge between the Governments of the United Kingdom and of India for purposes in which both are interested."

* Par. Return [C. 3086-1], 1881, p. 144. Minute, 29-4-75.

What we shall have to do is, first to ascertain all the purposes in which both countries are interested by examining every charge in them, and how far each of them is respectively interested therein.

In my opinion there are some charges in which the United Kingdom is almost wholly or wholly interested. But any such cases will be dealt with as they arise.

After ascertaining such purposes and the extent of the interest of each country the next thing to do would be to ascertain the comparative capacity of each country, so as to fix the right apportionment according to such extent of interest and such capacity.

I shall just state here what has been already admitted to be the comparative capacity by high authorities. Lord Cromer (then Major Baring), as the Finance Minister of India, has said in his speech on the Budget (1882): "In England, the average income per head of population was £33; in France, it was £23; in Turkey, which was the poorest country in Europe, it was £4 per head." I may add here that Mulhall gives for Russia above £9 per head. About India, Lord Cromer says: "It has been calculated that the average income per head of population in India is not more than Rs. 27 a year; and though I am not prepared to pledge myself to the absolute accuracy of a calculation of this sort, it is sufficiently accurate to justify the conclusion that the taxpaying community is exceedingly poor. To derive any very large increase of revenue from so poor a population as this is obviously impossible, and, if it were possible, would be unjustifiable." "But he thought it was quite sufficient to show the extreme poverty of the mass of the people." I think the principles of the calculation for India and the other countries are somewhat different; but that, if necessary, would be considered at the right time. For such large purposes with the Commission has to deal these figures might be considered enough for guidance. I then asked Lord Cromer to give me the details of his calculations, as my calculations, which, I think, were the very first of their kind for India, had made out only Rs. 20 per head per annum. Though Rs. 27 or Rs. 20 can make but very small difference in the conclusion of "extreme poverty of the mass of the people," still to those "extremely poor" people whose average is so small, and even that average cannot be available to every individual of them, the difference of so much as Rs. 7, or nearly 33 per cent., is a matter of much concern. Lord Cromer himself says: "He would ask honourable members to think what Rs. 27 per annum was to support a person, and then he would ask whether a few annas was nothing to such poor people."

Unfortunately, Lord Cromer refused to give me his calculations. These calculations were, I am informed, prepared by Sir David Barbour, and the results embodied in a Note. I think the Commission ought to have this Note and details of calculations, and also similar calculations, say for the last five years or longer, to the latest day practicable. This will enable the Commission to form a definite opinion of the comparative capacity, as well as of any progress or otherwise in the condition of the people, and the average annual production of the country.

The only one other authority on the point of capacity which I would now give is that of Sir Henry Fowler as Secretary of State for India. He said*:

---

* Budget Debate 15/8/64.

"Now, as to the revenue, I think the figures are very instructive. Whereas in England the taxation is £2 11*s*. 8*d*. per head; in Scotland, £2 8*s*. 1*d*. per head; and in Ireland, £1 12*s*. 5*d*. per head; the Budget which I shall present to-morrow will show that the taxation per head in India is something like 2*s*. 6*d*., or one-twentieth the taxation of the United Kingdom and one-thirteenth of that of Ireland." And that this very small capacity of 2*s*. 6*d*. per head is most burdensome and oppressive is admitted on all hands, and the authorities are at their wits' ends what to do to squeeze out more. So far back as 1870* Mr. Gladstone admitted about India as a country, "too much burdened," and in 1893,† he said: "The expenditure of India and especially the Military expenditure is alarming."

Sir David Barbour said‡: "The financial position of the Government of India at the present moment is such as to give cause for apprehension." The prospects of the future are disheartening."§

Lord Landsdowne, as Viceroy, said ‖: "We should be driven to lay before the Council so discouraging an account of our Finances, and to add the admission, that, for the present, it is beyond our power to describe the means by which we can hope to extricate ourselves from the difficulties and embarrassments which surround us." "My Hon'ble friend is, I am afraid, but too well justified in regarding our position with grave apprehension." "We have to consider not so much the years which are past

---

* Hansard, vol. 201, p. 521, 10/5/1870.
† Hansard, vol. 14, p. 622, 30/6/1893.
‡ Par. Return 207, of 1893, Financial Statement, 23/3/93.
§ Ib., para. 28.
‖ Par. Return 207, of 1893, Financial Statement, 23/3/93.

and gone as those which are immediately ahead of us, and if we look forward to these, there can be no doubt that we have cause for serious alarm." *

"Many such confessions can be quoted. And now when India is groaning under such intolerable heavy expenditure, and for the relief of which, indeed, this very Royal Commission has come into existence, the utmost that can be squeezed out of it to meet such expenditure is 2*s*. 6*d*. per head. Thus, by the statement of Sir H. Fowler as Secretary of State for India, the relative capacity of poor India at the utmost pressure is only one-twentieth of the capacity of the prosperous and wealthy United Kingdom. But there is still something worse. When the actual pressure of both taxations as compared, with the respective means of the two countries is considered, it will be found that the pressure of taxation on "extremely poor" India is much more heavy and oppressive than that on the most wealthy country of England.

Even admitting for the present the overestimate of Lord Cormer of Rs. 27 income, and the underestimate of Sir H. Fowler about 2*s*. 6*d*., revenue raised, the pressure of percentage of the Indian Revenue, as compared with India's means of paying, is even then slightly higher than that of the United Kingdom. But if my estimates of means and revenue be found correct, the Indian pressure or percentage will be found to be fifty or more per cent. heavier than that on the United Kingdom.

You have noticed a similar fallacy of regarding a smaller amount to be necessarily a lighter tax in the Irish Royal Commission.

---

* Par. Return 207, of 1893, p. 110. Financial Statement, 23/3/93.

"2613.* You went on to make rather a striking comparison between the weight of taxation in Ireland and Great Britain, and I think you took the years 1841 to 1881. In answer to Mr. Sexton, taking it head by head, the incidence of taxation was comparatively very light I may say in 1841, and very heavy comparatively in 1881?—Yes.

"2614. I would ask you does not that want some qualification. If you take alone without qualification the incidence of taxation upon people, leaving out of view entirely the fact whether the people have become in the interval poorer or richer, will you not get to a wrong conclusion? Let me give you an instance of what I mean. I will take such a place as the Colony of Victoria. Before the gold discoveries you had there a small, sparse, squatting population, probably very little administered, and paying very few taxes. Probably in such a case you would find out that the incidence of taxation at that time was extremely small?—Yes.

"2615. But take it thirty or forty years later when there was a greater population, and what I am now dwelling upon, an improvement in wealth, you would find out that the incidence of taxation was very much heavier per head; for instance, perhaps *5s.* per head at first, and perhaps £2 in the second; but it would be wrong to draw the conclusion from that fact that the individuals were relatively more heavily taxed at the later period than the first. Would it not?"

Similarly, it would be wrong to draw the conclusion that the individuals of England were more heavily taxed than those of India, because the average of the former was £2 *11s. 8d.*, and that of the latter was *2s. 6d.* An

* Par. Return [c. 7720-1], 1895. Lord Welby.

elephant may carry a ton with ease, but an ant will be crushed by a quarter ounce.

Not only is India more heavily taxed than England to supplying its expenditure, but there is another additional destructive circumstance against India. The whole British taxation of £2 11*s*. 8*d*. per head returns entirely to the *people themselves* from whom it is raised. But the 2*s*. 6*d*. so oppressively obtained out of the poverty-stricken Indians does not all return to them. No wonder that with such a destructive and unnatural system of "the administration and management of expenditure" millions perish by famine and scores of millions, or—as Lord Lawrence said (1864)—"the mass of the people, enjoy only a scanty subsistence." Again in 1873, before the Select Committee of the House of Commons, Lord Lawrence said: "The mass of the people of India are so miserably poor that they have barely the means of subsistence. It is as much as a man can do to feed his family or half-feed them, let alone spending money on what may be called luxuries or conveniences." I was present when this evidence was given, and I then noted down these words. I think they are omitted from the published report, I do not know why and by whom. In considering therefore the administration and management of expenditure and the apportionment of charge for common purposes, all such circumstances are most vital elements, the importance of the attention to which cannot be over-estimated.

The *Times* of 2nd July last, in its article on "Indian Affairs," estimates the extent and importance of the work of the Commission as follows:

"Great Britain is anxious to deal fairly with India. If it should appear that India has been saddled with charges which the British taxpayer should have borne, the British taxpayer will not hesitate to do his duty. At present we are in the unsatisfactory position which allows of injurious aspersions being made on the justice and good faith of the British nation, without having the means of knowing whether the accusations are true or false. Those accusations have been brought forward in the House of Lords, in the House of Commons, and in a hundred newspapers, pamphlets and memorials in India. Individual experts of equal authority take opposite sides in regard to them. Any curtailment of the scope of the Royal Commission's enquiry which might debar reasonable men from coming to a conclusion on these questions would be viewed with disappointment in England and with deep dissatisfaction throughout India."

Now, what are the "accusations" and "injurious aspersions" on the justice and good faith of the British nation? Here are some statements by high authorities as to the objects and results of the present system of the administration and management of expenditure of British Indian revenues.

Macaulay pointed out:

"That would indeed be a doting wisdom, which, in order that India might remain a dependency, would make it a usless and costly dependency—which would keep a hundred millions of men from being our customers in order that they might continue to be our slaves."*

Lord Salisbury says: "India must be bled."†

Mr. Bright said:

"The cultivators of the soil, the great body of the population of India, are in a condition of great impoverishment, of great dejection, and of great suffering."‡

"We must in future have India governed, not for a handful of Englishmen, not for that Civil Service whose praises are so constantly sounded in this House. You may govern India, if you like, for the good of England, but the good of England must come through the channels of the good of India. There are but two modes of gaining anything by our connexion with

* Hansard, vol. 19, p, 533, 10/7/1833.

† Par. Return [c. 3086-1], 1881.

‡ House of Commons, 14/6/1858.

India. The one is by plundering the people of India, and the other by trading with them. I prefer to do it by trading with them. But in order that England may become rich by trading with India, India itself must become rich." *

Now, as long as the present system is what Mr. Bright characterises by implication as that of plundering, India cannot become rich.

"I say that a Government put over 250,000,000 of people, which has levied taxes till it can levy no more, which spends all that it can levy, and which has borrowed £100,000,000 more that all that it can levy—I say Government like that has some fatal defect, which, at some not distant time, must bring disaster and humiliation to the Government and to the people on whose behalf it rules." †

Mr. Fawcett said:

"Lord Metcalf had well said that the bane of our system was that the advantages were reaped by one class and the work was done by another." ‡

Sir George Wingate § says with regard to the present system of expenditure:

"Taxes spent in the country from which they are raised are totally different in their effect from taxes raised in one country and spent in another. In the former case the taxes collected from the population . . . are again returned to the industrious classes. . . . But the case is wholly different when the taxes are not spent in the country from which they are raised. . . They constitute. . . . an absolute loss and extinction of the whole amount withdrawn from the taxed country . . . . might as well be thrown into the sea. . . . Such is the nature of the tribute we have so long exacted from India. . . . From this explanation some faint conception may be formed of the cruel, crushing effect of the tribute upon India." "The Indian tribute, whether weighed in the scales of justice, or viewed in the light of our own interest, will be found to be at variance with humanity, with common sense, and with the received maxims of economic science."

---

* House of Commons, 24/6/1858.

† Speech in the Manchester Town Hall, 11-12-1877.

‡ Hansard, vol. 191, p. 1841, 5/5/1868.

§ "A Few Words on our Financial Relations with India." (London, Richardson Bros., 1859.)

Lord Lawrence, Lord Cromer, Sir Auckland Colvin and others declare the extreme poverty of British India, and that after a hundred years of the administration of expenditure by the most highly-praised and most highly-paid service in the world—by administrators drawn from the same class which serves in England.

Sir John Shore, as already stated, predicted a hundred years ago that under the present system the benefits are more than counterbalanced by its evils.

A Committee of five members * of the Council of the Secretary of State for India said, in 1860, that the British Government was exposed to the charge of keeping promise to the ear and breaking it to the hope; and Lord Lytton † said, in 1878, the same, with greater emphasis, in a Minute which it is desirable the Commission should have.

Lord Lytton said ‡:

"The Act of Parliament is so undefined, and indefinite obligations on the part of the Government of India towards its Native subjects are so obviously dangerous, that no sooner was the Act passed than the Government began to devise means for practically evading the fulfilment of it. Under the terms of the Act, which are studied and laid to heart by that increasing class of educated Natives whose development the Government encourages without being able to satisfy the aspirations of its existing members, every such Native, if once admitted to Government employment in posts previously reserved to the covenanted service, is entitled to expect and claim appointment in the fair course of promotion to the highest post in that service. We all know that these claims and expectations never can or will be fulfilled We have had to choose between prohibiting them and cheating them, and we have chosen the least straightforward course.

* Sir J. P. Willoughby, Mr. Mangles, Mr. Arbuthnot, Mr. MacNaughton, Sir E. Perry.

† Report of the first Indian National Congress, p. 30.

‡ I believe this to be in a Minute 30/5/1878 (?) to which the Government of India's Despatch of 2/5/1878 refers. Par Return [C. 2376, 1870, p. 15].

The application to Natives of the competitive examination system—as conducted in England—and the recent reduction in the age at which candidates can compete are also many deliberate and transparent subterfuges for stultifying the Act, and reducing it to a dead letter. Since I am writing confidentially, I do not hesitate to say that both the Governments of England and of India appear to me, up to the present moment, unable to answer satisfactorily the charge of having taken every means in their power of breaking to the heart the words of promise they had uttered to the ear."

The Duke of Argyll said *

"I must say that we have not fulfilled our duty or the promises and engagements which we have made."

When Lord Northbrook pleaded † (1883) the Act of Parliament of 1833, the Court of Directors' explanatory despatch and the great and solemn Proclamation of 1858, Lord Salisbury in reply said: "*My lords, I do not see what is the use of all this political hypocrisy.*" ‡

The Act for which Macaulay said: "I must say that to the last day of my life I shall be proud of having been one of those who assisted in the framing of the Bill which contains that clause;" the clause which he called "that wise, that benevolent, that noble clause," and which Lord Lansdowne supported in a noble speech as involving "the hapiness or misery of 100,000,000 of human beings," and as "confident that the strength of the Government would be increased; and the great and most solemn proclamation of the Sovereign on behalf of the British nation are, according to Lord Salisbury, "political hypocrisy!" Can there be a more serious and injurious aspersion on the justice and good faith of the British nation?

The Duke of Devonshire pointed out that it would

* Speech in House of Lords, 11/3/1869.

† Hansard, vol. 277, p. 1792, 9/4/1883.

‡ *Ib.*, p. 1798.

not be wise to tell a patriotic Native that the Indians shall never have any chance "except by their getting rid in the first instance of their European rulers.* "

From the beginning of British connection with India up to the present day India has been made to pay for every possible kind of expenditure for the acquisition and maintenance of British Rule, and Britain has never contributed her fair share (except a small portion on few rare occasions, such as the last Afghan War) for all the great benefits it has always derived from all such expenditure and "bleeding" or "slaving" of India. And so this is a part of the important mission of this Commission, to justly apportion charge for purposes in which both countries are interested.

Such are some of the "accusations" and "injurious aspersions being made on the justice and good faith of the British nation," while truly "Great Britain is anxious to deal fairly with India." Justly does the *Times* conclude that any curtailment of the Royal Commission's enquiry which might debar reasonable men from coming to a conclusion on these questions would be viewed with dissappointment in England and with deep dissatisfaction throughout India."

The *Times* is further justified when Sir Henry Fowler himself complained of "a very strong indictment of the British Government of India" having been "brought before the House and the country." † And it is this indictment which has led to the enquiry.

On the 10th of this month the *Times*, in a leader on the conduct of the Transvaal with regard to trade and

* House of Commons, 23/8/1883.
† House of Commons, 15/8/1894.

franchise, ends in these words: "A man may suffer the restriction of his liberty with patience for the advancement of his material prosperity. He may sacrifice material prosperity for the sake of a liberty which he holds more valuable. When his public rights and his private interests are alike attacked the restraining influences on which the peace of civilised societies depends are dangerously weakened."

So, when the Indian finds that the present administration and management of expenditure sacrifice his material prosperity, that he has no voice in the administration and management of the expenditure of his country, and that every burden is put upon his head alone—when thus both "his public rights and private interests are alike attacked the restraining influences on which the peace of civilised societies depends are dangerously weakened."

Sir Louis Mallet ends his Minute of 3rd February, 1875, on Indian Land Revenue with words which deserve attention as particularly applicable to the administration, management, and necessity of Indian expenditure.* He says:

> "By a perpetual interference with the operation of laws which our own rule in India has set in motion, and which I venture to think are essential to success—by a constant habit of palliating symptoms instead of grappling with disease—may we not be leaving to those who come after a task so aggravated by our neglect or timidity that what is difficult for us may be impossible for them"?

I understand that every witness that comes before the Commission will not be considered as of any party, or to support this or that side, but as a witness of the Commission coming for the simple object of helping the

* Par. Return [c. 3086-1], 1881, p. 135.

Commission in finding out the actual whole truth of every question under consideration.

I shall esteem it a favour if, at the next meeting, you will be so good as to place this letter before the Commission. I may mention that I am sending a copy to every member of the Commission, in order that they may be made acquainted beforehand with its contents.

Yours truly,

DADABHAI NAOROJI.

II.

Dear Lord Welby,—I now submit to the Commission a further representation * upon the most important test of the present "Administration and Management of Expenditure," *viz.*, its results.

Kindly oblige me by laying it before the Commission at the next meeting. I shall send a copy of it to every member of the Commission. As the reference to the Commission embraces a number of most vital questions —vital both to England and India—I am obliged to submit my representation in parts. When I have finished I shall be willing, if the Commission think it necessary, to appear as a witness to be cross-examined upon my representations. If the Commission think that I should be examined on each of my representations separately, I shall be willing to be examined.

In the Act of 1858 (see. LIII) Parliament provided that among other information for its guidance the Indian authorities should lay before it every year "A Statement prepared from detailed Reports from each Presidency and District in India, in such form as shall best exhibit the Moral and Material Progress and Condition of India in each such Presidency." Thereupon such Reports were ordered by the Government of India to be prepared by the Government of each Presidency.

As a beginning the Reports were naturally imperfect in details. In 1862, the Government of India observed: "There is a mass of statistics in the Administration Reports of the various Local Governments . . . . but they are not compiled on any uniform plan . . . so as to show

* Submitted to the Welby Commission on 9th January, 1896.

the statistics of the Empire" (Fin. Con., June, '62). The Statistical Committee, which the Government of India had organised for the purpose, prepared certain Forms of Tables, and after receiving reports on those forms from the different Governments made a Report to the Government of India, with revised Forms of Tables (Office Memorandum, Financial Department, No. 1043, dated 28/2/66). The members of this Committee were Mr. A. Grote, president, and Messrs. G. Campbell, D. Cowie, and G. Smith.

I confine myself in this statement to the tables concerning only the material condition of India, or what are called "Production and Distribution."

The following are the tables prescribed :—

PRODUCTION AND DISTRIBUTION.

FORM D.—AGRICULTURE.

Under a former Section provision is made for information regarding soils so far as nature is concerned, and we have now to do with what the soil produces, and with all that is necessary to till the soil, all of which is embraced under the heads—Crop, Stock, Rent, and Production.

CROPS CULTIVATED IN ACRES, ACTUAL OR APPROXIMATE.—I.

Name of District.	Rice	Wheat	Other Food Grains	Oil Seeds	Sugar	Cotton	Opium	Indigo	Fibres	Tobacco	Tea	Coffee	Vegetables, etc., etc.
Total													

STOCK.—2.

District	Cows and Buffaloes	Horses	Ponies	Donkeys	Sheep and Goats	Pigs	Carts	Ploughs	Boats
Total									

RATES OF RENT AND PRODUCE.—3.

Average Rent per Acre for Land suited for

District	Rice	Wheat	Inferior Grains	Indigo	Cotton	Opium	Oil Seeds	Fibres	Sugar	Tobacco
General Average										

Average Produce of Land per Acre in lbs.

District	Rice	Wheat	Inferior Food Grains	Indigo	Cotton	Opium	Oil Seeds	Fibres	Sugar	Tobacco	Tea	Coffee, etc., etc.
General Average												

FORM E.

Price of Produce and labour at the end of the year.

PRODUCE.—1.

Price of Produce per maund of 80 lbs.

District	Rice	Wheat	Linseed	Jute	Cotton	Sugar	Salt	etc., etc.
General Average								

Prices—*continued.*				Labour.—2.						
				Wages per diem.						
Plough Bullocks, each	Sheep, each	Fish, per seer	Iron, per maund, etc., etc.	District	Skilled	Unskilled	Cart per day	Camel per day	Donkeys per score per day	Boat per ditto
				General average						

Note.—The general character of the staple of the district should be stated as "Cotton, Indigenous," "Cotton, New Orleans," "Sugar, Raw," "Sugar, Refined," "Salt, Rock," "Salt, Samber Lake," and so on.

FORM F.

Mines and Quarries.

Where Situated	Mineral Produced	Number of Mines	Annual Produce	Remarks

FORM G.—MANUFACTURES.

	Class of Manufactures.								
	Silk	Cotton	Wool	Other Fibres	Paper	Wood	Iron	Brass and Copper	Building, etc., etc.
Number of Mills and Manufactories ...									
Private Looms or Small Works									
Number of Workmen in Large Works :									
Female ...									
Male ...									
Number of Workmen in Small Works or Independent Artizans									
Number of European Superintendents in Large Works									
Value of block in ditto									
Estimated Annual Outturn of all Works ...									
Total ...									

It will be seen from these tables that they are sufficient for calculating the total "production" of any province, with such additions for sundry other produce as may be necessary, with sufficient approximacy to accuracy, to supply the information which Parliament wants to know about the progress or deterioration of the material condition of India.

Sir David Barbour said, in reply to a question put by Sir James Peile :—

> "2283. It does not by any means follow that people are starving because they are poor ?—Not in the least. You must recollect that the cost of the necessaries of life is very much less in India than it is in England."

Now, the question is, whether, even with this "very much less cost" of the necessaries and wants of life, these necessaries and wants of life even to an absolute amount, few as they are, are supplied by the "production of the year." Sir D. Barbour and others that speak on this point have not given any proof that even these cheap and few wants are supplied, with also a fair reserve for bad seasons. It is inexplicable why the Statistical Committee failed to prescribe the tables for the necessary consumption—or, as the heading of Form D. called "Distribution"—if they really meant to give Parliament such full information as to enable it to judge whether "the mass of the people," as Lord Lawrence said, "lived on scanty subsistence" or not. The Statistical Committee has thus missed to ask this other necessary information, *viz.*, the wants of a common labourer to keep himself and his family in ordinary, healthy working condition—in food, clothing, shelter, and other necessary ordinary social wants. It is by the comparison of what is *produced* and what is *needed* by the people even for the absolute necessaries of life (leave alone any luxuries) that anything like a fair idea of the condition of the people can be formed. In my first letter to the Secretary of State for India, of 24th May, 1880, I have worked out as an illustration all the necessary tables both for "production" and "distribution," *i.e.*, absolute necessaries of life of a common labourer in Punjab.

If the demands of Parliament are to be loyally supplied (which, unfortunately, is almost invariably not the attitude of Indian authorities in matters concerning the welfare of the Indians and honour of the British name depending thereon) there is no reason whatever why the information required is not fully furnished by every province. They have all the necessary materials for these tables, and they can easily supply the tables both for "production" and "distribution" or necessary consumption, at the prices of the year of all necessayy wants. Then the Statistical Department ought to work up the average per head per annum for the whole of India of both "production" and "distribution." Unless such information is supplied, it is idle and useless to endeavour to persuade the Commission that the material condition of the people of British India is improving. It was said in the letter of the Secretary of State for India to me of 9th August, 1880, that in Bengal means did not exist of supplying the information I desired. Now that may have been the case in 1880, but it is not so now; and I cannot understand why the Bengal Government does not give the tables of production at all in its Administration Report. The only table, and that the most important one, for which it was said they had not the means, and which was not given in the Administration Report, is given in detail in the "Statistical Abstract of British India for 1893-4" (Parl. Ret. [C. 7,887] 1895), pp. 141-2.

No. 73.—CROPS UNDER CULTIVATION IN 1893-4 (P. 141).

Administration—Bengal.

ACRES.

Rice.	Wheat.	Other Food Grains (including Pulses).	Other Food Crops.	Sugar-cane.	Coffee.
38,200,300	1,620,200	11,636,000	3,130,900	1,083,400	......

ACRES—*continued.*

Tea.	Cotton.	Jute.	Other Fibres.	Oil Seeds.	Indigo.
110,800	201,280	2,228,200	207,100	3,253,000	614,200

ACRES—*continued.*

Tobacco.	Cinchona.	Miscellaneous.	Total area under crops.	Deduct area cropped more than once.	Actual area on which crops were grown.
730,500	2,900	424,900	64,444,200	10,456,900	53,987,300

Then, at page 142, there is also given total area under crops—of area under irrigation—64,444,200 acres. Certainly, if they can know the total area, they can ascertain the average of some of the principal crops.

Then as to the crops per acre of some of the principal produce, they can have no difficulty in ascertaining, and the prices are all regularly published of principal articles of food. There can be no difficulty in obtaining the prices of all principal produce. The whole matter is too important to be so lightly treated. The extreme importance of this information can be seen from the fact that Parliament has demanded it by an Act, and that Sir Henry Fowler himself made a special and earnest challenge about the condition of the people. He said in his speech on 15th August, 1894, when he promised the Select Committee :—

> "The question I wish to consider is whether that Government, with all its machinery as now existing in India, has or has not promoted the general prosperity of the people in its charge; and whether India is better or worse off by being a Province of the British Crown."

And this is the question to which an answer has to be given by this Commission—whether the present administration and management of the military and Civil Expenditure incurred in both countries, "has or has not," as one of its results, "promoted the general prosperity of the people" of British India; or is, or is not, the result of this administration and management of expenditure "scanty subsistence" for the mass of the people as admitted by Lord Lawrence, and "extreme poverty" as stated by Lord Cromer, Sir Auckland Colvin, and Sir David Barbour among the latest Finance Ministers—a poverty compared with which even the most oppressed and misgoverned Russia is prosperity itself, the income of which is given by Mulhall as above £9 per head per annum, which Lord Cromer gives the income of British India as "not more than Rs. 27 per head per annum," and I calculate as not more than Rs. 20 per head per annum. Even this wretched income, insufficient as it is, is not all enjoyed by the people, but a portion never returns to them, thereby continuously though gradually diminishing their individual capacity for production. Surely, there cannot be a more important issue before the Commission as to the results of the administration and management of expenditure, as much or even more for the sake of Britain itself than for that of India.

Before proceeding further on the subject of these statistics it is important to consider the matter of the few wants of the Indian in an important aspect. Is the few wants a reason that the people should not prosper, should not have better human wants and better human enjoyments? Is that a reason that they ought not to produce as much wealth as the British are producing here? Once the Britons were wandering in the forests of this country, and their wants were few; had they remained so for ever what would Britain have been to-day? Has not British wealth grown a hundred times, as Macaulay has said? And is it not a great condemnation of the present British administration of Indian expenditure that the people of India cannot make any wealth—worse than that, they must die off by millions, and be underfed by scores of millions, produce a wretched produce, and of that even somebody else must deprive them of a portion!

The British first take away their means, incapacitate them from producing more, compel them to reduce their wants to the wretched means that are left to them, and then turn round upon them and, adding insult to injury, tell them: "See, you have few wants; you must remain poor and of few wants. Have your pound of rice—or, more generously, we would allow you two pounds of rice—scanty clothing and shelter. It is we who must have and would have great human wants and human enjoyments, and you must slave and drudge for us like mere animals, as our beasts of burden." Is it that the mass of the Indians have no right or business to have any advancement in civilisation, in life and life's enjoyments, physical, moral, mental and social? Must they always live to the brute's level—must have no social expenses—is that all extravagance, stupidity, want of intelligence, and what not? Is it seriously held, in the words of Lord Salisbury: "They (the Natives of India) know perfectly well that they are governed by a superior race" (*Hansard*, vol. 277, 9/4/83, page 1798), and that that superior race should be the masters, and the Indians the slaves and beasts of burden? Why the British-Indian authorities and Anglo-Indians generally (of course with honourable and wise exceptions) do every mortal thing to disillusion the Indians at the idea of any superiority by open violation and dishonour of the most solemn pledges, by subtle bleeding of the country, and by obstructing at every point any step desired by the British people for the welfare of the Indians. I do hope, as I do believe, that both the conscience and the aspirations of the British people, their mission and charge, which it is often said Providence has placed in their hands, are to *raise* the Indians to their own level of civilisation and prosperity, and not to degrade themselves to the lowness of Oriental despotism and the Indians to mere helots.

I may here again point out some defects in these statistics so as to make them as accurate as they can possibly be made, in supplying the Commission with the necessary information. It is surprising that Indian highly-paid civilians should not understand the simple arithmetic of averages; and that they should not correct the mistake even after the Secretary of State for India forwarded my letter pointing out the mistake.

The mistake is this. Supposing the price of rice in one district is Re. 1 per maund, and in another district Rs. 3 per maund, then the average is taken by simply adding 3 and 1 and dividing by 2, making it to be Rs. 2 per maund, forgetting altogether to take into account the quantities sold at Rs. 3 and Re. 1 respectively. Supposing the quantity sold at Re. 1 per maund is 1,000,000 maunds and that sold at Rs. 3 is only 50,000 maunds, then the correct average will be :—

	Maunds.		Rs.		Rs.
	1,000,000	×	1	=	1,000,000
	50,000	×	3	=	150,000
Total...	1,050,000				1,150,000

which will give Re. 1-1-6 per maund, instead of the incorrect Rs. 2 per maund, as is made out by simply adding 1 and 3 and dividing by 2.

In my "Poverty of India" I have given an actual illustration (*supra* pp. 3-4). The average price of rice in the Administration Report of the Central Provinces for 1867-8 was made out to be, by the wrong method, Rs. 2-12-7, while the correct price was only Rs. 1-8. Also the correct average of produce was actually 759 lbs. per acre, when it was incorrectly made out to be 579 lbs. per acre. Certainly there is no excuse for such arithmetical mistakes in information required by Parliament for the most important purpose of ascertaining the result of the British Administration of the expenditure of a vast country.

In the same way averages are taken of wages without considering how many earn the different wages of $1\frac{1}{2}$, 2, 3 or more annas per day and for how many days in the year.

In the Irish Commission you yourself and the Chairman have noticed this fallacy.

Witness, Dr. T. W. GRIMSHAW.

Question 2925. (Lord Welby): Do you take a mean price? —I take a mean price between highest and lowest.

2926. (Chairman): An arithmetical mean price without reference to the quantities?—Yes.

2927. (Lord Welby): For instance, supposing for nine months there had been a low price, and the remaining three a high price, the mean would hardly represent a real mean, would it?—You are correct in a certain sense. . . . .

TRADE.—Totals are taken of both imports and exports together and any increase in these totals is pointed out as proof of a flourishing trade and increasing benefit when in reality it is no such thing, but quite the reverse altogether. I shall explain what I mean.

Suppose a merchant sends out goods to a foreign country which have cost him £2,000. He naturally expects to get back the £1,000 and some profit, say 15 per cent.; *i.e.*, he expects to receive back £1,150. This will be all right; and suppose he sends out more, say £2,000 worth, the next year and gets back his £2,300, then it is really an increasing and profitable trade. But suppose a merchant sent out goods worth £1,000 and gets back £800 instead of £1,150 or anything above £1,000; and again the second year he sent £2,000 worth and got back £1,600. To say that such a trade is a flourishing or profitable trade is simply absurd. To say that because the total of the exports and imports of the first year was £1,800, and the total of the exports and imports in the second year was £3,600, that therefore it was a cause for rejoicing, when in reality it is simply a straight way to bankruptcy with a loss of £200 the first year, and £400 the second year (leaving alone profits), and so on. Such is the condition of British India. Instead of getting back its exports with some profit, it does not get back even equal to the exports themselves, but a great deal less every year. Why then, it may be asked, does India not go into bankruptcy as any merchant would inevitably go? And the reason is very simple. The ordinary merchant has no power to put his hand in other persons' pockets, and make up his losses. But the despotic Government of India, on the one hand, goes on inflicting on India unceasing losses and drain by its unnatural administration and management of expenditure, and, on the other hand, has the power of putting its hands unhindered into the pockets of the poor taxpayer and make its account square.

While the real and principal cause of the sufferings and poverty of India is the deprivation and drain of its resources by foreigners by the present system of expenditure, the Anglo-Indians generally, instead of manfully looking this evil in the face, ignore it and endeavour to find all sorts of other excuses. It is very necessary that the Commission should have the opportunity of fairly considering those excuses. Now, one way I can deal with them would be for myself to lay them down as I understand them; or, which is far better, I should deal with them as they are actually put forth by some high Anglo-Indian official. As I am in a position to do so, I adopt the second course. A high official of the position of an Under-Secretary of State for India and Governor of Madras, Sir Grant Duff, has already focussed all the official reasons in two papers he contributed to the *Contemporary Review*, and I have answered them in the same *Review* in 1887. I cannot therefore do better than to embody my reply here, omitting from it all personal remarks or others irrelevant to the present purpose. In connexion with my reply, I may explain here that it is because I have taken in it £1 = Rs. 10 that the incidence of taxation is set down as 6*s*. per head per annum, while Sir H. Fowler's estimate only 2*s*. 6*d*. per head at the present depressed exchange and excluding land-revenue. Sir H. Fowler's excludes land revenue from the incidence as if land revenue, by being called "rent," rained from heaven, and was not raised as much from the production of the country as any other part of the revenue. The fact of the matter is that in British India as in every other country, a certain portion of the production of the country is taken by the State, under a variety of names —land tax or rent, salt revenue, excise, opium, stamps, customs, assessed taxes, post office surplus, law and justice surplus, etc., etc. In some shape or other so much is taken from the production, and which forms the incidence of taxation. The evil which India suffers from is not in what is raised or taken from the "production" and what India, under natural administration, would be able to give two or three times over, but it is in the manner in which that revenue is spent under the present unnatural administration and management of expenditure whereby there is an unceasing "bleeding" of the country.

My reply to Sir Grant Duff was made in 1887. This brings some of the figures to a later date than my correspondence with the Secretary of State for India. Single-handed I have not the time to work out figures to date, but I shall add afterwards some figures which I have already worked out for later than 1887. I give below my reply to Sir Grant Duff as I have already indicated above.

All the subjects treated in the following extracts are the direct consequences of the present system of "the administration and management of expenditure in both countries." It is from this point of view that I give these extracts. (See my reply, in August and November, 1887, to Sir Grant Duff, *supra*, pp. 231-272.)

I give below some of the latest figures I already have to compare the results of the administration of expenditure in India with those of other parts of the British Empire.

TEN YEARS (1883-1892).

Countries.	Imports (including Gold and Sliver.)	Exports (including Gold and Silver.)	Excess of Imports over Exports.	Percentage of Trade Profits
	£	£	£	
United Kingdom (Par. Ret. [C. 7,143] 1893.)	4,247,954,247	3,203,603,246	1,044,351,001	32
Australasia ...	643,462,379	582,264,839	61,197,540	10·5*
North American Colonies ...	254,963,473	205,063,294	49,900,179	24·4
Straits Settlements... (Par. Ret. [C. 7, 144] 1893.)	204,613,643	181,781,667	22,831,976	12·5

* Australasia is a large gold and silver exporting country. Profits on this are a very small percentage. The profits on other produce or merchandise will be larger than 10·5 per cent., and it should also be borne in mind that Australasia, like India, is a borrowing country, and a portion of its exports, like that of India, goes for the payment of interest on foreign loans. Still, it not only pays all that interest from the profits of trade, but secures for itself also a balance of 10·5 per cent. profits, while India must not only lose all its profits of trade but also Rx. 170,000,000 of its own produce. Were India not "bleeding" politically it would also be in a similar condition of paying for its loans and securing something for itself out of the trade profits.

CAPE OF GOOD HOPE AND NATAL. I cannot give figures as the gold brought into the Colonies from Transvaal is not included in the imports; while exports include gold and silver.

NATAL. In this also goods in transit are not included in imports, although included in exports.

BRITISH INDIA. Far from any excess of imports or trade profits, there is, as will be seen further on, actually a large deficit in imports (Rx. 774,099,570) from the actual exports (Rx. 944,279,318). Deficit from its own produce (Rx. 170,179,748)—18 per cent.

INDIA.

Particulars of the Trade of India and the losses of the Indian people of British India; or, The Drain.

TEN YEARS (1883-1892). (Return [C. 7,193,] 1893.)

India's total Exports, including Treasure.	
Rx. 944,279,318	
„ 188,855,863	Add: as in other countries, say 20 per cent. excess of imports or profits (U. K. is 32 per cent.)
Rx. 1,133,135,181	or the amount which the imports should be. But
„ 774,099,570	only are the actual imports.
Rx. 359,035,611	is the loss of India for which it has not received back a single farthing either in Merchandise or treasure.

Now, the question is what has become of this Rx. 359,000,000 which India *ought* to have received but has not received.

This amount includes the payment of interest on railway and other public works loans.

Owing to our impoverishment, our utter helplessness, subjection to a despotism without any voice in the administration of our expenditure, our inability to make any capital, and therefore, forced to submit to be exploited by foreign capital, every farthing of the above amount is a loss and a drain to British India. We have no choice; the whole position is compulsory upon us. It is no simple matter of business to us. It is all simply the result of the despotic administration of expenditure of our resources.

Still, however, let us consider these loans as a matter of business, and see what deduction we should make from the above amount.

The loans for public works during the ten years (Par. Ret. [c. 7193] 1893, p. 298) are:—Rx. 34,350,000 (This is taken as Rs. 10 = £1—p. 130), or £34,350,000. This amount is received by India, and forms a part of its imports.

The interest paid during the ten years in England is £57,700,000. This amount, being paid by India, forms a part of its exports. The account, then, will stand thus:—

India received or imported as loans £34,350,000 in the ten years. India paid or exported as interest £57,700,000, leaving an excess of exports as a business balance £23,350,000, or, say, at average 1*s*. 4*d*. per rupee Rx. 37,360,000.

This export made by India in settlement of public works loans interest account may be deducted from the above unaccounted amount of Rx. 359,000,000, leaving a balance of Rx. 321,640,000 still unreceived by India.

The next item to be considered is public debt (other than for public works). This debt is not a business debt in any possible way. It is simply the political burden put upon India by force for the very acquisition and maintenance of the British Rule. It is entirely owing to the evil administration of expenditure in putting every burden on India. Make an allowance for even this forced tribute.

The public debt of India (excluding public works) incurred during the ten years is £16,000,000, (p. 298), of which, say, £8,000,000 has interest to be paid in London. (I do not know how much is raised in India and how much in England. I think I asked the India Office for this, but it is difficult to get definite information from it.) The interest paid in London during the ten years is £28,600,000. This forms part of the exports of India. The £8,000,000 of the debt incurred during the ten years form part of the imports of India, leaving a balance of, say, £21,000,000. On public debt account to be further deducted from the last balance of unaccounted loss of Rx. 321,640,000, taking, £21,000,000, at 1*s.* 4*d.* per rupee will give about Rx. 33,000,000, which, deducted from Rx. 321,640,000, will still leave the unaccounted loss or drain of Rx. 288,000,000. I repeat that as far as the economic effect on India of the despotic administration and management of expenditure under the British Rule is concerned, the whole amount of Rx. 359,000,000 is a drain from the wretched resources of India.

But to avoid controversy, allowing for all public debt (political and commercial), there is still a clear loss or drain of Rx. 288,000,000 in ten years, with a debt of £210,000,000 hanging round her neck besides.

Rx. 288,000,000 is made up of Rx. 170,000,000 from the very blood or produce of the country itself, and Rx. 118,000,000 from the profits of trade.

It must be also remembered that freight, insurance,

and other charges after shipment are not calculated in the exports from India, every farthing of which is taken by England. When these items are added to the exports the actual loss to British India will be much larger than the above calculations. I may also explain that the item of stores is accounted for in the above calculations. The exports include payment for these stores, and imports include the stores. The whole of the above loss and burden of debt has to be borne by only the Indian taxpayers of *British India*. The Native States and their capitalists, bankers, merchants, or manufacturers and the European capitalists, merchants, bankers, or manufacturers get back their full profits.

In the above calculation I have taken 20 per cent. as what ought to be the excess of imports under natural circumstances, just as the excess of the United Kingdom is 32 per cent. But suppose I take even 15 per cent. instead of 20 per cent., then the excess of imports would be, say, Rx. 311,000,000 instead of nearly Rx. 359,000,000. From this Rx. 311,000,000, deduct, as above, Rx. 37,000,000 for public works account and Rx. 33,000,000 for political public debt account, their will still be a loss or drain of Rx. 241,000,000 in ten years.

Strictly considered in India's helpless condition, there has been a drain of its wealth to the extent of Rx. 360,000,000 in the ten years.

But, as I have said, to avoid all futile controversy, after allowing fully for all debt, there is still a drain of Rx. 241,000,000 or Rx. 24,000,000 a year during the ten years.

But it must be also remembered that besides the whole of the above drain, either Rx. 359,000,000, or

Rx. 241,000,000, there is also the further loss of all that is consumed in India itself by foreigners so far, to the deprivation and exclusion of the children of British India.

Now, let it be once more understood that there can be no objection to any capitalist, or banker, or merchant, or manufacturer going to India on his own account and making any profits there, *if we are also left free to do our best in fair competition*, but as long as we are impoverished and made utterly helpless in our economic condition by the forced and unnatural present system of the administration and management of expenditure, the whole profits of foreigners (European or Indian) is British India's irreparable loss.

The moral, therefore, of this phenomenon is that Sir John Shore's prediction of 1787, about the evil effect of foreign domination by the adoption of the present system of the administration and management of expenditure, is amply and deplorably fulfilled. Truly has Macaulay said: "The heaviest of all yokes is the yoke of the stranger." It cannot be otherwise under the existing administration and management of expenditure. What an enormous sum, almost beyond calculation, would British India's loss amount to in the present century (leaving alone the last century of unparalleled corruption, plunder, and oppression by Europeans) when calculated with compound interest! A tremendously "cruel and crushing" and destructive tribute indeed!

With regard to the allegation that the fall in exchange has stimulated exports from India, here are a few figures which tell their own tale :—

Exports in	1870-1.	Rx. 64,690,000
"	1890-1.	Rx. 102,340,000

or an increase of about 60 per cent. This is the increase in the 20 years of the fall of exchange.

Now take	1850 exports...	£18,700,000
„ „	1870 „	£64,690,000

i.e., an increase of nearly 3½ times. Was this increase owing to fall in Exchange? There was then no such fall in Exchange. And what good was this increase to India? As shown above, in ten years only she has been drained to the extent indicated, besides what is eaten in the country by those who are not her children. The increase in trade, excepting that of Native and Frontier States, is not natural and economic for the benefit of the people of *British* India. It is mostly only the form in which the increasing crushing tribute and the trade-profits and wants of foreigners are provided by the poor people of British India, the masses of whom live on scanty subsistence, and are ill-fed, ill-clothed, and ill-habited hewers of wood and drawers of water for them.

But there is another most important consideration still remaining.

While British India is thus crushed by a heavy tribute which is exacted by the upper classes and which must end in disaster, do the British industrial people, or the great mass, derive such benefit as they ought to derive, with far greater benefit to England itself, besides benefitting India?

Here is this wretched result so far as the producers of British and Irish produce are concerned, or the British trade with India is concerned.

In 1893, all British and Irish produce exported to all India is only £28,800,000 for a population of 285,000,000 or 2*s*. per head per annum. But a large portion of this goes to the Native States and frontier territories. British Indian subjects themselves (221,000,000) will be found to take hardly a shilling or fifteen pence worth per head per annum. And this is all that the British people export to British India. If British India were more righteously treated and allowed to prosper, British produce will be exported to British India as much or a great deal more than what the British people are exporting to the whole world. A word to our Lancashire friends. If they would open their eyes to their true interests, and give up squabbling about these wretched cotton duties, they would see that a market of 220,000,000 people of British India, besides the 64,000,000 of the Native States, will require and take (if you take your hand off their throat), more than Lancashire will be able to supply. Look at the wretched Lancashire trade with the poverty-stricken British Indians :—

In 1892-3 India imported yarn £2,683,850 }
Manufactures £22,942,015 } —£25,625,865.

for a population of 285,000,000, or about 1*s*. 9*d*. per head per annum. But if you deduct Native States and Frontier States, it will possibly be 1*s*. per head for British India. Why should it not be even £1 or more per head if British India be not "bled"? And Lancashire may have £250,000,000 or more of trade instead of the wretched £25,000,000. Will Lancashire ever open its eyes and help both itself and India to be prosperous?

Argument of Population

Increase from 1881 to 1891 :—

	Increase.	Population per Square Mile.
England and Wales ...	11·6 per cent. ...	500
British India ...	9·7 ,, ...	230

In 1801, the population of England and Wales

(Mulhall's Dictionary, p. 444) was 8,893,000, say 9,000,000.

In 1884, the population was 27,000,000 (Parl. Ret [c. 7, 143], 1893), or three times as much as in 1801.

The income of England and Wales (Mul., p. 320) in 1800 was £230,000,000.

In 1884, while the population increased to 27,000,000 or three times that of 1801, the income increased to £976,000,000 (Mul., p. 321), or nearly 4½ times that of 1810.

The population of England and Wales (Mul., p. 444) in 1672, was 5,500,000. The income in 1664 (Mul., p. 320) was £42,000,000.

In 1884, (Mul., p. 321), population 27,000,000, increased five times; income £976,000,000, increased more than twenty-three times.

In comparison with earlier times Macaulay said (*Supra*, p. 269): "While our numbers have increased tenfold, our wealth has increased hundredfold."

These facts do not show that increase of population has made England poorer. On the contrary, Macaulay truly says "that the advantages arising from the progress of civilisation have far more than counterbalanced the disadvantages arising from the progress of population."

Why, then, under the administration of the "greatest" and most highly-paid service in the world, derived from the same stock as the administrators of this country, and, as Mr. Bright says, "whose praises are so constantly sounded in this House," is India, after a long period at present the most "extremely poor" country in the world? And yet how can the result be otherwise under the existing administration and management of expenditure, based upon the evil principle that "India must be bled ?" The fault is not of the officials. It is the evil and outrageous system of expenditure, which cannot but produce such pernicious and deplorable results, which, if not remedied in time, must inevitably bring about a retribution the extent and disaster of which can hardly be conceived. Officials over and over again tell us that the resources of India are boundless. All the resources of civilisation have been at their command, and here is this wretched and ignominious result—that while England has gone on increasing in wealth at a greater progress than in population, India at this moment is far poorer than even the misgoverned and oppressed Russia, and poorer even than Turkey in its annual production, as Lord Cromer pointed out in 1882.

I think I need not say anything more upon the first part of our Reference. If I am required to be cross-examined on the representations which I have submitted, I shall then say whatever more may be necessary for me to say.

I have shown, by high authorities and by facts and figures, one result of the existing system of "The administration and management of the Military and Civil Expenditure incurred under the authority of the Secretary of State for India in Council, or of the Government of India"—*viz.*, the most deplorable evil of the extreme poverty of the mass of the people of British India—suicidal and dishonourable to British name and rule, and destructive and degrading to the people of British India, with a "helot system" of administration instead of that of British citizenship.

The following remarks in a leader of the *Times* of 16th December, 1895, in connection with the Transvaal, is, short of compulsory service, applicable with ten times more force to the British Rule of British India. The *Times* says:—

"The time is past even in South Africa when a helot system of administration organised for the exclusive advantage of a privileged minority can long resist the force of enlightened public opinion. If President Kruger really possesses any of those statesmanlike qualities which are sometimes ascribed to him, he will hasten to accept the loyal co-operation of these *Ouitlandres*, who have already done so much and who are anxious to do more for the prosperity and progress of the South African Republic."

I would apply this to British India. The time is past in British India when a "helot system of administration," organised for the exclusive advantage of a privileged minority, and existing to the great dishonour of the British name for a century and a half, can long resist the force of enlightened public opinion, and the dissatisfaction of the people themselves. If the British statesmen of the present day possess those statesmanlike qualities which the statesmen of 1833 showed about India—to "be just and fear not," which the great Proclamation of 1858 proclaimed to the world, and which Sir H. Fowler so lately (3/9/95) described as having "the courage of keeping our word"— they will hasten to accept the loyal co-operation of the people of India, with whose blood mainly, and with whose money entirely, has the British Indian Empire been both built up and maintained; from whom Britain has drawn thousands of millions, or untold wealth calculated with interest; who for British righteousness would return the most devoted and patriotic loyalty for their own sake, and whose prosperity and progress, as Lord Roberts said, being indissolubly bound up with those of Britain, would result in largely increasing the prosperity of the British people themselves, in the stability of the British

Rule and in the redemption of the honour and good name of Britain from the dishonour of many broken pledges. The deplorable evil result of the present "administration and management of expenditure," in violation of solemn pledges, is so subtle, so artistic, so unobservably "bleeding," to use Lord Salisbury's word, so plausibly masked with the face of beneficence, and being unaccompanied with any open compulsion or violence to person or property which the world can see and be horrified with, that, as the poet says :—

> "Those lofty souls have telescopic eyes,
> That see the smallest speck of distant pain,
> While at their feet a world of agony,
> Unseen, unheard, unheeded, writhes in vain."

—*Great Thoughts*. 31/8/95.

Even a paper like the *Pioneer* of Allahabad (21/9/95) which cannot be accused of being opposed to Anglo-Indian views, recognises that India "has also perhaps to undergo the often subtle disadvantages of foreign rule." Yes, it is these, "*subtle* disadvantages of foreign rule" which need to be grappled with and removed, if the connection between India and England is to be a blessing to both, instead of a curse. This is the great and noble task for our Commission. For, indeed, it would be wise to ponder whether and how far Lord Salisbury's—a statesman's—words at the last Lord Mayor's dinner, apply to British India. He said :—

> "That above all treaties and above all combinations of external powers, 'the nature of things' if you please, or 'the providence of God.' if you please to put it so, has determined that persistent and constant misgovernment must lead the Government which follows it to its doom ; and while I readily admit that it is quite possible for the Sultan of Turkey, if he will, to govern all his subjects in justice and in peace, he is not exempt, more than any other potentate from the law that injustice will bring the highest on earth to ruin."

The administration of expenditure should be based

on this principle, as Sir Louis Mallet (c. 3086—1) 1881, p. 142, has said :—

"If India is to be maintained and rendered a permanent portion of the British Empire, this must be accomplished in some other way than by placing our future reliance on the empirical arts of despotism" and not on those low motives of making India as simply an exploiting ground for our "boys" as Sir C. Crossthwaite desired when he had the candour of expressing the motive of British action when speaking about Siam at the Society of Arts (vol. 39—19/2/92—p. 286). All that gentleman cared for was this. "The real question was who was to get the trade with them and how we could make the most of them, so as to find fresh markets for our goods and *also employment for those superfluous articles of the present day, our boys*" (the italics are mine), as if the whole world was created simply for supplying markets to the one people, and employment to their boys. Still, however, you can have ten times more trade than you have at present with India, far more than you have at present with the whole world, if you act on lines of righteousness, and cast off the second mean motive to enslave other people to give employment to your "boys," which certainly is not the motive of the British people. The short of the whole matter is, that under the present evil and unrighteous administration of Indian expenditure, the romance is the beneficence of the British Rule, the reality is the "bleeding" of the British Rule. Under a righteous "administration of expenditure," the reality will be the blessing and benefit both to Britain and India, and far more trade between them than we can form any conception of at present.

Yours truly,

DADABHAI NAOROJI.

III

THE APPORTIONMENT OF CHARGE BETWEEN THE GOVERNMENTS OF THE UNITED KINGDOM AND OF INDIA.*

DEAR LORD WELBY,—I now request your favour of laying before the Commission this letter of my views on the second part of the Reference, *viz.*, "The apportionment of charge between the Governments of the United Kingdom and of India for purposes in which both are interested."

The word England, or Britain, is always used by me as embracing the United Kingdom.

I do not know whether there is any portion of the Indian charge (either in this country or in India) in which Britain is not interested. The one chief object of the whole expenditure of Government is to govern India in a way to secure internal law and order and external protection. Now, in both internal law and order and external protection, the interests of Britain are as great or rather greater than those of India. That India is protected from lawlessness and disorder is unquestionably a great boon and benefit to it. But orderly or disorderly India shall always remain and exist where it is, and will shape its own destiny somehow, well or badly. But without law and order British Rule will not be able to keep its existence in India. British Rule in India is not even like Russian Rule in Russia.

---

* Submitted to the Welby Commission on 15th February, 1896.

However bad and oppressive the latter may be, whatever revolution or Nihilism there may occur, whatever civil wars or secret disasters may take place, the Russians and their Rulers remain all the same in Russia; only that power changes from one hand into another, or from one form into another. Only a few days ago (18th January, 1896) the Russian Tsar, styling himself "Emperor and Autocrat of all the Russias," issued a Manifesto for his Coronation as follows:—

"By the grace of God we, Nicholas II, Emperor and Autocrat of all the Russias, etc., make known to all our faithful subjects that, with the help of the Almighty, we have resolved to place upon ourselves the Crown, in May next, in the Ancient Capital of Moscow, after the example of the pious Monarchs our forefathers, and to receive the Holy Sacrament according to established usage; uniting with us in this Act our most beloved consort the Empress Alexandra Feodorovna.

"We call upon all our loyal subjects on the forthcoming solemn day of Coronation to share in our joy and to join us in offering up fervent prayers to the Giver of all good that He may pour out upon us the gift of the Holy Spirit, that He may strengthen our Empire, and direct us to the footsteps of our parent of imperishable memory, whose life and labours for the welfare of our beloved fatherland will always remain a bright example.

"Given at St. Petersburg, this first day of January in the year of Our Lord 1896, and the second year of our reign.

"NICHOLAS."

—The *Times*, 20th January, 1896.

Now, blood is thicker than water. Notwithstanding all the autocratic oppression that the Russian people may have suffered for all past time, every soul will rise to the call, and rejoice in the joy of the occasion. And, whether the present system of government and power endures or vanishes, the Russian Rule—whatever form it takes—will always be Russian, and for the Russians.

Take England itself. It beheaded one king, banished another, turned out its Parliament at the point of the bayonet, had civil wars of various durations, and disasters. Whatever was the change, it was English Rule for Englishmen. But the British in India is quite a different thing. They are aliens, and any disaster to them there has entirely a different result. In the very first paper that was read before the East India Association of London (2/5/1867) I said :—

"No prophet is required to foretell the ultimate result of a struggle between a discontented two hundred millions and a hundred thousand foreign bayonets. A drop of water is insignificant, but an avalanche may sometimes carry everything before it. The race is not always to the swift A disaffected nation may fail a hundred times, and may rise again; but one or two reverses to a foreigner cannot but be fatal. Every failure of the Natives, adding more burdens, will make them the more impatient to throw off the foreign yoke."

Can the British Sovereign call upon the Indians as she can call upon the British people, or as the Russian Tsar can call upon the Russians, to share in her joy ? Yes, on one condition. The people of India must feel that though the English Sovereign and people are not kindred in birth and blood, they are kindred in sympathetic spirit, and just in dealing; that, though they are the step-mother, they treat the step-children with all the affection of a mother—that the British Rule is their own rule. The affection of the Indian people is the only solid foundation upon which an alien rule can stand firm and durable, or it may some day vanish like a dream.

To Britain all the law and order is the very breath of its nostrils in India. With law and order alone can it live in India. Let there arise disorder and violence tomorrow, and what will become of the small number of Europeans, official and non-official, without even any direct battles or military struggle ?

If a thoroughly intelligent view of the position of Britain in India is taken the interests of Britain are equally vital, if not far more vital, in the maintenance of good and satisfactory government, and of law and order, than those of India; and, in a just view, all the charge or cost in both countries of such good government and law and order in India should be apportioned between the two countries, according to the importance of respective interests and to the proportion of the means or capacity of each partner in the benefit.

Certainly, no fair and just-minded Englishman would say that Britain should have all the gain, glory and every possible benefit of wealth, wisdom, and work of a mighty Empire, and the price or cost of it should be all burdened on the shoulders of India.

The correct judgment upon our second part of the reference will depend upon the fundamental principle upon which the British Administration ought to stand.

1. Is British Rule for the good of both India and Britain, and a rule of justice and righteousness? or,

2. Is the British Rule solely for the benefit of Britain at the destruction of India—or, in other words, the ordinary rule of foreign despotism, "the heaviest of all yokes, the yoke of the stranger" (Macaulay).?

The first is the avowed and deliberate desire and solemn promise and pledge of the British people. The second is the performance by the servants of the British nation—the Indian authorities—in the system of the administration adopted and relentlessly pursued by them.

The present British-Indian system of administration would not take long to degenerate and run into the Russian system and troubles, but for the check and drag of the British public wish, opinion, and voice.

Now, my whole argument in this representation will be based on the first principle— *viz.*, the good of both

India and England and justice and righteousness. I would, therefore, dispose of the second in a brief manner—that the second (England's benefit and India's destruction) is not the desire of the British people.

It has been the faith of my life, and it is my faith still, that the British people will do justice to India.

But, however, as unfortunately the system based on the second principle—the system which Lord Salisbury has described as of "bleeding" and "hypocrisy"—exists, it is desirable to remember the wise words of Lord Salisbury himself, uttered not long ago when he said (Lord Mayor's dinner on 9th November last): "'The nature of things' if you please, or 'the providence of God' if you please to put it so, has determined that persistent and constant misgovernment must lead the government which follows it to its doom . . . . that injustice will bring the highest on earth to ruin." The Duke of Devonshire has pointed out that the result of the present system would be to make the Indians to come to the conclusion that the Indians shall never have any chance "except by their getting rid in the first instance of their European rulers."

The question is, do the British people desire such a system, to exercise only the right of brute force for their sole benefit? I for one, and I can say without any hesitation that all the educated and thinking Indians do not believe so. It is their deep faith and conviction that the conscience of the British people towards India is sound, and that if they once fully understood the true position they would sweep away the whole present unrighteous system. The very fact that this Commission is appointed for the first time for such a purpose, *viz.*, to deal out fairly between the two countries an "apportionment of charge for purposes in which both are interested" is sufficient to show the awakening consciousness and desire to do justice and to share fairly the costs as well as the benefits. If further public indication was at all needed the *Times*, as I have quoted in my first representation, has put it very clearly: "Great Britain is anxious to deal fairly with India. If it should appear that India has been saddled with charges which the British taxpayer should have borne the British taxpayer will not hesitate to do his duty." I would not, therefore, pursue any further the assumption of the second principle of selfishness and despotism, but continue to base my remarks upon the basis of the first principle of the desire and determination of the British people for justice and righteousness towards India.

I have stated above that the whole cost of administration is vital to the very existence of the British Rule in India, and largely essential to the prosperity of the British people. Lord Roberts, with other thoughtful statesmen, has correctly stated the true relation of the two countries more than once. Addressing the London Chamber of Commerce he said: "I rejoice to learn that you recognise how indissolubly the prosperity of the United Kingdom is bound up with the retention of that vast Eastern Empire." (*Times* 25/5/93.) And again, at Glasgow, he said "that the retention of our Eastern Empire is essential to the greatness and prosperity of the United Kingdom." (*Times*, 29/7/93.) And further he also clearly points out upon what such an essential retention ultimately depends. Does it depend upon tyranny, injustice, bleeding, hypocrisy, "plundering," upon imposing the relations of master and slave upon large, well equipped and efficient armies; on the unreliable props of brute force? No! He says, "But however efficient and well equipped the army of India may be, were it indeed absolute perfection, and were its numbers considerably more than they are at present, our greatest strength must ever rest on the firm base of a united and contended India." Sir William Harcourt said in his speech (House of Commons, 3/9/95), "As long as you have the people of India your friends, satisfied with the justice and policy of your rule, your Empire will be safe."

Professor Wordsworth has said (*Bombay Gazette*, 3/3/83): "One of the greatest Englishmen of the last generation said that if ever we lost our Indian Empire we should lose it like every other we had lost, or were about to lose, by alienating the affections of the people."

Am I not then justified in asking that it is right and just, in order to acquire and preserve the affections of the people, that the cost of that administration which is essential to your "greatness" and your "prosperity," by which your prosperity is indissolubly bound up with that of India, and upon the secureness and law and order of which depends your very existence in India and as a great Empire, should be fairly shared by the United Kingdom?

Leaving this fair claim to the calm and fair consideration of this Commission and to the sense of justice of the British people, I take a less strict view of the duty of England. It is said that India should make all such payments as she would make for her government and her internal and external protection even if there were no British Rule and only its own Native Rule.

Now, suppose this is admitted, what is the position? Certainly in that case there will be no employment of Europeans. The present forced, inordinate, and arbitrary employment of Europeans in both the civil and military services in both countries is avowedly, entirely and solely owing to British Rule and *for British purposes and British interests*—to maintain British supremacy. If there were no British Rule there would be no Europeans employed by the Natives rulers. India accordingly may pay for every Indian employed, but justice demands that the expenditure on Europeans in both countries required for the sole interests of British Rule and for British purposes should be paid by the British exchequer. I am not going to discuss here whether even British Rule itself needs all the present civil and military European agency. On the contrary, the civil element is their greatest weakness, and will be swept away in the time of trouble from discontent and disaffection; and the military element, without being either efficient or sufficient in such crises, is simply destructive to India, and leading to the very disaster which is intended to be averted or prevented by it. Be this as it may, this much is clear: that the whole European agency, both civil and military, in England and in India, is distinctly avowed and admitted to be for the interests of England, *i.e.*, to protect and maintain her supremacy in India against internal or external dangers. Lord Kimberly has put this matter beyond all doubt or controversy, that the European services are emphatically for the purpose of maintaining British supremacy. He says (dinner to Lord Roberts by the Lord Mayor—*Times*, 13th June, 1893):—

"There is one point upon which I imagine, whatever may be our party politics in this country, we are all united; that we are resolutely determined to maintain our supremacy over our Indian Empire. That I conceive is a matter about which we have only one opinion, and let me tell you that that supremacy rests upon three distinct bases. One of those bases, and a very important one, is the loyalty and good-will of the native Princes and population over whom we rule. Next, and not less important, is the maintenance of our European Civil Service, upon which rests the foundation of our administration in India. . . . . Last, not because it is the least, but because I wish to give it the greatest prominence, we rest also upon the magnificent European force which we maintain in that country, and the splendid army of Native auxiliaries by which that force, is supported. . . . . Let us firmly and calmly maintain our position in that country; let us be thoroughly armed as to our frontier defences, and then I believe we may trust to the old vigour of the people of this country, come what may, to support our supremacy in that great Empire.,

Now, this is significant: while Lord Kimberley talks all these grand things, of resolute determination, etc., etc., to maintain British supremacy, and for all British purposes, he does not tell at whose cost. Is it at British cost, as it is for British purposes, or even any portion of that cost? He has not told the British public openly that it is for every farthing at the cost of the Indians, who are thus treated as mere slaves—all the gain, glory and Empire "ours," and all the burden for the Indian helots! Then, as I have already said, the second and third bases—the European civil and military services—are illusory are only a burden and destruction to India, without being at all a sufficient security in the time of any internal and external trouble, and that especially the civil service is suicidal to the supremacy, and will be the greatest weakness. Then it may also be noticed in passing that Lord Kimberley gives no indication of the navy having anything important to do with, or make any demand on, India.

However, be all this as it may, one thing is made clear by Lord Kimberley, that, as far as Britain is concerned, the only motive which actuates her in the matter of the second and third bases—the European civil and military services—is her own supremacy, and nothing else; that there can be no difference of opinion in Britain why European services in both countries are forced upon India, *viz.*, solely and entirely for British purposes and British interests, for "the resolute determination to maintain *our* supremacy."

I would be, therefore, asking nothing unreasonable, under the Reference to this Commission, that what is entirely for British purposes must in justice be paid for by the British people, and the Indian people should not be asked to pay anything. I, however, still more modify this position. Notwithstanding that the European services, in their present extent and constitution, are India's greatest evil and cause of all its economic miseries and destruction, and the very badge of the slavery of a foreign domination and tyranny, that India may consider itself under a reasonable arrangement to be indirectly benefited by a certain extent of European agency, and that for such reasonable arrangement India may pay some fair share of the cost of such agency employed in India. As to all the State charges incurred in this country for such agency, it must be remembered that, in addition to their being entirely for British purposes, they are all, every farthing, earned by Europeans, and spent every farthing, in this country. It is a charge forced upon India by sheer tyranny, without any voice or consent of India. No such charge is made upon the Colonies. The Colonies office building and establishment is all a charge upon the British Exchequer. All charges, therefore, incurred in this country for the India Office and its establishment, and similar ones for State purposes, should under any circumstances be paid from the British Exchequer.

I shall put, briefly, this moderately just "apportionment of charge" in this way :—

India and England should pay all salaries which are to be paid to their own people, within their own limits, respectively—*i.e.*, England should pay for all Englishmen employed in England, and India should pay for all Indians employed in India; and as to those of one country who are employed in the other country—*i.e.*, Englishmen employed in India, and Indians employed in England—let there be some fair and reasonable apportionment between the two countries—taking, as much as possible, into consideration their respective benefits and capacity of means.

As to pensions, a reasonable salary being paid during service in India, no pensions need follow; so that, when Europeans retire from India, there should be no charge on England for pensions, the employees having made their own arrangements for their future from their salaries.

By this arrangement India will not only pay all that it would pay for a government by itself, supposing the English were not there, but also a share in the cost in India for what England regards as absolutely necessary for her own purpose of maintaining her Empire in India.

I may say a few words with regard to the navy. On no ground whatever of justice can India be fairly charged any share for the navy, except so far as it falls within the principle stated above, of actual service in Indian harbours.

1. The whole navy as it exists, and as it is intended

to be enlarged, is every inch of it required for the protection and safety of this country itself—even if Britain had no Empire—for its own safety—for its very existence.

2. Every farthing spent on the navy is entirely earned by Englishmen; not the slightest share goes to India, in its gain, or glory, or employment, or in any way.

3. In the time of war between England and any European Powers, or the United States, the navy will not be able to protect British commerce itself.

4. There is no such thing, or very insignificant, as Indian foreign commerce or Indians' risk in what is called British Indian foreign commerce. The whole of what is called British Indian foreign trade is entirely first British risk and British capital. Every inch of the shipping or cargo on the seas is British risk of British East India banks, British marine insurance companies, and British merchants and ship-owners and manufacturers. Any person who has any knowledge of how the whole of what is called British Indian foreign trade is carried on will easily understand what I mean.

5. No European Power will go to attack India from the sea, leaving the British navy free to pursue it.

6. Suppose there was no English navy to pursue, Lord Roberts' united and contented, and therefore patriotic India will give such an irresistible Indian force at the command of Britain as to give a warm reception to the invader, and drive him back into the sea if he ever succeeded in landing at all.

With regard to the absolute necessity to the United Kingdom itself for its *own safety* of the whole navy as it exists and is intended to be increased, there is but one universal opinion, without any distinction of parties. It will be easy to quote expressions from every prominent politician. It is, in fact, the great subject of the day for which there is perfect unanimity. I would content myself, however, with a few words of the highest authority in the realm under the Sovereign, the Prime Minister, and also of the Chancellor of the Exchequer. Lord Salisbury said in his Brighton speech :—

"But dealing with such money as you possess . . . . then the first claim is the naval defence of England. I am glad that you welcome that sentiment. . . . . It is our business to be quite sure of the safety of this island home of ours whose inaccessibility is the source of our greatness, that no improvement of foreign fleets, and no combination of foreign alliances, should be able for a moment to threaten our safety at home . . . . . We must make ourselves safe at sea whatever happens. . . . . . But after all, safety—safety from a foreign foe—comes first before every other earthly blessing, and we must take care in our responsibility to the many interests that depend upon us, in our responsibility to the generations that are to succeed us, we must take care that no neglect of ours shall suffer that safety to be compromised."

Sir M. Hicks-Beach, the Chancellor of the Exchequer, so late as 28th January last (the *Times*, 29/1/96), said emphatically and in a fighting mood : "We must be prepared. We must never lose the supremacy of the sea. Other nations had not got it, and could afford to do without it : but supremacy of the sea was vital to our very existence."

With such necessity for England's own safety, whether she had India or not, any burden to be placed on India can only be done on the principle of the right of might over our helplessness, and by treating India as a helotdom, and not in justice and fairness. Yes : let India have complete share in the *whole* Imperial system, including the Government of this country, and then talk of asking her to contribute to Imperial expenses.

Then will be the time to consider any such question as it is being considered in relations with Ireland, which enjoys, short of Home Rule, which is vital to it, free and full share in the whole Imperial gain and glory—in the navy, army, and civil services of the Empire. Let all arrangements exist in India as they exist here for entrance into all the Imperial Services here and elsewhere, and it will be time and justice to talk of India's share in Imperial responsibilities. Certainly not on the unrighteous and tyrannical principle of all gain and glory, employment, etc., for England, and share of cost on India, without any share in such gain, glory, employment, etc.

As to the bugbear of Russian invasion. If India is in a contented state with England, India will not only give an account of Russia, but will supply an army, in the most patriotic spirit, large enough to send Russia back to St. Petersburg. India will then fight for herself in fighting for Britain. In satisfied India Britain has an inexhaustible and irresistible store of fighting power, enough and more to fight Britain's battles all over the world, as it has been doing. Lord Beaconsfield saw this and showed it by bringing Indian troops to Malta. Only *pay honestly* for what you take, and not dishonourably or tyrannically throw burdens upon India for your own purposes and interests. *With* India Britain is great and invincible; without India Britain will be a small Power. Make India feel satisfaction, patriotism, and prosperity under your supremacy and you may sleep securely against the world. But with discontented India, whatever her own fate may be—may be subjected by Russia or may repel Russia—England can or will have no safe position in India. Of course, as I have said before, I am arguing on the assumption that justice is to be dealt out by this Commission to both countries on the basis of the might of right. If that is not to be the case, and right of might is to be the deciding principle, if the eternal moral force is not to be the powers, but the ephemeral brute force is to be the predominant partner, then of course I have no argument. All argument, then, will be idle breath at present till nature in time, as it always does, vindicates and revenges itself, and unrighteousness meets with its doom.

Our Commission has a great, holy, and patriotic task before it. I hope it will perform it, and tell the British people the redress that is justly due to India. The very first and immediate justice that should be done by England is the abolition of the Exchange Compensation—which is neither legal nor pay it herself; inasmuch as every farthing paid will be received by English people and in England. It is a heartless, arbitrary, and cruel exaction from the poverty of India, worse than Shylocky—not only the pound of flesh of the bond, but also the ounce of blood. As to the general question of apportionment, I have stated the principle above.

Now, another important question in connexion with "apportionment of charge" has to be considered, *viz.*, of any expenses incurred outside the limits of India of 1858.

I shall take as an illustration the case of North-West frontier wars. Every war, large or small, that is carried on beyond the frontiers of 1858 is distinctly and clearly mainly for Britain's Imperial and European purposes. It is solely to keep her own power in India.

If it were not for the maintenance of her own power in India and her position in Europe she would not care a straw whether the Russians or any other power invaded India or took it. The whole expenditure is for Imperial and European purposes. On 11th February, 1880, Mr. Fawcett moved the following Amendment to the Address in reply to the Queen's Speech (*Hansard*. vol. 25, p. 453):—

"But humbly desire to express our regret that in view of the declarations that have been made by your Majesty's ministers that the war in Afghanistan was undertaken for Imperial purposes, no assurance has been given that the cost incurred in consequence of the renewal of hostilities in that country will not be wholly defrayed out of the revenues of India."

Mr. Fawcett then said (*Hansard*, volume: 250. p. 454):—

"And, fourthly, the most important question, as far as he was able to judge, was who was to pay the expenses of the war. ...... It seemed to be quite clear that the expenses of the war should not be borne by India, and he wished to explain that so far as India was concerned this was not to be regarded as a matter of generosity but of justice and legality......The matter must be decided on grounds of strict justice and legality........ (P. 457.) It was a remarkable thing that every speech made in that House or out of it by ministers or their supporters on the subject showed that the war was a great Imperial enterprise, those who opposed the war having always been taunted as being "parochial" politicians who could not appreciate the magnitude and importance of great Imperial enterprises........ (P. 458.) He would refer to the speeches of the Viceroy of India the Prime Minister, and the Secretary of State for Foreign Affairs upon the subject.........In December, 1878, the noble earl* warned the peers that they must extend their range of vision, and told them that they were not to suppose that this was a war which simply concerned some small cantonments at Dacca and Jellalabad, but one undertaken to maintain the influence and character not of India, but of England in Europe. Now, were they going to make India pay the entire bill for maintaining the influence and character of England in Europe?

* The Prime Minister.

............His lordship treated the war as indissolubly connected with the Eastern question............Therefore it seemed to him (Mr. Fawcett) that it was absolutely impossible for the Government, unless they were prepared to cast to the winds their declarations, to come down to the House and regard the war as an Indian one ....All he desired was a declaration of principle and he would be perfectly satisfied if some one representing the Government would get up and say that they had always considered this war as an Imperial one, for the expenses of which England and India were jointly liable."

Afterwards Mr. Fawcett said (p. 477) :—

"He was entirely satisfied with the assurance which had been given on the part of the Government that the House should have an opportunity of discussing the question before the Budget was introduced, and would therefore beg leave to withdraw his amendment."

In the House of Lords, Lord Beaconsfield emphasised the objects to be for British Imperial purposes (25/2/80—*Hansard*, vol. 250, p. 1,094) :—

"That the real question at issue was whether England should possess the gates of her own great Empire in India . . . we resolved that the time has come when this country should acquire the complete command and possession of the gates of the Indian Empire. Let me at least believe that the Peers of England are still determined to uphold not only the Empire but the honour of this country."

So it is clear that the object of all the frontier wars, large or small, was that "*England* should possess the gates of *her own* great Empire," that "*this country* should acquire the complete command and possession of the gates of the Indian Empire," and uphold not only the Empire, but also "the honour of this country." Can anything be more clear than the Imperial character of the frontier wars?

Mr. Fawcett, again, on 12/3/80, moved (*Hansard*, vol. 251, p. 922) :—

"That in view of the declarations which have been officially made that the Afghan war was undertaken in the joint interests

* The Marquess of Salisbury.

of England and India, this House is of opinion that it is unjust to defray out of the revenues of India the whole of the expenditure incurred in the renewal of hostilities with Afghanistan."

Speaking on this motion, Mr. Fawcett, after referring to the past declarations of the Prime Minister, the Secretary of State for Foreign Affairs, and the Chancellor of the Exchequer, quoted from the speech of the Viceroy soon after his arrival (p. 923) :—

"I came to India, and just before leaving England for India I had frequent interviews with Lord Salisbury, the then Indian Secretary, and I came out specially instructed to treat the Indian frontier question as an indivisible part of a great Imperial question mainly depending for its solution upon the general policy of Her Majesty's Government. . . ."

And further on Mr. Fawcett said (p. 926) :—

"What was our policy towards self-governed Colonies and towards India not self-governed ? In the self-governed Colony of the Cape we had a war for which we were not responsible. Who was to pay for it ? It would cost the English people something like £5,000,000. In India, there was a war for which the Indian people were not responsible—a war which grew out of our own policy and actions in Europe—and we are going to make the Indian people, who were not self-governed and were not represented, pay every sixpence of the cost."

And so Lord Salisbury, as Secretary of State for India, and the Viceroy had cleared up the whole position—"to treat the Indian frontier question as an indivisible part of a great Imperial question, mainly depending for its solution upon the general policy of Her Majesty's Government," and the Indian people having no voice or choice in it.

Mr. Gladstone, following Mr. Fawcett, said (p. 930) :—

"It appears to me that, to make such a statement as that the judgment of the Viceroy is a sufficient expression of that of the people of India, is an expression of paradox really surprising, and such as is rarely heard among us......(P. 932.) In my opinion my hon'ble friend the member for Hackney has made good his case............Still, I think it fair and right to say that, in my opinion, my hon'ble friend the member for Hackney has completely made good his case. His case, as I understand it, has not received one shred of answer............(P. 933.) In the speech of the Prime Minister, the speech of Lord Salisbury, and the speech of the Viceroy of India, and, I think my hon'ble friend said, in a speech by the Chancellor of the Exchequer, this Afghan war has been distinctively recognised as partaking of the character of an Imperial war...........But I think not merely a small sum like that, but what my right hon'ble friend the Chancellor of the Exchequer would call a solid and substantial sum, ought to be borne by this country, at the very least...........(P. 935.) As regards the substance of the motion, I cordially embrace the doctrine of my hon'ble friend the member for Hackney. There is not a constituency in the country before which I would not be prepared to stand, if it were the poorest and most distressed in the land, if it were composed of a body of men to all of whom every addition of a farthing for taxes was a sensible burden, and before them I would be glad to stand and plead that, when we have made in India a war which our own Government have described as in part an Imperial war, we ought not for a moment to shrink from the responsibility of assuming at least a portion of the cost of that war, in correspondence with that declaration, instead of making use of the law and argument of force, which is the only law and the only argument which we possess or apply to place the whole of this burden on the shoulders of the people of India.

The upshot of the whole was that England contributed £5,000,000 out of £21,000,000 spent on this war, when one would have naturally expected a "far more solid and substantial" sum from rich England, whose interest was double, both Imperial and European. But the extent of that contribution is not the present question with me. It is the principle that "the Indian frontier question is one indivisible part of a great Imperial question, mainly depending for its solution upon the general policy of Her Majesty's Government," and that, therefore, a fair apportionment must be made of all the charge or cost of all frontier wars, according to the extent of the interest and of the means of each country.

Coming down to later times, the action of Mr. Gladstone on 27th April, 1885, to come to the House of Commons to ask for £11,000,000—and the House accepting his proposal—on the occasion of the Penjdeh incident, is again a most significant proof of the Imperial character of these frontier wars. He said (*Hansard*, vol. 297, p. 859):—

> "I have heard with great satisfaction the assurance of hon'ble gentlemen opposite that they are disposed to forward in every way the grant of funds to us to be used as we best think for the maintenance of what I have upon former occasions described as a National and Imperial policy. Certainly, an adequate sense of our obligations to our Indian Empire has never yet been claimed by any party in this country as its exclusive inheritance. In my opinion he will be guilty of a moral offence and gross political folly who should endeavour to claim on behalf of his own party any superiority in that respect over those to whom he is habitually opposed. It is an Imperial policy in which we are engaged."

Lastly, last year (15/8/95) the present leader of the House of Commons (Mr. Balfour) in his speech referred to "a serious blow to *our* prestige;" "that there are two and *only two* great powers they (the tribesmen) have to consider," "*to us*, and *to us*, alone, must they look as a suzerain power." "To depend upon the British throne." (The italics are mine.) So it is all "ours" and "us" for all gain and glory and Imperial possession, and European position—except that India must be forced to pay the bill. Is this the sense and conscience of *English Justice* to make India pay the whole cost of the Chitral war or any frontier war?

Though the real and principal guiding motive for the British Government for these frontier wars is only Imperial and European for "its resolute determination" of keeping its possession of India and position in Europe, still India does not want to ignore its indirect and incidental benefit of being saved from falling into Russia's hands, coupled with the hope that when British conscience is fully informed and aroused to a true sense of the great evils of the present system of administration, these evils will be removed. India, therefore, accepts that these frontier wars, as far as they may be absolutely necessary, involves Indian interests also, and would be willing to pay a fair share according to her means.

India, therefore, demands and looks to the present Commission hopefully to apportion a fair division for the cost of all frontier wars in which India and England have and had purposes of common interest. This whole argument will apply to all wars, on *all* the frontiers of India—East, West, North, or South. With reference to all wars outside *all* the frontiers of India and in which India has no interest, Britain should honestly pay India fully for all the services of men or materials which she has taken and may take from India—not, as in the Abyssinian War, shirk any portion. Sir Henry Fowler, in his speech in the House of Commons (22/1/93), said:—"I say on behalf of the English people, they want to deal with Ireland, not shabbily but generously." I believe that the English people wish to deal with India also justly and generously. But do their servants, the Indian authorities, act in that way? Has not India greater claims than even Ireland on the justice and the generosity of the English people? Inasmuch as the Irish people have the voice of their own direct representatives in Parliament on their own and Imperial affairs, while India is helpless and entirely at the mercy of England, with no direct vote of her own, not only in Parliament, but even in the Legislative Councils in India, on any expenditure out of her own revenues. Ireland not only has such voice, but has a free and complete share in all the gain and glory of the British Empire. An Irishman can occupy any place in the United Kingdom or India. Can an Indian occupy any such position, even in his own country, let alone in the United Kingdom? Not only that, but these authorities not only do not act justly or generously, but they treat India even "shabbily."

Let us take an illustration or two. What is it if not shabby to throw the expenses of Prince Nassarulla's visit upon the Indian people! There is the Mutiny of 1857. The causes were the mistakes and mismanagement of your own authorities; the people had not only no share in it, but actually were ready at your call to rise and support you. Punjab sent forth its best blood, and your supremacy was triumphantly maintained, and what was the reward of the people? You inflicted upon the people the whole payment to the last farthing of the cost of that deplorable event, of your own servants, making. Not only then was India unjustly treated, but even "shabbily." Let Lord Northbrook speak: House of Lords (15/5/93—*Debates*, vol. xii. p. 874):—

"The whole of the ordinary expenses in the Abyssinian expendition were paid by India. * Only the extrordinary expenses being paid by the Home Government, the argument used being that India would have to pay her troops in the ordinary way, and she ought not to seek to make a profit out of the affair. But how did the Home Government treat the Indian Government when troops were sent out during the Mutiny? Did they say, 'we don't want to make any profit out of this'? Not a bit of it. Every single man sent out was paid for by India during the whole time, though only temporary use was made of them, including the cost of their drilling and training as recruits until they were sent out."

Can anything be more "shabby," not to use a stronger word? Here you send troops for your own very existence. The people help you as best they can, and

* With it India had nothing to do, and yet Britain did not pay all expenses.

you not only not pay even any portion of the expenditure but reward the people for their loyalty with the infliction of not only the whole expense and additional burdens but even as shabbily as Lord Northbrook discloses. Is this the way by dealing unjustly and shabbily with the people that you teach them and expect them to stand by you in the time of trouble! And still more, since then, you have in a marked way been treating the people with distrust, and inflicting upon them unnecessarily and selfishly a larger and more expensive army to be paid for as wholly and as shabbily as the army of the Mutiny—*viz.*, including the cost of a portion of the cost of their drilling and training as recruits until they are sent out, though all the troops are in this country and they form an integral part of the British Army. And the whole expenditure of the frontier war including Chitral is imposed upon the Indian people, though avowedly incurred for Imperial and European purposes, excepting that for very shame, a fourth of the cost of the last Afghan War was paid from the British Exchequer, thanks to Mr. Fawcett. In fact, the whole European army is an integral part of the British Army, India being considered and treated as a fine training ground for the British Army, at any expense, for English gain, glory, and prestige, and as a hunting ground for "our boys," and as a point of protection for British Imperial and European position, leaving Indians the helotry or the proud privilege of paying for everything to the last farthing, without having the slightest voice in the matter! The worst of the whole thing is that having other and helpless people's money to spend, without any check from the British taxpayer, there is no check to any unnecessary and extravagant expenditure.

Now, even all these unjust inflictions for the Mutiny, and all past tyranny were considered somewhat, if not fully, compensated by that great, noble, and sacred with invocation of Almighty God, Proclamation of 1858, by which it was proclaimed to India and to the world that the Indian subjects were raised to an equality with the British subjects in their citizenship and British rights. And is that solemn pledge kept? Not a bit of it. On the contrary, all such pledges are pronounced by Lord Salisbury as "hypocrisy," by Lord Lytton as "cheating" by "deliberate and transparent subterfuges," "and by breaking to the heart the word of promise they had uttered to the ear," by a Committee of the Council of the India Office itself as "keeping promise to the ear and breaking it to the hope," and by the Duke of Argyll as "we have not fulfilled our promises."

Can it be expected that by such methods of financial injustice and violation of pledges can be acquired the affection of the people upon which mainly and ultimately depends, as many a statesman has said the stability of the British supremacy?

At Glasgow, on November 14, 1895, Mr. Balfour said: "You all remember that the British Army—and in the British Army I include those Native soldiers, fellow subjects of ours, who on that day did great work for the Empire of which they are all citizens."—This is the romance. Had Mr. Balfour spoken the reality, he would have said: "Include those Native soldiers, the drudges of ours, who on that day did great work for the Empire of which they are kept-down subjects." For, does not Mr. Balfour know that, far from being treated as "fellow subjects" and "citizens of the Empire," the Indians have not only to shed their blood for the Empire, but even *to pay every farthing* of the cost of these wars for "our Empire" and "our European position," that no pledges, however solemn and binding, to treat Indians as "fellow subjects" or British citizens have been faithfully kept either in letter or spirit, that however much these Indians may be brave and shed their blood for Imperial purposes or be made to pay "cruel and crushing tribute" they are not allowed any vote in the Imperial Parliament or a vote in the Indian Legislative Councils on their own financial expenditure, that their employment in the officering of the army, beyond a few inferior positions of Subadar Major or Jamadar Major, etc., is not at all allowed, that they are distrusted and disarmed—are not allowed to become volunteers—that, every possible obstacle is thrown and "subterfuge" resorted to against the advancement of the Indians in the higher positions of all the Civil Services, and that the simple justice of allowing Indians an equality to be simultaneously examined in their own country, for *Indian* services, decided by Act and Resolution of Parliament and solemnly pledged by the great Proclamation, is resisted by every device and subterfuge possible unworthy of the English character. Is it not a mockery and an insult to call the Indians "fellow subjects and citizens of the Empire" when in reality they are treated as under-heel subjects ?

Here are Rs. 128,574,590, or nearly Rs. 129,000,000 spent from April, 1882, to March, 1891 (Parl. Return, 91 of 1895), beyond "the West and North-West frontiers of India," after the disastrous expenditure of £21,000,000 in the last Afghan War (of which only a quarter was paid by the British Exchequer). Every pie of this nearly Rs, 129,000,000 is exacted out of the poverty-stricken Indians, and all for distinctly avowed Imperial and European British purposes. I do not know whether the Rs. 129,000,000 includes the ordinary pay of all the soldiers and officers employed in the Frontier Service, or whether it is only the extraordinary military expenditure that is included. If the ordinary pay is not included, then the amount will be larger than Rs. 129,000,000. And these are "our fellow subjects" and "our Imperial citizens"! To shed blood for Imperial purposes and to pay the whole cost also!

Lord George Hamilton said at Chiswick (*Times*, 22/1/96): "He hoped that the result of the present Government's tenure of office would be to make the British Empire not merely a figure of speech, but a living reality." Now, is not this as much romance as that of Mr. Balfour's, instead of being a "living reality"? All the questions I have asked for Mr. Balfour's expressions apply as forcibly to the words of the present Secretary of State for India, who ought to know the real despotically subjected position of the people of British India, forming two-thirds of the Empire. Yes, the British Empire can be made a "living reality" of union and devoted attachment, but not under the present system of British Indian administration. It can be, when in that system, justice, generosity, fair apportionment of charges, and honour, and "courage of keeping the word" shall prevail over injustice, helotdom, and dishonour of open violation of the most solemn words of honour.

Now, Mr. Chamberlain, at Birmingham (*Times*, 27/1/96), said in reference to the African Republic :—

"Now, I have never denied that there is just cause for discontent in the Transvaal Republic. The majority of the population there pay nine-tenths of the taxation, and have no share whatever in the government of the country. That is an anomaly which does not exist in any other civilized community, and it is an anomaly which wise and prudent statesmanship would remove. I believe it can be removed without danger to the independence of the Republic, and I believe until it is removed you have no permanent guarantee against future internal disturbances."

Do not these words apply with ten times force to the case of India, and is not that wise and prudent statesmanship which is preached here required to be practised in connexion with the greatest part of the British Empire? I venture to use Mr. Chamberlain's words :—

"I believe (the anomaly) can be removed without danger to the stability of the British power, or, rather, with devoted and patriotic attachment of the British connexion; and I believe that until it is removed you have no permanent guarantee against future internal disturbances."

The *Times* (1/2/96) in a leader on Lord Salisbury's speech before the Non-Conformist Unionist Association, in a sentence about the Outlanders, expresses what is peculiarly applicable to the present position of India. It says :—

"The Outlanders in the Transvaal—not a minority, but a large majority—are deprived of all share of political power and of the most elementary privileges of citizenship, because the dominate class, differing from them in race and feeling, as Lord Salisbury says, 'have the government and have the rifles."

The Indians must provide every farthing for the supremacy of the minority of "the dominant class," and should not have the slightest voice in the spending of that every farthing, and find every solemn pledge given for equality of British citizenship flagrantly broken to the heart in letter and in spirit. And why? Is it because, as Lord Salisbury says, "they have the Government and have the rifles;" or as Mr. Gladstone said about India itself, " the law and argument of force, which is the only law and argument which we possess or apply." This Commission has the duty, at least so far as a fair apportionment of charge is concerned, to redress this great wrong.

Do the British Indian authorities really think that the Indians are only like African savages, or mere children, that, even after thousands of years of civilisation, when the Britons were only barbarians; after the education they have received at the blessed British hands, producing, as Lord Dufferin said, " Native gentlemen of great attainments and intelligence" (Jubilee speech); they do not see and understand these deplorable circumstances of their true position of degradation and economic destruction? Or do these authorities not care, even if the Indians did understand, as long as they can mislead the British people into the belief that all is right and beneficient in British India, when it is really not the case?

But the faith of the Indians in the conscience of the British people is unbounded and unshakeable, and the little incidents of bright spots keep up that faith, such as the justice of not burdening the Indian people with the cost of the Opium Commission, and—even though inadequate and partial—the payment of one-fourth of the cost of the last Afghan War. It is these acts of justice that consolidate the British Rule and tend towards its stability.

I believe now, as I have always believed, that the English people wish and want to deal with India justly and generously. When I say that, I believe in the British character of fair play and justice, it is not a sentiment of to-day or yesterday. In the very first political speech of my life, made as far back as 1853, at the formation of the Bombay Association, on the occasion of the Parliamentary Enquiry on Indian Affairs for the renewal of the Company's Charter I said :—

> "When we see that our Government is often ready to assist us in everything calculated to benefit us, we had better, than merely complain and grumble, point out in a becoming manner what our real wants are...... If an Association like this be always in readiness to ascertain by strict enquiries the probably good or bad effects of any proposed measure, and whenever necessary to memorialise Government on behalf of the people with respect to them, our kind Government will not refuse to listen to such memorials."

And under that belief the Bombay Association, the British Indian Association of Bengal, and the Madras Association, memorialised the then Select Committee on Indian affairs—for redress of grievances.

Now, after not very short of nearly half a century of hopes and disappointments, these are still my sentiments to-day—that with correct and full knowledge the British people and Parliament will do what is right and just.

I may here take the opportunity of making a remark or two about the wide extent of the scope of the enquiry of this Commission in the first part of the Reference.

Lord Cranborne, soon after having been Secretary of State for India, said (24/5/67) in reference to the powers of the Council of the Secretary of State for India :—

> "It possesses by Act of Parliament an absolute and conclusive veto upon the Acts of the Government of India with reference to nine-tenths, I might almost say ninety-nine hundredths, of the questions that arise with respect to that Government. Parliament has provided that the Council may veto any despatch which directs the appropriation of public money. Everyone knows that almost every question connected with Government raises in some way or other the question of expenditure."

The first part of the Reference to this Commission thus embraces "almost every question connected with Government" "ninety-nine hundredths of the questions that arise with respect to that Government."

This view is fully confirmed by the enquiry by the Select Committee of 1871-4. The reference to it was "to enquire into the Finance and Financial Administration of India," and our first reference is fully of the same scope and character. Now, what was the extent of the subjects of the enquiry made by that Committee? The index of the proceedings of the four years (1871-4) has a table of contents headed: "Alphabetical and Classified List of the principal headings in the following Index, with the pages at which they will be found." And what is the number of these headings? It is about 420. In fact, there is hardly a subject of Government which is not enquired into.

Yours truly,

DADABHAI NAOROJI.

IV.

THE RIGHT RELATIONS BETWEEN BRITAIN AND INDIA.*

DEAR LORD WELBY,—I have to request you kindly to put before the Commission this further representation from me on the subjects of our enquiry. This will be my last letter, unless some phase of the enquiry needed any further explanation from me.

Looking at the first part of the enquiry from every point of view, with regard to the administration and management of expenditure, we come back again and again to the view expressed by the Duke of Devonshire and Sir William Hunter and others. The Duke of Devonshire has said: "If the country is to be better governed, that can only be done by the employment of the best and most intelligent of the Natives in the service." Sir William Hunter has said: "But the good work thus commenced has assumed such dimensions, under the Queen's Government of India that it can no longer be carried on or even supervised by imported labour from England except at a cost which India cannot sustain. . . . If we are to govern the Indian people efficiently and cheaply, we must govern them by means of themselves, and pay for the administration at the market rates of Native labour."

From all I have said in my previous representations it must have been seen that the real evil and misery of

* Submitted to the Welby Commission, 21st March, 1896.

the people of British India does not arise from the *amount* of expenditure. India is capable, under natural circumstances, of providing twice, three times or more the expenditure, as the improvement of the country may need, in attaining all necessary progress. The evil really is in the way in which that expenditure is administered and managed, with the effect of a large portion of that expenditure not returning to the people from whom it is raised—in short, as Lord Salisbury has correctly described as the process of "bleeding." No country in the world (England not excepted) can stand such bleeding. To stop this bleeding is the problem of the day—bleeding both moral and material. You may devise the most perfect plan or scheme of government, not only humanly but divinely perfect—you may have the foreign officials, the very angels themselves—but it will be no earthly good to the people as long as the bleeding management of expenditure continues the same. On the contrary, the evil will increase by the very perfection of such plan or scheme for improvements and progress. For, as improvements and progress are understood to mean, at present, it is more and more bleeding by introducing more and more the foreign bleeding agency.

The real problem before the Commission is not how to nibble at the expenditure and suggest some poor reductions here and there, to be put aside in a short time, as is always done, but how to stop the material and moral bleeding, and leaving British India a freedom of development and progress in prosperity which her extraordinary natural resources are capable of, and to treat her justly in her financial relations with Britain by apportioning fairly the charge on purposes in which both are interested. Or, to put the problem in its double important bearings, in the words of an eminent statesman, "which should at once afford a guarantee for the good government of the people, and for the security of British rights and interests" (Lord Iddesleigh), as will be seen further on. I am glad to put before the Commission that this problem has been not merely enunciated, but that, with the courage of their convictions, two eminent statesmen have actually carried it out practically, and have done that with remarkable success. I am the more glad to bring forward this case before the Commission, as it also enables me to adduce an episode in the British Indian administration on the conduct of the Indian authorities in both countries and other Anglo-Indian officials, which reflects great credit upon all concerned in it—and as my information goes, and as it also appears from the records, that her Majesty personally has not a little share in this praise, and in evoking a hearty Indian gratitude and loyalty to herself. This episode also clearly indicates or points to the way as to what the true natural relations should be between Britain and India, with a result of the welfare and prosperity of both, and the security and stability of British supremacy.

In my previous letters I have confined myself to the evil results—suicidal to Britain and destructive to India—of the present unnatural system of the administration and management of expenditure and the injustice of the financial relations between the two countries, loudly calling for a just apportionment of charge for purposes in which both are interested.

Without dwelling any further on this melancholy aspect, I shall at once proceed to the case to which I have alluded above, and in connexion with which there have been true statesmanlike and noble declarations made as to the right relations between Britain and India as they ought to exist. This case is in every way a bright chapter in the history of British India. The especially remarkable feature of this case is that notwithstanding the vehement and determined opposition to it from all Indian authorities for some thirty-six years, after this wise, natural, and righteous course was decided upon by Her Majesty and the Secretary of State for India of the time, all the authorities, both here and in India, carried it out in the most loyal, earnest, and scrupulous manner and solicitude worthy of the British name and character—in striking contrast with the general conduct of these authorities, by which they have almost always frustrated and made dead letters of Acts and Resolutions of Parliament and royal proclamations and most solemn pledges on behalf of the British people by all sorts of un-English "subterfuges," "cheating devices" (Lytton), "hypocrisy" (Salisbury), "non-fulfilment of pledges" (Duke of Argyll, Lytton, and others), etc., in matters of the advancement and elevation of the Indian people to material and moral prosperity, and to real British rights and citizenship. Had they fortunately shown the same loyalty and true sense of their trust to these Acts and Resolutions of Parliament, to the solemn proclamations and pledges, as have been shown in the case I am referring to, what a different, prosperous, and grateful India would it have been to-day, blessing the name of Britain, and both to its glory and gain. It is not too late yet. It will be a pity if it ever becomes too late to prevent disaster.

On 22nd January, 1867, Lord Salisbury (then Lord

Cranborne and Secretary of State for India) said (*Hansard*, vol. 185, p. 839):—

"But there are other considerations, and I think the hon'ble gentleman (Sir Henry Rawlinson) stated them very fairly and eloquently. I do not myself see our way at present to employing very largely the Natives of India in the regions under our immediate control. *But it would be a great evil if the result of our dominion was that the Natives of India who were capable of Government should be absolutely and hopelessly excluded from such a career.* The great advantage of the existence of Native States is that they afford an outlet for statesmanlike capacity such as has been alluded to. I need not dwell upon the consideration to which the hon'ble gentleman so eloquently referred, but I think *that the existence of a well-governed Native State is a real benefit, not only to the stability of our rule.* but because, more than anything, it raises the self-respect of the Natives and forms an ideal to which the popular feelings aspire. . . . . Whatever treaties or engagements may be entered into, I hope that I shall not be looked upon by gentlemen of the Liberal Party as very revolutionary if I say *that the welfare of the people of India must override them all.* I quite admit the temptations which a paramount power has to interpret that axiom rather for its own advantage than its own honour. There is no doubt of the existence of that temptation, but that does not diminish the truth of the maxim." [The italics are mine.]

On 24th May, 1867, Lord Iddesleigh (then Sir Stafford Northcote and Secretary of State for India) said (*Hansard* vol. 187, p. 1068):—

"He believed that the change in education in India, and the fact that the Natives now saw what their system of government was and is, had told most beneficially on that country. He had, therefore, confidence that we might establish a state of things in Mysore which would have a happy effect on the administration of the country. What had taken place in other parts of India? Travancore forty years ago was in as bad a state as Mysore, yet its administration under British influence had so greatly improved that Travancore was now something like a model Native State. *Our Indian policy should be founded on a broad basis. There might be difficulties; but what we had to aim at was to establish a system of Native States which might maintain themselves in a satisfactory relation.* Keeping the virtues of Native States, and getting rid, as far as possible, of their disadvantages. We must look to the great *natural* advantages which the government of a Native State must *necessarily* have. Under the English system there were advantages which would probably never be under Native Administration—regularity, love of law and order and justice."

Had Lord Iddesleigh lived he would have with pleasure seen that the advantages he refers to are being attained in the Native States; and in Mysore itself, as well as in several other States, they have been largely already attained. And under the eye of the British Government there is progress everywhere. Lord Iddesleigh proceeds:—

"But native Administration had the advantage in *sympathy between the governors and the governed.* Governors were able to appreciate and understand the prejudices and wishes of the governed; especially in the case of Hindu States, the religious feelings of the people were enlisted in favour of their governors instead of being roused against us.* He had been told by gentlemen from India that nothing impressed them more than walking the streets of some Indian town, they looked up at the houses on each side and asked themselves, 'what do we really know of these people—of their modes of thought, their feelings, their prejudices —and at what great disadvantage, in consequence, do we administer the government.' The English Government must necessarily labour under great disadvantages, † and *we should endeavour as far as possible to develop the system of Native government to bring out Native talent and Statesmanship, and to enlist in the cause of government all that was great and good in them.* Nothing could be more wonderful than our Empire in India; but we ought to consider on what conditions we hold it and how our predecessors held it. The greatness of the Mogul Empire depended on the liberal policy that was pursued by men like the great Emperor Akbar and his successors availing themselves of Hindu talent and assistance, and identifying themselves as far as possible with the people of the country. They ought to take a lesson from such circumstances. *If they were to do their duty towards India they could only discharge that*

* The same can be said about the Muhammedans and other people.

† The greatest of them is the economic evil which Lord Salisbury has truly called the bleeding of the country.

duty by obtaining assistance and counsel of all who are great and good in that country. It would be absurd in them to say that there was not a large fund of statesmanship and ability in the Indian character. They really must not be too proud. They were always ready to speak of the English government as so infinitely superior to anything in the way of Indian Government. But if the Natives of India were disposed to be equally critical, it would be possible for them to find out weak places in the harness of the English administration. The system in India was one of great complexity. It was a system of check and counter checks, and very often great abuses failed to be controlled from want of a proper knowledge of and sympathy with the Natives." [The italics are mine.]

On the same day Lord Salisbury, supporting Lord Iddesleigh, said, (*Hansard*, vol. 187. p. 1073) :—

The general concurrence of opinion of those who know India best is that a number of well-governed small Native States are in the highest degree advantageous to the development of the political and moral condition of the people of India. The hon'ble gentleman (Mr. Laing) arguing in the strong official line seems to take the view that everything is right in British territory and everything dark in Native territory. Though he can cite the case of Oudh, I venture to doubt if it could be established as a general view of India as it exists at present. If Oudh is to be quoted against Native Government, the Report of the Orissa Famine, which will be presented in a few days, will be found to be another and far more terrible instance to be quoted against English Rule. *The British Government has never been guilty of the violence and illegality of Native Sovereigns. But it has faults of its own, which though they are far more guiltless in intention, are more terrible in effect.* Its tendency to routine; its listless heavy heedlessness, sometimes the result of its elaborate organisation; a fear of responsibility, an extreme centralisation—all these results, traceable to causes for which no man is culpable, *produce an amount of inefficiency which when reinforced by natural causes and circumstances, creates a terrible amount of misery.* All these things must be taken into consideration when you compare our elaborate and artificial system of government with the more rough and ready system of India. In cases of emergency, unless you have men of peculiar character on the spot, the simple form of Oriental government will produce effects more satisfactory than the more elaborate system of English Rule. I am not by this denying that our mission in India is to reduce to order, to civilise and develop the Native Governments we find there.* But I demur to that wholesale condemnation of a system of government which will be utterly intolerable on our own soil, but which has grown up amongst the people subjected to it. It has a fitness and congeniality for them impossible for us adequately to realise, but which compensate them to an enormous degree for the material evils which its rudeness in a great many cases produces. I may mention as an instance what was told me by Sir George Clerk, a distinguished member of the Council of India, respecting the Province of Kathiawar, in which the English and Native Governments are very much intermixed. There are no broad lines of frontier there, and a man can easily leap over the hedge from the Native into the English jurisdiction. Sir George Clerk told me that the Natives having little to carry with them were continually in the habit of migrating from the English into the Native jurisdiction, but that he never heard of an instance of a Native leaving his own to go into the English jurisdiction. This may be very bad taste on the part of the Natives; but you have to consider what promotes their happiness, suits their tastes, and tends to their moral development in their own way. If you intend to develop their moral nature only after an Anglo-Saxon type, you will make a conspicuous and disastrous defeat." [The italics are mine.]

In the above extract, Lord Salisbury says that the inefficiency reinforced by natural causes and circumstances creates a terrible amount of misery. These natural causes and circumstances which create the terrible amount of misery are pointed out by Lord Salisbury himself, as Secretary of State for India, in a Minute (29/4/75). He says "the injury is exaggerated in the case of India, where so much of the revenue is exported without a direct equivalent." And that under these causes and circumstances, the result is that "India must be 'bled," so that he truly shows that though under the British Rule there is no personal violence, the

* This is being actually done. Every effort is being made to bring the administration of the Native States to the level of the organisation of the British system which is not a little to the credit of the British Government.

present system of the administration of expenditure cannot but create and does "*create a terrible amount of misery.*"

Further, the crude and defective system of administration under the old system of Native rule is all changed and cannot apply to the present administration in British India. Any alteration that may be deemed necessary to be made for remedying this "terrible amount of misery," would not involve in British India any alteration at all in the existing developed plan or system of the organisation of the administration.

Now, the moral of the above extracts from the speeches of Lords Salisbury and Iddesleigh is clear. Under the present system of administration of government and expenditure and unjust financial relations, in the very nature of things, there is a perpetual and inevitable result of terrible misery, of slavery (Macaulay), absolute hopelessness of higher life or career, despair, self-abasement, without any self-respect (Salisbury), extreme destitution and suffering (Bright), extreme poverty (Lawrence, Cromer, Barbour, Colvin), degradation (Monroe), etc., etc. And as a consequence of such deplorable results, an inherent and inevitable "danger of the most serious order" (Lord R. Churchill) to the stability of British supremacy. British Rule under such circumstances can only continue to be a foreign crushing tyranny, leading the people to yearn (the Duke of Devonshire) to get rid of their European rulers, etc., etc.

On the other hand, (Salisbury) "the existence of a well-governed Native State is a real benefit, not only to the stability of the British Rule, but more than anything it raises the self-respect of the Natives and forms an ideal to which the popular feeling aspires." And "that a number of well-governed small Native States are in the highest degree advantageous to the development of the political and moral" (I may add, the material) "condition of the people of India." Lord Iddesleigh says on the same lines: "What we had to aim at was to establish a system of Native States which might maintain themselves in a satisfactory relation." And what is of far more importance, he actually inaugurated the great experiment, by which he proposed to solve the great problem, "which should at once afford a guarantee for the good government of the people and for the security of British rights and interests," and to which I desire to draw the attention of the Commission. In short, the lesson of the extracts is that the British Indian administration as it exists at present is positively and seriously dangerous to the British supremacy, and of terrible misery to the people; while a system of Native States will raise the people, and at the same time firmly secure the stability of the British supremacy and largely conduce to the prosperity of both countries—Britain and India.

Now comes the great merit—which will always be remembered by Indians with deep gratitude—of these two Statesmen (Salisbury and Iddesleigh). They did not rest satisfied with mere declaration of fine and great sentiments and then sleep over them, as has been done on many an occasion to the misfortune of poor India. No, they then showed that they had the courage of their convictions and had confidence in the true statesmanship of their views. In this good work Her Majesty took a warm interest and encouraged them to carry it out. The result was the memorable—and ever to be remembered with gratitude—despatch of 16th April, 1867, of Lord Iddesleigh, for the restoration of Mysore to the Native rule, notwithstanding thirty-six years of determined opposition of the authorities to that step (Parl Ret. 239, 30/4/67).

And now I come to the episode to which I have referred above, and about which I write with great gratification and gratitude, of the conduct of all the authorities in both countries and of all the Anglo-Indian officials who had any share in this good work, backed as I have said already, by the good-hearted and influential interest and support of Her Majesty herself. They may have made some errors of judgment, but there was universally perfect sincerity and loyalty to the trust. Among those concerned (and whose names it is a pleasure to me to give) were, as Secretaries of State for India, Lord Iddesleigh, the Duke of Argyll, Lord Salisbury, Viscount Cranbrook, and the Duke of Devonshire (from 1867 till 1881, when the late Maharaja was invested with power); as Viceroys, Lord Lawrence, Lord Mayo, Lord Northbrook, Lord Lytton, and Lord Ripon; and lastly, the Chief Commissioners and other officials of Mysore. The chief merit in the conduct of all concerned was this. Lord Iddesleigh laid down in his despatch of 16th of April, 1867:—

"Without entering upon any minute examination of the terms of the Treaties of 1799, Her Majesty's Government recognise, in the policy which dictated that settlement, a desire to provide for the maintenance of an Indian dynasty on the throne of Mysore, *upon terms which should at once afford a guarantee for the good government of the people and for the security of British rights and interest.* Her Majesty is animated by the same desire, and shares the views to which I have referred. . . . . Her Majesty desires to maintain that family on the throne in the person of His Highness's adopted son. . . . . It is therefore the intention of Her Majesty that the young Prince should have the advantage of an education suitable to his rank and position and calculated to prepare him for the duties of administration." [The italics are mine.]

This being once settled, though against all previous opposition, and necessitating the withdrawal of Europeans from the Services, all the authorities and officials concerned, to their honour and praise, instead of putting any obstacles in the way, or trying to frustrate the above intentions, discharged their trust most loyally, and with every earnestness and care and solicitude to carry the work to success. The Blue-books on Mysore from the despatch of 16th April, 1867, to the installation of the late Maharaja in 1881, afford a bright chapter in the history of British India, both in the justice, righteousness, and statesmanship of the decision, and the loyalty and extreme care of every detail in carrying out that decision—with success and satisfactory results in both objects set forth in the despatch, *viz.*, "*the good government of the people, and the security of British rights and interests.*"

I wish the India Office would make a return on Mysore relations and affairs up to date, in continuation of Ret. No. 1 of 1881 (c. 3026), to show how the good and creditable work has been continued up to the present time. I think I need not enter here into any details of this good work from 1867 to 1881 of the British officials; the Blue-books tell all that. Of the work of the late Maharaja from 1881 till his death at the end of 1894, it would be enough for me to give a very brief statement from the last Address of the Dewan to the Representative Assembly held at Mysore on 1st October, 1895, on the results of the late Maharaja's administration during nearly fourteen years of his reign, as nearly as possible in the Dewan's words. The Maharaja was invested with power on 25th March, 1881. Just previous to it, the State had encountered a most disastrous famine by which a fifth of the population had been swept away and the State had run into a debt of 80 lakhs of rupees to the British Government. The cash balance had become reduced to a figure insufficient for the ordinary requirements of the administration. Every source of revenue was at its lowest, and the severe retrenchments which followed had left every department of State in an enfeebled condition. Such was the beginning. It began with liabilities exceeding the assets by 30¾ lakhs, and with an annual income less than the annual expenditure by 1¼ lakhs. Comparing 1880-1 with 1894-5, the annual revenue rose from 103 to 180½ lakhs, or 75·24 per cent., and after spending on a large and liberal scale on all works and purposes of public utility, the net assets amounted to over 176 lakhs in 1894-5, in lieu of the net liability of 30¾ lakhs with which His Highness's reign began in 1881.

	Rs.
In 1881, the balance of State Funds was ...	24,07,438
Capital outlay on State Railways ...	25,19,198
Against a liability to the British Government of ...	80,00,000

Leaving a balance of liability of Rs. 30¾ lakhs.

On 30th June, 1895:

Assets—

(1)	Balance of State Funds ...		... 1,27,23,615
(2)	Investment on account of Railway Loan Repayment Fund ...		... 27,81,500
(3)	Capital outlay on Mysore-Harihar Railway		... 1,48,03,306
(4)	Capital outlay on other Railways		... 41,33,390
(5)	Unexpended portion of Capital borrowed for Mysore-Harihar Railway (with British Government) ...		... 15,79,495
			3,60,21,306

Liabilities—

(1)	Local Railway Loan ...	Rs. 20,00,000	
(2)	English Railway Loan ...	„ 1,63,82,801	
			1,83,82,801
	Net Assets		... Rs. 1,76,38,505

ADD OTHER ASSETS—

Capitial outlay on orginal Irrigation Works ... Rs. 99,08,935.

Besides the above expenditure from current revenue, there is the subsidy to the British Government of about Rs. 25,00,000 a year, or a total of about Rs. 3,70,00,000 in the fifteen years from 1880-1 to 1894-5, and the Maharaja's civil list of about Rs. 180,00,000, during the fifteen years also paid from the current revenue. And all this together with increase in expenditure in every department. Under the circumstances above described, the administration at the start of His Highness's reign was necessarily very highly centralised. The Dewan, or the Executive Administrative head, had the direct control, without the intervention of departmental heads of all the principal departments such as the Land Revenue, Forests, Excise, Mining, Police, Education, Mujroyi, Legislative. As the finances improved, and as department after department was put into good working order and showed signs of expansion, separate heads of departments were appointed for Forests and Police in 1885, for Excise in 1889, for Mujroyi in 1891, and for Mining in 1894. His Highness was able to resolve upon the appointment of a separate Land Revenue Commissioner only in the latter part of 1894. Improvements were made in other departments—Local and Municipal Funds, Legislation, Education, etc. There are no wails which unfortunately the Finance Ministers of British India are obliged to raise, year after year, of fall in Exchange, over-burdening taxation, etc., etc.

And all the above good results are side by side with an increase of population of 18·34 per cent. in the ten years from 1881 to 1891, and there is reason to believe that during the last four years the ratio of increase was even higher. During the fourteen years the rate of mortality is estimated to have declined 6·7 per mille.

But there is still the most important and satisfactory feature to come, *viz.*, that all this financial prosperity was secured not by resort to new taxation in any form or shape. In the very nature of things the present system of administration and management of Indian expenditure in British India cannot ever produce such results, even though a Gladstone undertook the work. Such is the result of good administration in a Native State at the very beginning. What splendid prospect is in store for the future, if, as heretofore, it is allowed to develop itself to the level of the British system with its own Native Services, and not bled as poor British India is.

Lord Iddesleigh is dead (though his name will never be forgotten in India, and how he would have rejoiced !), but well may Her Majesty, Lord Salisbury, and all others concerned in it, and the British people, be proud of this brilliant result of a righteous and statesmanlike act, and may feel secure of the sincere and solid loyalty, gratitude, and attachment of the rulers and people of Mysore to the British supremacy.

Here, then, is the whole problem of the right and natural administration of expenditure, etc., and stability of British supremacy solved, and that most successfully, by Lords Salisbury and Iddesleigh. It is now clear, by actual facts and operation, that the present system of expenditure, in all aspects of the administration of British India, is full of evil to the people and danger to British supremacy, while, on the other hand, "a number of well-governed Native States," under the active control and supremacy of Britain, will be full of benefit and blessing both to Britain and India and a firm foundation for British supremacy. And all this prophecy of Lords Salisbury and Iddesleigh has been triumphantly fulfilled. Lord Iddesleigh set to himself the problem "which should at once afford a guarantee for the good government of the people and for the security of British rights and interests," and most successfully solved it.

The obvious conclusion is that the only natural and satisfactory relations between an alien supremacy and the people of India can be established on this basis alone. There are these obvious advantages in these relations:—

The British supremacy becomes perfectly secure and founded upon the gratitude and affection of the people, who, though under such supremacy, would feel as being under their own rulers and as being guided and protected by a mighty supreme power.

Every State thus formed, from the very nature of its desire for self-preservation, will cling to the supreme power as its best security against disturbance by any other State.

The division in a number of States becomes a natural and potent power for good in favour of the stability of the British supremacy. There will be no temptation to any one State to discard that supremacy, while, on the other hand, the supreme Government, having complete control and power over the whole Government of each State, will leave no chance for any to go astray. Every instinct of self-interest and self-preservation, of gratitude, of high aspirations, and of all the best parts of human nature, will naturally be on the side and in favour of British supremacy which gave birth to these States. There will be an emulation among them to vie with each other in governing in the best way possible, under the eye and control of the supreme Government on their actions, leaving no chance for misgovernment. Each will desire to produce the best Administration Report every year. In short, this natural system has all the elements of consolidation of British power, of loyalty, and stability, and of prosperity of both countries. On the other hand, under the present system, all human nature and instincts are against you, and must inevitably end in disintegration, rebellion, and disaster. No grapes from thistles! Evil will have its nemesis. I hope and pray that this Commission will rise to the height of its mission, and accomplish it to the glory of this country and the prosperity of both.

I must not be misunderstood. When I use the words "Native States," I do not for a moment mean that these new States are to revert to the *old* system of government of Native rule. Not at all. The system of all departments that exists at present, the whole mode of government, must not only remain as it is, but must go on improving till it reaches as nearly as possible the level of the more complete mode of British government that exists in this country. The change to be made is, that these States are to be governed by Native agency, on the same lines as at present, by employing, as the Duke of Devonshire says, "the best and most intelligent of the Natives," or as Lord Iddesleigh says, "all that was great and good in them."

One question naturally presents itself. Are new dynastic Indian rajahs to be created for these new States? That is a question that men like Lord Salisbury himself and the Indian authorities are best able to answer. There may be difficulties in dynastic succession.

If so, the best mode of the headship under some suitable title of these States may be by appointment by Government, and aided by a representative Council. This mode has certain evident advantages, *viz.*, questions of dynastic succession may be avoided, Government will be free to secure the best man for the post, and Government will then have complete control over the States, especially with an English Resident, as in all Native States at present. If thought necessary, this control may be made still more close by having at the beginning for some time an English joint-Administrator instead of a Resident.

Sir Charles Dilke has, in one of his letters to me, said :—

> "I also agree as to reduction of Europeans (so far as the non-military people go). Indeed, I agree *without* limit, and would substitute for our direct rule a military protectorate of Native States, as I have often said."

In another letter to me, which is published in the September number of *India*, in 1893, Sir Charles dwells upon the same subject at some length, proposing to follow up the case of Mysore and to divide India into a number of Native States.

With regard to the financial relations between Britain and India, whether for military or civil charges, I have already expressed my views in my last representation. I would not, therefore, make any further remarks here.

Once this natural and righteous system of government by Native States is adopted, so as to make the administration of expenditure fully productive of good results to both countries, I may with every confidence hope that the authorities, as in the case of Mysore, will loyally and scrupulously do their best to carry out the plan to success by establishing in India every necessary machinery for preparation, examinations, and tests of character and fitness of the Indians "to (as Lord Iddesleigh says) develop the system of Native government, to bring out Native talent and statesmanship, and to enlist in the cause of government all that was great and good in them."

The prevention and cure of the evils of the present material and moral bleeding, arising from the existing system of the administration and management of expenditure, from unjust financial relations between the two countries, and for the redemption of the honour of this country from the dishonour of the violation of the most solemn and binding pledges, are absolutely necessary, if India is to be well governed, if British supremacy is to be made thoroughly stable, and if both countries are to be made prosperous by a market for trade of nearly 300,000,000 of civilised and prosperous people.

I do not here consider any other plan of Government to secure effectively the double object laid down by Lord Iddesleigh, because I think the plan proposed and carried out by him is the most natural and the best, and most secure for the continuance of British supremacy.

I also do not enter into any details, as all possible difficulties of details, and the means by which they were overcome, are all recorded in the Mysore Blue Books.

I submit to the Commission that unless the patriotism and prosperity of the people of India are drawn to the side of British supremacy, no plan or mode of government, under the existing system of expenditure, will be of any good either to British supremacy or to the Indian people. Evil and peril to both is the only dismal outlook. On the other hand, a number of Native

States, according to the noble views and successful work of Lords Salisbury and Iddesleigh, will contribute vastly both to the gain and glory of the British people, to vast expansion of trade, and to the prosperity and affection of the hundreds of millions of the human race.

If India is thus strengthened in prosperity, and patriotically satisfied in British supremacy, I cannot feel the least fear of Russia ever dreaming of invading India. Without any military help from England, and without any large European Army, India will be all sufficient in itself to repel any invasion, and to maintain British supremacy for her own and Britain's sake.

I hope earnestly that this Commission will, as Sir Louis Mallet has urged, grapple with the disease of the evil results of the present system of expenditure, instead of, like other past Commissions and Committees, keeping to the habit of merely palliating symptoms. I do not much intervene in examining details of departmental expenditure, such examination at proper intervals, as used to be the case in the time of the Company, serves the important purpose of keeping the Government up to mark in care of expenditure. But unless the whole Government is put on a natural basis, all examinations of details of departmental expenditures will be only so much "palliating with symptoms," and will bring no permanent good and strength either to the Indian people or to the British supremacy.

I offer to be cross-examined on all my representations.

As before, I shall send a copy of this to every member of the Commission.

Yours truly,

DADABHAI NAOROJI.

V.

THE CAUSES OF DISCONTENT.*

DEAR LORD WELBY,—I request you kindly to put before the Commission this representation on the subjects of our enquiry.

Nobody can more appreciate the benefits of the British connexion than I do—Education in particular, appreciation of, and desire for, British political institutions, law and order, freedom of speech and public meeting, and several important social reforms. All these are the glory of England and gratitude of India. I am most sincerely ready to accord my gratitude for any benefit which Britain can rightly claim.

But, while looking at one side, justice demands that we look at the other side also. And the main object of this Commission is to see the other side of the system of the administration and management of expenditure and right apportionment.

It must be remembered that while education and law and order have been beneficial to the Indians of British India they were also most essential to the very existence of the British in India. Only that while the benefits have been to both Britain and British India, the cost has been *all* exacted from the Indians.

The British Empire in India is built up entirely with the money of India, and, in great measure, by the blood of India. Besides this, hundreds of millions, or, more probably, several thousands of millions (besides

* Submitted to the Welby Commission, 31st January, 1897.

what is consumed in India itself by Europeans and their careers of life) of money, which the British have unceasingly, and ever increasingly, drawn from British Indians, and is still drawing, has materially helped to make Britain the greatest, the richest, and most glorious country in the world—benefiting her material condition so much that, even when there is a general and loud cry of depression in agriculture, etc., the Chancellor of the Exchequer is rejoicing that his income tax is marvellously increasing; while British India in its turn is reduced to "extreme poverty" and helotry.

Will the India Office be good enough to give us a Return of the enormous wealth which Britain has drawn out of India during the past century and a half, calculated with ordinary British commercial 5 per cent. compound interest, leave alone the 9 per cent. ordinary commercial rate of interest of British India? What a tale will that Return tell! The India Office must have all the records of the India House as well as its own.

I give a few figures that are available to me. The best test of this drain from British India is (1) that portion of produce exported out of British India for which nothing whatever has returned to her in any shape, either of merchandise or treasure; (2) the profits of her whole exports which she never got; (3) that portion of the exports which belongs to the Native States, and which the Native States get back, with their due profits, are included in the total imports, and are therefore not included in the "net exports." For No. (1) I have the following authoritative figures for only 45 years (1849-50 to 1894-5, "Statisical Abstract of British India," No. 30, 1895, p. 299). Will the India Office supply previous figures?

This table shows that British India sent out, or exported her produce to the extent of £526,740,000, for which she has not received back a single farthing's worth of any kind of material return. Besides this loss or drain of actual produces, there is (No. 2) the further drain of the profits on an export of £2,851,000,000, which, taken at only 10 per cent., will be another £285,000,000—which British India has not received—subject to the deduction of portion of (No. 3), *viz.*, the profits of the Native States. To this has to be added the profits which Indian foreigners (*i.e.*, the capitalists of Native States) make in British India, and carry away to their own States. Freight and marine insurance premiums have to be taken into account, for whether for exports from, or imports into, India, these items are always paid in England. It is necessary to know how these two items are dealt with in the Returns of the so-called trade of British India. In ordinary circumstances, one may not complain if a foreigner came and made his profits on a fair and equal footing with the people of British India. But British India is not allowed such fair and equal footing.

First, the unrighteous and despotic system of Government prevents British India from enjoying its own produce or resources, and renders it capitalless and helpless. Then, foreign capitalists come in and complete the disaster, sinking the people to the condition of the hewers of wood and drawers of water. The enormous resources of India are all at the disposal and command of these foreigners.

In understanding correctly the tables to which I refer, it must be borne in mind that all the loans made to India form a part of the imports, and are all already paid for and included in that portion of the exports which is equal to the total imports, the "net exports" in the table being, *after* allowing for *all* imports, including loans. Otherwise, if these loans were deducted from the imports, the "next exports" will be so much larger. The position of the exploitation by the foreign capitalists is still worse than I have already represented. Not only do they exploit and make profits with their own capital, but they draw even their capital from the taxation of the poor people themselves. The following words of Sir James Westland in the telegram of the *Times* of 18th December last will explain what I mean.

"Sir J. Westland then explained how closely connected the Money Market of India was with the Government balances, almost all the available capital employed in commerce practically being in those balances.........A crore and a half which under normal conditions would have been at headquarters in Calcutta and Bombay and been placed at the disposal of the mercantile community for trading purposes."

The Bank of Bengal and Chamber of Commerce "pressed the Government to take up the question of the paper currency reserve as urgently as possible, and pass a Bill without delay to afford relief to commerce." So, the European merchants, bankers, etc., may have Indian taxes at their disposal, the profits of which they may take away to their own country! The poor wretched taxpayers must not only find money for an unrighteous system of Government expenditure but must also supply capital to exploit their own resources.

The reference to this Commission is to enquire into expenditure and apportionment. I am fully convinced, and my representations fully prove it, that if the system of the administration and management of expenditure and the apportionment were based on principles of righteousness, honesty, honour, and unselfishness, the political peculiarities of India are such as would produce an abiding attachment and connexion between the two countries, which will not merely be of much benefit to British India but of vastly more benefit to the British themselves than at present. Hence, my extreme desire that the connexion should continue and I can say truly that, in a spirit of loyalty both to India and to the British Empire, I have devoted my life to strengthening this connexion. I feel it therefore my duty (though a painful one) to point out candidly the causes which, in my opinion, have weakened, and are weakening more and more, this connexion, and, unless checked, threaten to destroy it.

I. The un-English, autocratic and despotic system of administration, under which the Indian people are not given the slightest voice in the management of their own expenditure. It is not creditable to the British character that they should refuse to a loyal and law-abiding people that voice in their own affairs which they value so much for themselves,

II. The unrighteous "bleeding" of India, under which the masses have been reduced to such "extreme poverty" that the failure of one harvest causes millions upon millions to die from hunger, and scores of millions are living on "scanty subsistence." What Oriental despotism or Russian despotism in Russia can produce a more deplorable result?

III. The breach or evasion by subterfuges of solemn pledges and proclamations issued by Her Majesty and the British nation, and the floating of such Acts and Resolutions of Parliament as are favourable to Indians. Such proceedings destroy the confidence of the Indian people in the justice of British Rule. To sum up, these and other errors in administration have had the effect of inflicting upon India the triple evil of depriving the people of Wealth, Work, and Wisdom, and making the British Indians, as the ultimate result, "extremely poor," unemployed (their services which are their property in their own country, being plundered from them) and degradingly deteriorated and debased, crushing out of them their very humanhood.

Before I proceed further. let me clear up a strange confusion of ideas about prosperous British India and poverty-stricken British India. This confusion of ideas arises from this circumstance. My remarks are for British India only.

In reality there are two Indias—one the prosperous, the other poverty-stricken.

(1) The prosperous India is the India of the British and other foreigners. They exploit India as officials, non-officials, capitalists, in a variety of ways, and carry away enormous wealth to their own country. To them India is, of course, rich and prosperous. The more they can carry away, the richer and more prosperous India is to them. These British and other foreigners cannot understand and realise why India can be called "extremely poor," when they can make their life careers; they can draw so much wealth from it and enrich their own country. It seldom occurs to them, if at all, what all that means to the Indians themselves.

(2) The second India is the India of the Indians—the poverty-stricken India. This India, "bled" and exploited in every way of their wealth, of their services, of their land, labour, and all resources by the foreigners, helpless and voiceless, governed by the arbitrary law and arguments of force, and with injustice and unrighteous-

ness—this India of the Indians becomes the "poorest" country in the world, after one hundred and fifty years of British Rule, to the disgrace of the British name. The greater the drain the greater the impoverishment, resulting in all the scourges of war, famine and pestilence. Lord Salisbury's words face us at every turn, "Injustice will bring down the mightiest to ruin." If this distinction of the "prosperous India" of the slave-holders and the "poverty-stricken India" of the slaves be carefully borne in mind, a great deal of the controversy on this point will be saved. Britain can, by a righteous system, make both Indias prosperous. The great pity is that the Indian authorities do not or would not see it. They are blinded by selfishness—to find careers for "our boys."

To any appeals the ears of the British Indian authorities are deaf. The only thing that an Indian can do is to appeal to the British *people*. I must explain. I have no complaint against the British people. The Sovereign, the British people, and Parliament have all in one direction done their duty by laying down the true and righteous principles of dealing with India. But their desires and biddings are made futile by their servants, the Indian authorities in both countries. For these reasons my only resource, is to appeal to the British people and to this Commission to cause the order of her Majesty and of Parliament to be carried out.

It is not needful for me to repeat my views, which I have given in my five previous representations, which have been in the hands of the Commission from nine to fifteen months, and in which I have dealt with both the injustice and the evils and the remedy of the present system of expenditnre and apportionment, and it remains for the Commission to cross-examine me on all the six representations.

I would add here a few more remarks arising from some of the evidence and other circumstances.

Indians are repeatedly told, and in this Commission several times, that Indians are partners in the British Empire and must share the burdens of the Empire. Then I propose a simple test. For instance, supposing that the expenditure of the total Navy of the Empire is, say, £20,000,000, and as partners in the Empire you ask British India to pay £10,000,000, more or less; British India, as partner, would be ready to pay, and therefore, as partner, must have her share in the employment of British Indians and in every other benefit of the service to the extent of her contribution. Take the Army. Suppose the expenditure of the total Army of the Empire is, say, 40,000,000. Now, you may ask £20,000,000, or more or less, to be contributed by British India. Then, as partners, India must claim, and must have, every employment and benefit of that service to the extent of her contribution. If, on the other hand, you force the helpless and voiceless British India to pay, but not to receive, a return to the extent of the payment, then your treatment is the unrighteous wicked treatment of the slave-master over British India as a slave. In short, if British India is to be treated as a partner in the Empire, it must follow that to whatever extent (be it a farthing or a hundred millions) British India contributes to the expenses of any department, to that extent the British Indians must have a share in the services and benefits of that department—whether civil, military, naval or any other; then only will British India be the "integral part" of, or partner in, the Empire. If there be honour and righteousness on the side of the British, then this is the right solution of the rights and duties of British India and of both the references to this Commission. Then will the Empire become a true Empire with an honest partnership, and not a false Empire and an untrue partnership. This is the main, principal question the Commission has to clear up. This will fully show the true nature and solution of both the expenditure and apportionment. I appeal to the British people. When I have been personally observing, during forty years, how the British people are always on the side of the helpless and the oppressed; how, at present, they are exerting every nerve, and lavishing money, to save the thousands of Armenians, then I cannot believe that the same people will refuse to see into the system of expenditure adopted by their own servants, by which not merely some thousands or hundred thousands suffer, but by which millions of their own fellow-subjects perish in a drought, and scores of millions live underfed, on scanty subsistence, from one end of the year to the other. The so-called Famine Relief Fund is nothing more or less than mere substerfuge of taxing the starving to save the dying. This fund does not rain from heaven, nor does the British Exchequer give it. If the Government spend, say £5,000,000, on the present famine they will simply squeeze it out of the poverty-stricken surviving taxpayers, who would in turn become the victims of the next drought.

The British people stand charged with the blood of the perishing millions and the starvation of scores of millions, not because they desire so, but because the authorities to whom they have committed the trust betray that trust and administer expenditure in a manner based upon selfishness and political hypocrisy, and most disastrous to the people. There is an Indian saying: "Pray strike on the back, but don't strike on the belly."

Under the native despot the people keep and enjoy what they produce, though at times they suffer some violence on the back. Under the British Indian despot the man is at peace, there is no violence; his substance is drained away, unseen, peaceably and subtly—he starves in peace and perishes in peace, with law and order! I wonder how the English people would like such a fate I say, therefore, to the British people, by all means help the poor Armenians, but I appeal to you to look home also, and save the hundreds of millions of your own fellow-subjects, from whom you have taken thousands of millions of wealth, and obtained also your Indian Empire, entirely at their cost and mainly with their blood, with great careers for thousands of yourselves at our cost and destruction.

The great question is not merely how to meet a famine when it occurs—by taxing the poor people—but how to prevent the occurrence of the famine. As long as the present unrighteous system will prevail there will be no end of the scourges of India. We are thankful for the benefit of the knowledge of "Western civilisation." But what we need is the deeds of *Western righteousness and honour* to stop the famine and to advance the prosperity of both countries. With relation to the present famine I have to make one or two remarks.

For the famine of 1878, the British help amounted to the magnificent sum of about, I think, £700,000. On the other hand, the British public have to remember that they have been drawing, by the unrighteous system of the authorities, every year 30 to 40, or more times, £700,000 from poor India; or say from the time of the last famine they have drawn from India, and added to their own wealth, some £400,000,000 or more (leaving alone what they have been draining for a century and a half), and if they now give even £4,000,000 or £5,000,000 in the present distress, it will be but 1 or 2 per cent. of what they have obtained from India during the last eighteen years. It is a duty of the British people to give in abundance from the great, great abundance they have received. As far as the poor people of India are concerned, they will receive whatever you would give with deep gratitude in their dire extremity.

The second fact is, what the British people will readily and early give will have a double blessing. They will, in the first instance, save so many lives, and in the next place save the poor survivors from so much taxation, which otherwise the Government would exact every farthing of, for whatever Government would spend from the revenue. The novel, loud and vain boast of the Government of India having resources to meet the famine simply means this, that every farthing of the whole famine expenditure (bad or good) by the Government, will be, by their despotic power, squeezed out of the wretched people themselves by taxation in which they have not the slightest voice. Never was there a false trumpet blown than the boast of the Government to be able to cope with the famine "with its own resources." Of course, the resources of despotism are inexhaustible, for, who can prevent it from taxing as much as it likes? It is a wonder to me that they do not feel ashamed of talking of "their own resources," when it all means so much more squeezing of a squeezed and helpless people

And especially when they not only, Shylock-like, take the whole pound of their large salaries, but also the ounce of blood of their illegal and immoral exchange compensation!

Amongst the most favourite excuses of the Anglo-Indians is, that the extreme poverty of the people and the disasters of famines are owing to increase of population. I have dealt with this subject in my third representation, and I want to say a few words more. The point to which I want to draw attention here is, that Anglo-Indians, official or non-official of every kind, are not at all competent to pronounce any judgment upon the causes of poverty and disasters of famines. For, they themselves are the accused, as the cause of all the evils, and they cannot be judges to try themselves. Their own deep interest is concerned in it. Let them withdraw their hand from India's throat, and then see whether the increase in population is not an addition to its strength and production instead of British-made famines and poverty. Then it will also be seen that the hundreds of millions of British India, instead of being afflicted with all sorts of evils, will become your best customers and give you a *true* trade—more than your present trade with the whole world.

I now refer to a strange sign of the times. By an irony of fate, and as an indication of the future, and after 150 years of British connexion and rule, Russia—to whom the Anglo-Indians always point as a threat—offers generous sympathy and aid to starving and dying British subjects. I do not pretend to know Russia's mind, but any one can see what the effect of this, aided by the emissaries, might be on India. "See how kind and generous the Russians are, and give us help." It will be further pointed out, "See, not only are the Russians sympathetic with you, but their great Emperor himself has published in his book, words of condemnation of the rule which sucks away your life-blood." The *Times* of 10th December last, in its leader on the Russo-Chinese Treaty says:—"Russia, we may be sure, will pursue her own policy and promote her own interests." "Russia is bent upon developing her vast Asiatic Empire." But the blind Indian authorities would not see that England would not have any chance to hold her own in India without the true (not lip-loyal) attachment of the Indian people. Is it possible for any sane man to think that any one nation can hold another in slavery and yet expect loyal devotion and attachment from it? It is not nature, not human nature. It has never happened and will never happen. Righteousness alone can exalt and be enduring. Events are moving fast. The time is come when the question must be speedily answered, whether India is to be a real partner and strength to England, or a slave and a weakness to England—as it has hitherto been. How much of the future destiny of the British Empire and India depends upon this, a man of an unbiassed mind can think for himself. India forms five-sixths of the population of the British Empire.

I put one question, which I have often put, and which is always ignored or evaded. Suppose the British people was subjected to the same despotic treatment of expenditure by some foreign people, as India is by the British Indian authorities, would the British people stand it a single day without rebelling against it? No, certainly not; and yet, can the British people think it righteous and just to treat the Indians as the Indian authorities do—as mere helpless and voiceless slaves. Macaulay has truly said that:

"that would indeed be a doting wisdom which, in order that India might remain a dependency, would make it a useless and costly dependency, which would keep a hundred millions (now 225,000,000) from being our customers in order that they might continue to be our slaves."

The question of remedy I have already dealt with in my last representation, and I would not have said more here. But as the *Times* of 8th December last, in its article on "Indian Affairs," confirms, by actual facts and events, the wisdom and statesmanship of Lords, Salisbury and Iddesleigh in their one great work of righteous and wise policy, I desire to quote a few words. Fortunately, it is the very Mysore State to which this righteous and wise act was done. The *Times* says:—

"The account which Sir Sheshadri Iyer rendered to it of his last year's stewardship is one of increasing revenue, reduced taxation, expenditure firmly kept in hand, reproductive public works, and a large expansion of cultivation, of mining and of industrial undertakings. The result is a surplus which goes to swell the previous accumulation from the same source."

Can the present system of British administration and management of the expenditure ever produce such results? Never. A dozen Gladstones will not succeed.

Continuous and increasing "bleeding" can only reduce strength and kill. The *Times'* article concludes with the words:—

"A narrative such as Sir Sheshadri Iyer was able to give to the Representative Assembly of Mysore makes us realise the growth of capital in the Native States, and opens up new prospects of industrial undertakings and railway construction in India on a silver basis."

Can this be said of British India? No. I shall quote one other extract.

"One of the Bombay Chiefs, after some experience of railway making in his own and adjoining territories, struck out a new departure at the beginning of the present year. He conceived the idea of public loans to be issued for railway construction by one Feudatory Prince to another on the guarantee of the revenues of the borrowing State. The first transaction in which this principle is completely carried out was a loan of two million rupees by H. H. Sir Bhagvat Sinhji, the ruler of Gondal, to H.H. Jasvant Sinhji, the ruler of Jamnagar, on the 8th of January, 1896."

Now, anybody who knows Jamnagar, knows that with ordinary good management it will not be long before that State is in a position to pay off its debts, just as the good management of Mysore was able to do, and the good management of Gondal has enabled its ruler to lend such an amount. This loan by Gondal, it must be remembered, is in addition to building its own railway in its own territory from its own revenue, without any loan, or help, or additional taxation.

No one can rejoice more than myself that Native States which adopt ordinary good management go on increasing in prosperity in strong contrast with the system of the British management of expenditure. This is fully confirmatory of the words of Lords Salisbury and Iddesleigh as to what should be done for the British India's prosperity. I have quoted these words in my last representation. And some of them are worth quoting here once more. Lord Salisbury said :—

"The general concurrence of opinion of those who know India best is that a number of well-governed small Native States are in the highest degree advantageous to the development of the political and moral condition of the people of India . . . . . . But I think the existence of a well-governed Native State is a real benefit, not only to the stability of our rule, but because more than anything it raises the self-respect of the Natives, and forms an ideal to which the popular feelings aspire."

Referring to the several phases of the British Rule,

he sums up that they produce an amount of inefficiency which, when reinforced by natural causes and circumstances, creates a terrible amount or misery. It might also be noted that the richest provinces and most important seaports are now British. So the people of British India should be much more prosperous than those living in the inferior districts left to Native Chiefs. Yet in British India is the "terrible amount of misery," after a rule of 150 years by the most highly-trumpeted and most highly paid services. Lord Iddesleigh not only agreed with the best course indicated by Lord Salisbury, but actually put it fully into operation with the confidence that the course he took would "at once afford a guarantee for the good government of the people, and for the security of British right and interests." And after an experience of fifteen years, the writer in the *Times* is able to express such highly favourable opinion as I have quoted above.

Another favourite argument of some Anglo-Indians is the want of capacity of the Indians. In the evidence last year this was referred to once or twice. There is a paper of mine in the journals of the East India Association on that subject, but I do not want to trouble the Commission with it. It is the old trick of the tyrant not to give you the opportunity of fair trial, and to condemn you offhand as incapable. The Indians are put to the iniquitous handicap to come over to this country for the civil services in their own country, and from the Army and Navy they are entirely excluded from the commissioned ranks; and all this in complete violation of the most sacred pledges and Acs of Parliament. I will not, however, trouble the Commission with any further remarks on this all-important subject. It is enough for me to put before the Commission the article in the *Times* of 5th October last on Indian affairs as the latest honest expression of a well-known Anglo-Indian, as there have been many already from time to time from other Anglo-Indians. I put this article as an appendix.

In question 13,353, Lord Wolseley said "there never was an India until we made it"; and in question 12,796, Sir Ralph Knox says, "My own view is that England has made India what she is." I acknowledge the correctness of these statements, *viz.*, an India to be exploited by foreigners, and the most wretched, the poorest, the helpless, without the slightest voice in her own expenditure, perishing by millions in a drought, and starving by scores of millions; in short, "bleeding" at every pore and a helotry for England. It is not England of the English people who have made India what she is. It is the British Indian authorities who have made her what she is.

And now I shall give some account of the process by which this deplorable result was begun to be achieved. I give the character of the process in authoritative words—words of the Court of Directors, the Bengal Government, and Lord Clive—disinterred and exposed by the Committee of 1772.

First, I shall give a few words of the Court of Directors:—

"A scene of most cruel oppression" (8/2/1764). "That they have been guilty of violating treaties, of great oppression and a combination to enrich themselves" (Court of Directors' Letter, 26/4/1765). "The infidelity, rapaciousness, and misbehaviour of our servants in general." "Every Englishman throughout the country . . . . exercising his power to the oppression of the helpless Native." "We have the strongest sense of the deplorable state . . . . from the corruption and capacity of our servants, and the universal depravity of manners throughout the settlement," "by a scene of the most tyrannic and oppressive conduct that ever was known in any age or country" (17/5/1766).

Now, a few words of Lord Clive and Bengal letters :—

"Rapacity and luxury." "It is no wonder that the lust of riches should readily embrace the proffered means of its gratification, or that the instruments of your power should avail themselves of their authority, and proceed even to extortion in those cases where simple corruption could not keep pace with their rapacity." "Luxury, corruption, avarice, and rapacity" "to stem that torrent of luxury, corruption and licentiousness," "the depravity of the Settlement," "shameful oppression and flagrant corruption," "grievous exations and oppressions." The "most flagrant oppressions by members of the Board." "An administration so notoriously corrupt and meanly venal throughout every department," "which, if enquired into, will produce discoveries, which cannot bear the light . . . . but may bring disgrace upon this nation, and at the same time, blast the reputation of great and good families."

Such were the first relations between England and India, and the manner in which India was being made what she is.

Change came—corruption and oppression were replaced by high salaries. It is so easy and agreeable to give once's own countrymen high salaries at other people's expense—the drain remains going on heavier and heavier. What the drain in the last century was generally estimated at—something like three or five millions a year—has now become, perhaps, ten times as much. Would the India Office be good enough to give a correct statement?

Adding insult to injury, the Indians have often flaunted in their face the loans made to them, which are perhaps not one-twentieth of what is taken away from the wretched country, and which further drains the country in the shape of profits and interest. And the capitalists also are supposed to benefit us by using us as hewers of wood and drawers of water, and taking away from the country the profits of the resources of that country, and thus we lose our own wealth, services, and experience, helplessly; and yet we are told by some we are getting immensely prosperous. May the British people never meet our fate!

After I had finished the above I attended the meeting at the Mansion House. I do not in any way blame the speakers; but what a humiliating confession it was about the treatment of India by England. The only wonder is that those who made this confession did not seem to be conscious of its humiliation and unrighteousness. On the contrary, they took it with a complacency as if it was a merit of the Indian authorities. But Nature spoke the truth of the great wrong through them. Here is a people, who if they pride themselves —and justly pride—upon anything, it is their love of liberty, their determination to submit to no despotic master, who beheaded one king and banished another to preserve and maintain their government, with the voice of the people themselves, who sing that Britain shall never be a slave, whose fundamental boast is that they regard "taxation without representation is tyranny," and that they would resist any such tyranny to a man. These people, it is confessed from a platform in the very centre of the struggle for liberty, proclaimed with a *naivete* and functuousness that they deliberately in India deprived the hundreds of millions of people of this very right of humanhood for which they are so proud of themselves, that they reduced the people of India from humanhood to beasts of burden, depriving them of every voice whatsoever in their own affairs, and that they deliberately chose to govern them as the worst despots—the foreign despots about whom Macaulay has said that "the heaviest of all yokes is the yoke of the stranger." And it is this yoke of the worst despotism they imposed upon India, with all its most horrible evils of exploitation and all the scourges of this world. A Briton would not be a slave, but he would make hundreds of millions of others his slaves!—the greatest crime that any one nation can commit against another. And yet these Anglo-Indians are so callous to their own British instincts and character, that they proclaimed from the platform, with every complacency, that they had deliberately committed the unhumanising wrong, without feeling the least blush of shame, and to the disgrace and humiliation of their own nation, the British people, though the British people never desired such un-English unrighteousness towards the people of India; on the contrary, they always desired and proclaimed, by the most solemn pledges and Acts of Parliament, that the Indians shall be British citizens, with all the rights and duties of British citizenship, exactly like those which the British people themselves enjoy. Never was there a more condemnatory confession than in those speeches, that with the results of the terrible famine and plague they were bringing out more and more the bitter fruits of their unrighteous system in the administration of expenditure in the deaths of millions by famine and in the starvation of scores of millions.

The other day an Anglo-Indian military officer, talking about the immigration of the persecuted Jews in this country, held forth with the greatest indignation why these wretched Jews should come to this country and deprive our poor workingmen of their bread.

Little did he think at the time that he himself was an immigrant forced upon the Indian people by a despotic rule, and was depriving them, not of the bread of one person, but perhaps of hundreds, or thousands, of the poor workingmen of India.

I felt thankful from the bottom of my heart to the Lord Mayor for that meeting. It brought out two things—a satisfactory assurance to the Indian people that the British people are feeling for their distress, and are willing to help; and a lesson to the British people which they ought to take to heart, and for which they should do their duty, that their servants have deliberately adopted an un-English and unrighteous course, and deprived hundreds of millions of human beings of the very thing which the British people value most above all things in the world—their own voice in their own affairs; their highest glory above all other nationalities in the world. They call us fellow-citizens, and they must make their word a reality, instead of what it is at present, an untruth and a romance—simply a relationship of slaveholder and slave.

I shall sum up my representations by reading before the Commission a brief note of my propositions at the commencement of my examination, leaving the Commission to cross-examine me afterwards. I shall also lay before the Commission certain other papers bearing upon our enquiry.

Yours truly,

DADABHAI NAOROJI

VI.

ADMISSION OF NATIVES TO THE COVENANTED CIVIL SERVICE. *

DEAR LORD WELBY,—I now give my statement on the Admission of Natives to the Covenanted Civil Service in India, as promised by me at the meeting of the Commission on 21st July last, and request you to place it before the Commission. I shall send a copy to the members.

If required, I shall give any further statement I can on any particular point that may require to be more elucidated. I shall be willing to be cross-examined if required.

The first deliberate and practical action was taken by Parliament in the year 1833.

All aspects of the whole question of all services were then fully discussed by eminent men; and a Committee of the House made searching enquiry into the whole subject.

I give below extracts from what was said on that occasion, and a definite conclusion was adopted.

I am obliged to give some of the extracts at length, because it must be clearly seen on what statesmanlike and far-seeing grounds this conclusion was arrived at.

The italics all through are mine, except when I say that they are in the original.

* Submitted to the Welby Commission, November 3rd, 1897.

East India Company's Charter,

Hansard, Vol. XIX, Third Series, p. 169.

July 5th, 1833.

The MARQUESS OF LANSDOWNE :—

"But he should be taking a very narrow view of this question, and one utterly inadequate to the great importance of the subject, which involved in it the happiness or misery of 100,000,000 of human beings, were he not to call the attention of their lordships "to the bearing which this question and to the influence which this arrangement must exercise upon the future destinies of that vast mass of people." He was sure that their lordships would feel, as he indeed felt, that their only justification before God and Providence for the great and unprecedented dominion which they exercised in India was in the happiness which they communicated to the subjects under their rule, and in proving to the world at large and to the inhabitants of Hindustan that the inheritance of Akbar (the wisest and most beneficent of Mahomedan Princes) had not fallen into unworthy or degenerate hands. Hence it was important that when the dominion of India was transferred from the East India Company to the King's Government they should have the benefit of the experience of the most enlightened councillors, not only on the financial condition of our Empire in the East but also on the character of its inhabitants. He stated confidently, after referring to the evidence given by persons eminently calculated to estimate what the character of the people of India was, that they must, as a first step to their improved social condition, be admitted to a larger share in the administration of their local affairs. On that point their lordships had the testimony of a series of successful experiments and the evidence of the most unexceptionable witnesses who had gone at a mature period of their life and with much natural and acquired knowledge to visit the East. Among the crowd of witnesses which he could call to the improvable condition of the Hindu character he would select only two; but those two were well calculated to form a correct judgment, and fortunately contemplated Indian society from very different points of view. Those two witnesses were Sir Thomas Monro and Bishop Heber. He could not conceive any two persons more eminently calculated to form an accurate opinion upon human character, and particularly upon that of the Hindu tribes. They were both highly distinguished for talent and integrity, yet they were placed in situations from which they might have easily come to the formation of different opinions—one of them being conversant with the affairs of the East from his childhood and familiarised by long habit with the working of the system, and the other being a refined Christian philosopher and scholar going out to the East late in life, and applying in India the knowledge which he had acquired here to form an estimate of the character of its inhabitants. He held in his hand the testimony of each of those able men, as extracted from their different published works, and with the permission of the House he would read a few words from both. Sir T. Monro, in speaking of the Hindu character, said: 'Unless we suppose that they are inferior to us in natural talent, which there is no reason to believe, it is much more likely that they will be duly qualified for their employments than Europeans for theirs—because the field of selection is so much greater in the one than in the other. We have a whole nation from which to make our choice of Natives, but in order to make choice of Europeans we have only the small body of the Company's Covenanted servants. No conceit more wild and absurd than this was ever engendered in the darkest ages: for what is in every age and every country the great stimulus to the pursuit of knowledge but the prospect of fame or wealth or power? Or what is even the use of great attainments if they are not to be devoted to their noblest purpose, the service of the community, by employing those who possess them according to their respective qualifications in the various duties of the public administration of the country? Our books alone will do little or nothing; dry, simple literature will never improve the character of a nation. To produce this effect it must open the road to wealth and honour and public employment. Without the prospect of such reward no attainments in science will ever raise the character of a people.' That was the sound practical opinion of Sir T. Munro, founded on his experience acquired in every part of India, in every department of the public service. Bishop Heber during his extensive journey of charity and religion through India, to which he at length fell a martyr, used these remarkable expressions: 'Of the natural disposition of the Hindu I still see abundant reason to think highly, and Mr. Bayley and Mr. Melville both agreed with me that they are constitutionally kind-hearted, industrious, sober, and peaceable; at the same time that they show themselves on proper occasions a manly and courageous people.' And again: 'They are decidedly by nature a mild, pleasing, and intelligent race, sober, parsimonious, and, where an object is held out to them, most industrious and persevering.' Their lordships were therefore justified in coming to the same conclusion—a conclusion to which, indeed, they must come if they only considered the acts of this people in past ages—if they only looked at the monuments of gratitude and piety which they had erected to their benefactors and friends—for to India, if to any country, the observation of the poet applied:—

'Sunt hic etiam sua præmia laudi,
Sunt lacrymæ rerum, et mentem mortalia tangunt.'

But, however much civilisation had been obscured in those regions, whatever inroads foreign conquest and domestic superstition had made upon their moral habits, it was undeniable that they had still materials left for improving and ameliorating their condition; and their lordships would be remiss in the performance of the high duties which devolved upon them if they did not secure to the numerous Natives of Hindustan the ample development of all their mental endowments and moral qualifications. "It was a part of the new system which he had to propose to their lordships that to every office in India every Native, of whatsoever caste, sect, or religion, should by law be equally admissible, and he hoped that Government would seriously endeavour to give the fullest effect to this arrangement, which would be as beneficial to the people themselves as it would be advantageous to the economical reforms which were now in progress in different parts of India."

* * * * *

(*Page* 174, *July 5th*, 1833)—"And without being at all too sanguine as to the result of the following of those principles without calculating upon any extension of territory through them, he was confident "that the strength of the Government would be increased by the happiness of the people over whom it presided, and by the attachment of those nations to it."

Vol. XIX., Third Series, p. 191,
July 5th, 1833.

Lord Ellenborough :—

"He felt deeply interested in the prosperity of India and when he was a Minister of the Crown, filling an office peculiarly connected with that country, he had always considered it his paramount duty to do all in his power to promote that prosperity. He was as anxious as any of His Majesty's Ministers could be to raise the moral character of the Native population of India. He trusted that the time would eventually come, though he never expected to see it, when the Natives of India could, with advantage to the country and with honour to themselves, fill even the highest situations there. He looked forward to the arrival of such a period, though he considered it far distant from the present day; and he proposed, by the reduction of taxation, which was the only way to benefit the lower classes in India, to elevate them ultimately in the scale of society, so as to fit them for admission to offices of power and trust. To attempt to precipitate the arrival of such a state of society as that he had been describing was the surest way to defeat the object in view. He never, however, looked forward to a period when all offices in India would be placed in the hands of Natives. No man in his senses would propose to place the political and military power in India in the hands of the Natives.

"The Marquess of Lansdowne observed that what the Government proposed was that all offices in India should be by law open to the Natives of that country.

"Lord Ellenborough said such was precisely the proposition of Government, but our very existence in India depended upon the exclusion of the Natives from military and political power in that country. We were there in a situation not of our own seeking, in a situation from which we could not recede without producing bloodshed from one end of India to the other. We had won the Empire of India by the sword, and we must preserve it by the same means, doing at the same time everything that was consistent with our existence there for the good of the people."

Macaulay fully answers Lord Ellenborough.

Vol. XIX, Third Series, p. 533.

July 10th, 1833.

Mr. Macaulay :—

"I have detained the House so long, Sir, that I will defer what I had to say in some parts of this measure—important parts, indeed, but far less important as I think than those to which I have adverted, till we are in Committee. There is, however, one part of the Bill on which, after what has recently passed elsewhere, I feel myself irresistibly impelled to say a few words. I allude to that wise, that benevolent, that noble clause, which enacts that no Native of our Indian Empire shall, by reason of his colour, his descent, or his religion, be incapable of holding office. At the risk of being called by that nickname which is regarded as the most opprobrious of all nicknames by men of selfish hearts and contracted minds—at the risk of being called a philosopher—*I must say that, to the last day of my life, I shall be proud of having been one of those who assisted in the framing of the Bill which contains that clause.* We are told that the time can never come when the Natives of India can be admitted to high civil and military office. We are told that this is the condition on which we hold our power. We are told that we are bound to confer on our subjects—every benefit which they are capable of enjoying?—no—which it is in our power to confer on them?—no—but which we can confer on them without hazard to our own domination. "Against that proposition I solemnly protest as inconsistent alike with sound policy and sound morality."

"I am far, very far from wishing to proceed hastily in this most delicate matter. I feel that, for the good of India itself, the admission of Natives to high office must be effected by slow degrees. 'But that when the fullness of time is come, when the interest of India requires the change, we ought to refuse to make that change lest we should endanger our own power—this is a doctrine which I cannot think of without indignation. Governments, like men, may buy existence too dear. "Propter vitam vivendi prodere causas," is a despicable policy either in individuals or in States. In the present case, such a policy would be not only despicable, but absurd." The more extent of empire is not necessarily an advantage. To many Governments it has been cumbersome; to some it has been fatal. It will be allowed by every statesman of our time that the prosperity of a community is made up of the prosperity of those who compose the community, and that it "is the most childish ambition to covet dominion which adds to no man's comfort or security." To the great trading nation, to the great manufacturing nation, no progress which any portion of the human race can make in knowledge, in taste for the conveniences of life, or in the wealth by which those conveniences are produced, can be matter of indifference. It is scarcely possible to calcutate the benefits which we might derive from the diffusion of European civilisation among the vast p:pulation of the East. "It would be, on the most selfish view of the case, far better for us that the people of India were well governed and independent of us, than ill-governed and subject to us"—that they were ruled by their own kings, but wearing our broad cloth, and working with our cutlery, than that they were performing their salaams to English Collcetors and English Magistrates, but were too ignorant to value, or too poor to buy, English manufactures. To trade with civilised men is infinitely more profitable than to govern savages. "That would indeed be a doting wisdom, which, in order that India might remain a dependency, would keep it a useless and costly dependency—which would keep a hundred millions of men from being our customers in order that they might continue to be our slaves.

"It was, as Bernier tells us, the practice of the miserable tyrants whom he found in India, when they dreaded the capacity and spirit of some distinguished subject, and yet could not venture to murder him, to administer to him a daily dose of the pousta, a preparation of opium, the effect of which was in a few months to destroy all the bodily and mental powers of the wretch who was drugged with it, and to turn him into a helpless idiot.

"That detestable artifice, more horrible than assassination itself, was worthy of those who employed it. It is no model for the English nation. We shall never consent to administer the pousta to a whole community—to stupefy and paralyse a great people, whom God has committed to our charge, for the wretched purpose of rendering them more amenable to our control. What is that power worth which is founded on vice, on ignorance, and on misery—which we can hold only by violating the most sacred duties which as governors we owe to the governed—which as a people blessed with far more than an ordinary measure of political liberty and of intellectual light, we owe to a race debased by three thousand years of despotism and priestcraft? We are free, we are civilised to little purpose, if we grudge to any portion of the human race an equal measure of freedom and civilisation.

"Are we to keep the people of India ignorant in order that we may keep them submissive? Or do we think that we can give them knowledge without awakening ambition? Or do we mean to awaken ambition and to provide it with no legitimate vent? Who will answer any of these questions in the affirmative? Yet one of them must be answered in the affirmative by every person who maintains that we ought permanently to exclude the Natives from high office. "I have no fears. The path of duty is plain before us; and it is also the path of wisdom, of national prosperity, of national honour.

"The destinies of our Indian Empire are covered with thick darkness. It is difficult to form any conjecture as to the fate reserved for a State which resembles no other in history, and which forms by itself a separate class of political phenomena. The laws which regulate its growth and its decay are still unknown to us. It may be that the public mind of India may expand under our system till it has outgrown that system; that by good government we may educate our subjects into a capacity for better government, that, having become instructed in European knowledge, they may, in some future age, demand European institutions. Whether such a day will ever come I know not. But never will I attempt to avert or to retard it. Whenever it comes, it will be the proudest day in English history. To have found a great people sunk in the lowest depths of slavery and superstition, to have so ruled them as to have made them desirous and capable of all the privileges of, citizens would indeed be a title to "glory all our own." The sceptre may pass away from us. Unforeseen accidents may derange our most profound schemes of policy. Victory may be inconstant to our arms. But there are triumphs which are followed by no reverses. There is an empire exempt from all natural causes of decay. Those triumphs are the pacific triumphs of reason over barbarism; that empire is the imperishable empire of our arts and our morals, our literature, and our law."

Vol. XIX, Third Series, p. 536.
July 10, 1833.

Mr. WYNN:—

"In nothing, however, more unreservedly did he agree with the hon'ble member than in the sentiments which he so forcibly impressed on the House at the close of his speech. "He had been convinced, ever since he was first connected with the affairs of India, that the only principle on which that Empire could justly or wisely or advantageously be administered was that of admitting the Natives to a participation in the government, and allowing them to hold every office the duties of which they were competent to discharge.' That principle had been supported by the authority of Sir Thomas Munro, and of the ablest functionaries in India, and been resisted with no small pertinacity and prejudice. It had been urged that the Natives were undeserving of trust, that no dependence could be placed on their integrity, whatever might be their talents and capacity, which no one disputed. Instances were adduced of their corruption and venality—"but were they not the result of our conduct towards them?" Duties of importance devolved upon them without any adequate remuneration either in rank or salary. There was no reward or promotion for fidelity; and why then complain of peculation and bribery. "We made vices and then punished them; we reduced men to slavery and then reproached them with the faults of slaves."

Vol. XIX Third Series, p. 547.
July 10th, 1833.

Mr. CHARLES GRANT, in replying, said :—

" He would advert very briefly to some of the suggestions which had been offered in the course of this debate. Before doing so, he must first embrace the opportunity of expressing not what he felt, for language could not express it, but of making an attempt to convey to the House his sympathy with it in its admiration of the speech of his hon'ble and learned friend the member for Leeds—a speech which, he would venture to assert, had never been exceeded within those walls for the development of statesmanlike policy and practical good sense. It exhibited all that was noble in oratory, all that was sublime, he had almost said, in poetry—all that was truly great, exalted, and virtuous in human nature. If the House at large felt a deep interest in this magnificent display it might judge of what were his emotions when he perceived in the hands of his hon'ble friend the great principles he had propounded to the House glowing with fresh colours and arrayed in all the beauty of truth.

* * * * *

" If one circumstance more than another could give him satisfaction it was that the main principle of this Bill had received the approbation of the House, and that the House was now legislating for India and the people of India on the great and just principle that in doing so the interests of the people of India should be principally consulted, and that all other interests of wealth, of commerce, and of revenue, should be as nothing compared with the paramount obligation imposed upon the legislature of promoting the welfare and prosperity of that great Empire which Providence had placed in our hands.

* * * * *

" Convinced as he was of the necessity of admitting Europeans to India, he would not consent to remove a single restriction on their admission unless it was consistent with the interests of the Natives. Provide for their protection and then throw open wide the doors of those magnificent regions and admit subjects there—not as aliens, not as culprits, but as friends. In spite of the difference between the two peoples, in spite of the difference of their religions, there was a sympathy which he was persuaded would unite them, and he looked forward with hope and eagerness to the " rich harvest of blessings which he trusted would flow from the present measure."

Page 624, *July 12th 1833.*

Mr. WYNN :—

"He could not subscribe to the perfection of *the* system that had hitherto prevailed in India; for, he could not forget that the Natives and half-castes were excluded from all employment in situations where they could be more effective than Europeans and at a much smaller cost. "The principle of employing those persons he considered to be essential to the good Government of India," and he could not applaud that system which had been founded on a violation of that principle."

Vol. XX., Third Series, p. 223,
August 5th, 1833.

Duke of WELLINGTON :—

"Then with respect to the clause declaring the Natives to be eligible to all situations. Why was that declaration made in the face of regulation preventing its being carried into effect? It was a mere deception. It might, to a considerable extent, be applicable in the capitals of the Presidencies; but, in the interior, as appeared by the evidence of Mr. Elphinstone, and by that of every respectable authority, it was impracticable. He certainly thought that it was advisable to admit the Natives to certain inferior civil and other offices; but the higher ones must as yet be closed against them, if our Empire in India was to be maintained."

After such exhaustive consideration from all political, imperial, and social aspects, the following, "*that wise, that benevolent, that noble clauses,*" was deliberately enacted by the Parliament of this country—worthy of the righteousness, justice, and noble instincts of the British people in the true British spirit.

3 and 4 William IV., cap. 85. 1833.

"That no native of the said territories, nor any natural-born subject of his Majesty resident therein, shall, by reason only of his religion, place of birth, descent, colour, or any of them, be disabled from holding any place, office, or employment under the said Company."

Ret. C—2376, 1879, p. 13.

"The Court of Directors interpreted this Act in an explaining despatch in the following words:—

"The Court conceive this section to mean that "there shall be no governing caste in British India"; that whatever other tests of qualification may be adopted, distinction of race or religion shall not be of the number; that no subject of the King, whether of Indian or British or mixed descent, shall be excluded from the posts usually conferred on Uncovenanted servants in India, *or from the Covenanted Service itself*, provided he be otherwise eligible."

After this explanation by the Court of Directors, how did they behave?

During the twenty years of their Charter, to the year 1853, they made the Act and their own explanation a complete dead letter. They did not at all take any steps to give the slightest opportunity to Indians for a single appointment to the Covenanted Civil Service, to which my statement chiefly refers; though the British people and Parliament are no party to this unfaithfulness, and never meant that the Act should remain a sham and delusion.

Twenty years passed, and the revision of the Company's Charter again came before Parliament in 1853; and if anything was more insisted on and bewailed than another, it was the neglect of the authorities to give effect to the Act of 1833. The principles of 1833 were more emphatically insisted on. I would just give a few extracts from the speeches of some of the most eminent statesmen in the debate on the Charter.

Hansard, Vol. 120, p. 865.
April 19th, 1852.

Mr. GOLBEURN:—

"Sir Thomas Munro had said—There is one great question to which we should look in all our arrangements, namely what is to be the final result of our government on the character of the people, and whether that character will be raised or lowered. Are we to be satisfied with merely securing our power and protecting the inhabitants, leaving them to sink gradually in character lower than at present, or are we to endeavour to raise their character? It ought undoubtedly to be our aim to raise the minds of the Natives, and to take care that whenever our connection with India shall cease, it shall not appear that the only fruit of our dominion had been to leave the people more abject than when we found them. It would certainly be more desirable we should be expelled from the country altogether, than that our system of government should be such an abasement of a whole people."

Hansard, Vol. 121, p. 496.
May 11th, 1852.

Lord MONTEAGLE, in presenting a petition to the House of Lords, said :—

"But a clause recommended or supported as he believed by the high authority of Lord William Bentinck was made part of the last Charter Act of the 3rd and 4th William IV, and affirmed the principle of an opposite policy. It was to the following effect: . . . . Yet notwithstanding his authority, notwithstanding likewise the result of the experiment tried and the spirit of the clause he had cited, there had been a practical exclusion of them from all 'Covenanted Services,' as they were called, from the passing of the last Charter up to the present time."

Hansard, Vol. 127, p. 1,184.
June 3rd, 1853.

Mr. BRIGHT :—

"Another subject requiring close attention on the part of Parliament was the employment of the Natives of India in the service of the Government. The Right Hon'ble Member for Edinburgh (Mr. Macaulay), in proposing the India Bill of 1833 had dwelt on one of its clauses, which provided that neither colour nor caste nor religion nor place of birth should be a bar to the employment of persons by the Government; whereas, as matter of fact, from that time to this no person in India had been so employed who might not have been equally employed before that clause was enacted; and from the statement of the Right Hon'ble gentleman the President of the Board of Control, that it was proposed to keep up the Covenanted Service system, it was clear that this most objectionable and most offensive state of things was to continue. Mr. Cameron, a gentleman thoroughly versed in the subject, as fourth Member of Council in India, President of the Indian Law Commission, and of the Council of Education for Bengal—what did he say on this point? He said: "The statute of 1833 made the Natives of India 'eligible to all offices' under the company. But during the twenty years that have since elapsed not one of the Natives has been appointed to any offices except such as they were eligible to before the statute."

Hansard. Vol. 128, p. 759, 1853.

MACAULAY said :—

"In my opinion we shall not secure or prolong our dominion in India by attempting to exclude the Natives of that country from a share in its government." (*Contemporary Review*, June, 1883, p. 808.)

Hansard, Vol 128, p. 986.
June 30th, 1853.

Mr. RICH :—

"But if the case as to the Native military was a strong one, it was much stronger as to civilians. It had been admitted that ninety-five per cent. of the administration of justice was discharged by Native judges. Thus they had the work, the hard work; but the places of honour and emolument were reserved for the Covenanted Service—the friends and relatives of the directors. Was it just that the whole work, the heat and labour of the day, should be borne by Natives and all the prizes reserved for Europeans? Was it politic to continue such a system? They might turn up the whites of their eyes and exclaim at American persistence in slavery. There the hard work was done by the negro whilst the control and enjoyment of profit and power were for the American. Was ours different in India? What did Mill lay down European control—Native agency. And what was the translation of that? 'White power, black slavery.' Was this just, or was it wise? Mill said it was necessary in order to obtain respect from the Natives. But he (Mr. Rich) had yet to learn that injustice was the parent of respect. Real respect grew out of common service, common emulation, and common rights impartially upheld. We must underpin our Empire by such principles, or some fine morning it would crumble beneath our feet. So long as he had a voice in that House it should be raised in favour of admitting our Native fellow subjects in India to all places to which their abilities and conduct should entitle them to rise."

Hansard, Vol. 129, p. 581.
July 21st, 1853.

Mr. MONCTON MILNES :—

"Objectionable as he believed many parts of the Bill were, he considered this was the most objectionable portion, and from it, very unhappy consequences might arise. When the Natives of India, heard it proclaimed, that they had a right to enter the service of the company, they would by their own intelligence and ability render themselves qualified for that service, if they only had the means of doing so. Then one of the two consequences would follow. They would either find their way into the service, or else the company would have arrayed against them a spirit of discontent on the part of the whole people of India, the result of which it would be difficult to foresee. He did not see on what principles of justice, if they once admitted the principle of open competition, they could say to the Natives of India they had not a perfect right to enter the service."

Hansard, Vol. 129, p. 665.
July 22nd, 1853.

Mr. J. G. PHILLIMORE quotes Lord William Bentinck :—

"'The bane of our system' is not solely that the Civil Administration is entirely in the hands of foreigners, but the holders of this monopoly, the patrons of these foreign agents, are those who exercise its directing power at home; that this directing power is exclusively paid by patronage, and that the value of the patronage depends exactly upon the degree in which all the honours and emoluments of the State are engrossed by their clients to the exclusion of the Natives. There exists, in consequence, on the part of the home authorities, an interest in the Administration precisely similar to what formerly prevailed as to commerce, 'and directly opposed to the welfare of India'."

Though open competition was introduced, the monopoly of the Europeans and the injustice and injury to the Indians was allowed to continue by refusing to the Indians simultaneous examinations in India as the only method of justice to them, as will be seen further on.

Mr. Rich and Lord Stanley (the late Lord Derby) then emphatically put their fingers upon this black plague-spot in system of British Rule.

Hansard. Vol. 129, p. 682.
July 22, 1853.

Mr. RICH raised the question whether or not the Natives were to be admitted to *the Company's Covenanted Service.* He said :—

"As regarded employment in the public service, the Natives were placed in a worse position by the present Bill than they were before. The intention of the Act of 1833 was to open the services to the Natives; and surely now, when our Indian Empire was more secure than it was at that time, it was not wise to deviate from such a line of policy. His object was that all offices in India should be effectively opened to Natives, and therefore he would not require them to come over to this country for examination, as such a condition would necessarily entail on Natives of India great expense, expose them to the risk of losing caste, and thereby operate as a bar against their obtaining the advantages held out to all other of Her Majesty's subjects. The course of education through which the youth of India at present went at the established colleges in that country afforded the most statisfactory proof of their efficiency for discharging the duties of office. . . . .

"This was not just or wise, and would infallibly lead to a most dangerous agitation, by which in a few years that "which would now be accepted as a boon would be wrested from the Legislature as a right." They had opened the commerce of India in spite of the croakers of the day "Let them now open the posts of government to the Natives, and they would have a more happy and contented people."

Hansard, Vol. 129, p. 684.
July 22nd, 1835.

Lord STANLEY :—

"He could not refrain from expressing his conviction that, in refusing to carry on examinations in India as well as in

England—a thing that was easily practicable—the Government were, in fact, negativing that which they declared to be one of the principal objects of their Bill, and confining the civil service, as heretofore, to Englishmen. "That result was unjust, and he believed it would be most pernicious."

Hansard, Vol. 129, p. 784.
July 25th, 1853.

Lord STANLEY.

"Let them suppose, for instance, that instead of holding those examinations here in London, that they were to be held in Calcutta. Well, how many Englishmen would go out there—or how many would send out their sons, perhaps to spend two or three years in the country on the chance of obtaining an appointment! "Nevertheless, that was exactly the course proposed to be adopted towards the Natives of India."

Hansard, Vol. 129, p. 778.
July 25th, 1853.

Mr. BRIGHT said :—

"That the motion now before the Committee involved the question which had been raised before during these discussions, but which had never been fairly met by the President of the Board of Control, namely, whether the clause in the Act of 1833, which had been so often alluded to, had not up to this time been altogether a nullity. If any doubt had been entertained with respect to the object of that clause, it would be removed by reference to the answers given by the then President of the Board of Control to the hon'ble member for Montrose and to the speech of the right hon'ble gentleman the present member for Edinburgh (Mr. Macaulay), in both of which it was distinctly declared that the object was to break down the barriers which were supposed to exist to the admission of the Natives as well as Europeans to high offices in India. And yet there was the best authority for saying that nothing whatever had been done in consequence of that clause. He (Mr. Bright) did not know of a single case where a Native of India had been admitted to any office since that time, more distinguished or more highly paid than he would have been competent to fill had that clause been not passed."

Hansard, Vol. 129, p. 787,
July 25th. 1853.

Mr. MONCTON MILNES said :—

" He thought the Bill was highly objectionable in this respect that while it pretended to lay down the generous principle that no condition of colour, creed or caste was to be regarded as a disqualification for office, it hampered the principle with such regulations and modifications as would render it all but impossible for the Natives to avail themselves of it. The Bill in this respect was a delusion and would prove a source of chronic and permanent discontent to the people of India."

Hansard, Vol. 129, p. 788.
July 25th, 1853.

Mr. J. G. PHILLIMORE said :—

" He also feared that the Bill would prove delusive, and that although it professed to do justice to the Natives the " spirit of monopoly would still blight the hopes and break the spirits of the Indian people. While such a state of things continued India would be attached to this country by no bond of affection," but would be retained by the power of the Army and the terror of the sword. He implored of the Committee "not to allow such an Empire to be governed in the miserable spirit of monopoly and exclusion."

Will the present statesmen ever learn this truth? Is it a wonder that the British people are losing the affections of the Indian people ?

Hansard, Vol. 129, p. 1,335.
August 5th, 1853.

Earl GRANVILLE :—

" I for one, speaking individually, have never felt the slightest alarm at Natives, well-qualified and filled for public employments, being employed in any branch of the public service of India."

Thus began the second chapter of this melancholy history with the continuation of the same spirit of selfishness which had characterised the previous twenty years, with the clear knowledge of the gross injustice to the Indians by not allowing them the same facility as was allowed to English youths, by simultaneous examinations in India and England. This injustice continued till the second chapter ended in the Mutiny of 1857, and the rule passed from the Company to the Crown.

The third chapter from that time began again with the revival of great hopes—that, however unfortunate and deplorable the Mutiny was, one great good sprang from that evil. The conscience of the British people was awakened to all previous injustice and dishonour brought upon them by their servants, and to a sense of their own duty. A new era opened, brighter far brighter, than even that of the Act of 1833.

Not only was the Act of 1833 allowed to continue a living reality, at least in word, but in directing the mode of future services the Act of 1858 left it comprehensively open to adopt any plan demanded by justice. It did not indicate in the slightest degree prevention or exclusion of Indians from *any* service or from simultaneous examinations in India and England, or of any mode of admission of Indians into the Covenanted Civil Service, or of doing equal justice to all Her Majesty's natural-born subjects. I shall show further on the interpretation by the Civil Service Commissioners themselves.

The sections of the Act of 1858 are as follows :—

1.—21-22 Vic., cap. 106, "An Act for the better government of India" (2nd August, 1858). Section 23 provides that :—

"With all convenient speed after the passing of this Act, regulations shall be made by the Secretary of State in Council, with the advice and assistance of the Commissioners for the time being acting in execution of Her Majesty's Order in Council of Twenty-first *May*, One thousand, eight hundred, and fifty-five, 'for regulating the admission of persons to the

Civil Service of the Crown,' for admitting all persons being natural-born subjects of Her Majesty (and of such age and qulification as may be prescribed in this behalf) who may be desirous of becoming candidates for appointment to the Civil Services of *India* to be examined as candidates accordingly, and for prescribing the branches of knowledge in which such candidates shall be examined, and generally for regulating and conducting such examinations under the superintendence of the said last-mentioned commissioners, or of the persons for the time being entrusted with the carrying out of such regulations as may be from time to time established by Her Majesty for examination certificate, or other test of fitness in relation to appointments to junior situations in the Civil Services of the Crown, and the candidates who may be certified by the said Commissioners or other persons as aforesaid to be entitled under such regulations shall be recommended for appointment according to the order of their proficiency as shown by such examinations, and such persons only as shall have been so certified at aforesaid shall be appointed or admitted to the Civil Services of *India* by the Secretary of State in Council: Provided always, that all regulations to be made by the said Secretary of State in Council under this Act shall be laid before Parliament within fourteen days after the making thereof, if Parliament be sitting, and, if Parliament be not sitting, then within fourteen days after the next meeting thereof."

2.—The same Act, Cap. 106, Sect. 34, provides :—

"With all convenient speed after the commencement of this Act, regulations shall be made for admitting any persons "being natural-born subjects of Her Majesty" (and of such age and qualifications as may be prescribed in this behalf) who may be desirous of becoming candidates for cadetships in the Engineers and in the Artillery, to be examined as candidates accordingly, and for prescribing the branches of knowledge in which such candidates shall be examined, and generally for regulating and conducting such examinations."

Though this Section does not impose any disability on an Indian—for it provides for "any persons being natural-born subjects of Her Majesty"—yet an Indian is totally excluded from such examination. As I have already placed before the Commission my correspondence with the War Office, I need not say more.

3.—Sections 35 and 36 provide :—

"Not less than one-tenth of the whole number of persons to be recommended in any year for military cadetships (other than cadetships in the Engineers and Artillery) shall be selected according to such regulations as the Secretary of State in Council may from time to time make in this behalf from among the sons of persons who have served in India in the military or civil services of Her Majesty, or of the East India Company."

"Except as aforesaid, all persons to be recommended for military cadetships shall be nominated by the Secretary of State and Members of Council; so that out of seventeen nominations the Secretary of State shall have two and each Member of Council shall have one; but no person so nominated shall be recommended unless the nomination be approved of by the Secretary of State in Council."

In these sections also there is no exclusion of Indians.

But the Sovereign and the people did not rest even with such comprehensive enactments by Parliament. They explicitly emphasised and removed any possible doubt with regard to the free and equal treatment of all Her Majesty's natural-born subjects without any distinction of race, colour, or creed.

Thus, on the 1st November, 1858, followed the great and glorious Proclamation by the Sovereign on behalf of the British people: our complete "great charter" of our national and political rights of British citizenship and of perfect equality in all the services of the Sovereign—a proclamation the like of which had never been proclaimed in the history of the world under similar circumstances.

Here are the special clauses of that Proclamation :—

"We hold ourselves bound to the Natives of our Indian territories by the "same obligations of duty which bind us to all our other subjects," and those obligations, by the blessing of Almighty God, we shall "faithfully and conscientiously" fulfil."

"And it is our further will that, so far as may be, our subjects, of whatever race or creed, be freely and impartially admitted to offices in our service, the duties of which they may be qualified, by their education, ability, and integrity, duly to discharge."

"In their prosperity will be our strength, in their contentment our security, and in their gratitude our best reward. And may the God of all Power grant to us, and to those in authority under us, strength to carry out these our wishes for the good of our people."

Such was the noblest Proclamation of 1858. What more could we ask, and what bonds of gratitude and affection, and what vast benefits to both countries, were expected to tie us to the connection with Britain by a loyal and honourable fulfilment of it?

Yes, I was in Bombay when this glad—I may almost say divine—message to India was proclaimed there to a surging crowd. What rejoicings, what fireworks, illuminations, and the roar of cannon! What joy ran through the length and breadth of India, of a second and firm emancipation, of a new British political life, forgetting and forgiving all the past evil and hoping for a better future! What were the feelings of the people! How deep loyalty and faith in Britain was rekindled! It was said over and over again: Let this Proclamation be faithfully and conscientiously fulfilled, and England may rest secure and in strength upon the gratitude and contentment of the people—as the Proclamation had closed its last words of prayer.

Now, when I look back to-day to that day of joy, how I feel how all this was doomed to disappointment, with the addition of some even worse features, of dishonour, injustice, and selfishness. However, I must proceed with the sad tale.

Not long after Her Majesty's Proclamation of 1858, a Committee was appointed by the Secretary of State for India of the following members of his own Council:

Sir J. P. Willoughby, Mr. Mangles, Mr. Arbuthnot, Mr. Macnaghten, and Sir Erskine Perry, all Anglo-Indians. This Committee made its report on 20th January, 1860, from which I give the following extracts on the subject of the pledge of the Act of 1833:—

"2. We are in the first place "unanimously" of opinion that it is not only just, but expedient, that the Natives of India shall be employed in the administration of India to as large an extent as possible consistently with the maintenance of British supremacy, and have considered whether any increased facilities can be given in this direction.

"3. It is true that, even at present, no positive disqualification exists. By Act 3 and 4 Wm. IV, cap. 85, sec. 87, it is enacted 'that no Native of the said territories nor any natural-born subject of His Majesty resident therein shall, by reason only of his religion, place of birth descent, colour, or any of them, be disabled from holding any place, office, or employment under the said Company.' It is obvious, therefore, that when the competitive system was adopted, it could not have been intended to exclude Natives of India from the Civil Service of India.

"4. Practically, however, they are excluded. The law declares them eligible, but the difficulties opposed to a Native leaving India and residing in England for a time, are so great that, as a general rule, it is almost impossible for a Native successfully to complete at the periodical examinations held in England. "Where this inequality removed, we should no longer be exposed to the charge of keeping promise to the ear and breaking it to the hope."

"5. Two modes have been suggested by which the object in view might be attained. The first is, by allotting a certain portion of the total number of appointments declared in each year to be competed for in India by Natives, and by all other natural-born subjects of Her Majesty resident in India. The second is to hold simultaneously two examinations, one in England and one in India, both being, as far as practicable, identical in their nature, and those who compete in both countries being finally classified in one list according to merit, by the Civil Service Commissioners. The Committee have "no hesitation in giving the preference to the second scheme," as being the "fairest", and the most in accordance with the principles of a general competition for a common object.

"6. In order to aid them in carrying out a scheme of this nature, the Committee have consulted the Civil Service Commission, and, though the favour of Sir Edward Ryan, they have obtained a very able paper, in which the advantages and disadvantages of either plan are fully and lucidly discussed. They would solicit your careful consideration of this document and will only, in conclusion, add that, in the event of either of the plans being adopted, it will be requisite to provide for the second examination of successful competitors in India, as nearly as possible resembling that now required in England. The Civil Service Commissioners do not anticipate much difficulty in arranging for this. The committee, however, are decidedly of opinion that the examination papers on which the competition is to proceed in India and England should be identical; but they think, in justice to the Natives, that three colloquial Oriental languages, should be added to the three modern European languages, so as to give the candidates the opportunity of selection."

I asked the Indian Office to give me a copy of the "very able paper" of the Civil Service Commission above referred to. The India Office refused to give it to me. I was allowed to see it in the India Office, and I then asked to be allowed to take a copy of it myself there and then. This even was refused to me. I ask this Commission that this Report be obtained and be added here.

The above forms a part of the Report, the other part being a consideration of the advantages and disadvantages of an "exclusive" Covenanted Civil Service. With this latter part I have nothing to do here. The first part quoted above about the admission of Natives into the Covenanted Civil Service was never as far as I know published.

It is a significant fact that the Report of the Public Service Commission on the two subjects of the so-called "Statutory" Service and simultaneous examinations being in accordance with (what I believe and will show further on) the determined foregone conclusions of the

Government of India and the Secretary of State, was published and is being repeatedly used by Government in favour of their own proceedings, while the Report of 1860 of the Committee of five Members of Council of the Secretary of State for India was not only never published by Government as far as I know, but even suppressed in the Return made in 1879 on "Civil Service" (Return C. [2376] 1879). Even the Public Service Commission has not given, I think, the Report of 1860.

No action was taken on this part of the Report of 1860. This Report was made thirty-seven years ago, and even so early as then it was considered, and strongly recommended, that simultaneous examinations was the only way of redeeming the honour of England and of doing justice to India. The Report was suppressed and put aside, as it did not suit the views of the Secretary of State for India, who himself had appointed the Committee.

Thus, the new stage of the Proclamation of 1858, with all the hopes and joy it had inspired, began so early as 1860 to be a grievous disappointment and a dead letter, just as dead as the Act of 1833.

The next stage in this sad story is again a revival of hope and joy in a small instalment of justice by a partial fulfilment of all the pledges of 1833 and 1858. This was a bright spot in the dark history of this question, and the name of Sir Stafford Northcote will never be effaced from our hearts.

Sad to say, it was to be again darkened with a disappointment of a worse character than ever before. On August 13th, 1867, the East India Association considered the following memorial proposed by me, and adopted it, for submission to Sir Stafford Northcote (Lord Iddesleigh), the then Secretary of State for India :—

"We, the members of the East India Association, beg respectfully to submit that the time has come when it is desirable to admit the Natives of India to a larger share in the administration of India than hitherto.

"To you, Sir, it is quite unnecessary to point out the justice, necessity, and importance of this step, as in the debate in Parliament, on May 24th last, you have pointed out this so emphatically and clearly that it is enough for us to quote your own noble and statesmanlike sentiments. You said: 'Nothing could be more wonderful than our Empire in India; but we ought to consider on what conditions we hold it and how our predecessors hold it. The greatness of the Mogul Empire depended upon the liberal policy that was pursued by men like Akbar availing themselves of Hindu talent and assistance and identifying themselves as far as possible with the people of the country. He thought that they ought to take a lesson from such a circumstance, and if they were to do their duty towards India they could only discharge that duty by obtaining the assistance and counsel of all who were great and good in that country. It would be absurd in them to say that there was not a large fund of statesmanship and ability in the Indian character' (*Times* of May 25th, 1867).

"With these friendly and just sentiments towards the people of India we fully concur, and therefore instead of trespassing any more upon your time, we beg to lay before you our views and the best mode of accomplishing the object.

"We think that the competitive examination for a portion of the appointments to the Indian Civil Service should be held in India, under such rules and arrangements as you may think proper. What portion of the appointments should be thus competed for in India we cannot do better than leave to your own judgment. After the selection is made in India, by the first examination, we think it essential that the selected candidates be required to come to England to pass their further examinations with the selected candidates of this country.

"In the same spirit, and with kindred objects in view for the general good of India, we would ask you to extend your kind encouragement to Native youths of promise and ability to come to England for the completion of their education. We believe that if scholarships tenable for five years in this country were to be annually awarded by competitive examination in India to Native candidates between the ages of fifteen and seventeen, some would compete successfully in England for the Indian Civil Service, while others would return in various professions to India; and where by degrees they would form an enlightened and unprejudiced class, exercising a great and beneficial influence on Native society, and constituting a link between the masses of the people and their English rulers.*

"In laying before you this memorial we feel assured, and we trust that you will also agree with us, that this measure, which has now become necessary by the advancement of education in India, will promote and strengthen the loyalty of the Natives of India to the British Rule, while it will also be a satisfaction to the British people to have thus by one more instance practically proved its desire to advance the condition of their Indian fellow-subjects, and to act justly by them.

"We need not point out to you, Sir, how great an encouragement these examinations in India will be to education. The great prizes of the appointment will naturally increase vastly the desire for education among the people."

A deputation waited on Sir Stafford Northcote on 21st August, 1867, to present the petition. In the course of the conversation, Colonel Sykes explained the objects; and after some further conversation Sir Stafford Northcote said:—

"He had the question under consideration, and had conversed with Sir Herbert Edwards and others on it, and Sir Herbert had furnished him with a paper on it. Two plans were suggested—the one proposed that appointments should be assigned for competition in India, the other that scholarship should be given to enable Natives to come to finish their education in England. The first would manifestly be the most convenient for the Natives themselves; but it was urged in favour of the second that it would secure a more enterprising class than the first—men with more backbone—and he admitted the force of that. Moreover, he quite saw the advantage to India of a more efficient class which had had an English training. He took a very great interest in the matter, and was inclined to approve both proposals. He was corresponding with Sir J. Lawrence and the Indian Government on the

* This clause was an addition proposed by Sir Herbert Edwards.

subject" ("Journal of the East India Association," Vol. I., pp. 126-7).

In 1868, Sir Stafford Northcote, in paragraph 3 of his despatch, Revenue No. 10, of 8th of February, 1868, said as below :—

"This is a step in the right direction, of which I cordially approve, but it appears to me that there is room for carrying out the principle to a considerable extent in the regulation provinces also. The Legislature has determined that the more important and responsible appointments in those provinces shall be administered exclusively by those who are now admitted to the public service solely by competition; but there is a large class of appointments in the regulation as well as in the non-regulation provinces, some of them scarcely less honourable and lucrative than those reserved by law for the Covenanted Civil Service, to which Natives of India have certainly a preferential claim, but which, as you seem to admit, have up to this time been too exclusively conferred upon Europeans. "These persons, however competent, not having entered the service by the prescribed channel, can have no claim upon the patronage of the Government, none, at least, that ought to be allowed to override the inherent rights of the Natives of the country; and therefore, while all due consideration should be shown to well-deserving incumbents, both as regards their present position and their promotion, there can be no valid reason why the class of appointments which they now hold should not be filled, in future, by Natives of ability and high character."

I only note this here as what Sir Stafford Northcote had prescribed and instructed the Government of India for the Uncovenanted Services, but which instructions have also been made a dead letter as usual—I do not in this statement discuss this branch of the subject, *viz.*, the Uncovenanted Service, except for some short reference to some subsequent grievous events. I content myself with an expression of the Duke of Argyll on what Sir Erskine Perry describes in his "Memorandum" addressed to Lord Salisbury on 9th December, 1876, as "the vicious practice, supposed to be rapidly growing up in India, of appointing Englishmen to all the well paid uncovenanted offices." The Duke of Argyll in his despatch (10th March, 1870, Financial) said :—

"The principle which Her Majesty's Government steadily kept in view throughout the discussion on these furlough rules is, that the Uncovenanted Service should be principally reserved for the Natives of the country, and that superior appointments, which require English training and experience, should be made as heretofore in England. And they look with great disfavour on the system which appears to be growing up in India of appointing Englishmen in India to situations that ought only as a rule to be filled by civilians by open competition."

All such instructions, as usual, are thwarted by what Lord Lytton calls "subterfuges" and great ingenuity.

While Sir Stafford Northcote was considering, muttering, and preparing to bring into action the petition of the East India Association, Mr. Fawcett, raised the subject in the House of Commons. Referring to simultaneous examinations for the Covenanted Service, he said :—

Hansard, Vol. 191, pp. 1,839-40.
May 8th, 1868.

"There would be no difficulty in carrying out this plan. . . . . His proposal was that there should be examinations at Calcutta, Madras and Bombay, that there should be the same papers and the same test as in London, and the successful candidates, whether English or Native, should spend two years in this country. To this he had reason to believe, from memorials he had received from Calcutta and Bombay, the Natives would not object, though they naturally objected to coming over to England in the first instance without any guarantee of success. . . . . All they asked for was to be subjected to precisely the same trial as the English. . . . . With reference to their alleged inferiority of character he had asked what would be the effect on English character if we, having been subjected, were debarred from all but the meanest offices of the State. Our civilisation and our literature would be destroyed. Nothing would save us from debasement. It was an indisputable fact that many Natives competent to govern a Province were fulfilling the humblest duties at salaries less than was received by the youngest member of the Indian Civil Service. Lord Metcalf had well said that the bane of our system was that the advantages were reaped by one class and the work was done by another. . . . . Sir Bartle Frere, in one of his despatches, said he had been much struck with the fact that the ablest exponents of English policy and our best coadjutors in adapting that policy to the wants of the various nations occupying Indian soil were to be found among the natives who had received a high-class English education."

Hansard, Vol. 191, p. 1843.
May 8th, 1868.

Mr. FAWCETT moved :—

"That this House whilst cordially approving of the system of open competition for appointments in the East India Civil Service, is of opinion that the people of India have not a fair chance of competing for these appointments, as long as the examinations are held nowhere but in London; this House would therefore deem it desirable that simultaneously with the examination in London, the same examination should be held in Calcutta, Bombay and Madras."

I may here remark that at this time and till 1876 the Report of the five Councillors of the India Office of 1860, which I have given before, was not known to anybody outside, and Mr. Fawcett could not have known anything about it.

In the same speech from which a passage is extracted in the Memorial of the East India Association, Sir Stafford Northcote has said :—

"The English Government must necessarily labour under great disadvantages, and 'we should endeavour' as far as possible to develop the system of Native government, to bring out Native talent and statesmanship, and to enlist in the cause of government all that was great and good in them."

The outcome of the petition of the East India Association, Mr. Fawcett's motion, and Sir Stafford Northcote's favourable reception of the petition, was that Sir Stafford Northcote introduced a clause in his Bill entitled, "the Governor-General of India Bill" to grant the first prayer of the petition; and the Governor-General, Lord Lawrence, published a Resolution on 30th June, 1868, to grant the second prayer of the Memorial, and some scholarships were actually commenced to be given. But by a strange fatality that pursues everything in the interests of the Indians, the scholarships were soon abolished.

I do not enter into any detalis of this incident, as it affects only in an indirect manner and to a very small extent the question I am considering, *viz.*, the admission of Indians, in the Covenanted Civil Service.

I revert to the clause introduced by Sir Stafford Northcote in 1868. As this clause will come further on in the course of correspondence, I do not repeat it here.

This clause was subsequently passed in 1870, under the Duke of Argyll as Secretary of State, who communicated it to the Government of India by a despatch of 31st March, 1870. The Government of India being dilatory, as it is generally the misfortune of Indian interests, the Duke of Argyll in his despatch of 18th April, 1872, reminded the Government of India about rules required by the Act, as follows:—

"Referring to the 6th section of 33rd Victoria, cap. 3, I desire to be informed whether Your Excellency in Council has prescribed the rules which that Act contemplates for the regulation of the Admission of Natives to appointments "in the Covenanted Civil Service" who have not been admitted to that service in accordance with the provisions of the 32nd section of the 21st and 22nd Victoria, cap. 106."

The dilatoriness of the Government of India continuing, the Duke of Argyll again reminded the

Governor-General of India in a despatch of 22nd October, 1872 :—

"I have not received any subsequent communication from Your Excellency's Government on the subject, and therefore conclude that nothing has been done, although I addressed your Government on the subject on 18th April last."

These two reminders were not known to the public until a Return was made in 1879 [C—2,376].

Three years passed after the enactment of the clause, and the public not knowing of anything having been done, the East India Association felt it necessary to complain to the Duke of Argyll on the subject.

The following is the correspondence between the East India Association and Mr. Grant Duff in 1873, giving his Grace's speech, and a brief account of the events from 1867 to 1873 :—

EAST INDIA ASSOCIATION,
20, Great George Street, Westminster, London.
September, 1873.

To

M. E. GRANT DUFF, Esq., M. P.,
Under-Secretary of State for India,
India Office.

"SIR,—By the direction of the Council of the East India Association. I have to request you to submit this letter for the kind consideration of his Grace the Secretary of State for India.

"On the 21st August, 1867, this Association applied to Sir Stafford Northcote, the then Secretary of State for India, asking that the competitive examination for a portion of the appointments to the Indian Civil Service should be held in India, under such rules and arrangements as he might think proper, and expressing an opinion that, after the selection had been made in India by the first examination, it was essential that the selected candidates should be required to come to England to pass their further examinations with the selected candidates for this country.

"Sir Stafford Northcote soon after introduced a clause in the Bill he submitted to Parliament, entitled 'The Governor-Generel of India Bill.'"

"The enactment of this Bill continued in abeyance, until, under the auspices of his Grace the present Secretary of State, it became law on the 25th March, 1870, as 'East India (Laws and Regulations) Act.' Moving the second reading of the Bill on the 11th March, 1869, his Grace, in commenting upon clause 6, in a candid and generous manner made an unreserved acknowledgment of past failures of promises, non-fulfilment to an adequate extent, as follows :—

"'I now come to a clause—the 6th—which is one of very great importance involving some modification in our practice, and in the principles of our legislation "as regards the Civil Service in India." Its object is to set free the hands of the Governor-General, under such restrictions and regulations as may be agreed to by the Government at home, "to select, for the Covenanted Service of India, Natives of that country," although they may not have gone through the competitive examination in this country. It may be asked how far this provision is consistent with the measures adopted by Parliament for securing efficiency in that service; but there is a previous and, in my opinion, a much more important question which I trust will be considered—how far this provision is essential to enable us to perform our duties and fulfil our pledges and professions towards the people of India. . . . .

"'With regard, however, "to the employment of Natives in the government of their country in the Covenanted Service" formerly of the Company, and now of the Crown, I must say that we have not fulfilled our duty, or the promises and engagements which we have made.

"'In the Act of 1833, this declaration was solemnly put forth by the Parliament of England: "And be it enacted that no Native of the said territories, nor any natural-born subject of His Majesty resident therein, shall, by reason only of his religion, place of birth, descent, colour, or any of them, be disabled from holding any place, office, or employment under the said Company."

"'Now I well remember that in the debates in this House in 1853, when the renewal of the Charter was under the consideration of Lord Aberdeen's Government, my late noble friend Lord Monteagle complained, and I think with great force, that while professing to open every office of profit and employment under the Company or the Crown to the Natives of India, we practically excluded them by laying down regulations as to fitness which we knew Natives could never fulfil. If the only door of admission to the Civil Service of India is a competitive examination carried on in London, what chance or what possibility is there of Natives of India acquiring that fair share in the administration of their own country which their education and abilities would enable them to fulfil, and therefore entitle them to possess? I have always felt that the regulations laid down for the competitive examinations rendered nugatory the declaration of the Act of 1833; and so strongly has this been felt of late years by the Government of India that various suggestions have been made to remedy the evil. One of the very last—which, however, has not yet been finally sanctioned at home, and respecting which I must say there are serious doubts—has been suggested by Sir John Lawrence, who is now about to approach our shores, and who is certainly one of the most distinguished men who have ever wielded the destinies of our Indian Empire. The palliative which he proposes is that nine scholarships—nine scholarships for a Government of upwards of 180,000,000 of people!—should be annually at the disposal for certain Natives, selected partly by competition and partly with reference to their social rank and position, and that these nine scholars should be sent home with a salary of £200 a year each, to compete with the whole force of the British population seeking admission through the competitive examinations. Now, in the first place, I would point out the utter inadequacy of the scheme to the ends of the case. To speak of nine scholarships distributed over the whole of India as any fulfilment of our pledges or obligations to the Natives would be a farce. I will not go into details of the scheme, as they are still under consideration; but I think it is by no means expedient to lay down as a principle that it is wholly useless to require Natives seeking employment in our Civil Service to see something of English society and manners. It is true that in the new schools and colleges they pass most distinguished examinations, and as far as books can teach them, are familiar with the history and constitution of this country; but there are some offices with regard to which it would be a most important, if not an essential, qualification that the young men appointed to them should have seen something of the actual working of the English constitution, and should have been impressed by its working, as any one must be who resides for any time in this great political society. Under any new regulations which may be made under this clause, it will, therefore, be expedient to provide that Natives appointed to certain places shall have some personal knowledge of the working of English institutions. I would, however, by no means make this a general condition, for there are many places in the Covenanted Service of India for which Natives are perfectly competent, without the necessity of visiting this country; and I believe that by competitive examinations conducted at Calcutta, or even by pure selection, it will be quite possible for the Indian Government to secure able, excellent, and efficient administrators.

"The clause thus introduced, in a manner worthy of an English generous-minded nobleman, and passed into law, is as follows:—

"'6. Whereas it is expedient that additional facilities should be given "for the employment of Natives of India, of proved merit and ability, in the Civil Service of Her Majesty in India," be it enacted that nothing in the "Act for the Government of India," twenty-one and twenty.two Victoria, chapter one hundred and six, or in the "Act to confirm certain appointments in India, and to amend the law concerning the Civil Service there," twenty-four and twenty-five Victoria, chapter fifty-four, or in any other Act of Parliament, or other law now in force in India, shall restrain the authorities in India by whom appointments are or may be made to offices, places, and employments "in the Civil Service of Her Majesty in India," from appointing any Native of India to any such office, place, or employment although such Native shall not have been admitted to the said Civil Service of India in manner in section thirty-two of the first-mentioned Act provided, but subject to such rules as may be from time to time prescribed by the Governor-General in Council, and sanctioned by the Secretary of State in Council, with the concurrence of a majority of members present; and that, for the purpose of this Act, the words "Natives of India" shall include any person born and domiciled within the dominions of Her Majesty in India, of parents habitually resident in India, and not established there for temporary purposes only; and that it shall be lawful for the Governor-General in Council to define and limit from time to time the qualification of Natives of India thus expressed; provided that every Resolution made by him for such purpose shall be subject to the sanction of the Secretary of State in Council, and shall not have force until it has been laid for thirty days before both Houses of Parliament.'

"It is now more than three years since this clause has been passed, but the Council regret to find that no steps have apparently yet been taken by His Excellency the Viceroy to frame the rules required by it, so that the Natives may obtain the due fulfilment of the liberal promise made by His Grace.

"The Natives complain that, had the enactment referred to the interests of the English community, no such long and unreasonable delay would have taken place, but effect would have been given to the Act as quickly as possible," and they further express a fear that this promise may also be a dead-letter. *

"The Council, however, fully hope that further loss of time will not be allowed to take place in promulgating the rules required by the Act. The Natives, after the noble and generous language used by His Grace, naturally expect that they will not be again doomed to disappointment, and most anxiously look forward to the promulgation of the rules—to give them, in some *systematic* manner, 'that fair share in the administration of their own country which their education and abilities would enable them to fulfil, and therefore entitle them to posses," not only as a political justice, but also as a national necessity, for the advancement of the material and moral condition of the country.

"I remain, Sir, your obedient Servant,

"W. C. PALMER, Capt.

"*Acting Honorary Secretary of the East India Association.*"

"India Office, London,

October 10*th*, 1873.

"SIR,—I am directed by the Secretary of State for India in Council to acknowledge the receipt of your letter of the 2nd October, relative to the provisions of the 33rd Victoria cap. 3, section 6; and to inform you that the subject is understood to be under the consideration of the Government of India, the attention of which has been twice called to it.

"2. The Duke of Argyll in Council will send a copy of your letter to the Government of India, and again request the early attention of that authority to that subject."

I am, Sir, your obedient Servant,

(Sd.) M. E. GRANT DUFF.

"THE ACTING HONORARY SECRETARY,

East India Association."

---

* To our misfortune and to the dishonour of the authorities, it has been made a dead letter.

Such is the candid confession of non-performance of duty and non-fulfilment of solemn pledges for thirty-six years, and the renewed pledge to make amends for past failures and provide adequate admission for the future for at least some share in the administration of our own country. The inadequacy is clearly shown by the ridicule of nine scholarships for 180,000,000 souls, and the proposal to adopt means for the abolition of the monopoly of Europeans. When was this confession and this new pledge made? It was to pass the 6th clause of Act 33 Vic., cap. 3. The clause was passed on 25th March, 1870, one year after the above speech was made, and nearly three years after it was first proposed. Twice did Sir C. Wingfield ask questions in the House of Commons, and no satisfactory reply was given. At last the East India Association addressed the letter which I have given above to the India Office, and from the reply it will be seen how slow our Indian authorities had been, so as to draw three reminders from the Secretary of State.

With regard to the remark in the letter as to the complaint of the Natives that, "had the enactment referred to the interests of the English community, no such long and unreasonable delay would have taken place," I need simply point to the fact of the manner in which the Coopers Hill College was proposed and carried out promptly and with no difficulty raised, as is always raised against Indian interests.

In 1879, the India office made a Return [C—2,376] on the ("Civil Service"). In this Return, after the despatch of the Secretary of State for India of 22nd October 1872, no information is given till the Government of India's despatch of May 2nd, 1878.

In this Return as I have said already, the Report of the Committee of the five members of the Council of the Secretary of State of 1860, recommending that simultaneous examinations was the only fair way of redeeming the honour of the British name and doing justice to the Indians, was suppressed. There is a despatch of the Government of India of 1874, which Sir E. Perry in his memorandum describes as follows :—

"Nearly two years afterwards (20th August, No. 31 of 1874) the Government of India replied to this despatch, transmitting rules, but noticing very jejunely the principal question raised by his Grace. Rules were finally suggested for adoption by the Secretary of State, those originally transmitted being deemed by him, under legal advice, to place too narrow a construction on the statute" (Public Despatch to India, No. 131 of 20th of August, 1874).

These documents also have no place in the Return. Who knows what other inconvenient documents also may have not appeared. This is always the difficulty in Indian matters for Indian interests. The public can never know the whole truth. The Government put forward only such information as they like, and the public is left in the dark, so as not to be in a position to judge rightly. The way of the Indian authorities is first to ignore any Act or Resolution of Parliament or Report of any Committee or Commission in favour of Indian interests. If that is not enough, then to delay replies. If that does not answer, then openly resist, and by their persistence carry their own point unless a strong Secretary of State prevents it. But, unfortunately, to expect a strong and just Secretary of State on behalf of Indian Interests is a rare good fortune of India, because he changes so often and is mostly in the hand of the Anglo-Indian members of his Council and other Anglo-Indian officials of the India Office. If any Committee or Commission really want to know the whole truth, they must do what the Committee of 1772 did—to have "every" document on the subject under consideration to be produced before them. What an exposure that Committee of 1772 made of the most outrageous, most corrupt, and most tyrannical misconduct of the Government and officials of the day.

I may also mention that the despatch of the Duke of Argyll (10th March, 1870, Financial), to which I have already referred, has also not been given in the Return.

Of course, I am not surprised at these suppressions. It is our fate, and the usual ways of a despotic regime. But why I mention this is that the public are misled and are unable to know the true state of a case in which Indian interests are involved; the public cannot evolve these suppressions from their inner consciousness.

And still the outside public and the non-official witnesses are sometimes blamed for not supplying criticisms on the statements made by the officials of Government!

Again, there is the despatch of Lord Salisbury of 10th February, 1876, not given in the Return. Sir E. Perry, referring to this despatch, says:—

"Lord Salisbury decided the matter once for all in his despatch of 10th February, 1876, Financial, in which he quoted the Duke of Argyll's despatch of 1870 *(Supra)*, and after stating that he concurred in the views thus expressed, he proceeded to lay down precise rules by which the appointment of Englishmen in India to the higher Uncovenanted offices should in future be restricted."

Now, I cannot say whether all these suppressed documents were satisfactory or not, or whether they are published in some other place; but when the India Office omits such information in a Return on the subject itself, what are we to do? And if we criticise upon imperfect information, the authorities come down upon us denouncing in all sorts of ways for our wrong statements, exaggerations, inaccuracies, and what not.

The next despatch that the Return gives is that of the Government of India of 2nd May, 1878. It was in connexion with this dispatch that Lord Lytton wrote a note dated 30th May. In this note he had the courage to expose the whole character of the conduct of Indian authorities in both countries since the passing of the Act of 1833, denouncing that conduct as consisting of deliberate, transparent subterfuges, and dishonourable, as making promises to the ear and breaking them to the hope. Here are Lord Lytton's own words, referring to the Act of 1833 :—

"The Act of Parliament is so undefined, and indefinite obligations on the part of the Government of India towards its Native subjects are so obviously dangerous, that no sooner was the Act passed than the Government "began to devise means for practically evading the fulfilment of it." Under the terms of Act which are studied and laid to heart by that increasing class of educated Natives whose development the Government encourages, without being able to satisfy the aspirations of its existing members, every such Native if once admitted to Government employment in posts previously reserved to the Covenanted Service is entitled to expect and claim appointment in the fair course of promotion to the highest post in that service.

"We all know that these claims and expectations never can or will be fulfilled. We have had to choose between prohibiting them and cheating them: and we have chosen the last straightforward course. The application to Natives of the competitive examination system as conducted in England, and the recent reduction in the age at which candidates can compete, are all so many deliberate and transparent subterfuges for stultifying the Act and reducing it to a dead letter. Since I am writing confidentially I do not hesitate to say that both the Governments of England and of India appear to me, up to the present moment, unable to answer satisfactorily the charge of having taken every means in their power of breaking to the heart the words of promise they had uttered to the ear."

I admire the English candour and courage with which this humiliating confession is made. But I protest that so far as the people, the Parliament and the Sovereign are concerned, it is an injustice to them to put the dishonour and the disgrace of subterfuges to their charge. It is a libel upon the statesmen of 1833, that they said so many deliberate falsehoods intentionally when they contended for the justification of the clause for equality in such noble and generous and English spirit and terms. It is a gross libel on the Sovereign and the people of this country that the Proclamation of 1858, so solemnly promulgated, calling God to witness and to help, was all hypocrisy, an intentional mockery and delusion. I protest against this assumption. The truth I believe to be is that the Sovereign, the Parliament and the people of this country sincerely meant what they said—but that their servants, the executive authorities in both countries, uncontrollable and free to follow their own devices in their original spirit of selfishness and oppression with which they commenced their rule in India, frustrated the highest and noblest desires of the Sovereign and the people by "deliberate and transparent subterfuges to attain their own selfish ends"—which on one occasion an Anglo-Indian very *naively* confessed in these remarkable words. In a debate at the Society of Arts, 19th February, 1892, upon Siam, Sir Charles Grossthwaite said:—

"The real question was who was to get the trade with them, and how we could make the most of them so as to find fresh markets for our goods and "also employment for those superfluous articles of the present day," *our boys*". So the whole reason of the existence of the world is market for British capitalists and employment for "*our boys.*"

In India, this greed for the monopolising of profits of trade, and of the employment of "our boys," is the chief key to the system of all the actions of an unsympathetic, selfish rule as it is at present made by the executive authorities. Not that it need be so. A righteous system can be adopted, as many a statesman has declared, by which both England and India may be blessed and benefited, and for which purpose the Indians have been crying all along in the wilderness. Let the saddle of the present evil system be on the right horse. The Sovereign, the Parliament and the people have done all that could be desired. The only misfortune is that they do not see to their noble wishes and orders being carried out, and leave their servants to "bleed" India of all that is most dear and necessary to the human existence and advancement—wealth, wisdom and work—material and prosperity. Reverting to Lord Lytton's true confession, that the executives have "cheated" and "subterfuged," frustrated and dishonoured all Acts and Resolutions of Parliament and the most solemn Proclamations of the Sovereign, one would think that after such confessions some amends will be made by a more honourable course. Far from it. This despatch of 2nd May, 1878, will remain one of the darkest sections in this sad story instead of any contrition or reparation for the past evil.

What did the Government propose in this despatch? To destroy everything that is dearest to the Indian heart—his two great Charters of 1833 and 1858, the Act of a partial justice of 1870—to murder in cold blood the whole political existence of equality of Indians as British citizens which—at least by law, if not by deed or action of the authorities—they possessed, and make them the *hsparia* of the high public service.

Mark! by the Act of 1870, the Indians were to have a distinct proportion of appointments (which was fixed by the Government of India to be about one-fifth, or about 7 every year) in the *Covenanted Civil Service*—, which meant that in the course of 25 to 30 years, the duration of the service of each person, there would gradually be about 180 to 200 Indians admitted into the Covenanted Civil Service. This was most a bitter pill for the Anglo-Indians, official and non-official, to swallow. The Government resorted to every subterfuge to ignore and with passive resistance to make the Act a dead letter. This not succeeding, they deliberately proposed to throw aside all Acts, Resolutions, and Proclamations—all pledges and laws of equality—and to establish a "close Native Civil Service" that is to say to deprive the Natives once and for ever of any claim to the whole higher Covenanted Services, and *by law* shut up in a lazaretto of a miserable close service.

And what was to be *this close* service? Not even to the extent to which the Act of 1870 led to the hope of the share in the Covenanted Civil Service—but only to propose to assign certain fixed appointments now held by the Covenanted Service, and to rob the Uncovenanted Service of some of their appointments to cast them into this service; that is to say, in reality to make a "pariah" service of a small number of Covenanted Service employments—about 90 or so (the Uncovenanted being alrealy the Indian's own)—in place of what the Act of 1870 would have entitled them, to the extent of 180 or more, and to be eligible to the *whole* Covenanted Service employment; and what is still worse, and exhibits the inner spirit, that even this miserable so-called "close" service was not to be entirely reserved for the

Indians, but, as I understand, a door is left open for Europeans also to get into it. And still more, the Government of India so mercilessly wanted to put the badge and stamp of inferiority and exclusion upon the Indians at large and rob them of their only consolation, their only hope and charter, that they already possessed by law and by pledges, of equality of British citizenship with the British subjects of this country. But there is something still worse: the Government cooly proposed not only not to give them simultaneous examinations in India, but to deprive them even of the right they now possess of competing for the Covenanted Service in this country itself.

Were the Government of India gone mad? The Government of India said, in cold blood, that "the ordinary Covenanted Civil Service should no longer be open to Natives;" thus proposing insidiously that the Acts of 1833 and 1870 and the Proclamation should be thrown to the winds. So these Acts and the Proclamations of the Sovereign upon which hangs all our devoted loyalty, all our hopes and aspirations (though in all conscience most mercilessly disregarded) all that is at all good and great in the British name in India, all that is to be swept away by a new un-British and tyrannical legislation! The whole despatch is so distressful, so full of false blandishments, that I cannot venture to say anything more about it. The wonder is that on the one hand Lord Lytton exposes the "subterfuges" and dishonour of the Executive, and himself and his colleagues sign such a despatch of 2nd May, 1878. And what is still more curious is this; about seventeen months before this despatch, on 1st January, 1877, at the Delhi Assemblage, on the assumption of the title of Empress of India, Lord Lytton on behalf of Her Majesty said:—

"But you the Natives of India, whatever your race and whatever your creed, have a recognised claim to share *largely* with your English fellow-subjects according to your capacity for the task, in the administry of the country you inhabit. *This claim is founded on the highest justice.* It has been repeatedly affirmed by British and Indian statesmen and by the legislation of the Imperial Parliament. It is recognised by the Government of India as binding on its honour and consistent with all the aims of its policy;" and all such "highest justice" and all this "binding on honour" ended in this extraordinary despatch of 2nd May, 1878! It is the most dismal page in the whole melancholy affair about the Covenanted Service.

But the further misfortune is that since the despatch of 2nd May, 1878, the whole heart and soul of the Government is directed in the spirit of the despatch, and though they have not attempted to alter legislation, they have by persistence and devices most ingeniously carried out their own object, and made the Acts of 1833 and 1870, and the great Proclamations, more shams and delusions. With trumpet tongues they have proclaimed to the world that the miserable "*close* service" was an extraordinary and generous concession, when in reality we are plundered of what we already possessed by the Act of 1870, and our political position is reduced to the condition of political pariahs.

I do not enter here into a discussion of the un-English and subtle procedure by which we are deprived of the so-called "statutory service," which had secured for us no less than a complete and free admission into the whole Covenanted Civil Service, to the number which had been at the time considered for a beginning as a fair proportion of about one-sixth or one-fifth of the total number of this service.

There is one other important reason why I do not pursue any more the criticisms upon this despatch. The Secretary of State himself found it impossible to swallow it, summarily disposed of its fallacies, hollowness, brushed it aside, and insisted upon carrying out the Act of 1870.

Now before going further, I have to request the commission to bear in mind that the Government of India had, by this despatch, most earnestly and laboriously committed themselves to a "close Native service," and it will be seen that they bided their time and left no stone unturned, by any means whatever, to attain ultimately their object.

As I have said above, Lord Cranbrook, the then Secretary of State, would not swallow the preposterous despatch, and put down his foot against such openly violating all honourable and solemn pledges of the Sovereign and Acts of Parliament.

Lord Cranbrook in his despatch of 7th November, 1878, said in reply :—

"6. But your proposal of a close Native service with a limited class of high appointments attached to it, and your suggestions that the Covenanted Civil Service should no longer be open to Natives, involve an application to Parliament which would have no prospect of success, and which I certainly would not undertake. Your lordship has yourself observed that no scheme would have a chance of sanction which included legislation for the purpose of repealing the clause in the Act of 1833 above quoted, and the obstacles which would be presented against any attempt to exclude Natives from public competition for the Civil Service would be little less formidable.

"10. It is, therefore, quite competent to your lordship's Government to appoint every year to the Civil Service of India any such number of Natives as may be determined upon, and the number of Covenanted civilians sent out from this country will have to be proportionately decreased. The appointments should in the first instance, be only probationary, so as to give ample time for testing the merit and ability of the candidates.

"11. It appears to me that the advantages of such a simple scheme will be obvious :—

"(i) It will undoubtedly be much more popular with the Natives, as it will place them on a footing of social equality with the Covenanted civilian.

"(ii) Inasmuch as it will exclude no civilian at present in India from any office which he has a moral claim to expect it will avoid any clashing with the vested interests of the Civil Service.

"(iii) It will avoid the necessity of any enhancement of salaries of Uncovenanted officers which is now proposed, not because such enhancement is necessary, but from the necessity of creating a class of well-paid appointments to form sufficient prizes for a close Native service.

"And lastly, it pursues the same system of official training which has proved so eminently successful in India."

Thus foiled in the monstrous attempt to inflict upon the Indians the most serious political disaster, the Government of India whined and lay low to wait their opportunity, and as compelled, and with bad grace, made the required rules one year after the despatch of 2nd May, 1878.

With their despatch of 1st May, 1879, the Government of India sent the rules, and explained in para. 8 of the despatch the proportion of Indians they proposed to select :

"The proposed statutory Rules, in brief, provide that a proportion not exceeding one-sixth of all the recruits added to the Civil Service in any one year shall be Natives selected in India by the local Governments."

I give here the rules proposed :

"No. 18.

"RULES for the APPOINTMENT OF NATIVES OF INDIA to offices ordinarily held by members of Her Majesty's Covenanted Civil Service in India.

"In exercise of the power conferred by the Statute 33 Vict., chap. 3, section 6, the Governor-General in Council has been pleased to make the following rules, which have been sanctioned by the Secretary of State in Council with the concurrence of a majority of members present:—

"I.—Each Local Government may nominate persons who are Natives of India within the meaning of the said Act, for employment in Her Majesty's Covenanted Civil Service in India within the territories subordinate to such Government. Such nominations shall be made not later than the first day of October in each year. No person shall be nominated for employment in the said service after he has attained the age of twenty-five years, except on grounds of merit and ability proved in the service of Government, or in the practice of a profession.

"II.--Nominations under the foregoing rule shall, if approved by the Governor-General in Council, be provisionally sanctioned by him. The total number of nominations so sanctioned in any year shall not exceed one-fifth of the total number of recruits appointed by Her Majesty's Secretary of State to the said service in such year; provided that the total number of such nominations sanctioned in each of the years 1879, 1880, and 1881 may exceed the said proportion by two. On sanction being given by the Governor-General in Council the nominee shall be admitted on probation to employment in the said service; such admission may be confirmed by the Governor-General in Council but shall not be so confirmed until the Local Government have reported to the Governor-General in Council that the probationer has acquitted himself satisfactorily during a period of not less than two years from the date of his admission, and that he has, unless specially exempted by the Governor-General in Council, passed such examinations as may from time to time be prescribed by the Local Government subject to the approval of the Governor-General in Council. In case of persons admitted under these rules after they have attained the age of twenty-five years, the Governor-General in Council may confirm their admission without requiring them to serve for any period of probation.

"III.—Persons admitted under these rules to employment in the said service shall not, without the previous sanction of the Governor-General in Council in each case, be appointed to any of the undermentioned offices, namely:—

"Members of a Board of Revenue.

"Secretaries to the several Governments and Administrations in India.

"Chief Magisterial, or Chief Revenue, Officers of Districts.

"Commissioners of Divisions, or of Revenue.

"IV.—Persons admitted under these rules to employment in the said service shall ordinarily be appointed only to offices in the province wherein they were first admitted. But the Governor-General in Council may transfer from one province to another a person finally admitted to employment in the said service.

"V.—Any person admitted under these rules may, with the previous sanction of the Governor-General in Council, be declared by the Local Government to be disqualified for further employment in the said service."

Two comments suggest themselves with regard to these rules—when read with the light that the Government of India's whole heart was in the "close Native service"— and that, therefore, to carry out loyally the Act of 1870 was naturally against their grain.

At the very beginning they began to nibble at the Statute of 1870 and proposed in Rule III, not to put Natives on the same footing with Europeans with regard to all high offices. On this unworthy device I need not comment, as the Secretary of State himself struck out this Rule III, without much ceremony.

Now, whether intentionally or unintentionally, the rules had been so framed that had the Government of India sat down to devise the most effective means of bringing discredit and failure on the service under the Act of 1870, they could not have done better or worse than these rules. These Indian civilians were to be the colleagues of and to do the duties with the best educated and severely tested (educationally, physically, and morally) English youths. Particular care was taken not to prescribe any systematic compulsory rules for such high test and for obtaining recruits worthy of being included in such a highly trained service as the Covenanted Civil Service, of which these Indians were to be an integral part and in which service they were to be exactly on the same footing as English civilians. This was the crux and spirit of the whole matter; the rules simply made the matter one of patronage and back-door influence. It needs no stretch of the imagination to see that such a course could lead only to one result, as it has always done, *viz.*, failure. It was absurd to expect that such Indian civilians should prove as successful and efficient as the English civilians so well prepared. This was the first covert blow given by the Government of India at the very birth of the operation of the Act of 1870, and unfortunately Lord Cranbrook did not see his ingenious device.

The Commission can hardly realise the intensity of the gratitude of the Indians to Sir Stafford Northcote for proposing, and the Duke of Argyll for passing, the clause in the Act of 1870, and not less intense was their gratitude to Lord Cranbrook and to Sir Erskine Perry who co-operated with him, for the determination with which Lord Cranbrook overcame all strenuous opposition and the blandishments of the Government of India of their own good-will and justice to the Indians; and he compelled that Government to give effect to the Act of 1870.

The clause was at last given effect to, though with great reluctance and under compulsion, after ten long years. This is generally the case. For all Indian interests the officials always require long and most careful and most mature consideration, till by lapse of time the question dies. Under Lord Cranbrook this clause had better fortune, but only to end in utter and more bitter disappointment to the Indians, and to add one more dishonour to the British name. The first appointments under the clause, though after a delay of ten years, again infused a new life of loyalty and hope in the justice of British people, throughout the length and breadth of India. It was a small instalment, but it was a practical instalment, and the first instalment of actual justice. And it was enough, for an ever disappointed and unjustly treated people, to rejoice, and more so for the future hope of more justice and of righteous rule, little foreseeing to what bitter disappointment they were to be doomed in the course of the next ten years! The first appointments were made under the rules in 1880. Now, we come to the next melancholy stage.

The immediate development of the compulsion on the Government of India to carry out the clause of 1870—coupled with the fear of the possible effect of the despatch of Sir Stafford Northcote of 8th February, 1868, to restrict employment of Europeans to those only who pass the examination here, and to insist upon the inherent rights of the Indians to all appointments—was to produce a sullenness of feeling and great vexation among the Anglo-Indian body generally (with, of course, honourable and noble exceptions).

I do not enter, as I have already said, upon the latter question of the Uncovenanted Service. I mention it here simply because it added to the anger of the Anglo-Indians against the noble policy of men like Sir Stafford Northcote. I confine myself to the said story about the admission of Indians in the Covenanted Civil Service.

Well, the so-called "statutory" service was launched in 1880. It was called by a distinctive name "statutory" as if the whole Covenanted Service was not also a "statutory" service, and as if the clause of 1870 was not simply for full admission into the whole Covenanted Service. But what is in a name? The Government of India knew the value of creating and giving a distinct name to the service so that they may with greater ease kill it as a separate service; and at last, kill it they did. The Anglo-Indians, official and non-official, were full charged with sullenness and anger, and with the spark of the "Ilbert Bill" the conflagration burst out.

Here I may point out how shrewdly Lord Salisbury, while fully approving the clause of 1870, had prophesied the coming storm. On the debate on the clause in 1870. Lord Salisbury had said :—

"Another most important matter is the admission of Natives to employments under the Government of India. I think the plan of the noble Duke contained in this Bill is, I believe, the most satisfactory solution of a very difficult question."

And after so fully accepting the clause, he said :—

"One of the most serious dangers you have to guard against is the possibility of *jealousy* arising from the introduction of Natives into the service."

Owing to this jealousy ten years elapsed before any action was taken on the Act of 1870, and that even *under compulsion* by Lord Cranbrook. Before three years after this effect was given to the clause, Lord Salisbury's prophecy. was fulfilled. Explosion burst out over the Ilbert Bill.

I cannot enter here into the various phases of the excitement on that occasion, the bitter war that raged for some time against Indian interests. I content myself with some extracts from the expression of Lord Hartington (the Duke of Devonshire) upon the subject. It clearly proves the action of the *jealousy* of the Anglo-

Indians. Lord Hartington said (speech, House of Commons, August 23, 1883) :—

"It may by some be thought sufficient to say, that the Anglo-Indian, whatever may be his merits, and no doubt they are great, is not a person who is distinguished by an exceptionally calm judgment."

Hansard, Vol. 283, p. 1818.
August 23rd, 1883.

"I could quote passages in letters in the Indian papers in which it is admitted that the agitation was directed against the policy of the Home Government in providing appointments for Native civilians while there are many Europeans without appointments. . . . . I believe that the cause of the prevalent excitement is to be found, not in this measure, but in the general course of policy that has been pursued both by this Government and the late Government. It has been the policy of Government for some years past to impress upon the Government of India the desirability of obtaining the assistance of the Native population as far as possible in the government of that country. Over and over again that policy has been inculcated from home. In 1879, a Resolution was passed which limited appointment of the value of Rs. 200 a month to officers of the army and to Natives. That restriction has been rightly enforced, and has met with "all kinds of opposition from non-official classes of Europeans, who think that all the appointments must be reserved for them." The same spirit was shown when it was determined that admission to the Engineering College at Roorki should be confined to Natives. . . . . Agitation of the same character has been seen before when there was just as little foundation for it. Lord Macaulay, Lord Canning, and other Anglo-Indian statesmen experienced the same kind of opposition from Anglo-Indians; but all these reproaches have recoiled, not against the statesmen with regard to whom they were uttered, but against the persons uttering themselves. . . , .

"There is a further reason, in my opinion, why this policy should be adopted, and that is that it is not wise to educate the people of India, to introduce among them your civilisation and your progress and your literature, and at the same time to tell them they shall never have any chance of taking any part or share in the administration of the affairs of their country, except by their getting rid, in the first instance, of their European rulers. Surely, it would not be wise to tell a patriotic Native of India that. . . .

"Whatever difference of opinion there may be, there can, in my opinion, be very little doubt that India is insufficiently governed at the present time. I believe there are many districts in India in which the number of officials is altogether insufficient, and that is owing to the fact that the Indian revenue would not bear the strain if a sufficient number of Europeans were appointed. The Government of India cannot afford to spend more than they do in the administration of the country, " and if the country is to be better governed that can only be done by the employment of the best and most intelligent of the Natives in the service."

It was on this occasion that Lord Salisbury made the confession that all the pledges, proclamations, and Acts to which Lord Northbrook had referred was all "political hypocrisy." The reasons which Lord Salisbury assigned were not accurate, but I cannot strike off into a new controversy now. It is enough for me to say that, as I have already said, I protest against placing this "hypocrisy" at the door of the people, Parliament, and Sovereign of this country. It lies on the head of the servants, the executives in both countries. It is they who would ruin the Empire by their "hypocrisy" and selfishness.

At last, however, the agitation of the Ilbert Bill subsided. The eruption of the volcano of the Anglo-Indian hearts stopped, but the anger and vexation continued boiling within as the cause of the explosion still remained. And the Government of India were biding their time to carry out that most un-English scheme of the despatch of 2nd May, 1879, to create a *pariah* lazaretto to consign these *pariahs* thereto.

Owing to the persistence of Lord Cranbrook the appointments under the Act of 1870 had begun in 1880, and continued to be made, *i.e.*, about six or seven Indians continued to be admitted in the Covenanted

Civil Service. The main cause of the explosion having continued, and the Government of India having set its heart upon its own scheme, a new departure and development now arose. The question at the bottom was how to knock the "statutory service" on the head, and put down effectively the cry for simultaneous examinations. The explosion under the excuse of the Ilbert Bill did not effect that object, and so, according to Lord Lytton's confession of the general conduct of the Executive, something also should be done.

We now enter upon the next stage of this sad story. I shall place some facts and any fair-minded Englishman will be able to draw his own conclusions. Before I do so certain preliminary explanation is necessary.

In India, when the authorities are decided upon certain views which are not likely to be readily accepted by the public, a Commission or Committee comes into existence. The members are mostly officials or ex-officials—English or Indians. Some non-officials, English or Indians or both, are sometimes thrown in, selected by the Government itself. It is a well understood thing that in all matters officials are bound always to take and support the Government views. The ex-officials are understood to be bound by gratitude to do the same. If anyone takes an independent line, either in a Commission or Committee, or in his own official capacity, and displeases the Government, I cannot undertake to say with instances what happens.

Perhaps, some Anglo-Indians themselves may feel the sense of duty to supply some instances from their own experience. Almost by accident an instance has just come back before me in the *Champion*, of Bombay, and which gives the incident almost in the author's (Mr. Robert H. Elliot) words : " Mr. Geddes came before the Finance Committee (1871-74), and that the members thought it well worth examining him is evidenced by the fact that he was examined at very great length. Here was a chance for Duff : he thought he would do a very clever thing, and as Mr. Geddes had introduced into his financial pamphlet some views of rather a novel description, and had, besides, made use of some rather out-of-the-way illustrations, this gave a good opportunity for putting questions in such a way as was calculated to cast ridicule on Mr. Geddes, and depreciate the value of the important points he had brought out. But this was far from being all. It was intimated pretty plainly to Mr. Geddes that his opinions ought to be in harmony with the Government he served, and here Mr. Geddes said that he certainly ought to be in harmony with the Government if there was any spirit of harmony in it. Mr. Geddes was clearly not to be put down, and Duff thought he would try something more severe. 'You hold an appointment in the Government, do you not?' 'Yes,' said Mr. Geddes. 'And do you expect to return to that post?' asked Duff. 'Now, my dear John,' continues the author, you will not find that question in the report, for the simple reason that it was ordered to be expunged." Would some Anglo-Indian kindly give us some information of what afterwards became of Mr. Geddes ? I would not trouble the Commission with my own treatment before the same Committee, which was anything but fair, because, like Mr. Geddes, I had something novel to say. I would only add that an important and pointed evidence of Lord Lawrence, on the wretchedness and extreme poverty of India, was also suppressed in the Report.

The officials have therefore to bear in mind to be in harmony with Government or think of their posts—and I suppose the ex-officials have also to bear in mind that there is such a thing as pension.

Here is one more instance. When Mr. Hyndman published his "Bankruptcy of India," Mr. Caird at once wrote to the *Times* contradicting him. The India Office soon after sent him to preside over the Famine Commission. He, though at first much prejudiced by Anglo-Indian views, and going to bless the Government, returned cursing. He made a report on the condition of India, and that being contrary to official views, O! how Government laboured to discredit him!

Lastly, Commissions or Committees report what they like. If they are in the expected harmony with Government, all is well. But anything which Government does not want or is contrary to its views is brushed aside. Reports of Commissions must be in harmony with the views of the Government. If not, so much the worse for the Commissioners; and this is what has actually happened with the Public Service Commission, which I am now going to touch upon as the next stage in this sad history of the fate of Indians for services in their own country.

When I came here in 1886, I paid a visit to Lord Kimberley, the Secretary of State for India. I had been favoured with more than an hour's conversation, mainly on the two topics of "statutory service" and simultaneous examinations, and I found him a *determined*, decided opponent to both, and completely, to our misfortune, saturated with Anglo-Indian views—not seeming to realise at all the Indian side. He urged to me all the Anglo-Indian stock arguments, and I saw what he was really aiming at—the very thing which Lord Cranbrook had summarily rejected—the scheme of the Government of India of the despatch of 2nd May, 1878, the close service.

From that interview I saw clearly what the "Public Service Commission" was for—that the abolition of the "statutory" service, the suppression of the cry for simultaneous examinations, and the adoption of the scheme of 2nd May, 1878, were determined, foregone conclusions.

Soon after my conversation with Lord Kimberley, I happened to be on the same boat with Sir Charles Turner on my way to Bombay. Sir Charles Turner was going out by appointment by Lord Kimberley to join the Public Service Commission. I at once prepared a short memorandum, and gave it to him. Afterwards, in the course of the conversation, he told me that he had certain instructions from Lord Kimberley. Sir Charles Turner, of course, could not tell me, whatever they may have been. But I could not help forming my own conclusions from what I had myself learnt from Lord Kimberley himself in my conversation with him. Sir Charles Aitchison was the President of the Commission, and he, as Lieutenant-Governor of the Punjab, made a representation to the Commission, in which he expressed his clear opposition to the simultaneous examinations. About the "statutory" service he had already most strongly objected two years before the appointment of the Commission, in a very inaccurate and hasty argument and on very imperfect information. In a country like India, governed under a despotism, where, under present circumstances, service under and favour of Government is to many the all in all, what effect must declarations of the head of the province, and the well-known decided views of the Government itself, produce upon the invited witness—not only official, but non-official also—can hardly be realised by Englishmen, who have their government in their own hands.

The third important member's—Sir Charles Crossthwaite—view, as I have already indicated, seemed the anxiety about "our boys."

There were among the members of the Commission—

8 European officials.
1 Indian official.
3 Indian ex-officials.
1 Non-official European, the General Secretary of the Behar Indigo Planters' Association. (It would be worth while to know what share the planters had taken in the Ilbert Bill agitation.)
1 Eurasian.
2 Indian non-officials, one of whom, I think, never attended the Commission till it met for Report.

Mr. Kazi Shahabu-din, before he joined the Comission, distinctly told me that he was dead against both questions, "statutory" and simultaneous. It was all very good, he said to me, to *talk* of eternal principles and justice and all that, but he was determined not to allow the Hindus to advance. The views of Sir Syed Ahmad Khan were no secret as being against simultaneous examinations and statutory service. I am informed that Mr. Nuhlkar and Mr. Mudliar were sorry for their action in joining in the Report, and Mr. Romesh Chandra Mitra has, I think, expressed some repudiation of his connection with the Report of the Commission. The Raja of Bhinga only joined the Commission at the Report.

Our misfortune was, as I saw at that time, the three Hindu members did not, I think, fully realise how a deathblow was being struck at the future political and administrative advance and aspirations of the Indians; and how, by an insidious and subtle stroke all pledges and Acts of Parliament, and Proclamations—the very breath of our political life—the hope and anchor of our aspirations and advance were being undermined and swept away. I have also already pointed out the *determination* of the Government of India since their letter of 2nd May, 1878, not only to stop further advance, but even to take away what they, the Indians, already had.

I was a witness before this Commission. I fully expected that as I was considered one of the chief complainants in these matters, I would be severely examined and turned inside out. But the Commission, to my surprise, carried on with me more of an academical dabate than a serious practical examination, and seemed wishful to get rid of me quickly, so much so, that I was forced to request that a Memorandum which I had placed before them should be added to my evidence on several points.

I may here explain that simultaneous examinations was by far the most important matter, and, if granted, would have dispensed with the necessity of the "statutory" service. The chief fight was for simultaneous examinations.

First, as far as the "statutory" service is concerned here is the extraordinary result. In the instructions, the object of the Commission was stated, "broadly speaking," "to devise a scheme which may reasonably be hoped to possess the necessary elements of *finality*, and to do *full justice* to the claims of the Natives of India *to higher and more extensive* employment in the public service"; and in this the Governor-General in Council fully and cordially agreed.

This was the promise, and what is the performance? The admission of one-sixth Indians into the Covenanted Service we already possessed by law—and in operation. We were already eligible to all Uncovenanted Services. Full justice, and still higher and more extensive employment were promised—and what did we actually get? We were deprived of what we already by law (of 1870) possessed; and instead of giving us "full justice" it deprived us of all our hopes and aspirations to be admitted to an equality of employment with British officials; and we were coolly, mercilessly, despotically, and illegally consigned to a small pariah service, open to Europeans also—which had been *already schemed and firmly determined upon ten years before* in the despatch of 2nd May, 1878—in utter and dishonourable violation of the Acts of 1833 and 1870, and three gracious Proclamations. This is the way in which the Public Service Commission has carried out its object to devise a scheme to possess elements of finality and to do full justice to the claims of the Natives to *higher* and *more extensive* employment in the public service.

Now, with regard to simultaneous examinations, the conduct of the Public Service Commission seems to be still more extraordinary. Why they actually reported as far as I can see, in opposition to the weight of evidence, I cannot understand. Mr. William Digby has analysed the evidence in a letter to Lord Cross, of 8th May, 1889, and I append that part of his letter. I asked the Secretary of State to inform me whether Mr. Digby's analysis was correct or not, but the information was not given me.

There is again a curious coincidence between the action of Lord Lytton and Lord Dufferin which I may intervene here.

Of Lord Lytton I have already mentioned about the contrast between his speech at the Delhi Durbar in January, 1877, and his action in the despatch of 2nd May, 1878.

On 4th October, 1886, was started the Public Service Commission, and in the beginning of the very next year, 1887, on the occasion of the Jubilee, Lord Dufferin said in his Jubilee speech :—

"Wide and broad, indeed are the new fields in which, the Government of India is called upon to labour, but no longer as afore-time need it labour alone. Within the period we are reviewing, education has done its work, and we are surrounded on all sides, by Native gentlemen of great attainments and intelligence, from whose hearty, loyal, and honest co-operation we may hope to derive the greatest benefit. In fact, to an administration so peculiarly situated as ours, "their advice, assistance, and solidarity are essential to the successful exercise of its functions." Nor do I regard with any other feelings than those of approval and good-will their natural ambition to be more extensively associated with their English rulers in the administration of their own domestic affairs."

At the same time the Empress of India thus emphasises her great Proclamation of 1858 :—

"It had always been, and will always be, her earnest desire to maintain unswervingly the principles laid down in the Proclamation published on her assumption of the direct control of the Government of India."

And these two declarations of hope and justice came to what end? Within two years, as I have already said, Lord Cross, with a ruthless hand, snatched away from us the small instalment of justice which Sir S. Northcote had done to us, consigned us to a small "pariah service," and destroyed virtually all our charters and aspirations.

I now come to the last dark section of this sad chapter, which also shows that, to our misfortune, we have had nothing but bitter disappointments—since 1833—nothing but "subterfuges" and "political hypocrisy" up to the present day.

Propose anything for the benefit of Europeans and it is done at once. The Royal Engineering College at Coopers Hill and the Exchange Compensation Allowance are two notorious instances, the latter especially heartless and despotic. The Government of India has distinctly admitted that the compensation is illegal. It knew also that it would be a heartless act towards the poverty-stricken people of India. But, of course, when European interests are concerned, legality and heart go to the winds; despotism and force are the only lay and argument. Here is another curious incident connected both with examinations and Europeans.

As I have already placed before the Commission my papers on the entire exclusion of Indians from military and naval examinations, either here or in India, I will not say anything more. The curious incident is this:—

The War Office would not admit Indians to examinations even in this country, and on no account simultaneously in India. But they allowed Europeans to be examined directly in India. St. George College, Massoori, examined its boys. A boy named Roderick O' Connor qualified for Sandhurst from the college in 1893. Two boys named Herbert Roddy and Edwin Roddy had also passed from that college.

On 2nd June, 1893, the House of Commons passed the Resolution to have simultaneous examinations in England and India for all the services for which the examinations are at present held in England alone.*

Had such a Resolution been passed for any other department of State it would have never dared to offer resistance to it. But with unfortunate India the case is quite different.

The Resolution of 2nd June, 1893, having been carried, the Under-Secretary of State for India (Mr. Russell said (*Hansard*, vol. 17, p. 1035): "It may be in the recollection of the House that in my official capacity it was my duty earlier in the Session to oppose a Resolution in favour of simultaneous examinations. But the House of Commons thought differently from the Government. *That once done* I need hardly say that *there is no disposition on the part of the Secretary of State for India or myself to thwart or defeat the effect of the vote of the House of Commons* on that Resolution.

"We have consulted the Government of India, and have asked them as "to the way" in which the Resolution of the House "can best be carried out." It is a matter too important to be carried out without the advice of the Indian Government, and at present impossible to state explicitly what will be done."

Now, the Commission will observe that the Government of India was to be consulted as to *the way* in which

---

* "All open competitive examinations heretofore held in England alone for appointments to the Civil Services of India shall henceforth be held simultaneous both in India and England, such examinations in both countries being identical in their nature, and all who compete being finanlly classified in one list according to merit."

the Resolution was to *be best carried out, and not as to whether it was to be carried out or not nor to thwart or defeat it.* What did the Prime Minister (Mr. Gladstone) say:

"The question is a very important one, and has received the careful consideration of Government. That have determined that the Resolution of the House should be referred to the Government of India without delay, and that there should be a prompt and careful examination of the subject by that Government, who "are instructed" to say in "what mode" in their opinion, and under what conditions and limitations the Resolution 'could be carried into effect."

It must be observed again that the Government of India were to be instructed to say *by what mode the Resolution could be carried into effect.*

After such declarations by two important officials what did the Secretary of State do?

Did he loyally confine himself to these declarations? We know that Lord Kimberley (who was then the Secretary of State) was dead against simultaneous examinations. He knew full well that the Government of India was well known to the world *to be as dead against any such interest of the Indians.* Sir James Peile in his minute even said as much. And yet in a very clever way, the Indian Office adds a sentence to its despatch, virtually telling the Government of India to resist altogether. The last sentence added to the despatch was:—

"3. I will only point out that it is indispensable that an adequate number of the members of the Civil Service shall always be Europeans and that no scheme would be admissible which does not fulfil that essential condition."

And further, that there should remain no doubt of the real intention of this sentence, six members of the Council wrote vehement minutes emphatically indicating that the Government of India should resist—not obey the instruction as to what mode should be adopted to carry out the Resolution. And thus, knowing full well what the Government of India's views were, knowing also that the Resolution was passed *notwithstanding the opposition of the Government*; knowing also that Mr. Russell had distinctly told the House of the acceptance by the Government of what the House decided, and promising on behalf of the Secretary of State, as well as himself, *not to thwart or defeat the Resolution*, Lord Kimberley sent the Indian lamb back to the Government wolf, as if the Resolution of the House was not of the slightest consequence, and the Governments here and in India were supreme and above the House of Commons. They had always done this for two-thirds of a century to every Act or Resolution of Parliament, or the Sovereign's Proclamations.

With such open suggestion and encouragement from the Secretary of State and his councillors, and with their own firm determination not to allow the advancement of the Natives by simultaneous examination—even having only lately snatched away from the hands of the Indians the little instalment of justice that was made by Sir Stafford Northcote and the Duke of Argyll, and was approved by Lord Salisbury—what could be expected in reply to such a despatch. Of course, the Government of India resisted with a will, tooth and nail, as they had always done.

At first, the Government of Madras was one for justice. And then, in the vicious circle in which all Indian interests are usually cleverly entangled, the Government here made that very resistance of the Indian Government a subterfuge and excuse for itself—that as the Government of India refuses they could not carry out the Resolution! And the House of Commons had, as usual on Indian matters, one more disregard and insult.

And thus was one more disappointment—the bitterest of all the 64 years of disappointments the people of India have suffered. And yet there are men who raise up their hands in wonder that there should be any dissatisfaction among the Indians, when they themselves are the very creators of this discontent and great suffering.

I have referred to Lord Kimberley's actions, which showed how he was actuated from the very beginning. Now even *before* the despatch was sent to India, Lord Kimberley himself showed his full hand and let the Government of India know, by anticipation, his entire resistance to the Resolution within nine days of the passing of the Resolution on 2nd June, 1893, and ten days *before* the despatch was sent to India. He said (dinner to Lord Roberts by the Lord Mayor—*Times*, 13th June, 1893) :—

"There is one point upon which I imagine, whatever may be our party politics in this country, we are all united ; that we are resolutely determined to maintain our supremacy over our Indian Empire. That I conceive is a matter about which we have only one opinion, and let me tell you that that supremacy rests upon three distinct bases. One of those bases, and a very important one, is the loyalty and good-will of the Native Princes and population over whom we rule. Next, and not less important, is the maintenance of our "European" Civil Service, upon which rests the foundation of our administration in India. . . . Last, not because it is the least, but because I wish to give it the greatest prominence, we rest also upon the magnificent European force which we maintain in that country, and the splendid army of Native auxiliaries by which that force is supported. . . . Let us firmly and calmly maintain our position in that country ; let us be thoroughly armed as to our frontier defences, and then I believe we may trust to the old vigour of the people of this country, come what may, to support our supremacy in that great Empire."

Now, if it was as he said, there was only one opinion

and such resolute determination, why on earth was all the fuss and expense of a Public Service commission made? If European service was a resolute determination, was it not strange to have the subject of simultaneous examinations taken up at all by the Commission on grounds of *reason*, when it was a resolute, despotic, foregone conclusion? And why was the statutory service disturbed when it had been settled by Northcote, Argyll, and Salisbury and Parliament as a solution of compromise?

Now, we must see a little further what Lord Kimberley's speech means. It says, "One of those bases, and a very important one, is the loyalty and good-will of the Native Princes and population over whom we rule." Now, the authorities both in England and India do everything possible to destroy that very loyalty and good-will, or, as it is often called, contentment, which these authorities profess to depend upon. I cannot say anything here about the Native Princes. But what about the good-will of the Native population! Is it productive of loyalty and good-will (will a Briton be similarly content) to tell the Indians, "you will be kept down with the iron heel upon your neck of Europen services—military and civil—in order to maintain our power over you, to defend ourselves against Russian invasion, and thereby maintain our position in Europe, to increase our territory in the East, and to violate all our most solemn pledges. And all this at *your* cost, and mostly with your blood, just as the Empire itself has been built up. We have the power and for our benefit; and you put your Parliament and your Proclamations into your pocket." Queer way of producing contentment and loyalty!

This is a strange superiority over the despotic old

Indian system! It is seldom a matter of the slightest thought to our authorities as to who should pay for these European services and for the outside wars, and what the consequences are of the "bleeding."

In connexion with India generally, the Englishman (with some noble exceptions) deteriorates from a lover of liberty to a lover of despotism, without the slightest regard as to how the Indians are affected and bled. He suddenly becomes a superior, infallible being, and demands that what he does is right, and should never be questioned. (Mr. Gladstone truly called the "garment and law of force"* as the law and argument of the present Anglo-Indian rule). "Our boys" is his interest. The "boys" of others may go to the dogs, perish or be degraded for what he cares.

This is what the Anglo-Indian spirit of power, selfishness, and despotism (strange products of the highest civilisation) speaks through the mouth of the heads. How this spirit, if continued, will recoil on this country itself, there cannot be for Englishmen themselves much difficulty to understand.

My remarks about Lord Kimberley are made with much pain. He is one of the best Englishmen I have ever met with. But our misfortune is this. Secretaries of State (with few exceptions) being not much conversant with, or students of, the true Indian affairs, place themselves in the hands of Anglo-Indians. If, fortunately, one turns out capable of understanding the just claim of the Indians and does something, some successor under the everlasting influence of permanent officials subverts the justice done, and the Indian interests perish with all their dire consequences. A Sir Stafford Northcote gives, a Lord Cross snatches away.

It will be seen that the very claim now put forward by the Indian authorities of having done a great favour by the "Provincial Service" is misleading and not justified. On the contrary, we are deprived of what we already possessed by an Act of Parliament (1870) of admission into the *full Covenanted* Civil Service to the extent of about 180 or 200 appointments, while what is given to us with much trumpeting is a miserable "close pariah service" of about 95 Covenanted specific appointments, and that even not confined to Indians, but open to Europeans also, and so devised that no regular admission (as far as I know) on some organised system and tests is adopted, and I understand it to be said that some twenty or thirty years will elapse before the scheme will come into some regular operation. Can there be a greater blow and injustice to the Indians and a greater discredit to the authorities? But what is worst of all is that insidious efforts are made to undermine and destroy all our charters of equal British citizenship with the people of this country.

Lord Kimberley's speech in support of the present system is the best justification of what Macaulay had said that "the heaviest of all yokes is the yoke of the stranger." If this speech meant anything, it meant that the British yoke over India should be as heavy a foreign yoke as could be made. For, he does not say a word that if England employs the European Agency for its own sake he should think it just that England should pay for it, or, at least, the greater portion or half of it. Any such act of justice does not seem to occur to the Anglo-Indian "Masters." India alone must bleed for whatever the Master wills. And Britain cares not as it has nothing to pay. Worse still, the masters do not seem to care what deterioration of character and capacity is caused to the Indians.

As to the fitness and integrity of the Indians in any kind of situation—military or civil—there is now no room for controversy, even though they have not had a fair trial they have shown integrity, pluck, industry, courage and culture, to a degree of which the British people may well be proud, as being the authors of it. I have already touched upon the point of fitness in one of the statements.

About loyalty. In the despatch of 8th June, 1880, the Government of India itself said, "To the minds of at least the educated among the people of India—and the number is rapidly increasing—any idea of the subversion of British power is *abhorrent* from the consciousness that it must result in the wildest anarchy and confusion."

The fact is that because India asks and hopes for *British* rule on *British* principles, and not un-British rule on un-British principles of pure despotism aggravated by the worst evils of a foreign domination, that the educated are devotedly loyal, and regard their efforts for this purpose as their highest and best patriotism. Nothing can be more natural and sensible.

SUMMARY.

In 1833, a noble clause was passed by Parliament—everything that the Indians could desire. Had the Executives loyally and faithfully carried out that clause, India would have been in the course of more than sixty years a prosperous and contented and deeply loyal country, and a strength and a benefit to the British Empire to an extent hardly to be conceived or realised at present, when, by an opposite course, India is afflicted with all the horrors and misery to which humanity can possibly be exposed. After 1833, twenty years passed but nothing done. Fresh efforts were made in Parliament to put the Indians on the same footing as British subjects, by simultaneous examinations in this country and India. Stanley, Bright, Rich and others protested to no purpose; the violation of the Act of 1833 continued.

Then came the great and glorious Proclamation of the Queen in 1858, and a new bright hope to the Indians; but not fulfilled up to the present day. In 1860, a Committee of five members of the Council of the Secretary of State pointed out the dishonour of the British name, and reported that simultaneous examinations were the best method to do justice to the Act of 1833—to no purpose; the Report was suppressed and the public knew nothing about it. In 1867, the East India Association petitioned for the admission into the Covenanted Civil Service of a small proportion of Indians. Sir Stafford Northcote admitted the justice of the prayer, and proposed a clause to give a partial fulfilment of the Act of 1833. The Duke of Argyll passed it. Lord Salisbury approved of it, but pointed out how the jealousy of the Anglo-Indians would wreck it—a prophecy which was not long to be fulfilled.

The Government of India resisted tooth and nail, and made some outrageous proposals in the despatch of 2nd May, 1878. It was then that Lord Lytton, in a minute, admitted the ignoble policy of subterfuges and dishonour upon which the Executives had all along acted since 1833.

A strong and justly inclined Secretary (Lord Cranbrook) persisted, brushed aside all resistance and plausibilities, and compelled the Government of India to give effect to the clause. The Government of India, with bad grace and very reluctantly, made the rules—cleverly drawn up to throw discredit upon the service—the worst part was rejected by Lord Cranbrook; but an insidious device remained, and the appointments were begun to be made. The Anglo-Indians boiled with rage, and the explosion on the Ilbert Bill was the open declaration of war. Lord Salisbury on that occasion confessed that the conduct of the Executive all along was merely "political hypocrisy."

The agitation subsided, but the appointments having remained to be continued the boiling under the crater continued, and, instead of exploding, the Government resorted to other devices and gained their settled object with a vengeance—the report of the Public Service Commission confirmed the foregone conclusions against the Statutory Service and simultaneous examinations.

The statutory service of full eligibility and of about 200 employments in the course of thirty years in the whole Covenanted Service was abolished, and the wretched scheme of May 2nd, 1878, established instead.

The whole position has been thrown back worse than it ever was before.

A Conservative (Sir Stafford Northcote) proposed, and a Liberal (Duke of Argyll) passed the Act of 1870 to do some justice. A Conservative (Lord Cranbrook) insisted upon carrying it out. A Liberal (Lord Kimberley) began to undermine it, and another Conservative (Lord Cross) gave it the deathblow—though, to the humiliation of the House of Commons, the Act remains on the Statute Book. What faith can the Indians have on any Act of Parliament? To-day something given, to-morrow snatched away; Acts and Resolutions of Parliament and Proclamations notwithstanding.

Once more Parliament did justice and passed the Resolution, in 1893, for simultaneous examinations, to share the same grievous fate as all its former enactments. And the Indian Executive thus stands proclaimed the supreme power over the heads of all—Parliament, people, and Sovereign.

The whole force and object of the two references to our Commission is to reply to Sir Henry Fowler's most important challenge, and that reply mainly depends upon the consideration of the way in which the clauses in the Acts of 1833 and 1870 and the Proclamations are dealt with.

Sir Henry Fowler's challenge is this: "The question I wish to consider is, whether that Government, with all its machinery as now existing in India, has, or has not, promoted the general prosperity of the people of India, and whether India is better or worse off by being a province of the British Crown; that is the test."

I may here give a few extracts as bearing upon the subject and its results. I am obliged to repeat a few that I have already cited in my previous statements.

Sir William Hunter has said:—

"You cannot work with imported labour as cheaply as you can with Native labour, and I regard the more extended employment of the Natives not only as an act of justice but "as a financial necessity"...........I believe that it will be impossible to deny them a larger share in the administration. ....The appointments of a few Natives annually to the Covenented Civil Service will not solve the problem...........If we are to govern the Indian people efficiently and cheaply we must govern them "by means of themselves" and pay for the administration at the market rates of Native labour............ Good work thus commenced has assumed such dimensions under the Queen's Government of India that it can no longer be carried on, "or even supervised, by imported labour" from England, except at a cost which India cannot sustain."

* * * * *

"I do not believe that a people numbering one-sixth of the whole inhabitants of the globe, and whose aspirations have been nourished from their earliest youth on the strong food of English liberty, can be permanently denied a voice in the government of the country."

Lord Salisbury has said: "But it would be a great evil if the result of our dominion was that the Natives of India who were capable of government should be absolutely and hopelessly excluded from such a career."

Now that it is emphatically declared that all professions of equality of British citizenship were only so much hypocrisy—that India must be bled of its wealth, work, and wisdom, that it must exist only for the maintenance of British Rule by its blood, its money, and its slavery—England and India are face to face; and England ought to declare what, in the name of civilisation, justice, honour, and all that is righteous England means to do for the future. The principles of the statesmen of 1833 were: "Be just and fear not;" the principles of the present statesmen appear to be: "Fear and be unjust." Let India know which of the two is to be her future fate. However mighty a Power may be, justice and righteousness are mightier far than all the mightiness of brute force. Macaulay has said: "Of all forms of tyranny I believe that the worst is that of a nation over a nation." And he has also said: "The end of government is the happiness of the people." Has the end of Indian government been such, or all a "terrible misery," as Lord Salisbury has truly characterised it? Let the question be honestly answered.

The statesmen of 1833 accepted that "the righteous are as bold as a lion." But the authorities seem to have always forgotten it or ignored it; and political cowardice has been more before their eyes.

Lord Salisbury has said many more truths, but I have mentioned them before.

Mr. Gladstone has said :—

"It is the predominance of that moral force for which I heartily pray in the deliberations of this House, and the conduct of our whole public policy, for I am convinced that upon that predominance depends that which should be the first object of all our desires as it is of all our "daily official prayers," namely, that union of heart and sentiment which constitutes the two bases of strength at home, and therefore both of strength and good fame throughout the civilised world."

Again :

"There can be no more melancholy, and in the last result, no more degrading spectacle upon earth than the spectacle of oppression, or of wrong in whatever form, inflicted by the deliberate Act of a nation upon another nation. . . . .

"But on the other hand there can be nobler spectacle than that which we think is now drawing upon us, the spectacle of a nation deliberately set on the removal of injustice, deliberately determined to break—not through terror, and not in haste, but under the sole influence of duty and honour—determined to break with whatever remains still existing of an evil tradition, and determined in that way at once to pay a debt of justice, and to consult by a bold, wise and good Act, its own interest and its own honour."

These extracts refer to Ireland. They apply with ten times the force to India.

With regard to India, he has fully admitted that there the law and argument of England was "the law and argument of force." Lord Randolph Churchill realised the true position of the evil foreign domination of England in India under the present system. He said :—

"The position of India in relation to taxation and the sources of the public revenues is very peculiar, not merely from the habits of the people, and their strong aversion to change, which is more specially exhibited to new forms of taxation, "but likewise from the character of the government, which is in the hands of foreigners, who hold all the principal administrative offices and form so large a part of the Army." The impatience of the new taxation which will have to be borne wholly as a consequence of "the foreign rule imposed on the country," and virtually to meet additions to charges arising outside of the country, would "constitute a political danger," the real magnitude of which, it is to be feared, is not at all appreciated by persons who have no knowledge of or concern in the Government of India, but what those responsible for that Government have long regarded "as of the most serious order."

The East India Company, in their petition against change of government, said :—

"That your petitioners cannot contemplate without dismay the doctrine now widely promulgated that India should be administered with an especial view to the benefit of the English who reside there; or that in its administration "any advantage should be sought for Her Majesty's subjects of European birth," except that which they will necessarily derive from their superiority of intelligence, and from the increased prosperity of the people, the improvement of the productive resources of the country and the extension of commercial intercourse."

The course, however, during the administration by the Crown, has been to regard the interests of Europeans as the most important, and paramount, and generally every action is based upon that principle, with little concern or thought what that meant to the people of India at large.

Everything for the benefit of Indian interests is the romance, any everything for the benefit of the British and "cruel and crushing tribute" from Indians is the reality.

The edifice of the British-Rule rests at present upon the sandy foundation of Asiatic despotism, injustice, and all the evils of a foreign domination, as some of the best English statesmen have frequently declared; and the more this edifice is made heavier by additions to these evils, as is continuously being done, by violation of pledges and exclusion of Indians from serving in their own country, with all its natural evil consequences the greater, the more devastating and complete, I am grieved to foresee, will be the ultimate crash.

The question of remedy I have already dealt with in one of my representations to the Commission.

In a letter in the *Times* of September 28 last, Bishop Tugwell quotes an extract from the *Times* with regard to the African races. How much more forcibly does it apply to India, to whom the people of England mostly owe the formation and maintenance of the British Indian Empire, and who for their reward receive "terrible misery" and "bleeding."

The *Times* says :—

> "The time has long passed away when we were content to justify our rule by the strong hand alone. We should no longer hold our great tropical possessions with an easy conscience did we not feel convinced that our tenure of them is for the advantage, not of ourselves only, but of the subject peoples."

Can a fair-minded, honest Englishman say that he has his easy conscience with regard to India, after the wars, famine and pestilence which have been devastating that illfated country, after a British Rule of a century and a half ?

Macaulay has said, in 1833 :—

> "'Propter vitam vivendi perdere causas' is a despicable policy either in individuals or States. In the present case such a policy would not only be despicable but absurd."

After describing from Bernier the practice of miserable tyrants of poisoning a dreaded subject, he says :—

> "That detestable artifice, more horrible than assassination itself, was worthy of those who employed it. It is no model

for the English nation. We shall never consent to administer the pousta to a whole community—to stupefy and paralyse a great people—whom God has committed to our charge, for the wretched purpose of rendering them more amenable to our control."

Lord Hartington said in 1883:—

"It is not wise to educate the people of India, to introduce among them your civilisation and your progress and your literature, and at the same time to tell them shall never have any chance of taking any part or share in the administration of the affairs of their country, except by their getting rid in the first instance of their European rulers. Surely, it would not be wise to tell a patriotic Native of India that."

This naturally suggests the question of the future of India with regard to Russia. This is rather a wide subject, and somewhat indirectly connected with this statement. But I may say here that there are, in my thinking, certain features in the Indian rule of great plausibility, which the Russians, by their emissaries, will urge upon the mind of the masses of the Indians, when they are in any spirit of discontent, with great effect against the English. Nor need I enter on the speculation whether Russia would be able to make a lodging in India. These are matters which every Englishman is bound to consider calmly. The English people and Parliament should not wait to consider them till it is too late. My whole fear is, that if the British people allow things to drift on in the present evil system, the disaster may come to both countries when it is *too late* to prevent or repair it.

My whole earnest anxiety is that righteous means may be adopted by which the connection between the two countries may be strengthened with great blessings and benefits to both countries. I speak freely, because I feel strongly that it is a thousand pities that a connection that *can* be made great and good to both countries is blindly being undermined and destroyed with detriment to both. My previous statements have clearly shown that. The whole question of the *blessing* or *curse* of the connection of England and India upon both countries rests mainly upon the honourable and loyal fulfilment of the Act of 1833 and the Proclamation of 1858, or upon the dishonour of the non-fulfilment of them: "Righteousness alone will exalt a nation; Injustice will bring down the mightiest to ruin."

I conclude with my earnest hope and prayer that our Commission will pronounce clearly upon all the vital questions involved in their two references on which I have submitted my views.

One last word of agony. With the dire calamities with which we have been overwhelmed, and in the midst of the greatest jubilation in the word, in which we took our hearty share, in spite of those calamities, we have not, as far as I know, got the word of our greatest hope and consolation—a repetition of the most gracious Proclamation of 1858, of equality of British citizenship, which we received on the assumption of the Imperial title and on the Jubilee, nor of anything of its application.

Yours truly,

DADABHAI NAOROJI.

VII.

INDIANS IN THE INDIAN CIVIL SERVICE.*

A

In proposing for your adoption this memorial,† I am glad that I have a very easy task before me, unless I create some giants of my own imagination to knock them down, for on the principle of the memorial I see on all hands there is but one opinion. Beginning with our gracious Sovereign, she has emphatically declared with regard to the natives of India (in a proclamation dated the 1st of November, 1858), "We hold ourselves bound to the natives of our Indian territories by the same obligations of duty which bind us to all our other subjects, and those obligations, by the blessing of Almighty God, we shall faithfully and conscientiously fulfil." Then referring to this particular point, the proclamation goes on, "It is our further will, that so far as may be, our subjects, of whatever race or creed, be freely and impartially admitted to offices in our service, the duties of which may be qualified by their education, ability, and integrity duly to discharge." That being the gracious declaration of the will and pleasure of our Sovereign,

* (Paper read before an evening Meeting of the East India Association, at London, Tuesday, August 13th, 1867. Lord Lyveden in the Chair.)

† "We, the members of the East India Association, beg respectfully to submit that the time has come when it is desirable to admit the natives of India to a larger share in the administration of India than hitherto."

let us pass next to the opinion of Parliament upon the subject. The opinion of Parliament has been all long decisive upon this matter. As far back as 1833, in the Act of that year, it was distinctly declared, "That no native of the said territories, nor any natural-born subject of His Majesty, resident therein, shall, by reason only of his religion, place of birth, descent, colour, or any of them, be disabled from holding any place,

---

"To you, sir, it is quite unnecessary to point out the justice, necessity, and importance of this step, as in the debate in Parliament, on May 24 last, you have pointed out this so emphatically and clearly, that it is enough for us to quote your own noble and statesmanlike sentiments. You said—'Nothing could be more wonderful than our empire in India; but we ought to consider on what conditions we held it, and how our predecessors held it. The greatness of the Mogul empire depended upon the liberal policy that was pursued by men like Akbar, availing themselves of Hindu talent and assistance, and identifying themselves as far as possible with the people of the country. He thought that they ought to take a lesson from such a circumstance, and if they were to do their duty towards India they could only discharge that duty by obtaining the assistance and counsel of all who were great and good in that country. It would be absurd in them to say that there was not a large fund of statesmanship and ability in the Indian character.'—(*Times*, 25th May, 1867.) With these friendly and just sentiments towards the people of India we fully concur, and therefore, instead of trespassing any more upon your time, we beg to lay before you our views as to the best mode of accomplishing the object.

"We think that the competitive examinations for a portion of the appointments to the Indian Civil Service should be held in India, under such rules and arrangements as you may think proper. What portion of the appointments should be thus competed for in India we cannot do better than leave to your own judgment. After the selection is made in India, by the first examination, we think it essential that the selected candidates be required to come to England to pass their further examinations with the selected candidates of this country.

"In the same spirit, and with kindred objects in view for the general good of India, we would ask you to extend

office, or employment under the said Company;" and on every occasion when Parliament has had the matter before it, there has scarcely been any opposition to the principle enunciated by this memorial. Again, up to the latest day, during the past three or four debates in Parliament which have taken place this year, we have seen the same principle emphatically declared; even in last night's debate we find the same again brought forward in a prominent way by some who are friends to India, and who also wish well to England. While we have this testimony on the part of our Sovereign and Parliament, we find that the press upon this matter at least is unanimous. So far back as 1853, in commenting upon the petition presented by

---

your kind encouragement to native youths of promise and ability to come to England for the completion of their education. We believe that if scholarships, tenable for five years in this country, were to be annually awarded by competitive examination in India to native candidates between the ages of 15 and 17, some would compete successfully in England for the Indian Civil Service, while others would return in various professions to India, and where by degrees they would form an enlightened and unprejudiced class, exercising a great and beneficial influence on native society, and constituting a link between the masses of the people and their English rulers.

"In laying before you this memorial we feel assured, and we trust that you will also agree with us, that this measure, which has now become necessary by the advencement of education in India, will promote and strengthen the loyalty of the natives of India to the British Rule, while it will also be a satisfaction to the British people to have thus by one more instance practically proved its desire to advance the condition of their Indian fellow-subjects, and to act justly by them.

"We need not point out to you, sir, how great an encouragement these examinations in India will be to education. The great prizes of the appointments will naturally increase vastly the desire for education among the people."

the Bombay Association, I find a large proportion of the press here admitted the justice and truth of the complaints made by the natives of India, as to the exclusiveness adopted in the civil service at the time, and urging that the natives should be to a suitable extent introduced into the enjoyment of the higher places of responsibility and trust. And recently, in commenting upon the debates that have taken place in Parliament, which I have just referred to, the press has been equally unanimous in reference to this subject. As far as Parliament and the press are any indication of the opinions of the people, we can say the people are at one on this subject. As far as my personal knowledge is concerned, during the twelve years I have been here, or while I was in India, I must confess that I have always found every Englishman that I have spoken to on the subject, admitting its justice, and assuring me that England will always do its duty towards India. I have been sometimes told that some civilians, perhaps, do not like it but I should not do the injustice to say that I recollect any instance in which such an opinion has been expressed to me. The testimony of all eminent men in the Indian service is in favour of giving all necessary facilities for the admission of natives of India to the civil service, as well as that of all those eminent statesmen here who have made India their study. The interest that the natives feel in this subject I need not at all enlarge upon; that can be at once conceived by their presence here; the interest they would feel in the Government of India by having the responsibilities of that administration on their own heads, speaks for itself; and at the same time the strength it would give to the British Rule is also a matter of the greatest importance. Lastly, I find that the present Government itself has emphatically declared on this point. In the words I have quoted in the memorial, Sir Stafford Northcote has distinctly stated, "Nothing could be more wonderful than our empire in India; but we ought to consider on what conditions we held it, and our predecessors held it. The greatness of the Mogul empire depended upon the liberal policy that was pursued by men like Akbar availing themselves of Hindu talent and assistance, and identifying themselves as far as possible with the people of the country. He thought that they ought to take a lesson from such a circumstance, and if they were to do their duty towards India, they could only discharge that duty by obtaining the assistance and counsel of all who were great and good in that country. It would be absurd in them to say that there was not a large fund of statesmanship and ability in the Indian character." With such complete testimony on the principle of this memorial, I think I was quite justified in saying at the beginning that my task was a very easy one. This last extract, again, enables me to dispose of another point, namely, as to the capacity of the Natives of India for administration and for high education. I may at once leave that alone, because at this time of day after the education which has been received by the natives of India after the results as shown by the university examinations, and with the actual facts of the efficiency of the services rendered by the natives of India, whenever they are employed in any office of responsibility and trust, it would be simply ridiculous on my part to try to prove to you their capacity for administration and for study, and their high character. The importance and justice of introducing natives of India into the administration to a proper extent, has been urged by various eminent men at different times before committees of the Houses of Parliament. If I had considered it necessary, I could have collected a volume of such extracts. I need only glance at this point, namely the assistance which the Government of India would derive from the native element being introduced into it. With the best intentions, Englishmen cannot understand the natives of India as a body; their feelings, their ways of thought, and their original education, are so different, that with the best intentions on the part of Englishmen, they very often fail in pointing out the exact remedies for any complaints made by the natives; but if the natives of India were introduced to a proper extent into the administration of the country, naturally their own countrymen would have more sympathy with them. Those native administrators would know where the exact difficulties were, and many of the problems of the present day, to grapple with which all the energies of our English administrators are taxed in vain, would be solved most easily. We would then have the sympathy of the natives with the British Rulers, and one of the results of such a concession to the natives would be gratitude on their part, which would form a strong foundation for the upholding of the British Rule in India. And when I advocate that which would have a tendency to uphold the British Rule in India, it is not for the sake of the English, but for the sake of the natives themselves. They have every reason to congratulate themselves on being under the British Rule, after the knowledge they have now derived, and are every day deriving, of the benefits of it. I come, then, to the practical part of the memorial itself. At present the arrangement is that the civil service examination is open to all British subjects; and under that arrangement, no doubt, the natives of India can come here and they have come here, and undergone the competitive examination (one has passed, and is now serving in India). But if we refer back to the gracious words of our Sovereign, that the natives of India be admitted "freely and impartially," the question naturally arises whether under the present arrangement that declaration and that assurance is practically given effect to. The difficulty on the face of it is this, that the natives are put to the disadvantage of coming over here and remaining here for several years. The risk of losing a sum of money which perhaps thy cannot afford, is in itself a disadvantage sufficient to require some change in the arrangement. But, supposing even some few were willing to come here and to compete in the examination, it is not desirable that only those few should be admitted into the civil service which requires that those serving in it, whether native or English, should be of the highest talents. We do not want those having the longest purses only, but what we want is—in the words of Sir Stafford Northcote—the assistance and counsel of all who are great and good in the country; and we cannot attain that object unless we have a competitive examination which would enable *all* the best men of India to compete for appointments in the Indian Civil Service. Such are the men who ought to be introduced into that service. Therefore, putting aside all the disadvantages that the native is put to in coming over to this country, and which are in themselves sufficient to require that some alteration should be made in the present arrangement, the very best interests of the service require that some competition should take place in India whether at an earlier stage or at a later stage; and that a selection should be made, not only of those who can afford to spend a few thousands to come here, but of those who possess the *best* talent among the people. I have nothing more to say than to refer to the plan I have suggested in the memorial, and I have left it as general as possible, because, with the evidence before us of the interest which Sir Stafford Northcote has taken in the subject, and the emphatic manner in which he has expressed his views as to the necessity and justice of introducing the native element into the service, I can, with the utmost confidence, leave any of the details that would be best suited for the purpose to himself. The natives of India are willing to submit to any standard; if they could not come up to the standard required by the service, it would be their own fault, and nobody would have any right to complain; but as long as they can assert that they would be able to stand any standard of examination which they may be reasonably subjected to, it is only just and proper that they should have the opportunity given them. Take, for instance, the case of the fair trial given to the natives for acquiring high education. There were no B.A.s or M.A.s before. The universities being established, we know the result, that the natives have fully vindicated their intellect. And they only ask a fair trial for the civil service. I am desirous, that instead of taking up more of your time, the members present should discuss this fully, and I therefore conclude as I began with the words of our Sovereign, "In their prosperity will be our strength, in their contentment our security, and in their gratitude our best reward;" and my only prayer is, that a reward nobler than that which has ever been attained by any nation, or any individual, may be earned by our British Rulers.

In the proposal made by me, the examination takes place in India, just as it takes place here; the candidates that pass in India are exactly on the same footing as what are called selected candidates in England. After passing the competitive examination, there are what are called further examinations here, and it is for those further examinations here that I wish those natives to come here, which would be no hardship on them; the utmost sacrifice which they might be required to make, if the Government would not assist them, would be the voyage home; if the Government would pay that, then there would be no hardship, because, as soon as they come here they begin to prepare for their further examination; they get the first year £100, and the second year £200, and then, if they show the necessary proficiency in the subjects they are required to study, there is no competition and no rejection afterwards; they have only to show that they have spent two years in the necessary studies, having in view the special duties required of them in India; so that there is no risk of their being rejected. The competitive examination in India would be what it is here, and after they passed that they would be admitted as selected candidates. As I am on my legs, allow me to add to what I have already said, that there is no practical difficulty in what is proposed. The whole thing is embraced in the rules published by the Secretary of State for India every year; the Secretary of State for India has only to decide as to what proportion of natives it would be advisable to introduce into the civil service, and then to send out instructions to the local government to institute examinations of the same character and under the same rules that are followed here, under which examinations the candidates would be selected; the number may be five or ten, or I should be satisfied if there were two for Bengal and one for each of the other presidencies. Those examinations would take place there under the same rules and the same arrangements under which they take place here. The best on the list would become the selected candidates, and when once they become selected candidates there would be no risk of failing in the competition. There are no practical details to propose; the arrangement of the whole thing is already practically carried out. The simple question for the Secretary of State to decide being, what proportion of the appointments should be competed for in India, it would be, I think, more proper on the part of this Association to leave that to Sir Stafford Northcote and the Council. They are best able to judge as to that, and I have every confidence that they would do that which is right. The manner in which justice has been done in the case of Mysore makes me perfectly confident that we have a Government not only willing to make professions, but willing to *do* what they profess. As I did not contemplate that any details should be proposed, except simply that a certain proportion of appointments to be decided on by the Secretary of State should be competed for in India, the managing committee, to whom this proposal was referred, thought wisely that we might at once go to the whole Association itself, and we have done so. If the Association are inclined to adopt the proposal of the noble chairman, of referring the matter back to a committee, I do not say anything against it, but there is nothing to be considered; the whole thing is ready cut and dried. There are only two points to be decided by Sir Stafford Northcote: first, whether a certain number of appointments should be competed for in India or not, and next, what proportion of the appointments should be so competed for. With regard to the various remarks which have been made by Mr. Hodgson Pratt, I agree with the full force of them. When he, some years ago, was anxious to promote the plan of bringing over to England young men to be educated, I endeavoured to contribute my humble mite to that endeavour. All I say upon the remarks he has addressed to you is this, that he attaches a little too much importance to an independent body of natives in India who had received their education in England, and who would spread themselves in all the different departments of life, being the only means by which the tone of society, and the status of the whole population would be raised; for, we must not forget that, attaching to the administration of the country itself, there are responsibilities that must be incurred; and when a native is introduced into the administration he comes under a responsibility which an outsider cannot appreciate. If we had only a body of independent educated natives we should have nothing but agitation; there would be no counterpoise to it, there would be no men trained under the yoke of responsibility, who would tell them that there were such and such difficulties in the way of the administration. I have considered this matter very carefully for a long time. I have taken the utmost possible trouble to induce my friends to come over here for their education, and most of the twenty-five who have been referred to are under my care. I have taken that responsibility, because I feel strongly upon the point. I have taken that guardianship for the past twelve years with no little anxiety to myself, but I am glad to say that those young men have behaved most admirably, never having given me cause to complain, and the character that has been given of them, whether by the gentlemen with whom they have been residing, or by the professors of their college, has been that they have been very steady and very good. But in this way we cannot get the *best* talent. Therefore I hope that it will not be considered by the Association that I have brought forward this question inconsiderately and immaturely. I do not see the necessity of troubling a Committee to go into it again. Here I have my proposal in some detail :—" First examination for the Civil Service of India, to be held in India." (I would be satisfied even with a few to begin with ; I suggest five.) " Five candidates shall be selected every year as follows :—2 from Bengal, 1 from Bombay, 1 from Madras, 1 from the North-West Provinces and the Punjab. The examination shall be held in each of the above territories, under the instruction of the local government, in the subjects, and according to the rules adopted from time to time by the Civil Service Commissioners for the first competition examination in England. The highest in rank shall be deemed to be selected candidates for the civil service of India. The selected candidates shall, within three months of the announcement of the result of the examination, proceed to England, and the local government shall pay the passage money. After arrival in England these selected candidates shall be subject to the rules and terms for the subsequent 'further examination,' etc., like the selected candidates of England." If it is necessary for a plan to be attached to the memorial, here is one. I admit the force of the remark made by Mr. Hodgson Pratt, that mere education in colleges and universities is not enough, that there are other qualifications necessary. But though I do not agree with those who say that the education given in India does not raise the moral as well as the intellectual character of the pupil, still I purposely make it essential that those natives who are selected for the service should come over to England for those two years, in order that they may acquire all the benefits in England which Mr. Hodgson Pratt so ably described. As to the competitive system, it must be recollected that it has been established as being the best system that can be adopted for arriving at the qualities and capabilities of a man. If the Council think that there ought to be a standard of proficiency at the oar or at cricket, let them establish such a standard; I daresay the natives of India would be quite prepared to try a hand at bowling or at the oar with the natives of England; only, let every one be put on an equal footing. We no longer select men for the service in India according to the system of patronage; we know how that system worked in former times—how proprietors joined together to get their nephews in. I do not refer to past grievances; let the past be the past, we have enough to be thankful for; we select our best men in the best way in our power, by a competitive examination, and though, in a competition of 200 for 50 or 60 situations, there is some chance of an incompetent man getting in, by cramming or by some accident, still, where there is a competition of 100 or 1,000 for only one or two places, the chances are infinitesimally small that anybody who does not possess the highest order of intellect will be able to take those prizes. I beg to submit to our President, with very great deference, that the proposal I have made has been carefully considered. I have consulted several gentlemen who are deeply interested in the matter, and I hope our noble President will support me in approving of this memorial, with the addition which Sir Herbert Edwardes has made, to which I have no objection; it gives the memorial a wider scope, and meets the other difficulty which our noble President suggested as to the expense. It is desirable, instead of simply allowing a few young men to enter the Civil Service, that we should also carry out a comprehensive principle of giving some opportunity to natives of entering upon other independent departments. I fully agree that the assistance proposed by Sir Herbert Edwardes' amendment should be held out to the youths of India; we want the best talent of the country brought here; therefore, I propose that Sir Herbert Edwardes' addition should be embodied in the memorial. Our noble President has said that this memorial does not properly come within the province of this Association. With every deference, I beg to differ from his Lordship. The very basis upon which this institution has been formed is, as expressed by the second rule, the promotion, by all legitimate means, of the interests and welfare of India generally. If the object and purpose of the Association is simply to supply information, I do not see that the Association can do any very great good; but if the Association takes up one subject after another, considerately and carefully, as our noble President suggests, and does actual practical good to the various interests of India, the Association then will have fulfilled its mission of bringing India and England together, doing justice to India, informing the people of this country of all that is necessary to be known by them in relation to Indian matters, and suggesting to them what they, in the situation in which Providence has placed them, as rulers of India, ought to do towards India. If the Association has not been formed to attain those objects, I do not see what good it can do. We may read papers here and have a pleasant discussion on them, and go away with the feeling that we have had a very successful meeting; but if we are to end there, what good shall we have done? What is the object of all our discussion? It is to take such practical steps as may influence the people of this country, and as may influence the Government to rectify existing evils, the rectifying of which would have the effect of consolidating the British Rule in India, to the great benefit of both England and India.

B. *

GENTLEMEN,—Since our deputation waited on the Secretary of State for India with the Memorial † relative to the Indian Civil Service, I find several objections urged from different quarters; and, as I see that Mr. Fawcett is going to move a Resolution, I beg to submit for your consideration my views on those objections. They are, as far as I have met with, principally these :—

1. That the natives are not fit, on account of their deficient ability, integrity, and physical power and energy.

2. That Europeans would not like to serve under natives.

3. That native officials are not much respected by the natives, and that when a native is placed in any position of eminence, his fellow-countrymen all around him are ready to backbite and slander him.

4. That natives look too much to Government employment, and do not show sufficient independence of character to strike out for themselves other paths of life.

5. That though natives may prove good subordinates, they are not fit to be placed at the head of any department.

6. That natives who seek for admission into the Civil Service should be Anglicised.

7. That natives ought not to be put in positions of power.

8. That the places obtained by the natives will be so many lost to the English people.

---

* Paper read before a meeting of the East India Association, London, Friday, April 17th, 1868. E. B. Eastwick, Esq. C.B., F.R.S., in the Chair.

† Appendix B.

9. That natives are already largely employed.

To avoid confusion, I give hereafter the replies to these objections separately, but it is necessary to guard against being drawn into a discussion of these objections, and thereby missing the *real* point at issue. Whatever may be the weight or value of these objections, they are now altogether beside the question. The real position of the question at present is simply this: That, notwithstanding *all these* and other such objections, after a searching inquiry, and after taking them all into very careful consideration, Parliament has decided and publicly enacted "That no native of the said territories (India), nor any natural-born subject of His Majesty resident therein, shall, by reason only of his religion, place of birth, descent, colour or any of them, be disabled from holding any place, office, or employment under the said Company." This enactment by Parliament in the year 1834 was again confirmed in distinct, honest and emphatic terms by our gracious Sovereign in the year 1858: "We hold ourselves bound to the natives of our Indian territories by the same obligation of duty which bind us to all our other subjects, and those obligations, by the blessing of Almighty God, we shall faithfully and conscientiously fulfil. . . . . It is our further will that, so far as may be, our subjects, of whatever race or creed, be freely and impartially admitted to offices in our service, the duties of which they may be qualified by their education, ability, and integrity duly to discharge." The test of qualifications, character and health are laid down. Now, the question simply is, whether these solemn Royal declarations, and enactments of Parliament are to be *fairly* and *honestly* carried out, or whether they are only to be a mockery and a delusion as far as the British subjects in

India are concerned. This is the whole question. I have not the least doubt that the intentions of our Sovereign and Parliament are honest, and the only course open is, not to subject any one class of British subjects to greater difficulties and sacrifices than another. Every obstacle left or thrown in the way of the natives of India is equivalent to making the Royal word and Parliamentary enactment, as far as they are concerned, a dead letter and a mockery. The only way in which natives of India can be put on an honestly equal footing with Englishmen is by holding examinations in India also. I trust that in the debate in Parliament this real point at issue will not be lost sight of, and will be distinctly pronounced upon.

The questions which will have to be necessarily discussed in connection with this point are—first. Whether it is practicable to hold examinations in India. It is evident that there can be no insurmountable difficulty. I need hardly take up your time on this point, as you are all well aware that there are competent staffs of examiners in India. I would only throw out one or two suggestions. If it be considered necessary that *all* the candidates both of this country and of India should be subjected to the *same* examination, papers for both written and *vivâ voce* examinations can be sent from here, to be opened in India in the examination rooms on the same day as they are opened here; and in the case of the *vivâ voce* examinations (whether papers are sent or not, or questions additional to those given in the papers are put by the examiner for obtaining fully the object of the *vivâ voce* examinations), if the examiners are required to write down all the questions put and answers given, with such remarks as may occur to them as to the manner of the replies of each candidate, the Commissioners here will be well able to control the whole examination, and bring it to a common standard. If, on the other hand, the Government of India be left to carry out the examination in India, there will be no difficulty whatever in finding a competent staff of examiners. It is neither desirable, nor should it be expected by the natives, that the English portion of the service should not be larger than the native; and a small portion of the annual appointments left to be competed for in India, is all, I think, that they can at present fairly ask. In that case the latter plan of leaving to the Government of India to conduct the examinations would be preferable. The chief objection to this latter plan is that by a separate examination a native may come in who may be inferior to the English candidates rejected here. To avoid this difficulty, either the first plan of "same papers" must be adopted; or, if the Government of India adopt a sufficiently high standard of examinations and a high minimum, considering that the number of appointments will be very small indeed compared with the number of candidates who are likely to compete in such a large population, the successful candidates will not only be comparatively, but absolutely, good and superior men. Again, on the other hand, the chief objection to the "same examination for all" is that as the number of candidates will be in the course of time much larger in India than here, on account of the immensely larger population from which they will come, there is some chance that the Commissioners may find a much large number of natives coming high than the Secretary of State may think desirable to give appointments to, If, therefore, any natives are then rejected and their English inferiors are selected, the cry of injustice will naturally arise, which contingency ought, I think, to be avoided. Upon the whole, therefore, I think leaving the examination to the Government of India, with a sufficiently high standard, will be the most practicable plan, as the chance is very slight of inferior men passing in a very large competition. Again, whether the examinations should be held in some one place only, or at all the Presidency towns, is another question. This can be well left to the Viceroy. Each Presidency is so large a country by itself that, if a distribution of the appointments were made among them, the work of the examiners will be ample, and the civil servants being thus drawn from the different localities of India, a larger and more varied experience will be introduced into the service than if they were all or most of them drawn from one province only, which I think will be an advantage. These details, however, had better be left to the judgment of the Secretary of State.

As to the general character of the candidates, the certificates will be mostly from the English heads of their colleges, about whom certainly nobody can object that they would not be as conscientious and honest as the heads of the colleges here. The weight of any other certificates that may be produced by the candidates can easily be judged of by the examining authorities. In short, Government may adopt such rules as they may deem necessary to get the Indian candidate of the same level with the English, whether in acquirements, *character, physical energy*, or in any other particular. If the natives fail in coming up to a fair standard, it would be their own fault; *they only ask a fair trial.* Now suppose any inefficient person by some accident found admission into the service (which is very unlikely in a large competition for a very few places), or suppose that after admission the integrity of any was not found satisfactory; there is no difficulty for Government in discharging such a person. By his appointment once he does not become a permanent fixture. Nor is it incumbent upon Government to promote any servant who does not prove his fitness for promotion. So there is no reason whatever why the enactment of Parliament or the proclamation of our Sovereign should not be fairly carried out, and the mere bugbear of the fear that some native *employé* may misbehave himself be allowed to interfere with a necessary act of justice and policy.

As to the locality for the examinations, Clause XXXII of the Act of 1858 does not fix any. The Secretary of State for India is not prevented from holding examinations where he may think necessary.

The second question will be the necessary expenditure, but it is only natural and quite evident that the natives would only be too glad to have any necessary portion of the revenue devoted to such purposes.

I need not here do more than simply state that the two requests made in our memorial have been by some confounded with each other as alternatives, but you are aware they are not so. The very wording of the second request and the speech of Sir H. Edwardes shows that the two requests have two different objects, the first to give a fair, free, and impartial chance to the natives to enter the Indian Civil Service on the same footing as Englishmen, and the second to send out natives in various independent professions to India, "where by degrees they would form an enlightened and unprejudiced class, exercising a great and beneficial influence on native society, and constituting a link between the masses of the people and their English rulers."

When I moved the memorial, I did not go further into this matter than pointing out that our Sovereign and the Parliament, and the press as representing the people of this country, and the present Government were of the one opinion which is expressed in the words I have quoted before from an Act of Parliament and from the proclamation of our Sovereign. Even now the press of this country, while commenting on the Blue Book of the comparison of the British and Native Rule, have almost unanimously declared that a fair field for the aspiration of natives of ability and character is one of the most important was of the British Rule, both to make it beloved as well as efficient. I also then urged that the best interest of the service required that the first competition for selection should take place in India, in order that selection of qualified natives may not be made from a small body only, but to select the *best* talent and character from the *whole* talent and character of the country.

With such a clear case of law, justice, and necessity, we may think, and properly too, that I should have nothing more to say, and that my paper should end here. So I had thought on the occasion of proposing the memorial, but as some objections have been since started from quarters, no matter of whatever character, and as it is likely that some members of Parliament may desire to know the value of these objections, though, as I have explained before they are all now quite irrelevant, I discuss them one by one.

1. "That the natives are not fit, on account of their deficient ability, integrity, and physical power and energy.

The reports of the education department of India and of the administrative departments show what the abilities and acquirements of the natives are, and how offices of trust and responsibility hitherto entrusted to educated Indians have been discharged by them.

The testimony as to the ability and intelligence of the natives is now complete, that the intellect of the natives of India is equal to that o' any other people. Its ancient literature speaks for itself, and the result of modern education is that its universities declare, year after year, that their work is successful, and that graduates begin to number by hundreds, and undergraduates by thousands. I shall revert to this point again shortly, in connection with the question of integrity.

With regard to the general integrity and character of the whole nation, it would be too long to go over the ground I have once treated in my paper on the European and Asiatic races. Nor is it at present necessary for me to do so, as the question now before us is not the indiscriminate employment of natives generally in high offices of trust and responsibility, but only of that class which proves itself qualified by its high education, ability, and character. Now, it would be a strange commentary on the educational results of the English colleges in India (which are very justly regarded, both by the English nation and the natives, as one of the greatest boons and blessings conferred by England upon India), and on the character of all English intellectual, moral, and scientific literature, if the highly educated youths of these colleges did not also attain to high moral character. But as in the immutable order of nature a good seed can never produce bad fruit, especially in a soil that has once proved itself fertile, it is not the fact that the education of these colleges does not raise the sense of moral duty of the students. I might here reason out a long argument to show why the natives ought to be and are as good as any other people under similar circumstances; but, as any length of argument or number of assertions will not carry conviction home to those who have now to pronounce on this point so completely as a few actual facts, I applied my self to this task. Before I give you the result, I have to make one observation. I do not do this in any spirit of recrimination, or ill-feeling, nor do I wish to urge the delinquencies of any one class as any justification for those of another; but it is only in simple fairness and justice that I ask English gentlemen to make proper allowances. Those gentlemen who so often cast stones at the want of integrity and the corruption of the natives should not forget how some Englishmen in India, in former days, were suddenly transformed into rich Nawabs; how Mr. Drake got his Rs. 2,80,000, or how a number of others got their lakhs to side with one or other of the contending native princes, to the tune of some millions sterling within nine years, from 1757 to 1766,* and how, after selling their power and influence in India in the above manner, the Company bought their power in the English legislature, by bribing in the legislature to something like £90,000 in the year 1693;† how the Company's servants cheated their own masters; how, in Mr. Mills' words, in one matter, "the conduct of the Company's servants upon this occasion furnishes one of the most remarkable instances upon record of the

* Mills' 'British India,' vol. iii., ed. 1826, p 326.

† Ibid, vol. i., ed. 1826, p. 115.

power of interest to extinguish all sense of justice, and even of shame."* It is natural for gentlemen who have received a high education, and who begin their Indian service or life with high pay or profits, and high prospects, to feel indignant at the bribery and curruption of the poor people with low education, low pay or profits, and low prospects, and exclaim how can such things be. But if those gentlemen would only observe a little more around themselves, observe the amount of fraud and "doing" in this metropolis, if they would only remember the cry very recently raised against butchers and grocers, and discounts for servants, the convictions for false weights, the puffs of advertisements, the corruption among the "independent and intelligent electors" and their respectable corruptors, that, as said above, English gentlemen bought and sold power, and that several Englishmen from the lower classes are not behaving quite creditably in India now, etc., they will then see that such things not only can be, but *are* to be found even in this country under similar circumstances, learn to make allowances for similar phenomena among other people, and agree in the "decided conviction" expressed by the Court of Directors,† that "we have no right to calculate on them (the natives) resisting temptations to which the generality of mankind in the same circumstances would yield."

The real question now, gentlemen, is whether, when natives are as highly educated as Englishmen, they attain to the same character for integrity or not, whatever may be the difference of opinion about the character of the whole nation, or native agency generally.

---

* Ibid, vol. iii., ed. 1826, p. 300.

† Letter to Bengal Government, dated 23rd July, 1824.

I have collected a large amount of testimony with regard to native agency. Here I have in my hand a pamphlet of ninety-five pages, entitled 'Evidences relating to the Efficiency of Native Agency in India, published under the superintendence of the British India Society, reprinted with a supplement by the British Indian Association, Calcutta, 1853.' This pamphlet contains a collection of the testimony of Indian officials up to 1853. We have further in the Parliamentary reports of the same year a large amount of evidence on the same subject, and also a good deal scattered over in different works, or in periodical literature. But for our present purpose nearly the whole of this mass of evidence is inapplicable; and therefore useless to lay before you. All this evidence has been chiefly upon the question of native agency *generally*, but the present question is not the efficiency and integrity of the natives generally, but of the particular body who can pass the ordeal of a high examination and produce satisfactory testimony of character. I therefore thought proper to request several Indian officials now resident in this country to give me their opinion. I addressed the following letter :—

"I shall be exceedingly obliged if you would kindly give me your opinion as to the efficiency and integrity of the educated natives employed in the various departments of the Indian service in offices of trust and responsibility."

To this inquiry several gentlemen have kindly replied. I give you all these replies in Appendix A, and leave you to judge for yourselves. Out of the testimony already published I give you a few extracts only in the same appendix, which directly bear upon the present question. It will be observed that the appended testimony represents *all* parts of India. Sir W. Denison's opinion appears unfavourable. He admits that there *are*, even though as exceptions, some natives who *are* serving the state with efficiency. Now, it is only for men like these, and who can also prove their character, no matter whether they are few or many, that our memorial asks for free admission. It is only those natives who can prove their ability by passing through a severe ordeal, and who can also prove their character by satisfactory testimony (and not natives indiscriminately), that we ask admission for. And even after such natives are admitted, if any is found wanting, either in efficiency or integrity, there is nothing to prevent Government from dismissing him. Nor is Government bound to promote, unless satisfied with the merits of any servant. Against Sir W. Denison's opinion representing Madras, we have, on the other hand, a different opinion from Lord Harris, Sir C. Trevelyan, General Briggs, and Mr. Edward Maltby. On a fair estimate of the whole evidence, I venture to conclude that the educated natives of India, when employed in the public service, *have* proved their efficiency and integrity. My humble testimony may be worthless, especially in a matter in which I am one of the petitioners; but I think I may at least say what I conscientiously believe, that as a native, and therefore having good opportunity of knowing the private character of the educated natives of the Bombay Presidency, many of whom were my students, fellow-students, friends, acquaintances, or fellow-labourers in public movements (without undertaking to give an opinion as to their efficiency, though I know well their ability), I conscientiously believe that their integrity is undoubted, and that they are actuated by a true and genuine sense of moral duty in their good conduct and public spirit. Among them a spirit of condemning any lapse of duty, to the want of which, among natives generally, Sir R. Wallace alludes, is getting very strong, and the severest reproach that any one administers to another is to tell him that he did not behave in a way worthy of his education. The feeling among them is very strong, that their high education demands from them a high moral character, and a performance of their duties. I can give extracts of open censure from the native press. Our present rulers may well be proud of such result of their educational establishments, and point to it as one of their strongest claims upon our loyalty and gratitude. It only now remains for our rulers to let such results bear good fruit, instead of running into discontent and mischief, by giving a fair and reasonable scope for the talent evolved. The question is simple: either the natives must be allowed to have a fair share in the administration of the country, or the nation must be kept ignorant, and the rulers take the chances of the results of such ignorance and hatred for foreign rule combined therewith.

I am glad to say that as far as I am aware of the views of some of the English principals and professors of the colleges in the Bombay Presidency, they are the same with mine, and it is with much pleasure I find that Sir A. Grant, the present Director of Public Instruction, has distincly recorded his opinion as follows. In his report as Principal of Elphinstone College.* for 1862-63, he says, "As far as my experience goes, nothing can be more untrue than the common notion that English education is injurious to the moral principle of natives.

* Bombay Education Report, 1862-63, p. 94

In the College, I have invariably found that students improve in trustworthiness and respectability in direct ratio to their improvements as scholars." Any doubts about the physical energy or pluck of the candidates can easily be removed by requiring any test for the purpose. Certainly, the people with whose assistance, as the native army, the British Indian Empire has been mostly built up, cannot be pronounced as wanting in physical power and energy. They ought to have a fair trial. From the political cause of long subjection to foreign rules, and several religious and social causes, it cannot be denied that the people of several portions of India are enervated, —those of Lower Bengal I am told especially; and some Englishmen, observing the effeminacy of these people have drawn the general conclusion with regard to all India. But about this very people Mr. Anstey told us the other day*: "Who were the Sikhs when their prophet first found them out? Poor miserable starving fugitives from Bengal, of whom their great founder, knowing well the stuff from which Asiatics were made, looking with a prophetic eye into the future, said, 'I will teach the sparrow to strike the eagle.' In comparison with the great dignity of Aurungzebe, it was the sparrow as compared to the eagle, and in less than a century the sparrow did strike the eagle."

Let, therefore, the natives once feel that it is time for them to shake off this effeminacy, and that, under the blessing and ægis of the British Rule, there is full scope for the head, heart and hand, and I have no doubt they will prove themselves worthy of the power and civilization they once possessed, and of the blessing of the

* Journal of the East Indian Association, No. 2, p. 182.

new regeneration now bestowed upon them by the light of the higher enlightenment and civilization of the West by their British rulers.

In short, whatever may be the value of the objection as to the efficiency, integrity, and energy of the natives, the very fact that none can find admission into the service who are not qualified as required, removes the objection altogether. I once more wish to impress that it is not only the willingness of a native to be examined that will find him admission into the examination-room, but he will have to prove to the satisfaction of Government that he is a person of character, in the same way as the candidate is required to do here; that his futher promotion will be entirely in the hands of Government, and his failure will bring dismissal.

2. "That Europeans would not like to serve under natives."

This I cannot help considering as a libel on the English character. I have a much higher opinion of it than to believe that Englishmen are not capable of appreciating and respecting true merit. Moreover, facts disprove this objection. The native judges of the high as well as the subordinate courts, and natives in any other position of eminence, are respected by English subordinates. Englishmen serve both here and in India native masters with every respect. In the Bombay dockyard, Englishmen served under native superiors. In short, it would be strange if it were otherwise, for Englishmen are especially alive to merit. Why, if there be any Englishmen in the service, who should be so lost to their sense of duty and appreciation of true merit as to be reluctant to serve under natives of merit, they do not deserve to be in the service at all.

3. "That native officials are not much respected by the natives, and are envied and slandered."

This objection can only be the result of the ignorance of the feelings of the natives towards officials of real merit, be they Englishmen or natives. The gratification of seeing their own countrymen rise in dignity and honour is naturally as great among the natives as among any other people. That narrow minded or interested people will envy others is a trait which can be met with as much among any other people as among the natives of India. Only some weeks ago I read in the *Hindu Reformer* of Bombay, of 15th January last, "We hail with excessive joy the selection of Mr. Mhadeo Govind Ranade, M.A., LL.B., Niayadhish of Kolapore, to fill the chair of English Literature and History in the Elphinstone College. . . . . The honour which is thus conferred on Mr. Ranade is as much deserved by him as it is suggestive of his superior accomplishments as a scholar, and we have not the slightest doubt that it will cause much satisfaction to all who take an interest in the cause of the education of the youth of this Presidency." This is a fair specimen of the feelings of the natives towards their countrymen of merit. I can give more extracts if necessary. When I was appointed Professor of Mathematics in the same College, I can candidly say that I think I was looked upon with very kindly feelings by my countrymen around me generally, as well as by the students of the College and the masters of the school departments. The feelings of my European colleagues were so kind towards me that I shall always remember them with pleasure and gratitude.

Turning to official testimony, I think none can be more satisfactory and complete than the following :—

In one of the Government Gazettes of Calcutta, of last year, the following paragraph appeared: "The Governor-General in Council has received, with sincere regret, official intimation of the death of the Hon'ble Shamboonath Pundit, one of the Judges of Her Majesty's High Court at Fort William. The Hon'ble the Chief Justice in communicating this intelligence to the Governor-General has said: 'So far as Mr. Justice Shamboonath Pundit was concerned, the experiment of appointing a native gentleman to a seat in the High Court has succeeded. He had a considerable knowledge of his profession, and a thorough acquaintance with the natives. I have always found him upright, honourable, and independent, and I believe that he was looked up to by his countrymen with respect and confidence.' The interest which both in India and England attaches to the experiment of placing a native gentleman in the highest judicial situation in the country has induced the Governor-General in Council to make public the opinion of the Honourable the Chief Justice, in which His Excellency entirely agrees."

Certainly, the above extracts prove anything but envy. They also disprove the first objection as to the ability and character of the natives. Sir A. Grant is no ordinary judge of scholarship, and that *he* should appoint a native as Professor of English Literature and History speaks volumes. The testimony of the Governor-General and the Chief Justice about Pundit Shamboonath speaks for itself.

The Court of Directors say, "The ability and integrity of a large and increasing number of the native judges to whom the greater part of the civil jurisdiction in India is now committed, and the high estimation in which many among them are held by their fellow countrymen," etc.*

The North-West Provinces report that the Courts of Honorary Magistrates appear to possess the confidence of the people.†

4. "That natives look too much to Government employment, and do not shew sufficient independence of character to strike out for themselves other paths of life."

This is also contrary to facts, and has its origin in superficial observation, or in the knowledge of particular localities. That they should look to Government appointments, and wish to aspire to a share in the administration of their own country, is only as natural with them as with Englishmen here. Until lately there were very few openings for educated men. The legal profession being now open to them, many are going to it. The medical profession is availed of as far as it can be, in spite of the prejudices against dissection. But except at the Presidency and some other large towns, an educated doctor can hardly get practice suited to his position; the number, therefore, of well-educated practitioners who can at present pursue this profession with profit is limited. The fact that European doctors chiefly confine themselves to the Presidency and some few other towns, shows that the field for educated medical men is not yet very large. The educated theological profession has yet to be created, except among native Christians. The Gujurati Hindus of India have been merchants from time immemorial, and they are still as enterprising as ever. There is a large internal commerce carried on by the natives. Many among educated natives would gladly become

* 'Educational Despatch of 1854', p. 77.

† 'Return, Moral, etc., Progress, 1867', p. 88.

merchants, or follow other professions, if they had the requisite capital or means. During the years 1862-64, when there was such a rush for trade and speculation, many natives left Government service. The manufacturers of England, especially textile, have broken down very much the corresponding industries of India; and now, as the establishment of manufactories is a question of large capital, it is naturally shut to those who do not possess it. Still, several natives get employment in such as are established. In railways and other works they are ready to be employed. Besides, civil and marine engineering is adopted by several.

In short, this objection may be answered briefly in this way—that there are only about 400 natives in Government service at a salary above £300 per annum and upwards (see Return 201-206, 1858, 223; sec. ii, 1859). What do all those other thousands of natives do who are also earning as much? So far as the native finds an independent opening, he does not fail to take advantage of it. I know from my experience of the educated natives of the Bombay Presidency, that they are very glad to have independent careers.

So far was I convinced of this and of the necessity of affording facilities for new careers, that I made an attempt in 1864 to adopt some means to enable highly talented natives to continue their studies for professional careers *after* completing their college education. One of the natives of Bombay offered a lakh, and some others Rs. 1,75,000 for two fellowships of Rs. 200 and Rs. 300 per month respectively, and asked Government to contribute as much; but unfortunately the offer was not accepted by Government.

In addition to these fellowships, which were intended to encourage high education and high independent careers, there was also started for the less educated, and the enterprising spirits generally, a "Students' Loan Company," to lend money at moderate interest to persons wishing to visit England and other places, to complete their education or to learn any trade, art, or profession. The Rs. 300 fellowship and the Students' Loan Company were intended for the benefit of all India. The commercial crash broke down all these proposals. I don't think that there can be any question that the natives do *not* look to Government employments any more than the people of any other country in similar circumstances. Supposing, however, for argument's sake, that there was among the natives some tendency to look a little too much to Government employments, that certainly can be no good reason that they should therefore be debarred from aspiring to a reasonable extent to a share in the service of their own country when *qualified* by their ability and character. It is said that this tendency was observed in Lower Bengal, but, even in that part of India, the tendency, if it ever existed to any unreasonable extent, is now changing. The body of independent barristers, solicitors, and vakils, doctors, and merchants shows that even the Bengalees are not blind to the advantages of independent careers as they become open to them.

5. "That, though natives may prove good subordinates, they are not fitted to be placed at the head of any department."

Without giving a fair trial, such an objection is, to say the least, very unreasonable. Besides, the objection is not borne out by facts. In many instances in which natives have been put in positions of trust and responsibility, they have shown themselves equal to their duties, as you must have seen from the evidence I have read to you. If, in any case, Government found inefficiency, there could be no difficulty in removing it, just as it does with English servants. Moreover, after getting admission into the service, the natives would not be put at the head all at once. They will have to show their efficiency, and to work their way up; and Government will have every opportunity of testing whom they can trust and whom not with higher positions.

6. "That natives who seek for admission into the Civil Service should be first Anglicised."

The education that natives receive in India is in itself a process of Anglicising them, with this advantage, that they retain the sympathy and knowledge of their own country; and if a native is required to visit this country after his selection by the first competition, the object of the visit to this country will be realized. If it be thought that two years' visit to this country is not enough, there can be no difficulty in arranging and requiring the native successful candidates to spend a little longer time here; because the reasons why English candidates are required to go to India at an early age do not apply to the natives, as the natives do not require to be acclimatized, nor do they require the same time to learn the character, thoughts and habits of the people that foreigners do.

I do not mean to say that young boys should not also be brought here for education. But there are many difficulties and troubles for taking care of them. Unless good care is taken to keep them within the charm of the circle of good society, there is some danger of evil instead of good resulting. When those educated in India come here at a mature age, everything they see is novel to them, every moment of their sojourn here is valuable, and spent in comparisons; they return to India *enthusiastic*, and do much good. We know what good a Karsandas Moolji or a Dosabhoy Framjee has done to their country by their visits here. Now, it is not to be understood that the objections given above to very young boys coming here, or what I have said in favour of visits at a greater age, apply generally. There are some youths under my care for several years, who, I am sure, will do credit to themselves and benefit to their country. I give the above *pros* and *cons* not as a speculation, but the actual result of my experience during the past twelve years, during which time a good many youths have been under my care, coming here at different ages, from about ten to twenty-one. Upon the whole, I think that the necessity of coming here at an early age cannot be reasonably urged against holding examinations in India. There is much to be said in favour of both early and late visits to this country, and the best course will be to have a proper proportion of both. As I shall point out hereafter, there are strong objections urged to making compulsory any visit at all to this country, either before or after selection, on account of the caste difficulty for the Hindus, who form the majority of the native population.

7. " That natives ought not to be put in positions of power."

If the British Rule is to be based on willing consent and sincere loyalty, it is necessary that means be adopted to give the natives an interest in and a gratitude for the British Rule, by giving them a reasonable share and voice in the administration of the country. If

India is a trust for the good of India, that trust ought to be faithfully discharged. It is rather strange that there should ever have been at this day a necessity to ask whether the British or Native Rule was more liked by the natives. The question should have been by this time put beyond all doubt. There is no comparison between law above sovereign and sovereign above law. I must wait for another opportunity to give my views fully on this subject. If, instead of fearing to give a reasonable share of power to the natives, our rulers would do what remains to be done, they may well challenge the whole world to say whether they have not acted nobly. Unless the people are taught what British Rule and machinery of administration are, and are brought up with the idea that the British Rule is a blessing to them, it is simply unreasonable to hope that they could appreciate what they do not understand. We may as well expect the blind to appreciate a painting. If with this knowledge, by national education, is associated a gratification of the high aspirations and patriotic feelings of the educated native for a voice and share in the government of his country, and if the material prosperity of the mass is promoted by a bold policy for public works to develop the resources of the country, and if the princes and the aristocracy be sure of good faith with them, and receive the benefit of good advice, Britian may well point to its handiwork with pride, and India may for ever remember with gratitude the hand that raised it. If, in consideration of the interest which England has to retain her power in India, it gave India the benefit of all her influence and credit, by guaranteeing the Indian debt, the relief to India of some two millions a year will go for to the attainment of the other objects. Great indeed would that statesman be, the benefactor of India, who would achieve this glorious work of regenerating a nation of 200 millions. If the British don't prove better rulers, why should they be in India? However, be the value of the above remarks what it may, one thing is certain, that among the remedies pointed out, and those I think as necessary to make the British Rule popular and beloved, this one at least, of giving freely and impartially to the natives a share in the administration of the country, is admitted on all hands by those who have given their opinions to the Viceroy, and their reviewers in the Press and Parliament. I will just remark here that, in connection with the necessity of giving a voice in the application of the revenues, the very modest proposal made in a petition by the British Indian Association of Calcutta, reported in the *Times of India* Summary of 7th March last, will, I hope, have due consideration from the Secretary of State for India.

That there is no danger in entrusting power to educated natives is proved by the well-known fact that they understand and appreciate *most* the benefits of English Rule, and, in the words of Sir B. Frere: "And now, wherever I go, I find the best exponents of the policy of the English Government, and the most able coadjutors in adjusting that policy to the peculiarities of the natives of India, among the ranks of the educated natives," etc., etc.' I also showed this at some length in my paper on "England's Duties to India."

8. "That the places obtained by the natives will be so many less to the English people."

The mere statement of this objection is its own condemnation as to its selfishness and want of a due sense of justice, statesmanship, and the high moral responsibilities of the British in India. It is the plain duty of Government to secure the most efficient service they can, and for that purpose let the words proclaimed in the name of the Sovereign be honestly fulfilled, "that as far as may be our subjects, of whatever race or creed, be *freely* and *impartially* admitted to offices in our service, the duties of which they may be qualified by their education, ability, and integrity to discharge." To compel the natives to come to England for competition for service in their own country is no more reasonable, free, are impartial, than it would be to compel Englishmen to go to India or Australia for admisson into the Civil Service in England.

9. "That natives are already largely employed."

The facts, however, are these. There are above 1,700 Europeans in the covenanted services in India at a cost of above three millions per annum, at a salary of from £240 to £25,000 per annum (Return 116 to 1860). There are 849 Europeans and Anglo-Indiana in the uncovenanted service, at salaries of £300 and upwards; while of natives there are only about 600 at a salary at and above £240 a year (Return 201—vi. 1858, 223, sec. ii., 1859), of whom about 350 are between £240 and £360 per annum. This return will also show how very few —only about a dozen—natives there are at salaries at and above £840 a year. Since these returns there have been some few more high positions given to the natives, but I cannot say whether there is yet any or more than one or two above the salary of £2,000 per annum.

In my remarks of course I don't mean to say that there are not and, would not hereafter be, found black sheep among the educated natives as among any other people, but that in a fair trial the natives will come up to the average of ability and honesty of any other people.

There is only one more point to which I wish to draw your attention. To the Hindu the caste question is socially of great importance till the system is broken down. It may be said that a candidate for the Civil Service ought to show that he has the moral courage to break through such trammels. This he would do by his visit to this country *after* his selection, but it is certainly not reasonable to expect that any one should subject himself to great sacrifices both of money and social position on the risk of the uncertain result of his venture. If he succeeds in his competition in India, he acquires a certain position of respect, and he can then well undertake the journey to this country with the £100 for the first year, and £200 for the second year, which will be allowed to him by Government, with the double object of completing his qualifications and of giving a finish to his education, and of dealing with the trammels of caste with advantage. It is not proper to sneer at the cowardice of submitting to the caste system. The English even now have their trammels in other shapes, as of fashions, society, etc., and had till very lately their exclusive guilds. The English ought also not to forget at what cost reformations have taken place in Europe, and what previous preparation of the revival of knowledge has been necessary, and has led to them. The Hindu institution of caste has a growth of centuries and over a people numbering above a hundred and fifty millions. It is so intimately mixed with some of the most important social relations of births, deaths, and marriages, that due allowance ought to be made for the difficulties and sacrifices of overcoming its difficulties.

Some English and native gentlemen, with much effect, urge that the Hindus should not be subjected to this sacrifice at all, by being required to come to this country even *after* selection. When I consider the advantages of travelling in foreign countries, which is so much considered of for the youth of this country even, when I see the necessity of the natives in high positions being able to deal with English officials on a footing of equality in the knowledge of the world, especially of the English world, I cannot help still urging that the visit to this country after the selection should be insisted on: though I think the first Hindus coming here, even *after* the selection, will have to put up with much inconvenience and sacrifice, and be something of martyrs in a good cause.

I am also emboldened to adhere to this opinion by finding that some of the native papers of Bombay, conducted by *Hindus* themselves, have also expressed their views that the visit to this country after selection is desirable. Moreover, in the petition from the Bombay Association, adopted at a large and influential meeting at the house of its President, the Hon'ble Mr. Munguldass Nathoobhoy, and by his advice being extensively signed by *all* classes of natives, it is also proposed, "that if necessary they (the selected candidates) may be required to proceed to England to receive a course of special training, prescribed by the existing regulations, for which there are greater facilities in Europe than in India." Besides, though there may be some inconveniences to the first native civilians, the respectability of their position, and the certainty of the number of such officials increasing every year, will give them in time sufficient weapons to fight their battles against losing caste. Also, if I am not mistaken in my impression, I think the following circumstance has already met the difficulty, or at least prepared the way for the visitors to this country, *after* their selection, being able to deal with some ease and power with the question of losing caste. I remember, whether from reading or from conversation I cannot tell, that His Highness the Holkar intended to send some pundits to this country. He called a meeting of the learned Brahmins, and asked their opinion. It was decided in that assembly, that persons going abroad for *State* purposes do not lose caste, because in the glory and height of Hindu power, ambassadors went to different courts for State purposes. If so, that will be just the proper argument for *selected* candidates. After their selection, being servants of the *State*, and being required by their Sovereign to visit this country for qualifying themselves for State purposes, they cannot lose caste.

It is said by some that if Government grant the second part of our memorial, by conferring scholarships upon youths after a certain competition, those youths will be able to study for the service and compete here; and the object of opening the service freely and impartially to the natives of India will be gained. Nothing can be a greater mistake, I think. Now, it must be borne in mind that the scholarships are intended to leave the scholars holding them free to pursue whatever professional study they like, in order especially to create an independent class of educated native gentlemen. If the stipend of these scholarships is sufficient to enable youths to come here, its natural effect will be that most of them will prefer other independent professions, as certain in-their results, to studying for the Indian service with the risk of failure, and the want of opportunity to learn any profession afterwards. Then to the Hindu the failure in the competition here will be the greatest injury possible; for having first incurred the penalties of losing caste, and the displeasure of his friends, the mark of failure on his forehead, no matter whether deserved or not, would render him an object of ridicule among his countrymen. Such an amount of sacrifice it is utterly unreasonable and cruel to exact. But after he is selected in India, and is sure of his position, it is reasonable for important purposes that some sacrifice and inconvenience should be asked from him. There is another way in which mere dependence upon this scholarships will not secure the free admission of the *best* talent of the country. We must remember that it is not the horse who makes the best start that always wins. So by this plan of scholarships, if even all studied for the Indian service, contrary to the real object, the State will be spending money upon good starters only, whether they may ultimately succeed or not. But by allowing the competition in India, the State without this expenditure gets the actual winners of the race in a competition of a large number, who have proved their mental calibre as well as their character, by their stay through a trying college course and by fulfilling all the conditions of ability and character for admission, and who at an advanced age can be left by their friends to act as they like, and are able to take care of themselves. While the boys are very young, many parents would be unwilling to allow their sons to go to a distant country out of their own care, and thus again the area of selection for the scholarships will be much limited, but young men at the age required for the competition are more free to act and more able to take care of themselves. So that we then have a competition among all those who have proved talent and character. You will see, therefore, that though these scholarships may remove the obstacle of money, there are, in the case of the Hindus especially —who, it must be borne in mind, form the principal population of India—other most serious obstacles, which can only be dealt with by transferring the examination for a portion of the selection to India.

The Governor-General in his Resolution last year admits that "he is fully alive to the urgent political necessity that the progress of education has created, for opening up to natives of ability and character a more important, dignified, and lucrative sphere of employment in the administration of British India ;" and as the remedy, His Excellency recognizes the eligibility of natives for only some higher grades in the non-regulation provinces. First of all the natural effect of this will be that those serving and living in those provinces will very likely have in time the little benefit thus held out, while in the regulation provinces—those in which education has advanced most—the natives of which have the greatest claim for a share in the administration as British subjects of long standing, should be required to incur all the sacrifices and risks (which to the Hindu are of no ordinary order) involved in a visit to this country for several years as youths. If the political necessity is so emphatically admitted by the Viceroy, I do not see how it is possible to rest satisfied with offering a few situations in the non-regulation provinces. Mark again, it is only to men of ability and character. If so, how can anything short of a free competition in India give a satisfactory fulfilment to this political necessity and an honest performance of the promise of our gracious Sovereign?

Such honest and candid declarations of necessity and justice, when followed by poor and inadequate fulfilment, naturally create dissatisfaction and irritation.

It is said that high appointments in the uncovenanted service may be given to natives in the regulation provinces also; but if qualified natives are to be trusted with such high appointments in the uncovenanted service, in regulation or non-regulation provinces, why are they unfit to enter the covenanted service? Certainly, no one means to say that high uncovenanted appointments require less trustworthiness, responsibility, respect, or confidence than covenanted appointments. Has the word "uncovenanted" such a charm that it at once removes all those objections which are urged against the free and impartial admission of qualified natives into the covenanted service? If the declarations of Government are sincere, of which I have no doubt, then I see no escape for the honest fulfilment of the words of our Sovereign and Parliament from holding examinations in India, as proposed by us, so as to put *all* Her Majesty's subjects on a fairly equal footing.

Again, in the uncovenanted service also, the principle of appointment or promotion should be fitness, no matter whether the right person be European or native, only that the principle should be honestly adhered to.

It is sometimes urged that natives do not learn for learning's sake. It is strange anybody could be expected to appreciate a thing before he knows what it is. Educated natives fully appreciate learning.

I hope, gentlemen, I have satisfied you that educated natives have already shown ability and character as among any other people (and which is tacitly admitted by the Viceroy himself), and that the only honest way of fulfilling the promise of our Sovereign and Acts of Parliament, of securing the best talent for the service, and of increasing the loyalty and gratitude of India, is by giving a free admission to such natives of ability and character by competition in India.

You will have observed that I have not entered into any discussion of the great benefit to the administration and of the encouragement and inducement to high education, not only among the people generally, but among the higher and aristocratic classes, by the granting of our petition. The whole of India will by this concession be quite electrified. But as on this point there is no doubt or question, it is unnecessary for me to take up your time nor could I enter on it fully in this paper.

Now, gentlemen, I have said my say, and leave to you to say or act as you think proper. I conclude by moving the Resolution of which I have given notice :—

"That a letter be addressed to the Secretary of State for India, with a copy of this paper, to request him to take it into his consideration, and in reply to Mr. H. Fawcett's motion, to accede to the memorial presented on 21st August last by a deputation from this Association."*

* Appendix B.

C.*

The whole Indian problem in all its aspects, material, moral, industrial, educational, political, etc., will be solved only when means are adopted to check the annual disastrous drain of the produce of India and to bring it within reasonable and moderate limits. I have gone into the details of this subject in my papers on "The Poverty of India," and in the Correspondence with the Secretary of State for India on the "Condition of India." I shall add here only, one more testimony of the highest financial authority, the late Finance Minister, Sir E. Baring, on the extreme poverty of India, and corroborating my calculation of the very low income of this country as compared with the worst European country—Turkey. Here is this emphatic testimony in addition to the opinions given in my "Poverty of India," Part I., especially of Lords Lawrence and Mayo, and of Mr. Grant Duff as Under-Secretary of State for India, with regard to all India, at page 278. Sir E. Baring in his Budget speech of 18th March, 1882, says:—

"It has been calculated that the average income per head of population in India is *not more than rupees 27 a year*, † *and though I am not prepared to pledge myself to*

---

* Revised Memorandum on the most important Reforms needed by India. (Submitted for the consideration of the last and present Viceroys, and some other high Officials in India in 1884.)

† I make not more than rupees 20. I requested Sir E. Baring to give me his calculations, either to correct mine or his, but I am sorry he declined. However this difference is a matter of not much consequence, as it makes but very little difference in proving the *extreme poverty* of India. (The italics are mine.)

the absolute accuracy of a calculation of this sort, it is sufficiently accurate to justify the conclusion that the tax-paying community is *exceedingly poor*. To derive any very large increase of revenue from so poor a population as this is obviously impossible, and if it were possible, would be unjustifiable."

Again, in the discussion on the same Budget, he said, after repeating the above statement of rupees 27 per head per annum:—

". . . But he thought it was quite sufficient to show the *extreme poverty* of the mass of the people. In England, the average income per head of population was £33 per head; in France, it was £23; in Turkey, which was the poorest country in Europe, it was £4 per head. He would ask honourable members to think what rupees 27 per annum was to support a person, and then he would ask whether a few annas was nothing to such poor people."

This was stated in connection with salt duty. It must be remembered that rupees 27 (or my rupees 20) is the average income, including that of the richest, or all various disproportionate distribution that takes place among all grades of people, while the average of the lower classes only will be very poor indeed.

The whole problem of India is in a nutshell. *Never* can a foreign rule be anything but a curse to any country, except so far as it approaches a native rule.

Hoping that my papers will be carefully studied, I confine myself here to the remedy of the evil in its practical form. I may explain here that a part of the drain I complain of is not to be laid *directly* at the door of Government. It is in the hands of the natives to prevent it if they could and would. I mean the employment of non-official professional agency, such as barristers, solicitors, engineers, doctors, etc. Though not *directly*, the English official agency *indirectly* compels natives to employ such European non-official agency. English officials in power generally, and naturally, show more sympathy with and give greater encouragement to English professional men. The result is that the portion of the drain caused by the non-official Europeans is as much, though indirectly the result of Government or official action, as the other portion of the drain. The remedy, therefore, I am proposing, will influence the whole drain.

This remedy is in the power of the English Parliament only. It is (though at first sight it is not so readily apparent) the transference of examinations to India for services in all the civil departments—civil, medical, engineering, forest, telegraph, or any other. Canada, Australia, or the Cape, are not compelled to go to England for their services. Over India alone does England impose its despotic will in this one respect. This, in fact, is *the* one important act of the British nation, which is now un-English and unjust, and which mars and nullifies all the other blessings (which are not few) conferred by it upon India. Let England be just to India and true to itself in this one respect, and honestly, according to the Queen's proclamation, and declarations of British statesmen and Acts of Parliament, let the natives have free scope to serve in their own country, and every other measure for the purposes of good government and administration, or for improving the material and moral condition of India, which at present generally fails or produces poor and doubtful results, will be crowned with success. Every matter will then fall into its natural groove, and the effect on every thing will be marvellous. Private efforts will receive natural and immense impetus for providing all higher education, leaving Government to devote itself, with far ampler means than at present, to primary education as in England. So will railways and all public works and all private enterprise receive a rapid and successful development. And, above all, will be this most important result—that the growing prosperity of India will lead to a *truly great and extensive trade between England and India*, far outweighing the present benefit to England at the sacrifice of and misery to India.

Of course, when examinations for *all* the higher services in *all* the civil departments are transferred to India, the ruling and controlling offices should be mainly reserved for Englishmen, such as the Viceroy, the Governors and their Councillors, the Chief Secretaries, and Board of Revenue (if such boards be of any use) and chief heads of departments. Admission of any natives to any such appointments should be entirely in the gift of the Government, as a special reward for some high and exceptional services and deed of loyalty. In the military department, the English should have the chief share, leaving some fair scope for the warlike races, to draw and attach them to the side of the British Rule. It will never do to repress all military ambition altogether. This will be a great mistake.

The subject of the confidence which our British rulers ought to show towards their subjects, and thereby beget and acquire the sincere confidence of the subjects in response, both by trusting them with reasonable military position, and by allowing and encouraging volunteering, under some well-considered principles and rules, is too important and extensive to be adequately treated in a short space. I can only say that it deserves our rulers' serious consideration. The open want of confidence by the British rulers is a weakness to them, and cannot but in time lead to evil.

If the examinations, as a first step, are not altogether transferred to India, simultaneous examinations at least ought to be held in India for *all* the services. This great reform and justice to India is absolutely necessary. This alone will be a fair fulfilment of the promises of the Act of 1833, of the gracious proclamation of 1858, and of the various declarations made from time to time by English statesmen and Governments. At least, for simultaneous examinations in India and England, the India Office itself has unequivocally admitted its justice and necessity. I give below an extract from a Report of a Committee of the India Council (consisting of Sir J. P. Willoughby, Sir Erskine Perry, Mr. Mangles, Mr. Arbuthnot, and Mr. Macnaghten) made to Sir C. Wood (Lord Halifax) on 20th January, 1860. The Report says:

"2. We are in the first place unanimously of opinion that it is not only just, but expedient, that the natives of India shall be employed in the administration of India to as large an extent as possible, consistently with the maintenance of British supremacy, and have considered whether any increased facilities can be given in this direction.

"3. It is true that, even at present, no positive disqualification exists. By Act 3 and 4, Wm. IV., c. 85, s. 87, it is enacted 'that no native of the said territories, nor any natural born subject of His Majesty resident therein, shall by reason only of his religion, place of birth, descent, colour or any of them, be disabled from holding any place, office, or employment under the said Company.' It is obvious, therefore, that when the competitive system was adopted, it could not have been intended to exclude natives of India from the Civil Service of India.

"4. Practically, however, they are excluded. The law declares them eligible, but the difficulties opposed to a native leaving India and residing in England for a time are so great, that as a general rule, it is almost impossible for a native successfully to compete at the periodical examinations held in England. Were this inequality removed, we should no longer be exposed to the charge of keeping promise to the ear and breaking it to the hope.

"5. Two modes have been suggested by which the object in view might be attained. The first is, by allotting a certain portion of the total number of appointments declared in each year to be competed for in India by natives, and by all other natural-born subjects of Her Majesty resident in India. The second is to hold, simultaneously, two examinations, one in England and one in India, both being, as far as practicable, identical in their nature, and those who compete in both countries being finally classified in one list, according to merit, by the Civil Service Commissioners. 'The Committee have no hesitation in giving the preference to the second scheme as being the fairest and the most in accordance with the principles of a general competition for a common object'."

This principle ought to apply to *all* the services.

Now, I say let Government lay down *any* test—mental, moral and physical—and the natives cannot and would not object being on equal terms with the English candidates. It may also be arranged that every successful candidate in India be required to go to England and study for two years more with the successful candidates of England in their respective departments; or any other arrangement may be adopted by which the successful candidates of India may derive the benefit of two years' residence and study in England in the department in which they have competed successfully. India will be but too happy to have a portion of its revenue devoted to this purpose.

Till this most important, "just and expedient" and

"fairest" measure is adopted, England can never free itself from the charge of "*keeping promise to the ear and breaking it to the hope*," and India can never be satisfied that England is treating her justly and honestly.

But I earnestly submit that this is not merely a question of "justice and expediency," though that is enough in itself for this reform, but that it is absolutely necessary for the *far larger necessity* of the material and moral prosperity of India—for the chief remedy of the present "*extreme poverty*" of India—if English Rule is really and honestly meant to be a just rule and a blessing to this country. My earnest desire and intense interest in this great reform to hold examinations in India, solely, or, at least, simultaneously, for all the services in the Civil Departments (with some fair scope in the military) do not arise simply from the motive of seeing an opening made for the gratification of the natural ambition of educated natives to serve in their own country, but more for the solution of the great question—the question of questions—whether India is to remain poor, disloyal, and cursing England, or to become prosperous, loyal, and blessing England.

Coming to the uncovenanted services, both higher and lower, they must also be reduced to some system of examination, based upon some clear and just principles. The system worked by the Civil Service Commissioners in England for subordinate servants for all the different departments of State may well provide a model for these examinations, according to the higher and lower wants of all the departments for their uncovenanted servants. It will be the best way to secure servants *most fitted* and *best prepared* for their respective departments, and to give to every subject of Her Majesty a free and fair scope and justice according to his merits, relieving Government from the obloquy that is often cast upon it for injustice or favouritism in its appointments.

Next to this great reform for examinations solely or simultaneously in India for all the covenanted services, and for all the uncovenanted in India alone, is the important question of introducing due representation and reform in the Legislative Councils in India. But I consider the first reform as of such *paramount importance* that I do not mix up the second and some others with it here.

VIII.

THE EUROPEAN AND ASIATIC RACES.*

I feel very thankful to Mr. Crawfurd and the Council for allowing me to make a few observations upon Mr. Crawfurd's paper, "on the European and Asiatic Races."

Mr. Crawfurd tells us, in illustration of the mental inferiority of the Asiatics, that in the seminaries at eighteen the native is left far behind by the European, and never after recovers his lost ground. What are the facts? Only a few mails ago, *The Friend of India* tells us, that at the Calcutta University there were then above 1,200 candidates for entrance; that 447 underwent the first examination, and that 120 had applied to compete for the B.A. degree. The *Friend* remarks, "These examinations are assuming a Chinese magnitude, and present a spectacle at once curious and gratifying." The result of my own experience as a teacher and professor for ten years in the Elphinstone Institution, and of my observations for ten years more, is entirely contrary to Mr. Crawfurd's statement. Gambier, Perry, Lewin, Sims, Warden, and others, have given similar opinions in their evidence before Parliament. The mistake made by Mr. Crawfurd is one of those which foreign travellers and writers are very apt to fall into from superficial observation and imperfect information.

When English seminaries were first opened in India, boys were principally sent there with the object

* (Read before the Ethnological Society, London, March 27th, 1866, Observations on the Paper read by John Crawfurd, Esq., F.R.S.)

of acquiring a sufficient knowledge of the English language to enable them to get a situation in Government offices, or to talk and write English. The consequence was, that for some time these seminaries did not produce any scholars, the pupils generally leaving on attaining their main object. With the imperfect education with which they usually left school, and falling again in the society of their own equally or more ignorant countrymen, they were not able to continue their studies. Those Englishmen, however, who watched their progress, but did not understand the cause, wondered at such a result, and concluded that the native youth was incapable of progress after eighteen. There is another circumstance which unfortunately aggravated the mischief; the custom of early betrothal and marriage among the natives. The pupils, therefore, were often fathers before they were eighteen or twenty, and the necessity of supporting a family soon drove them from school to service.

For those who take a real interest in the natives of India, I cannot do better than refer them to that mass of interesting evidence given before Parliamentary Committees by interested and disinterested persons, and I have no doubt that any impartial and candid inquirer will find that the natives of India are not below the average of the head and heart of any other nation in the world.

This evidence was given in 1853 and 1858; but since that time the progress in education and several other matters has been so marked, though not very great, that even this evidence has become obsolete in some particulars. No careful observer will now make the statement that the Hindu is not capable of keeping up his studies after leaving college, much less that he falls back at eighteen and never regains his lost ground. The very fact that the Hindus were even capable of producing a vast and varied literature in all departments of human knowledge, shows beyond all doubt that the capacity to study all life is not wanting. The fertile soil is there, but neglected. Let it have its proper cultivation, and it will again show the same fruit.

Lastly, as Sir C. Trevelyan very justly remarks, what is said about the natives takes place in some degree in all countries, even in England, and as a remedy, he says,—"The main thing required is, to open to them a proper field of mental and moral activity in after life . . . and we should encourage a wholesome mental activity in the pursuits of literature, science, and the fine arts . . . all the avenues of employment in the service of the state should be opened to them.* They have very considerable administrative qualities, great patience, great industry, and great acuteness and intelligence."†

I do not know whether the remarks made by Mr. Crawfurd on Asiatic literature and the dearth of great names are based upon his own personal knowledge of all these literatures or on the authority of others who possess such knowledge, or on the assumption that, because Mr. Crawfurd does not know them, therefore they do not exist. Mr. Crawfurd himself admits that there have been some conquerors, lawgivers, and founders of religious sects. I suppose such names as Christ, Mahomed, Zoroaster, Manu, Confucius, Cyrus, Akbar, Fardoosi, Hafiz, Sadi, Kalidas, Panini, Abool Fazil, and

* Lords' Committee, 1853, ques. 6644.

† Ib. 6605.

a host of others, are such as any nation may be proud of. The Royal Asiatic Society has a descriptive catalogue of 163 manuscripts in their library of 100 distinct Persian and Arabic works on the single subject of history. Sir W. Jones thinks * Persia has produced more writers of every kind, and chiefly poets, than all Europe put together. He mentions a manuscript at Oxford of the lives of 135 of the finest Persian poets.†

Mr. Crawfurd speaks disparagingly of the *Shanameh*, as consisting "of a series of wild romances of imaginary heroes, and of such slender merit that no orientalist has ever ventured on presenting it in a European translation." I hope Mr. Crawfurd has read it, or as authority for what he says. In my humble opinion, from what little I know of it, it is a work of great poetic merit.‡ Sir W. Jones, after giving the palm of superiority to Homer, asserts a very great resemblance between the works of these extraordinary men; and admits that both drew their images from nature herself, and both possessed, in an eminent degree, that rich and creative invention which is the very soul of poetry.§

He considers the characters in it as various and striking; the figures bold and animated, and the diction everywhere sonorous, yet noble; polished, yet full of fire.|| Sir J. Malcolm thinks that the most fastidious European reader will meet with numerous passages of exquisite beauty in the noble epic poem of Firdoosi;

---

* Vol. x., p. 349.

† I have given the opinions of others as closely as possible in their own words.

‡ Dr. Julius Mohl informs me that he has already published four volumes of the text and translation; the fifth is nearly ready for publication, and the sixth is printing.

§ Vol. x., p. 355. || Ibid. 354.

that some of the finest scenes are described with simplicity and elegance of diction, and that to those whose taste is offended with hyperbole, the tender part of his work will have most beauty.* Sir W. Jones considers that the Persian language is rich, melodious, and elegant; that numbers of admirable works have been written in it, by historians, philosophers, and poets, who found it capable of expressing, with equal advantage, the most beautiful and the most elevated sentiments.† With reference to the ridiculous bombast of the Persian style, he remarks, that though there are bad writers, as in every country, the authors who are esteemed in Persia are neither slavish in their sentiments, nor ridiculous in their expressions.

Upon Mr. Crawfurd's remarks as to the absence of any literature or history among the Persians before the Arabian conquest, let us see what Sir John Malcolm says. He says: the Arabs, in their irritation at the obstinate resistance of the Persians for their independent religion, destroyed their cities, temples, etc., etc. And the books, in which were written whatever the learned of the nation knew either of general science, or of their own history, and religion, were, with their possessions, devoted to destruction. He refers, as a parallel, to the fate of Greek and Roman manuscripts, to show how few the works of a conquered and despised nation like Persia, would be saved amid the wreck to which that kingdom was doomed.

He further says:—"We know from sacred history, that the deeds of the Kings of Persia were written in a book styled the chronicles of that kingdom; and we are told by a Grecian author, who was at the court of

* Vol. ii., p. 539. † Vol. v., p. 165.

Artaxerxes Mnemon, that he had access to volumes which were preserved in the royal archives."*

I need not take up your time with more extracts on the merits of other poets. Mr. Fraser, after naming Nizami, Omar Keyormi, Oorfi, and Rudki, says he might cite a hundred others as high examples of genius. Lastly we must bear in mind, that a large amount of Asiatic and European Literature may have been lost in that deplorable act of destruction of the Alexandrian Library by Omar.

In Arabic literature, to the *Arabian Nights*, at least, I hope Mr. Crawfurd accords some merit; for, according to his test of merit the work is translated in European languages, and extensively read, too. Chrickton's *History of Arabia* gives an account of a varied and

* Mr. Ed. B. Eastwick, in reply to my inquiries as to his opinion upon the extracts I have given from Sir W. Jones and Sir John Malcolm on Persian Literature, etc., says:—

"I thoroughly agree in the opinions expressed of Firdausi, and of the Persian poets, by Sir W. Jones and Sir J. Malcolm. The narratives of events in the *Shanameh* are not so unnatural, hyperbolic, or absurd as those in the *Iliad*, and the 'curisa felicitas verborum' cf the Persian poet is little, if at all, inferior to that of Homer. Mr. C. cannot be aware that M. Mohl has translated the *Shanameh* into French and that Atkinson has rendered some portions into English. If Arabic and Persian were taught in our schools, as Greek and Latin are, we should have as many and as careful translations of the *Shanameh* as of the *Iliad*. It is not the slender merit of the poet, but our ignorance of Persian, that has made the dearth of translations. As yet we have only dipped into Persian poetry. No Europeans can pretend to have explored that ocean of literature."

I am sorry that my very slight knowledge of French prevents me from studying, for the present, the annual reports of Dr. Julius Mohl; but I give below, an extract from his letter to me, which I think gives the Eastern literature its proper place in the history of man.

"Oriental literature can only take its place in the universal literature of mankind, when intelligent historians show its vast Arabian literature. He thinks Europe indebted to the Arabs for some of her most valuable lessons in science and arts. He also gives the names of more than half-a-dozen female poetesses and philosophers.

Professor Max Müller thinks that the achievements of the Brahmins in grammatical analysis, which date from six centuries before Christ, are still unsurpassed by any nation.* Colebrook thinks that among the infinity of volumes on Nyaya, there are compositions of very celebrated schoolmen,† and that the Hindu writings abound in every branch of science. Sir W. Jones strongly recommends to Europeans the study of Indian medical works. He says there are many works on music, in prose and verse, with specimens of Hindu airs in a very elegant notation, that the Sanscrit prosody is easy and beautiful, that there are numerous astronomical works, and that wherever we direct our attention to Hindu literature, the notion of *infinity* presents itself, from which we may gather the fruits of science without loading ourselves with the leaves.

No doubt there may be much leaves and branches,

value for history in its largest sense—history of the developement of the human race, its ideas, its manners, etc.; and show too, how large has been the past of the East, and how great in some respects its influence. This is gradually being done, in proportion as translations and researches on special subjects put the materials in the hands of thinking people. It is, above all, the history of religion, of legislation, of philosophy, and of poetry, which will show the importance of Oriental literature; but it is slow work, and cannot be otherwise, by the nature of the case. Greek and Latin literature will always prevail in Europe; our minds have been moulded upon them, and they are nearest to us; but this does not extinguish the claim of the East to take its place. I have said this over and over, in my annual reports to the Asiatic Society."

* Science of Language, p. 80.

† Religion and Philosophy of the Hindus, p. 167.

or much trash, in this vast forest of literature, but we know also what amount of trash is daily poured upon us in the present day.

Sir W. Jones ventures to affirm that the whole of Newton's *Theology*, and part of his *Philosophy*, may be found in the *Vedas*, which also abound with allusion to a force of universal attraction.* With regard to the Sanscrit language, he says, whatever be its antiquity, it is of wonderful structure, more perfect than the Greek, more copious than the Latin, and more exquisitely refined than either.† With all the above opinions of Sir W. Jones Dr. T. Goldstucker concurs.

Horace Wilson thinks it probable that in fiction much of the invention displayed on the revival of letters in Europe was referable to an Indian origin; ‡ that enough has been ascertained to determine the actual existence in Sanscrit or in vernacular translations from it of a very extensive literature of fiction, in which many of our European acquaintances are at once to be recognised,§ and that the Hindus occupy an early and prominent place in the history of fiction: || that in speculations upon the nature of the superior being and man, the Hindus traverse the very same ground that was familiarly trodden by the philosophers of Greece and Rome.¶ He also remarks:—"That in medicine, as well as in astronomy and metophysics, the Hindus once kept pace with the most enlightened nations of the world; and that they attained as thorough a proficiency in medicine and surgery as any people whose acquisitions are recorded, and as indeed was practicable, before anatomy was made known to us by the discoveries of

* Vol. iii., p. 246. † Vol. iii., p. 34. ‡ Vol. iii., p. 156.
§ Vol. v., p. 108. || Vol. iii, p. 159. ¶ Vol. ii., p. 115.

modern inquirers. That surgery (as well as other departments of medical science) was once extensively cultivated and highly esteemed by the Hindus."

Lastly, I appeal to Professor Goldstucker, whether Sanscrit literature was not important enough to warrant the formation of the Sanscrit Text Society, headed by His Royal Highness the Prince of Wales.

Further development was checked by the frequent invasions of India by, and the subsequent continuous rule of, foreigners of entirely different character and genius, who, not having any sympathy with the indigenous literature—on the contrary, having much fanatical antipathy to the religion of the Hindus—prevented its further growth. Priesthood, first for power and afterwards from ignorance, completed the mischief, as has happened in all other countries.

Mr. Crawfurd tells us that the Asiatics are untruthful, very inferior in morals, and have no fidelity to engagements.* Beginning with the ancient Persians, Zoro-

* Mr. Crawfurd says : "In morals there has ever existed a wide difference between Europeans and Asiatics. Truth, the basis of all morality, has never distinguished the races of India. In Europe, fidelity to engagements has been in esteem even in rude times, and increased with the advance of civilization. Not so in Asia, for it may safely be asserted that there the most civilized nations are found to be the last truthful, among whom may be named the Persians, the Hindus, and the Chinese. Integrity is most prevalent among the educated classes in Europe; but with the more civilized, the want of it pervades all classes in Asia. The European maxim that 'honesty is the best policy' is not recognised by the more civilized people of Asia ; on the contrary, finesse is substituted. It is only among Asiatic nations of the second order of civilization (Mr. C. knows only them, it appears), such as Burmese, Malays, etc., that we find an adherence to truth, and even they become demoralised in the attainment of power. The difference in morals between Europeans and Asiatics seems to have belonged to all ages.'

aster, hundreds of years before Christ, taught, "I understand truth-telling exalted; all the days of the holy man are with thoughts of truth, words of truth and deeds of truth. Those that tell untruths and do wicked actions shall not receive the reward of life from Hormuzd. To speak true words is true excellence; in the treasures of religion exalt truth above all. What is the high religion?—that which promotes my holiness and truth, with good thought, word, and deed. In this house may. . . . prevail words of truth over words of lie.—Punish the breakers of promise, and those that induce others to break their promise."* Coming down in the course of time to the third century of the Christian era, Ardai Viraf, a high priest, holds out the punishment of hell, among others, to the following:—

"The man who used false weights and measures took full weight and return false, who adulterated his goods by mixing water with milk, to men who were liars and talebearers. The crime of lying being the most displeasing in the sight of God: even the most trivial and innocent falsity being a heinous sin. The man who was a bearer of false witness; who was fraudulent and deceitful; who, though he kept his word and rigorously performed his agreement with those of his own sect and faith, yet held it no sin to break his faith with those of a different persuasion; this, in the eye of Omnipotence, being a heinous sin, and the keeping of a promise even with an enemy being a duty inculcated."

Mr. Pope, the translator, of Ardai Viraf, concludes with the following remark, "that the philosophers will rejoice to find them (the modern Parsees) neither defi-

* My paper on the Parsee religion read before the Liverpool Literary and Philosophical Society.

cient in virtue or morality." Mr. Rawlinson says, "that in their (Zoroastrian) system, truth, purity, piety and industry were the virtues chiefly valued and inculcated."

Coming down to the latest times, the Parsee children are taught as religious lesson to speak the truth, and not to tell untruths nor to commit treachery.

The above is the testimony of the religious literature of the Persians. Let us see what the foreigners have said of them. Greek testimony about Persians is to be taken with care and caution. When we see that in the nineteenth century, gentlemen of learning and authority, with every means of obtaining correct information available, commit such mistakes as the one I have pointed out before, about the educational capacity of the natives of India, and make statements contrary to well known facts, how much more necessary is it to sift carefully the testimony of a hostile people given at a time when intercommunication was rare and difficult, and the character and manners of the two people very different. Even good Greek testimony, however, is in the favour of the Persians. Herodotus says, "Their sons are carefully instructed . . . . to speak the truth." He also says "They hold it unlawful to talk of anything which is unlawful to do; the most disgraceful thing in the world they think is to tell a lie, the next worse to owe a debt, because, among other reasons, the debtor is obliged to tell lies." *

Next, there is the testimony of the inscriptions in which lying is taken as the representative of all evil. Darius's successors are exhorted not to cherish but to cast into utter perdition the man who may be a liar, or

* Rawlinson's Herodotus, vol. ii., p. 222.

who may be an evil doer.* The modern Parsees are admitted by Mr. Crawfurd himself, as well as others, as a trustworthy and truthful race.

Of the modern Mahomedan Persians of Persia I do not know much. But I may say this much, that if they be truthful, Mr. Crawfurd's statement, then, is incorrect; if untruthful, Mr. Crawfurd's conclusion of his paper is so far upset. For, the present untruthful Persians, being the descendants of an old truth-speaking race, the difference in the character is no proof of difference of race, and that external circumstances have great influence in modifying a nation's character.

About the Hindus I can speak, both from personal knowledge and from other testimony, that Mr. Crawfurd's charge against them is unfounded. This mistake also arises from causes I have alluded to before—superficial observation and hasty conclusions. Fortunately, there are many who have studied the native character more carefully. Not to take up much of your time, I refer you to the evidence given before Parliament, 1853 and 1858, and I think that a careful and candid examination of that evidence will, satisfy anybody, that the general character of the natives of India is as good as that of any other people.

I shall very briefly refer to some of this testimony here. Beginning with the early writers, Strabo testifies to the truthfulness and virtue of the Hindus. † Arrian also describes the Hindus as truthful, saying, "and indeed none of the Indians were ever accused of that crime (falsehood)."‡ Coming down to later times, Abool Fazil, the celebrated Mahomedan minister of Akbar,

* Ib. note 7. † Vol. iii. p., 106.
‡ Vol. ii., c. xii., p. 206.

describes the Hindus in the sixteenth century as lovers of justice, admirers of truth, grateful, and of unbounded fidelity.* Coming down still later to the present time, Sir G. Clerk thinks the morality among the higher classes of Hindus of a high standard, and of the middle and lower classes remarkably so. He thinks there is less immorality than in many countries of Europe.† Sir E. Perry tell us, that offences against property and crimes generally are less frequent in the island of Bombay than in any similar community in Europe, and that it is the opinion of the Hindus that native morality suffers by coming into close contact with the English—the pristine simplicity and truthfulness of the native village disappears in drunkenness, intrigue, and a litigious spirit supervening,‡ and that their commercial integrity has always been famous.§

This commercial integrity is mentioned by Strabo also, who says that "they make their deposits, and confide in one another."‖ It is a fact at the present day, that transactions of great value take place between natives, for which there is no further evidence than the entry in the books of the seller. I do not suppose there is any parallel to this in Europe.

Colonel D. Sims considers the natives not inferior to the people of other countries in point of honesty, and even veracity, and says that people are apt to judge of the natives of India by those whom they find about the precincts of the different courts of justice, where,

---

* J. Crawfurd's Researches, vol. ii., p. 139.
† Report of Select Committee, 1853, Ques. 2278.
‡ Bird's-eye View of India, p. 77.
§ Report of Select Committee, 1853, Ques. 2582.
‖ Vol. iii., p 105.

temptations to mendacity being many, the atmosphere is unfavourable to truthfulness, as is probably the case in any other countries under the same circumstances. * When Mr. Fowler, a planter, gained the confidence of his labourers by his fair dealings with them, everything went on smoothly, and he was never in any part of the world where he had less trouble with his labourers †

Horace Wilson tells us not to imagine that the Hindus are ignorant of the foundations of all morality, or that they do not value truth, justice, integrity, benevolence, charity, to all that lives, and even the requital of evil with good; that these duties are all repeatedly enjoined, and Hindu authorities commend as earnestly as those of any other language. ‡

The complaint often made about untruthfulness of natives, has, I think, this cause. There are several professional experts about the courts who sell their evidence. The judge is very often not sufficiently familiar with the vernacular; some of the subordinates in the court being most wretchedly paid, yield to the temptation of bribery, and these three causes combined together make the task of the judge sometimes difficult, and every instance of successful perjury naturally encourages it more. The obvious remedy, one would think, would be that if proper severe examples were made of the prejurers, instead of merely raising up the cry of untruthfulness against the

* Report of Select Committee, 1853, Ques. 8548-9.

† Colonization Committee, Ques. 5742-4—In Mr. Justice Phear's opinion, "the character of the average oral testimony 'in the Guildhall of London, and that of the same in the Townhall of Calcutta, were on a par." And the Hon'ble. Mr. Campbell fully admits that it was the courts which were to blame for the character of native testimony. (*Native Opinion*, Bombay, 25th March, 1866.)

‡ Vol. ii., p. 109.

whole nation, their number, if at all unusual, would soon be reduced.

The other cause of the Hindus being sometimes denounced as untruthful, is the following clauses in the *Institutes of Menu* :—

Chap. iv., 138. "Let him say what is true, but let him say what is pleasing; let him speak no disagreeable truth, nor let him speak agreeable falsehood. This is a primeval rule."

139. "Let him say 'well and good,' or let him say 'well' only; but let him not maintain fruitless enmity and altercation with any man."

Chap. viii., 103. "In some cases, a giver of false evidence from a pious motive, even though he knows the truth, shall not lose his seat in heaven: such evidence wise men call the speech of the gods."

104. "Whenever the death of a man, *who had not been a grievous offender*, either of the servile, the commercial, the military, or the sacerdotal class, would be occasioned by true evidence, *from the known rigour of the king, even though the fault arose from inadvertence or error*, falsehood may be spoken: it is even preferable to truth." (The italics in all extracts from Menu are from the commentators on Menu.)

It must be remembered that these are laws for a state of society entirely different from your present one; the will or wisdom of the sovereign is the practical law of the land. I do not propose here to read a dissertation on truth, but I may simply, as parallel to the above extracts from the works of a Hindu legislator, refer to what is said by some of the European thinkers of modern times. Bentham allows, 1, falsehoods to avoid mischief, the case of misdirecting a murderer; 2, falsehoods of humanity, the case of physicians; 3, falsehoods of urbanity, an exaggerated compliment. In these cases, or at least in the first two, he says, "falsehood is a duty; in other cases it may be allowable, as in all those in which the person addressed has no right to know the truth. This would embrace most of the cases discussed by Grotius and Puffendorf." Instead of making any further quotations, I refer you to an article in the *Saturday Review* of July 2nd, 1864, on "Lying," from which the above extract is taken.

I give in a note below extracts from the *Institutes of Menu* to show how highly truth and virtue are valued among the Hindus.* Dr. Goldstucker kindly writes to me to say, that in Rigveda and Yajurveda "the necessity of speaking truth and avoiding untruth is emphasised in the most beautiful language, but unfortunately there are as yet no translations of these texts."

Mr. Crawfurd admits the commercial integrity among native merchants. Dealings in money, however, produce the greatest temptations to dishonesty, and when the commercial portion of a nation can stand this ordeal well, one would think it must tell much in favour of the general character of a people.

---

* Chap. iv., para. 175. Let a man continually take pleasure in truth, in justice, in laudable practices, and in purity; let him chastise those whom he may chastise, in a legal mode; let him keep in subjection his speech, his arm, and his appetite.

Para. 237. By falsehood the sacrifice becomes vain.

Para. 256. All things have their sense ascertained by speech; in speech they have their bases; and from speech they proceed; consequently, a falsifier of speech falsifies everything.

This is somewhat similar to Bentham's description of truth, in his *Theory of Legislation* (p. 260): "Every instance of our lives we are obliged to form judgments and to regulate our conduct according to facts, and it is only a small number of these facts which we can ascertain from our own observation. Then results an absolute necessity of trusting to the reports of others. If there is in these reports a mixture of falsehood, so far our judgments are erroneous, our motives wrong, our expectations misplaced. We live in restless distrust, and we do not know upon what to put dependence. In one word, falsehood includes the principle of every evil, because in its progress it brings on at last the dissolution of human society."

Mr. Crawfurd denies integrity even to the educated classes. I do not hesitate to give a direct contradiction to this statement. From my actual acquaintance and experience of the educated natives in the Bombay Presidency, I can with confidence assert, in Mr. Crawfurd's own words, that integrity is most prevalent among them as among the educated in Europe. This

---

Para. 255. For he, who describes himself to worthy men, in a manner contrary to truth, is the most sinful wretch in this world: he is the worst of thieves, a stealer of minds.

Chap. vi., para. 92. Content, returning good for evil, resistance to sensual appetites, abstinence from illicit gain, purification, coercion of the organs, knowledge of Scripture, knowledge of the Supreme Spirit, veracity, and freedom from wrath, form their tenfold system of duties.

Chap. vii., 26. Holy sages consider as a fit dispenser of criminal justice, that king who invariably speaks truth, who duly considers all cases, who understands the sacred books, who knows the distinction of virtue, pleasure, and riches.

Chap. viii , para. 79 The witnesses being assembled in the middle of the court-room, in the presence of the plaintiff and the defendant, let the judge examine them, after having addressed them altogether, in the following manner :—

Para. 80. What ye know to have been transacted in the matter before us between the parties reciprocally, declare at large and with truth, for your evidence in this cause is required.

Para. 81. A witness who gives evidence with truth, shall attain exalted seats of beatitude above and highest fame here and below: such testimony is revered by Brahma himself.

Para. 82. The witness who speaks falsely, shall be fast bound *under water*, in the *snaky* cords of Varuna, and be wholly deprived of power to *escape torment* during a hundred transmigrations; let mankind, therefore, give no false testimony.

Para. 83. By truth is a witness cleared from sin; by truth is justice advanced: truth must, therefore, be spoken by witnesses of every class.

Para. 84. The soul itself is its own witness; the soul itself is its own refuge; offend not thy conscious soul, the supreme internal witness of men!

Para. 85. The sinful have said in their hearts: "None sees us." Yes; the gods distinctly see them; and so does the spirit within their breasts.

mistake about the integrity of the educated is also like that about the capacity for education. There are many youths who know how to speak and write English without being educated, and Englishmen often confound them with the educated.

Polygamy.—The Parsees are strictly monogamists. The old and young, the most bigoted orthodox and the most liberal, all agree in their abhorrence of bigamy. They prevailed with Government to make bigamy crim-

---

Para. 89. Whatever places of torture have been prepared for the slayer of a priest, for the murderer of a woman or of a child, for the injurer of a friend, and for an ungrateful man, those places are ordained for a witness who gives false evidence.

Para. 90. The fruit of every virtuous act, which thou hast done, O good man, since thy birth, shall depart from thee to dogs, if thou deviate in speech from the truth.

Para. 91. O friend of virtue, that supreme spirit, which thou believest one and the same with thyself, resides in thy bosom perpetually, and is an all-knowing inspector of thy goodness or of thy wickedness.

Para. 92. If thou beset not at variance, by speaking falsely, with Yama, or the subduer of all, with Vaivaswata, or the punisher with that great divinity who dwells in thy breast, go not on a pilgrimage to the river Ganga, nor to the plains of Curu, for thou hast no need of expiation.

Para. 93. Naked and shorn, tormented with hunger and thirst and deprived of sight, shall the man, who gives false evidence, go with a potsherd to beg food at the door of an enemy.

Para. 94. Headlong, in utter darkness, shall the impious wretch tumble into hell, who, being interrogated in a judicial inquiry, answers one question falsely.

Para. 95. He who in a court of justice gives an imperfect account of any transaction, or asserts a fact of which he was no eye-witness, shall receive pain *instead of pleasure*, and resemble a man who eats fish *with eagerness*, and swallows the sharp bones.

Para. 96. The gods are acquainted with no better mortal in this world, than the man of whom the intelligent spirit which pervades his body, has no distrust, when he prepares to give evidence.

inal among them. I am not able to refer to the books, but I have a strong impression that there is nothing in the religious literature of the Old Persians indicative of the prevalence or sanction of polygamy among them. It is the most universal belief among the modern Parsees that they have always been monogamists, and they con-

---

Para. 97. Hear, honest man, from a just enumeration in order, how many kinsmen, in evidence of different sorts, a false witness kills, or incurs the guilt of killing.

Para. 193. That man who, by false pretences, gets into his hands the goods of another, shall, together with his acomplices, be punished by various degrees of whipping or mutilation, or even by death.

Para. 257. Veracious witnesses, who give evidence as the law requires, are absolved from their sins; but such as give it unjustly, shall each be fined two hundred panas.

Chap. x., para. 93. Avoiding all injury to animated beings, veracity, abstaining from theft, and from unjust seizure of property, cleanliness, and command over the bodily organs, form the compendious system of duty which Menu has ordained or the four classes.

Chap. iv., para. 170. Even here below an unjust man attains no felicity; nor he whose wealth proceeds from giving false evidence; nor he who constantly takes delight in mischief.

Chap. v., para. 109. Bodies are cleansed by water; *the mind is purified by truth*; the vital spirit, by theology and devotion; the understanding, clear knowledge.

Chap. ii., para. 97. To a man contaminated with sensuality, neither the Vedas, nor liberality, nor sacrifices, nor strict observances, nor pious austerities, ever procure felicity.

Chap. vii., para. 13. Let the king, prepare a just compensation for the good, and a just punishment for the bad: the rule of strict justice let him never transgress.

Chap. viii., para. 111. Let no man of sense take an oath in vain, that is, not in a court of justice, on a trifling occasion; for the man who takes an oath in vain, shall be punished in this life and in the next.

Para. 86. The guardian deities of the firmament, of the earth, of the waters, of the human heart, of the moon, of the sun, and of fire, of punishment after that, of the winds, of night, of both twilights, and of justice, perfectly know the state of all spirits clothed with bodies.

sider concubinage, also, a sin. Greek testimony, however, is against the Persians in this matter. But at the same time, the Greek best authority lays the blame upon the Greeks themselves, for Herodotus tells us, "as soon as they (Persians) hear of any luxury they instantly make it their own, and hence, among other novelties, they have learnt unnatural lust from the Greeks. Each of them has several wives and a still larger number of concubines." It appears, then, that we have to thank our good friends, the European Greeks, for this unnatural lust. The magi of the Medes are charged with worse institutions than polygamy by some Greek authorities, but Mr. Rawlinson says, "whether it had any real foundation in fact is very uncertain."*

The *Desatir*, which in some parts is, according to some, of great antiquity, and according to others only a work about three hundred years old, but, withal, the work of an Asiatic, says: "Marry only one woman and do not look with a wicked eye on or cohabit with any other woman." This fact deserves much consideration. Had the Persians been originally polygamists, it is strange that, during their residence in India for 1,200 years in the midst of the Hindus and Mohammedans, who are more or less polygamists, they should have so strictly preserved their monogamic character.

I asked Professor Spiegel to point out any texts in the religious literature of the Parsees for or against ploygamy.

He replied: "As far as my knowledge goes, there is no instance of polygamy in the religious literature of the Parsees. It is said that Zerdusht had three wives, but he had them successively. I share with you the conviction

* Vol. iii., p. 131.

that the majority of the Parsees were at all times monogamists, although, perhaps, indulgences have been granted to kings and other individuals of high station." In another reply to further inquiry from me, about these indulgences, he repeats that there is not a single text of the *Avesta* or the later *Parsis*, which alluded to polygamy, and that the indulgences he referred to were upon Greek and Latin authority.

Moreover, Sir J. Malcolm thinks, "There is every reason to believe that the manners of the ancient inhabitants of Persia were softened, and in some degree refined, by a spirit of chivalry which pervaded throughout that country from the commencement till the end of the Kayanian dynasty. The great respect in which the female sex was held was no doubt the principal cause of the progress they had made in civilization; these were at once the cause of generous enterprise and its reward. It would appear that in former days the women of Persia had an assigned and an honourable place in society, and we must conclude that an equal rank with the male creation, which is secured to them by the ordinance of Zoroaster, existed long before the time of that reformer." I can say, in confirmation of this, that even among the old and most orthodox in the present Parsee society, the above remarks on the respect to the female sex are true, and to the best of my recollection, I can confirm the remark of the equality of rank of the female and male creation by the ordinance of Zoroaster.

Mr. Rawlinson also thinks the Aryan races seem in old times to have treated women with a certain chivalry, which allowed the development of their physical powers, and rendered them specially attractive alike to their own husbands and to the men of other nations.

The existence of polygamy among the Hindus cannot be denied, but on reading the *Institutes of Menu*, I think that any one will be satisfied that, short of a perfect equality with man, and strict monogamy, woman has high consideration shown her. Menu says: " When females are honoured then the deities are pleased; but when they are dishonoured, then religious acts become fruitless" (chap. iii. 56). The duties enjoined to husbands and wives are as good as those of any other people. They are summed up in the following words:—" Let mutual fidelity continue to death (chap. ix. 101); this, in few words, may be considered as the supreme law between husband and wife." I give below a few more extracts.*

Strabo says of the Hindus, "and the wives prostitute themselves unless chastity is enforced by compulsion." This bears evident mark of a hasty conclusion from some partial observation. Domestic matters are always most difficult to be ascertained by a foreigner. Certainly, the people who not only considered chastity a high virtue, as I have already shown, but even a

*Para. 58. On whatever houses the women of a family, not being duly honoured, pronounce an imprecation, those houses, with all that belong to them, utterly perish, as if destroyed by a sacrifice for the death of an enemy.

Para. 60. In whatever family the husband is contented with his wife and the wife with her husband, in that house will fortune be assuredly permanent.

Para. 28. From the wife alone proceed offspring, good household management, solicitous attention, most exquisite caresses, and that heavenly beatitude which she obtains for the names of her ancestors, and for the husband himself.

Para. 165. While she who slights not her lord, but keeps her mind, speech, and body devoted to him, attains his heavenly mansion and by good men is called sàdshiré, or virtuous.

power, and represented it so in the drama, cannot be charged with such degradation.

Damayante, on being insulted by a hunter in the forest, uttered loud her curse of wrath :—

> "As my pure and constant spirit swerves not from Nishadha's Lord,
> Instant so may this base hunter lifeless fall upon the earth !
> Scarce that single word was uttered, suddenly that hunter hold
> Down upon the earth fell lifeless, like a lightning-blasted tree."*

On the subject of chivalry among the Hindus, Sir Bartle Frere, in a speech at the distribution of prizes to the girls' schools of the Students' Literary and Scientific Society of Bombay, says to the natives around him, after alluding to the spirit of chivalry and its effects in Europe. "There is no doubt that our ancestors regarded the female portion of the community as the great, almost the chief instruments in bringing back civilisation to Europe. I wish all my native friends to recollect, that this spirit, although if manifested chiefly there, was not confined to Europe. If they read any history of Rajputana, they will see that this spirit was a desire to make them as far as possible equal to this. This spirit is essentially the spirit of the Hindu races—a spirit wich subdued India and drove out the barbarous tribes of those days, and formed such communities that they are now, after the duration of many centuries, still vigorous and still able to oppose to us a vital power, which in spite of this government and its forces, can command the respect of all who go among them."†

Lastly, I beg to draw Mr. Crawfurd's attention to

* Story of Nala, p. 35.

† Stud. Lit. and Scientific Society's Report, 1864-5.

the phenomenon of Mormonism among European races of the nineteenth century.

It is a matter much to be regretted that gentlemen, like Mr. Crawfurd, make sweeping denunciations against the character of the Asiatics. They naturally provoke recriminations like the following, with all their mischievous consequences.

A Parsee gentleman, during his residence in this country for nearly eight years, disgusted with these sweeping charges, used to say :—'Look at all the mass of untruths in the daily advertisements and puffs; in the daily language of shop-keepers; how much swindling is there in the concoction of companies for the benefit of the promoters only; see what the book on facts, failures, and frauds discloses: what extremely watchful care one is obliged to have in his dealings in the city, where every kind of scoundrelism is so rife; how many manufactures always give you the best article only, at any price; how cleverly flaws are found in contracts; how artizans always require more time for wage-work than for job; how often you get goods different from patterns and samples; and he asked what grounds are there for Europeans to boast of higher commercial morality than that of the natives of India?' He asked: 'Look at the number of immoral haunts in London, read the account of *Life in Liverpool*, see the social evil and street immorality, cases of unfaithfulness in domsetic life, great immorality wherever numbers of the two sexes work together, the amount and character of crime disclosed by police and law reports, and election corruption, and all this among a highly civilised people? Is there not more reason for humiliation than boasting on the part of Europeans as to their morality? See the constant changes of views in the papers about Indian matters as it suits the purpose of the writer at the moment; the mode in which India has been acquired :—

> "War, disguised as Commerce, came."
> Won an empire, lost a name.

'When it suits their purpose the Hindus are described as most loyal, obedient, civilised, etc.; at other times they are cowardly wretches, disloyal, ungrateful, barbarous. They first give a bad name, and then cry out to hang them. They draw millions every year from India, and in return abuse its people, carrying not so much for it as for a rotten English borough. They yield with the greatest reluctance and difficulty any of the just rights and privileges demanded by the natives. Look at that iniquitous annexation policy in spite of treaties; see how the cost of the Afghan war is clapped on the shoulders of India; their whole aim being how to get most money from India.' Reasoning in this way he concluded, 'the only God the English worshipped was gold; they would do anything to get it,' and he illustrated this by saying, 'that if it were discovered that gold existed in human blood, they would manage, and with good reasons to boot, to extract it from thence.'

He said 'the English boast of fair play, etc., and yet see with what different measures they deal it out sometimes to the European and native; with what flagrant injustice was Dr. Colah treated; how bullying they are towards the weak, and very polite and reasonable with the strong. Coercion alone, it seems, makes them do what is right.' He said that as long as an Englishman wanted anything he was the very embodiment of politeness, but the object gained, he was no more the same person, and pointing to the treatment of

India generally, he thought gratitude was not a very prominent trait in the English character.

They pay native officials most wretchedly, and yet claim from them as efficient and honest service as they get from the highly-paid English officials, forgetting how rife corruption was among themselves in the days of small pay and much service. They complain of the untrustworthiness of native servants, but in their innocence they do not know how cleverly English landladies and servants manage to have their pickings and discounts.

Studying the English character in this manner, the gentleman formed his opinion that the English were the most hypocritical, the most selfish and unprincipled people, and had no right to boast of higher morality and integrity. Now, if such evidence as Mr. Crawfurd relies upon be conclusive as to the character of the natives of India, I do not see how this Parsee gentleman's conclusions cannot be also admitted as proved. Strange to say, the principal argument that was flung at our face against our attempt some sixteen years ago to establish female schools, was the state of English society, which the objectors, from superficial observations, urged was not highly moral, as female education afforded opportunities of secret intrigue and correspondence. I trust it is not such kind of evidence that will be considered sufficient by any thinking man to traduce whole nations.

When we left India in 1855 to come over here to open the first Parsee firm, the principal advice given by our European friends was to be exceedingly careful in our business in the city against the many rogues we should meet with there. "In India," said some one, "we keep one eye open; in England, you must keep both eyes wide open."

In the cause of truth and science I do not in the least object to the proclamation of truth regardless of consequences; but I appeal to Mr. Crawfurd himself, and to Englishmen, whether, in the instance of the natives of India, the case at the worst is but doubtful, such wholesale abuse of the whole nation from persons of position and authority in science is not much to be deplored; it creates ill-feeling and distrust, excites recrimination, and engenders a war of races.

India, gentlemen, is in your power and at your mercy; you may either give it a helping hand and raise it to your political and enlightened condition, to your eternal glory or keep it down with the foot of the tyrant upon its neck to your eternal shame! The choice is in your power, and, as I am happy to believe that, true to English nature, the first course is chosen, though not yet very energetically pursued, is it not very necessary, for men of weight or influence, not to say or do anything to mar this great and good work?

Abuse from persons like Mr. Landon of Broach, or Mr. Jeffries of the East Indian Association, natives care not for. The natives know the men and their motives; but disinterested gentlemen of weight and authority ought to ponder well upon their responsibilities. I do not mean to say that you should not point out to the natives of India their real faults and shortcomings—in fact, you cannot do a better act of friendship; but pointing out real faults is different from traducing indiscriminately. I may demand, in the words of Horace Wilson, "Let whatever they urge be urged in charity."

In my remarks about the general moral character of the Parsees and Hindus, I do not mean to be understood that they are models of perfection; they have no doubt their fair share of black sheep also, and their faults arising from centuries of foreign rule and more or less oppression; but judging from the experience of some past years, there is every hope of the faults being corrected by education.

The intercourse between the Europeans and native is not, except in few instances, of that frankness and confidence which alone can enable them to judge of each other rightly. Coupled with this, they very often misunderstand each other; and the Englishman, generally being an educated man, judges of every native by the high standard of his own enlightenment and civilisation. The result is often anything but a right conclusion, and hasty generalisation. Every wrong act of the native is at once condemned as innate in the native; similar acts of Europeans are of course only individual delinquencies, or capable of explanation!

There is nothing strange in the natives feeling shy and misunderstanding the rulers. The other day the Welsh farmers did not fill up Government returns about cattle, after deliberation, on the ground that Government wanted to tax cattle.

There is no doubt that owing to a colder and more bracing climate, the enjoyment of free institutions for centuries, the advantages of high educational establishments and high moral culture, free public opinion, and the advancement in material prosperity and mode of life by the discoveries of physical science and mineral resources, the modern Englishman is, in his physical and mental development, in his pluck and public spirit, in literature, science and arts, superior to the modern Hindu ground down and depressed as he is by centuries of foreign rule and oppression, and possessing less advantages of climate and food for personal vigour. But the very fact that the Hindu has under all such unfortunate circumstances preserved his character for morality and virtue, for high commercial integrity, for his bravery and military aptitude, and that he has at one time produced his vast ancient lore shows that there is no want of capacity, and that, under the influence of British Rule rightly administered, and reinvigorated by modern western civilization, he may once more regain his former high position among mankind.

At present he has not yet fully recovered from the staggering blow of the most extraordinary revolution by which a small nation in the far west has become a ruler of his vast country. He does not yet quite understand his new rulers. He is only just beginning to see dimly that after all he has perhaps some reason to congratulate himself for the change. The higher classes, the rulers now displaced or still remaining, are in a bewildering state of mind. They lying prostrate, with all their energies fled, and smarting at their fallen condition, cannot be naturally expected to reconcile themselves suddenly to the loss of their power, and to find themselves, once rulers of millions, now of less importance than an ordinary English official, and sometimes treated with injustice or indifference. The revolution in all its aspects, military, political, social, or intellectual, is so extraordinary and unparalleled in the history of mankind, that it cannot but be a work of time before a people, numbering two hundred millions, though now a fallen, but once a highly civilised nation, can be reconciled and assimilated to the new order of things. Under these circumstances, coupled with some unfortunate social barriers between the rulers and the ruled, the ignorance of each other's language, and the little interest shown by Englishmen, the Englishman and the native of India are still at a wide distance from each other, and know therefore little of each other's true merits and faults. The time, however, I hope will come, when, as some who have taken a real interest in the people have already done, the English people will with better knowledge think well of the natives of India. It will be the fault of the rulers themselves if they do not find the Hindus a loyal and a grateful people, and capable of the highest degree of civilisation. Even Abool Fazul, the minister of the greatest Mahommedan ruler of India, has borne high testimony for them. Unfortunately, the mischief of distance between the Englishman and natives is aggravated by the conduct of a class of Englishmen in India, who, either from interested motives or from pride of superiority, always run down the natives, and keep up an ill-feeling between the races. Sometimes some English gentlemen claim ten or twenty years' experience who have hardly been on intimate terms, or have familiarly conversed, with as many natives, or have hardly learnt to speak as many sentences in the language of the natives as the number of years they claim experience for; and such gentlemen constitute themselves the infallible judges of the character of the people. Perhaps, a paralled to this to some extent is to be found in the accounts about Englishmen themselves given by European foreigners. When Englishmen are incorrectly described for these foreigners, they of course open their whole artillery of ridicule upon such ignorance, and yet it does not always occur to them that in their judgment on natives of India, with less mutual acquaintance, they may be as much, if not more, egregiously mistaken.

There are several peculiar difficulties in India in the way of rapid progress. Education permeates the mass very slowly on account of many different languages; the efforts of the educated to improve their countrymen remain confined within small limits, while in this country an idea in the *Times* is known over the whole length and breadth of the land within twenty-four hours, and the whole nation can act as a man.

The natives are sometimes charged with want of moral courage. We have only to look at the difference of treatment by the Bombay Government between a native and an English judge—I mean Mr. Manockjee Cursetjee and Mr. Anstey—and one may ask what result can be expected from such circumstances.

However, though such unfortunate circumstances do now and then occur, the educated are beginning to learn that the rights of intellect and justice are the same for all, and that, though often snubbed and discouraged, they may rely upon the ultimate triumph of truth and justice.

Lastly, I think Mr. Crawfurd's treatment of this important subject is one-sided, and not judicial and scientific. The paper professes to draw a conclusion from certain facts, but to me it seems the facts are selected for, and adapted to, a foregone conclusion. All explanatory causes of difference are made light of and thrown into the background, and all tending to prove the conclusion brought most forcibly into the foreground. The whole reasoning is that, because there is a diversity in the intellectual, moral and physical character of various nations, they must therefore have separate origins, but the premises do not warrant the conclusion; moreover, there are several assumptions which are not correct.

In one place, a comparison is made between different countries, and it is assumed that the greater the natural resources, the greater must be the development; while a most important feature in human nature,—"necessity the mother of invention,"—greater difficulties compelling greater exertions, and calling forth the exercise of higher powers, and the bracing effects of colder climates, are ignored. In one place, the Phœnicians, Jews, and Mamelukes are taken over to the European side as they seem to disturb the argument.

Mr. Crawfurd alludes to the bad government in Asia as their own creation, as if bad governments had never existed in Europe, and no European kingdoms or empires had to thank bad goverments and degeneracy for their fall.*

One principal objection to Mr. Crawfurd's paper is an unfair camparison between the old Asiatic civilisation and the modern European civilisation, with all the impetus given to its material advancement by the discoveries of physical science, both in the arts of war and peace. The ancient civilisation of both continents may be a legitimate subject of comparison. The Asiatics after their fall from the first civilisation, had not new blood and vigour brought to them. The Goths and other wild tribes, mainly derived from Asiatic races, permanently settled in and brought new vigour to Europe, and created a new civilisation in it with the advantages of groundwork of the old civilisation. It would be interesting to make a fair comparison between the old civilisa-

* In the nineteenth century, and in the very heart of Europe, a king claims "divine right" and a minister sets all law and justice at defiance. Poland and the Duchies are a strange commentary upon the political justice of Europe. Has not Italy till very lately groaned under bad governments ?

tions of the two continents and between the modern condition of the people among whose ancestors the old civilisations prevailed. But to compare a hand armed with an Armstrong gun with an unarmed one and thence to draw the conclusion of superior strength and warlike spirit of the former, may be complacent, but does not appear to me to be fair.

Differences in the conditions of nations and their various peculiarities, arising from differences of political, physical, and social circumstances, and these circumstances reacting upon each other, require careful study and due allowance before attributing any share to innate difference.

I do not mean to undertake here the solution of the most difficult problem of the unity or plurality of races, or of maintaining or denying what may legitimately follow from Mr. Crawfurd's conclusions, that there are as many distinct races with distinct orgins as there are countries or even provinces with peculiarities of their own. I leave to ethnologists to say whether the present philological and physical researches which Mr. Crawfurd has altogether ignored, and other ethonological inquiries, lead to the conclusion of the unity or plurality of races, or whether more light is still necessary upon the subject.

I shall only make a few remarks suggested by the paper. The races of Europe present a large variety in their size, from the Highlanders to the Laps. The Asiatic races have their Afghans, of the large size, and other races of different sizes. Herodotus writes: * "For, in boldness and warlike spirit the Persians were not a whit inferior to the Greeks;" in another place he

* Vol. iv., p. 354.

says:* "And in the mid battle, when the Persians themselves and the Sacæ had place, the barbarians were victorious, and broke and pursued the Greeks in the inner country." In the comparison between the Greeks and Persians, Herodotus accounts for the inferiority of the latter in dificiency of discipline and arms only.

Rawlinson, in his *Five Monarchies*, judges from the sculptures that the ancient Aryan race is a noble variety of the human species—tall, graceful, and stately; physiognomy handsome and somewhat resembling the Greek; and that on the authority of Xenophon and Plutarch the Median and Tromen Persians were remarkable for their stature and beauty. Palgrave calls the Arabs of inhabited lands and organised governments one of the noblest races on earth.† A large portion of the Sikhs and Afghans, and large numbers of Brahmans in Central India, have fair complexions and fine features.

We must not also forget, in comparisons of nations, the part which accident, or commonly called luck, plays. We know what part storms played in the defeat of the navy of Xerxes and of the armada of the Spaniards.‡ The European lives in a colder and bracing climate. I do not suppose the innate physical character of any European race will enable it to preserve its vigour and strength intact on the plains of India for a long time.

* Vol. iii., p. 405. † Vol. i., p. 24.

‡ Now, a single law sometimes fixes the character of a nation for a time for good or evil. What extraordinary changes have been wrought since the recognition of free trade by this nation! I do not suppose Mr. Crawfurd means the English of the past generation were a different race, because they were protectionists, less tolerant, and in several other respects different from the present generation.

The European, says Mr. Crawfurd, enjoys walking, the Asiatic prefers sitting. The Asiatic, when here, enjoys walking as much as any European can do, for he must walk in this climate to preserve his health. The European in India, after the fatigue and heat of the day, often prefers sitting in a cool breeze. With the European dress, and in this climate, sitting with his legs tucked up under him, becomes, irksome to the Asiatic also. The rigidity of the muscle of the European is much modified in India. I suppose it is a well-known fact to ethnologists that animals are capable of acquiring a large variety of physical characters in different climates, though originally of the same stock. Mr. Crawfurd's statement, that the Jews of Asia are substantially Persian among Persians, Arab among Arabs, and difficult to distinguish from Hindus among Hindus, and that their social advancement in Europe is with the people of the community among which they dwell, tends rather against his theory, showing that external circumstances have modified the character of a people within historic times.

In estimating the character of a people, we must not forget that sometimes single events have given a peculiar direction to their character and history. Had it not been for taxed tea, we do not know whether there would have been a United States now. Had the confederates been victorious, what would have been the future history of the United States and of Slavery? Had Britain been connected with the Continent of Europe, it is probable that it might have had a different history, either a large European empire, or a province of some other. What change was wrought in the character of the Britons when they complained. " The Picts drive us to the sea, and the sea drives us to the Picts ?" Was that change in character, the result of external influence of the Roman civilisation and Government or not ?

The one-sided and partial treatment of the subject by Mr. Crawfurd is best illustrated by the comparison made between Greece and the island of Java. The wide difference between the climate and products of the two countries is admitted, but the legitimate conclusion of its effects in stimulating or checking exertion are ignored ; the rest of the comparison might as well not have been made.

The Guzerati-speaking Hindus are eminently commercial, and carry on the most extensive foreign commerce, while just on the other side of the Ghauts and in Concan the Martha-speaking Hindus are quite uncommercial, except so far as some inland trade is concerned. Whether these may be considered as two distinct races by Mr. Crawfurd or not I cannot say, but there is this marked difference in their character, arising, to a great extent, from local and historical circumstances, the Guzerat people having commercial connections with Arabia and the West from ancient times.

Again, in Western India there is even now a marked difference in the educational, and therefore intellectual condition of the Mahomedans and Hindus of Concan ; though thay have the same physiognomy, speak the same language, and, in fact, are originally the same people, there are not half a dozen of these Mahomedans attending the English seminaries, while the Hindus swarm in numbers. Should this state of things continue for some length of time, the difference in the characters of these two portions will be so great that, according to Mr. Crawfurd's theory, I suppose they will have to be put down as two distinct races.

I wish I had more time to examine more fully the several points I have touched upon, and also to examine a few more statements of Mr. Crawfurd's paper, especially about Hindu astronomy, music, and architecture and Chinese literature and character. The ethnologist should study man in all his bearings, and make due allowances for every cause of disturbance. Mr. Crawfurd's conclusion may be right or wrong, but, with every deference to him, all I wish to submit to the Society is that the evidence produced is not only not sufficient but defective in itself, inasmuch as it is superficial, and several statements are not quite correct.

I have not made these remarks for the pleasure of objecting, or simply for the sake of defending the Asiatics; truth cannot be gained, and I hope I shall be the last person to deny it wherever it is proved to exist, no matter in howsoever unpleasant a form. The sole business of science, as I understand it, is to seek the truth and to hail it wherever it is found, and not to bend and adapt facts to a foregone conclusion.

IX

SIR M. E. GRANT DUFF ON INDIA.*

I offer some observations on Sir Grant Duff's reply to Mr. Samuel Smith, M. P., in this *Review*. I do so not with the object of defending Mr. Smith. He is well able to take care of himself. But of the subjects with which Sir Grant Duff has dealt, there are some of the most vital importance to India, and I desire to discuss them.

I have never felt more disappointed and grieved with any writings by an Englishman than with the two articles by Sir Grant Duff—a gentleman who has occupied the high positions of Under-Secretary of State for India and Governor of Madras. Whether I look to the superficiality and levity of his treatment of questions of serious and melancholy importance to India, or to the literary smartness of offhand reply which he so often employs in the place of argument, or to the mere sensational assertions which he puts forward as proofs, I cannot but feel that both the manner and matter of the two articles are in many parts, unworthy of a gentleman of Sir Grant Duff's position and expected knowledge. But what is particularly more regrettable is his attitude towards the educated classes, and the sneers he has levelled against higher education itself. If there is one thing more than another for which the Indian people are peculiarly and deeply grateful to the British nation, and which is one of the chief reasons of

* Contemporary Review, August, 1887.

their attachment and loyalty to British Rule, it is the blessing of education which Britain has bestowed on India. Britain has every reason to be proud of, and to be satisfied with, the results, for it is the educated classes who realise and appreciate most of the beneficence and good intentions of the British nation; and by the increasing influence which they are now undoubtedly, exercising over the people, they are the powerful chain by which India is becoming more and more firmly linked with Britain. This education has produced its natural effects, in promoting civilisation and independence of character—a result of which a true Briton should not be ashamed and should regard as his peculiar glory. But it would appear that this independence of character and the free criticism passed by the educated classes on Sir Grant Duff's acts have ruffled his composure. He has allowed his feelings to get the better of his judgment. I shall have to say a few words on this subject hereafter.

Sir Grant Duff asks the English tourists, who go to India "for the purpose of enlightening their countrymen when they come home"—"Is it too much to ask that these last should take the pains to arrive at an accurate knowledge of facts before they give their conclusions to the world?" May I ask the same question of Sir Grant Duff himself? Is it too much to ask him, who has occupied high and responsible positions, that he, as far more bound to do so, should take the pains to arrive at an accurate knowledge of facts before he gives his conclusions to the world? Careless or mistaken utterances of men of his position, by misleading the British public, do immeasurable harm, both to England and India.

Of the few matters which I intend to discuss there is one—the most important—upon which all other questions hinge. The correct solution of this fundamental problem will help all other Indian problems to settle themselves under the ordinary current discussions of every day. Before proceeding, however, with this fundamental question, it is necessary to make one or two preliminary remarks to clear away some misapprehensions which often confuse and complicate the discussion of Indian subjects.

There are three parties concerned—(1) The British nation, (2) those authorities to whom the Government of India is entrusted by the British nation, and (3) the Natives of British India.

Now, I have no complaint whatever against the British nation or British Rule. On the contary, we have every reason to be thankful that of all the nations in the world it has been our good fortune to be placed under the British nation—a nation noble and great in its instincts; among the most advanced, if not the most advanced, in civilization: foremost in the advancement of humanity in all its varied wants and circumstances; the source and fountainhead of true liberty and of political progress in the world; in short, a nation in which all that is just, generous and truly free is most happily combined.

The British nation has done its part nobly, has laid down, and pledged itself before God and the world to a policy of justice and generosity towards India, in which nothing is left to be desired. That policy is complete and worthy of its great and glorious past and present. No, we Indians have no complaint against the British nation or British Rule. We have everything from them to be grateful for. It is against its servants, to whom it has entrusted our destinies, that we have something of which to complain. Or rather, it is against the system which has been adopted by its servants, and which subverts the avowed and pledged policy of the British nation, that we complain, and against which I appeal to the British people.

Reverting to the few important matters which I desire to discuss, the first great question is—What is Britain's policy towards India? Sir Grant Duff says: "Of two things one: either we mean to stay in India and make the best of the country—directly for its own advantage, indirectly for that of ourselves and of mankind at large, or we do not." Again, he says: "The problem is how best to manage for its interest, our own interest, and the interest of the world. . . . ." Now, if anybody ought to know, Sir Grant Duff ought, that this very problem, exactly as he puts it and for the purposes he mentions, has been completely and exhaustively debated, decided upon, and the decision pledged in the most deliberate manner, in an Act of Parlimament more than fifty years ago, and again most solemnly and sacredly pledged more than twenty-five years ago. Sir Grant Duff either forgets or ignores these great events. Let us see, then, what this policy is. At a time when the Indians were in their educational and political infancy, when they did not and could not understand what their political condition then was or was to be in the future, when they had not uttered, as far as I know, any complaints, nor demanded any rights or any definite policy towards themselves, the British nation of their own accord and pleasure, merely from their own sense of their duty towards the millions of India and to the world, deliberately declared before the world what their policy should be towards the people of India. Nor did the British people do this in any ignorance or want of forethought or without the consideration of all possible consequences of their action. Never was there a debate in both Houses of Parliament more complete and clear, more exhaustive, more deliberately looked at from all points of view, and more calculated for the development of statesmanlike policy and practical good sense. The most crucial point of view—that of political danger or of even the possible loss of India to Britain—was faced with true English manliness; and the British nation, through their Parliament, then settled, adopted, and proclaimed to the world what their policy was to be—*viz.*, the policy of justice and of the advancement of humanity.

I can give here only a very few extracts from that famous debate of more than half a century ago—a debate reflecting the highest glory on the British name.

Sir Robert Peel said :—

"Sure I am at least that we must approach the consideration of it with a deep feeling, with a strong sense of the responsibility we shall incur, with a strong sense of the moral obligation which imposes it upon us as a duty to promote the improvement of the country and the welfare and well-being of its inhabitants, so far as we can consistently with the safety and security of our dominion and the obligations by which we may be bound . . . . ."

The Marquess of Lansdowne, in the House of Lords, said :—

"But he should be taking a very narrow view of this question and one utterly inadequate to the great importance of the subject, which involved in it the happiness or misery of one hundred millions of human beings, were he not to call the attention of their Lordships to the bearing which this question and to the influence which this arrangement must exercise upon the future distinies of that vast mass of people. He was sure that their Lordships would feel, as he indeed felt, that their only justification before God and Providence for the great and unprecedented dominion which they exercised in India was in the happiness which they communicated to the subjects under their rule, and in proving to the world at large, and to the inhabitants of Hindoostan, that the inheritance of Akbar (the wisest and most beneficent of Mahomedan princes) had not fallen into unworthy or degenerate hands. . . . ." His Lordship, after announcing the policy intended to be adopted, concluded: "He was confident that the strength of the Government would be increased by the happiness of the people over whom it presided, and by the attachment of those nations to it."

Lord Macaulay's speech is worthy of him, and of the great nation to which he belonged. I have every temptation to quote the whole of it, but space forbids. He calls the proposed policy "that wise, that benevolent, that noble clause," and he adds :—

"I must say that, to the last day of my life, I shall be proud of having been one of those who assisted in the framing of the Bill contains that clause . . . . Governments, like men, may buy existence too dear. 'Propter vitam vivendi perdere causes' is a despicable policy either in individuals or States. In the present case such a policy would be not only despicable but absurd. . . . . To the great trading nation, to the great manufacturing nation, no progress which any portion of the human race can make in knowledge, in taste for the conveniences of life, or in the wealth by which those conveniences are produced, can be a matter of indifference . . . To trade with civilised men is infinitely more profitable than to govern savages. That would indeed be a doting wisdom, which, in order that India might remain a dependency, would make it a useless and costly dependency—which would keep a hundred millions of men from being our customers in order that they might continue to be our slaves. It was, as Bernier tells us, the practice of the miserable tyrants whom he found in India, when they dreaded the capacity and spirit of some distinguished subject, and yet could not venture to murder him, to administer to him a daily dose of the pousta, a preparation of opium, the effect of which was in a few months to destroy all the bodily and mental powers of the wretch who was drugged with it, and to turn him into a helpless idiot. The detestable artifice, more horrible than assassination itself, was worthy of those who employed it. It is no model for the English nation. We shall never consent to administor the pousta to a whole community, to stupify and paralyse a great people whom God has committed to our charge, for the wretched purpose of rendering them more amenable to our control. . . . . I have no fears. The path of duty is plain before us; and it is also the path of wisdom, of national prosperity, of national honour. . . . . To have found a great people sunk in the lowest depths of misery and superstition, to have so ruled them as to have made them desirous and capable of all the privileges of citizens, would indeed be a title to glory—all our own. The sceptre may pass away from us. Unforeseen accidents may derange our most profound schemes of policy, Victory may be inconstant to our arms. But there are triumphs which are followed by no reverses. There is an empire exempt from all natural causes of decay. Those triumphs are the pacific triumphs of reason over barbarism; that empire is the imperishable empire of our arts and our morals, our literature and our law."

Now, what was is that was so deliberately decided upon—that which was to promote the welfare and well-being of the millions of India, involve their happiness or misery, and influence their future destiny; that which was to be the only justification before God and Providence for the dominion over India; that which was to increase the strength of the Government and secure the attachment of the nation to it; and that which was wise, benevolent and noble, most profitable to English trade and manufacture, the plain path of duty, wisdom, national prosperity and national honour, and calculated to raise a people sunk in the lowest depths of misery and superstition to prosperity and civilisation? It was this "noble" clause in the Act of 1833, worthy of the British character for justice, generosity and humanity: "That no Native of the said territories, nor any natural-born subject of His Majesty resident therein, shall, by reason only of his religion, place of birth, descent, or any of them, be disabled from holding any place, office or employment under the said Company.

I now ask the first question. Is this deliberately declared policy honestly promised, and is it intended by the British nation to be honestly and honourably fulfilled; or is it a lie and a delusion, meant only to deceive India and the world? This is the first clear issue.

It must be remembered, as I have already said, that this wise and noble pledge was given at a time when the Indians had not asked for it. It was of Britain's own will and accord, of her own sense of duty towards a great people whom Providence had entrusted to her care, that she deliberated and gave the pledge. The pledge was given with grace and unasked, and was therefore the more valuable and more to Britain's credit and renown. But the authorities to whom the performance of this pledge was entrusted by the British nation did not do their duty, and left the pledge a dead letter. Then came a time of trouble, and Britain triumphed over the Mutiny. But what did she do in that moment of triumph? Did she retract the old, great and noble pledge? Did she say, "You have proved unworthy of it, and I withdraw it." No! True to her instincts of justice, she once more and still more emphatically and solemnly proclaimed to the world the same pledge, even in greater completeness and in every form. By the mouth of our great Sovereign did she once more give her pledge, calling God to witness and seal it and bestow His blessing thereon; and this did the gracious Proclamation of 1858 proclaim to the world:—

"We hold ourselves bound to the Natives of our Indian territory by the same obligations of duty which bind us to all our other subjects; and those obligations, by the blessing of Almighty God, we shall faithfully and conscientiously fulfil.

"And it is our further will that, so far as may be, our subjects of whatever race or creed, be freely and impartially admitted to offices in our service, the duties of which they may be qualified by their education, ability, and integrity duly to discharge.

"In their prosperity will be our strength, in their contentment our security, and in their gratitude our best reward. And may the God of all power grant to us and to those in authority under us strength to carry out these our wishes for the good of our people."

Can pledges more sacred, more clear, and more binding before God and man be given?

I asked this second question. Are these pledges honest promises of the British Sovereign and nation, to be faithfully and conscientiously fulfilled, or are they only so many lies and delusions? I can and do expect but one reply: that these sacred promises were made honestly, and honourably fulfilled. The whole Indian problem hangs upon these great pledges, upon which the blessings and help of God are invoked. It would be an insult and an injustice to the British nation, quite unpardonable in me—with my personal knowledge of the British people for more than thirty years—if I for a moment entertained the shadow of a doubt with regard to the honesty of these pledges.

The third question is—whether these pledges have been faithfully and conscientiously fulfilled. The whole position of India is this: If these solemn pledges be faithfully and conscientiously fulfilled, India will have nothing more to desire. Had these pledges been fulfilled, what a different tale of congratulation should we have had to tell to-day of the prosperity and advancement of India and of great benefits to and blessings upon England. But it is useless to mourn over the past. The future is still before us.

I appeal to the British nation that these sacred and solemn promises should be hereafter faithfully and conscientiously fulfilled. This will satisfy all our wants.

This will realize all the various consequences, benefits and blessings which the Statesmen of 1833 have foretold, to England's eternal glory, and to the benefit of England, India and the world. The non-fulfilment of these pledges has been tried for half a century, and poverty and degradation are still the lot of India. Let us have, I appeal, for half a century the conscientious fulfilment of these pledges, and no man can hesitate to foretell, as the great Statesmen of 1833 foretold, that India will rise in prosperity and civilization, that "the strength of the Government would be increased by the happiness of the people over whom it presided, and by the attachment of those nations to it." As long as fair trial is not given to these pledges it is idle, and adding insult to injury, to decide anything or to seek any excuses against us and against the fulfilment of the pledges.

If this appeal is granted, if the British nation says that its honest promises must be honestly fulfilled, every other Indian question will find its natural and easy solution. If, on the other hand, this appeal shall go in vain—which I can never believe will be the case—the present unnatural system of the non-fulfilment of the great policy of 1833 and 1858 will be an obstacle and a complete prevention of the right and just solution of any other Indian question whatever. From the seed of injustice no fruit of justice can ever be produced. Thistles will never yield grapes.

I now come to the second important question—the present material condition of India as the natural result of the non-fulfilment of the great pledges. Mr. Samuel Smith had remarked that there was among the well-educated Natives "a widespread belief that India is getting poorer and less happier," and he has subsequently expressed his own impressions: "The first and deepest impression made upon me by this second visit to India is a heightened sense of the poverty of the country." Now, to such a serious matter, what is Sir Grant Duff's reply? First, a sneer at the educated classes and at higher education itself. Next, he gives a long extract from an address of the local reception committee of the town of Bezwada, in which, says the address, by means of an anicut, "at one stroke the mouths of a hungry and dying people have been filled with bread, and the coffers of the Government with money." Now, can levity and unkindness go any further? This is the reply that a great functionary gives to Mr. Smith's serious charge about the poverty of India. What can the glowing, long extract from the address of the committee of Bezwada mean, if Sir Grant Duff did not thereby intend to lead the British public into the belief that, because the small town of Bezwada had acknowledged a good thing done for it, therefore in *all* India all was happy and prospering? However, Sir Grant Duff could not help reverting, after a while, to the subject a little more seriously, and admitting that "there is in many parts of India frightful poverty." What, then, becomes of the glowing extract from the Bezwada address, and how was that a reply to Mr. Smith's charge? However, even after making the admission of the "frightful poverty in many parts of India," he disposses off-hand of the grave matter—remarking that other people in other countries are also poor, as if that were a justification of "the frightful poverty in many parts of India," under a rule like that of the British, and conducted by a service the most highly praised and the most highly paid in the world. Sir Grant Duff, with a cruel levity, only asks two or three questions, without any proof of his assumptions and without any attention to the circumstances of the comparisons, and at once falls foul of the educated classes, as if thereby he gave a complete reply to the complaint about the poverty. Now, these are the three questions he puts :—"The question worth answering is: Do the Indian masses obtain, one year with another, a larger or smaller amount of material well being than the peasantry of Western Europe?" and he answers himself: "Speaking of the huge province of Madras, which I, of course, know best—and I have visited every district in it—I think they do ...." They "do" what? Do they obtain a larger or smaller amount? His second question is: "But is there not the same, and even worse, in our own country?" And lastly, he brings down his clincher thus:—"As to our system 'draining the country of its wealth,' if that be the case, how is it visibly increasing in wealth?" And he gives no proof of that increased wealth. Thus, then, does Sir Grant Duff settle the most serious questions connected with India. First, a sneer at educated men and higher education, then the frivolous argument about the town of Bezwada, and afterwards three off-hand questions and assertions without any proof. In this way does a former Under-Secretary of State for India, and only lately a ruler of thirty millions of people, inform and instruct the British public on the most burning Indian questions. We may now, however, see what Sir Grant Duff's above three questions mean, and what they are worth, and how wrong and baseless his assertions are.

Fortunately, *Mr.* Grant Duff has already replied to *Sir* Grant Duff. We are treated by Sir Grant Duff to a long extract from his Budget speech of 1873. He might have as well favoured us, to better purpose, with an extract or two from some of his other speeches. In 1870 Mr. Grant Duff asks Sir Wilfred Lawson a remarkable question during the debate on Opium. He asks: "Would it be tolerable that to enforce a view of morality which was not theirs, which had never indeed been accepted by any large portion of the human race, we should grind an already poor population to the very dust with new taxation?" Can a more complete reply be given to Sir Grant's present questions than this reply of Mr. Grant Duff: that the only margin that saves "an already poor population" *from being ground to the very dust* is the few millions that are obtained by poisoning a foreign country (China).

Again *Mr.* Grant Duff supplies another complete reply to *Sir* Grant Duff's questions. In his Budget speech of 1871, he thus depicts the poverty of India as compared with the condition of England—"one of the countries of Western Europe" and the "our own country" of his questions. Just at that time I had, in a rough way, shown that the whole production or income of British India was about Rs. 20 (40*s.*) per head per annum. Of this Mr. Grant Duff made the following use in 1871. He said: "The position of the Indian financier is altogether different from that of the English one. Here you have a comparatively wealthy population. The income of the United Kingdom has, I believe, been guessed at £800,000,000 per annum. The income of British India has been guessed at £300,000,000 per annum. That gives well on to £30 per annum as the income of every person of the United Kingdom, and only £2 per annum as the income of every person in British India. Even our comparative wealth will be looked back upon by future ages as a state of semi-barbarism. But what are we to say of the state of India? How many generations must pass away before that country has arrived at even the comparative wealth of this?"

But now Sir Grant Duff ignores his own utterances as to how utterly different the cases of England and India are. Mr. Grant Duff's speeches having been received in India, Lord Mayo thus commented upon it and confirmed it:—

"I admit the comparative poverty of this country, as compared with many other countries of the same magnitude and importance, and I am convinced of the impolicy and injustice of imposing burdens upon this people which may be called either crushing or oppressive. Mr. Grant Duff in an able speech which he delivered the other day in the House of Commons, the report of which arrived by the last mail, stated with truth that the position of our finance was wholly different from that of England. 'In England,' he stated, 'you have comparatively a wealthy population. The income of the United Kingdom has, I believe, been guessed at £800,000,000 per annum; the income of British India has been guessed at £300,000,000 per annum: that goes well on to £30 per annum as the income of every person in the United Kingdon, and only £2 per annum as the income of every person in British India.' I believe that Mr. Grant Duff had good grounds for the statement he made, and I wish to say, with reference to it, that we are perfectly cognisant of the relative poverty of this country as compared with European States."

Here, again, is another answer to Sir Grant Duff's questions, by the late Finance Minister of India. Major (Sir) E. Baring, in proof of his assertion of "the extreme poverty of the mass of the people" of British India, makes a comparison not only with "the Western countries of Europe" but with "the poorest country in Europe." After stating that the income of India was not more than Rs. 27 per head, he said, in his Budget speech of 1882: "In England, the average income per head of population was £33 per head; in France it was

£23; in Turkey, which was the poorest country in Europe, it was £4 per head."

It will be seen, then, that *Mr.* Grant Duff and a higher authority than *Sir* Grant Duff have already fully answered Sir Grant Duff's questions. The only thing now remaining is whether Sir Grant Duff will undertake to prove that the income of British India has now become equal to that of the Western countries of Europe; and if so, let him give us his facts and figures to prove such a statement—not mere allusions to the prosperity of some small towns like Bezwada, or even to that of the Presidency towns, but a complete estimate of the income of *all* British India, so as to compare it with that of England, France, or "Western countries of Europe."

I may say here a word or two about "the huge province of Madras, which," says Sir Grant, "I, of course, know best, and I have visited every district in it." We may see now whether he has visited with his eyes open or shut. I shall be glad if Sir Grant Duff will give us figures to show that Madras to-day produces as much as the Western countries of Europe.

Sir George Campbell, in his paper on tenure of land in India, says, from an official Report of 1869, about the Madras Presidency, that "the bulk of the people are paupers." I have just received an extract from a friend in India, Mr. W. R. Robertson, Agricultural Reporter to the Government of Madras, who says of the agricultural labourer:—

"His condition is a disgrace to any country calling itself civilised. In the best seasons the gross income of himself and his family does not exceed 3*d.* per day throughout the year, and in a bad season their circumstances are most deplorable. . . .

I have seen something of Ireland, in which the condition of affairs bears some resemblance to those of this country, but the condition of the agricultural population of Ireland is vastly superior to the condition of the similar classes in this country."

There cannot be any doubt about the correctness of these views; for, as a matter of fact, as I have worked out the figures in my paper on "The Poverty of India," the income of the Madras Presidency in 1868-69 was only about Rs. 18 per head per annum.

Such is the Madras Presidency, which Sir Grant Duff has visited with his eyes apparently shut.

I shall now give a few statements about the "extreme poverty" of British India, by persons whose authority would be admitted by Sir Grant Duff as far superior to his own. In 1864 Sir John (afterwards Lord) Lawrence, then Viceroy, said: "India is on the whole a very poor country; the mass of the population enjoy only a scanty subsistence." And again, in 1873, he repeated his opinion before the Finance Committee that the mass of the people were so miserably poor that they had barely the means of subsistence. It was as much as a man could do to feed his family, or half-feed them, let alone spending money on what might be called luxuries or conveniences. In 1881 Dr. (Sir W.) Hunter, the best official defender of the British Indian Administration, told the British public that 40,000,000 of the people of British India "go through life on insufficient food." This is an official admission, but I have no moral doubt that, if full enquiries were made, twice forty millions or more would be found "going through life on insufficient food;" and what wonder that the very touch of famine should destroy hundreds of thousands or millions. Coming down at once to the latest times, Sir E. Baring said, in his finance speech in 1882:—

"It has been calculated that the average income per head of population in India is not more than Rs. 27 a year; and, though I am not prepared to pledge myself to the absolute accuracy of a calculation of this sort, it is sufficiently accurate to justify the conclusion that the tax-paying community is *exceedingly poor*. To derive any very large increase of revenue from so poor a population as this is obviously impossible, and if it were possible would be unjustifiable."

Again, in the course of the debate he repeated the statement about the income being Rs. 27 per head per annum, and said in connection with salt revenue: "But he thought it was quite sufficient to show the *extreme poverty of the mass of the people.*" Then, after stating the income of some of the European countries, as I have stated them before, he proceeded: "He would ask honourable members to think what Rs. 27 per annum was to support a person, and then he would ask whether a few annas was nothing to such poor people." I asked Sir E. Baring to give me his calculations to check with mine, but he declined. But it does not matter much, as even "not more than Rs. 27" is *extreme poverty of the mass of the people.* Later still the present Finance Minister, in his speech on the Income Tax, in January 1886, described the mass of the people as "men whose income at the best is barely sufficient to afford them the sustenance necessary to support life, living, as they do, upon the barest necessaries of life."

Now, what are we to think of an English gentleman who has occupied the high and important positions of an Under-Secretary of State for India and Governor of the thirty millions of Madras, and who professes to feel deep interest in the people of India, treating such grave matters as their "extreme poverty" and "scanty subsistence" with light-heartedness like this, and coolly telling them and the British public that the people of Bezwada were gloriously prosperous, and that there, "at one stroke, the mouths of a hungry and dying people have been filled with bread and the coffers of the Government with money!"

I shall now give a few facts and figures in connexion with the condition of India, and with some of the other questions dealt with by Sir Grant Duff. First, with regard to the poverty to which Mr. Samuel Smith referred. Sir Grant Duff may rest assured that I shall be only too thankful to him for any correction of my figures by him or for any better information. I have no other object than the truth.

In my paper on "The Poverty of India". I have worked out from official figures that the total income of British India is only Rs. 20 (40*s*, or, at present exchange, nearer 30*s*.) per head per annum. It must be remembered that the mass of the people cannot get this average of Rs 20, as the upper classes have a larger share than the average; also that this Rs. 20 per head includes the income or produce of foreign planters or producers, in which the interest of the natives does not go further than being mostly common labourers at competitive wages. All the profits of such produce are enjoyed by, and carried away from the country by, the foreigners. Subsequently, in my correspondence with the Secretary of State for India in 1880, I placed before his lordship, in detailed calculations based upon official returns, the income of the most favoured province of the Punjab and the cost of absolute necessaries of life there for a common agriculture labourer. The income is, at the outside, Rs. 20 per head per annum, and the cost of living Rs. 34.

No wonder then that forty or eighty millions or more people of British India should "go through life on insufficient food." My calculations, both in "The Poverty of India" and "The Condition of India" (the correspondence with the Secretary of State), have not yet been shown by anybody to be wrong or requiring correction. I shall be glad and thankful if Sir Grant Duff would give us his calculations and show us that the income of British India is anything like that of the Western countries of Europe.

I give a statement of the income of the different countries from Mulhall's "Dictionary of Statistics":—

Countries.	Gross earnings per inhabitant.	Countries.	Gross earnings per inhabitant.
England	... £41	Belgium	... £22·1
Scotland	... 32	Holland	... 26
Ireland	... 16	Denmark	... 23·2
United Kingdom	... 35·2	Sweeden and Norway	16·2
France	... 25·7	Switzerland	... 16
Germany	... 18·7	Greece	... 11·8
Russia	... 9 9	Europe	... 18
Austria	... 16·3	United States	... 27·2
Italy	... 12	Canada	... 26·9
Spain	... 13·8	Australia	... 43·4
Portugal	... 13·6		

The table is not official. In his "Progress of the World" (1880), Mulhall gives—Scandinavia, £17; South America, £6; India, £2. What is then poor India's whole income per head? Not as even much as the United Kingdom pays to its revenue only per head. The United Kingdom pays to revenue nearly 50*s.* per head when wretched India's whole income is 40*s.* per head, or rather, at the present exchange nearer 30*s* than 40*s.* Is this a result for an Englishman to boast about or to be satisfied with, after a century of British administration? The income of British India is only a third of that of even the countries of South America! Every other part of the British Empire is flourishing except wretched India.

Sir Grant Duff knows well that any poverty in the countries of Western Europe is not from want of wealth or income, but from unequal distribution. But British India has her whole production or income itself most wretched. There is no wealth, and therefore the question of its right distribution, or of any comparison with the countries of Western Europe or with England is very far off indeed. Certainly a gentleman like Sir Grant Duff ought to undersand the immense difference between the character of the conditions of the poor masses of British India and of the poor of Western Europe, the one starving from scantiness, the other having plenty, but suffering from some defect in its distribution. Let the British Indian administration fulfil its sacred pledges and allow plenty to be produced in British India, and then will be the proper time and occasion to compare the phenomena of the conditions of Western Europe and British India. The question at present is, why, under the management of the most highly paid services in the world, India cannot produce as much even as the worst governed countries of Europe. I do not mean to blame the individuals of the Indian services. It is the policy, the perversion of the pledges, that is at the bottom of our misfortunes. Let the Government of India only give us every year properly made up statistical tables of the whole production or the income of the country, and we shall then know truly how India fares year after year, and we shall then see how the present system of administration is an obstacle to any material advancement of India. Let us have actual facts about the real income of India, instead of careless opinions like those in Sir Grant Duff's two articles.

Instead of asking us to go so far as Western Europe to compare conditions so utterly different from each other, Sir Grant Duff might have looked nearer home, and studied somewhat of the neighbouring Native States, to institute some fair comparison under a certain similarity of circumstances. This point I shall have to refer to in the next article, when dealing with a cognate subject. Sir Grant Duff says: "I maintain that no country on the face of the earth is governed so cheaply in proportion to its size, to its population and to the difficulties of government." Surely, Sir Grant Duff knows better than this. Surely, he knows that the pressure of a burden depends upon the capacity to bear it: that an elephant may carry tons with ease, while a child would be crushed by a hundredweight. Surely, he knows the very first axiom of taxation—that it should be in proportion to the means of the taxpayer. Mulhall very properly says in his Dictionary: "The real incidence of all taxation is better shown by comparison with the people's earnings." Let us see facts. Let us see whether the incidence in British India is not *heavier than that of England itself.* The gross revenue of the United Kingdom in 1886 is £89,581,301; the population in 1886 is given as 36,707,418. The revenue per head will be 48*s.* 9*d.* The gross revenue of British India in 1885 is (in £1 = ten rupees) £70,690,000, and population in 1881, 198,790,000—say roundly, in 1885, 200,000,000. The revenue of the United Kingdom does not include railway or irrigation earnings; I deduct, therefore, these from the British Indian revenue. Deducting from £70,690,000, railway earnings £11,898,000, and irrigation and navigation earnings £1,676,000, the balance of gross revenue is £57,116,000 which taken for 200,000,000, gives 5*s*. 8½*d*—say 5*s*. 8*d*.—per head. Now, the United Kingdom pays 48*s*. 9*d*. per head from an income of £35·2 per head which makes the incidence or pressure of 6·92 per cent. of the income. British India pays 5*s*. 8*d*. out of an income of 40*s*., which makes the incidence or pressure of 14·3 per cent. of the income. Thus, while the United Kingdom pays for its gross revenue only 6·92 per cent. out of its rich income of £35·2 per head, British India pays out of its scantiness and starvation a gross revenue of 14·3 per cent. of its income ; so that, wretchedly weak and poor as British India is, the pressure, upon it is more than doubly heavier than that on the enormously wealthy United Kingdom ; and yet Sir Grant Duff says that no country on the face of the earth is governed so cheaply as British India, and misleads the British public about its true and deplorable condition. But what is worse, and what is British India's chief difficulty is this : In England, all that is paid by the people for revenue returns back to them, is enjoyed by them, and fructifies in their own pockets ; while in India, what the people pay as revenue does not all return to them, or is enjoyed, by them, or fructifies in their pockets. A large portion is enjoyed by others, and carried away clean out of the country. This is what makes British India's economic position unnatural.

I give below the incidence of a few more countries :—Percentage of expenditure to income : Germany, 10·7 ; France, 13·23 ; Belgium, 9·5 ; Holland, 9·61 ; Russia, 10·1 ; Denmark, 5·17 ; United States, 3·9 ; Canada, 5·0 ; Australia, 16·2. But in all these cases, whatever is spent returns back to the people, whether the percentage is large or small.

The Budget Estimate of 1887-88 is nearly £77,500,000, so the percentage of incidence will increase still higher. Sir Grant Duff's object in this assertion is to justify the character and prove the success of the present British Indian policy. It will be hereafter seen that this very argument of his is one of the best proofs of the failure of this policy and of the administration based upon it. Sir Grant Duff says: "Mr. Smith proceeds to admit that India has absorbed some £350,000,000 sterling of silver and gold in the last forty years, but makes the very odd remark that, although English writers consider this a great proof of wealth, it is not so regarded in India." To this, what is Sir Grant Duff's reply? Of the same kind as usual: mere careless assertions, and a fling at the misrepresentation about the educated classes. He says:—

> "It may suit A or B not to regard two and two as making four, but arithmetic is true, nevertheless; and there is the bullion, though doubtless one of the greatest boons that could be conferred upon India would be to get the vast dormant hoards of gold and silver which are buried in the ground or worn on the person brought into circulation. Can that, however, be hoped for as long as the very people whom Mr. Smith treats as exponents of Native opinion do their utmost to excite hostility against the British Government?"

To avoid confusion I pass over for the present without notice the last assertion. It will be seen further on what different testimony even the highest Indian authorities give upon this subject. With regard to the other remarks, it is clear that Sir Grant Duff has not taken the pains to know what the Natives say, and what the actual state of the matter is, with regard to these economic conditions. The best thing I can do to avoid useless controversy is to give in my second article a series of facts and official figures, instead of making bare assertions of opinion without any proofs, as Sir Grant Duff says. These economic questions are of far greater and more serious importance, both to England and India, than Sir Grant Duff and others of his views dream of. These facts and figures will show that British India has not received such amounts of gold and silver as is generally supposed, or as are more than barely adequate to its ordinary wants. The phenomenon of the import of bullion into British India is very much misapprehended, as will be shown in my second article; and Sir Grant Duff's assertions are misleading, as such meagre, vague, and off-hand assertions always are. By the present policy British India is prevented from acquiring any capital of its own, owing to the constant drain from its wretched income, and is on the verge of being ground down to dust. Such foreign capital as circulates in British India carries away its own profits *out* of British India, leaving the masses of its people as poor as ever, and largely going through life on insufficient food.

I shall now consider the important questions of trade bullion, population, drain, etc., to which Sir Grant Duff has referred. As promised in my first article, I shall at once proceed to give official facts and figures, which will enable the public to judge for themselves.

I begin with the question of the trade of British India. What is the true trade of British India? The trade returns of British India, as published in Blue Books, both in England and India are misleading to those who do not study them with certain necessary information to guide them. What are given as trade returns of British India are not such really, as I explain below.

The exports of the produce of a country form the basis of its trade. It is in return for such exports, together with ordinary commercial profits, that the country receives its imports. I shall first analyse the so-called exports of British India. A large portion of them, together with their profits, never return to British India in any shape, either of merchandise or treasure; though in every true trade all exports with their profits ought so to return. The present exports of British India consist of—

1. The exports of produce belonging to the Native States.

2. The exports of produce belonging to the territories beyond the land frontiers.

3. The exports of the produce belonging to European or other foreign planters or manufacturers, the profits of which are enjoyed in and carried away out of the country by these foreigners, and do not belong to or become a portion of the capital of the people of British India. The only interest the people have in these exports is that they are the labourers, by whose labour, at poor wages, the resources of their own country are to be brought out for the profit of the foreigners, such profit not to remain in the country.

4. Remittances for "home charges," including interest on public debt held in England, and loss in exchange, and excluding interest on debt which is incurred for railways and other productive works.

5. Remittances for interest on foreign debt incurred for railways and other productive public works. What in this case the lenders get as interest is all right; there in nothing to comlpain of in that. In other countries, beyond the interest to be paid to the lenders, the rest of

the whole benefit of such loans remains to the people of the country. This, however, is not the case with British India.

6. Private remittances of Europeans and other foreigners to their own countries for their families, and on account of their savings and profits. These remittances, together with item four, and what the foreigners enjoy in the country itself, are so much deprivation of the people, and cause the exhausting annual drain out of the very poor produce or income of British India. This is India's chief evil.

7. The remainder are the only *true* trade exports of the produce belonging to the people of British India.

Let us now examine the actual figures of the so-called exports of British India, say for 1885. For easier understanding I give the figures in sterling, taking the conventional £1 = Rs. 10. The amount of merchandise exported is £83,200,528. This, however, consists of not only domestic produce and manufactures of all India, but also foreign merchandise re-exported. I do not include treasure in these exports, for the simple reason that the gold or silver is not produced in India, but is simply a re-exportation out of what is imported from foreign parts. I take all my figures from the statistical abstracts published among Parliamentary returns, except when I mention any other source. I take, then, exports of merchandise to be £83,200,528. We must first know how much of this belongs to the Native States. The official trade returns give us no information on this important point, as they should. I shall therefore make a rough estimate for the present. The population of all India is nearly 254,000,000, out of which that of the Native States is 55,000,000, or about

21·5 per cent.; or say, roundly, one-fifth. But the proportion of their exports will, I think, be found to be larger than one-fifth. All the opium exported from Bombay comes from the Native States. A large portion of the cotton exported from Bombay comes from the Native States. According to Hunter's "Imperial Indian Gazetteer," one-sixth of such cotton comes from Kathiawad alone. To be on the safe side, I take the total of exports of the Native States to be one-fifth only —*i.e.*, £16,600,000. Next, the export of merchandise from the frontier countries is about £5,300,000. I may roughly take only one-quarter of this as exported out of India. That will be £1,300,000.

The exports of coffee, indigo, jute manufactures, silk, tea, etc., which are mostly those belonging to foreign planters and manufacturers, amount to about £11,500,000. I cannot say how much of this belongs to Native planters, and not, to foreigners. I may take these exports as £10,000,000.

Remittances made for "home charges" (excluding interest on railway and productive works loans) including interest on public debt and loss in exchange, come to about £11,500,000.

Remittances for interest on foreign loans for railways and other public works are about £4,827,000. I cannot say how much interest on the capital of State railways and other productive works is paid in England as part of the interest paid on "debt" (£2,612,000). If I take debt as £162,000,000, and capital laid out on productive works £74,000,000, the proportion of interest on £74,000,000 out of £2,612,000 will be about £1,189,000. If so, then the total amount of interest on *all* railways and public works will be about £6,000,000, leaving all other home charges, including exchange and interest or public debt as £11,500,000, as I have assumed above.

Private remittances of Europeans and other foreigners for their families, and of savings and profits, and for importing merchandise, suitable for their consumption, may be roughly estimated at £10,000,000, though I think it is much more.

The account, then, of the *true* trade exports of British India stands thus :—

Total exports of all India and Frontier States . . .		£83,200,000
Native States	£16,600,000	
Frontier Territory	1,300,000	
European planters	10,000,000	
Home charges	11,500,000	
Interest on all railways and public works loans	6,000,000	
Private remittances	10,000,000	
		55,400,000
The true trade exports of the people of British India.		£27,800,000

Or say, roundly, £30,000,000 for a population of nearly 200,000,000, giving 3*s*. per head per annum. If proper information could be obtained, I believe this amount would turn out to be nearer £20,000,000 than 300,000,000 for the *true* trade exports of the people of British India. To be on the safe side, I keep to £30,000,000. I must be remembered that this item includes all the re-exports of foreign merchandise, which have to be deducted to get at the true exports of domestic produce.

Is this a satisfactory result of a century of management by British administrators? Let us compare this result with the trade exports of other parts of the British Empire. As I have no information about the foreign debt of those parts, for the interest of which they may have to export some of their produce, I make allowance for their *whole* public debt as so much foreign debt. This, of course, is a too large allowance. I take interest at 5 per cent., and deduct the amount from the exports. I am, therefore, evidently under-estimating the exports of the other parts of the British Empire. As the exports of British India include re-exports of foreign merchandise, I have taken the exports of all other countries, in a similar way, for a fair comparison. No deduction for any payment of interest on foreign debt is made for the United Kingdom, as it is more a lender than a borrower. I cannot give here the whole calculation, but only the results and they are these :—

Countries.	True trade exports per head (1885). s. d.
The United Kingdom.	149 4
Australia (including bullion and specie which it produces) ...	271 0
Natal	28 8
Cape of Good Hope (exclusive of diamonds) ...	35 5
North American Colonies	70 5
West India Islands ...	75 4
British India only ...	3 0

Let us next take some of the foreign countries, and see how wretched British India's trade is when compared with even them. For a few of the foreign countries I can get particulars of their public debt, but not of that portion of it which is foreign debt. I have taken the amount of the *whole* public debt, and allowed 5 per cent. interest on it, to be deducted from the exports, as if it were all foreign debt. In this way I have under-estimated the true trade exports. These countries I mark with an asterisk ; those marked † include bullion. For these I cannot get separate returns for merchandise only. In the case of the United States the figure is really a great under-estimate, as I take its foreign debt as equal in amount to its whole public debt, and also as I take interest at 5 per cent. I cannot get particulars of the foreign debts, if they have any, of other countries, and some allowance will have to be made for that. But in all these cases the amount of exports is so large, as compared with the paltry figure of British India, that the contrast remains most striking :—

Countries.	Exports per head. s.	d.	Countries.	Exports per head. s.	d.
*Russian Empire ...	12	0	Austro-Hungarian Empire ...	47	0
*Norway ...	61	7	†Roumania ...	27	0
Sweden ...	61	6	†Greece ...	39	9
*Denmark ...	97	5	Egypt ...	38	9
German Empire ...	107	2	*United States ...	55	6
Holland ...	348	1	†Mexico ...	20	1
*Belgium ...	375	2	†Chili ...	149	0
*France ...	68	7	†Argentine Republic .	90	8
†Portugal ...	33	9	†Uruguay ...	198	2
Spain ...	36	5	Japan ...	3	8
*Italy ...	17	9	British India ...	3	0

Even Japan, only so lately opened up, is exporting more than British India.

After seeing how poor the *true trade* exports are of the people of British India from the point of view of British India's interests, let us next examine the matter from the point of view of *England's* interest. What benefit has England's trade derived, after possessing and administering British India for more than a hundred years, under a most expensive administration, with complete despotic control over it, the people having no voice and no control of any kind. Has British India so improved as to become an important customer for British goods? There was no protection, no heavy duties to hamper British imports, as in other parts of the British Empire itself, or in foreign countries. And yet we find that British India is by far the most wretched customer for British produce or manufactures. Here are the facts:—The total of the exports of British produce from the United Kingdom to India is, for the year 1885, £29,300,000. As I have explained before about exports from India, that they are not all from British India, so also these exports from the United Kingdom to India are not all for British India, though they enter India by British Indian ports. These British exports have to be distributed among—(1) Native States; (2) frontier territories; (3) consumption of Europeans; (4) railway and Government stores; and (5) the remainder for the Natives of British India. Let Government give us correct information about these particulars, and then we shall be able to know how insignificant is the commercial benefit England derives from her dominion over British India. I shall not be surprised if it is found that the real share of the people of British India in the British exports is not half of the £29,300,000 imported into India. It must be remembered that whatever is received by the Natives States and the frontier territories is in *full* return, with the ordinary profits of 15 per cent., for their exports to the United Kingdom. Their case is not like that of British India. They have no such exhausting drain as that of British India, beyond paying the small tribute of about £700,000. If I take £15,000,000, as British produce received for the consumption of the Native subjects of British India, I think I am on the safe side. What is this amount for a population of 200,000,000? Only 1*s*. 6*d*. per head. Take it even at 2*s*. per head if you like, or even £25,000,000, which will be only 2*s*. 6*d*. per head. What a wretched result *for four-fifths of the whole British Empire!* The population of British India is 200,000,000, and that of the rest of the British Empire outside India, including the United Kingdom, about 52,000,000.

I now compare the exports of British produce to British India with those to other parts of the British Empire and to other foreign countries. I give the results only :—

BRITISH EMPIRE.

EXPORTS OF BRITISH PRODUCE PER HEAD FOR 1885.

To Countries.	s.	d.	To Countries.	s.	d.
British India 1s. 6d. or	2	6	Ceylon	3	10
North American Colonies	30	8	Mauritius	14	2
West Indian Island and Guiana ...	37	10	Cape of Good Hope and Natal	45	8
British Honduras ...	66	7	West African Settlements	57	3
Australasia	155	8	Possessions on the Gold Coast	13	10
Straits Settlements ...	86	10			

Some deductions may have to be made from these figures.

What a sad story is this! If British India took only £1 per head, England would export to British India alone as much as she exports at present to the *whole* world (£213,000,000). What an amount of work would this give to British industries and produce! Will the British merchants and manufacturers, open their eyes? Will the British working men understand how enormous their loss is from the present policy, which involves besides a charge of dishonourable violation of sacred promises that clings to the British name? If India prospered and consumed British produce largely, what a gain would it be to England and to the whole world also! Here, then, will be Sir Grant Duff's "India's interest, England's interest, and the world's interest" to his hearts content, if he will with a true and earnest heart labour to achieve this threefold interest in the right way.

Let us next take other foreign countries with most or all of which England, I think, has no free trade, and see how British India stands the comparison even with them :—

EXPORTS OF BRITISH PRODUCE PER HEAD

To Countries.	s.	d.	To Countries.	s.	d.
British India	2	6	Russia (perhaps partly supplied through intermediate countries)	0	11½
Germany	7	3	Greece	10	1
France	7	11	*Turkey in Europe	16	8
Sweden and Norway	10	8	*Turkey in Asia	3	10
Denmark and Iceland	19	4	Egypt	10	2
Holland (this may be supplying some portion of Central Europe)	44	3	United States	8	9
Belgium (do. do.)	28	3	*Central America	4	7
Portugal	8	0	*Brazil	10	5
Spain	3	9	Uruguay	54	0
Italy (perhaps partly supplied by intermediate countries)	4	9	Argentine Republic	31	8
Austrian territory do.	0	8	Chili	12	4
			Japan	1	1

Japan, so lately opened, has commenced taking 1*s*, 1*d*. worth per head. These figures tell their own eloquent tale. Is it too much to expect that, with complete free trade and British management, and all "development of resources," the prosperity of British India ought to be such as to consume of British produce even £1 per head, and that it would be so if British India were allowed to grow freely under natural economic conditions ?

In the first article I referred to the capacity of British India for taxation. Over and over again have British Indian financiers lamented that British India cannot bear additional taxation without oppressiveness. Well, now what is the extent of this taxation which is already so crushing that any addition to it would "grind British India to dust"? It is, as I have shown in the first article, after squeezing and squeezing as much as

* Whitaker's Almanac.

possible, only 5*s*. 8*d*. per head per annum, and according to the present budget a little more—say 6*s*. Let us see what the capacity for taxation of other parts of the British Empire and of other foreign countries is, and even of those Native States of India where anything like improved government on the British Indian system is introduced. I give results only :—

BRITISH EMPIRE.

GROSS REVENUE PER HEAD PER ANNUM.

Countries.	s.	d.	Countries.	s.	d.
British India	6	0	Cape of Good Hope	53	1
United Kingdom	48	9	North American Colonies	31	7
Ceylon	8	6	West India Islands	23	1
Mauritius	40	5	British Guiana	32	2
Australia	139	8			
Natal	29	10			

FOREIGN COUNTRIES.

GROSS REVENUE PER HEAD PER ANNUM.

Countries.	s.	d.	Countries.	s.	d.
Russia in Europe	24	5	Austro-Hungary	40	6
Norway	23	6	Italy	39	10
Sweden	19	8	Greece	37	7
Denmark	26	11	Servia	16	3
German Empire	13	6	Bulgaria	12	3
Prussia	41	2	Roumania	20	3
Saxony	22	8	Egypt (proper)	30	11
Grand Duchy of Oldenburgh	18	6	United States (different) States have their separate revenue besides)	26	10
Saxe-Coburg and Gotha	17	0	Mexico	15	3
Bavaria	44	9	Brazil	26	1
Würtenburg	27	8	Guatemala	24	0
Grand Duchy of Baden	27	2	Nicaragua	18	9
Grand Duchy of Hesse	21	8	Salvador	29	8
Alsace-Lorraine	24	8	Orange Free State	36	9
Holland	47	1	Persia	8	7
Belgium	45	7	Republic of Peru	18	2
France	73	6	All territory directly under Turkey	13	3
Portugal	31	6			
Spain	41	10			
Switzerland	12	2			

N.B.—Some of the above figures are worked out of Whitaker's Almanac, 1886.

It will be seen that British India's capacity for paying taxation is very poor indeed compared to that of any other country of any consequence. Of the above figures I cannot say which may be oppressive to the people. I give this as a fact, that these people pay so much for being governed. But it must be further borne in mind that every farthing of what these people pay returns back to them, which is not the case with British India. Can it be said of any of these countries that one-fifth or one-third of its people goes through life on insufficient food from sheer poverty of only 40*s.* income, and not from imperfect distribution?

I shall next take the case of some of the Native States of India. I have taken some, where during the minorities of the Princes, English officials have administered the State and put them into order and good government. The capacity for taxation which I give below is not the result of any oppressive taxation, but of the natural developments by improved government, and of the increasing prosperity of the people. I give instances in the Bombay Presidency that I know, and of which I have been able to get some particulars.

GROSS REVENUE PER HEAD (£1 = Rs. 10.)

		s.	*d.*			*s.*	*d.*
Baroda	...	12	8	Gondal	...	18	0
Cutch	...	7	11	Morbi	...	17	2
Bhavnagar	...	12	6	Wadhwan	...	18	10

These States have no debts. Baroda, Bhavnagar, and Gondal have built and are extending their own railways, and all have built and are building their own public works from revenue, and have good balances. Baroda has a balance in hand of £2,100,000, equal to eighteen months' revenue; Cutch has £140,000, equal to eight months' revenue; Bhavnagar has £560,000, equal to two years' revenue; and Gondal has £150,000, equal to fifteen months' revenue. I give only one or two short extracts from official statements. Sir W. Hunter, in his "Imperial Gazetteer," says about Bhavnagar in connection with Kathiawar: "Bhavnagar has taken the lead in the material development of her resources, and is the first State in India which constructed a railway at her own expense and risk." I may say that Gondal did the same in conjunction with Bhavnagar, and Baroda had done that long before. In handing over the rule of Gondal to the Prince on the completion of his minority, Major Nutt, the British Administrator, and in charge of the State at the time, says with just pride and pleasure, in reference to the increase of revenue from £80,000 in 1870 to £120,000 in 1884: "One point of special interest in this matter is, that the increase in revenue has not occasioned any hardship to Gondal subjects. On the contrary, never were the people generally—high and low, rich and poor,—in a greater state of social prosperity than they are now." The Bombay Government has considered this "highly satisfactory."

At the installation of the present Chief of Bhavnagar, Mr. Peile, the Political Agent, describes the State as being then "with flourishing finances and much good work in progress. Of financial matters I need say little; you have no debts, and your treasury is full." When will British Indian financiers be able to speak with the same pride, pleasure, and satisfaction? "No debt, full treasury, good work in progress, increase of revenue, with increase of social prosperity, for high and low, rich and poor." Will this ever be in British India under the present policy? No.

There are some other States in Kathiawar in which higher taxation per head than that of British India is paid by the people, though I do not know that it is said that there is oppressive taxation there. I may instance Junagadh as 11*s.* per head, with £500,000 balance in hand, equal to fifteen months' revenue; and Nawanagar as 16*s.* 3*d.* per head, and gradually paying off some debt. I have no doubt that Native States will go on rapidly increasing in prosperity as their system of government goes on improving. I know from my own personal knowledge as Prime Minister of Baroda for one year that that State has a very promising future indeed. There are several other Native States in India in which the gross revenue per head is higher than that of British India. All the remaining first and second class Kathiawar States are from 8*s.* to 13*s.* per head; Gwalior, 7*s.* 8*d.*; Indore, 13*s.* 5*d.*; Bhurtpore, 8*s.* 8*d.*; Dholepur, 8*s.* 10*d.*; Tonk, 7*s.*; Kotah, 11*s.* 4*d.*; Jallawar, 8*s.* 10*d.* Only just now Sindia lends £3,500,000 to the British Government; Holkar, I think, has lent £1,000,000 for the Indore railway.

There cannot be much oppression in these States, as the Political Agents' vigilance and superintendence, and the fear of the displeasure of Government, are expected to prevent it.

Then Sir Grant Duff maintains that no country on the face of the earth is governed so cheaply as British India. In the first place, this is a fiction, as the heaviness of burden on poverty-stricken British India is more than double than that on the enormously rich England; and secondly, Sir Grant Duff's object is to show that this cheapness is a proof of the success of the present British Indian policy. But, on the contrary, the facts and figures I have given above about British India's wretched income and capacity for taxation, its insignificant trade, and the very paltry commercial benefit to England, are conclusive proofs of anything but success in improving the prosperity of the people. Moreover, for the so-called cheapness, it is no thanks or credit to Government. It is not of choice that Government takes only 6*s*. per head. On the contrary, it is always longing, ever moaning, and using every possible shift to squeeze out more taxation if it can. By all means make British India capable of paying even 20*s*. per head (if not 50*s*. per head, like England) for revenue, without oppression and misery; or make its income £20 per head, if not £41, like that of England; and then fairly claim credit for having raised to some material extent the prosperity of British India. Let us have such *results*, instead of tall talk and self-complacent assertions. Had Government given us year after year correct information about the actual income and condition of the people of British India, Britain would then have known the deplorable results of the neglect of, and disobedience to, her deliberate and sacred mandates.

Again, Sir Grant Duff's boast of the cheapness of government is wrong, even in the misleading sense in which he maintains it. He tries to show that because British India pays only 6*s*. per head, it is therefore the most cheaply governed country on the face of the earth—*i.e.*, no other country pays a less amount per head. But even in this he is not quite accurate. He would have found this out had he only looked about in India itself, and he would have saved himself the surprise which he expresses at Mr. Smith being startled when he (Mr. Smith) was told that taxation was lighter in Native

States than in British India. As a matter of fact, there *are* some Native States in which the revenue per head is lighter than the British India. Whether that is a desirable state of affairs or not is another question ; but when he twits Mr. Smith he should have ascertained whether what Mr. Smith was told was at all correct or not. There *are* some of the Native States where the gross revenue is very nearly as low as or even less than 6*s.* per head: Hyderabad, 6*s.* 4*d.*; Patiala, 6*s.* 4*d.*; Travancore, 5*s.* 8*d.*; Kolhapur, 5*s.* 6*d.*; Mysore, 4*s.* 10*d*; Dungapore, 2*s.*; Marwar, 4*s.* 10*d.*; Serohi, 2*s.* 3*d.*; Jeypore, 4*s.* 3*d.*; Banswara, 3*s.* 8*d.*; and Kishengarh, 4*s.* 10*d.* Travancore is known as a well-governed country. £15,000 of its revenue is interest on British Indian Government securities, and it holds a balance in hand in Government securities and otherwise of £564,000—equal to nearly eleven months' revenue. Jeypore has the reputation of being a well-governed State. There are similarly even some foreign countries outside India which are as "cheaply governed" as British India: United States of Columbia, 5*s.* 10*d.* Republic of Boliyia, 5*s.* 11*d.*

Sir Grant Duff refers to the absorption of gold and silver and to hoarding. What are the facts about British India? In my "Poverty of India" I have treated the subject at some length. The total amount (after deducting the exports from imports) retained by India during a period of eithty-four years (1801 to 1884), including the exceptionally large imports during the American war, is £455,761,385. This is for *all* India. The population at present is 254,000,000. I may take the average of eighty-four years roughly—say 200,000,000. This gives 45*s.* 6*d.* per head for the whole eighty-four years, or 6½*d.*

per head per annum. Even if I took the average population as 180,000,000, the amount per head for the eighty-four years would be 50*s*. or 7*d*. per head per annum. Of the United Kingdom I cannot get returns before 1858. The total amount of treasure retained by the United Kingdom (after deducting export from imports) is, for twenty-seven years from 1858 to 1884, £86,194,937. Taking an average of 31,000,000 of populatfon for twenty-seven years, the amount retained for these twenty-seven years is 55*s*. 7*d*. per head, or very nearly 2*s*. 1*d*. per head per annum; while in India for more than three times the same period the amount is only 45*s*. 6*d*. per head, or 6½*d* per head per annum. France has retained from 1861 to 1880 (Mulhall's Dictionary) £208,000,000; and taking the population — say 37,000,000—that gives 112*s*. per head in twenty years, 5*s*. 7*d*. per head per annum.

Sir Grant Duff ought to consider that the large amount of bullion is to be distributed over a vast country and a vast population, nearly equal to five-sixths of the population of the whole of Europe; and when the whole population is considered what a wretched amount is this of gold and silver—*viz*., 6½*d*. per head per annum—received for all possible wants! India does not produce any gold or silver. To compare it with Europe—Europe retained in ten years, 1871-1880 (Mulhall, "Progress of the World," 1880), £327,000,000 for an average population of about 300,000,000 or 21*s*. 10*d*. per head, or 2*s*. 2*d*. per head per annum. India during the same ten years retained £65,774,252 for an average population of, say, 245,000,000; so that the whole amount retained for the ten years is about 5*s*. 4*d*., or only 6½*d*. per head per annum, against 21*s*. 10*d*. and 2*s*. 2*d*. respectively of

Europe. This means that India retained only one-fourth of what Europe retained per head per annum during these ten years. It must be further remembered that there is no such vast system of cheques, clearing-houses, etc., in India, as plays so important a part in England and other countries of Europe. Wretched as the provision of 6½*d.* per head per annum is for *all* wants—political, social, commericial, etc.—there is something far worse behind for British India. All the gold and silver that I have shown above as retained by India is not for British India only, but for the Native States, the frontier territories, and the European population; and then the remainder is for the Native population of British India. We must have official information about these four divisions before we can form a correct estimate of what British India retains. The Native States, as I have said before have no foreign drain except the small amount of tribute of about £700,000. Some frontier territories receive something instead of paying any tribute. These States therefore receive back for the exports of their merchandise, and for the ordinary trade profits on such exports, full returns in imports of merchandise and treasure, and this treasure taken away by the Native States and frontier territories forms not a small portion of what is imported into India. It must also be considered how much metal is necessary every year for waste of coin and metal and for the wants of circulating currency. When Government can give us all such information, it will be found that precious little remains for British India beyond what it is compelled to import for its absolute wants. I hope England does not mean to say that Englishmen or Englishwomen may sport as much as they like in ornaments or personal trinkets or jewellery; but that the wretch of a Native of British India, their fellow-subject has no business or right to put a few shillings' worth of trinkets on his wife or daughter's person; or that Natives must simply live the lives of brutes, subsist on their "scanty subsistence," and thank their stars that they have that much.

I will now try to give some indication of what bullion British India actually retains. Mr. Harrison gave his evidence before the Parliamentary Committee of 1871-74 that about £1,000,000 of fresh coinage was more than sufficient to supply the waste of coin or metal. Is it too much to assume that in the very widespread and minute distribution, over a vast surface and a vast population, of small trinkets or ornaments of silver, and their rough use, another million may be required to supply waste and loss? If only a pennyworth per head per annum be so wanted, it would make a million sterling. Next, how much goes to the Native States and the frontier territories? Here are a few significant official figures as an indication: The "Report of the external land trade and railway-borne trade of the Bombay Presidency for 1884-85" (p. 2), says of Rajputana and Central India—"The imports from the external blocks being greater than the exports to them, the balance of trade due by the Presidency to the other provinces amounts to Rs. 12,01,05,912, as appears from the above table and the following." I take the Native States from the table referred to.

EXCESS OF IMPORTS IN BOMBAY PRESIDENCY.

From Rajputana and Central India ...	Rs.	5,55,46,753
,, Berar	,,	1,48,91,355
,, Hyderabad	,,	8,67,688
Total ...	Rs.	7,13,05,796

Or £7,130,579. This means that these Native States have exported so much more merchandise than they have imported. Thereupon the Report remárks thus :—"The greatest balance is in favour of Rajputana and Central India, caused by the import of opium from that block. Next to it is that of the Central Provinces. It is presumed that these balances are paid back *mainly in cash*" (the italics are mine). This, then, is the way the treasure goes; and poor British India gets all the abuse—insult added to injury. Its candle burns not only at both ends, but at all parts. The excessive foreign agency eats up in India and drains away out of India a portion of its wretched income, thereby weakening and exhausting it every year drop by drop, though not very perceptibly, and lessening its productive power or capability. It has poor capital, and cannot increase it much. Foreign capital does dearly all the work, and carries away all the profit. Foreign capitalists from Europe and from Native States make profits from the resources of British India, and take away those profits to their own countries. The share that the mass of the Natives of British India have is to drudge and slave on scanty subsistence for these foreign capitalists; not as slaves in America did, on the resources of the country and land belonging to the masters themselves, but on the resources of their own country, for the benefit of the foreign capitalists. I may illustrate this a little. Bombay is considered a wealthy place, and has a large capital circulating in it, to carry on all its wants as a great port. Whose capital is this? Mostly that of foreigners. The capital of the European exchange banks and European merchants is mostly foreign and most of the Native capital is also foreign—*i.e.*, that of the Native bankers and merchants from the Native States. Nearly £6,000,000 of the capital working in Bombay belongs to Native bankers from the Native States. Besides, a large portion of the wealthy merchants, though more or less settled in Bombay, are from Native States. Of course, I do not mean to say anything against these capitalists from Europe or Native States. They are quite free and welcome to come and do what they can. They do some good. But what I mean is, that British India cannot and does not make any capital, and must and does lose the profit of its resources to others. If British India were left to its own free development it would be quite able to supply all its own wants, would not remain handicapped, and would have a free field in competition with the foreign capitalist, with benefit to all concerned. The official admission of the amount of the drain goes as far as £20,000,000 per annum; but really it will be found to be much larger (excluding interest on railway and public works loans):—add to this drain out of the country what is eaten and enjoyed in the country itself by others than the Natives of the country, to the deprivation by so much of these Natives, and some idea can be formed of the actual and continuous depletion. Now, take only £20,000,000 per annum to be the extent of the drain, or even £10,000,000 per annum; this amount, for the last thirty years only, would have sufficed to build all the present and great many more railways and other public works. There is another way in which I may illustrate the burning of the candle at all parts. First of all, British India's own wealth is carried away out of it, and then that wealth is brought back to it in the shape of loans, and for these loans British India must find so much more for interest; the whole thing moving in a most vicious and provoking circle. Will nothing but a catastrophe cure this? Even of the railway, etc., loans the people do not derive the full benefit. I cannot go into details about this here. I refer to my correspondence with the Secretary of State for India.* Nor can I go here into the calculation, about the drain. I can only refer to my papers on "The Poverty of India" and "Condition of India."† Let Sir Grant Duff kindly show me where I am wrong in those papers, and I shall be thankful; or he will see that no country in the world, not even England excepted, can stand such a drain without destruction. Even in those days when the drain was understood to be only £3,000,000 per annum, Mr. Montgomery Martin wrote in these significant and distressing words‡ :—

> "The annual drain of £3,000,000 on British India has amounted in thirty years, at 12 per cent. (the usual Indian rate) compound interest, to the enormous sum of £723,900,000 sterling............ So constant and accumulating a drain, even in England, would soon impoverish her. How severe, then, must be its effects on India, where the wage of a labourer is from twopence to threepence a day! Were the hundred millions of British subjects in India converted into a *consuming* population, what a market would be presented for British capital, skill and industry!"

What, then, must be the condition now, when the drain is getting perhaps ten times larger, and a large amount besides is eaten up in the country itself by others than the people? Even an ocean would be dried up if a portion of its evaporation did not always return to it as rain or river. If interest were added to the drain, what an enormous loss would it be!

---

* *Supra*, pp. 193-196.

† *Supra*, pp. 33, 196-199.

‡ "Eastern India, 1838," vol. i., p. xii.

In the darkness of the past we see now a ray of light and hope when the highest Indian authority begins to perceive not only the material disaster, but even the serious "political danger" from the present state of affairs. I only hope and pray that Britain will see matters mended before disaster comes. Instead of shutting his eyes like an ostrich, as some persons do, the Secretary of State for India only last year, in his despatch of 26th January, 1886 to the Treasury, makes this remarkable admission about the consequences of the present "character of the government," of the foreign rule of Britain over India:—

"The position of India in relation to taxation and the sources of the public revenues is very peculiar, not merely from the habits of the people and their strong aversion to change, which is more specially exhibited to new forms of taxation, but likewise *from the character of the Government*, which is in the hands of foreigners, who hold all the principal administrative offices, and form so large a part of the Army. The impatience of new taxation, which would have to be borne wholly as a consequence of the foreign rule imposed on the country, and virtually to meet additions to charges arising outside of the country, would constitute a political danger the real magnitude of which, it is to be feared, is not at all appreciated by persons who have no knowledge of or concern in the government of India, but which those responsible for that government have long regarded as of the most serious order." [The italics are mine.]

This gives some hope. If, after the faithful adoption of the policy of 1833 and 1858, our material condition does not improve, and all the fears expressed in the above extract do not vanish, the fault will not be Britain's, and she will at least be relieved from the charge of dishonour to her word. But I have not the shadow of a doubt, as the statesmen of 1833 and the proclamation of 1858 had no doubt, that the result will be a blessing both to England and India.

A second ray of hope is this. Many Englishmen in

England are taking active interest in the matter. Mr. Bright, Mr. Fawcett, Sir C. Trevelyan, and others have done good in the past. Others are earnestly working now—Mr. Slagg, Mr. Wilson, Mr. Digby, Mr. S. Smith, Mr. Hyndman, and several others. A further ray of hope is in an increasing number of members of Parliament interesting themselves in Indian matters, such as Dr. Hunter, Mr. S. Smith, Dr. Clark, Mr. Cremer, Sir J. Phear, Sir W. Plowden, and many others; and we cannot but feel thankful to all who have taken and are taking interest in our lot. All unfortunately, however, labour under the disadvantage of want of full information from Government, and the difficulty of realising the feelings and views of the Natives. But still they have done much good. I must also admit here that some Anglo-Indians begin to realise the position. We owe much to men like Sir W. Wedderburn, Sir G. Birdwood, Major Bell, Mr. Ilbert, Mr. Cotton, and others of that stamp, for their active sympathy with us. Mr. Bright hit the blot as far back as 1853 in his speech of the 3rd of January: "I must say that it is my belief that if a country be found possessing a most fertile soil and capable of bearing every variety of production, and that notwithstanding the people are in a state of extreme destitution and suffering, the chances are that there is some fundamental error in the government of the country." It is not necessary to go far to seek for this fundamental error. It is the perversion of the policy of 1833, which in the more widened and complete form of 1858 is virtually still a dead letter.

Much is said about poor Natives wasting money in marriages, etc. I hope it is not meant that these poor wretches have no right to any social privileges or enjoyments, and that their business is only to live and die like brutes. But the fact of the matter is, that this is one of those fallacies that die hard. Let us see what truth the Deccan Riots Commission brings to light. The Report of that Commission says (page 19, para. 54): "The results of the Commission's enquiries show that undue prominence has been given to the expenditure on marriage and other festivals as a cause of the ryots' indebtedness. The expenditure on such occasions may undoubtedly be called extravagant when compared with the ryots' means; but the occasions occur seldom, and probably in a course of years the total sum spent this way by any ryot is not larger than a *man in his position is justified in spending on social and domestic pleasures*." (The italics are mine.) And what is the amount the poor ryot spends on the marriage of his son! Rs. 50 to 75 (£5 to £7 10*s.*) say the Commissioners.

Sir Grant Duff says: "We have stopped war, we are stopping famine. How are the ever-increasing multitudes to be fed?" Is not Sir Grant Duff a little hasty in saying, "We are stopping famine." What you are doing is to starve the living to save the dying. Make the people themselves able to meet famine without misery and deaths, and then claim credit that you are stopping famine. However, the true answer to the question, "How are the ever-increasing multitudes to be fed?" is a very simple one, if gentlemen like Sir Grant Duff will ever have the patience to study the subject. The statesmen of 1833 and of 1858 have in the clearest and most emphatic way answered this question. They knew and said clearly upon what the welfare and well-being of the hundreds of millions depended. They laid down unequivocally what would make British

India not only able to feed the increasing multitudes, but prosperous and the best customer of England; and Mr. Grant Duff's following kind question of 1871 will be fully answered; "But what are we to say about the state of India? How many generations must pass away before that country has arrived at even the comparative wealth of this (England)?" This benevolent desire of Mr. Grant Duff would be accomplished in no long time. This question of population, of "the ever-increasing multitudes," requires further examination. Macaulay, in his review of Southey's "Colloquies on Society," says:—

> "When this island was thinly peopled, it was barbarous; there was little capital, and that little was insecure. It is now the richest and the most highly civilised spot in the world, but the population is dense. . . . But when we compare our own condition with that of our ancestors, we think it clear that the advantages arising from the progress of civilisation have far more than counterbalanced the disadvantages arising from the progress of population. While our numbers have increased tenfold our wealth has increased hundredfold. . . . . If we were to prophesy that in the year 1930 a population of fifty millions, better fed, clad, and lodged than the English of our time, will cover these islands,. . . . many people would think us insane. We prophesy nothing; but this we say, if any person had told the Parliament which met in perplexity and terror after the crash in 1720, that in 1830, the wealth of England would surpass all their wildest dreams, ... that for one man of ten thousand pounds then living there would be five men of fifty thousand pounds, ... our ancestors would have given as much credit to the prediction as they gave to 'Gulliver's Travels.'"

I claim no prophecy, but the statesmen of 1833 have prophesied, and the Proclamation of 1858 has prophesied. Do what they have said, and their prophecies shall be fulfilled.

Now, let us see a few more facts. Because a country increases in population it does not necessarily follow that it must become poorer; nor because a country is densely populated that therefore it must be poor. Says Macaulay: "England is a hundredfold more wealthy while it is tenfold denser." The following figures speak for themselves:—

Countries.		Inhabitants per sq. mile about 1880.		Income per inhabitant (Mulhall's Dictionary of Statistics, 1886).
Belgium	...	487	...	£22·1
England	...	478 (1886)	...	41 (1882)
Holland	...	315	...	26
Italy	...	257	...	12
British India	...	229	...	2
Germany	...	217	...	18·7
Austria	...	191	...	16·3
France	...	184	...	25·7
Switzerland	...	184	...	16
Ireland	...	153 (1886)	...	16 (1882)
Denmark	...	132	...	26·2
Scotland	...	128 (1886)	...	32 (1882)
Portugal	...	126	...	13·6
Turkey	...	120 (Mulhall).		4 (Sir E. Baring)
Spain	...	85	...	13·8
Greece	...	69	...	11·8
Russia in Europe	...	41	...	9·9
Sweden	...	27 }	...	16·2
Norway	...	15 }		

The densest Province of British India is Bengal (443). Thus, here are countries denser and thinner than British India, but *every one* of them has a far better income than British India. Belgium, denser than the densest Presidency of British India, is eleven times more wealthy; England, as dense, is twenty times more wealthy. Here are some very thinly populated countries: Mexico, 13 per square mile; Venezuela, 4·7; Chilli, 8·8; Peru, 18·6; Argentine Republic, 2·6; Uruguay, 7·8; and several others. Are they therefore so much richer than England or Belgium? Here is Ireland, at your door, About its people the Duke of Argyll only a few weeks ago (22nd of April last), in the House of Lords, said: "Do not tell me that the Irish labourer is incapable of labour, or energy, or exertion. Place him in favourable circumstances, and there is no better workman than the Irishman. I have myself employed large gangs of Irishmen, and I never saw any navvies work better; and besides that, they were kind and courteous men." The population of Ireland is less than one-third as dense as that of England; and yet how is it that the income of England is £41 and that of Ireland only £16 per inhabitant, and that the mass of the people do not enjoy the benefit of even that much income, and are admittedly wretchedly poor?

British India's resources are officially admitted to be enormous, and with an industrious and law-abiding people, as Sir George Birdwood testifies, it will be quite able to produce a large income, become as rich as any other country and easily provide for an increasing population and increasing taxation, if left free scope.

Lastly, a word about the educated classes, upon whose devoted heads Sir Grant Duff has poured down all his vials of wrath. Here are some fine amenities of an English gentleman of high position: "Professional malcontents; busy, pushing talkers; ingeniously wrong; the pert scribblers of the Native Press; the intriguers; pushing pettifoggers, chatterboxes; disaffected cliques; the *crassa ignorantia*; little coteries of intriguers; silly and dishonest talk of Indian grumblers; politicising sophists threaten to be a perfect curse to India," etc.

I leave these flowers of rhetoric alone. Not satisfied even with this much, he has forgotten himself altogether, and groundlessly charged the educated classes—"who do their utmost to excite hostility against the

British Government," "who do their utmost to excite factitious disloyalty." I repel this charge with only two short extracts. I need not waste many words.

The following, from the highest authority, is ample, clear, and conclusive. The Government of India, in their despatch of the 8th of June, 1880, to the Secretary of State for India, bear this emphatic testimony: "To the minds of at least the educated among the people of India—and the number is rapidly increasing—any idea of the subversion of British power is abhorrent, from the consciousness that it must result in the wildest anarchy and confusion." Secondly, on the auspicious day of the Jubilee demonstration the Viceroy of India, in his Jubilee speech, says:—

> "Wide and broad indeed are the new fields in which the Government of India is called upon to labour—but no longer, as of aforetime, need it labour alone. Within the period we are reviewing, education has done its work, and we are surrounded on all sides by Native gentlemen of great attainments and intelligence, from whose hearty, loyal and honest co-operation we may hope to derive the greatest benefit. In fact, to an administration so peculiarly situated as ours their advice, assistance, and solidarity are essential to the successful exercise of its functions. Nor do I regard with any other feelings than those of approval and good-will their natural ambition to be more extensively associated with their English rulers in the administration of their own domestic affairs."

Look upon this picture and upon that!

Two Indian National Congresses have been held during the past two years—the second great one, at Calcutta, having 430 delegates present from all parts of India, and of all classes of the people; and what is it that both these Congresses have asked? It is virtually and simply the "conscientious fulfilment" of the pledges of 1833 and 1858. They are the pivot upon which all Indian problems turn. If India is to be retained to

Britain, it will be by men who insist upon being just, and upon the righteous fulfilment of the proclamation of 1858. Any one can judge of this from the kind of ovations given to Lord Ripon and Sir W. Wedderburn on their retirement.

Here, again, our gracious Empress in the year of her auspicious Jubilee once more proclaims to the world and assures us, in her response to the Bombay Jubilee Address last June, "It had always been, and will always be, her earnest desire to maintain unswervingly the principles laid down in the proclamation published on her assumption of the direct control of the government of India." We ask no more.

X.

EXPENSES OF THE ABYSSINIAN WAR.*

My Lord and Gentlemen,—In our views on Indian matters we shall sometimes agree and sometimes differ with the Indian Government. When we agree, we shall be only too glad to express our views accordingly. When we differ, either from looking at the subject from a different point of view, or from more or less information, we shall respectfully lay before the Government our views. In doing so, it cannot be supposed that our object is to set up an opposition party. On the contrary, our object is co-operation, as the aims both of the Government and of ourselves are the same, *viz.*, the good government and welfare of India. I believe that Government would rather be glad than otherwise to know our independent views, provided we always confine ourselves to a dispassionate and careful examination of their acts, and lay our reasons of difference before them in a becoming manner, especially making "measures, not men—arguments, not abuse," our rule of conduct. I hope, therefore, I shall not be misunderstood for laying before you my views, and you for expressing yours on the subject of this paper.

I beg to submit for your consideration that the decision of the Cabinet not to pay the ordinary pay of the Indian troops employed in the Abyssinian expedition is

* (Read before an Afternoon Meeting of the East India Association, London, Friday, November 29th, 1867, Lord William Hay, M.P., in the Chair.)

an injustice to India, and an injury to the prestige of England; that the decision is not only unfair in principle, but contrary to the reasonable practice of former days. I first examine whether there are any past events or precedents which can guide us to a just decision.

When the English Government was only one of many independent Indian Powers, and when temporary assistance like the present was needed from each other, on what principles was such assistance given and taken? I find that in these cases the English had acted on the fair and equitable principle that the party receiving assistance should pay the *whole* charge of the troops during the period of assistance. I shall not take up your time with many extracts, I shall give only three or four short ones. In the treaty with Hyder Alli 1769, it is provided (Article 2)—

"That in case either of the contracting parties shall be attacked, they shall, from their respective countries, mutually assist each other to drive the enemy out. The pay of such assistance of troops from one party to another to be after the following rates, *viz.* to every soldier and horseman fifteen rupees per month, and every sepoy seven and a half rupees per month. The pay of the sirdars and commandants to be as it shall be agreed on at the time."*

The treaty of 1770 contains similar stipulations, which are again confirmed in the treaty of 1792.

In the treaty of alliance with Bazalut Jung, 1779, it is provided (Article 4)—

"If the Nawab Shujah-ool-Moolk's territories be invaded by an enemy, we shall, besides the troops that are stationed with him, send such a sufficient force as we can spare to his assistance. The ordinary and extraordinary expenses of such troops, whatever they may amount to, shall be paid agreeably to the Company's established customs by the Nawab, who will sign the accounts."†

* Aitchison's Treaties, vol. v., p. 128.
† Aitchison's Treaties, vol v., p. 36.

Again, in the treaty with the Nizam, 1790 (Article 4)—

"If the Right Honourable the Governor-General should require a body of cavalry to join the English forces, the Nawab Asuph Jah and Pundit Prudhan shall furnish to the number of 10,000, to march in one month, etc. . . . . . the pay of the said cavalry to be defrayed monthly by the Hon'ble Company at the rate and on conditions hereafter to be settled."*

In the "Articles explanatory o fthe 3rd Article of the Treaty of Mysore, concluded in 1799," Article 3 provides—

"If it should at any time be found expedient to augment the cavalry of Mysore beyond the number of (4,000) four thousand, on intimation to that effect from the British Government, His Highness the Raja shall use his utmost endeavours for that purpose; but the *whole* expense of such augmentation, and of the maintenance of the additional numbers at the rate of (8) eight star pagodas for each effective man and horse while within the territory of Mysore, and of an additional sum or batta at the rate of (4) four star pagodas a month after the expiration of one month from the period of their passing the frontier of Mysore, as described in the 2nd article, shall be defrayed by the Hon'ble Company." †

Now, I ask why this reasonable and just practice should have been subsequently departed from. I hope the standard of fair play of the Crown is not to be inferior to that of the Company. Next, I ask a few questions. Suppose the tables were turned, and England sent some troops for India's assistance, will the English taxpayer and Parliament allow the assistance without charging India with the *whole* expense?—or rather, has the British Government ever given any assistance to the British Indian Government, or the British Indian Government to any native Power, of the sort without making the receiver of the assistance pay *fully*? Sup-

* Ibid., p. 44. † Ibid., p. 168.

pose some subjects of the Nizam were held in captivity by some Arab chief, and the Nizam, to liberate his subjects and to maintain his honour, deciding to send an expedition to Arabia, requested his allies, the British, to assist him temporarily with troops; would such assistance be given without charging the Nizam with the pay of the troops, as well as any extra expenses? If not, then on what grounds of equity or fair play should England now get the Indian troops without being charged for their pay? Why, instead of the British Government having ever given any assistance of the kind, it has a few accounts to settle with its conscience for having made India pay even more than what could be fairly due from it.

It is said that India will lose nothing. What is it that the troops are kept in India for? Whatever that is, that India loses. If it is nothing, then the army should be reduced by so much. If it is something, then India is not losing nothing. If the troops are required for security, then it is unfair that India should be deprived of that security, and yet be made to pay for it. The question resolves itself into this: Should the pay of the troops be allowed to be a saving to India or to England? For, if India is made to pay, it is so much a saving to England, and if England pays, India saves so much. Now, whether on the grounds of equity, or of need, or of ability, certainly India has the claim to be allowed to save what it can. England has always charged for everything she has given on similar occasions, so she should not now shrink from paying when it is her turn to do so. The need of India to save whatever it can, is greater than that of England. Famines, intellectual and physical, are its crying evils, and the weight of a large army keeps some of its urgent wants in abeyance. Lastly, England is the richer of the two, and well able to pay for what it receives. The very circumstance that England is able to avail herself of a ready made army, a very convenient base of operations, and the services of Indian officials, and of experienced Indian officials and of experienced Indian officers, is in itself a great advantage to the English taxpayer.

It is urged, that because the prestige of England is important, therefore India must contribute. But what prestige is it that England has and needs to maintain? Is it that England is poor in means and unfair in dealing, or that her resources are as great as her arm is strong, and that her sense of justice is above suspicion? Here England sends her envoys to Abyssinia, and finds in its ruler a troublesome customer. Her honour is insulted, and her representative is kept in captivity. The prestige which England has to maintain under such circumstances is to show that she is *herself* able to hold her own, from her own resources; not that she is so poor or unfair that she is unable or unwilling to pay for the very troops which are employed in vindicating her honour, and liberating her own representative, and help herself from the Indian purse. Can the world be blamed if they consider it strange that the England which is ready to spend some four millions or more for her honour should shrink to pay a few hundred thousands?

However, even the question of the few hundred thousand pounds is not of so much importance. A far more important question, of the principles of the financial relations between the two countries, is involved in the present course of the Cabinet: Who is the guardian of the Indian purse? and are the British Government and Parliament absolute masters and disposers of it, or is it a trust in their hands to be discharged on some equitable principles? I should think that in the present condition of the political relations of England and India, the Indian Secretary ought to be its natural guardian; that he ought, when English and Indian relations are to be adjusted, to act as if he were an independent Power, representing Indian interests, and negotiate with the Foreign Secretary on terms fair and equitable to both parties. If this position of the Indian Secretary is faithfully acted upon, India will have the satisfaction to know that they have some one here to protect them from any unjust treatment, Parliament being the ultimate Court of Appeal. The Indian Secretary, instead of offering to make a present to the English taxpayer from the Indian revenue, ought to protect it from any encroachment. India is unable to protect itself, and as the British Government and Parliament hold its purse in trust, it is the more necessary for them that they should not be generous to themselves with others' trust-money, but, on the contrary, adopt the only proper course of treating the trust with the strictest justice and care, especially in the relations with themselves.

Clause 55 of the Indian Government Act of 1858, runs thus:—

"Except for preventing or repelling actual invasion of Her Majesty's Indian possessions or under sudden and urgent necessity, the Revenues of India shall not, without the consent of both Houses of Parliament, be applicable to defray the expenses of any military operation carried on beyond the external frontiers of such possessions by Her Majesty's forces charged upon such revenues."

The evident object of this clause, I submit, is to prevent the application of Indian revenues except for Indian purposes, or otherwise the clause means nothing. If Indian revenues can be applied for the payment of troops beyond the Indian frontiers, then the clause becomes simply useless, for England then can use Indian troops under any circumstances, as the two grounds—*viz.* of Indian purposes, and of loan to England for her own wars—will embrace all cases.

I have now laid before you as briefly as possible my reasons why England should pay the *entire* expense of the Expedition, under any consideration, whether of justice and fair play or prestige, with the hope of eliciting an impartial discussion from you. Upon the necessity of the expedition, and when and how Englishmen should vindicate their honour, it is not for me to tell them. Among the nations most able to uphold their honour, the English have never held a second place. Their whole history, and their instinctive love of liberty and honour, are enough to satisfy the most sceptical that England is well able to take care of herself, and to know what her honour is and how to uphold it.

When I wrote this paper I could not know the reasons of the Government; therefore I must crave your indulgence while, in continuation of the paper, I make a few remarks on the debate of last night. But, in making those remarks, it is far from my intention to make any personal reflections on any speaker: Parliament has accepted the reasons, and decided upon the resolution; consequently any remarks I may make apply as much to Parliament itself as to any of the individual speakers. To make my remarks as few as possible, I shall just read a few extracts from some of the speeches of last night, which give nearly the pith of the whole argument, and give my views upon them. Sir S. Northcote said—"From the first moment that this expedition was thought about, early in the month of April last year, in reply to communications addressed to the Secretary of State in Council, we stated that we were willing to place the resources of India at the disposal of the Home Government, but must stipulate that, as the matter was one in which Indian interests were not concerned, India should not bear any portion of the charge. At that time it was clearly understood, though we did not put that into the despatch to the Treasury, that, though we were determined to resist any attempt to charge the revenues of India with any new burthen, we did not, to use a homely expression, want to make money by the transaction." This amounts to saying that India must pay under all circumstances. If Indian interests were concerned, then, of course, India must pay also; and if Indian interests were not concerned, then also India must pay for the troops in order "not to make money." Can this be considered right? Sir Stafford Northcote says—"It is said, and we have said it ourselves, that India has no interest in this matter. That is perfectly true if by 'interest' you mean material interest. But there are principles which should be upheld in the interest of both countries, even at the cost of blood and treasure, and one of them is this—that envoys of the Sovereign of this country should be protected by us. That is a leading principle of international law, and we should be untrue, not only to ourselves, but to the civilized world, if we fail to uphold it." If that principle is to be admitted, if the envoys of England are to be protected everywhere at the expense of India, then India could be made to share in the expenses of a European or American war. Also, in other words, if the United States dismissed an English ambassador, and insulted the dignity of the Crown, and if the Crown went to war with America, India must contribute for it; or if the Crown embarked in a European war, India must contribute. This, I trust, would not be allowed by Englishmen as just. Again, the interests of the Colonies are as much, or perhaps more, involved in this principle. What are they contributing to the present expedition? And would they be always ready to act according to the principle laid down in the extract I have read? Sir Stafford Northcote has been at great pains to show that the news about the Abyssinian captives, and the efforts made to release them, is carried to the natives of India, and that in undertaking this expedition the opinion of the people of India about the power and resources of England is most important to be taken into consideration. If it be considered so important that the prestige of England should not suffer in the slightest degree in the estimation of the natives of India, then that is just the reason why Parliament should not have passed the Resolution. For, it will be naturally thought that though the English Government admit that the war is for their own purposes, that it is for liberating their own captives, that it is for vindicating England's honour; yet they, while ready to spend five millions, or ten millions if necessary, to protect their country's honour, and to punish its insulters, take from India a little because India cannot help herself. That cannot increase the prestige of England in India; it is likely to have just the contrary effect, not only among the natives of India, but perhaps among all Asiatics.

Let us now consider the precedents brought forward by Government for what they propose to do now. We have the Persian war and the Chinese war referred to. There is one important difference between the precedents I have brought before you and those of the Government. In the precedents I have referred to there were two parties, both able to take care of themselves, who negotiated with each other, and who were able to strike the right balance between them; whereas in the case of Government precedents the holder of the purse was also its disposer, without any voice from the owner, and therefore the transactions themselves required examination. Even granting, for argument's sake, that former transactions were in just proportions, they are not at all applicable to the present expedition. The Persian war and the Chinese war do not bear analogy to this. In the Chinese and Persian wars we can, at least, trace some Indian concern—with the former commercial, with the latter political, the alleged necessity of arresting Russian progress; but Government itself acknowledges that, in the present expedition, Indian interests are not concerned. All these present complications have arisen without the India Office or the natives of India having anything to do with the matter. It is entirely the Foreign Office affair. Even at present it is the Foreign Secretary who takes the whole brunt of the battle in Parliament, and the only way in which India is brought forward is that it is the best agency through which the Foreign Secretary can accomplish his object of carrying on the war in the cheapest and most expeditious way possible. Sir Stafford Northcote says—"All that India undertakes to do is to lend her troops, without charge, as long as she can spare them. That is the principle upon which we have proceeded, and which, I contend, is a just and liberal one. I say it is just, because India really loses nothing whatever in point of money; she only continues to pay that which, if the expedition had not been ordered, she would still pay; and it is liberal, because India places at the disposal of Her Majesty forces which the Imperial Government could not obtain without paying for them." If to be prevented from saving when saving can be made, is not losing, then I do not know what losing means. Again, if India loses nothing, then how can there be any liberality? I have no doubt if England ever needed aid or liberality, India, from very gratitude to England for the position in which it now stands, ought, and would, strain every nerve to give it. But is the present such a case? The world naturally does not like trustees to be liberal to themselves. It is a matter of regret more on account of England herself, that she should present the spectacle of, on the one hand, being able and ready to spend any number of millions for her honour, and on the other of taking a few hundred thousand pounds from India for the pay of the very troops to be employed in vindicating that honour. However, had Government stopped at the argument of liberality, or sense of gratitude, or friendly feeling towards England, there would not have been much to complain of, and the natives perhaps, would have been glad to have been looked upon as friendly; but by citing precedents for justification, and arguing for rights, the question assumes a different aspect, and occasions the present discussion. Then the Government has taken very great pains to prove that after all what India has to pay is very little, and that if all the former precedents were followed, it would have had to pay more. But suppose it is a small affair, then it is a greater pity that they should have made so much fuss about it, and not paid this little themselves, and should not have taken this opportunity to show that they are as just as they are strong and rich. Sir Henry Rawlinson says—"Our system of Government in India was essentially for the maintenance of our power, and when we spoke of Indian interests we meant our own interest as the ruling power of India." If that is the case, and that is the guiding principle of the Government, then against such argument of the rights of might there can be no discussion. But I believe the English Government to be guided by the principles of justice and truth and not of the rights of might. Sir Henry Rawlinson says—"The Royal Navy now fulfilled gratuitously all the duties connected with the defence of India, that were formerly discharged by the Indian navy—a service which drew heavily upon the Imperial Exchequer; and in many instances the Home Government had sent out, at its own expense, expeditions of which the objects more nearly related to India than to the rest of the British Empire." I have no right to question the truth of that statement. I only say if it be true, and as it is also intimated by Mr. Gladstone, that India is better off in its financial relations with England, it is indeed a great pity that the natives of India should be allowed to remain under a false impression. If it be true that England has, on occasions, performed services for India to which India has not contributed, it is in the first place necessary, for the sake of justice to both parties, that the financial relations between the two countries in respect of those services should be fairly examined and adjusted; and next, if India has been so benefited as alleged by England, it is proper and just that India should know and feel that benefit, and knowing it be grateful for it. At present India is under the impression that England, having the purse, appropriates it at its own pleasure, and that unjust burthens have been placed upon her. As Sir Henry Rawlinson has not given us any instance of what he refers to, we are left in the dark; but against his statement there is one of another authority, equally, if not more important. Lord Cranbourne says—"At all events the special injustice of the course now about to be pursued consists in this—that when we employ English troops in India they are paid for out of the Indian revenues from the moment they land in that country; but when we employ Indian troops on English duty, we say that India must pay for them." I do not, of course, impute to Sir Henry Rawlinson, who has only lately given a signal instance of his sense of justice to India, that he would state anything that he did not thoroughly believe. I wish he had given the cases, for it is very desirable, for the sake of both countries, that the real state of the case, in regard to this matter, should be known. It is also necessary to know how far the Colonies, which also benefit by the Royal Navy, contribute to it. Then there is some stress laid upon this, that India benefits by this expedition: that by the expedition going from India, stores are brought there, and money is poured into the country; but nobody can seriously urge that, therefore, India must contribute to the expedition. I do not suppose that cotton merchants, or ship-owners, paid anything towards the American war because they benefited largely by its occurrence. The fact is, that

India is resorted to on this occasion in order that the interests of the English taxpayer may be served in the best possible manner. Lord Stanley distinctly stated that he referred to the Indian Secretary, and to the Indian authorities, in order to carry out the expedition in the most successful way. He found in India a ready machinery for carrying out the expedition. That induced the English Government to make India the basis of operations. In concluding my remarks I once more suggest that the discussion should be confined to the one point which I have brought before you, and I hope that we shall follow the advice of our noble Chairman, and not be guilty of any personalities, but shall confine ourselves entirely to the arguments of the case. It is my sincere conviction that Lord Stanley or Sir Stafford Northcote would never allow any injustice intentionally. All their acts would at once refute any contrary assumption. I take this opportunity of thanking Mr. Fawcett and the other twenty-two members, and the English press, for their advocacy of justice to India.

XI.

MYSORE.*

I trust the meeting will make some allowance for the imperfections of this paper, hurriedly prepared within two days; and by their own temperate, disinterested, and judicious discussion, make up its deficiencies.

It is discovered by Lord W. Hay that Lord Wellesley drew his pen through the words "heirs and successors," and it is therefore argued that Lord Wellesley therefore intended the subsidiary treaty to be only a personal one. The question then naturally arises, whether any alterations made in drafts can affect the actual compact ultimately agreed upon? Next, had Lord Wellesley any right to depart from the stipulations of the partition treaty, which is the sole authority for the subsidiary treaty? The very draft of the subsidiary treaty goes to show that the drawer of the treaty naturally felt that the subsidiary treaty was to be an hereditary treaty. If we accept the argument now based upon the new discovery in the British Museum, we are driven to the necessity of casting a reflection upon the character of Lord Wellesley. For leaving aside, for the present, the consideration and proper interpretation of the words "unnecessary and dangerous," this discovery, as it is proposed to be interpreted, would mean that a British statesman, knowingly and intentionally, just left *in* words

* (Read before a Meeting of the East India Association, London, Friday, July 5th, 1867. Sir James Fergusson, Bart, M.P., in the Chair).

enough to lull any suspicion, and left *out* words enough for some private ulterior motives. Here are the words left *in*: "A treaty of *perpetual** friendship and alliance" —and, "as long as the sun and moon shall endure;" just sufficient to lull any suspicion, and yet, behind the back of the other contracting party, "heirs" and such words are omitted, in order that when the opportunity came, advantage might be taken of the omission. I sincerely trust that the present English statesmen are not going to hold out this as an edifying and statesman-like course of conduct to be learnt by the natives from their enlightened English teachers. No, I do hope that a more reasonable and satisfactory explanation may be given of the discovery which Lord William Hay has brought to light. I shall revert to this point again further on. It is urged that the words "as long as the sun and moon shall endure" are only conventional terms; and in support of this, the following sentence is quoted from Sir T. Munro:—"The terms employed in such documents, 'for ever,' 'from generation to generation,' or in Hindu grants, 'while the sun and moon endure,' are mere forms of expression, and are never supposed, either by the donor or the receiver, to convey the durability, which they imply, or any beyond the will of the sovereign." On what authority or grounds this proposition is laid down I cannot say. If it means anything, it means that there are no such documents as were really intended to mean perpetuity by the donor and receiver. According to this proposition the British Government can make one clean swoop of all property possessed under any grants

* The italics in all the extracts are mine.

whatever; for even the words "generation to generation," and "for ever," are not safe from its grasp. Then again, were there ever perpetual grants made or not under the former rulers? and how could they ever be considered so if words like "for ever" and "from generation to generation" were meaningless? It is true that high-flown compliments, raising one to the seventh heaven, or becoming one's most humble servant or slave, are mere forms, but to say that words expressing the duration of an engagement mean nothing, is more than I ever knew among the natives. I wonder how such duration can or was ever expressed, if not by the words "during life," or "for ever," or "from generation to generation," etc. To me it appears that it is not correct to assume that both the receiver and the donor did not understand the words to mean what they said, but that the Hindu sovereign, being in the very nature of his position a despotic sovereign whose will *was* law, and *above* law, and at whose mercy lay, not only any grants, but even any property whatever of his subjects, as well as their lives, did sometimes confiscate by his will such grants, though originally intended to be perpetual. Such arbitrary exercise of power could not, however, make the contract the less binding, but there was no power above that of the will of the sovereign to compel him to abide by his contract; it was simply the power of might over right. But this treaty is not of a Hindu sovereign. It is drafted and made by Englishmen for an English sovereign. Is the English sovereign the same despotic ruler? Is it right for the Englishmen to boast of their superior political condition, in which the sovereign is no less subordinate to law and bound to good faith than the meanest subject, and yet, for a purpose like this, suddenly to sink down to the level of the despotic Hindu rulers? Whatever may have been the conduct of the Hindu rulers in such matters, certainly the English rulers ought to set a better example, especially in a case when they are parties to the words "as long as the sun and moon shall endure," not only in the Mysore treaty alone, but quite pointedly again in another treaty of 1807, explanatory of the third article of this very subsidiary Mysore treaty: by the words, "these four additional articles, which, *like the original treaty of Mysore*, shall be binding on the contracting parties as long as the sun and moon shall endure."

Such pointed expression of the duration of the treaty of Mysore, coupled with the words "treaty of *perpetual* friendship and alliance," at the very heading of the treaty itself must certainly make any English statesman who has the slightest consideration for the honour of his country's word, pause before trying special pleading. I appeal to you as Englishmen to say whether, had such pleas been put forward by a native ruler, the most indignant denunciations would not have been poured out, not only against himself but against the whole Hindu race? How loud and angry would have been the uproar of the virtuous indignation of the upright Englishmen against the innate depravity and treachery of the Hindu race? And yet it is calmly pleaded by English statesmen, that in their language, treaties made by themselves, when it suits the occasion, "perpetual" means "temporary," that the duration of the existence of the sun and moon means only a man's lifetime; and that "treaties" mean "deeds of gift." But, strange to say, as the sun and moon sometimes send a ray through the heaviest cloud, to assure poor mortals of their existence, the sun and moon of this treaty have sent one stray ray through the heaviest cloud. In the despatch of August 31, 1864, from Sir John Lawrence to Sir Charles Wood, it is said :—" By the favour of the British Government, and in the exercise of its sovereign right, acquired by conquest, the Maharaja was raised from a prison to the government of a large principality, *subject to conditions*; which, if fulfilled by him, would have been the safeguard of his authority, and the guarantee *of the continuance of a native rule* in Mysore." Now, I leave to you, gentlemen, that if this treaty was simply a personal treaty, what is meant by "subject to conditions which if fulfilled by him, would have guaranteed the continuance of a native rule in Mysore?" Are there, then, certain conditions in the treaty guaranteeing the continuance of a native rule in Mysore? Then what becomes of the personal character of the treaty?

Now, revert to the question, whether Lord Wellesley had a bad intention in drawing his pen through certain words, or whether he meant to do something consistent with a faithful performance of his obligations under "the partition treaty." The only explanation I can at present see of Lord Wellesley's proceedings, is this. There is no doubt in my mind that Lord Wellesley did not mean to act in bad faith; that in allowing the words perpetual, and about the sun and moon, to remain, he did mean what he said; but that his object in striking out the word "heir," etc., was to keep such full control over the native principality as to enable the English Government to oust any particular oppressive sovereign, and put some other in his place, or, in cases of disputed succession, that the English may be able to decide in favour of one or the other without being encountered by the difficulties which the word "heir" might occasion; that the word "unnecessary" in the margin means that as far as permanency of native rule was concerned, the words "perpetual" and "as long as the sun and moon shall endure," are sufficient; and that the word "dangerous" means the strong title which an "heir" may maintain, and thereby lessen the complete English control; and that according to practice a new treaty may be made with every successor, with such modifications as time and circumstances may require. I venture to offer this explanation for your consideration, leaving alone the question whether any departure from "the partition treaty" was justifiable. I cannot, however, persuade myself that a statesman like Lord Wellesley would be guilty of such a mean act as the present discovery of Lord William Hay is made to imply. I do not stand here as the advocate of either the Raja or the English. I wish only for justice and truth, be it on the one side or the other.

Much has been said about Lord Canning not having sent the adoption *sunud* to the Raja. Was Lord Canning justified in doing so? Did he do so as a punishment for the Raja's past offences? This is not the case, as the Raja was declared deserving of reward for his thorough loyalty. Two reasons are urged: first, it was because Lord Canning knew that the Raja intended to leave his territories to the English. By admitting this position, Lord Canning admitted the power of the Raja to bequeath; but it was subsequently urged that the treaty itself did not entitle him to any such adoption. Now, I ask, do English words mean one thing in one treaty and another thing in another treaty? If not, I request explanation for the following anomaly.

The treaty of 1805, with the Rajah of Travancore, is, *word for word*, in *all* its important portions bearing upon the present issue, the same with the treaty of Mysore. I give these portions in the Appendix.

Now, I trust it is a fair question to ask, why the very same words which in the Trvancore treaty entitled the Travancore Rajah to the adoption *sunud*, did not mean the same thing with the Mysore Rajah. The parallel, however, does not end here. The Rajah of Travancore, like the Rajah of Mysore, also incurred the displeasure of British Government, and the latter were going to assume the internal administration of the country. But the Rajah died. Nobody, however, then thought of interpreting the treaty of 1805 as a personal one, and the heir was allowed to succeed. The difference, then, in the cases of the Rajah of Mysore and that of Travancore, seems to be that the latter, by his death, made the treaty of 1805 an hereditary one, and the former, by living longer, has rendered, in some mysterious way, a similar treaty a personal one. It is pressed that Sir Stafford Northcote ought not to have reversed the policy and gone against the opinion of three Governor-Generals and two Secretaries of State. Sir Stafford can well be left to hold his own. He needs no defence at my poor hands. But I ask: Is it because the others were right that Sir Stafford should not have reversed their acts, or is it meant that even they were wrong, Sir Stafford should have abided by their decision? I know full well what English prestige means in India. In fact, it is the settled opinion of the natives for the English high character, that is your principal charm and spell over them. When once that is broken, half your strength is gone. But it is not by special pleadings, or persisting in a wrong course, that the prestige will be increased. Howsoever vehemently or authoritatively may assertions be made of honest decisions, the natives can think for themselves, and can know where there is real honesty and where there is sham. If Sir Stafford has subverted the decision of fifty governors-general and as many secretaries, if he has but done what is right, he will have increased your prestige far more than any amount of persistence in a wrong course. I trust the objectors on the ground of authority do not mean to contribute a wasp of an idea to Mr. Buxton's collection, that "the perpetration of a wrong is a justification for persisting in it." If the objectors mean that the former decision was right and Sir Stafford is wrong on merits, then let them discuss on merits only, instead of holding up the bugbear of high and many authorities.

Again, it must be remembered, that we look for authorities when the subject is exclusively a study for few students; when the materials for ordinary judgment are not sufficiently accessible, and when therefore decisions for action can only be based on authority, the number and positions of authorities are matters of importance; but as in the present case, when the materials are at the command of all who choose to see them, when Sir Stafford Northcote is exactly in the same position as any other individual, to judge for himself, how could mere priority of time give to the others an infallibility? On the contrary, Sir Stafford ought to be, if he make a right use of his opportunities, under a proper sense of responsibility, in a better position to decide rightly, having the views and arguments of his predecessors before him.

There is again the argument of the good of the people of Mysore. I hope I am not dead to a desire for the welfare of any people, and more especially of my own countrymen. The picture of an Englishman holding off the savage ruler from his victim is no doubt a very pretty and gratifying one, but unfortunately there is a little want of truth in it, and a little daub in it. First of all, the Rajah repeatedly offered to allow such arrangements for the welfare of the people as would be satisfactory to the British, and so there is no savage king tearing up his victim. But then, is not in that case the Rajah a mere puppet? How strangely does this exclamation come from persons who pride in their sovereign being not a despot, but subject to law and order, and guided by wise and able ministers. What constitutional sovereign is not a puppet, if to govern under fixed and well-regulated administration be to be a puppet? Besides, it is a strange reflection upon the British Government that with their control and influence they do not bring up the native princes in the way they should go. Besides there being some untruth in the picture, there is this daub. In the corner of the picture the natives of Sholapore and the assigned districts restored to the Nizam stand surprised at this turn of philanthropy. Now, is it possible for the native to increase his esteem and believe in your sincerity with such inconsistent conduct before him, notwithstanding the most vehement assertions of your desire for the good of the Mysoreans?

To destroy the native rule in Mysore it is pressed that as Englishmen have settled there, it ought to be taken into English possession. This I suppose is an invention of the nineteenth century. What a fine prospect this opens up of conquering the whole world without much trouble. Some Englishmen have only to go and settle in a country, and then the English Government has simply to say: "You see English people cannot be managed by you, therefore you should give up the country to us;" and there is a conquest! But, unfortunately for the inventor, those stupid fellows the French and other Continentals, the Americans and such others, won't see it.

Then again, is this an encouragement to the other native Rajahs to allow Englishmen to settle in their country, and derive the benefits of the contact of English enterprise and knowledge? If they take such a step the result is loss of rule, on the plea that Englishmen cannot be managed by natives. If they do not, then they are blamed for being apathetic, and indifferent to the best interests of their dominions and people.

The important question constantly arises: Who is to judge when the British Government and a native prince are at issue? How can the decision of the stronger party in its own favour be free from the suspicion of being interested? Cannot, when such important questions of the rights of Government arise, an important judicial commission of some of the best judges of this country be appointed to try the matter? I should think that, considering the confidence the natives of India have in the integrity, uprightness, and independence of English high judges, the natives would feel satisfied to have such issues tried by such impartial tribunals: otherwise the native, like anybody else, naturally thinks when the decision is against him, that injustice is done to him; and it is only when the justice of the decision is so clear as to be *entirely* above suspicion, that the British Government does not run the risk of being considered as having taken advantage of their might against right.

I have not here entered upon the general question of adoption, as in the present case the reason urged is that the Rajah is by the treaty itself not entitled to leave his territories even to his own son, any more than to his adopted son. Nor do I here enter into a discussion of the general question of annexation, nor into that of the rights of the Nizam, as the present decision of the Secretary of State renders this discussion unnecessary.

I would not take up much of your time upon the subject of the relative position of the Nizam and the British power at the time the subsidiary treaty was made, and the real source of that treaty. I shall simply quote a few sentences from two or three treaties, leaving you to draw your own inferences. In the treaty of 1790, between the English, the Nizam, and the Mahrattas, Article 6 says—

"The three contracting powers having agreed to enter into the present war, should their arms be crowned with success in the *joint* prosecution of it, an *equal* division shall be made of the acquisition of territory."

In the treaty with the Nizam of 1798, in the preamble it is said—"And the present juncture of affairs, and the recent hostile conduct and evil designs of Tippoo Sultan, so fully evinced by his sending ambassadors to the Isle of France, by his proposing to enter into a treaty, offensive and defensive, with the French republic against the English nation, and by actually receiving a body of French troops into his dominions, and immediately, rendering it *indispensably necessary* that effectual measures for the *mutual* defence of their respective possessions should be immediately taken by the three allied powers united in a defensive league against the aforesaid Tippoo Sultan," etc. etc.

In the treaty of 1880 with the Nizam occur these words :—

"Who, with uninterrupted harmony and concord having equally shared the fatigues and dangers of war and the blessings of peace, are, in fact, become one and the same in interest, policy, friendship, and honour.' "

The partition treaty of 1799 says—

" And whereas it has pleased Almighty God to prosper the just cause of the said *allies*, the Hon'ble English Company Bahadoor, and His Highness Nizam-ood-Dowla Ausuph Jah Bahadoor, with a continual course of victory and success, and finally to crown their arms by the reduction of the capital of Mysore, the fall of Tippoo Sultan, the utter extinction of his power, and the unconditional submission of his people; and, whereas the said *allies* being disposed to exercise the rights of conquest with the same moderation and forbearance which they have observed from the commencement to the conclusion of the late successful war, have resolved to use the power which it has pleased Almighty God to place in *their* hands for the purpose of obtaining reasonable compensation for the expenses of the war, and of establishing permanent security and general tranquillity for themselves and their subjects as well as for all the powers contiguous to their respective dominions. Wherefore a Treaty for the adjustment of the territories of the late Tippoo Sultan between the English East India Company Bahadoor, and His Highness the Nawab Nizamood-Dowlah Ausuph Jah Bahadoor, is now concluded by . . . . according to the undermentioned articles, which, by the blessings of God, 'shall be binding on the heirs and successors of the contracting parties as long as the sun and moon shall endure, and of which the conditions shall be reciprocally observed by the said contracting parties.' "

The above extracts show what the relative position of the English and Nizam was, and the last extract shows that " the partition treaty" was binding on both parties for ever.

This partition treaty binding, as above stated, on "heirs and successors" of the contracting parties, provides in Article 4 :—

" 'A separate government shall be established in Mysore ;' and for this purpose it is stipulated and agreed that the Maharajah Mysore Kishna Rajah Oodiaver Bahadoor, a descendant of the ancient Rajahs of Mysore, shall possess the territory hereinafter described upon the conditions hereinafter mentioned."

Again, in Article 5 :—

"The contracting powers mutually and severally agree that the districts specified in Schedule C, hereunto annexed, shall be ceded to the said Maharajah Mysore Kishna Rajah, and 'shall form the separate government of Mysore, upon the conditions hereinafter mentioned.'"

Article 8, again, throws some light on the relative position of the Nizam and the English :—

"Then the right to the sovereignty of the several districts hereinbefore reserved for eventual cession to the Peishwa Rao Pundit Prudhan Bahadoor, shall 'rest jointly' in the said 'English East India Company Bahadoor, and the said Nawab Nizam-ood-Dowlah Ausuph Jah Bahadoor who will either exchange them with the Rajah of Mysore for other districts of equal value more contiguous to their respective territories, or otherwise arrange and settle respecting them, as they shall judge proper."

Article 9 gives the conditions referred to in Article 5, and is the authority of the subsidiary treaty.

So the facts are these : A *separate* government of Mysore was to be formed, and which stipulation is binding on the heirs and successors of the contracting parties. The question then simply is : Was Lord Wellesley justified in introducing anything into the subsidiary treaty that would in any way destroy the "separate government of Mysore," or anything beyond the condition contained in Article 9 as to the provision for a subsidiary force?

This is Article 9 :—

"It being expedient, for the effectual establishment of Maharajah Mysore Kishna Rajah in the Government of Mysore, that His Highness should be assisted with a suitable subsidiary force, it is stipulated and agreed that the whole of the said force shall be furnished by the English East India Company Bahadoor, according to the terms of a separate treaty to be immediately concluded between the said English East India Company Bahadoor and His Highness the Maharajah Mysore Kishna Rajah Oodiaver Bahadoor."

In accordance with Article 9 of the partition treaty, given above, the subsidiary treaty was made, and the preamble simply recites the same purpose, as it in honesty ought.

The heading begins with the words; "A treaty of perpetual friendship and alliance;" then the preamble says in accordance with the partition treaty:—

"Whereas it is stipulated in the treaty concluded on the 22nd of June, 1799, between the Hon'ble English East India Company Bahadoor and the Nawab Nizam-ood-Dowlah Ausuph Jah Bahadoor, for strengthening the alliance and friendship subsisting between the said English East India Company Bahadoor, His Highness Nizam-ood-Dowlah Ausuph Jah Bahadoor, and the Peishwa Rao Pundit Prudhan Bahadoor, and for effecting a settlement of the territories of the late Tippoo Sultan, 'that a separate government shall be established in Mysore,' and that His Highness Maharajah Mysore Kishna Rajah Oodiaver Bahadoor shall possess certain territories, specified in Schedule C, annexed to the said treaty, and that, for the effectual establishment of the government of Mysore, His Highness shall be assisted with a suitable subsidiary force, to be furnished by the English East India Company Bahadoor; wherefore, in order to carry the said stipulations into effect, and to increase and strengthen the friendship subsisting between the said English East India Company and the said Maharajah Mysore Kishna Rajah Oodiaver Bahadoor, this treaty is concluded by Lieutenant-General George Harris . . . . and by His Highness Maharajah Mysore Kishna Rajah Oodiaver Bahadoor, 'which shall be binding upon the contracting parties as long as the sun and moon shall endure."

Nothing can be clearer than the preamble, distinctly based upon the partition treaty, which binds for ever the English for a "separate government in Mysore," and providing for a suitable force. And yet this is the treaty which is endeavoured to be made personal, and by which some Englishmen have created a right of annexation.

Let us see the treaty further on. The very first

article treats the two parties on an equality of duties, like two independent powers:—

> The friends and enemies of either of the contracting parties shall be considered as the friends and enemies of both.

Further articles relating to the question are given in the Appendix.

I shall make only one more short extract, which shows the assumption of power by the British Government was not to be perpetual, but temporary. These are the words in Article 5:—

> "Provided always, that whenever and that *so long as* any part or parts of His said Highness's territory shall be placed and shall remain under the exclusive authority and control of the East India Company," etc., etc.

I leave now to you, gentlemen, to say whether the subsidiary treaty could, under all these circumstances, be considered as a simple personal treaty, and that the English have the right to annex Mysore on the death of the Rajah?

This paper is written by me not for complaint, but for thanksgiving. To Sir Stafford Northcote, as well as to Lord Cranbourne and the few Councillors who sided with them, sincere thanks are due not only from the natives of India, but even from Englishmen, for having to the former done an act of justice—or if you will have it, a proper and politic act of generosity—and for the latter, vindicated and maintained to the natives of India and to the world the character of the English nation for justice and liberality.

What gratitude and admiration such noble words as the following from Sir S. Northcote deserve, needs no comment from me:—" And we should endeavour as far as possible to develop the system of native government, to bring out native talent and statesmanship, and to enlist in the cause of government all that was great and good in them."

The following letter was addressed to Lord William. Hay in connection with the above subject:—

32, GREAT ST. HELEN'S, LONDON,
8th July, 1868.

MY LORD,

I again take this opportunity of thanking you for pointing out to me without hesitation what you considered as an oversight on my part. I have no object in this matter except truth and justice. We may now see whether I have really made any mistake. You will please first remember that the words "perpetual," or "for ever," or "as long as the sun and moon shall endure," or words of that character, are not admitted by you as of any consequence in giving to the treaty a permanent character. You want the words "heirs and successors," or either of them, to make the Mysore Treaty a permanent one.

In the Travancore Treaty of 1795 the word "heirs" does not occur anywhere. The word "successors" does occur often; but, as you will see below, in the Treaty of 1805 *great care* is taken not only to strike out this word "successors," or any other words of similar import, but even pointedly to describe the Rajah of Travancore as one of the contracting parties, as "His Highness the Rajah of Travancore *for himself,*" which words "for himself" are not used even in the Mysore Treaty. This itself would be sufficient to show that if the subsidiary Mysore Treaty was a personal one, the Travancore Treaty of 1805 was especially, by the special wording of that treaty, a still more personal one for the Rajah with whom that treaty was concluded.

Now, if under the 5th Article of the Mysore Treaty the English were entitled to take the administration of Mysore into their own hands and afterwards to claim that the country should not be restored because the Mysore Treaty was a personal one, it was the more logical, that as the Treaty of 1805 was concluded by the Rajah of Travancore "for himself," and as the special stipulation made "*by himself*" was infringed by the Rajah, that therefore under the treaty his country should have been annexed. I say that this single circumstance of the words "for himself" would have been enough, according to the argument adopted with Mysore case, to annex Travancore to British India, which was not done.

But I proceed further, and show that the Travancore Treaty of 1805 was, *with all possible care*, made to correspond in every possible way with the Mysore Treaty, and whatever may have been Wellesley's objects (which it is not at present my purpose to search for), it is clear that the Rajah of Travancore was put in the same position as the Rajah of Mysore, or if anything in a worse one, by the words "for himself."

In the preamble of the Treaty of 1795* the Rajah, as a contracting party, is described not only by his own name, but is further described as "the *reigning Rajah* of Travacore," while in that of the Treaty of 1805 the Rajah, as a contracting party, is described simply as "His Highness the Rajah of Travancore *for himself*."

Article 2 of 1795 is modified by Article 1 of 1805. It will be seen in this that while in the Treaty of 1795 the words used are "the country of the said Rajah or of his successors," in that of 1805 the words "His successors" are omitted.

Article 3 of 1795 is modified by Article 3 of 1805. It will be seen that in the Article 3 of 1795, "The Rajah of Travancore doth engage for himself and *his successors*," while in Article 3 of 1805 the words "his successors" are omitted, and only "His Highness engages to pay," and only "His said Highness further agrees."

Article 4 of 1795 is modified by Articles 3 and 4 of 1805. It will be seen that while in Article 4 of 1795 the stipulations are on behalf of "the Rajas and his successors," in the corresponding Articles 3 and 4 of the Treaty of 1805 the words "his successors" are omitted, and instead of "the Rajah and his successors" the words are only "the said Maharajah" or "His Highness."

Article 5 and 6 of the Treaty of 1795 are modified in the 7th and 8th Articles of the Treaty of 1805. Now, it will be observed, that while in the Articles of 1795 the Rajah is described, "the Rajah present and *future*," "the Rajah or his successors," and "the reigning Rajah of Travancore *for the time being*," in Articles 7 and 8 of 1805, we have neither "Rajahs future," nor "his successors," nor "reigning for the time

---

* See Appendix, in which both the Treaties of 1795 and 1805 are given.

being," but only "His Highness Maharajah Ram Rajah Bahadoor," "His said Highness," or "His Highness."

Article 7 of the Treaty of 1795 is repealed by Article 2 of 1805. Now, in the Article 7 of 1795 we have "the *said reigning* Rajah *for the time being*," while in the 2nd Article of 1805 we have only "Ram Rajah Bahadoor." I do not suppose it was intended, or that it has been, or that it is likely to be, so acted upon, that after the death of this Ram Rajah Bahadoor of the Treaty of 1805 "his successors" would, by the 7th Article of the Treaty of 1795, cancelled, as above shown, be made to pay again what was released and discharged in this Article 2 of 1805.

Article 9 of the Treaty of 1795 is altered by the Articles 5 and 6 of the Treaty of 1805. Now, it will be seen, that while in Article 9 of 1795 there are the words "Rajah or his successors' country" in the Articles 5 and 6 of 1805, the words are only "the possessions of His Highness Ram Rajah Bahadoor," or "His Highness."

The above Articles 5 and 6 of 1805, are the most important Articles by which the British Government came to have *any right*, to interfere in the administration of the country, and in providing for this new right, Wellesley not only omitted the words "successors, etc.," but adopted almost entirely the language, word for word, of the stipulations of the Mysore Treaty. This right of interference is essentially the provision of the Treaty of 1805, and can be exacted in terms of that treaty only, without reference to any previous treaty, for previous treaties have nothing to say on this point; and so far as any interference is concerned, it is with Ram Rajah "for himself," as the contracting party, that the arrangement was made by Wellesley.

Now, is it a fair inference or not, that by so deliberately and carefully omitting in every Article of the Treaty of 1805 the words "successors," "for the time being," "Rajahs in future," etc., Wellesley deliberately intended to bring the position of the Rajah of Travancore to the level of the Rajah of Mysore? And it is not also fair to infer, that had part of Article 9 and Article 11 of 1795 which are the only Articles (out of the few which have not been modified) that contain the word "successors" by implication or directly, been also modified or repeated in the Treaty of 1805, the word "successors" would have been deliberately and carefully struck out? If not, then why were they struck out throughout the *whole* of the Treaty of 1805. However, whether you admit this inference or not, what does the Article 9 of the Treaty of 1805, from which you quoted, amount to? It cannot certainly renew and confirm what is altered in the Treaty of 1805. It renews and confirms that part of the Treaty of 1795 which is not modified in that of 1805. Now, there are only part of Article 9 and the Article 11, which contain directly, or by implication, the word "successors," to which this confirmation can be of any consequence for the present argument (if the confirmation is at all such as you suppose, which is not the case, as I shall show hereafter). But I ask again whether, had these clauses been at all touched in the Treaty of 1805, Wellesley would have allowed the word "sucessors" to remain? However, be this as it may, for whom does the Article 9 of 1805 "confirm and renew" the remaining Article of 1795? It is distinctly for the "contracting parties." And who are the contracting parties? The Indian contracting party of the Treaty of 1805 is not, as in the Treaty of 1795, the "Rajah and successors," or "Rajahs future," or "for the time being," but only "His Highness the Rajah of Travancore for himself," and nobody else any more than I.

Now, what I say is this, be the intentions of Wellesley what they may, they were the same with regard to the Rajahs of Travancore and Mysore, and the two treaties are on the same footing; and that this is clear by his having so carefully and deliberately expunged the words successors, etc., in *every* Article in the Treaty of 1805, by adopting the very phraseology of the Mysore Treaty in that of 1805, as far as possible, and by "confirming" in the 9th Article, for the *contracting parties*" only, and not for "successors," etc.

I hope, therefore, you will now be satisfied that I have not been inaccurate in my statement, and that I had carefully compared the Treaties of 1795 and 1805; and I am correct in stating, and in accordance with the Travancore Treaty of 1805 and the Mysore subsidiary Treaty, the Rajahs of Mysore and Travancore were deliberately put on the same footing by Wellesley whatever that footing was.

As you do not desire any controversy upon the merits of the Mysore case annexation, etc., I do not enter into that discussion, and content myself with the simple remark, that in my humble opinion your remarks on that subject are refutable.

I remain, yours truly,

DADABHAI NAOROJI.

LORD WILLIAM HAY.

XI.

THE FEAR OF RUSSIAN INVASION.*

The common error of persons who discuss the possibilities of Russian invasion of India is to ignore the most important element in the problem, namely, the attitude of the people of British India and of the Native States. This attitude may be either hostile or favourable to British Rule. If it is favourable, there is nothing more to be said. Then the British position is invulnerable. But if, on the contrary, there is any likelihood of its being hostile, any argument based upon considerations which ignore that possibility falls to the ground. In that case will the European army be engaged in resisting Russia or in protecting the European population, scattered all over India, who will be the first and immediate victims of such hostilities? And if the native army sympathise with the hostile feeling of their countrymen, what will be the consequences? Moreover, if any discontent is known to exist among the Indian people, Russia knows well how, by her emissaries, to fan this discontent, and, as in Ireland, the British Government made use of Irish traitors to betray their country, it may be expected that some Indians out of that vast population will be ready to do Russia's work. Russia will bide her time till discontent has fully developed itself, ready to burst into a conflagration. Then Russia not only can, but will, invade India, whether with success or not is another question, but with the result of

* Reprint from "India," September, 1895.

the destruction of British Rule, crushed as it would then be between external invasion and internal trouble. What I want Englishmen to consider is whether such an unfortunate contingency is possible or not and if possible, to take that most vital element into account in their discussions of the problem.

Let us consider what the probability or possibility is under the present system of British Indian Administration. I repeat the views of British and Anglo-Indian statesmen for a hundred years as to the true character of the present system, saying nothing about the oppression and corruption of the previous period. Sir John Shore (1787) pointed out that whatever might be the increased industry of the people, the benefits of it would be more than counterbalanced by the evils of the present system. The natural inference from this view is that the effect of the system must be impoverishment. This prophecy has been fulfilled. In 1833, Macaulay characterised the system as that of holding Indians as slaves and keeping them too poor to be able to buy British goods. (1837) Mr. F. Shore described the system as a sordid system of misrule to which the interests of millions had been sacrificed for the benefit of the few, and of grinding extortion which effected impoverishment to an extent almost unparalleled. (1858) Mr. Bright referred to the system as plundering India. (1859) Sir George Wingate characterised the system as exacting a cruel and crushing tribute. (1864) Lord Lawrence (Viceroy) stated that the mass of the people enjoyed only a scanty subsistence. To come down to later days, (1875) Lord Salisbury (Secretary of State for India) pointed out that the injury was exaggerated in the case of India, where so much of the revenue was exported without a direct equivalent, and declared the policy of the system to be that India must be bled. (1880) Sir William Hunter considered that forty years hence the British people would have an Indian Ireland multiplied fifty-fold on their hands. (1882) Lord Cromer (Finance Minister) described the people of India as extremely poor. (1886) Lord Randolph Churchill (Secretary of State for India) described the system as constituting a political danger which the Government had long regarded as of the most serious order. (1886) Sir Auckland Colvin (Finance Minister) said that the income of the mass of the people, at the best, was barely sufficient to afford them the sustenance necessary to support life. I need not say anything about the complete confusion in which India is at present.

The natural consequences of this system are the opium trade, poisoning a vast nation, the salt tax, oppressive exaction of revenue, general extreme poverty, destruction of millions by famine, and the starving, underfed condition of some scores of millions.

Can any man in his senses doubt for a moment that the inevitable result of such a state of affairs must be discontent? Could anything be more foolish than hiding the head under the sand, as the statesmen of the present day are doing, thinking that Indians do not see and understand the evil system with which British India is afflicted?

I need not say much about the possible attitude of the native princes. They are, from a clear sense of their own interests, thoroughly loyal to British supremacy. But the Indian Foreign Office and political agencies unfortunately are keeping up chronic interference, and have again begun nibbling at the power of the princes, as in the fifties, short of annexation. If the princes become hostile, the fault will lie entirely at the door of the present system. Otherwise these princes have every reason to desire the supremacy of the British hand.

Next, the British word is coming to command less confidence in the mind of Indians. The people generally cannot quite clearly make the distinction between the British people and their servants, the Anglo-Indian authorities both here and in India. Though the British people and Parliament have repeatedly laid down the policy of righteousness, Anglo-Indian authorities have persistently, barefacedly, and perversely ignored and thwarted the Resolutions and Acts of Parliament and the most solemn pledges and Proclamations. No department here would dare to ignore a Resolution or Act of Parliament on matters concerning this country. But there is hardly a Resolution, an Act of Parliament, a Proclamation, or a pledge for the promotion of the true welfare of the Indians which the Anglo-Indian authorities have not ignored, resisted, and made a dead letter. A Viceroy (Lord Lytton, 1878) confesses that the Indian authorities had used every device, deceit, and subterfuge to defeat the policy of the British people and Parliament. Lord Salisbury (1883) declared that all pledges, voluntary acts, etc., were so much political hypocrisy. Such, at present, are the dark colours with which the servants of the British people have covered their good name.

Again, to the expenditure of the Indian revenues, by which Great Britain derives the benefit of the greatest empire the world has ever seen, she does not contribute a single farthing from the British Exchequer. All must be paid by the Indians as British helots. Further, the birth-right of British subjects is—"taxation without representation is tyranny." But the Indians have no voice in the raising or disbursement of their revenues. What is worse still, they are treated with distrust as candidates for the higher civil or military services. In the latter they have no share at all. Under these circumstances is it reasonable, is it common sense, to expect loyalty and hearty patriotic support from Indians in a time of trouble?

Now, I ask Englishmen to take into account in their problem this most vital element: if the system of the present despotism, drain, and distrust are continued, sooner or later, perhaps sooner, if Indain human nature is like all other human nature, great trouble will ensue, whether Russia can invade or not. Invasion by Russia sinks into insignificance compared with the troubles that the British Indian system itself is storing up. I have been crying in the wilderness for a long time. But I have faith in the British people, and if they set themselves to consider these questions there is hope that the position of affairs in India may yet mend before it is too late. Vast and great forces are rapidly developing themselves through one of the several beneficent acts of the British people themselves—the dissemination of education (though at India's own expense). It is for British statesmen to draw these forces to their own side before they turn against them. If the internal problem is satisfactorily solved, we may quite contentedly leave Russia to her own devices. Indians, if trusted instead of being distrusted, if satisfied with British Rule as a rule of righteousness and beneficence, will fight for British Rule as for their own hearths and homes as patriots.

The British people and Parliament have been making the most solemn pledges for more than sixty years by Resolutions, by Acts of Parliament, and by Proclamations in the name of the British people, and by the mouth of the Sovereign. The Indian authorities, on the other hand, have been violating these pledges in letter and in spirit with unblushing openness. The British people have pledged themselves to treat Indians as British subjects. But the British Indian system actually treats them as mere subjects of a foreign despotic rule. Can any Englishman in his senses be blind to the consequences of such conduct?

Afflicted as India is with the impoverishing European Services, and with the indirect help of these Services in enabling other Europeans and European capital to exploit India in every possible way for their own benefit, what can be expected from the Indians? I say again, and say it with all earnestness, that the present system of administration and the financial treatment of India is full of most serious danger.

Indian reformers are very properly fighting the "forward" frontier policy tooth-and-nail. But even if the Cabinet decided to-day to put an end to it, that would be a relief from only a part of the aggravation of the principal Indian evil. The progress of events in India is tending to an inevitable catastrophe. The Indian National Congress is exerting itself to check this tendency.

Our efforts must not be confined to the question of the "forward" frontier policy. Of course, it would be a great and immediate gain to check it, but the danger of internal rebellion and external invasion would remain the same. On the other hand, if India were treated righteously, if she prospered, and felt it a patriotism to be loyal to British supremacy, both the present "forward" policy and the danger of a foreign invasion would vanish of themselves. No truer words have been uttered than those of Lord Roberts when he said: "However efficient and well equipped the army of India may be, were it indeed absolute perfection, and were its numbers considerably more than they are at present, our greatest strength must ever rest on the firm base of a united and contented India." Yet, strange to say, Lord Roberts himself advocates the wasting of money, energy and life on the "forward" policy, and the violation of the solemn pledges of the British to the Indian people, thereby adopting the most effective means of producing a disunited and discontented India. Let there be a contented, and not distressed, British India, and Englishmen may snap their fingers at any external danger.

DADABHAI NAOROJI.

XII

THE INDIAN TRIBUTE.

The following is the full text of a letter sent by Mr. Dadabhai Naoroji to the *Daily News* :—

22, Kennington Road, S. E.,
April 3, 1905.

SIR,—In the *Daily News* of 31st ultimo a correspondent, "A Reader," asks for information about the yearly drain of £30,000,000 from India. Will you kindly allow me to give it? I have given this explanation two or three times before, as may be seen in my book; but I now bring the figures up to date.

Any drain from, or addition to, the wealth of a country in connection with other countries takes place through the channel of commerce. I give an approximate calculation.

In order to have a fair average, I take figures for ten years; but I leave out the years 1899-1900 and 1900-1, as these two years were those of famine in India, and were, therefore, not of average normal condition.

I take United Kingdom for the same ten years, *viz.*, 1892 to 1899 and 1902 and 1903. (The latest figures available are till 1903. Parl. Ret. Cd. 2192—1904.)

The total imports of the United Kingdom for these ten years (merchandise and treasure) are £4,988,919,359.

The total exports for the same period (merchandise and treasure) are £3,421,478,153.

This shows an excess of imports over exports, or, in other words, the profits on the exports as £1,567,441,206. That is to say, the United Kingdom received back the whole amount of its exports (£3,421,478,153), and also over and above that £1,567,441,206 more as an addition to its wealth by all its international transactions with foreign countries during the ten years.

Thus, the United Kingdom made a profit of 45·8 per cent. over its exports.

I would make, however, the following allowance:—

The total profit of £1,567,441,206 includes, taking roughly, £300,000,000 in ten years of the political drain of India. Deducting this £300,000,000 from the above profit leaves the net profit of its transactions with other countries as £1,267,441,206 independently of the drain from India. This deduction reduces the percentage of the profit of the United Kingdom from 45·8 to 37 per cent. on its own exports.

I now take India. (Parl. Ret. Cd. 2299—1904.) The total exports (including Native States) of merchandise and treasure during the ten years are Rx. 1,180,665,000. To this must be added freight and insurance on exports to the United Kingdom, because they are paid in the United Kingdom, and not included in the invoices and official returns. This was the case when I was in business in the city. I do not know how the case is for exports to other countries, so I do not add this item. I take roughly for freight and insurance on exports to the United Kingdom from India for the ten years at 5 per cent. The amount of exports is Rx. 364,948,240, and 5 per cent. on it will be Rx. 18,247,412. This addition will make the total of exports from India to be Rx. 1,180,665,000, plus Rx. 18,247,412, = Rx. 1,198,912,412.

The next item to be considered is the profit on the total exports. Though the profits of the United Kingdom, as stated above are 37 per cent., I take for India a profit of only 20 per cent. The total, therefore, of exports and profit will be for the ten years Rx. 1,198,912,412 plus profit 239,782,482, = Rx. 1,438,694,894.

This, then, is the amount equal to which India ought to have imported under normal circumstances like those of the United Kingdom.

But India has not imported this amount, but only a much less amount of Rx. 923,205,000, leaving a drain or deprivation of Rx. 515,489,894 in the ten years.

Taking the present exchange of Rs. 15 to £1, this drain in ten years amounts to £343,659,920, or, say, average of £34,000,000 every year.

If the exports and imports of the Native States are excluded, the drain from British India will be larger than £34,000,000 a year. Besides this, there is the burden of foreign debt inflicted on India without India's voice.

Now, one thing must be carefully borne in mind—that the people in India have not the slightest voice in the administration which is producing such disastrous results. The rule is absolute despotism.

Here, then, is a strange and sad contrast. The United Kingdom and India are governed by the same government, with the result of bringing to the United Kingdom an addition to its wealth, as profits of its exports, in ten years, of £1,267,441,206, and, on the other hand, causing to India in the same ten years a deprivation and loss of £343,659,920.

Not only this. The loss to India must be measured by how much more India would have benefited had this enormous drain of the ten years and all drain of previous years been at India's own disposal and fructified in the Indians' pockets. It must be further remembered that what Europeans consume in India itself, to the deprivation of the Indians, is not included in this drain. Truly has Macaulay said: "Of all forms of tyranny I believe that the worst is that of a nation over a nation."

The present evil system of the government of India is that kind of tyranny.

Yours faithfully,

DADABHAI NAOROJI.

XIII.

MESSAGE TO THE BENARES CONGRESS.

22, Kennington Road, London, S.E.
November 26, 1905.

MY DEAR GOKHALE,—I should have much liked to be present at the Twenty-First Congress. It is the last before coming of age, when it is time to look back over the past and consider the future.

Looking back fifty-two years to the year 1853, when the first the three political associations had their birth—*viz.*, the British Indian Association of Bengal, the Madras Association, and the Bombay Association—we see how limited our political ideas and aspirations of that time were. The extent and causes of the increasing poverty of India, we had hardly and clear conception of, nor had we fully realised our rights and duties as free British citizens. Like all beginnings this was small, but it was sound and healthy in the circumstances and knowledge of the time. I can say this as I was present at the inauguration of the Bombay Asssociation, and have taken part in it and in its subsequent work.

Of these three the British Indian Association has preserved its existence till to-day doing much good work. The Bombay Association, after several years of good work, came to a close, but was revived and after some years was succeeded by the present active Bombay Presidency Association. I think the Madras Asssociation had also similar chequered career, and is now represented by the present active Madras Mahajana Sabha. There were some Provincial Associations also formed in time, as the Poona Sarvajanik Sabha and others. Now, what was the result in brief of all this our first awakening and work? The work done by these Associations and the seeds sown by them during thirty-two years, till 1885, produced their fruit in a larger conception of our political condition and knowledge, and what was of still greater importance —a closer union among all classes, creeds, and races of the whole country—results of which at our political birth in 1853 there was not much clear idea or anticipation. And, further, the development of the political ideas and forces carried with it an impetus mainly upon ourselves. We need a body of half a dozen at least, if not a dozen, of enthusiastic and well-qualified Indians for the work of the Committee here, and of propagandism by our organ, literature and lectures, to be permanent residents in England. These may be either well educated and competent well-to-do men who can live on their own means, or the well-to-do should supply the means to enable such well-qualified men to live here. Our success must depend upon our own proper men and sufficient means.

Indians must make up their minds for large sacrifices, both personal and pecuniary. In England itself we have object-lessons. Taking one instance only, of the Abolition of the Corn Laws: many men, like Bright and Cobden, worked devotedly and the League raised, if I am not mistaken, funds of two millions to fight the cause.

This for one cause only. How many movements for reforms of one kind and another are now going on here with devoted men and women and large means. Our work is of the utmost importance and of the greatest difficulty—the emancipation, freedom, and prosperity of some 300,000,000 of mankind—and in proportion to the importance does it demand from us the most strenuous devotion and large sacrifices. Yes, the Japanese people, high and low, made such sacrifices and the world knows the result and is the better for it to-day. Should we fail!

To sum up. We require, on the one hand, to inspire the people of India at large with the desire of attaining and enjoying their birth-and-pledged rights and the absolute necessity of freedom and self-government like that of the colonies for their material and moral development, progress, and prosperity. Without self-government the Indians can never get rid of their present drain, and the consequent impoverishment, misery, and destruction. No palliative of any kind whatever, no mere alteration and tinkering of the mechanical machinery of a demonstration, can and will do any good at all. The drain can only be stopped by the Government, by the people themselves. To be prosperous, India must govern itself like the colonies. Here are remarkable and true words uttered by Sir Henry Campbell Bannerman only three days ago (on the 23rd):—" good government could never be a substitute for government by the people themselves." Our need, therefore, is the utmost for governmemt by the people themselves.

Self-government is the only remedy for India's woes and wrongs. For this purpose we must strengthen this Congress, our great body, representative of all India, to go on making every possible effort to accomplish this end, which is quite practicable, as I have already said, and has been already successfully carried out very far by British rulers themselves as far back as thirty-eight years ago, in the case of Mysore.

Yours sincerely,

DADABHAI NAOROJI.

Dadabhai's Birthday Messages

I.—"EMANCIPATION AND ELEVATION OF INDIA."

Mr. Dadabhai Naoroji's message in 1911 was as follows:—

I offer my most heartfelt thanks to all friends in India, England and South Africa who have sent me their kind congratulations and good wishes on my 87th birthday.

I am very sorry that two assassinations have taken place this year when every day is bringing us accumulating evidence of better days coming.

Whether these assassinations are political or not Lord Minto had already said in his Simla speech of 14th October last year:—

> I absolutely deny that should further outrage occur they can be taken as symbolical of the general political state of India. They cannot justly be assumed to cast a slur upon the loyalty of the people.

In December next there will happen the greatest as well as the most propitious event in the history of this great country.

His Majesty the King Emperor, in his speech from the Throne on February 6th of this year, himself graciously gave us the glad news:—

> It is my intention when the solemnity of my Coronation has been celebrated to re-visit my Indian Dominion and there to hold an assemblage in order to make known in person to my subjects my succession to the Imperial Crown of India.

What can be more gratifying, encouraging and full of promise to the people of India than that His Majesty the King-Emperor in Company with Her Majesty the Queen-Empress should pay his first visit to India after his Coronation and establish India's important position in the British Empire! And what hopeful prospects this visit opens out for the future good of India!

Among their precious and gracious words and acts we have first the speech at Bombay on 9th November, 1905, when His Majesty as Prince of Wales declared 'Love' and 'Affection' for the Indian people and 'an increased and abiding interest in India's wants and problems' and next the speech at the Guildhall on 25th May, 1906, when he expressed 'wide sympathy' and 'an earnest desire and efforts to promote the well-being, and to further the best interests of every class.'

During the past sixteen months of the present reign we have had Their Majesties' gracious words and acts full of vast importance and significance. But all these gracious words and acts, it is impossible for me to embody in this statement. I shall state a few only.

I may, however, point out here that Their Majesties have already symbolized and established the equality and importance of India in the Empire by introducing at the Coronation in several ways the position of India —as among the Banners, on the King's Stols, in the Queen's Robe and on the floor of the Abbey; and also on the new Indian coin.

First.—His Majesty's message of 8th May, 1910, to Lord Minto in which His Majesty says:—

The prosperity and happiness of my Indian Empire will always be to me of the highest interest and concern as they were to the late King-Emperor and Queen-Empress before me.

Soon afterwards in the message of 23rd May, 1910, to the Indian people, His Majesty the King-Emperor gave his most gracious assurance :—

> Queen Victoria of revered memory addressed her Indian subjects and the heads of Feudatory States when she assumed the direct Government in 1858, and her august son, my father of honoured and beloved name, commemorated the same most notable event in his Address to you fifty years later. These are the charters of the noble and benignant spirit of Imperial rule and by that spirit in all my time to come I will faithfully abide.

These glorious and gracious declarations and pledges fortify our faith and expectation in the British word of honour, and I look forward with complete confidence that the pledge of Parliament and the Proclamation of our two last great and beloved Sovereigns—our great charters—will now be fully fulfilled by His Majesty the present King-Emperor as he has graciously said that 'in all my time to come I will faithfully abide.' In the fulfilment of these charters will be the accomplishment of His Majesty's highest interest and concern in the prosperity and happiness of his Indian Empire.'

May I be permitted to indicate what I consider the most important and immediately urgent steps to secure the prosperity and happiness of the Indian people and fulfil faithfully in their broad scope and spirit pledges of Parliament and of the gracious Royal Proclamations?

'After the reform of the Councils, for which our most grateful acknowledgments are due to Lord Morley and Lord Minto, I would place first simultaneous examinations in England and India for all the Indian services with the ultimate object of Indians being trained for self-government under British supremacy like that of the Colonies with the same rights and responsibilities.

Then, and then only, the great problem of sufficient revenue for all wants, of sufficient means for the great masses and of the ultimate high mission of England, will ever be solved.

Second.—If there is one thing more than another which entitles Britain to the glory of the everlasting gratitude of the Indian people it is giving them education in general and English education and knowledge of British institutions, British character, civilization and efforts for liberty, in particular. To complete this great boon it is very needful for the masses to have free compulsory elementary education supplemented by a system of advancing higher very promising youths. It is impossible to gauge the extent and variety of benefits that may accrue from this. In this connection, I may mention a personal incident of gratification, and gratitude. I bless the Government and people of Bombay of my early days, that as far as I remember I have received free my school education and my college education with additional benefit of a scholarship.

The King-Emperor in his letter of 29th June, 1911, to his people, says :—

> Believing that this generous out-spoken sympathy with the Queen and myself is under God our surest source of strength, I am encouraged to go forward with renewed hope. Whatever perplexities or difficulties may be before me and my people, we shall all unite in facing them resolutely, calmly and with public spirit confident that under Divine guidance the ultimate outcome will be to the common good.

It is our great good fortune that His Excellency Lord Hardinge, who is now at the beginning of his Viceroyalty, has the same earnest sympathy and good will towards us as Their Majesties. Just to quote one sentence from his speech at Simla on 3rd May, 1911:—

I trust that India may be happy and my administration successful, but this time alone can show and my brief experience has been enough to satisfy me that the next few years will be very strenuous, and the shade of my grandfather would rise to reproach me if I did not use every power that in me lies in an earnest endeavour to set forward my great charge in the path of progress, prosperity, peace and happiness.

Under such fortunate and hopeful circumstances I feel confident that we can well look forward to the emancipation and elevation of India during the reign of the King-Emperor who is coming amongst us with such great good will and lofty purpose.

DADABHAI NAOROJI.

VERSOVA,
6th September, 1911.

II.—FUTURE HOPE FOR INDIA—SELF-GOVERNMENT

Mr. Dadabhai Naoroji never lost hope for Self-Government for India. So late as 1912 he addressed the following message of hope to the people of India on the occasion of his 88th birthday :—

Versova, 6th September, 1912.

I offer my most heartfelt thanks to all friends in India, England and South Africa, who have sent me their kind congratulations and good wishes on my 88th birthday on 4th instant.

I am deeply grieved at the death of Mr. A. O. Hume. He was a true and whole-heartedly devoted friend and benefactor of India. Indians can and will never forget deep debt of gratitude which they owe to him.

The great and glorious event in Indian History—the Announcement in India in person by His Majesty the King-Emperor, on the Coronation of His Majesty—has taken place with entire satisfaction to all and great hopefulness to the Indian people.

Let us now calmly consider what this most auspicious event leads us to expect for the future for the Indian people.

His Majesty has most graciously and feelingly expressed many times the most earnest desire for the prosperity of the Indian people. I give here only a few extracts.

We earnestly pray that God's blessing may rest upon our Indian Empire, and that peace and prosperity may be ever vouchsafed to its people.

Six years ago I sent from England to India a message of sympathy. To-day in India I give to India the watchword of hope. On every side I trace the signs and stirrings of new life.

Their interests and well-being will always be as near and as dear to me as those of the millions of my subjects in other quarters of the Globe. * * * May the Almighty ever assist me and my successors in the earnest endeavour to promote the welfare and to secure to it the blessings of prosperity and peace.

These gracious words show clearly that there is an intensely earnest and sincere desire in the hearts of Their Majesties to secure and promote the prosperity of the Indian people and to hold their interests and well-being as near and as dear to them as those of the millions of their subjects in other quarters of the Globe. And that reading between the lines of all the incidents, despatches, and events of this ever-memorable visit of Their Majesties, it seems that there is also thought out and determined upon a new evolution to secure the prosperity of the Indian people.

Be my thought about the evolution as it may, there can be no question about the earnest desire of Their Majesties to hold the Indian people as near and as dear to them as the Colonies and to secure to them the blessings of prosperity and peace.

The question then arises how to secure this benign and glorious result.

It is our great good fortune that the true reply to this question is given to us practically by the British Government itself in the notable instance of the Restoration of Mysore to the glory of the British name and to the credit of Lord Salisbury and Lord Iddesleigh with the benign approval and influence of the great good Queen.

I give below some extracts from my letter of 21st March, 1896 to the Lord Welby Royal Commission which will show that the Restoration of Self-Government to the people themselves restored prosperity to Mysore and similarly will prosperity be restored to all other parts of British India as Their Majesties so earnestly desire.

Letter of 21st March, 1896 to the Welby Royal Commission :—

I am glad to put before the Commission that this problem has been not mearly enunciated, but that, with the courage of their conviction, two eminent statesmen have actually carried it out practically, and have done that with remarkable success. The result was, the memorable and ever to be remembered with gratitude despatch of 16th April, 1867 of Lord Iddesleigh for the Restoration of Mysore to the Native rule notwithstanding thirty-six years of determined opposition of the authorities to that step. * * *

This being once settled, though against all previous opposition and necessitating the withdrawal of Europeans from the services, all the authorities and officials concerned to their honour and praise, instead of putting any obstacles in the way or trying to frustrate the above intentions, discharge their trust most loyally and with every earnestness and care, and solicitude to carry the work to success. The Blue Books on Mysore from the despatch of 16th April, 1867 to the installation of the late Maharaja in 1881 is a bright chapter in the History of British India. * * *

I think I need not enter here into any details of this good work from 1867 to 1881 of the British officials. The Blue Books tell all that. Of the work of the late Maharaja from 1881 till his death at the end of 1894, it would be enough for me to give a very brief statement from the last address of the Dewan to the Representative Assembly held at Mysore on 1st October, 1895, on the results of the late Maharaja's Administration during nearly fourteen years of his reign, as nearly as possible in the Dewan's words. The Maharaja was invested with power on 25th March 1881. Just previous to it, the State had encountered a most disastrous famine by which a fifth of the population had been swept away, and the State had run into a debt of 80 lakhs of rupees to the British Government. The cash balance had become reduced to a figure insufficient for the ordinary requirements of the Administration. Every source of revenue was at its lowest and the severe retrenchments which followed had left every department of State in an enfeebled condition. Such was the beginning. It began with liabilities exceeding the assets by 30⅜ lakhs, and with an annual income less than the annual expenditure by 1¼ lakhs. Comparing 1880-1 with 1894-5, the annual revenue rose from 103 to 180¼ lakhs, or 72·2 per cent., and after spending on a large and liberal scale on all works and purposes of public utility, the nett assets amounted to over 176 lakhs in 1894-5 in lieu of the nett liability of 30⅜ lakhs with which His Highness's reign began in 1881.

	Rs.
In 1881 the balance of State funds was	24,07,438
Capital outlay on State Railways	15,19,128
Against a liability to the British Government of ...	80,00,000

Leaving a balance of liability of Rs. 30 lakhs.

On 30th June 1895:

Assets :—

(1)	Balance of State Funds	1,27,23,615
(2)	Investment on account of Railway Loan Repayment Fund	27,81,500
(3)	Capital outlay on Mysore Harihar Railway ...	1,48,03,306
(4)	Capital outlay on other Railways	41,33,390
(5)	Unexpended portion of Capital borrowed for Mysore Harihar Railway (with British Government)	15,79,495
		3,60,21,306

Liabilities :—

(1)	Local Railway Loan ...	20,00,000	
(2)	English Railway Loan ...	1,63,82,801	
			1,83,82,801
	Net Assets		1,76,38,505

Add other assets :—

Capital outlay on original irrigation works	99,08,935	

Besides the above expenditure from current revenue there is the subsidy to the British Government of about 25,00,000 a year, or a total of about Rs. 3,75,00,000 in the fifteen years from 1880-1 to 1884-5, and the Maharaja's civil list of about Rs. 1,80,00,000, during the fifteen years also paid from the current revenue. And all this together with increase in expenditure in every department. Under the circumstances above described, the Administration at the start of His Highness's reign was necessarily very highly centralised. The Dewan, or the Executive Administrative Head, had the direct control, without the intervention of departmental heads of all the principal departments, such as the Land Revenue, Forest, Excise, Mining, Police, Education, Mujroyi, Legislative. As the finances improved, and as department after department was put into good working order and showed signs of expansion, separate heads of departments were appointed for Forests and Police in 1885, for Excise in 1889, for Mujroyi in 1891, and for Mining in 1894. His Highness was able to resolve upon the appointment of a separate Land Revenue Commissioner only in the latter part of 1894. Improvements were made in other departments Local and Municipal Funds, Legislation, Education, etc.

And all the above good results are side by side, with an increase of population of 18·34 per cent. in the ten years from 1881 to 1891, and there is reason to believe that during the last four years the ratio of increase was even higher. During the fourteen years the rate of mortality is estimated to have declined 6·7 per mille.

But there is still the most important and satisfactory feature to come *viz.*, that all this financial prosperity was secured not by resort to new taxation in any form or shape.

Such is the result of good administration in a Native State at the very beginning. What splendid prospect is in store for the future if, as heretofore, it is allowed to develop itself to the level of the British system with its own native services.

I stop my extracts here as the point I desire to make in this letter is to show how by self-government may be attained the most earnest desire of Their Majesties :—*viz.*, securing to the Indian people the blessings of prosperity and peace.

I may however just remark here that the same remedy of self-government applies to all other questions Political, Agricultural, Social, Commercial, Industrial Educational, etc., is everything depends upon prosperity.

A great responsibility rests on Mysore to turn to the best account its good future not only for its own sake but for the sake of all India.

Having said so much as above, and without entering into the consideration of the events and incidents of the past sixteen years, since my letter to the Royal Commission was written in 1896, which have so happily ended in the auspicious announcement of the Coronation in India by Their Majesties themselves, may I not indulge in the "Hope" that before long St. George of England will bear aloft the glorious Standard of the mighty British Empire including India with her many self-governing, free and prosperous peoples enjoying rights and responsibilities akin to those of the Colonies. That indeed would be a proud day for the country under the all-speading "Chhatra" of benign Britain.

DADABHAI NAOROJI.

III.—INDIA AND THE WAR.

On the outbreak of the great war in Europe, in August 1914, Mr. Dadabhai Naoroji, as the acknowledged leader of the Indian nation, addressed a letter to the Indian public pointing out the supreme duty of his countrymen at such a crisis. After an expression of sympathy in the sad bereavement of His Excellency the Viceroy, caused by the death of Lady Hardinge, the venerable patriarch continued :

What calamity to the world is at present happening? War in Europe. What is an Indian's place in it? We are a people of the British Empire. Let us see what our duty and position are. If ever India expects to attain again the former glory on the advanced character and scale of the modern British civilisation of liberty, humanity, justice and all that is good, great and divine, it shall be at the hands of the British people and as self-governing members of the British Empire. We are all British Citizens of the great British Empire and that is at present our greatest pride.

On the other hand is Britain engaged in the present great struggle for some selfish purpose for the extension of her own dominion and power? No. It is simply for keeping her word of honour and for righteously discharging a solemn obligation for the peace and welfare of the minor and weak powers. Fighting as the British people are at present in a righteous cause, to the good and glory of human dignity and civilisation, and moreover being the beneficent instruments of our own progress and civilisation, our duty is clear to do anything to support Britain's fight with our life and property.

I have all my life been more of a critic than a simple praiser of the British Rule in India, and I have not hesitated to say some hard things at times. I can, therefore, speak with most perfect candour and sincerity what the British character is, what the civilisation of the world owes to the British people for benefits in the past, as well as for benefits to come. Yes, I have not the least doubt in my mind that every individual of the vast mass of humanity of India will have but one desire in his heart, *viz.*, to support to the best of his ability and power the British people in their glorious struggle for justice, liberty, honour and true humane greatness and happiness.

The Princes and the peoples of India have made already spontaneous efforts and until the victorious end of this great struggle, no other thought than that of supporting wholeheartedly the British Nation should enter the mind of India.

IV.—DADABHAI'S LAST BIRTHDAY MESSAGE.

The 91st birthday of Dadabhai Naoroji was celebrated with befitting enthusiasm all over India. Among the countless messages that were pouring in at "Versova," on the morning of Saturday the 4th September, 1915, was one from His Excellency Lord Hardinge who wired :—

I send you warm congratulations and heartiest good wishes on your 91st birthday and hope that your life may be prolonged for many years as a bright and enduring example to others.

Mr. Naoroji sent the following reply :—

I am deeply touched with your warm congratulations and heartiest good wishes on my 91st birthday, and thank you sincerely and heartily for the same. I hope, this world's strife will terminate soon and successfully. I am sure that India will continue its devotion and loyalty to our Sovereign and will receive justice and equality of citizenship with other parts of the Empire.

His Excellency the Governor of Bombay also sent a congratulatory message. In reply to the numerous greetings from the Press and platform, Mr. Naoroji sent the following epistle :—

I have been overwhelmed with congratulations and good wishes from friends and admirers in various parts, and I take this opportunity to thank them most heartily, as also all the numerous public bodies who held congratulatory meetings in Bombay, Calcutta, Madras and other centres in connection with my 91st birthday.

Times are critical and it behoves every unity of the vast population under British Rule in India to give every loyal assistance in order that Victory, to the arms of the Allies who are fighting the battle of freedom and in the cause of humanity, may be assured at an early date.

England by her undaunted courage and unity of action has maintained her place among the nations, and has sent an example to the world, and all India must feel, as I do feel, intense satisfaction for her ultimate success in the near future.

There was, besides, a special feature in regard to the last birthday greetings. A deputation of ladies of Bombay waited upon Mr. Dadabhai Naoroji at his residence on the morning of the 4th September. The deputation was a fairly representative one, consisting of Hindu, Moslem and Parsi ladies. Mrs. Sarojini Naidu, the gifted poetess from Hyderabad, addressed the G. O. M. in a graceful speech. Mrs. Jamnabhai Sakhai, of the Gujarati Streemandal, read an address congratulating Mr. Dadabhai on the auspicious event. In the course of his reply, Mr. Naoroji touched appropriately on the Memorial to the Right Hon'ble Mr. Austen Chamberlain, on the education of the girls and the women of India and observed :—

I am glad my good friend Sir William Wedderburn and many others are presenting a memorial to Mr. Chamberlain, the Secretary of State for India, on the subject of the education of girls and women in India. Let India support this movement whole-heartedly and I have great hopes that something substantial will be done to accelerate the progress of female education in India. Let the result of this be what it may; it is we the people of India who must do all what we can for this all important matter.

In fact Mr. Naoroji's tender and loyal championship of women and women's education is but one aspect of a life of what Mrs. Sarojini Naidu so aptly called, "one long and noble consecration to the Motherland."

APPENDIX—A.

EVIDENCE BEFORE THE ROYAL COMMISSION ON THE ADMINISTRATION OF THE EXPENDITURE OF INDIA.

Mr. DADABHAI NAOROJI, a Member of the Commission, examined.

Will you state what public position you have held, and what opportunities you have had of becoming practically acquainted with public affairs relating to India, and to what class of questions you have given special attention?—From my early days I have been associated with those who have been working for the social, political, and material improvement of India, and was a member of various reform associations in Bombay, sometimes as president and secretary; in 1851, I founded the "Rast Goftar," a cheap weekly journal in Bombay, of which I was proprietor and editor. After some years' service in the Educational Department, I was in 1854 appointed Professor of Mathematics and Natural Philosophy in the Elphinstone College, being the first Indian appointed to a professor's chair. In 1853, I was one of the founders of the Bombay Association, and at the inauguration I declared my political creed of faith in the conscience and justice of the British people. In 1855, I and two other Parsi gentlemen opened the first Indian business firm in England, in London and Liverpool, and I remained in business as a merchant and commission agent till 1881. In 1867, I, with others, founded the East India

Association in London, and induced some leading Indian Princes to subscribe an endowment for it. In 1869, we founded the Bombay Branch of the East India Association, and some years subsequently, the Bombay Presidency Association. In 1873, I gave evidence before Mr. Fawcett's Select Committee on Indian Finance. In 1874, I was Dewan, or Prime Minister, of Baroda. In 1875-6 and afterwards in 1881 to 1885 I was a member of the Town Council of Bombay, and in 1885-6, I was appointed a member of the Legislative Council of Bombay. In 1885, I was one of the founders of the Indian National Congress and presided over the Meeting at Calcutta in 1886. In 1892, I was returned M.P. for Central Finsbury, and was a member of the House of Commons till 1895. In 1893, I visited India to be President over the Ninth Indian National Congress at Lahore, and on the occasion was accorded a reception of a marked kind in various parts of India. For the last 40 years I have paid special attention to the material condition of the masses in India, and have published books, pamphlets, and speeches setting forth my views on the subject.

In what form would you prefer to give your evidence?—I have handed in to the Commission six printed statements. These statements contain the facts, figures, and authorities upon which I rely, and I am prepared to be cross-examined upon them.

The statements which you have put in deal with a variety of subjects which perhaps hardly fall within the scope of the reference to us. Of course, you are aware our Commission only permits us to inquire into the administration, management and apportionment of expenditure, and I should like to ask you to let it be understood between yourself as a witness and the Commission that you are prepared to limit yourself within reasonable bounds to the instructions of the Commission?—Oh, I am quite within the instructions of the Commission in what I have said and in what I propose to say.

Perhaps you could place before us in some concise form the leading facts and figures upon which you rely in those statements?—The headings under which my evidence falls are: the Administration of Expenditure, the Apportionment of Charge and Practical Remedies. Upon each of those headings I am prepared to state categorically my most important contentions on behalf of India.

Will you state your propositions with reference to the first heading you mentioned, the Administration of Expenditure ?—Yes. I consider that the Act of 1833, confirmed by the pledges contained in the Queen's Proclamation of 1858, conferred upon Indians a right to their full claim and share of public employment and emoluments and voice in their own expenditure, in order to secure their happiness and prosperity and good government, and attachment to British Rule, and the prosperity of the British people themselves. I maintain that the administration of Indian expenditure is not conducted according to the principles thus laid down and that the non-fulfilment of these pledges has produced poverty and degradation; the inherent and essential defect of British Administration being the financial, political, and intellectual drain, which is inseparable from a remote foreign dominion exercised in disregard of the sound principles above stated. In my six statements I set forth the facts of India's poverty, as shown by the comparative production and consumption of each Province, by calculating the average production of Indian per head, by analysing the trade returns, and by reference to the small amount of revenue obtained after exhausting all sources of taxation. I maintain that the impoverishment and degradation of British India has been caused by the compulsory employment of costly foreign official agencies and foreign capital (represented by the public debt, political and commercial) beyond the means of the taxpayer, resulting in a drain from British India, financial, political, and intellectual—aggravated by heavy frontier Imperial war expenditure—and that, indirectly, the foreign dominion has caused a further drain by creating a practical monopoly in favour of foreign private capital, which reaps the advantage of British India's material resources.

That is a general statement from your point of view upon the administration of India; but it does not give us your opinion of the questions more immediately before us, namely, upon the different branches of expenditure, to explain the details of which we have had before us the official witnesses.

Have you anything to state upon those branches of expenditure, and upon the official evidence that has been placed before us?—Yes. Shall I wait until later, or shall I give my views now?

I will take the question, if you wish it, later; I am only anxious at the present moment to know how far you intend, by the answer you have given, to express your opinion upon the administration of expenditure?—Yes, that is the general answer I have given; shall I go now to the question of the machinery?

I think, if you are prepared to go on with that subject, perhaps you had better take it at this point?—Very well, I will give such criticisms as I can offer upon the administrative machinery of the expenditure of India. When in August 1894 we asked for an inquiry, Sir Henry Fowler said that a very strong indictment of the British Government of India had been brought before the House and the country (15th August, 1894). And then Sir Henry Fowler, when promising a Select Committee, himself challenged: "The question I wish to consider is whether that Government, with all its machinery, as "now existing in India, has, or has not, promoted the general "prosperity of the people in its charge: and whether India is "better or worse off by being a Province of the British "Crown." And this is the question to which an answer has to be given by this Commission, whether the present machinery of administration and management of the military and civil expenditure incurred in both countries "has or has not," as one of its results, "promoted the general prosperity of the people" of British India. I say that it has not promoted the general prosperity of the people. In the statements I have given in I have considered every aspect of this fact, which was the most important point of the inquiry. The most important criticism, therefore, to which this machinery is subject is that it is based on the basis of foreign domination. This is its worst evil. It is a machinery for what Lord Salisbury very correctly calls bleeding. However perfect the mere rules of the work to be done by the officials may be, the system or machinery is a crushing machinery. It produces in the words of Lord Salisbury a "terrible amount of misery." The machinery not only "bleeds" directly, but by the economic exhaustion of the people, leaves the resources of the country entirely at the mercy and disposal for exploitation by foreign capitalists. I have in my six statements shown this fully. India cannot afford to be governed by this crushing machinery. The Duke of Devonshire and Sir William Hunter have quite truly pointed out that India must be governed by its own native labour and at native rates. In the rates, although with equal efficiency, there will be at least one-third saving according to Government's own scale, but I feel that more saving can be made. In reality, the employment of a native is a whole saving to the country, inasmuch as it provides a native, and the money remains in the country to fructify in the people's own pocket, instead of its being consumed and carried away by somebody else. This machinery inflicts the triple calamity of depriving the Indians of wealth, employment, and experience.

How do you propose to improve the machinery in the way you desire?—One of two ways, or partly both ways, must be adopted to improve this machinery and remove its chief fundamental evil. Both these ways I have already indicated. 1. That native labour must replace foreign labour; and, 2. If any amount of foreign labour is considered as absolutely necessary as it is insisted on, as being necessary for the maintenance of British Rule in India, and British Supremacy in the East, the British Government ought, in justice, pay a share for its common interest with that of India. The machinery may be divinely perfect in its rules, but in its constitution or personnel it has a deep evil, and this evil ought to be remedied if Britain is to be a blessing and a benefit both to India and itself. At present this machinery renders Britain an evil to India instead of a benefit and blessing. I have not much intervened in examining details of departmental expenditure which have been examined with much trouble by the Chairman, and so also the question of financial control. Such examination at proper intervals, as used to be the case in the time of the Company, serves the important purpose of keeping the Government up to mark in case of expenditure. But unless the whole administration of expenditure is put on a natural basis, all examinations of details of departmental expenditures, etc., will be only so much "palliating with symptoms," and will bring no permanent good and strength either to the Indian people or to the British Supremacy. However much you may change the rule or system of work, as long as this evil lasts as at present there cannot be good or beneficial government of India. My statements fully prove this. As this Return (192 of 1892) on the salaries shows, there are about Rx. 15,000,000 paid annually for salaries, etc., above Rx. 1,000 per annum. Add to this all that is paid to the European soldiers, and in a rough way it can be said that about 18 or 20 millions of rupees are paid to Europeans every year. I asked for the correct amount but have not obtained it. Economically it is a loss to Indians, and more especially the portion that goes clean out of the country as savings and pensions and salaries paid in this country. I take an instance: Suppose a European servant draws a salary of Rs. 1,000 a month. He uses a portion of this for all his wants of living, comfort, etc., etc. All this consumption by him is at the deprivation of an Indian who would and could, under right and natural circumstances, occupy that position, and enjoy that provision. This is the first partial loss to India, as, at least, the services enjoyed by the European are rendered by Indians as they would have rendered to any Indian occupying the position. But whatever the European sends to England for his various wants, and whatever savings and pension he ultimately, on his retirement, carries away with him, is a complete drain out of the country, crippling her whole material condition and her capacity to meet all her wants, a dead loss of wealth together with the loss of work and wisdom, *i.e.*, the accumulated experience of his service. Besides, all State expenditure in this country is a dead loss to India. This evil of bleeding must be removed from the present machinery of administration of expenditure as I have said, by treating India fairly for common purposes and by substituting native labour for foreign or European labour. The Rx. 20,000,000 are not by themselves the only evil. They return in the shape of capital and drain away a great deal more.

I beg your pardon. Would you explain that statement more fully?—There is regularly a transfer of a large portion of this Rx. 20,000,000 to this country adding to its capital; a portion of that again comes back to India as capital. Well, we are left entirely helpless, because we cannot make any capital, and, therefore, the foreign capitalist exploits, or uses to his benefit, all the resources of the country and carries away so much more in profits, in interests, and in every way. If we were free to accumulate our own capital fully we should be able then to compete on equal and fair terms with the foreign capital coming in, and there would be perhaps more benefit than evil by the foreign capital. At present we suffer it as an evil because we are helpless and on the ground, and foreign capital comes in and develops the resources for their benefit, and carries away the whole profit that is obtained out of those resources. We are simply used as common labourers, mere hewers of wood and drawers of water. That is the only position to which we are reduced.

That goes a little bit beyond my question. I understand the ground upon which you base your opinion, but I do not quite connect it with this Rx. 20,000,000. Do you think that a soldier who receives his part of the Rx. 20,000,000 immediately lends it out in India again, and do you make that a grievance?—No, it comes indirectly in the usual economic way.

I want to connect it with this particular Rx. 20,000,000. I want to connect it with the soldiers' or civilians' pay, and I cannot follow you when you say that the soldier with his 1*s*. a day or 1*s*. 6*d*. a day, and the civilian with so many rupees a month lays it out so that it returns in the shape of capital and drains away a great deal more. I confess that I am unable to connect the two things?—It does not do it directly, but the economical result of that is that a large portion of the capital of the wealth of India is drained to this country and goes back to the other country in the shape of capital not exactly ear-marked that it is the 1*s*. of the soldier or that it is the 100*l*. of the civilian that exactly formed that capital, it all comes into the great reserve of the capital of this country and from it again the capitalist takes it away back.

And, therefore, you do think it an evil if the soldier, out of his large surplus income, invests it in any Indian securities, that is a mischief to India, is it?—The evil is in this way, that India therefore is unable to make any capital to make any benefit out of its own resources. The foreign capitalist comes in, both European as well as native—there are capitalists from Native States—and works up those resources and carries away the profit out of the country again. It is so much additional loss to the country on account of its helplessness. The original cause being these Rx. 20,000,000 drawn from them.

And the deduction which I must draw from that is that the investment by the soldier of his surplus pay in Indian securities is an evil to India?—Yes, in a way, I say that it comes indirectly.

I only want to follow that—that you regard the investment by the soldier of his surplus pay in Indian securities as an evil to India?—It comes in indirectly, it is economically an evil.

To illustrate your meaning, if there is a gold mine in Mysore which yields 10 per cent., the Indians there, having no accumulated capital, are not able to undertake that enterprise, and this 10 per cent. profit goes to English capitalists instead of to Indian capitalists, so that India gets no benefit from her gold mines. That, I understand, is the sort of idea?—Yes, and so with regard to all resources.

I was under the impression that that was the meaning in Mr. Naoroji's mind. Only you observe that he connects it with the particular payments made to the soldier and civilian; and it seemed to me that to connect the question of investment of capital with the surplus pay of the soldier and the civilian, and with what they do with that surplus pay, is really building too big an over-structure on a narrow foundation. If Mr. Naoroji puts it to us in the form in which you have put it to him, we should understand it. I only want to make quite clear what he means with regard to this particular Rx. 20,000,000.

It is a pure assumption that India is helpless and has no capital?—That is what I have proved in my six statements.

No, you have asserted it—not proved it I think?—But it is there.

Would you consider the fact that almost every year in India

four or five crores of rupees are raised as a public loan? How much of that comes from the Native States, we should like to know.

But you do not know how much?—Well, that is what I want to know from the India Office and from the Government of India. I shall have a remark to make about our not knowing certain things further on.

Yes?—But, with regard to that, when you consider that out of the 300 millions of people in the general poverty, of course there is a small portion that has some little capital and that very little capital comes out in some way of investment. That certainly does not enable India to go in freely with all its own resources to develop its own resources for its own benefit as Sir William Wedderburn has just pointed out. It is in this that we are not able to develop our own resources, which we would otherwise do if we were not deprived of this money every year.

What evidence have you as to the accumulation of capital in India before the time of British Rule?—India has been well known to be a rich country before the time of British Rule, that it is its own riches that has brought all these invasions upon it, otherwise I do not think that the English would have come there had they thought that they would get no benefit out of going to India and merely to go on a quixotic expedition in order to save India from destruction or anything of that kind. And, besides that, the very fact that such an amount of wealth has been drawn from India shows that it has a capacity for producing if it is only allowed to enjoy what it produces.

One question more about this Rx. 20,000,000?—Yes.

I want to be perfectly fair on the subject. You speak of this Rx. 20,000,000 as if it went to England and was then returned in the shape of capital to India; but is it not the case that a very large amount of it is spent on the spot in India by the civil servant and by the soldier?—Yes.

And therefore, are you right in putting it forward that Rx. 20,000,000 comes to England and goes back again in the shape of investment?—No, I do not put the whole Rx. 20,000,000 as going to England. I first explained how a portion of it is spent in India; that portion is still to a certain extent to the detriment of an Indian, who would have taken his place; but that portion is spent there so far, with the loss that it is not enjoyed by an Indian but by a European.

I do not want to press this unduly, but would you not, therefore, modify your statement, " that Rx. 20,000,000 are not of "themselves the only evil; they return (that is the Rx. 20,000,000) " in the shape of capital to drain away great deal more "?—Yes I take the Rx. 20,000,000 as representing the whole evil, not simply for what passes out of the country, but what is also consumed in the country by somebody else other than the Indian, but it is the actual amount of capital; of course I mean that the actual amount of capital that goes clean out of the country is what is left after allowing for what is spent there, so far as among the Indians themselves—I do not mean to say that the whole of the Rx. 20,000,000 goes bodily out of the country entirely; I do not mean that.

Well, but that it is your statement?—Oh, yes.

You would probably wish to modify that?—I think I have modified it; in fact, I have shown that this is the partial loss, and the other, which goes out of the country is the entire loss. Oh yes, that may be clearly understood; it is clear on the face of it. Shall I go on?

Yes?—The present machinery of foreign domination of government is most destructive in every way. If England were subjected to such machinery, notwithstanding all its present great wealth, it would be, like India, impoverished before long. The one other necessity to improve the machinery is that the people themselves must have a voice in its conduct. Till the people themselves have a voice, it is simply an Oriental despotism, and India does not derive that blessing which it has a right to demand from Britain of a constitutional government in place of a despotic government of the worst kind; "the heaviest of all yokes is the yoke of the stranger" as Macaulay has truly said. Then the present machinery requires to be improved by the employment of native labour, by a fair share in the expenditure, of all that is insisted as necessary of foreign element in the services to maintain British Rule, and to give to the Indians the true and the only important blessing of the British Rule, the Right of British Citizenship, of having a voice in its own expenditure, thereby fulfilling all the solemn pledges and Acts of Parliament which the British people by every honour are bound to fulfil, and which have been so far dishonourably ignored and not fulfilled by the Executive Governments in both countries. I feel bound to repeat, that if the machinery of a number of Native States, as suggested by Lords Salisbury and Iddesleigh, be carried out, all the requirements of Britain's best interests and India's best interests will be fully realised and fulfilled. I do sincerely hope that this Commission will see their way to an improvement of the present machinery, in a way beneficial both to England and India. I may add here my agreement to what I have already quoted from Sir Wm. Hunter: "But the good work thus commenced "has assumed such dimensions under the Queen's Govern-"ment of India that it can no longer be carried on or even "supervised by improved labour from England, except at a "cost which India cannot sustain," . . . "40 years here-"after we should have had an Indian Ireland multiplied fifty-"fold on our hands. The condition of things in India com-"pels the Government to enter on these problems. Their "solution and the constant demand for improvement in the "general executive, will require an increasing amount of "administrative labour. India cannot afford to pay for that "labour at the English rates, which are the highest in the "world for official service. But she can afford to pay for it "at her own native rates, which are perhaps the lowest in the "world for such employment." "You cannot work with "imported labour as cheaply as you can with native labour, "and I regard the more extended employment of the natives "not only as an act of justice but as a financial necessity." "The appointment of a few natives annually to the Covenant-"ed Civil Service will not solve the problem. . . . If we "are to govern the Indian people efficiently and cheaply we "must govern them by means of themselves, and pay for "administration at the market rates of native labour." This, I say, is a fair statement of the principal imperfections and evils of the present machinery, which must be improved as suggested. This peculiar inherent evil, or fundamental error, in the present British Indian administration and management of expenditure, and its consequences have been foretold more than 100 years ago by Sir John Shore (1787): "Whatever "allowance we make for the increased industry of the subjects "of the State, owing to the enhanced demand for the produce "of it (supposing the demand to be enhanced), there is reason "to conclude that the benefits are more than counterbalanced "by evils inseparable from the system of a remote foreign "dominion." And it is significantly remarkable that the same inherent evil in the present system of administration and management of expenditure has been, after nearly 100 years, confirmed by a Secretary of State for India. Lord Randolph Churchill has said in a letter to the Treasury, (1886): "The position of India, in relation to taxation and the "sources of the public revenues, is very peculiar, not merely "from the habits of the people and their strong aversion to "change, which is more especially exhibited to new forms of "taxation, but likewise from the character of the Govern-"ment, which is in the hands of foreigners who hold all the "principal administrative offices, and form so large a part of "the Army."

Might I interrupt you, is that true that you have just read, "who hold all"?—Hold all the principal administrative offices.

All?—Yes, that at least is the assertion of the Secretary of State, but there are a few Natives now, I think, in those appointments—very few—such as a few Chief Justices.

A few Chief Justices?—I mean the judges, and there has been some little advance in the application of what was incorrectly called the Statutory Service; but they have put an end to that.

Well "all" is not correct, then?—All the highest offices is certainly correct.

That has been much qualified, has it not?—Well, it is qualified to a very small extent in regard to some of the inferior offices; still, I have quoted what the Secretary of State says.

But the judges are not administrative departments?—No, not administrative nor executive.

All the principal administrative offices?—Yes, all the principal administrative offices. "The impatience of new taxation "which would have to be borne wholly as a consequence of "the foreign rule imposed on the country, and virtually to "meet additions to charges arising outside of the country, "would constitute a political danger, the real magnitude of "which it is to be feared is not all appreciated by persons "who have no knowledge of or concern in the Government "of India, but which those responsible for that Government "have long regarded as of the most serious order." Lord Salisbury, as Secretary of State for India, put the same inherent evil in this manner: "The injury is exaggerated in the case "of India, where so much of the revenue is exported without a "direct equivalent." And he indicates the character of the present system of the administration and management of expenditure as being that "India must be bled." I need not say more upon this aspect of the inherent evil of the present system and machinery of expenditure. I give these opinions in these words as I agree with them, and as very significant as coming from high authority. Almost in words of prophecy Sir David Barbour and Lord Lansdowne uttered these words only four years ago on the present machinery of Government. Sir David Barbour said: "The financial position of the Government of India at the present moment is such as to give cause for apprehension." "The prospects of the future are "disheartening." Lord Lansdowne, as Viceroy, said: "We "should be driven to lay before the Council so discouraging an "account of our finances, and to add the admission, that, for "the present, it is beyond our power to describe the means by "which we can hope to extricate ourselves from the difficulties "and embarrassments which surround us." "My honourable "friend is, I am afraid, but too well justified in regarding our "position with grave apprehension." "We have to consider not "so much the years which are past and gone as those which "are immediately ahead of us, and if we look forward to these "there can be no doubt that we have cause for serious "alarm." And now within four years, India is visited by the greatest and direst calamity as was feared. When will there be an end of these calamities? Sir George Wingate says, with which I agree, with regard to the present system of expenditure: "Taxes spent in the country from which they are raised "are totally different in their effect from taxes raised in one "country and spent in another. In the former case the taxes "collected from the population . . . are again returned to "the industrious classes. . . . But the case is wholly "different when the taxes are not spent in the country from "which they are raised. . . . They constitute . . . an "absolute loss and extinction of the whole amount withdrawn "from the taxed country . . . might as well be thrown into "the sea. . . . Such is the nature of the tribute we have so "long exacted from India. . . . . From this explanation "some faint conception may be formed of the cruel crushing "effect of the tribute upon India." "The Indian tribute, whether "weighed in the scales of justice, or viewed in the light of our "interest will be found to be at variance with humanity, with "common sense, and with the received maxims of economic "science." This is my criticism on the most vital aspects of the present machinery of the administration of expenditure. It is destructive to India, and will be disastrous to England, and cannot promote the general prosperity of the people. My statements have been in the hands of the Commission from 9 to 15 months (the sixth being about 6 or 7 weeks), and I cannot but trust that the Commission will have fully examined them, and know my views on the most important references to them; *viz.*, the administrative machinery of expenditure and the apportionment of charges for common purposes. Now, coming direct to some of the incidence of the machinery. I say there is one thing very unfortunate in the Government of India; in both countries there is great disinclination to give information, especially if it is likely to tell against them. Even such information as Parliament prescribes and the Government of India itself tabulates. In the Act of 1858 (Section LIII), Parliament provided that, among other information for its guidance, the Indian authorities should lay before it every year "a statement prepared from detailed reports from each "Presidency and district in India, in such form as shall best "exhibit the moral and material progress and condition of "India in each such Presidency." Thereupon such reports were ordered by the Government of India to be prepared by the Government, of each Presidency. As a beginning the reports were naturally imperfect in details. In 1862, the Government of India observed: "There is a mass of statistics "in the Administration Reports of the various Local Govern- "ments . . . . but they are not complied on any uniform plan ". . . . so as to show the statistics of the Empire (Fin. "Con., June 1862)." The Statistical Committee, which the Government of India had organised for the purpose, prepared certain forms of tables. And after receiving reports on those forms from the different Governments made a report to the Government of India, with revised forms of tables (Office Memorandum, Financial Department, No. 1,943, dated 28th February, 1866). The members of this Committee were Mr. A. Grote, President, and Messrs. G. Campbell, D. Cowie, and G. Smith. Now, if all these tables of the different departments were fully and carefully given, in the Annual Administration Reports, the non-official public and, for the matter of that, the officials themselves would be able to judge correctly the character of the efficiency or inefficiency of the departments. But the non-official public and Parliament have no means afforded them by the Government to understand and judge fairly the working of the whole machinery. The machinery of every department is a monstrosity, a huge heavy weight of lead, of high salaries to a few Europeans at the top, and the undermachinery from which all work originates is very weak, underpaid, and offering every temptation to corruption and oppression, and consequently both insufficient and inefficient, or worse than inefficient, as in the case of the police. If India were allowed the benefit of its own production, instead of being bled unceasingly, it is capable of giving as full resources to Government as this country is. But this is not allowed. Compare the expenditure incurred in this country to enjoy efficiency of administration and protection, with the wretched provision in India, because India is not allowed to enjoy its own. And consequently the whole machinery of Government is unworthy of an English administration. All this great imperfection and discredit would become clear to the public if the administration reports gave all the information which Parliament has asked, subject to such improvements as may be suggested from time to time. This is the chief reason why the non-official public in India are unable to criticise this machinery. Criticism presupposes knowledge and information of the subject, and this cannot be got. If we criticise without precise information, from general belief, we are at once come down upon as reckless, attacking Government without knowledge, ill-informed agitators, and what not, when really the head and front of the offence is the Government itself. I shall read the comparison I have made between the expenditure of this country and of India to show that with India's poor expenditure on India's benefit (after the bleeding), makes inefficiency and insufficiency of Government as a matter of course. The Duke of Devonshire, Lord Salisbury, Sir William Hunter, and others are perfectly justified in their views about the inefficiency and insufficiency of Government of India. And then I have got this table of comparison between the expenditure incurred here for the sake of efficiency and the expenditure we can only provide it from very poor resources in India, which, of course, must naturally be insufficient and inefficient in Government. Am I to read all the figures or only just give the ultimate result?

Perhaps you will take the course that you think best for the Commission?—Very well. The United Kingdom, 1896—I have taken this from the Statistical Abstract Return, No. C. 8209 of 1896—United Kingdom expenditure—I exclude interest, because it does not form a part of the administration or protection—civil list, and civil administration list, £21,251,357.; army, £18,459,800. Navy I exclude, because we have no Navy, except a small marine expenditure, and therefore I do not think it just to put that in. Charges for the collection of revenue, £13,119,000.; total expenditure for administration and protection, excluding the Navy and interest —£52,830,157.; or £53,000,000. for a population of 39,465,730, say, 40,000,000. This gives £1. 6*s* 6*d*. per head, excluding the Navy and interest. On the side of British India: the statistical abstract of British India, Return C. 8238 of 1896; the figures are for 1894-5—I exclude interest also. Post office, telegraph, and mint. Rx. 2,466,175; salaries and expenses of civil departments, Rx. 14,835,209; miscellaneous civil charges, Rx.6,065,705; famine relief and insurance, Rx. 610,235; buildings and roads, Rx. 5,352,801; army services, Rx. 24,096,091; special defence works, Rx. 217,867; provincial expenditure defrayed from provincial balances, Rx. 560,860; direct demands on revenue, Rx. 9,722,041; deduct refunds, Rx. 280,555; the total amounts to Rx. 63,646,429, or, say, 640 million rupees, for nearly six times the population; for a population of 230 millions; and taking the population of 1891 as 221,172,952, and adding 4 per cent. for the subsequent four years, gives a total of 230,091,870—say, 230 millions population. The expenditure, therefore, per head comes to 2 rupees 12 annas per head as compared with £1. 6*s*. 6*d*. in the United Kingdom.

And what deduction do you draw from that?—What is the impression it leaves on your mind; and what is the impression you wish to convey to the Commission?—The impression left on my mind, and what I wish to impress on the Commission, is, that resources of British India are so very poor that Government cannot get more with all the taxation than 2 rupees and 12 annas per head for administration and protective charges. Consequently, necessarily this Government should be very inefficient, while here the fact that for efficient and good government the public are willing and are able to give £1 6*s*. 6*d*. per head shows that the Government of British India naturally throws a great deal of discredit upon the Government of India for the poor resources that they have at their command for giving efficient and sufficient government.

I ask that question with reference to this point; you are comparing the rich country and the poor country?—Yes.

You have dwelt very much upon the wealth of England, and very much upon the poverty of India; and yet from your putting those two totals together, it looked as if you thought it an evil that the administration in India did not cost more?—What I want to conclude is that the administration of India is very imperfect and very inefficient on account of its resources being so poor, caused by the foreign domination system, and the unnatural system which is introduced, or which is worked in India.

But I want to follow you out. Would you advocate a larger

expenditure on administration in India?—Yes; I advocate that India should be left to be benefited by its own resources; and India would be able to give a great deal more for governing purposes, and be more efficiently governed than what it is at present. The cause of its being in such an unfortunate plight is that the system of machinery adopted there is a very unnatural and a very unfortunate one.

Then what is your conclusion; that if India was independent, would the independent Government double, treble, quadruple, quintuple the taxation in order to bring the expenditure to something more like the expenditure in England?—If India is allowed to keep its own resources to itself I am quite confident that India would be quite able to supply all the necessary funds as they are supplied here.

That is to say, that, if India were independent she would have to raise something like Rx. 300,000,000?—Very well.

And you really think that if India was independent, she could do that without damaging her own resources?—If India is allowed to retain all its resources whilst being dependent upon British Rule, because it is a great blessing—the British Supremacy—for various reasons; but if India is allowed to retain its resources instead of being bled by this foreign domination, India would be quite able to pay, if necessary, Rx. 200,000,000.

That is to say, that you are using that expression "if India was independent" because that is the easiest way of putting it?—You may put it in that way to illustrate the case.

That the Indian Governments in that day without doing harm to India, could quintuple the present taxation?—I cannot go so far as to say that it would quadruple or sextuple it; but still, I have no doubt that it would supply all the necessary funds for efficient government.

I want to get at your standard. You are holding up to us a comparison between the expenditure in England of £1 6*s.* 6*d.*, and the expenditure in India of 2 rupees and 12 annas?—Yes.

And your evidence would lead us, I think, to think that India, under a happier state of things, would emulate, in order to get a thoroughly good administration, the expenditure per head which obtains in this country?—Yes.

I want to give you the opportunity of qualifying the statement if you think it necessary. It leads to this, that in some shape or other you are to get out of India, which you say is a poor country, say, five times the present revenue. It is a question of the difference between the £1 6s. 6d. and those 2 rupees 12 annas a head, which, I think, take it up very closely to Rx. 300,000,000. That is multiplying its present revenue by six or seven. Do you think that a poor country, if it were only under an independent Government, could raise that amount of money without impairing its resources?—With this British Supremacy, what is poor now would become rich if it is allowed to keep its own benefits. The only qualification I have to make, whether she will need even so much money as England requires for efficiency, is this: that labour there and efficient labour and native labour would be so much cheaper, a good deal cheaper, than what it is here, and the result would be that perhaps if we did not require Rx. 200,000,000 or Rx. 300,000,000 or as many times as the difference now exists; but certainly India would be quite capable of supplying as much as may be necessary for its own efficient and sufficient government; that I have not the least doubt whether it would be 150,000,000 or 200,000,000 or 150,000,000, I have not the least fear that India's resources would be found quite equal to the necessities of its wants.

You see the practical remedy which you have indicated to us as a means of arriving at this result is that, whereas Rx. 20,000,000 is now spent upon European soldiers and European civilians, that amount should be spent upon Indians, that is to say that Indians should receive this Rx. 20,000,000; but, supposing that was done, that would not supply anything like the difference which would be necessary to raise the two rupees up to a level of £1 6s. 6d. per head, and therefore you would have to find the difference by some other method?—If what is taken out of the country is saved to the country its economical effect would be to enrich the country.

But you cannot enrich it more than the sum?—No. This sum remaining in the country will economically provide far better effects than it does at present. It is not the saving of the Rx. 20,000,000 only, it would be the saving of all the reproduction, fructification of the money in the country itself.

But that Rx. 20,000,000 laid out there could only produce a certain interest?—It is not all interest, it is developing the resources of the country which might quintuple and make the riches of the country far greater than what they are. It will make, in fact, the country rich if all that is drawn away from India is saved in it and becomes its own resources. It is the capital, the blood of the country.

May I interpret it in this way, that if that Rx. 20,000,000 was left in Indian pockets it would produce every year Rx. 300,000,000, and that gain, realised by laying out those Rx. 20,000,000 in India, would enable the Indian Government to raise the rate of taxation from 2 rupees 12 annas a head to something like £1 6*s*. 6*d*. It is a very large deduction. I am delighted to hear that India is so rich that laying out Rx. 20,000,000 would produce in a year between Rx. 200,000,000 and Rx. 300,000,000?—Of course it will not produce it in a year, but it will first have to fill up the gap of all that has been drawn away, and it will raise it gradually to that rich condition which it is capable of. Of course to say that these Rx. 20,000,000 saved this year will enable the Government of India to have Rx. 200,000,000 for the purposes of Government cannot be thought of. Of course I never meant that, but if those Rx. 20,000,000 or Rx. 30,000,000, or whatever it is that is drawn from India, is saved to it, it will gradually work its economical effect in enriching India every year by increased foreign trade, by increased production, and in that manner will make it strong enough and rich enough to give the Government of India such resources as may be necessary to their heart's content.

I am only anxious to bring out clearly, Mr. Naoroji, what you mean by it in order to give you an opportunity of making any modification of the statements which you have just given us in evidence?—Yes.

Because at present it certainly, I think as it stands, would sound rather drawing wide deductions from small premises. You point out to us that India is a very poor country, you go on to say that, if she was independent, you would quintuple her expenditure in order to bring her up to somewhere near the standard that you suggest it should be or to the English standard, and you produce that result by proposing that a comparatively small sum in salaries and pay, which now goes to Europeans, should go to Indians?—Yes. It is not the amount that is so much the difficulty. If the people get back what they give, as here, India can give in time all that may be necessary, Rx. 200,000,000 or Rx. 300,000,000.

And you think that that comparatively small sum kept in India would result, perhaps in a few years, in this enormous sum in order to raise the expenditure of India to something like the level of the English expenditure?—I thank you very much for pointing out the likely misunderstanding which would arise, and therefore I have given the modifying answers, so that it may not be misunderstood. Then I have given an illustration here. I have taken just one instance of public education in which I have also worked out those figures which come to for primary education alone; here 4*s.* 6*d.* per head of the population, while in British India it comes to about one anna and half-a-pie per head. I just point out my object in bringing this illustration was not to point out that the figures must be equal, but that there is a great disparity on account of certain causes which I lay stress upon.

And I think that you do not lay stress upon the word "independent" which the Chairman used?—No, I do not at all.

You mean that if a suitable system is adopted it will tend greatly to prosperity; it will allow of much heavier taxation and sufficient taxation?—Quite right; that is what I mean.

And that the present system is as though the people were to consume the seed corn which is needed for next harvest, it will produce destitution even though sowing that seed corn may not immediately produce prosperity. I think that is the drift of your evidence?—Yes.

In using the phrase "independent Government," I was only wanting to get out your view, Mr. Naoroji, that if the English Government were removed, and, therefore, if the great evil which is pressing on India in your view were removed, India under a better system of administration would be able to work in the direction of the model which you have put before us; namely, the amount of expenditure in this country ?– Of course. What I mean is that I for one, certainly do not wish to sever the connection with Britain. On the contrary it is my extreme desire that the connection with Britain may last a very long time for the benefit of both countries; it is for that reason alone that I am struggling; if it were otherwise, I think I had better remain quiet.

Then may we take that as giving your views upon the machinery of administration? Upon the machinery of administration,

There is nothing you would like to add to that ?—No. I do dot think I have got anything to add here.

I mean that is a general statement of your views?—A general statement.

But I would bring it before you that it hardly touches the subjects that have been before us and upon which Indian officials have placed very full information before us; namely, the analysis of the different branches of public expenditure in India. Beyond your comment upon the small amount spent in education, do I understand that you do not wish to offer any criticisms upon the description they have given of Indian administration in all its branches ?—No, I do not offer any criticism upon those details for the simple reason that I confine myself especially to the important point for which I asked the Commission and for which Sir Henry Fowler said that he wanted to prove that there was prosperity or not from the machinery of the Government as it existed. I therefore applied myself fully to prove that point that it did not promote prosperity. I therefore did not apply myself to the little details for two reasons first that you cannot get information from the public records of any kind so as to go very minutely into precise figures, and for the present purpose for which this Commission, as far as I was concerned, was asked was the important purpose of the principles upon which the whole Government expenditure was conducted, and these principles being unnatural any discussion upon the details of the different departments will benefit nothing excepting perhaps proposing a reduction here and a reduction there which is soon forgotten and which is the fate of all the previous Commissions that have generally taken place, and as I know of the Financial Committee of 1871-4. I purposely, therefore, wanted to bring out as prominently as possible this fundamental evil difficulty, by the removal of which both England and India may benefit.

Then may we take it that you confine your recommendation for reform of Administration in India to the doing away with the European element—I do not want to put this in an antagonistic manner, but merely to get out your view?—No.

From your evidence I gather that your remedy is to do away with the European element in India and replace that element by an Indian Army and by an Indian Administration—no Europeans being employed in the Army, no Europeans being employed in the Administration—that I should gather to be your view?—No. I can explain what I mean; I do not mean that there should be no Europeans at all in the Army, nor in the Civil Administration. What I want to say is—even Lord Ripon put it as the irreducible minimum—that as far as possible every native added in the service will be a gain to the Administration of the country and that if any portion of Europeans is considered as absolutely necessary it is on the ground of the maintenance of the British Rule; otherwise there will be no necessity as far as the British Government or the British people are concerned. In that case, I say in fairness, if they went for the common purpose, and I admit that is a benefit to India also, that in fairness the expenditure incurred upon the European portion—the irreducible minimium—should be fairly divided between the two countries instead of putting the whole burden upon India. As to the employment of every Indian, of course, India ought to pay and should be very prepared to pay.

You put your suggestion before us as a means of raising the expenditure of India to something like a level of the expenditure of England. As far as possible the Europeans in the Army and the Europeans in the Administration should be replaced by Indians. The mere fact of paying an Indian, you look upon it, instead of a European would have such a fructifying effect that in the course of a certain number of years it would enable the Indian Government to raise taxation up to almost the level of the English taxation. But you go further, and you say wherever Europeans are employed that England should repay. Therefore the position would be this, that supposing, we will say, that only one-fourth of the present force were retained of Europeans that would cost something like Rx. 5,000,000. I am now taking the figures of Rx.20,000,000 as the total that will be paid by England to India by your view, and that would be the sole immediate cash benefit?—Immediate benefit, yes.

Beyond that Rx. 15,000,000 would be paid to Indians, and that left in the Indian pocket would produce this enormous interest or fructifying power, which would enable the Indian Government within a few years to raise the expenditure per head from 2 rupees 12 annas to something like £1. 6*s*. 6*d*. per head?—Sticking to that comparison between the two as I have brought in this table as an illustration, I do not think it is fair to me. What I mean there is that India, if left to such resources as I am mentioning, will be able to supply all its wants, and that the cheaper rate of labour every demand required of themselves; but I say if it requires Rx. 200,000,000 or if it requires Rx. 150,000,000 to be more efficient and sufficient to give that, Indian resources are quite enough to meet all its wants, provided those resources remain in its hands.

That is the object with which I asked these questions?—Yes.

You placed this before us as a model?—Yes, as an illustration.

And your evidence after that, I think, pointed very much to this—you were giving the cost of the English Administration at home as a type, and you considered that something of the kind should be the object of administration in India. The increase of taxation which that involves in so poor a country, is, of course, very startling. I wanted to be quite sure that there was no modification in the case that you are putting before us that you would wish to make?—Yes.

Now, I understand that you modify it so far as this, that you do not put the £1. 6*s*. 6*d*. as an absolute type?—No.

But, of course, you do leave it that a very large increase of expenditure is necessary in India for Indian purposes?—Yes.

And therefore that considerable means ought to be found for that purpose; but the one practical remedy which you suggest is, that a certain number of Europeans who are now employed in India should be replaced by Indians?—Yes. The principle which I approve is that which was declared by the Duke of Devonshire, who said: "If the country is to be "better governed, that can only be done by the employment of "the best and most intelligent of the natives in the service," and as pointed out by Sir W. W. Hunter, "if we are to govern "the people of India efficiently and cheaply, we must govern "them by means of themselves, and pay for the administration "at the market rates of native labour." An administration conducted on these principles will stop the material, political, and intellectual drain from India.

And I think you are able to illustrate the general problem to which the Chairman has referred, the wonderful improvement in the case of Mysore, which was handed over to native rule in a condition of great financial difficulty, and which is now able to raise a large revenue and to do a great deal for the public good. and yet is in a prosperous financial condition. It is not to the mere interest profit out of sums invested, but to a more economical and suitable method of administration that you look for the prosperity which will bear the additional expenditure. Is that not so?—Yes. In the case of the Mysore State this method was adopted by Lords Salisbury and Iddesleigh "as a guarantee for the good government of the people, and for the security of British rights and interests." This experiment, though disapproved by the Anglo-Indian authorities, was loyally and effectively carried out by them, and proved a brilliant success, resulting in a contented people, a full treasury, moral and material progress, and attachment to British Supremacy. It is a brilliant episode in British Indian History. Similarly British India will be prosperous and contented if the same principles are followed, local administration being entrusted to competent native officials under European control, co-operating with representative assemblies.

I understand that it is your desire that British Rule in India should be continued and strengthened?—I gladly recognise the benefits of British Rule, especially as regards law and order, education, and freedom of the press and public meeting; but I believe that British power and influence are much weakened by the refusal to administer expenditure in a way so as to give the people justice and a voice in their own affairs, by the consequent "extreme poverty" of the masses, and by the non-fulfilment of the solemn pledges given by Parliament and the Crown, of equal opportunity in the public service to all subjects of Her Majesty; and I sincerely desire to see British Rule strengthened on the lines most beneficial to the people both of India and of Britain.

Then, before we pass on to apportionment, I would call your attention to one point, Mr. Naoroji. We have a proverb here, "take care of the pence and the pounds will take care of themselves." That argument does not apply in India, does it? Your evidence does not deal with the reform of the administration in its details?—Taking care of the pence and an examination like this which you have so very carefully and with much trouble carried out has its use. What I want to point out was that that alone by itself will not remove that general condition of the poverty of India, and all the bad effects of the present system of administration, unless we go into the question of the principles upon which the whole administration of expenditure is based.

Quite so?—And I wanted to impress upon the Commission particularly that they must fully treat India on righteous principles, and if that is once settled a great deal of the difficulty would be removed; the whole Indian problem will be solved; and there would be time enough then to go into the details which will be a matter of necessity, as here, every year, there is an examination of the details of Government in the discussion on the Budget.

Quite so. You have put before us your general view of the manner in which the reform of the administration should be effected and its results. The Commission, I think, might regard the remedies you propose as outside their powers—but within our powers we have had a very exhaustive examination of the detafls of adminstration, and I was anxious to know whether in the course of that examination you had any views to express upon the different branches of the public service as they have been brought before us. It is only by going into those details that economy can be effected; I rather gather from you that you are not prepared to offer us any suggestions or criticisms upon this evidence which has been placed before us?—No; I do not enter into the criticism of the details, as I have already explained that, with the best results that may be obtained there is very much of this criticism that would not touch the chief evil and the real evil of the whole matter; and so far as the Government of India is concerned, taking the things as they are, they are doing what they can to a very great extent, and I do not find much fault with them as far as the machinery is adopted by them subject to all humam imperfections as they have. An examination like this of details at regular intervals something like what it was every 20 years in the case of the East India Company might be very important to check any unnecessary expense, or any extravagance in expenditure, and that also has been discussed during the last Financial Committee. On the present occasion my chief contention, and I wanted particularly to keep aloof from the details for the very reason that I may direct the Commission as pointedly as possible to going to the root of the whole evil, so that there may be some permanent benefit, and therefore I am not prepared to go into the criticism of the details. I did that deliberately and I may say generally, as I said just now that the Government of India avoiding the question of the evil of this principle of administration they are doing as well as they can, with all human imperfectjons and requiring criticism from time to time. They are doing their work with a sufficient desire to administer in the best way possible. I am quite willing to give them that credit, that the officials are doing what they can, even under very disadvantageous and evil circumstances.

And does not that somewhat justify my quoting the proverb about the pence? Is it not worth taking care of the pennies?—Only that these points will all again come back when the Government of India falls into its own regime, and there will be no good done. And that was my own personal course that I have taken. I do not know; my other friends may be able to go into some criticism of details here.

You have been critical upon the Indian administration and you have stated that the information, I think, was not forthcoming which would enable you more effectually to criticise Indian administration?—Yes, that is true; that is the great want.

But has not this commission given you a very fair opportunity for obtaining that information. We have had the responsible Indian officials before us?—Yes.

And was not that a far better opportunity to cross-examine them and elicit from them this information which is wanting, rather than after the time to say that examination is difficult because the information is not forthcoming?—Yes; but the information that has come before the Commission is of that kind, especially from the official point of view, is a one-sided information to a large extent necessarily to justify their own way of procedure. We have not that information which would enable us to know behind the scenes what is wanting in it. Only we should have in order to criticise, and that is a great disadvantage for every non-official witness that he cannot criticise, because he has not a full knowledge and a complete knowledge, and he does not know what to ask. It is for the Government of India to give this information as is asked by the Committee of the Government of India and by Parliament, and we would then be able to criticise more effectually and more precisely what decrease, or what extravagance, or what waste has taken place in any particular department, or in any particular way.

I think, Mr. Naoroji, a man who has given so much attention to these subjects as you have evidently done from the papers which you have laid before us, is in a position, when he is put face to face with the official witnesses to elicit from them those weak points upon which they have not given us, in his opinion, full information?—We have not got such information as would enable us to know what the weak points are. The official witnesses really do not point out what their weak points are, and we are not able to point out those weak points for the simple reason that we have no information, or very imperfect information which would not help.

If you have no information, is it quite fair to make a general attack on Indian administration?—The general attack is perfectly justified from the results. The results show that the very nature of the administration with the poor resources at the command of the Government, that the Government must be inefficient and insufficient, and the general attack I made is not so much upon the Government as officials, but upon the system upon which they are working, that system being an evil system. They cannot help but do what of course would produce unsatisfactory results. I have not the least wish to attack the Government of India or the officials, because I do not believe they themselves would do any evil. It is the cause of the evil system upon which they are working, and which requires to be considered and modified so that they themselves may be able to do their work with greater satisfaction to themselves as well as with greater satisfaction to the people. That is the principle which I wanted specially and principally to bring forward.

Of course, the point to which I am directing your attention is this. We have had a large amount of evidence before us of an official character; and we have done our best on the Commission not only to get the best official evidence, but also the evidence of high officers who have held posts in India, and who are above the ordinary official witnesses. In addition we have been anxious to learn native opinion upon the subject: and here a very large field of examination has been opened upon which, I think, every opportunity has been given in bringing over witnesses from India to undergo examination; every fair demand for information has been fairly met, and at the end of it I am anxious to learn from you whether, from a native point of view and as representing native opinion, you have any criticism to offer upon the subject more immediately interesting to us, namely, administrative management of expenditure in its details?—If this question of the greatest importance upon which I insist is put aside, and if simply the machinery as it is taken, supposing it to be, as it were, machinery in which that evil did not exist, I have not much criticism to offer myself. I do not think it so much necessary that I need go into very great detail in order to point out any defects in any particular department.

With regard to what you say of not being able to get the information of certain definite facts, can you give the Commission a note of the points on which you had asked for information, and you have not got it, and points on which you desire information from the India Office or the Indian Government, can you give a statement to that effect?—I can give it at once just now; to say that if all the tables which are proposed by the Government of India were fully filled up for any particular year, we shall be able to offer a good deal of criticism.

Yes: but will you just give a form that you wish filled up, and then I have no doubt the Chairman will consider whether they can be obtained?—Yes, I can do that if the India Office would be good enough to give us the Report of that Committee which settled the tables, and from those tables—those tables are the very tables that they have not placed before the Commission.

What tables are those?—The tables that were fixed by this Committee of Sir George Campbell and others, and what the different administrative officials give in their Administrative Reports, and if those tables were supplied with the information I think, it would be good for the Government itself as well as for the public to understand each other, and a good deal of misunderstanding and misapprehension will then be removed, and then the statement I can lay partly as I pointed out in one instance already in my Report with regard to the agricultural tables a factor of depreciation. I have got those tables at page 4 of my statement of the 9th January, 1896, and as they were prescribed by this Committee, and if this information is fully given, we should be able very well to ascertain what the capacity, and what the condition of the people is. This is only one set of tables, and there are tables with regard to the Judicial Department, and with regard to the Police Department, with all the departments, and if those tables were correctly and fully given of course, we have all the information. It is not that the information does not exist; this Commission would have been very much helped and we would have been very much helped, to help the Commission in the most effective manner possible.

Do you wish to ask Mr. Naoroji to put in such a paper?

I should like a note of that to be put in, and to state distinctly what is the information that you consider necessary?—Very good, I shall require, Sir James Peile, if I can be given a copy of the Report of this Committee with all the tables connected with it. I was obliged to go—even those few tables that I have made—I was kindly allowed to go to the India Office by Sir Charles Bernard, and to copy out some of those which I immediately required.

Has a copy been refused to you?—Yes, a copy has been refused, for this reason, that they have got it all bound up in one volume and no spare copy.

But you can come and consult it here?—So I went and copied what was required for this purpose. If a copy could be made by a clerk, or by the India Office, it would save me a great deal of trouble; if not, I will come and copy it all myself, in order to place it here.

You drew attention to the difference between the salaries payable to Europeans and to Natives, and seem to think that India would gain very much if the salaries were reduced to the native scale. Can you give any instance of the high salaries which you think would be saved if a system of native employees was introduced?—All the high positions are of such salaries that the Government of India does say that if any Indian is employed in any of those places two-thirds the salary would be quite enough for him, as a very liberal salary. The Government of India and the Secretary of State, has himself laid down this condition, that wherever an Indian is employed in place of a European, that two-thirds of the salary ought to be enough for him. That in itself at once saves one-third. But then I go further than that, even those two-thirds in its economical effect will be still of far greater benefit, as the one-third saved.

And is it the rule at present when a native is appointed to any one of those high positions that he receives two-thirds of the salary?—Yes, I think that is the rule now.

May I correct you?—Is it not?

No; that rule is now abolished. Under the Provincial Service there are special rates of salary lower than the European rates fixed for the natives, except in the highest appointments, such as the High Court, where a Native Judge gets the same salary as a European Judge?—Yes. What I say is that even in the highest positions a lower salary will be accepted by quite equally efficient men, even on the scale which the Government of India itself has laid down; but at present, of course, it produces to a certain extent dissatisfaction, for one official is paid at a very high salary for services of the same character done by a native. If the European official were also brought down to the same salary as the Indian there would be some fairness; that the salary is paid not according to the individual, but according to the services done; and if it is paid according to the services done, there will be a great deal of saving, not only two-thirds, but, I think less—at least this is my opinion—that these high salaries can be reduced with satisfaction both to the Government, as a relief to them, and to the Indians, that they have employment in their own country.

Does that apply to any very large number of appointments?—There are very few appointments yet given in that way.

But is there a very large number of these high appointments?—Yes.

To which high salaries are attached?—Yes.

Which could be reduced, do you think, if a Native Indian was employed?—Here we have got a Return which gives us the figures. I got them out. From what salary do you think I should begin in. Here is a Return from Rs. 1,000 per annum up to—well, take the salary of the Viceroy, £25,000. Then, as you go through, we go to the highest, the number, of course, is smaller, but the amount is very large. If you look at this, this will give you the exact figures, and we can work them out if you like.

But you think that below the very highest appointments there are salaries which are too high for the scale of work, either for the European or for the Native ?—Yes, there are to a very great extent—all those salaries. The very fact that the Government has determined, in regard to the Covenanted Civil Service especially, that any appointment now, except those that pass here with the other competitors, that they are kept, I think on the same level, but when the Statutory Service was passed, that is to say, the Service under the Act of 1870, the Government passed a rule that any appointments given to them should have two-thirds of the salaries paid to Europeans, and that regulates appointments under the Statutory Service; though the Act exists, its action is repealed by the Secretary of State himself, though Parliament required that a certain number of Indians should be every year appointed in India itself, and that Act of 1870 is now a dead letter.

Did you say a dead letter ?—It is a dead letter is the Act of 1870. The Provincial Service is now introduced, which really does not supply what this Act of 1870 meant.

Why ?—Why, because it does not come to the same level. In the Act of 1870, it was intended that the Indians appointed in India itself, without being required to come to this country were to be put exactly on the same footing as those who went from this country, in fact, they were to form an integral part of the Civil Service. Well, this went on for 10 years, and then the Secretary of State decided that no further appointments should be made in that way. In 1878, the Government of India urged very strongly not to act upon that Act, and to introduce what I may call the Provincial Service. The Secretary of State refused to do that; the Secretary of State wished that the Act should be carried out in its integrity, and then only after the Secretary of State's resistance the rules were made. For six years no notice whatever was taken of this Act, either here or in India.

For what six years ?—From 1870 to 1876. The Secretary of State, from here, several times reminded the Government of India to make rules, but they did not do it until they were pressed afterwards, and in 1878 they wrote a long despatch, trying to persuade the Secretary of State for India not to compel them to make these rules, and not to carry out the Act of 1870.

The Statute was passed in 1870, was it not?—The Statute was passed in 1870.

Are you aware that rules were prepared and sent here for approval in 1873?—Yes, that I became aware of when the Blue Book was published, but the rules that were sent were not received, as far as I can understand, were not adopted by the Secretary of State, and it was in 1876 or 1877.

Do you know why they were not adopted?—That I cannot say, because the information is not given in the Blue Book.

Well, I will give you the information. You could have had it at any time in the Report of the Public Service Commission? —Yes.

The difficulty was that the Law Officers of the Crown raised an objection to the rules proposed by the Government of India. Do you know when the next set of rules were proposed; you said nothing was done for six or eight years?—The next set of rules was proposed by Lord Cranbrook, who pressed those rules again.

What year?—That was again in 1877 or 1876.

No, in 1875, on the contrary?—I know; I have not even the despatch, I think.

Revised rules were drawn up by Lord Northbrook's Government in 1875?—Very well. I am very glad to have all that information.

Rules were proposed in 1873 and 1875; and then what next?—They were only settled in what year?

The rules were sanctioned in that year?—When was the Act brought into regular operation?

It was brought into regular operation in 1875?—Were there any elections or nominations made in 1875?

One or two, I believe?—No.

Yes?—I do not think—at least that is my knowledge—that no nominations were made.

Well, we differ?—I know I had none from the India Office. Every Member of the Council, when I complained to him that no notice was taken of the Act of 1870—that the rules were made and finally settled—I do not know whether it was in 1877 or 1878, and the very first nominations were made much later ; that is my information ; that is just our difficulty.

The rules were not finally settled, but a new set of rules was prepared in 1878, to give more thorough effect to the Statute ?—Very well, if the rules were made in 1878 to give thorough effect to the Statute.

More thorough?—Very well, more thorough; I am very glad. Then it is very strange that those rules were abolished, and the nomination entirely put an end to altogether ; why were they not carried out while the Statute was still standing ?

When were they abolished ?—The nomination continued, as far as I can remember, about 10 years.

And why were they abolished ?—That I do not know. The Government of India was determined, even in their despatch, that long despatch, I do not know whether it was in 1877 or 1878 ; they recommended very strongly that those rules should not be made, and that Provincial Service should be adopted.

That does not really concern the question ? — Yes ; it concerns this question.

I asked you why were they abolished ?—Why they were abolished is the thing.

Was it not that after the experience of a good many years it was found that the system introduced in 1879 did not work satisfactorily ?—Yes ; very well there is nothing strange in that ; it was actually foretold by people that it would not work, because the rules were not satisfactory.

Then in 1886 a Commission was appointed to consider the whole subject ?—Yes.

On which native members sat ?—Yes.

And they reported. And the consequence of their report was that a new system was adopted, which is now in force ?—Yes. I know that the Commission was appointed and that the Commission came to that conclusion. The fact of the matter is, and of course, I do not want to attribute any motives, but the effort of the Government of India was to have the rules that they themselves had suggested to the Secretary of State in that long despatch, to be somehow or other got into operation, and this Act of 1870 should not be carried out in its full extent.

The result of that was that first the rules were made very unsatisfactorily. Instead of making rules by which the nominations in India should be of the same standing, the same competence, and under the same tests of examinations; instead of that the rules made were to leave the Governments—the different Governments—to make their choice; and, in my opinion, without any satisfactory test of competence. Well, the result was that the rules were made which were very unsatisfactory, which were not as they ought to have been, and the result was naturally that discredit should be brought upon them. The rules themselves showed in their very face; whether there was the intention or not; but that that should be the result, where the nominations were made merely according to the ideas of the Government of the day, instead of having any public good test, just as it was, adopted here for the competitive examination.

The Government of India themselves tried in various ways to give effect to the Statute?—Yes.

And they have now introduced a new system which is on its trial, and which appears to have a satisfactory working?—Yes. Well, this new system they were determined to have.

That is all I wish to ask you?—That is quite right. I wish to say this, that this new system which is now introduced was the Government of India's desire many years before, publicly expressed in their public despatch, and they did try at least to carry that system of their own into effect and nullify the Act, as it was originally, no doubt. That is what I have to say.

Was not the object of the Act of 1870, to give promotion to higher offices to men of experience and qualifications already in the service who had shown their competency. Was not that the object of the Act?—That was a part of the object.

That was one of the objects of the Act?—Yes; that was one of them.

And the objection to the rules was that they allowed the Government of India to appoint young men of good family or otherwise without any qualifications at all?—Without any qualifications at all.

And that was the objection to the rules, and it was owing to that that public opinion in India considered that the Statutory Service was not successful ?—No.

But it would have been successful if it had been carried out, thoroughly in the spirit of the Act of 1870 ?—That is what I say.

But, however, you are willing to accept the proposal or the idea that if the natives were employed in any of those places the salaries could be very largely reduced ?—Yes ; certainly salaries could be reduced by one-third as it is already settled ; and I think that if a fair trial is given many thoroughly efficient persons would be able to accept these higher offices at less than two-thirds because the original standard is very high.

Mr. Dadabhai Naoroji, I suppose you stand by all that you have said in the pamphlets which you have printed for the instruction of the Commission ?—Yes.

I understand that your views may be summarised in this way, first, that India is so crushed with taxation and impoverished by the withdrawal of her wealth abroad, that the Indian people are ground to the dust and reduced to starvation ?—These are the words of authorities.

Secondly, that the European services,and the present forced inordinate and arbitrary employment of Europeans are India's greatest evil, and the cause of all its economic miseries and destruction ?—Yes.

And, thirdly, that the Government of India is an unrighteous system of selfishness and despotism ? Yes ; I have said that.

Carried on by the Anglo-Indian authorities in defiance of the desires and biddings of the British people and Parliament ?—Yes. Well, the desire of the British people in Parliament is distinctly pointed out by the Act of 1833, by the Proclamation of the Queen which is again repeated at the last Jubilee. There you have the whole policy of the British-people in Parliament set forth, and if that had been carried out, and even if it were now carried out, the whole difficulty would disappear, and the British Government would indeed be a great blessing to India, and India will not be a less blessing to England. That is what I say.

With regard to the taxation ; you are at considerable pains to prove that the taxation of India is exceptionally low, as compared with that of European nations, and of the Indian Native States?—I want to show there is a little misunderstanding; it is exceptionally low in amount, and far heavier in incidence and pressure than even British taxation, because of the incidence of taxation, as I have explained over and over again.

That would depend, of course, on the comparative poverty of the people?—Upon the comparative capacity and poverty of the people.

Yes?—That when you take the whole production over India and you take the whole production of this country, and compare the taxation in this country with the whole wealth and compare the taxation of India with their capacity you will find that the percentage of the incidence of that taxation in India is higher than the percentage of taxation as compared with the wealth of this country, with such information as we have got.

Well, it amounts to this, that the people being poor, the Government has kept the taxation of India extraordinarily low; but when you come to the incidence of taxation on wealth, and you allege increasing poverty, and crushing taxation, I want to know what proof you have of the capacity and wealth of the Indian people?—I first worked out the poverty of India, the total production of India mostly on official authority; this calculation has been before the public and I should have been very glad if any mistake had been pointed out. When Lord Cromer—Sir Evelyn Baring—gave his opinion as that the production of the country was 27 rupees per head per annum—while I have made it 20 rupees per head per annum which, however, will not make a very great difference,—however, I asked Sir Evelyn Baring, the present Lord Cromer, to give me that calculation so that I might see whether I had made a mistake, or who has made the mistake. Unfortunately that calculation was not given to me, and therefore I adhere to my resolution that the total production of India—British India—is on the average only 20 rupees per head per annum.

That is the total income of the people?—No; there is a little confusion, only the total production, actually the quantity of material wealth produced in the year by cultivation, by manufacturers, from the mines and so on, all these accumulated as the total wealth of the country produced during the year and calculated at the prices which are always published regularly. We will make out—and the whole process of calculation is given in my books—we make out that the average cost of about 20 rupees per head per annum.

Then, with a family of seven or eight, the production, not the income, would be Rs. 140, Rs. 160, and so on?—Yes, and it is not enough to keep them.

That is at best an assumption?—And it is by comparing the consumption I have given, not only the production; the production may be very small in amount, and yet if the requirements of consumption may also be comparatively small in amount there would be nothing to complain of; but they are not able to produce as much as would even satisfy their ordinary want of common labour. These figures also I have given there, and I have not up to this time had pointed out to me that they are wrong. I have had correspondence direct with the India Office—I laid down all this—and I have not had any reply to refute those figures from the India Office.

Do you think that calculations of that kind in a country like India are of any value whatever?—Even Lord Cromer himself has said that, for all practical purposes they are sufficiently approximate, we cannot expect them to the farthing; but at the same time in India we have this advantage, that Government has almost all the information it can require to calculate such a result as that. What the result really is of the annual wealth produced in the country which is not very easy here in this country, but there they being principal proprietors, as you may say, why they have all the details of land cultivation in every way. Then the Administration Reports also give, what manufacturers are done, what mines exist, and so on we have very substantial material to go upon in order to calculate from year to year what the real production is or the amount of wealth that is produced every year, and from which the State expenditure and taxation has to be paid, and were that taxation to return to the people as it returns here, notwithstanding such a large debt the interest comes back to the taxpayers, the whole tax that is raised comes back to the taxpayers, there is nothing to complain of, that is the difference.

Now as regards crushing taxation, I see here you take the taxation of 1886 of India and from that you deduce that the taxation comes to about 5s. 6d. a head. Well, in looking into the details of that year——?—Will you kindly tell me what page it is, and which report it is of mine?

It is page 27?—What date is it No. III?

I am not going into the pamphlet; the 9th of January is the date, but I am merely referring to it?—9th of January. Yes and what is the page?

The 27th page?—27, thank you. Yes, this pamphlet was written, it is a copy of the pamphlet that was written, in reply to Sir Grant Duff in those years.

On looking to the items that make up the taxation which you give there as about Rx. 57,000,000, the first item I remark on his Land Revenue, about Rx. 23,500,000?—What are my figures to which you refer?

I am not referring to any of your figures; I am referring to the details, the items, which make up your Rx. 57,000,000? —Rx. 57,116,000; I have got it only from public records, I have not created it myself.

No, I am not disputing it?—No.

The first item which makes up your total is the Land Revenue?—Yes.

Rx. 23,500,000.?—Yes.

You consider that to be taxation?—It is taken from the wealth of the country whether you call it taxation of rent, or anything; it does not matter at all as far as the economic condition is concerned. I think Lord Salisbury himself has discussed that point in one of his minutes, if I remember right, in which he says that you may call it taxation or you may call it rent, but he is more inclined to call it taxation, as so much taken off from the country for revenue purposes.

I do not wish to enter into any controversy as to the nature of the Land Revenue?—No; very well.

But I will just ask you one question, when a man is taxed is he taxed on his own property or income, or on the property of some other person?—On his own property.

On his own property ?—Yes.

Now is it not the fact that throughout all history a portion of the produce of the land in India has belonged to the Ruler or Crown ?—Yes.

In that case it does not belong to the producer ?—You take the principles of the despotic Government. I grant that as a fact. Go on; yes, I will answer that question if you like.

I am quite satisfied with your answer. Does not the British Land Revenue as it is now constituted represent the share which the former Native Governments used to own of the produce of the land ?—Yes; in its economic effect you may call it the property of Government or the property of the people, it is not of the slightest consequence, because in those days though Government took this half it used it on the government of the country, and every farthing of that half remained in the country. It is there that the difficulty lies; I do not care at all whether it is.

We are not on that point, at all events at present ? —That is the real purpose which we have to discuss.

The next item is opium ?—Well.

In that year it came to about Rx. 9,000,000. Now that is paid by China ?—That is paid by China; very well.

It is not a tax on India ?—No; it is so much, that is to say, that is actually, properly speaking, the property of the Indian people, which Government—

Certainly ?—Because it is their produce which brings this profit. Whether it is morally good or not is not the question; but it is the produce of the country which otherwise would have gone to the people. It is the profit of the people of India; the Government find it very convenient to have this for their government purposes.

It is a tax on that produce which is paid by China ?—Yes, that is true; that is the case with all trade, every trade. When you send goods to another country, you get a certain profit out of it, and that becomes the profit of the country.

Well, let us proceed. I think the home charges that year were about £14,000,000.; that at 1*s.* 7*d.* to the rupee is about Rx. 18,000,000, so that you see China paid half of those home charges ?—Yes, that is so ; India's profit ; that is so much gain in that direction.

And the public share, the national share of the land produce would more than cover the whole of the home charges ?—Yes ; but then why should India be deprived of that benefit ? That is no justification that somebody else should take it away if it is the produce of India—India must enjoy it.

We are not on that point now. If you would kindly just answer the question ?—Yes ; I am answering the question.

Now, from that Indian taxation fund which you have admitted to be exceptionally low, far lower than that of any other country ?—In amount, not in incidence.

Whether it is 6*s*. a head, as you say, or 2*s*. 6*d*. a head as Sir Henry Fowler makes it ?—Sir Henry Fowler makes it so ; that is the authority.

If you take away land revenue and opium, the remaining taxation comes to a very small amount ?—I do not think land revenue ought to be taken into account.

Is it not the fact that from that very low taxation fund the Government pays all the charges which devolve upon Government, namely, all the charges for the Army, both in India and in England, the contribution to the Navy, the whole cost of civil administration both in India and in England ; the interest on railway capital ?—Yes.

And the deficiency on the revenue account of railways, the interest of debt, all charges for pensions and leave allowances ; and also the cost of all stores, and all railway materials ?—Yes.

In fact every charge ?—Yes.

Is paid out of the very low rate of taxation which is levied by the Government ?—Yes.

And your grievance appears to be that out of that low rate of taxation about one-fourth in this year, 1886, was applied to the payment of home charges ?—Yes ; well.

These home charges are what you call tribute ?—Yes.

Now, is it the case that one single rupee from the Indian revenues goes into the British treasury as tribute ; that is to say, is applied otherwise than as a payment for something which is given in return ?—What is given in return. First of all my grievance has been again misunderstood. The grievance lies in this, that what is taken from the people as so much taxation in any shape whatsoever does not return to the people, but a portion of it goes away out of the country and impoverishes the country—that is the grievance. It is not of the slightest consequence, that the very fact that from a very small taxation the Government of India is obliged to carry on all these departments shows that these departments therefore naturally become very insufficient and inefficient; and the Secretaries of State, two Secretaries of State were perfectly justified in saying that this was an awful condition of things. That is the grievance.

What you have said is that this tribute, as you call it, is a portion of the produce exported out of British India, for which nothing whatever has returned to her in any shape?—Yes.

Now, I ask you whether there is any part of it that is not spent upon services or materials supplied to India?—Very good; it is only for necessary services. The services itself are our grievance, we are not only deprived of our money, but we are deprived also of our employment. We do not want those services.

Excuse me, that is not our point?—That is the main point.

The point is whether, rightly or wrongly, the money has not been paid for services or materials supplied to India?—The services are a portion of the tribute which we are compelled to pay. The services, and the money which is given for the services, both are our great grievances, that we are doubly injured both in the point of money and in the employment which belongs to us by right in our country should be taken away from us; and with it, therefore, the wisdom which is derived from that service, so that it is a grievance.

So that the irreducible minimum of Europeans is not to be paid for, is it?—First of all, there ought not to be so great a minimum as now exists. I explained that very clearly that the irreducible minimum, if considered by the British as absolutely necessary, it is for the sake of maintaining their rule in India and their position in the East, as well as their position in Europe. Well, therefore, all I say is, that we grant, though if I were to take it in its logical sequence I do not grant that it is absolutely necessary to have this irreducible minimum, with the exception of the few highest offices, in order to keep the control over India; but I grant for the sake of present purposes, and for practical purposes, that a certain number of Europeans may be considered absolutely necessary. Then I say—

We will come to that presently ?—If you will kindly allow me to finish. Then I say, if it is true that Europeans for certain purposes are required simply on account of the British Rule, then the British people ought to pay a fair share for that interest which they themselves have.

Now, next you contrast the British system of government with the system in the Native States ?—Yes.

Very much to the disadvantage of the British system?—Yes, the system of course. There is nothing to be said but against the bad system.

You say the Native States which adopt good management go on increasing in prosperity, in strong contrast with the system of the British management of expenditure ?—Yes.

And you give instances of the taxation in certain States which come to about 12 rupees, 18 rupees, and so on, per head, so that the taxation of the Native States is at least two or three times what it is in British India, or even more ?—It is more.

Twice or three times that of the native of British India ?—And yet he is better off.

That is what you say ?—And yet he is better off.

That has to be proved, I think, has it not ?—The proof lies on the very surface. First of all—

We shall come to that ?—I have given testimony; one testimony, I think, in regard to this in Bhownuggar.

I have seen what you refer to, and I do not think it proves it in the slightest degree ?—I have your own words that Bhownuggar had a full treasury, and so on.

I said it had a full treasury. Still, if you take three times the taxation from the people you can easily have a full treasury ?—Yes, but the whole people are much better off.

I did not say that, you assume it ?—What was the use of praising that State if this was not the meaning of it. You praised it because it was a good government.

Under a long British management it had a full treasury ?—True, but British management was Indian management.

Shall we go on?—Yes; I have to explain a little.

I have not asked you any question?—No; but it is in answer to that question we had just now.

What?—In regard to the comparison with Native States exacting greater taxation, and yet you say: How is it that they are prosperous?

I did not ask you that?—Oh, very well then.

You say the capacity for taxation in the Native States is not the result of any oppressive taxation, but the natural developments under improved government of the increasing prosperity of the people. Well, the first point is that the taxation is at least two or three times as high as that of British India?—Yes, and taxation here is I suppose, 20 times higher than in British India.

Now how is this taxation in Native States spent; have you ever heard of its being wasted upon unworthy favourites and in debauchery?—That may be, if the political agents do not do their duty; but that is no argument against the development of the prosperity of the people under this taxation.

Have you ever heard of the Native State revenues being hoarded?—Hoarded, yes; and they can afford to hoard.

You give the case of Scindia, for instance, who lent 3½ millions sterling to the British Government?—Yes, that is the British Government.

Where was that money produced from; was it not hoarded in vaults?—It was hoarded in vaults.

For many years?—Yes; and it was the fault of the Native State that it did so; but we are discussing the ordinary good management.

When the money was hoarded in vaults in that way, was it doing any good to the subjects of Scindia?—No, it was not doing any good; that was the fault of the Native State, and notwithstanding that the people were in better condition.

Now let me ask another question. Does any of the Native State revenue go outside the Native State, is it spent outside the State; for instance, there is a considerable item of tribute that goes out?—Yes, that is the only thing, and it is a very small item, it does not affect them very much; the whole thing is so very small.

The Mysore State pay 25 lakhs a year ?—25 lakhs, and yet they flourish.

You keep on assuming that as a fact ?—Yes, we have that point.

Mysore pays 25 lakhs ?—Yes.

That is as a subsidy for military aid ?—Yes.

For military protection. Therefore you see that the Mysore subject contributes a considerable sum towards the cost of the English Army ?—Yes, that might very well be considered, what might be a reasonable contribution to a portion of the Army.

That is not the point. He is, therefore, very much in the same position as the British Indian subject as regards contributing to the Army ?—Yes, but not exactly the same position.

Now do you not find in Native States European servants ?—Yes ; that is of their own choice.

We will take the Bhownuggar State ?—Yes.

I daresay you are aware that for the last 20 years the Head of the Public Works there has been a European with a family at home ?—Yes.

And that some of his sons are also employed ?—Yes.

Again, take the Native State Railways ?—Yes.

The Managers of the Native State Railways are Europeans living in Native States ?—Yes.

And the railway materials and the rolling stock have all been bought in England ?—I never made a complaint of that.

The Native Chiefs are in the habit of coming to Europe ?—Yes.

And spending large sums of money in England ?—Yes.

In all those ways a portion of the taxation of the Native States goes out and is spent abroad ?—Yes.

So that their position in that respect also is like that of British India ?—That is so very small compared with the system in British India, there is no comparison between the two.

There is no comparison between a Native State like Bhownuggar and the British Empire ?—Yes.

In size ; therefore neither should there be in the amount of revenue spent abroad ?—Then I am again misunderstood. What I say is this, that in the Native States you have the whole of the service from top to bottom, the natives themselves.

I have just shown you that you do not?—The whole of them are natives with the exception of such Europeans as a sort of investment they employ for benefit; and so for instance for the mills in Bombay. Actually I myself have sent from here managers.

We are discussing the Native States I think, if you do not mind?—It is the similarity of the incident that induced me to mention it; I will keep to the Native States. Therefore every farthing that is raised by the State is returned to the people, it remains in the country, it fructifies among the people naturally. I have been, of course, in Baroda, and I know a Native State.

But if Europeans are employed there that does not take place?—The Europeans are employed for special purpose of their own choice; here they are compelled to put upon us where it is unnecessary, where you can have Indians of the same efficiency to do that work.

But Europeans in Native States send their savings home just the same as Europeans in British India?—Yes, that is true, but the Native States do that of their own choice for their benefit; in the other case it is compulsory to an extent that the people cannot afford.

Now we come to a point in which you see a great advantage in the Native States, that is to say that they build and extend their own railways from revenue?—They have their revenue.

British India is not able to do that because they have no revenue?—They cannot, yes.

Do you think you are correct in that statement? Baroda has built its own railway.

That, while the Native States build their railways from revenue—— ?—Baroda has built it from revenue.

British India is not able to do so?—No, it cannot.

You think that is correct?—Yes, I think so.

Do you happen to remember a question in our evidence some time back in which it was shown that the British Government has spent Rx. 22,000,000 on railway and irrigation works out of revenue?—What is that compared with the whole debt.

I did not ask what it was compared—is that the evidence or not?—If you want to modify it in this way, that British India has from revenue spent some money on railways, of course I did not deny altogether.

Do you think that the Native States have spent anything like Rx. 22,000,000 on railways?—But Native States are not so big as British India.

Then, in proportion?—In proportion they have spent a good deal, and they are spending more every day.

How much, do you know?—One Native State has lent to another Native State for railway extension.

Can you tell us what amount Native States have spent on railways?—I would work it out if you want it.

You do not know?—I could not tell you off-hand.

But that is not all, besides the expenditure on railways and irrigation, the British Government has spent—I have taken it out for 10 years, 1885-6 to 1894-5, has spent immense amounts on roads and rest-houses, and all sorts of communications?—Yes.

And on other public improvements, water supply, and so on. Will you allow me to ask my question?—Yes, I am not interfering.

The total of expenditure from revenue on these for the 10 years, 1885-6 to 1894-5, amount to Rx. 43,000,000?—Yes. All that from that wretched taxation; all that from a small amount. You ought to have been able to do 10 times as much.

Will you allow me, that is spent by the British Government from revenue?—Yes.

So you are wrong in saying that the British Government is unable to find revenue for public works?—Yes; that is to the extent they ought to do.

That was not your remark?—I have said that in my evidence to-day; I have referred to that point. All this is from a poor revenue, therefore they ought to be able to if they were in the same condition as the Native States, then their expenditure would have been in such a large proportion.

I think it is plain, then, that the Native State subject is really in precisely the same position as the British Indian subject as regards the appropriation of his taxation to the interest on loans which they have in Mysore and the Nizam's Dominions, too; to the payment of Europeans employed by the States, and to payments made towards the cost of the British Army, as in the case of Mysore?—Yes.

I think all you have shown me is that a large revenue is raised, and not why the people are more prosperous?—Yes.

Do you recollect also that the Native States contribute largely to the British salt revenue?—Yes. Well, that shows, you see, that there is something drawn from other people which the people themselves are not able to supply.

The point I am making is that the Native State subject pays money to the salt revenue?—So much the worse.

Which money goes abroad?—So much the worse for the British Administration.

Again, they pay a portion of the duty on piece-goods?—Yes.

In all these ways they pay taxation?—Yes.

Which goes out of the Native State?—No. Still, as much as goes out of the State, they are still able to do that and be prosperous.

Well, I will take the point of prosperity. Will you allow me to ask you a question as to the testimony of your own eyes. You are a native of Western India?—Yes.

You know the districts of Kaira and Neriad?—Yes.

You know the magnificent cultivation of Neriad?—Yes.

Do you know also the Plains of Kathiawar?—Yes.

Contrasting those two, do you think the conditions of prosperity in Neriad are smaller than those in the Native States of Kathiawar?—Well, is it fair to compare a very fertile portion of the country with a portion of the country which is not so fertile? Leaving that alone; I have been in Baroda; I know something of the condition of Baroda, of the condition of the people of Baroda, its revenue, having administered that for a year; and I know that the Baroda people are much better off than the people of the neighbouring territory.

Baroda, again, is a particularly rich territory?—Very well then, if you compare it.

That is exactly my point. Do you not think the comparative prosperity of the people depends as much on the fertility of the lands they have to cultivate as on the form of government ?—If it is a fertile region and the political condition is good it will be still happier, still better.

The advantage of the political condition is that they pay three times as much taxation ?—Yes, it all comes back to them, while in our case one-third does not.

I have shown that it does not all come back to them ?—The very fact that so much is raised from them, and all that comes back to them.

You forget you have admitted Europeans ?—Very few Europeans, that are not worth considering.

Loans are raised; tribute is paid ?—The tribute is very small compared with the resources.

Now, as to the capacity for taxation not being the result of any oppressive taxation ?—It is oppressive taxation, because they are unable to pay it.

Will you kindly wait until you are asked a question ?—Yes.

I wish to contrast the British system as regards the land revenue with the Native State system. Are you aware that the Famine Commission, after very carefully examining the question, and with every advantage in access to statistics, brought out that the incidence of the British land revenue was about 7 per cent. of the gross produce; are you aware of that? —I am not aware of it, but I would take it from you. I believe you; yes.

Are you also aware that the ordinary system in the Native States is that the State—the Native Ruler takes one-half of the gross produce. You see, then, there is a considerable advantage there on the side of the British subject ?—Yes, and yet all that advantage is lost on account of the system of the Government.

That is your assumption ?—I simply mention the fact that the half—I take that for granted—though I know that in the British assessment it is a great deal more than 7 per cent.; but I do not question that point. I take the fact as you have placed it, but the chief point is, that though they may take half of the produce, or more or less, the produce, remains in the country. It is enjoyed by the country, every part of it.

I have ventured to show you that it does not?—Very well, you may say so, and the difficulty is that the exception of just this little portion of tribute that they pay; it is not large at all or weighing upon them, and they are increasing in prosperity, so that this tribute is almost not worth thinking of; but the prosperity, consists in this, the difference in the two rules consist in this, that in one case every farthing, as in this country, although it pays nearly £100,000,000, but all that £100,000,000, come to the people; in the other case one-fourth or so goes to other people and not to the Indians. There is the point. Of other comparisons I have no complaint to make.

Do you consider the British land revenue to be oppressive to the people?—Their taxation, I consider, is oppressive, simply from this point of view, that it becomes oppressive. The people's capacity for payment becomes less and less every year.

And that it reduces the people to a state of starvation? —Just so; it does.

Would you allow me to read a part of a speech made in India by Sir Syed Ahmed Khan of Aligarh?—He has his own views, and I have my own views.

In the course of the last month?—Yes.

He says, "Two very large classes of the population consist of zemindars and peasants. The amount of attention that is now given to the welfare of the peasantry is unparalleled in any former Indian kingdom. In those provinces in which the East India Company made a permanent settlement of the land the enormous increase of the wealth of the zemindars has been such that it is unnecessary for me to enlarge on it, but I wish to say something about the land revenue system in the provinces in which there is no permanent settlement. If you will study old histories you will find that the mode of assessment adopted by this great empire is far lighter and milder than that adopted by fomer rulers. The most famous of former land settlements was instituted by Shere Shah, and perfected by Akbar, and I wish, in a few words, to explain the difference between that system and the present one, so that everyone may understand it. It is this, that in the former system Government took a share of the whole produce of a village, and under the present Government a share of the whole produce is not taken, but a share only of the surplus after the peasants have received their dues. Hence, everyone can see how light and easy is the land settlement even in these provinces in which there is no permanent settlement. No one can deny that under this good administration every species of property, and especially landed properties, has immensely increased in value. These landed properties, which were formerly a burden on their owners, are now a source of profit and wealth, of honour and social distinction. The income from property has increased tenfold, so that he who formerly got Rs. 10 now gets Rs. 100, and the owner of an estate worth Rs. 10,000 has property now worth a lakh"?—Yes; so I answer, first of all, the proportion of people to whom he refers is but infinitesimally small. The large mass of the people suffer. This is what we complain of, both from starvation and famine; but with regard to the system of assessment, I would take for granted that it is a good system, that the system adopted by the British is a better systsm than the old rulers had; but the whole mischief comes in this, that whether it was a bad system or a good system in their old Government, and under their own kings, every farthing produced was taken by the State and returned to them, it remained in the country. The evil of this foreign domination is that it drains the country of a portion every year unceasingly, and there the whole difficulty lies. If some proper suitable remedy were applied to reduce that to its minimum extent—a fair tribute—we do not then object to pay the tribute, as it were, just as the Native States pay; but that could be brought within such dimensions as would enable India to make capital, so as to be able to stand on the same footing as any other country; it would be all right. As I said in answer to former questions, I do not want to object to the system of rules that are adopted for the sake of good government. I accept them. The difficulty lies the economical condition of the foreign domination, and that must be reduced to its lowest possible mischief, which cannot but be incidental to a foreign domination.

I have pointed out to you that what you call the drain amounts to about one-fourth of a very low rate of taxation?—Very well.

And that about one-half of that in the year we took was paid by China. Now I want to ask you with regard to another point; there seems to be some misunderstanding as to the return of the price and profits of exports? Yes.

You seem to be under the impression that the British Indian subject does not get back his full price and profits of his export; that some part is retained somewhere?—That is this what is taken away from the country.

Will you let me now just put a case. Suppose that a British Indian subject in Ahmedabad, and a Native State subject in Kathiawar adjoining, each sent home cotton worth ten sovereigns?—Yes.

Each of those men gets the full value of his ten sovereigns in rupees paid to him, does he not?—Yes.

Then the British Indian subject is not deprived of any part of his ten sovereigns?—Yes; I will explain that. The British Indian subject, is sending his ten sovereigns worth of produce; that produce is here intercepted by the India Office in sending him a bill.

Not the produce, I think?—That produce is sold, and the agent for the sale of that produce pays the British Indian subject by an India Office bill, and sends it out there to be paid not from the price that it is got here from that produce, but from the revenues of India that are drawn upon to meet that bill which is kept here. That is to say it is paid from the revenue. It requires to be understood clearly.

We are all perfectly aware of that, Mr. Naoroji. It is a convenient fiscal expedient?—No.

Yes?—I would not interrupt you.

It is a convenient fiscal expedient?—Yes.

That is to say, the Secretary of State, wanting the gold here for the Home charges, takes from the merchant the gold price of the Indian produce and he gives the merchant an order on the Indian Treasury for an equivalent amount of rupees?—Yes.

Does that in any way affect the profit of the native producer and exporter in India ?—Of course its effect is this, that as much as is intercepted here by the India Office in sending their bills off that price of the produce, does not itself return to India, but in its place that price of the produce is paid out of British revenue which, in the case of the Native States, is quite different, he gets back actually the return.

It really amounts to this, does it not, that that small portion of the low taxation fund is paid at home for material and service supplied to India from England ?—Very well, we come back to that again.

I do not wish to go into that. That is the fact, whether you think the services are worth it or not is another question. I say it is paid for in material or service supplied to India ?—That is the whole of my complaint.

That is the whole transaction ?—That is the whole of my complaint.

The money might be sent home to India, but the money, the gold, is kept here and the silver is obtained for it in India ?—Which must be paid in some shape or other.

Does that affect the native exporter of the produce itself ?—No, the native exporter is not affected.

That is all I wish to know ?—But then, at the same time, it is misleading if you stop there.

I beg your pardon, I do not think it is at all misleading ?—I must give my full answer, that the native exporter receives his money from the Indian Exchequer and not the money which is actually got by the sale of the goods. The sale of the goods, which means, therefore, that so much of the produce of the country entirely went out of the country without that material return in the shape of produce or bullion or in any shape.

But in the shape of service or materials ?—Then that service comes in. The service does not give us a grain of rice more, but then the service in itself again is a further complaint, a further grievance of ours.

The question I was asking you was as to the profits of the native exporter, you will admit that he gets back the whole of these profits ?—He must get his value; but at the same time, he does not get it from his own proceeds, he gets it from Indian revenues.

Never mind?—That makes all the difference.

Not the slightest?—That is what I complain of; else, I have no complaint whatever. The native gets this, but then what he has sent here is never returned except in the shape of services.

It is simply a convenient arrangement?—It is not a convenient arrangement, it is an economic drain.

You have admitted that the Native State subject and the Indian subject each get their full equivalent of the £10?—The native must get his £10, but in the one case—

And out of the £10 the Native State subject pays 12 or 18 rupees of taxes, and the British Indian subject pays half a crown?—Yes, because the Native Indian subject does get back his full price of the produce that he has sent, all the £10; and the British Indian subject, that is to say British India as a body economically does not get his own £10. That makes all the differences.

I want to ask you a few questions as to the agency employed in exporting; that is to say, the foreign merchant. You are particularly hard on him are you not?—In what way?

You grudge him what he eats?—I do not grudge him anything.

You said of him "he eats what the Indian would eat if he did not eat it"?—That is the Indian not employed.

Oh no, the merchant?—The merchant or the non-official?

What is the merchant in India? What is his business. Does he not export raw produce?—Yes.

And import English goods in return?—Quite right.

His gains are what—the interest on the capital he employs in that business?—Yes.

Do you not think that that is a benefit to India?—Under a self-governing country, if we were a self-governing country, or at least governed in the way I am describing, we would welcome the merchant, because we would have our own resources daily employed, and the merchant would have so much more, and he is quite welcome to come in there and use his capital, and get any profit himself in the perfect free trade, but our position is that we are helpless, our capital is taken away from us, we cannot make any capital, and the foreign merchant or the foreign capitalist comes in. He has a full monopoly, as it were, of the resources of the country, he benefits by it, and we are simply the hewers of wood and the drawers of water to them. That makes an entirely different position in the economical condition of India.

Does the foreign merchant pay taxes in the country?—He may pay taxes. It is nothing, the small amount he pays. It is all very good.

Does he spend largely on living and employ labour, and so on?—Yes, to his profit.

Has he any privileged position at all?—No, the economic condition is the thing in all these things.

I find, however, in one of your remarks you suppose that he has a certain privilege?—Oh, yes, he has. I can understand what you mean.

I should like to ask you about that?—Yes.

You say here: "The position of the exploitation by the foreign capitalists is still worse than I have already represented. Not only do they exploit and make profits with their own capital but they draw even their capital from the taxation of the poor people themselves. So that the European merchants, bankers, etc., may have Indian taxes at their disposal, the profits of which, they may take away to their own country"? —Yes.

What does that mean?—I have explained it thereto.

Oh, I see?—If you read further on in explanation I have quoted Sir James Westland himself.

Allow me to read Sir James Westland?—Yes, if you please.

You say "The following words of Sir James Westland in "the telegram of 'The Times' of the 18th December last, will "explain what I mean. Sir James Westland then explained "how closely connected the money market of India is with "the Government balances, almost the whole of the available "capital employed in commerce practically being in those "balances. . . . A crore and-a-half, which under normal "conditions would have been at headquarters in Calcutta and

"Bombay, had been placed at the disposal of the mercantile "community for trading purposes," and so on. Is it possible that you have confused these two different things, that is, the loan of money out of taxes to foreign merchants for trading purposes, and the supply of the currency by the Government for the trade generally?—No, this is quite a different thing. This simply means this: that a portion of the taxation or the money raised by taxation is or would have been available, as he says, at the disposal of commerce, and that means, therefore, that a portion of the taxation goes into the Banks; from these Banks European merchants mainly draw their credit, and use that money for their own business, which in reality is supplied to them as a capital from the taxation of the people.

Do you mean to say that the Government lends the taxes to the foreign merchants?—No, the Government does not lend. The Government gives it to the Banks, there is a certain amount of balance kept into the Banks. The merchants get the benefit of it because the Banks do not put it in a stocking, and put it away saying, "there is Government money, it must remain there." They use it, they lend it: they make a profit out of it, and that means that it goes mostly to those who are in the commercial world.

Do you really suppose that that amounts to lending the taxes to the merchants?—It is so really.

Lending the taxes?—Because it is from the taxes that that money is deposited in the Banks; where does that money come from?

Well, we will leave it there. Now I should like to say a few words about the civil administration. You are even harder upon the civil administration than you are upon the foreign merchant?—How; in what way, let me see?

Well, I will quote a few of your phrases. "The European civil and military services are a burthen and a destruction to India"?—Yes.

"The European services are India's greatest evil." "The present forced, inordinate, and arbitrary employment of Europeans." "A charge forced upon India by sheer tyranny"?—Yes.

" It is the British Indian authorities who have made India what she is, bleeding at every pore, and a helotry for England." " The sovereign, the British people and Parliament have done their duty by laying down the true and righteous principles of dealing with India, but their desires and biddings are made futile by their servants, the Indian authorities "?—Yes.

Now do you mean to say that you really believe that the English authorities in India are at liberty to disobey and set at defiance the orders of the English Government?—Why, your own Viceroy has acknowledged it in so many terms. Lord Lytton in his private minute says distinctly that of the two ways of saying straightforward to the Indian people that we shall not do this, or that. Instead of that we have deceived the people; we have adopted (I think the words are) transparent, deliberate subterfuge in all these matters.

Have you got that paper ?—It is in the statements. I will read the part itself.

Have you got the paper you are quoting—Lord Lytton's?—I will read it.

Have you got the whole of his confidential minute ?—No such confidential minute.

Has it ever been published ?—I do not know. I will tell you. The extract was brought forward publicly, by a Speaker in the first—I think it was the first—meeting of the Congress. It is in the very first Congress. It has been in the public prints all this time—12 years—and it has never been contradicted.

It was a confidential paper pilfered from the Viceroy?—That I do not know. I have nothing to do with that.

Will you answer this question ? Was the purport of that paper in favour of a larger employment of Indians in offices in India ?—It would have been very good if it had been published. I do not know.

Was it so or not ?—I do not know. This is the only extract out of the Despatch which has became public some way or other.

Now let us return to the question before us?—

Will you give an instance of a great public measure, in which the Viceroy and the Government officials in India have thwarted and defied the wishes and the orders of the English Government ?—Yes.

Give it then ?—This very Act of 1833 has been left a dead letter up to the present moment.

That is not at all to the point ?—Yes, but I want to show that.

I want you to show me some great measure ?—This is the great measure.

In which the Anglo-Indian authorities, the English authorities in India have defied, and resisted, and obstructed a great measure which the English Government wished to give effect to in India ?—That is just what I am answering, that the greatest of all measures, our very emancipation as you may say, our great charter, the Act of 1833 has been kept a dead letter up to the present time.

But is it not the case that whatever has been done in that matter has been done under the orders of the Secretary of State and the English Government ?—Very well. It is no consolation to me whether it is the Secretary of State or the Government of India. When I am talking of the authorities I talk of both.

No ; I beg your pardon, I quoted this to show that you were speaking of the English in India of whom you complained ?—I speak of the English altogether.

I beg your pardon, it is not so ?—Whatever the——

They are the public servants, the Indian authorities ?—Yes, the Indian authorities ; but I mean, of course, the Indian authorities in both countries.

You say, "British Indian authorities and Anglo-Indians " generally obstructing at every point any step desired by the " British people for the welfare of the Indians ?"—Yes. There it is. This illustration.. This is confirmed by Lord Lytton himself. Then there is the admission by the Duke of Argyll, showing that we have not fulfilled our promises, and I could make out a statement if you like.

And you condemn both the Anglo-Indians and also the Government at home ?—Oh yes, both.

But the Government at home is responsible to Parliament?—Very well.

And Parliament represents the English people?—Yes; and Parliament has passed the Acts.

And do you mean to say that the Indian Government can refuse to obey or ever have refused to obey any order sent out to them from the Cabinet and the Secretary of State at home?—But there are the facts.

Where?—This Act of 1833 has been disobeyed entirely. The Act of 1870 was disobeyed for six years and every effort was made not to carry it out.

I have shown already that it was not disobeyed for six years and you admitted it?—Very well. Then, again, I give the authority also.

Will you kindly answer the question about that Statute of 1870?—Yes.

Is it not the fact that nothing could be done under that Act without the sanction of the Secretary of State?—My complaint is about the Secretary of State as much as about the Government of India.

You say it is the English authorities in India?—No, Indian authorities. I mean, if I have not expressed it properly, my complaint is more against the India Office than against the Government of India. To take for instance this Resolution that was passed for simultaneous examination, why the Secretary of State and the Government of India resisted to the tooth, and they would not have it, though the Resolution was passed by the House of Commons.

But they may be quite right in the opinion of the British Government?—That is another affair. As to the disobedience of the Government of India or the Secretary of State to a Resolution passed, this is the instance; really the reasons are there before you. Whether they are good reasons or bad reasons is not the question now.

You have shifted your ground. Your statements were made about the British Indian authorities, and I wish to know whether it is true that they can act in defiance of the home authorities?—No, I never meant such a thing. I mean both British and Indian authorities. I mean both authorities over

India; I have repeatedly stated that, as well as in this country.

Let that rest there?—Very well then.

You have condemned these European services in these strong terms, I want to call your attention to the sort of work that they have done in India?—Yes.

India is a great exporter of raw produce, is it not?—Yes.

And what a country of that nature requiries is to be opened up by railways?—Yes.

Up to last December the Government had opened 20,000 miles of railway?—Quite.

Did the natives of India take any great part in promoting those railways?—Simply because they have not got the means, their means are taken away.

That is what you say?—Yes, that is what I say. If the people were able to invest their money in those railways they would be only too glad to do it.

We have had that a great many times. Now, with regard to commerce, I will just read, and it is as good as anything for the purpose, the remarks of Mr. Playfair in the Chamber of Commerce in Calcutta this month. He says, speaking of Her Majesty's reign and the increase of Indian trade during Her Majesty's reign: "The combined value of exports and imports, including treasure, in 1837 amounted to about 19 crores; it now exceeds 200 crores. The capital invested in cotton mills, exceeds 13 crores, and in jute mills 4 crores. The cornfields yield 3,000,000 tons annually, while the zea crop is valued at 24 crores. The progress which the country has made in the 60 years, during which its resources have been developed, communication improved, law and order maintained, and the protection of life and property assured, was described, as lending lustre to the Queen's reign." Then I will quote a few figures relating to the last seven or eight years. In four provinces, being the Punjab, Madras, the Central Provinces and Lower Burma, for which exact figures happen to be available—the average cultivation—cultivated acres, in 1886-9 was 72,215,000, in 1893-5 the average acreage was 80,915,000. The value of some of the principal exports, cotton, rice, wheat, oil, jute, tea and indigo in 1881-5 the average was Rx. 54,000,000 in 1891-5 it was Rx. 73,000,000 ?—Yes.

You see the increase which has taken place in the figures which I have quoted ?—Yes. But all this I have fully explained in my statements.

Now you will naturally say that the taxation also has greatly increased ?—Well, we are going into a subject which requires very careful examination, both with regard to the taxation, and we are not going into taxation; I am not allowed to go into that by our reference, or I would have gone into it.

I am merely wishing to give you a few figures as to the great increase of taxation, which is probably a question in which you take an interest ?—Yes.

I was taking the Queen's reign as before. I find that between 1839 and 1840 the average yearly taxation, was 18 crores; in 1896-97 it is 65 crores ?—That does not show that there is a natural increase of prosperity, it has been new taxation.

No, on the contrary, I suppose it would *prima facie* show that there had been a heavy increase of taxation ?—Yes, heavy and crushing.

I wish you to look at one or two items. The land revenue has increased from Rx. 12,000,000 to Rx. 26,000,000, that is an increase right off of Rx. 14,000,000 ?—Well, it is not a great matter, after so many years of increasing assessment.

Of course there are new provinces which have been added ?—Yes.

And, as I have just shown, an enormous additional acreage has come under assessment ?—Yes.

For instance, it amounts, as I have shown you, to 8,000,000 acres in 7 years in four provinces only ?—Yes. There is an increase of population also.

Then in opium there is an increase of from Rs 784,000 to Rx. 7,123,000 ?—Yes.

That 6,000,000 is got from China, as we have already agreed. In customs there is an increase of Rx. 4,000,000 and in excise an increase of Rx. 6,000,000 ?—Yes.

That is upon strong liquor generally ?—Yes.

In stamps there is an increase of 4,000,000 ?—Yes.

I suppose in none of those things would you find a specimen of "crushing taxation grinding India to the dust "?—How has that taxation increased? The nature of the taxation, the principles upon which it has enhanced that has to be considered and examined before you give any judgment upon these.

I have just been accounting for the increase of land revenue ?—Yes.

The increase of Chinese tribute ?—Yes.

And so on ?—Well, what I say is that the increase in the land revenue is an increased oppression; well, without going into the character and the examination of the increase of this land revenue, unless we go into a thorough examination of the way in which it has increased and the other increases, we cannot form a judgment generally that it is all favourable, because a more high figure is not necessarily good. We are precluded by our reference from going into taxation.

I have shown you that in 10 years there was an increase of over 8,000,000 acres in four provinces?—Yes, and there is an increase of population also.

Which came under assessment ?—Yes.

So that it is the growth of cultivation which largely accounts for the increase of the land revenue and also the increase of territory ?—All this require examination, which the Commission cannot go into.

But I think you know that as a fact?—If it is a fact we must go into it, and we cannot go into it here.

There is one item which I have not noticed, and which you have not noticed also—salt. The increase during the Queen's reign has been from Rx. 2,696,745 to Rx. 8,861,845 ?—Yes, by what increase of rate.

An increase of 6 millions of Rx.? Yes, and there is an increase in the rate of taxation.

That, I suppose, you would consider as an instance of heavy additional taxation ?—Yes, it is additional taxation, and it is more crushing to the poor people that it should ever be taxed at all.

It is a poor man's tax ?—It is the poor man's tax; he is not able to pay any tax. He is starving, he is dying off at the slightest touch, living on insufficient food.

The incidence of the salt tax has been lightened and not made more heavy during the last 30 or 40 years. Do you know that fact?—There is no need of doubting anything; if the fact is a fact you can put it here before the Commission. There is no need of doubting it. All I know is that there are 6,000,000 or 7,000,000 raised from salt, which is one of the most objectionable taxes that can be put upon these poor, wretched people.

The question is whether there is a crushing and increasing burden of taxation, crushing the life out of the people?—That is what I consider.

I wish to show that this salt tax, which is the most open to objection, is actually lighter than it was 30 or 40 years ago?—If it is actually lighter than that was 30 or 40 years ago, that is no consolation. It was very heavy.

Do you know what the price of a pound of salt is in India? I know in my own time what the price of salt was. I, myself, as a little boy, used to go to the salt store and used to buy it far cheaper than it is now.

Do you know what the price of salt is—a pound of salt?—Yes.

Well, what is it?—It is a tax added to its cost of production.

What is the price of a pound of salt in India?—I do not know the exact figure; I can find it out very easily.

I only wanted to know whether you knew?—I do not know just now; I cannot tax my memory immediately.

The price of a pound of salt in India is something over ½*d*; it is ·68 of a penny. The price of salt in London is ·75 of a penny; so that it is dearer in London than it is in India?—Yes, it is much worse for the Indians than in London, because the people have not the means of paying. Lord Cromer said, when talking of this: You say that one anna—it only costs one anna, or the addition is one anna; do you mean to say that one anna is not a matter of concern to people who are so extremely poor?

I quite agree with you that that is perfectly evident?—It is perfectly evident.

This is really the only tax the poor man pays?—They are not capable of paying it. They are starving, as you know.

I wish to point out the nature of the salt tax in India. It is generally looked upon as a rather arbitrary tax. The real fact in India is, is it not, that the Government sells the salt to the people?—Yes.

And charges a certain duty—at present 2 rupees 8 annas a maund, in addition to the cost price of production?—Yes.

With the result that, while the salt supplied is of very excellent quality—far better than it used to be—the price at which the salt is sold is less than it was 40 years ago; that is all I wish to bring out?—Yes, but all I wish to say is that, notwithstanding that, these people are so wretched that they cannot get enough of salt for themselves and for their cattle.

That is what you say?—Well, those are the facts.

Now, with regard to what you call the minimum which you want to sweep away—the minimum civil administration—you call it inordinate; "forced inordinate and arbitrary employment of Europeans"?—It is arbitrary because we have no voice in it.

Of course not?—Yes.

Are you aware that the higher administrative body, the Indian Civil Service, consists of less than 1,000 persons, of whom about 60 are natives?—Yes.

You grant that?—I know that.

Do you think that a large proportion for managing 300,000,000 of people?—It is the amount of money which is paid to them, and the economic effect of the large amount of money which is paid to them. It is not simply the men.

You think that too many?—Yes, certainly. It is the very cause of the whole grievance.

You would sweep them all away?—No, I would not sweep them all away. You may have your Viceroys and Governors, and a few Heads of Departments to have your whole control. There is no necessity for having this 1,000 Europeans.

Let us go on to the next official rank; the middle rank—Sub-Judges and Magistrates, and that class. I take the figure of the Public Service Commission Report, that is sufficiently near; the number of persons is 2,558?—Yes.

Of these 35 were Europeans?—Very well.

Thirty-five were domiciled Europeans, 104 were Europeans permanently resident in India and Eurasians?—Yes.

When you get to the next rank below that the whole are natives?—Of course all the lower places are given to Indians, because they cannot help it. It is at these low salaries Europeans could not be employed.

It is not necessary to attribute motives. I suppose it is a fact, is it not?—It is a fact. I do not say it is not, but it is the higher salaries that it takes away.

Are there Native Judges on the Benches of the High Court?—There are some few.

Are there Native Judges on the Benches in each High Court?—Yes.

Are there native gentlemen in the Legislative Councils?—Yes, that has nothing to do with the economical condition, and they do not get anything.

Are there Native Judges on the District Benches?—Yes, on the District Benches. Do you mean what are called District Judges, and who can be only employed from the Civil Service?

Yes?—Well, there are a few that, being entered into the Civil Service, are necessarily District Judges.

The Provincial Service comprises a considerable number of the district judgeships, which have been handed over to them in order that natives may be employed?—It is yet to be seen whether this Provincial Service which has destroyed the Statutory Service will fill up its place. We have been deprived of something like 200 situations given to us in the Civil Service by the introduction of this, what is called the Provincial Service; we lost instead of gained by it.

Would you take it from me, that in the North-West Provinces now, or very recently, two district judgeships having been placed in the provincial list, there are four native gentlemen filling the appointment of District Judge?—I am very glad, so far we have made very little progress but the progress would have been far greater had the Act of 1870 been kept intact, and the number of additions which was a partial instalment, what was given to us on my petition through the

East India Association by Sir Stafford Northcote. If that had been loyally and faithfully carried out by this time we should have had a much larger number.

Will you answer me this question? Has the general tendency of the British Government been to increase or decrease the employment of natives in public offices?—Well, there are two opinions upon it, and, of course, we are obliged to remain on general belief. There is an opinion prevalent in India among the Indians that wherever they can introduce an European they try to do it, notwithstanding the Despatch of Sir Stafford Northcote referred to, with regard to 200 rupees of salary, namely, that any appointment of 200 rupees of salary, or above that salary, should not be given as far as possible to an European, but to an Indian, except with the consent of the Secretary of State. But the actual practice, so far as I have heard, has been that situations are given to Europeans. The Secretary of State's consent is taken, and that really and properly speaking the Despatch is a dead letter, in which Sir Stafford Northcote had put very strong grounds. I have not got that Despatch, or I should have been glad to read it.

Do you know that in 1880 the recruitment for the Civil Service was decreased by one-sixth, in order to make room for natives?—For the Act of 1870.

Quite so?—But unfortunately then for 10 years there was such a deal of opposition to it, some way or other, that it was cut away.

What was cut away?—This one-sixth, had you gone on adding this one-sixth we should have been very glad.

I beg your pardon, the decrease of the Civil Servants has not been abolished?—The Statutory Service does not exist.

But the Provincial Service has taken its place?—The substitution of the Provincial Service was actually a loss to us from what was the Statutory Service.

I do not admit that at all. You have got the whole of the statutories so far?—That is so. Those that had been passed; but none after that—after that year.

Of course not?—The year 1838 or 1889.

The Provincial Service has been substituted?—The Provincial Service has been substituted on a different scale altogether.

The Provincial Service has been substituted ?—There was no reason why it should be substituted. The Statutory Service was a great gain to us, as an instalment, and as a part of the Civil Service. Had you gone on adding that one-sixth to the service every year in 30 years, 210 situations in the service would have been held by Indians in what is the Indian Civil Service.

A statutory civilian does not hold a position in the service, he is simply put into some appointment. He is not a member of the Indian Civil Service ?—That was the interpretation put upon it. The Act was passed in reference to our petition, and it was simply and solely an integral part of the Civil Service. The only difference was that—

Where is that, is it in the Act ?—Oh yes, the 6th Clause says that distinctly.

What does it say ?—That instead of Indians being required to come and pass their examination here, to get into the Civil Service—

That is not in the Statute of 1870 ?—Yes, the service, the Statutory Service is a wrong name given to it. Why the Civil Service itself is the Statutory Service, the whole of it.

There is not a word of that in the Statute; the Statute simply says that in order to increase the promotion of natives of approved merit and ability, a native may be appointed to any post without restriction ?—Yes, and then a certain portion is fixed, is it not.

No ?—A certain portion—one-sixth—or something of that sort is fixed.

No ?—And then the speeches will illustrate very largely what the Act says.

No; you are quite mistaken ?—One-sixth was prescribed in order that so many appointments should be made every year for the Civil Service.

Was that in the Act ?—Whether it is in the Act, or whether it is in the despatch, I am not able to say just now.

It is not in the Act; I have sent for the Act ?—We shall see the Act. If it is not, some way or other the rule was adopted, in fact, by the Government from 1880, I think as you said.

It was in 1880?—And they fixed a proportion of six and seven, say six and seven every year. Well, there, they at least made it as the proportion in which they should be nominated every year. What it ought to have been would have been that by a good strong test of competition they should have been selected. Instead of that they were nominated by the Government, and the whole of the statutory service was discredited in that manner. It does not exist now, and the provincial service was substituted for it which the Government of India was determined to have as early as 1877 or 1878. They did not then get it, and they at last got it by their own way.

You are aware that the statutory civilians are young gentlemen of good birth and station?—Yes, but they were not competent.

And that was found on the whole not to answer?—Yes.

And therefore the Statutory Service was abolished?—Yes.

And what promised to be a better system was substituted for it?—No, but there is an injustice done to the Statutory Service.

We need not go into that; that is another question?—Then what is the good of putting your question to me; I must answer that question.

The injustice done to the Statutory Service has nothing to do with the question?—Yes, because you referred to the Statutory Service just now, and said it was found unsatisfactory; but the reason was, that the Statutory Service was introduced in a way which was sure to fail; instead of simply going to have boys belonging to good families, one essential and most important necessity was that they should have been first found and tested as competent to hold such places. Well, that was not done.

Quite so. It was right to do away with such a system, was it not?—Yes; but then that system should not have been introduced. Well, at least, this was the suspicion in the mind of the Indians, that these rules were adopted without the test of competence, and that it was the object of the Government to throw discredit upon it and to try to get rid of it.

Do you attribute such a motive as that?—I do not attribute it myself; but that is the general feeling, and also this is a fact, that this is a general feeling among the Indians, that the rules were made, whether intentionally or unintentionally—the rules were not such as they ought to have been made.

I will read part of the Statute of 1870, Section 6. "Whereas it is expedient that additional facilities should be given for the employment of natives of India, of proved merit and ability, in the Civil Service of Her Majesty in India: Be it enacted that nothing in the 'Act for the Government on India,' 21 & 22 Vict. c. 106, or in the 'Act to confirm certain appointments in India and to amend the Law concerning the Civil Service 'there,' 24 & 25 Vict. c. 54, or in any other Act of Parliament or other law now in force in India, shall restrain the authorities in India by whom the appointments are or may be made to offices, places, and employments in the Civil Service of Her Majesty in India from appointing any native of India to any such office, place, or employment, although such native shall not have been admitted to the said Civil Service of India in manner in Section 32 of the first-mentioned Act provided, but subject to such rules as may be from time to time prescribed, by the Governor-General in Council, and sanctioned by the Secretary of State in Council, with the concurrence of a majority of members present; and that for the purposes of this Act the words 'natives of India' shall include any person born and domiciled within the dominion of Her Majesty in India, of parents habitually resident in India, and not established there for temporary purposes only; and that it shall be lawful for the Governor-General in Council to define and limit from time to time the qualifications of natives thus expressed; provided that every Resolution made by him for such purpose shall be subject to the sanction of the Secretary of State in Council, and shall not have force until it has been laid for 30 days before both Houses of Parliament?"—Those rules were made, which were unsatisfactory altogether. Unfortunately the Secretary of State, when the rules were made, did not pay attention to those rules, and they were unsatisfactory to us.

What you said about one-sixth and all that is not in the Statute ?—I will find out.

You did not find it in the Statute ?—I cannot lay my hand upon it at once, but the best proof of that is that the Government of India actually adopted a certain proportion, whether it was by a despatch from the Secretary of State for India or whether it was the Government of India's own decision I am not prepared to say, but there was the fact.

Are you aware of what were called the rules of 1879 ?—What are they, and what about them ?

The rule of 1879 was that in this intermediate or middle body of officials, subordinate magistrates and judges and so on, no European should be appointed to a place of 200 rupees and upwards if a native could be found fit to hold it ?—Yes.

Now was that provision in favour of the appointment of natives to that class ?—Yes, it was, for the lower class.

At the same time that one-sixth was deducted from the recruitment of the Civil Service ?—Yes, that was an independent provision.

Was not that in the direction of giving larger employment to natives ?—Then I have to ask that question, if you would kindly supply it to us—how many appointments have been made since that time ?

Since what time ?—Since the time that that despatch was written, that no appointment at 200 rupees salary should be given as far as possible, to Europeans, but to Indians, except with the consent of the Secretary of State ; I never have been able to get the information.

I can personally testify that the rule has been most rigidly observed ?—Very well, I am very glad to hear that, but I can tell you that the general impression among us is that it has not been strictly carried out.

That may be ?—And the Secretary of State has sanctioned, of course, whatever the Government of India said, and all such situations have not been given ; there was one complaint from Madras, if I remember rightly, of such an appointment which was irregular, and the Secretary of State actually put it back.

I have no doubt; that confirms what I say?—But I should be very glad indeed to be satisfied that that is done.

Might I put another point to you?—Yes.

The admission of natives to high offices has always been conditional, in a certain sense, from the first. For instance, in the Act of 1833 it is said that no native shall be excluded from office on account of his religion or his place of birth?—Yes.

It does not say that he is to be admitted to office on account of his religion?—He is not to be excluded; therefore he ought to have been given equal facilities.

Allow me to go on. In the Queen's Proclamation we find "that, so far as may be, Our subjects, of whatever race or creed, be freely and impartially admitted to offices in Our service, the duties of which they may be qualified, by their education, ability and integrity, duly to discharge?—Yes. quite right; that is all we ask.

Then when you get to the Statute of 1870, it provides for the promotion of natives of approved merit and ability?—True.

So you see the Government always has the same difficult task of deciding, in any case, whether a native candidate is qualified by education, ability, and experience for any particular office? Yes.

And that makes a considerable difficulty in carrying out the Statute of 1870?—There can be no difficulty whatever if the Government is determined to do it, for they have only to lay down the standard.

But they are determined to do it, and they have done so?—They have not done so. That is my complaint.

They have tried various expedients, and are now trying one which they hope will succeed?—They have not tried the right expedient.

That is your opinion?—That is what I point out to you. The expedient is just as they have done here; they ought to have laid down rules according to which the Indian candidates are examined, and whether physical, mental, or moral, there is the standard laid down there. Well, according to that standard, those Englishmen who come to that standard are elected in the same manner. Have the regular standard as high as you like, either mentally, morally, or physically; put it forward, and then let them come forward without any disabilities of being compelled to come to this distant country. Let them have equal facilities. We do not want anything more; we do not want any favouritism or any concession, but, let us all be treated exactly on the same footing, and on the same standard and then if we fail the fault will be ours. Let us have simultaneous examination upon the very same standard.

That is your view of the matter?—I can only give my view.

I want to ask you, generally, what it is that you want; do you wish to sweep away the whole English Civil Service?

I think when Mr. Naoroji says again and again that he does not wish to do it that he should not be asked this question.

I want to know what he says.

Mr. Chairman, I do not think, when Mr. Naoroji has only made a statement of that sort, it is a fair question.

I asked him whether he wishes to sweep away the whole Civil Service in India, which he describes as the destruction of India and its greatest evil?—Yes, as it is.

I want to know whether he wishes to get rid of it bodily?—There you misunderstand me. What I lay down in my fifth pamphlet, what I considered as the best means of governing India, is suggested by Lord Salisbury and Lord Iddesleigh themselves.

What proportion would you keep?—There is no proportion there; there you have first of all Native States, and that supreme power should be maintained there a certain contribution from all the States, just to keep a certain reasonable amount of the European Army; and in each Native State, as we will call it, you will have a political agent who will have a complete control over the work—call him a Governor, call him a subordinate, call him anything you like; this will supply the double purpose both of maintaining the supremacy in a very remarkable and in a very efficient manner, and that the same time the people will feel that they are governed by themselves.

I merely wish to ask whether you propose to retain any part of the Civil Service?—The European service? Only the highest portion, such as the Viceroy, the Governors, the Commander-in-Chief, leaving the Military alone if we are talking of the Civil Service, and the Lieutenant-Governors, or you may go one grade below as a beginning. Now I do not mean to say that all the Europeans are to be turned out; let there be, as in Mysore, gradually every European place being supplied by the Indian, till at last you come to these highest places which are really not the places of the Civil Service; let us have the whole Civil Service, leaving alone all the high level to Europeans as the controlling power. That I have always said.

Then you would have the Viceroys, the Governors, and the Lieutenant-Governors?—Lieutenant-Governors; these certainly.

No Englishmen beneath them?—I do not see any necessity for others; even if you go one grade lower for the sake of regularity in a practical way, you may begin with, say, one-half the Civil Service should be given to the Indians, and let the number be reduced from 1,000, as you said, to 500 or 400; that by itself would be a great relief.

And by degrees you would evict them all?—Then we may go on gradually higher up.

Then tell me about the Army; what would you do about that—the British Troops?—I am quite willing to say that Lord Roberts put it very properly: He says we have an Army, and he praised, that Army. I have not the least objection to that praise, but he said that after all the real strength of the British Rule depends upon the contentment of the people. If the people were contented, and if they are at your back, no matter when Russia or five Russias come to invade India; if the people are at your back you can raise an Army sufficient even to drive away Russia to St. Petersburg. But I am just going further—I am quite willing to allow that a certain portion of the British Army is absolutely necessary for the purpose of benefiting both England and India. Let there be a fair proportion of expenses divided between the two countries, because the European soldier of the European Army is wanted, especially for the sake of the British Rule. We grant that the continuance of the British Rule is also a benefit to us, and therefore we do not want to object to the European Army to a reasonable extent, and I will show that afterwards. Let the British people pay a share of it. Now, with regard to the whole Army, I do not see it is necessary. The number that was at the time of the transference to the Queen, say about 30,000 or say 40,000, may very well be kept, say, up to 40,000, and half share must be paid by the British on account of the mutual benefit for common purposes, and if the other plan is adopted of Native States being formed out of them, they contribute what share would be considered as reasonable as for common purposes, and then the whole thing will be as natural and as worthy of the English name and the English fame as can possibly be.

Yes. You heard Lord Ripon say that his Government had considered the question most carefully?—Yes. Very well.

And had arrived at the conclusion that the proportion necessary to maintain is one English soldier to two natives?—Yes because it is on account of the fear that is entertained that the soldiers cannot be depended upon; it is the fear of the people.

Of the soldiers?—I mean of the Indian soldier; it is the fear of the Indian soldier. We propose then—it is a question merely whether you are to act upon fear or upon confidence. If you act upon fear then there is no help; then, at least, you must pay a proper proportion for keeping such an European Army as you think necessary on account of that fear.

If you had a very small European Army do you think that you would have the means of preventing two sections of the Indian Army fighting one another, Mohammedans and Hindus for instance?—Again we are going back to the first proposition.

I said with a very small European Army?—Have that confidence in the people and the people will side with you and will regard it as your and their own interest.

I am not speaking of the people siding with you, but of the people fighting among themselves?—The people fighting among themselves is quite a different thing altogether from the Imperial purpose of keeping up the supremacy of the British Rule which, first of all, necessitates this employment of Europeans to an inordinate extent. If you, say that a certain amount of European Troops are necessary it is always from fear that the Indian Army will not behave properly. I am willing to grant the fear, and whatever they consider as the necessity either of the protection or the fear of the Indian soldier going wrong at any time, very well, all this arises from the necessity of maintaining British Rule in India and British Empire in the East. Well, therefore, I say that granting that an irreducible minimum, as Lord Ripon called it, granting that that is absolutely necessary, without controverting that point, I say that it is for the benefit of both, and therefore a share must be paid by the British Treasury. That is granting all the necessity that the British rulers may consider necessary to have Europeans there.

What I wanted to bring before you was this; suppose the English Civil Administration is reduced to half a dozen men, and the English Army is reduced to——?—Say 40,000.

Would England be able to keep the warlike races of India from invading the peaceful ones?—The warlike races of India have been there for thousands of years, the peaceful ones have been there for thousands of years, and the people themselves and they have not disappeared. They are now even perishing by millions. Take for instance, Europe, civilised highly advanced countries, they are armed to the teeth, one spark will throw them we do not know where.

But the history of India is that the people have been continually slaughtering each other?—What have you done here; what is the history of Europe? We do not want to go back, because we have learnt as you have learnt.

Is your receipt for reviving the prosperity of India to let loose the Pindaris?—Not necessarily; those days are gone; you have now introduced, and perhaps that is one reason that I say that your supremacy must remain there in a way in which the interest of every Native State will be to take care of itself and will therefore depend more upon you, and you will be more secure, you see. I have proposed my plan, and I do not want to go beyond my plan.

Do you remember what Sir Madava Rao, Prime Minister of Baroda, said to Lord Roberts on the subject of India for the Indians?—What did he say? I do not know.

He said it would be like loosing the bars of the cages of the Zoological Gardens and letting out the animals, that very soon they would all be dead except the tiger—the tiger was, I believe, the warlike people of Northern India?—Is this the result of 150 years of British Rule that we are not so civilised enough to observe law and order?

It would be the result of the suspension of British Rule?—The result of British Rule that we are yet unfit for law-abiding people?

Now, Mr. Dadabhai Naoroji, we have kept the Commission a long time. You and I are agreed on certain propositions—that it is a disadvantage—however inevitable it may be—that, people, or a continent of people, should be under the supreme control of foreigners who cannot, from the nature of the Indian climate, be permanently amalgamated with the Indian people, and that in those circumstances it is the duty of the Supreme Power to be careful that the cost of Government should not be unduly heavy on a poor population, and that natives of India should be admitted freely to all public offices for which they are fit?—Yes.

But we differ in that I have some regard to facts and possibilities, while you, as I think, indulge in visions and certainly in a great deal of strong condemnatory language. Do you not think that, considering the facts to which I have called your attention, and the evidence before the Commission, when you describe the Government of India as a selfish and despotic tyranny, crushing India to the dust by cruel and reckless taxation administered by the Civil and Military Services, which are the destruction of India and its greatest evil, when you describe Lord Elgin, Lord Lansdowne, Lord Dufferin, Lord Ripon, Lord Lytton, Lord Mayo, and Lord Canning as the agents of this selfish and despotic tyranny, defying and thwarting the desires and bindings of the British people and Parliament, so that India is bleeding at every pore and a helotry for England, do you not think you are, shall we say, somewhat overstating your case?—First of all, the words "poor people" is assumed there, or at least you understand it as if it is an actual natural necessary incident of the people; they are poor because of the system. When you make me say that Lord Mayo and Lord So-and-So and all the Viceroys and the Secretary of State are the agents of this tyranny—there, I say, I am misunderstood. They are merely working in a system which is evil and bad; they are working in a system; how far it is their fault, or their agent, it is quite a different thing. It is the system that is bad, and that makes very good men work on wrong lines, and therefore the result is that, on account of this foreign system, without giving the people of India such a position in its own Government as would make them prosperous, and, at the same time, benefit Britain, in that my complaint lies. The way in which you have put it just now is certainly unjust and unfair to me.

*. Well, I quoted your own words, and I will leave it there. We will now pass on to the question of the apportionment of the charge?—Yes.

Will you tell us what your suggestions or propositions will be upon that head?—Yes, my propositions are—(1) That it is the desire of the British people that British Rule should be one of justice and righteousness, for the benefit of both India and Britain, and not for the benefit of Britain only to the detriment of India, and that the financial relation in apportionment of charge should be as those between two partners, and not as those between master and slave. (2) That upon this equitable basis the apportionment of expenditure in which Britain and India are jointly interested should be according to extent of the interest, and according to capacity to pay. (3) That the creation and maintenance of British Imperial supremacy in India is a British interest of the first magnitude; yet, with a few exceptions, India has been unjustly charged with the whole cost of creating and maintaining the British Imperial supremacy, without Britain paying any portion, and without India being allowed to share in the advantages connected with that supremacy. (4) That law and order are beneficial to India, but they are also British interest, as a condition essential to the very existence and prosperity of British Rule. (5) That, assuming, as it is said, that India should bear all those charges for internal and external protection, which she would have to bear if British Rule did not exist, she should not bear the special cost of European agency so far as used solely to maintain British supremacy. And, moreover, that if British Rule did not exist, everyone employed will be an Indian and not an European. (6) That, as a practical arrangement, Britain should pay for all British employed in Britain, that India, should pay for all Indians employed in India, and that as regards British employed in India and Indians employed in Britain, there should be an equitable apportionment, according to respective benefit, and capacity to pay. To put it still more moderately, the payments to Europeans in both countries may be divided half-and-half between Britain and India. (7) That in the Army, Navy, and Civil Service, public employment, with its advantages and emoluments, should be proportioned to the charge; and in considering this point it should be borne in mind that in India Government employment monopolises in great part the sphere of private enterprise and the open professions as practised in Britain. (8) That the wars carried on beyond the Indian frontier of 1858 are, as stated by Lord Salisbury, "An indivisible part of a great Imperial question," and that therefore the cost should primarily be borne by the Imperial Exchequer, India contributing a fair share on account of, and in proportion to, indirect and incidental benefits accruing to her, and direct share in the Services. (9) That from April 1882 to March 1891, nearly Rx. 129,000,000 were spent from Indian revenues beyond the western and north-western frontiers of India, for avowedly Imperial purposes, and that a fair share of this amount should be refunded from the Imperial Exchequer, and similarly for the cost of the Burmese war.

Where do you get that 129 millions?—There is a return made.

What is the reference?—Return East India Military Expenditure beyond the frontier, No. 91 of 1895.

Perhaps you would just hand it to me. (Return handed in.)

Quite so. Would you go on?—Colonel H. B. Hanna in his book No. 3 "Backwards or forwards" gives at page 40 a table, and makes the total about Rs. 714,500,000, out of which the British Exchequer paid £5,000,000, towards the expenses of the Afghan war. Besides this amount he points out several omissions. I may put in this table with his remarks thereon in Chapter III.

Are there any further papers you would like to put in?—I desire to put in my correspondence with the War Office, the Admiralty, and the Civil Service Commissioners. In this I claim that neither the War Office nor the Admiralty had any authority or power to exclude Indians from the commissioned ranks.

What was the origin of this correspondence of yours with these three departments?—Questions were put in the Commission whether Indians were admissible in the Civil Service in this country, and, then I put a question or two, I think to Admiral Kennedy with regard to the admission of Indians in the Naval service. The answers were not quite positive and I thought proper to communicate with these three departments and find out exactly what the real condition is, and that made me carry on this correspondence which I am now putting before you.

It is quite irrelevant to our subject, your correspondence?—The employment of the service?

I am anxious to know what the object was, because the Commission must hereafter consider whether the correspondence is a correspondence which they would care to publish; therefore I will ask you what was the outcome of the correspondence—let me take first of all the Civil Service Commissioners?—The Commissioners have replied positively that the Civil Service is open to all the Indians in this country, excepting, of course, that they must come over here to be examined.

Yes?—Upon which I have put a short note saying that while for the Civil Service here every facility is given to the candidate, by examinations in Edinburgh and Dublin, that Indians should be compelled to come here for their examinations for service in their own country was not fair or just. That is a note that I have attached to it.

Your point there is that in order to qualify or to obtain admittance to the Civil Service in India, Indian gentlemen have to come over here to be examined?—Yes.

Did I not gather from some questions and answers that passed between Sir James Peile and yourself that there has been a Statute passed to enable Indian gentlemen to be admitted on certain conditions to the Civil Service in India without coming over here?—Yes, a portion of them.

I thought I also understood from Sir James Peile that the principle involved in that arrangement has been consistently carried out.

With regard to that appointment of natives in India, Yes? —What I meant to say is, that there is a Statute prescribing these appointments of a portion of the Civil Service, and rules were made and appointments were made; but after some nine or ten years that is abolished, so that the Statute is a dead letter now.

Then, in fact, the point at issue between you and the Civil Service Commissioners was that you object to the Indian candidates for appointments to the Indian Civil Service being brought over here?—Yes; that was not the correspondence; it is my note upon the reply that for the English Civil Service they are eligible.

They are eligible?—They are eligible; that is distinctly pointed out, which was doubtful.

May I also ask the upshot of the correspondence with the Admiralty?—The Admiralty—I was obliged to put the last interpretation myself, that in the commissioned offices Indians will not be admitted, and so is the reply also of the War Office. I discussed that the authority by which they had any power to make appointments did not authorise them to exclude the Indians positively and distinctly from these services.

But you say that the Regulations of the War Office and the Admiralty do exclude Indians?—They do exclude Indians —the War Office—which I demur to.

They do not specifically do it, but they say that it rests with the authorities here to say who is to be admitted.

They are not barred by Statute, but by Regulation?—No; the War Office regulations distinctly exclude them.

They do not mention natives ?—Oh yes, distinctly.

You think so ?—Oh yes ; the correspondence states it.

My recollection was that they reserved the power to say who was eligible ?—That is what I wanted to know from them; the Admiralty fenced with me in that respect and would not give me a decided answer, but the War Office regulations are clear; they are given to me there distinctly they must be Europeans or Europeans naturalised; any others are entirely excluded, and then the Admiralty replied that their rules were something like or approximately.

Would you read the passage in the War Office letter on which you build that conclusion ?—Oh yes, I will read it; "I am to acquaint you, in reply, that candidates for admission in the British Army must be of pure European descent, and are also required to be British-born or naturalized British subjects ; that is the Regulation."

I thought that had been altered ?—This is the latest I have got.

That is about a year ago, is it not? What is the date of that letter?—The date of this is the 10th June, 1896; they have not given us any further information. The correspondence is carried on up to the present day; there is a reply still standing which they have not yet given. Since that a good deal of correspondence has taken place, but they have never modified that.

You have referred to Mysore State. Are you able to develope and illustrate the views which are put forward as to government by the Native States ?—Yes. With regard to the Native States I agree with Lord Salisbury when he says: "The general concurrence of opinion of those who know India best is that a number of well-governed small Native States or in the highest degree advantageous to the development of the political and moral condition of the people of India." And Lord Iddesleigh similarly said: "Our Indian policy should be founded on a broad basis. There might be difficulties; but what we had to aim at was to establish a system of Native States which might maintain themselves in a satisfactory relation." Again, we should endeavour, as far as possible, to develop the system of native government to bring our native talent and statesmanship, and to enlist in the cause of Government all that was great and good in them." Entertaining these ideas, Lord Iddesleigh practically carried them out in restoring Mysore, on the distinct basis that "at once offered a guarantee for the good government of the people and for the security of British rights and interests," as I have already stated.

What advantages do you think would accrue from this arrangement?—The advantages from this arrangement will be these: The obvious conclusion is that the only natural and satisfactory relations between an alien supremacy and the people of India can be established on this basis alone. There are these obvious advantages in these relations. The British Supremacy becomes perfectly secure and founded upon the gratitude and affection of the people, who, though under such Supremacy would feel as being under their own rulers, and as being guided and protected by a mighty supreme power. Every State thus formed, from the very nature of its desire for self preservation, will cling to the supreme power as its best security against disturbance by any other State. The division in a number of States becomes a natural and potent power for good in favour of the stability of the British Supremacy. There will be no temptation to any one State to discard that supremacy, while, on the other hand, the Supreme Government, having complete control and power over the whole Government, of each State, will leave no chance for any to go astray. Every instinct of self-interest and self-preservation of gratitude, of high aspirations, and of all the best parts of human nature, will naturally be on the side and in favour of British Supremacy which gave birth to these States. There will be an emulation among them to vie with each other in governing in the best way possible, under the eye and control of the Supreme Government on their actions, leaving no chance for mis-government. Each will desire to produce the best Administration Report every year. In short, this natural system has all the elements of consolidation of British power, of loyalty, and stability, and of prosperity of both countries. The result of this arrangement, in the case of Mysore, has been most satisfactory from all sides. For the result in Mysore, I give a short statement from the Mysore Report of 1st October, 1895. Of the work of the late Maharaja from 1881 till his death at the end of 1894, it would be enough for me to give a very brief statement from the late address of the Dewan, to the Representative Assembly held at Mysore on 1st October, 1895, on the results of the late Maharaja's administration during nearly 14 years of his reign, as nearly as possible in the Dewan's words. The Maharaja was invested with power on 25th March, 1881. Just previous to it, the State had encountered a most disastrous famine, by which a fifth of the population had been swept away, and the State had run into a debt of 80 lakhs of rupees to the British Government. The cash balance had become reduced to a figure insufficient for the ordinary requirements of the administration. Every source of revenue was at its lowest, and the severe retrenchments which followed had left every Department of State in an enfeebled condition. Such was the beginning. It began with liabilities exceeding the assets by Rx. 307,500, and with an annual income less than the annual expenditure by Rx. 12,500. Comparing 1880—1 with 1894—5, the annual revenue rose from Rx. 1,030,000 to Rx. 1,805,000, or 75·24 per cent., and after spending on a large and liberal scale on all works and purposes of public utility, the net assets amounted to over Rx. 1,760,000 in 1894—5, in lieu of the net liability of Rx. 307,500 with which His Highness's reign began in 1881.

	Rx.
In 1881, the balance of State Funds was	240,743
Capital outlay on State Railways	251,919
Against a liability to the British Government of ...	800,000

Leaving a balance of liability of Rx. 307,500.

On 30th June, 1895 :—

Assets :

(1)	Balance of State Funds	1,272,361
(2)	Investment on account of Railway Loan Repayment Fund	278,150
(3)	Capital outlay on Mysore-Harihar Railways	1,480,330
(4)	Capital outlay on other Railways	413,339

		Rx.
(5) Unexpended portion of capital borrowed for Mysore-Harihar Railway (with British Government)		157,949
		3,602,129
Liabilities:	Rx.	
(1) Local Railway loan	200,000	
(2) English Railway loan	1,638,280	
		1,838,280
Net assets		1,763,849

And other assets :
Capital outlay on original irrigation works Rx. 990,893

Besides the above expenditure from current revenue, there is the subsidy to the British Government of about Rx. 250,000 a year, or a total of about Rx. 3,700,000 in the 15 years from 1880-1 to 1894-5, and the Maharaja's civil list of about Rx. 180,000 during the 15 years also, paid from the current revenue. And all this together with increase of expenditure in every department. Under the circumstances above described, the administration at the start of His Highness's reign was necessarily very highly centralised. The Dewan, or the Executive Administrative Head, had the direct control, without the intervention of departmental heads of all the principal departments, such as the Land Revenue, Forests, Excise, Mining, Police, Education, Mujroyi, Legislative. As the finances improved, and as department after department was put into good working order and showed signs of expansion, separate heads of departments were appointed for Forests and Police in 1885, for Excise in 1889, for Mujroyi in 1891, and for Mining in 1894. His Highness was able to resolve upon the appointment of a separate Land Revenue Commissioner only in the latter part of 1894. Improvements were made in other departments, local and municipal funds legislation, education, etc. There are no walls which, unfortunately, the Finance Ministers of British India are obliged to raise, year after year, of fall in Exchange, overburdening taxation, etc. And all the above good results are side by side with an increase of population of 18·34 per cent. in the 10 years from 1881 to 1891, and there is reason to believe that during the last four years the ratio of increase was even higher. During the 14 years the rate of mortality is estimated to have declined 6·7 per mille. But there is still the most important and satisfactory feature to come, *viz.*, that all this financial prosperity was secured not by resort to new taxation in any form or shape. In the very nature of things the present system of administration and management of Indian expenditure in British India cannot ever produce such results, even though a Gladstone undertook the work. Such is the result of good administration in a Native State at the very beginning. What splendid prospect is in store for the future if, as heretofore, it is allowed to develop itself to the level of the British system with its own native services, and not bled as poor British India is.

You had some personal knowledge of Mysore, had you not?—No, of Baroda I have personal knowledge.

Have you any later information about Mysore?—I have the latest report of Mysore, which is summarised in the "Times" of the 8th December 1896. The "Times," in its article on Indian affairs, confirms by actual facts and events the wisdom and statesmanship of Lords Salisbury and Iddlesleigh in their one great work of righteous and wise policy. Fortunately, it is the very Mysore State to which this righteous and wise act was done; therefore, I desire to quote a few words. The "Times" says: "The account which Sir Sheshadri Iyer rendered to it of his last year's stewardship is one of increasing revenue, reduced taxation, expenditure firmly kept in hand, reproductive public works, and a large expansion of cultivation of mining, and of industrial undertakings. The result is a surplus which goes to swell the previous accumulations from the same source." The "Times" article concludes with the words: "A narrative such as Sir Sheshadri Iyer was able to give to the Representative Assembly of Mysore makes us realise the growth of capital in the Native States, and opens up new prospects of industrial undertakings and railway construction in India on a silver basis." Then he has said about some other Native States, but I have not introduced that here. I have got this latest report, if the Commission would allow me to put in a statement out of it, like the one I have already given. I have cited other illustrations of Native States in my statements.

I think it probably would be best if you were to modify by those latest figures the figures which you have already given in your evidence?—I could give the latest figures in continuation of those.

You are giving us the examples of Mysore?—Yes.

It is no good giving us two sets of tables in regard to it. Can you not, with this latest report, correct the table you have already given us in evidence?—I could do, but there is this difference, that in the report which I have quoted here he went into the comments on the administration of the 15 years and gave the result up to 1894-5; in this last report, of course, he only goes, in the usual way, into the figures of receipts and expenditure of the year; he does not go again into a report of the administration of the 15 years.

Do the latter figures very much vary from the former?—They are not on those lines; the other figures are simply the results and expenditure in the usual way, a sort of budget.

We must bear in mind the danger of drowning the Commission in figures. You were giving us an instance of the working of a Native State; it is no use giving us two sets of tables in illustration of that. If you are satisfied with the figures you have given us for 1894-5—they appear to me to give the illustration which you desire to give—then I do not think it would be necessary to supplement them with other figures?—All right.

Would you take Mysore as a type of Native States generally?—Yes.

If I had, for instance, a list of the Native States before me here, and I were to put them to you one by one, would you quote each of them as a model State of the kind like Mysore?—Not every one of them—those that have introduced improvements in the way in which they have been introduced in Mysore—Baroda will be a very good illustration, as far as that goes.

One used to hear that Oudh was not a model kingdom? Oudh was not a model kingdom.

I have heard so. What security is there that such a state of things as occurred in Oudh, or something like it, may not occur in these Native States?—No, for the times are entirely changed, and the control which the British Government has even on the existing Native States is now of a different character altogether, and the management or the system of Government is more or less assimilated and brought to the system which exists in British India.

Then your contention is that repetition of such evils as those which led to the annexation of Oudh must be prevented by the precautions to be taken by the Supreme Government; that is, by the Indian Government?—In fact, the later improvements and the way in which the administration is introduced in all Native States.

Would you quote Hyderabad as a case of model government?—Well, I am not acquainted with the details of the Hyderabad Government, and therefore it would not be right for me to give any opinion upon it. My general impression is—and I may be wrong—that the State is not conducted in the way which would produce such results as Mysore has produced. It is more the defect of the administration than the possibility of results as good as the Mysore; but still I qualify it that I may be wrong, because I am speaking only from general impressions about that State.

In that case, if Hyderabad does not come up to the level of Mysore the supremacy of the British Government is not sufficient to secure in a Native State such good results?—If I am right in the impression, I think then it is evident that in that case the supremacy has not been exercised to the best advantage.

Now, leaving this point, you have put before us the practical remedy which you would recommend; that is to say, you have called our attention to the cost to India of Europeans. Have you any facts or practical figures on that subject which you would like to put before the Commission?—Yes, I leave the important suggestions I have made; I leave that consideration alone, and I come now to matters exactly as they are. First of all, Europeans. Here is Return 192 of 1892 of East India salaries. In the Civil Department the amount of annual salaries, Rs. 1,000 and upwards, is :—

	Rx.
	3 874,929
Public Works Department (Civil)	909,814
Absentee Allowances Civil Department	175,677
Public Works Department (Civil)	44,734
Pensions paid in India, Civil :—	
Europeans (Eurasians)	97,323
Public Works Department, Civil :—	
Europeans (Eurasians)	23,871
Total in India	5,126,348

in England. The amount for civil and military are not separate, which I may request to be supplied.

Are you suggesting that those figures should be supplied to enable you to give a complete statement of the sum which represents the cost of Europeans in India ?—Yes ; the two are mixed up, Civil and Military, only that the amounts might be separated, but I have just the total further on ; it does not matter much even if the information is not given, because my illustration stands just the same. Now what I urge is that the European Civil Service is distinctly alleged to be employed mainly for the maintenance of the British Rule. For a practical purpose at present I grant that the service is for the benefit of India also—as for the maintenance of the British Rule—and further, I do not press for the very weak capacity of India. I say the least that Britain can do in justice to India is to pay half of the salaries of the Europeans in the Civil Departments. The next figure I want to put is the expenditure on the European Army in India, and pensions and other disbursements in England.

Army Europeans.

	Rx.
For the Military Department, Annual Salaries	3,781,844
Public Works (Military)	171,075

	Rx.
Absentee Allowances, Military	234,900
Public works Military	7,089
Pensions paid in India :	
Pensions under Civil Regulations :	
Europeans (Eurasians)	8,839
Pensions under Army and Marine Regulations :	
Europeans (Eurasians)	101,697
Total—India ...	4,305,444

Paid in England—

The amounts, Civil and Army together, are £3,710,678 (including contributed) say at Rs. 15 per £, Rx. 5,566,01, grand total about 15 millions of Rx., to which is to be added the payments to European soldiers. What I urge is that the British Army is mainly for the maintenance of British Rule against internal or external troubles. But for present practical purposes I accept that the Army is for the benefit of India also, as for that of Britian; and I urge, therefore, that, leaving alone even the poverty in India, Britain in fairness to India should share the expenditure, say half and half, for what is a common purpose of equally vital importance to both. The Government of India correctly puts the position: "Millions of money have been spent on increasing the Army in India, on armaments and fortifications to provide for the security of India, not against domestic enemies, or to prevent the incursions of the warlike peoples of the adjoining countries, but to maintain the supremacy of British power in the East."

You have heard a good deal of evidence taken on the subject of existing Army charges. Would you not think it desirable to criticise what you have heard put before us with regard to the different branches of Army expenditure or have you any remarks or suggestions to make upon the question of appointment as it has been before us?—Apart from the important considerations to which I have already referred, and taking the question as it exists now I consider, as far as I can judge at present, that the Government of India has made out a fair case. I have heard the other side of the War Office and the Admiralty, and this I shall fairly consider and give my opinion on in the preparation of the Report.

Therefore, so far, in offering your evidence you do not wish to make any remarks upon those important questions? – No; I do not see the necessity of it, because the question has been very fairly and largely discussed, and the Government of India has put the case very fairly, as far as I could see it.

On that point you associate yourself with the Government of India?—Yes; I am quite satisfied with the fairness with which they have urged the question.

And you do not wish to go beyond them?—No, I do not wish to go beyond them.

Then do you wish to offer any remarks in connexion with the Navy?—Yes, with regard to the Navy, it is of absolute necessity to England whether there was rule in India or not. With regard to the absolute necessity to the United Kingdom itself for its own safety, of the whole Navy as it exists and is intended to be increased, there is but general opinion, without any distinction of parties. It will be easy to quote expressions from many prominent politicians. It is, in fact, the great subject of the day for which there is almost unanimity. I would content myself, however, with a few words of the highest authority in the realm under the Sovereign, the Prime Minister and also of the Chancellor of the Exchequer. Lord Salisbury said in his Brighton speech, I have not quoted the whole words, but just such words as apply here:

"But dealing with such money as you possess . . . that the first claim is the naval defence of England. I am glad that you welcome that sentiment. . . , . It is our business to be quite sure of the safety of this island home of ours whose inaccessibility is the source of our greatness, that no improvement of foreign fleets, and no combination of foreign alliances, should be able for a moment to threaten our safety at home. . . . . We must make ourselves safe at sea whatever happens. . . . . . But after all, safety, safety from a foreign foe, comes first before every other earthly blessing, and we must take care in our responsibility to the many interests that depend upon us in our responsibility to the generations that are to succeed us, we must take care that no neglect of ours shall suffer that safety to be compromised."

Sir M. Hicks-Beach, the Chancellor of the Exchequer, so late as 28th January last (the "Times" 29th January, 1896), said emphatically, and in a fighting mood: "We must be prepared. We must never lose the supremacy of the sea. Other nations had not got it and could afford to do without it, but supremacy of the sea was vital to our very existence."

The Irish Financial Relations Report at page 23, says:

"Sir Edward Hamilton has stated in his evidence that he did not believe that if Ireland ceased to exist, Great Britain's expenditure on the Army and Navy could be reduced (Ans. 8741-2). The enormous outlay on the Navy has become necessary in consequence of Great Britain's position as the first commercial power in the world, on account of her enormous trade with every part of the globe, and on account of the dependence of her inhabitants for subsistence on supplies from abroad, and on having a safe ocean communication."

Notwithstanding that such is the absolute necessity of England to have even more than its present Navy as a world-wide power, I am willing to allow that a fair share should be paid by India, for the vessels that are kept in the Indian waters, and which have been under consideration by the Commission. Well, that I have said in the question of partnership, and therefore I will not add here, that whatever is asked from us to contribute, to that extent we should have a share in the benefits of that service. It comes, in fact, next immediately—about partnership.

Considering the partnership between England and India, should not India take some share in all such charges as are required for Imperial common interests?—Yes. About the partnership between England and India, as it becomes an element in all questions of the relations between the two countries. The Indians are repeatedly told, and in this Commission several times, that Indians are partners in the British Empire and must share the burdens of the Empire. Then I propose a simple test. For instance, supposing that the expenditure of the total Navy of the Empire is, say, £20,000,000 and as partners in the Empire you ask British India to pay,

£10,000,000, more or less, British India, as partner, would be ready to pay, and, therefore as partner, must have her share in the employment of British Indians, and in every other benefit of the service to the extent of her contribution. Take the Army. Suppose the expenditure of the total Army of the Empire is, say, £40,000,000. Now, you may ask £20,000,000 or more or less to be contributed by British India. Then, as partners, India must claim, and must have, every employment and benefit of that service to the extent of her contribution. If, on the other hand, you force, the helpless and voiceless British India to pay, but not to receive a return to the extent of the payment, then your treatment is the unrighteous treatment of the slave-master over British India as a slave. In short, if British India is to be treated as a partner in the Empire it must follow that to whatever extent (be it a farthing or a hundred millions) British India contributes to the expense of any department, to that extent of the British Indians must have a share in the services and benefits of that department, whether civil, military, naval, or any other; then only will British India be the "integral part" of, or partner in, the Empire.

Have you any considerations to lay before the Commission on the subject of frontier expenditure?—Yes; according to the table of, and comment on, the expenditure on the frontier wars from Colonel Hanna's book. This expenditure, which is entirely Imperial—for the maintenance of British Rule against Russian invasion—is, say, roundly, about Rx. 80,000,000 or more, out of which £5,000,000 have been paid by England. I am not at all discussing the policy of these wars. All I simply say is that these frontier wars are avowedly for Imperial purposes, that both England and India must be considered as benefited by it, and the least that should be done in justice in India is to halve the expenditure, if not in the proportion of the capacity of India as compared with that of England.

I have here the highest declarations of the Imperial character of these wars. If the Commission would allow, I shall read them.

On 11th February 1880, Mr. Fawcett moved the following

amendment to the Address in reply to the Queen's Speech (Hansard, Vol. 250, p. 453).

"But humbly desire to express our regret that in view of the declarations that have been made by Your Majesty's ministers that the war in Afghanistan was undertaken for Imperial purposes, no assurance has been given that the cost incurred in consequence of the renewal of hostilities in that country will not be wholly defrayed out of the revenues of India."

Mr. Fawcett then said (Hansard, Vol. 250, p. 454):

"And, fourthly, the most important question, as far as he was able to judge, of who was to pay the expenses of the war. . . . It seemed to be quite clear that the expenses of the war should not be borne by India, and he wished to explain that so far as India was concerned this was not to be regarded as a matter of generosity, but of justice and legality. . . . . . The matter must be decided on grounds of strict justice and legality . . . . . . (p. 457): It was a remarkable thing that every speech made in that House, or out of it, by ministers or their supporters on the subject showed that the war was a great Imperial enterprise, those who opposed the war having always been taunted as being "parochial" politicians who could not appreciate the magnitude and importance of great Imperial enterprise. . . . . (p. 458): He would refer to the speeches of the Viceroy of India, the Prime Minister, and the Secretary of State for Foreign Affairs upon the subject. . . . . . In December, 1878, the noble earl * warned the peers that they must extend their range of vision, and told them that they were not to suppose that this was a war which simply concerned some small cantonments at Dakka and Jellalabad, but one undertaken to maintain the influence and character not of India, but of England in Europe. Now were they going to make India pay the entire bill for maintaining the influence and character of England in Europe. . . . . His lordship† treated the war as indissolubly connected with the

* The Prime Minister.

† The Marquess of Salisbury.

Eastern question. . . . . Therefore, it seemed to him (Mr. Fawcett), that it was absolutely impossible for the Government, unless they were prepared to cast to the winds their declarations, to come down to the House and regard the war as an Indian one. . . . . . All he desired was a declaration of principle, and he would be perfectly satisfied if someone representing the Government would get up and say that they had always considered this war as an Imperial one, for the expenses of which England and India were jointly liable."

Afterwards Mr. Fawcett said (p. 477):

"He was entirely satisfied with the assurance which had been given on the part of the Government that the House should have an opportunity of discussing the question before the Budget was introduced; and would, therefore, beg leave to withdraw his amendment."

In the House of Lords, Lord Beaconsfield emphasised the objects to be for British Imperial purposes (25th February 1880, Hansard, Vol. 250, p. 1,094):

"That the real question at issue was whether England should possess the gates of her own great Empire in India. . . . . We resolved that the time had come when this country should acquire the complete command and possession of the gates of the Indian Empire. Let me at least believe that the peers of England are still determined to uphold not only the Empire, but the honour of this country."

So it is clear that the object of all the frontier wars, large or small, was that "*England* should possess the gates of *her own*, great Empire," that "*this country* should acquire the complete command and possession of the gates of the Indian Empire," and uphold not only the Empire, but also "the honour of this country." Can anything be more clear than the Imperial character of the frontier wars?

Mr. Fawcett, again, on 12th March, 1880, moved (Hansard Vol. 251, p. 922):

"That in view of the declarations which have been officially made that the Afghan war was undertaken in the joint interests of England and India, this House is of opinion that it is unjust to defray out of the revenues of India the whole of the expenditure incurred in the renewal of hostilities with Afghanistan."

Speaking to this motion, Mr. Fawcett, after referring to the past declarations of the Prime Minister, the Secretary of State for Foreign Affairs, the Chancellor of the Exchequer, quoted from the speech of the Viceroy soon after his arrival (p. 923):

"I came to India, and just before leaving England for India I had frequent interviews with Lord Salisbury, the then Indian Secretary, and I came out specially instructed to treat the Indian frontier question as an indivisible part of a great Imperial question mainly depending for its solution upon the general policy of Her Majesty's Government.

And further on Mr. Fawcett said (p. 926):

"What was our policy towards self-governed colonies, and towards India, not self-governed? In the self-governed colony of the Cape we had a war, for which we were not responsible. Who was to pay for it? It would cost the English people something like £5,000,000. In India there was a war, for which the Indian people were not responsible—a war which grew out of our own policy and actions in Europe—and we are going to make the Indian people, who were not self-governed and were not represented, pay every sixpence of the cost."

And so, Lord Salisbury, as Secretary of State for India, and the Viceroy, had cleared up the whole position: "To treat the Indian frontier question as an indivisible part of a great Imperial question, mainly depending for its solution upon the general policy of Her Majesty's Government," and the Indian people having no voice or choice in it.

Mr. Gladstone, following Mr. Fawcett, said (p. 930):—

"It appears to me that, to make such a statement as that, the judgment of the Viceroy is a sufficient expression of that of the people of India, is an expression of paradox really surprising, and such as is rarely heard among us . . (p. 932): In my opinion my hon'ble friend the member for Hackney has made good his case . . Still, I think it fair and right to say that, in my opinion, my hon'ble friend the member for Hackney has completely made good his case. His case, as I understand it, has not received one shred of answer . . . . .

(p. 933): In the speech of the Prime Minister, the speech of Lord Salisbury, and the speech of the Viceroy of India, and, I think my hon'ble friend said, in a speech by the Chancellor of the Exchequer, this Afghan war has been distinctively recognised as partaking of the character of an Imperial war. . . . . . But I think not merely a small sum like that, but what my right hon'ble friend the Chancellor of the Exchequer would call a solid and substantial sum, ought to be borne by this country, at the very least . . . . . (p. 935): As regards the substance of the motion, I cordially embrace the doctrine of my hon'ble friend the Member for Hackney. There is not a constituency in the country before which I would not be prepared to stand, if it were the poorest and most distressed in the land, if it were composed of a body of men to all of whom every addition of a farthing for taxes was a sensible burden, and before them I would be glad to stand and plead that, when we have made in India a war which our own Government have described as in part an Imperial war, we ought not for a moment to shrink from the responsibility of assuming at least a portion of the cost of that war, in correspondence with that declaration, instead of making use of the law and argument of force, which is the only law and the only argument which we possess or apply to place the whole of this burden on the shoulders of the people of India."

The upshot of the whole was that England contributed £5,000,000 out of £21,000,000 spent on this war, when one would have naturally expected a "far more solid and substantial" sum from rich England, whose interest was double, both Imperial and European. But the extent of that contribution is not the present question with me. It is the principle that "the Indian frontier question is one indivisible part of a great Imperial question" mainly "depending for its solution upon the general policy of Her Majesty's Government," and that, therefore, a fair apportionment must be made of all the charge or cost of all frontier wars, according to the extent of the interest and of the means of each country.

Coming down to later times, the action of Mr. Gladstone on 27th April, 1885, to come to the House of Commons to ask for £11,000,000 and the House accepting his proposal, and on the occasion of the Penjdeh incident, is again a most significant proof of the Imperial character of these frontier wars. He said (Hansard, Vol. 297, p. 859):—

"I have heard with great satisfaction the assurance of hon'ble gentlemen opposite that they are disposed to forward in every way the grant of funds to us to be used as we best think for the maintenance of what I have upon former occasions described as a National and Imperial policy. Certainly, an adequate sense of our obligations to our Indian Empire has never yet been claimed by any party in this country as its exclusive inheritance. In my opinion he will be guilty of a moral offence and gross political folly who should endeavour to claim on behalf of his own party and superiority in that respect over those to whom he is habitually opposed. It it an Imperial policy in which we are engaged."

You lay great stress on the high authorities you quote, do you not, throughout your evidence?—Yes.

May I ask you, would you lay equal stress if I placed before you the same high authorities speaking in the other direction?—I lay stress upon high authorities in all matters which I have so thoroughly studied, and in which I agree with them. Of course, each authority has different opinions upon different subjects.

But if the same high authorities on another occasion spoke in a different sense would you lay equal stress upon them?—On the same subject.

On the same subject?—Well, I should be glad to see them.

You quote these high authorities, in support of your own position?—In support of my own views.

And strengthen your own views based on personal experience?—What I consider to be the right thing, of course.

There is this to be said, where great reliance is placed on the expression of opinion of a high authority, in all probability an equally high authority can be produced on the other side?—As Mr. Caine said, I produced authorities which are in support of my opinion.

I am only pointing out that high authorities may be found

on both sides; we should bear that in mind before we place absolute reliance upon what is said in political discussion?—Yes.

You are aware that there has been much discussion about the employment of the Indian Army outside of India; have you any remarks to make upon what has occurred before the Commission upon that head?—Yes. This can be answered in two ways. If the test I have just proposed of dividing the whole Imperial expenditure, and each deriving the benefit of the services in proportion to the contribution, then the whole Army and Navy becomes altogether Imperial, and may be used in any part of the world at common additional expenditure. Secondly, apart from such Imperial, partnership, whenever Indian forces are taken outside Indian limits, the expenses must be paid in full by the British Exchequer except when the interests are distinctly common, like that of the frontier wars as a protection for both against Russian invasion. In such case as I have already stated, expenses may be divided in some fair way, giving some consideration to the capacity of both. On the other hand, such wars as that of Abyssinia, and for the benefit of Egypt or the Cape Colony, no expenditure should be placed, ordinary or extraordinary, upon the Indian revenues. The only case which can come at all, outside of India, within purview of common purposes like the North-Western Frontier wars, is when the Suez Canal is actually threatened and has to be defended. Then, like common purpose, both India and Britain can make a fair share with some consideration for the poorer party. Aden should be considered as for Imperial purposes, and be divided in a similar way. With all other diplomatic or other expenses of Britain, India has no connection or interest, and should not be made to contribute. Now, sometimes this question of interest may not be so very obvious, and, in any such difference, some fair tribunal should be resorted to decide the difference. This question of tribunal has been already discussed in evidence, and I trust the Commission may be able to see their way to recommend some.

That, I think, completes your evidence, thank you, Mr. Naoroji.

Just one question on what you have said. You say that India and Britain should take a fair share when the Suez Canal is actually threatened and has to be defended. Do you not think that Australia and New Zealand, the Straits Colonies, and Hong Kong and Ceylon, ought also to take a fair share ?—Surely they ought to.

You do not discriminite between India and the other dependencies interested in the Suez Canal ?—They are as much interested in the Suez Canal as India is.

APPENDIX—B.

STATEMENT SUBMITTED

TO THE

INDIAN CURRENCY COMMITTEE OF 1898.

Washington House,
72, Anerley Park, S.E.
July 30, 1898.

MY DEAR SIR WILLIAM WEDDERBURN,—In accordance with the reply of the 5th inst. from the Currency Committee to your letter saying "they will, however, be glad to accord their best consideration to any written communication which you may desire to lay before them," I send you this statement, which you would be good enough to forward to them.

2. I may add that I am willing to submit to any cross-examination that may be considered necessary to test the correctness of my views, or to ask me other questions. You know that I have been in business in the City for twenty-five years as a merchant, and also as a commission agent; I have dealt with almost every kind of export and import between England and India. I have seen some commercial and monetary crisis, including that of "the Black Friday," when I think Messrs. Overend Gurney and Co., closed their doors.

3. Fall or rise in exchange does not in itself (other circumstances remaining the same) matter in true international trade, which adjusts itself automatically to the requirements of exchange. To establish this proposition by a detailed explanation of the mode of operations of Indian trade, I attach as Appendix A, some letters which I wrote to *The Times* and *The Daily News* in 1886.

4. Closing the mints or introducing a gold standard does not and cannot save a single farthing to the Indian taxpayers in their remittance for "Home Charges" to this country. The reason is simple. Suppose we take roundly £20,000,000 sterling to be the amount of the "Home Charges." The Indian taxpayers have to send as much produce to this country as is necessary to buy £20,000,000 not an ounce less, no matter whatever may be the rupee or whatever the standard (gold or silver) in India. England must receive £20,000,000 in gold or produce worth £20,000,000. The only way in which relief can come to the Indian taxpayers in these remittances is the rise in the prices of the Indian merchandise in this country, and not by any juggling with the currency laws of India.

5. The Government of India, in their despatch to the Secretary of State (Simla, November 6, 1878), themselves admit this in so many words :—

"66. Now, it is plain that so long as the amount of the so-called tribute is not changed the quantity of merchandise necessary to pay it will not change either, excepting by reason of a change of its value in the foreign country to which it goes." (c. 4868, 1886, p. 25.)

6. Closing of the mints, and thereby raising the true rupee, worth at present about 11*d*. in gold, to a false rupee to be worth 16*d*. in gold, is a covert exaction of about 45 per cent. more taxation all round from the Indian taxpayers, and at the same time of increasing the salaries of officials and other payments in India by Government to the same extent, and giving generally the advantage to creditors over debtors, the former being generally well-to-do and the latter the poorer classes, especially in the case of the money-lenders and the rayats.

7. The real and full effect of the closing of the mints must be examined by *itself*, irrespective of the effect of other factors. First of all, the closing of the mints was illegal, dishonourable, and a despotic act. It is a violation of all taxation Acts, by which there was always a distinct contract between the Government and the taxpayers based upon the fundamental principle of sound currency—*i.e.*, of a certain definite rupee. And what is that fundamental principle upon

which the currency, both of this country and of India, is based? The former is upon what is called the gold standard, and the latter the silver standard. Take this country first.

8. Here the whole currency is based upon a sovereign—a fixed unit of a certain quantity of gold, whatever its relative exchangeable value may be with all other commodities. A sovereign is nothing more or less than, or anything else but, 123·274 grains of gold of a certain fineness, with a stamp upon it, certifying to the world that it is what it professes to be, and that no restriction whatsoever was to be placed either on the market of gold or on the coining of gold. Any person may present 123·274 grains of gold, of standard fineness with the mintage (which, I think, is three halfpence on an ounce), and ask for a sovereign and will get it. It is not buying or selling gold; Government simply having fixed a unit of currency measure, stamps the unit that it is the proper unit. I should be surprised if Government here should even think of interfering with this unrestricted sale and coinage of gold, as the foundation of the sound currency of this country. The sovereign is the standard by which every other commodity, including silver, is measured in its exchangeable value, just as a foot is a standard measure of length, a gallon of liquid. The taxpayer's contract with the Government is that he is to pay in such unrestricted sovereigns, and every taxation law lays down the payment in such sovereigns.

9. Similarly about India—substitute 180 grains of standard silver, with 2 per cent. for mintage for a rupee, in place of 123·274 grains of gold, with three halfpence for every ounce of gold coined, for a sovereign, and all the above remarks apply word for word to the case of India, except that I should not be surprised at the Indian authorities playing any pranks, regardless of consequences to the Indian people, as long as they are considered favourable to the "interests," and are to be made at the cost of the Indians.

10. This is the true rupee—180 grains of standard silver

* I understand that there is no charge now. (Coinage Act of 1870, Sec. 8.)

at its market value, with nearly 4 grains more for mintage, is convertible into a rupee without any restriction either on the silver market or on the free coining of silver. It is in this true rupee that the taxpayer is legally bound to pay his taxes. Any interference with the fundamental principal and law of the rupee is illegal, immoral, or dishonourable.

11. Now comes the false rupee. The true rupee, in its relation to gold at the present market value of silver of 184 grains, is worth, say, about 11*d*. of gold. Government intervenes, abuses its power or duty to coin silver unrestrictedly, makes the rupee scarce and false, and forces it up to the value of 16*d*. of gold, or about 269 grains of silver (including mintage), which the rupee does not contain. And the taxpayer is compelled, by what Mr. Gladstone called "the argument and law of force," to pay his tax in this false rupee, under the false pretence of using the word "rupee" when this "rupee" is not one rupee but nearly one and a half rupee.

12. Let us now take the factor of closing the mints by *itself*. Suppose I go into the market with my produce to buy 184 grains of standard silver for which I am asked one maund of rice. I go to the mint and ask to coin this into a rupee which I have to pay to the Sircar for my tax. If I get the rupee, then it is all right. But no, the mint refuses to coin. It virtually tells me, "Bring 269 grains of silver (*i.e.*, worth 16*d* of gold) and you will get a rupee." I go into the market to get the rupee. The man who has the rupee tells me, "If you give me 269 grains of silver, or as much produce as would buy 269 grains of silver, I would give you the rupee." What alternative remains for me but to give as much of my rice, about 1½ maunds, to get this false "rupee," instead of only one maund to get the true rupee which I can get in the *same market* and at the *same time*? This is altogether independent of whatever the *actual* price of commodities may be.

13. If the actual price of rice does not show this fall, owing to the disguise of the false "rupee," it is not that the closing of the mints has not produced this decline, but that other fortunate factors have influenced the price, whose benefit is robbed away from me by the Government by the covert device of the closing of the mints. Otherwise I would have

received so much higher price for my produce than the actual price. The loss, therefore, to me is all the same, as I was forced to pay in my produce for 269 grains of silver to get the false "rupee" instead of at the *same moment* paying for 184 grains of silver to get the true rupee. These two different prices in merchandise for the false and the true rupee are demanded, as I have said above, at the *same time*, and in the same market, *i.e.*, the price of the false rupee, 45 per cent. higher than that of the true rupee, entirely irrespective of any general market rise or fall of price at any same time. If the actual price of rice be 1½ maunds for the false rupee, the price at the *same time* will be one maund for the true rupee, or for 184 grains of silver.

14. To test this in another way, let us take some commodity in the country itself upon which the factor of the closing of the mints produces its full effect in the actual market, and which is not materially affected by other commercial factors, which operate generally upon the general merchandise. Such a commodity, in India is gold. It is affected, not in merely foreign exchange or international relations, but in *Indian itself* as a commodity, like every other commodity. Say, I have a sovereign, and I want to sell it for rupees in India itself—not for exchange to foreign parts. If the "rupee" were the honest, true rupee of the market value of 184 grains of silver, I should get 22 such rupees for my sovereign, but at the false value of "rupee," *i.e.*, the market value 269 grains of silver, I actually get only 15 "rupees." This is the actual price of gold in India, a decline in the proportion of the false inflation of the false "rupee." This is the case with every commodity, as can be tested by offering produce for the true rupee of 184 grains of silver, and for the false rupee or 269 grains of silver at the *same time* and in the *same market*.

15. In addition to the higher taxation thus inflicted on the Indian taxpayers, by an irony of fate, the very "interests" (bankers, merchants, planters, foreign capitalists of all kinds, etc.) for whose behalf, besides that of Government itself, all this dislocation of currency was made, are now loudest in their cry for all the mischief caused also to them, and yet the authorities in both countries remain blind and infatuated

enough not to learn even by experience, and persist in a mischievous course.

16. In the Treasury letter of 24th November, 1879 (c. 4868, 1886, p. 31) to the India Office, my Lords say :—

"I. The proposal appears to be open to those objections to a token currency which have long been recognised by all civilised nations, *viz.*: That instead of being automatic, it must be, 'managed' by the Government, and that any such management not only fails to keep a token currency at par, but exposes the Government which undertakes it to very serious difficulties and temptations.

17. "2. It appears to my Lords, that the Government of India, in making the present proposal, lay themselves open to the same criticisms as are made upon Governments, which have depreciated their currencies. In general, the object of such Governments has been to diminish the amount they have to pay to their creditors. In the present case, the object of the Indian Government appears to be to *increase the amount they have to receive from their taxpayers.* My Lords fail to see any real difference in the character of the two transactions.

18. "...... If, on the other hand, it is the case that the value of the rupee has fallen in India, and that it will be raised in India by the operation of the proposed plan, that plan is open to the objection that *it alters every contract and every fixed payment* in India.

19. "This proposal is, in fact, contrary to the essential and well-established principle of the currency law of this country, which regards the current standard coin as a piece of a given metal of a certain weight and fineness, and which condemns as futile and mischievous every attempt to go behind this simple definition.

20. "It is perfectly true as stated in the despatch (paragraph 41), that the "very essence of all laws relating to the currency has been to give fixity to the standard of value as far as it is possible," but it is no less true that, according to the principles which govern our currency system, the best and surest way, and, indeed, the only tried and known way, of giving this fixity is to adhere to the above definition of current standard coin. A pound is a given quantity of gold, a rupee is a

given quantity of silver; and any attempt to give those terms a different meaning is condemned by experience and authority.

21. "3. If the present state of exchange be due to the depreciation of silver, the Government scheme, if it succeeds, may relieve:—

(1) The Indian Government from the inconvenience of a nominal re-adjustment of taxation in order to meet the loss by exchange on the home remittances:

(2) Civil servants and other Englishmen who are serving or working in India, and who desire to remit money to England:

(3) Englishmen who have money placed or invested in India which they wish to remit to England. *But this relief will be given at the expense of the Indian taxpayer*, and with the effect of increasing every debt or fixed payment in India, including debts due by *ryots to money-lenders*; while its effect will be materially qualified, so far as the Government are concerned, by *the enhancement of the public obligations in India, which have been contracted on a silver basis*.........

22. "If, then, a case has been made out, which my Lords do not admit, for an alteration of the currency law of India, the particular alteration which the Government of India, propose could not, in the opinion of the Treasury, be entertained until the doubts and objections which have suggested themselves to my Lords are answered and removed. These objections are founded on principles which have been long and ably discussed, and which are now generally admitted by statesmen and by writers of accepted authority to lie at the root of the currency system.

23. "It is no light matter to accept innovations which must say and undermine that system, and my Lords have therefore felt it their duty plainly—though they hope not inconsistently with the respect due to the Government of India—to express their conviction that the plan which had been referred to them for their observations is one which *ought not to be sanctioned* by Her Majesty's Government or by the Secretary of State." (Italics are mine.)

24. Can condemnation be more complete and convincing?

25. The introduction of a gold standard, while it will not save a single farthing or a single ounce of produce to the Indian taxpayer in his payment of "Home Charges," as already explained, will simply add more to his already existing grievous burdens to the extent of the heavy cost of the alteration, and injure him, Heaven knows in what other ways, as the events of the past five years have shown.

26. The whole basis of the action of the Government is, and was, the assumption that, as fall in exchange will necessitate increased burden of taxation, the closing of the mints and introduction of a gold standard will save the Indian taxpayer from any such additional burden of taxation which would otherwise arise enormously in the remittance of "Home Charges," and that it is imperatively necessary to establish a stable ratio between gold and silver. That the anxiety of the Government about increased burdens of taxation and its political dangers, and that to save the people from the former and the Government from the latter, were the professed motives of all the present currency laws, would be clear from Government's own despatches.

27. In order not to encumber the statement here with the extracts from those despatches, I give them as Appendix B.

28. Both these objects, *viz.*, saving people from additional taxation, and thereby Government from political danger, by the present proposals, and past currency legislation, are pure delusions. The Government might as well have tried to stop the action of gravitation, as to try against a natural law, that while gold and silver should fluctuate in value in relation to and like all other commodities, yet between themselves they could be made to keep up a fixed ratio, or to try to make a rupee which may be only worth 11*d.* or even 6*d.* of gold, become worth 16*d.* of gold, unless Government have found the philosopher's stone or have attained the divine power of creating something out of nothing.

29. It is not that the Government of India did not know this, or were not told this from the highest authority and other's and in distinct and emphatic terms. Of this I have already given (see *supra* 16 to 23 paras.) extracts from the despatch of the Treasury, of November 24th, 1879.

30. Notwithstanding the clear and emphatic views of the Treasury expressing "their conviction that the plan which had been referred to them for their observations is one which *ought not to be sanctioned by Her Majesty's Government, or by the Secretary of State,*" the Government of India and the India Office again opened the subject in another form.

31. Lord Randolph Churchill wrote to the Treasury on January 26th, 1886, and forwarded on March 17th, 1886, a letter from the Government of India, dated February 2nd, 1886 (c. 4868, 1886, pp. 3-5). To avoid repetition, I would not take extracts from these letters, as the reply of the Treasury embodies their views.

32. This reply of the Treasury is dated May 31st, 1886 (signed Henry H. Fowler) :—"6. As a result of this review of the inconveniences caused by the depression in the value of silver, the Government of India express their opinion .... Yet there remains one thing which is not beyond the posibility of human control, and that is 'the establishment of a fixed ratio between gold and silver.' The proposition thus stated as an undoubted axiom is, however, one of the most disputable and disputed points in economic science. My Lords may, in passing, compare with this statement the declaration recorded by Mr. Goschen, Mr. Gibbs, and Sir Thomas Seccombe as the representatives of Her Majesty's Government at the International Monetary Conference of 1878, that 'the establishment of a fixed ratio between gold and silver was utterly impracticable."

33. "The Indian Government further express their belief (paragraph 7) that it is possible to 'secure a stable ratio between gold and silver,' and that 'a serious responsibility will rest both on the Government of India and on Her Majesty's Government if they neglect any legitimate means to bring about this result.' It would, however, have been more satisfactory if the Indian Government had undertaken to explain the grounds of their confidence that a stable ratio between gold and silver can be established, and the methods by which this is to be accomplished......"

34. "8. In December 1878, Lord Cranbrook, then Secretary of State for India, forwarded to the then Chancellor of

the Exchequer (Sir Stafford Northcote), without any expression of opinion, two despatches from the Government of India, containing certain proposed remedies for the evils arising out of the depression in the value of silver which were then in full force. In the only one of those despatches to which reference need here be made, after *unfavourable* reference to previous suggestions—(1) that a gold standard and gold currency should be introduced into India; and (2) that the weight of silver in the rupee should be increased, it was proposed to limit the free coinage of silver at the Indian mints. The intention of this change was to introduce into India a gold standard, while retaining its native silver currency, the ratio between the currency unit (the rupee) and the standard (the sovereign) being fixed arbitrarily by the Government. The means for attaining this end are worked out in the despatch with great elaboration of detail." (Italics are mine.)

35. "9. This despatch and its proposals were submitted by Lord Cranbrook, on behalf of the Indian Government, and Sir Stafford Northcote, as Chancellor of the Exchequer, to a Committee consisting of Sir Louis Mallet, Mr. Edward Stanhope, M. P., Sir Thomas Seccombe, Mr. (now Sir Thomas) Farrer, Mr. (now Sir Reginald) Welby, Mr. Giffen, and Mr. Arthur Balfour, M. P. These gentlemen reported, on the 30th April, 1879—'That having examined the proposals contained in the despatch, they were unanimously of opinion that they could not recommend them for the sanction of Her Majesty's Government.'

36. "10. Subsequently on the 24th November, 1879, the Treasury replied in detail to the proposals of the Indian Government. In the first part of that letter, which summarises the case as stated in the despatch, I am to call the particular attention of the Secretary of State to the following passages which seem to apply with equal force to the present situation:—

37. "'My Lords need not point out that a change of the Currency Laws is one of the most difficult tasks which a Government can undertake, and that it is most unadvisable to legislate hastily and under the influence of the pressure of the moment, or of an apprehension of uncertain consequences,

upon a subject so complicated in itself and so important to every individual of the community, in its bearing upon the transactions and obligations of daily life.

38. "'It is not proved that increase or re-adjustment of taxation must necessarily be the consequence of matters remaining as they are, for nothing is said about reduction of expenditure, and equilibrium between income and expenditure may be regained by economy of expenditure as well as by increase of taxation. Further, the cost of increase of salaries may be met, or at least reduced, by a careful revision of establishments......

39. "'A perusal of the despatch leads to the conclusion that the Government of India are especially anxious to put an end to the competition of silver against their own bills as a means of remittance to India. But my Lords must ask whether this would be more than a transfer of their own burden to other shoulders; if so, who would eventually bear the loss, and what would be the effect on the credit of the Government and on the commerce of India?'"

40. The letter then further quotes the paragraphs, which I have already given before, pointing out that the relief wished for by the Government, "will be given at the expense of the Indian taxpayer."—(*Supra* para. 21.)

41. "The Treasury find no reason stated in the despatch of the Government of India in the present year, which induces them to dissent from the conclusions thus sent forth on the authority of Sir Stafford Northcote as to the results of any attempt artificially to enhance the gold price of silver...

42. "'13. ...... It has been the policy of this country to emancipate commercial transactions as far as possible from legal control, and to impose no unnecessary restrictions upon the interchange of commodities. To fix the relative value of gold and silver by law would be to enter upon a course directly at variance with this principle, and would be regarded as an arbitrary interference with a natural law, not justified by any present necessity.

43. "...... The observation of the Treasury in 1879, 'that nothing is said about reduction of expenditure,' seems to apply still more strongly to the existing situation, and it may be

safely concluded that the control of its expenditure is far more within the reach of a Government than is the regulation of the market value of the precious metals." (c. 4868, 1886, p. 12.)

44. Before proceeding further I may in passing point out that in 1876 the Government of India itself was against their present proposals, and, as my Lords of the Treasury say, they have urged no sound reasons to alter those views. I have not got the Government of India's despatch of 1876, but I quote from that of November 9, 1878 (c. 4868), 1886, p. 18.

45. "3. The despatch above referred to (October 13th, 1876) discussed in some detail............ The general result, however, was to point out that the adoption of a gold standard with a gold currency that should replace the existing silver would be so costly as to be impracticable, and would otherwise be open to objection ; ......

46. "4. The despatch notices also, *but only to reject it* the proposal that the Indian standard of value, and with it the exchange value of the rupee, might be raised by limiting the coining of silver in the future and by adopting a gold standard without a gold currency." (The italics are mine.)

47. " The Government of India, in their reply of February 9, 1877, to a Resolution of the Bengal Chamber of Commerce passed by them on July 15, 1876, said :—

"8. The value of no substance can serve as a standard measure of value unless its use as the material of legal tender currency is freely admitted. If, therefore, the free coinage of silver on fixed conditions were disallowed in India silver would no longer be the standard of value of India, but another standard would be substituted, namely, the monopoly value of the existing stock of rupees tempered by any additions made to it by the Government or illicitly. If no such conditions were made the value of the rupee will gradually but surely rise."

48. "9. The stamp of a properly regulated mint, such as the Indian Mints, adds nothing except the cost of manufacture and seigniorage to the value of the metal on which it is impressed, but only certifies to its weight and purity."

49. "10. A sound system of currency must be automatic or self-regulating. No civilised Government can undertake to determine from time to time by how much the legal-tender

currency should be increased or decreased, nor would it be justified in leaving the community without a fixed metallic standard of value even for a short time. It is a mistake to suppose that any European nation has rejected silver as a standard of value without substituting gold." (c. 7060, II, 1893, p. 337. Petition of the Indian Association to the House of Commons.)

50. And yet the Government forgot its "civilisation" and its "sound system," and inflicted upon poor India the penalty of its folly by the troubles of the past five years, and what is worse still, they want to persist in the same mischief.

51. Reverting to the above replies of the Treasury, after such complete condemnation by the Treasury of the proposals of the Government of India, the Indian authorities fought shy of the Treasury, and, after inviting a meaningless despatch to keep up appearances, left the Treasury severely alone, as far as I know, and adopted their own usual means to have their own way to rush, into their own foregone crude, and thoughtless legislation. The only wonder is that the Committee of 1893, while knowing all this and seeing all the pitfalls and serious consequences of the proposals allowed the Indian Government to have their own way, in the face of the emphatic rejection by the Treasury of these proposals.

52. To me the proceedings of the Indian authorities are nothing surprising. Whenever they make up their mind to do a thing they would do it—be the opposition what it may—be it of Parliament itself. Resolutions or Statutes of Parliament, or condemnation by the Treasury, are to them nothing. The usual process in such cases is to appoint a Commission or a Committee, put in Members, and have witnesses of their own choice, leaving, if possible, just a small margin for appearance of independence. Generally, they get their own foregone conclusions. If by some happy chance the Commission decided anything against their view so much the worse for the Commission. The report is pigeon-holed, never to see the light of day, or to ignore such part as is not agreeable. If thwarted (as in this instance by the Treasury), the Government keep quiet for a time, wait for more favourable opportunities, and are at it again, taking better care against another mishap.

53. Thus they took their own usual course, which has, as was clearly predicted at the time, launched us on the present sea of troubles.

54. What is stranger still is, that after the Treasury so distinctly condemned these proposals, they did not care to see that any contemplated rash and crude legislation was not inflicted on the Indian taxpayers. The fact seems to be that India is the vile body upon which any quacks may perform any vivisection, and try any cruel, crude, or rash experiments. What matters what is done to it? The Treasury, *i.e.*, the English taxpayer, has not to suffer in any way. India is our helot, she can be forced to pay everything. But they forget Lord Salisbury's *eternal* words—"injustice will bring down the mightiest to ruin."

55. The next natural question is—Why is it that fall in exchange should cause grievous troubles to India and not to any other self-governing, silver-using country? What is the real disease which creates all the never-ceasing pains of India? The reply is given by Lord Salisbury in four words, "India must be bled" under a system of "political hypocrisy." As long as this is the fate of India under an un-British system of Government, no jugglery, no loud professions of benevolence, no device of raising a rupee to what it is not worth, will cure India's sad fate and "terrible misery." (Lord Salisbury's words.)

56. I shall let the authorities themselves speak about the real cause of India's troubles. Lord Salisbury's view I have given above. The following extracts explain this view more explicitly and how it is effected. First, Lord Salisbury has explained that "the injury is exaggerated in the case of India, where so much of the revenue is exported without a direct equivalent."

57. And the literature of this very controversy itself supplied a clear explanation. Lord Randolph Churchill, as Secretary of State for India, explains how the "bleeding" and the drain of revenue is effected, and indicates also the final retribution—just as Lord Salisbury does, as already quoted by me. Lord Randolph Churchill, in his despatch to the Treasury of January 26th, 1886, (c. 4868) 1886, p. 4, says:—first—

58. "It need hardly be said that it is in consequence of the large *obligatory payments* which the Government of India has to make in England in gold currency that the fall in the exchange value of the rupee affects the public finances." (Italics are mine.)

59. And next he hits the nail on the head, and gives concisely and unmistakeably the real evil from which all India's woes flow.

60. He says :—"The position of India in relation to taxation and the sources of the public revenues is very peculiar, not merely from the habits of the people, and their strong aversion to change, which is more specially exhibited to new forms of taxation, but likewise *from the character of the Government, which is in the hands of foreigners, who hold all the principal administrative offices and form so large a part of the Army.* The impatience of new taxation, which would have to be borne *wholly as a consequence of the foreign rule imposed on the country, and virtually to meet additions to charges arising outside of the country,* would constitute a *political danger*, the real magnitude of which, it is to be feared, is not at all appreciated by persons who have no knowledge of, or concern in, the Government of India, but which those responsible for that Government have long regarded as of the most serious order." (The italics are mine.)

61. Here, then, is the real disease—"*The character of the Government, which is in the hands of foreigners*, who hold all the principal administrative offices, and form so large a part of the Army"—"the taxation which would have to be borne *wholly as a consequence of the foreign rule* imposed on the country, and virtually to meet additions to charges arising outside of the country."

62. And, it is remarkable that this was prophesied more than a hundred years ago by the highest Indian authority of the day.

Sir John Shore, in his famous minute in 1787 (Parliamentary Return 377 of 1812, para. 132), says :—

63. "Whatever allowance we may make for the increased industry of the subjects of the State owing to the enhanced demand for the produce of it (supposing the demand to be

enhanced), there is reason to conclude that the benefits are more than counterbalanced by *evils inseparable from the system of a remote foreign dominion*." (Italics are mine.)

64. These *evils of the system of a remote foreign dominion* must be faced by the British rulers before it is "too late." No jugglery of currency, or loud professions of benevolence, or the hundred and one subterfuges to which Indian authorities resort, will ever cure these evils—or put British Rule on a solid and safe foundation and relieve the Indian people of all these national, and political and moral degradations and debasement, and economic and material destruction. Give India true *British* Rule in place of the present *un-British* Rule, and both England and India will be blessed and prosperous.

65. Now, with regard to the immediate position—What is to be done now? Retrace the false step of 1893, taken in spite of the clear warnings of the Treasury and others, and against the "law of Nature." The opening of the mints to the unrestricted coining of silver will correct all the mischievous results that have flowed from the closing of the mints. And further, the true remedy, as pointed out by the Treasury, is a reduction of expenditure and readjustment of establishments.

66. It never occurs to the Indian authorities in both countries that the high salaries of officials may be reduced, say a third, and, as repeatedly urged by many a right-thinking man, Native agency should be substituted—except for the highest control—for the foreign agency, and that Britain should contribute its fair share of the expenditure, to the extent to which such expenditure is incurred for *its own purposes and benefits*, such as the European services and Imperial wars, etc. Of course, anybody can understand that it is hard for officials to cut their own salaries, and let the Indians to come by their own, or ask the British people to contribute a fair share. But this is the only remedy both for the preservation of English rule and for the prosperity of both England and India.

67. The opening of the mints will have immediate important effects. (1) The stringency of the money market and the consequent dislocation of trade, will be remedied. (2) The poor taxpayer will have to submit to such additional taxation only (after careful and earnest reduction of expend iture and

avoiding of suicidal and unnecessary wars) as will be absolutely necessary to meet the deficit caused by the natural fall of exchange, instead of a concealed enormous enhancement of the *whole* taxation of the country, under the disguise and by the creation of a false "rupee" by closing the mints, to the extent of the difference between the value of the true and false rupee (may be between 6*d*. and 16*d*., or nearly three times as much).

The Indian authorities must take the advice which the Treasury has given, and restore the currency law to its original purity and soundness.

68. The second proposal for a gold standard (with partial or full quantity of gold) must be abandoned. The Government of India have themselves condemned the proposal, as already stated, paragraph 45. What does it mean? It is most inopportune at present. It means that all the proportionate small quantity of silver that is in British India, and the proportionately large quantity that is in the Native States, must be forcibly (not by any natural economic cause but by the despotism of the State) deprived of a large portion of its present value by throwing a large quantity of it in the market, and buy a large quantity of gold at a still higher proportion of value by the large additional demand created by it. All this loss in cheapening silver, and dearer gold to be squeezed out of the poor, wretched, famished ryot of India.

69. The conversion of silver into gold standard cannot be carried out without great cost (see paragraph 45), which will be the highest cruelty and tyranny to inflict upon the "bloodless" and miserable and helpless people of India, and especially this infliction to be made on the false assumption that it will give relief from the burden of the remittances for "Home Charges," when it will do nothing of the kind, as stated by Government itself.

70. The step is not at all necessary for any economic purpose except that it will be a convenience to the foreign exploiter, official and non-official. A gold currency without gold (paragraph 46) and with an unrestricted silver currency is a delusion rejected by Government itself, and forcibly impressed by the Treasury.

71. I do sincerely hope and trust that this and all such heartlessness towards, and un-British treatment of, the wretched people of India will become a thing of the past, and a true *British* Rule may bring blessing and prosperity to both Britain and India.

72. I beg to give in Appendix C. a statement of December 11th, 1892, which I had submitted to the Currency Committee in 1892, from which it will be seen that I had then pointed out the objections to the proposals. I also beg to refer the Committee to my evidence before the same Committee on December 17th, 1892, (Chap. 7060, II, 1893, p. 106).

73. There are several other more or less minor questions. Suppose a ryot is paying Rs. 10, what will be taken from him in gold? Will it be at the rate at which the intrinsic value of the silver is at the time (at present 11*d.* may be 6*d.*), or will demand be made at the present false value of 1*s.* 4*d.*, or even in the despotic power, at the rate of 2*s.*, *i.e.*, £1 of the Rs. 10?

74. When gold currency is introduced what salary will be paid to the officials at 11*d.* or 6*d.* of whatever the market value of the rupee may be, or at 16*d.*, or even 24*d.*, of the despotic value of the "rupee," for every rupee of the salary—a rupee of 180 grains of silver. In other words, will it be £25 at 6*d.*, or about £46 at 11*d.*, or about £66 at 16*d.*, or £100 at 24*d.* for a present salary of Rs. 1,000, of a rupee of 180 grains?

75. There is the foreign merchant or capitalist of every kind always wanting to save himself in his trade-risks at the cost of the taxpayer, besides using to no small extent, or to the extent of the deposits of revenue in the banks, the revenues of the taxpayers, as his capital for his trade, and besides what is brought back to India out of the "bleeding" of India as his, the foreign capitalist's capital. Is Government going to inflict oppression upon the Indian taxpayer whenever these "interests" raise a cry and agitation for their selfish ends? Merchants and all sorts of foreign capitalistic exploiters and speculators must be left to themselves. It is no business of the State to interfere in their behalf at the cost of the Indian taxpayers; they know their business; they are able, and ought to be left to take care of themselves. They exploit the country with the Indians' revenue and "bleeding." That is bad enough

in all conscience—the profits are theirs, and the losses must be also theirs and not an additional infliction upon the Indian taxpayers.

76. The Government here dare not play such pranks with the taxpayers. In India the Government only thinks of the foreign "interest" (official and non-official) first, and of the subjects afterwards, if it ever thinks of the subjects at all, when foreign "interests" are concerned.

77. Lord Mayo has truly said: "I have only one object in all I do. I believe we have not done our duty to the people of the land. Millions have been spent on the conquering race which might have been spent in enriching and in elevating the children of the soil. We have done much, but we can do a geat deal more. It is, however, impossible, unless we spend less on the 'interests' and more on the people."

78. On another occasion he said: "We must take into account the inhabitants of the country—the welfare of the people of India is our primary object. If we are not here for their good, we ought not to be here at all."—The *Hindu* of 4th May, 1898. Sir W. Hunter's "Life of Mayo."

79. This is exactly the whole truth. It is the "interests" alone that the present selfish system and spirit of Government care for—and though that is some profit to England, it is most destructive to India. If, according to the noble words of Lord Mayo, the *people's* true welfare were made the object, England itself will be vastly more benefited than it is at present, and India will also be benefited and will bless the name of England, instead of cursing it as she now begins to do—shut your eyes to it as much as you like. Do as Lord Mayo says, and all difficulties of trade, taxation, finances, currency, famine, plague, unnecessary wars, and last, but not least, of *poverty and disaffection* will vanish. The past has been bad, "bleeding and degrading"; let the future be good yet—prospering and elevating. India then will be quite able to pay as much as may be necessary for healthy Government, and *all necessary* progress.

80. In the above remarkable and true words of Lord Mayo, you have the cause of all India's woes and evils, and all England's political dangers of "the most serious order,"

as well as the proper remedy for them. Will this Currency Committee rise to its duty and patriotism?

Yours truly,

DADABHAI NAOROJI.

Sir William Wedderburn,
Chairman of the British Committee of
The Indian National Congress,
84, Palace Chambers, Westminster, S. W.

APPENDIX A.—INDIAN EXCHANGES.

From the TIMES, *September 9th, 1886.*

SIR,—I hope you will kindly allow me to make a few observations upon Indian exchanges. I shall first describe the mode of operation of an export transaction from India. In order to trace the effect of the exchange only, I take all other circumstances to remain the same—*i.e.*, any other circumstances, such as of supply and demand, etc., which affect prices.

I take an illustration in its simplest form. Suppose I lay out Rs. 10,000 to export 100 bales of cotton to England. I then calculate, taking exchange into consideration, what price in England will enable me to get back my Rs. 10,000, together with a fair profit—say, 10 per cent.—making altogether Rs. 11,000. Suppose I take exchange at 2*s.* per rupee, and find that 6*d.* per lb. will bring back to me in remittance as much silver as would make up Rs. 11,000. I then instruct my agent in England to sell with a limit of 6*d.* per lb., and to remit the proceeds in silver, this being the simplest form of the transaction. The result of the transaction, if it turned out as intended, will be that the cotton sold at 6*d.* per lb. will bring back to me Rs. 11,000, and the transaction will be completed.

Now, I take a transaction when exchange is 1*s.* 4*d.* instead of 2*s.* per rupee. I lay out Rs. 10,000 for 100 bales of cotton, all other circumstances remaining the same. I calculate that I can get back my Rs. 10,000, and 10 per cent. profit, or Rs. 11,000 altogether, if my cotton were sold at 4*d.* per lb. Then I instruct my agent for a limit of 4*d.*, which, being obtained, and silver being remitted to me at the reduced price, I get back my Rs. 11,000.

The impression of many persons seems to be that, just as I received 6*d.* per pound when exchange was 2*s.* per rupee, I get 6*d.* also when exchange is only 1*s.* 4*d.* per rupee, and that, silver being so much lower, I actually get Rs. 16,500, instead of only Rs. 11,000. This, however, is not the actual state of the case, as I have explained above. When exchange is at 2*s.* per rupee, and I get 6*d.* per lb. for my cotton, I do not get 6*d.* per lb. when exchange is only 1*s.* 4*d.* per rupee, but I get only 4*d.* per lb.; in either case the whole operation is that I laid out Rs. 10,000 and received back Rs. 11,000. When exchange is 2*s.* I get 6*d.* of gold; when exchange is 1*s.* 4*d.* I do not get 6*d.* of gold, but 4*d.* of gold, making my return of silver, at the lower price, of the same amount in either case—*viz.*, Rs. 11,000.

I explain the same phenomenon in another form, to show that such alone is the case, and no other is possible. Supposing that, according to the impression of many, my cotton could be sold at 6*d.* per lb. when exchange is only 1*s.* 4*d.*—that is to say, that I can receive Rs. 16,500 back for my lay-out of Rs. 10,000, why my neighbour would be only too glad to undersell me and be satisfied with 40 per cent. profit in place of my 50 per cent. profit, and another will be but too happy and satisfied with 20 per cent., and so on till, with the usual competition, the price will come down to the natural and usual level of profits.

The fact is no merchant in his senses ever dreams that he would get the same price of 6*d.* per lb. irrespective of the exchange being either 2*s.* or 1*s.* 4*d.* Like freight, insurance, and other charges, he takes into consideration the rate of exchange, and settles at what price his cotton should be sold in order that he should get back his lay-out with the usual profit. This is what he expects, and he gains more or less according as the state of the market is affected by other causes, such as larger supply or demand, or further variation in exchange during the pendency of the transaction.

Taking, therefore, all other circumstances to remain the same, and the exchange remaining the same during the period of the completion of the transaction, the effect of the difference in the exchange at any two different rates is that when exchange is lower you get so much less gold in proportion, so that in the completion of the transaction you get back in either case your cost and usual profit. In the cases I have supposed above, when exchange is 2*s.* and price is 6*d.* per lb., then when exchange is 1*s.* 4*d.* the price obtained or expected is 4*d.* per lb. in both cases there is the return of Rs. 11,000 against a cost of Rs. 10,000.

I stop here, hoping that some one of your numerous readers will point out if I have made any mistake. It is very important in matters of such complicated nature as mercantile transactions that the first premises or fundamental facts be clearly laid down. If this is done a correct conclusion will not be difficult to be arrived at. I have, therefore, confined myself to simple facts. If what I have said above is admitted, I shall next explain the operation of imports into India, and then consider in what way India is actually affected by the fall in exchange or in the value of silver.

Yours faithfully,

DADABHAI NAOROJI.

National Liberal Club,
September 2nd.

APPENDIX B.

1. Government of India to Secretary of State, November 9th, 1878 :—

"12. . . . And bearing in mind the necessary fixity of much of the existing taxation, the difficulty of finding new sources of revenue, and the dissatisfaction caused by all increases of taxation, even by those for which there is the most urgent necessity, it is indisputable that the political inconvenience of this gradually increasing burden is extremely great, aggravated as it further is by the uncertainty of its amount and the impossibility, of foreseeing its fluctuations, which may at any moment become the cause of the most grave financial embarrassment."—(c. 4,868, 1886, p. 19.)

2. Now is it not very strange that the necessity of avoiding additional taxation is met by laying on as heavy a taxation as possible in the covert way of creating a false rupee?

3. "74. To this might further be added that the political risks of the present time, and the prospects they create of necessary additional taxation, which, if our proposals were adopted might be avoided wholly or to a great extent, or even be met by reduction of taxation, add force to the argument that if these changes are to be made, there would be special political advantage in making them now."—(P. 26.)

4. Now this beats everything. While by proposing the device of closing the mints, and giving a false value to the rupee, they are actually increasing the burden of taxation to the extent of the false increase of the value of the rupee, the Government, with an extraordinary *naivete*, say that their proposals will "*even be met by reduction of taxation*!" The Government of India has beaten itself!

5. India Office to Treasury, January 26th, 1886:—

"It is not, however, upon the large amount of the charge that Lord Randolph Churchill is desirous of dwelling, so much as upon the extreme difficulty in which the Government of India is placed in relating its finances, and the dangers that attend a position in which any sudden fall in the exchange may require the increased charge caused thereby to be met by additional taxation."—(c. 4,868, 1886, p. 4.)

6. "The imposition of additional taxation has always been a matter of much anxiety to the Indian Government, and the greatest objection has always been evinced to imposing such taxation in forms to which the people are unaccustomed, or to frequent changes, or to measures which give rise to fears of possible further changes and additional taxes."—(P. 4.) Is it for this reason that this covert way was discovered to impose heavy additional taxation?

7. Government of India to the Secretary of State for India, February 2nd, 1886 :—

"Speaking generally, the period of financial pressure to which we refer may be said to have extended from 1873-74 to 1880-81, and to have involved increased taxation, large reductions in public works expenditure, and a heavy addition to the gold debt held in England."—(c. 4,868, 1886, p. 6.)

8. "This state of affairs would be an evil of the greatest magnitude in any country in the world ; in a country such as India it is pregnant with danger."—(P. 7.)

And so the Government of India aggravate this state !

9. "If a stable ratio between gold and silver cannot be secured we must continue to add to the gold debt of India, though we are fully aware of the objections to borrowing largely in England in a time of peace, and view with apprehension the additional burden which will be imposed on India when borrowing in England ceases, and the remittances from India must be increased in order to pay the interest charge on an increased gold debt."—(P. 8.)

Is that the reason why Government goes on increasing this debt with a light heart ?

10. The words used by Lord Lytton's Government in a despatch dated November 9th, 1878, might be applied almost literally to the circumstances of the present day.

11. "At the present time when political events may throw upon India new burdens of unusual magnitude, the position of our Government in relation to this question assumes a character of extreme gravity. Whether, if such demands upon us arise, they would require us to have resort to increased taxation to provide additional resources for the service of the year, or to loans to meet sudden or unusual charges, or, as may be more probable, to a combination of the two, the anxiety that will attend our financial administration must be very great ; and if the holders of silver should under any combination of circumstances, throw any considerable quantity on the market, as is at all events possible, the consequences to India might be financially disastrous. How a sudden call to supply by taxation a million or more to provide for further loss by exchange, and one or two millions for war charges could be met, we are

at a loss to know ; yet that such demands might arise no one can say is so improbable as to remove them from a serious claim on our attention. The prospects of a loan in such a case would not be much more satisfactory. Any temporary relief obtained by borrowing in England would be more than compensated by the increased burdens created in the future, and the necessary tendency of things would be to go from bad to worse." (P. 10.)

12. So it appears that this "extreme gravity," "the anxiety," and going "from bad to worse" were the reasons why wars of Imperial interest were undertaken, and why the increasing burdens are going on! And why it is now decided that India and India alone should bear every burden?

13. Lord Randolph Churchill, in his letter to the Treasury of January 26th, 1886, says :—"It is not, however, upon the large amount of the charge that Lord Randolph Churchill is desirous of dwelling so much as upon the extreme difficulty in which the Government of India is placed in regulating its finances and the dangers that attend a position in which any sudden fall in exchange may require the increased charge caused thereby to be met by additional taxation."

14. These extracts are sufficient to show the anxiety of the Government for increasing burdens on the people, and political danger to Government; and the beauty of the whole thing is, that they have done and are doing the very things which they proclaimed loudly should not be done : increased both taxation with a light heart and political danger with a vengeance!

15. I shall add what was said on the passing of the Bill in 1893 :—

In the Legislative Council of June 26th, 1893, the Hon'ble Mr. Mackay, who was perhaps one of the most active persons in bringing about this legislation, said :—

"I am completely in accord with the provisions of the Bill just introduced by the Hon'ble Sir David Barbour, and with the greatest deference I venture to congratulate Your Excellency on having succeeded in bringing forward a measure which will have the effect, not only of restoring the finances of the country to a satisfactory condition, but which will also mpart to trade and commercial transactions that legitimate amount of certainty of which they have been deprived for the past twenty years. The measure at the same time relieves the country of that dread of additional and seriously disturbing taxation which has been weighing upon it for some time past."

His Excellency the President said :—

16. "I think, then, that I may sum up this part of the case by saying that it has now been established almost beyond controversy that to leave matters as they were meant for the Government of India hopeless financial confusion; for the commerce of India a constant and ruinous impediment; for the taxpayers of India the prospect of heavy and unpopular burdens; for the consumers of commodities a rise in the prices of the principal necessaries of life; and for the country, as a whole, a fatal and stunting arrestation of its development" . . . . "We earnestly hope that our proposals may be fruitful of good, that the commerce of India may be relieved from an impediment which has retarded its progress, that the Government of India may be enabled to meet its obligations without adding to the burdens of the taxpayer; and that capital will flow more freely into this country without the adventitious stimulus which we have hitherto been unable to refuse. We trust, finally, that in process of time sufficient reserves of gold may be accumulated to enable us to render our gold standard effective, and thereby to complete the great change towards which we are taking the first steps to-day. Time only can show whether all these hopes will be fulfilled or be disappointed."

17. Vain, unfortunate hope! A Currency Committee is sitting again. What was said by the Treasury and others has come to pass, and all the glowing prophecies of the Indian authorities based upon clear fallacies, have been falsified—and yet persistence in the same course!

———

APPENDIX C.

INDIA, JULY 1ST, 1893.—THE CURRENCY QUESTION.

STATEMENT SUBMITTED BY MR. DADABHAI NAOROJI TO THE CURRENCY COMMITTEE.

The questions of exchange and currency in connexion with India have, unlike those questions in other countries, two different branches, and it is very important to keep them distinctly in mind.

(1) Political. (2) Commercial.

(1) The political aspect entails upon British India the compulsory remittance of about £16,000,000 to this country every year (which will now be £19,000,000, as no more railway capital will be forthcoming to be used here instead of drawing on India). I am not discussing here the righteousness or otherwise of this state of affairs. It is the loss caused by the fall in exchange in the remittances of these (now) £19,000,000 which is the point under consideration. Otherwise the question of exchange would have no significance, as I have shown in my letters to the *Times* in September, 1886.

The proposal to introduce a gold currency into India is based on the argument that it would save all present loss to the people of India from the fall in exchange. It will do nothing of the kind. It will simply inflict greater loss and hardship on the wretched Indian taxpayer. I explain.

The Indian taxpayer, at the time when exchange was 2*s.* per rupee, was sending produce to England worth 16 crores of rupees to meet the payment of £16,000,000. Now, taking exchange, say roundly 1*s.* per rupee, he has to send produce worth 38 crores of rupees to meet the (present) remittance of £19,000,000—or at a double rate. To avoid the confusion of ideas that prevails through the present controversy, I would eliminate silver altogether from the problem and put it in another form—that when one rupee was equal to 2*s.* the Indian taxpayer sent, say, one million tons of produce to meet the £19,000,000 of Home Charges—when a rupee is 1*s.*, he has to send two million tons of produce to meet the same demand. Whether the currency be gold or silver or copper or lead will not be of the slightest consequence. The Indian taxpayer will have to send to this country as much produce, and not one ounce less, as would purchase £19,000,000—the only difference in the quantity of produce to be sent will depend solely on the rise or fall in gold. Only there will be on the poor taxpayer this additional infliction—that he will be saddled with the heavy cost of the conversion of the currency in gold; and gold becoming so much more in demand will still further rise, and the taxpayer will have to send so much more produce to meet the additional rise in the value of gold. All talk of saving to the Indian the present loss by fall in exchange is pure imagination.

Again, suppose a ryot is paying Rs. 10 as land tax. When gold currency is introduced, what will Government take from him in place of Rs. 10? Will Government demand at the supposed rate of 1*s*. per rupee—*i.e.*, ten shillings only—or will Government demand arbitrarily in its despotic power at the rate of the fictitious value of a rupee as two shillings and will take £1, or any amount at any higher rate above the intrinsic value of the rupee? Taking the gross revenue comprehensively, the total gross revenue is Rs. 850,000,000, what will Government take from the taxpayer when gold currency is introduced? Will it take at the present supposed rate of 1*s*. per rupee, *viz*., £42,500,000, or will it arbitrarily impose a double revenue at the rate of 2*s*. per rupee, so that from his present poor produce the taxpayer must sell double the produce to meet the demands of Government. If the latter, what a precious benefit will this be to the Indian taxpayer from the gold currency!

When gold currency is introduced what salary will be paid to the European official? Suppose he has a salary of Rs. 1,000 per month, will Government give him at the rate of 1*s*. per rupee, *i.e.*, £50, and will the official accept £50 for the rupees 1,000? Is not all the present strong agitation of the Anglo-Indian a clear reply that he will do nothing of the kind, but will continue his agitation till he gets £100 or something near it for his Rs. 1,000: or in other words get his salary doubled at a stroke, at the expense of the starving ryot? And has not Government already shown that it will yield to such agitation, and will be readily "liberal" to European demands at the sacrifice of the Indians? It has already yielded to the demands of the Uncovenanted Europeans and has given them a fixed exchange of 1*s*. 9*d*. per rupee for their furlough, no matter whether exchange is 1*s*. or even less, say 6*d*. Now the whole European service is agitating to get them 1*s*. 9*d*. or some other high fixed exchange, even to the extent of half their salary. Do these Anglo-Indians really want to exact from the starving ryot such high exchange when the rupee is worth perhaps a shilling or even sixpence? Who will pay this difference? Of course an arbitrary Government may oppress a people as much as they like, but will the British people and Parliament allow such a thing?

On the top of all this comes the merchant with his agitation for the gold currency, that he may be saved, at the sacrifice of the ryot, from his risks of trade. The profits of trade are for his pocket, but risks of a commercial disturbance must be met by the ryot? The poverty-stricken ryot must protect the well-to-do trader! God save India!

I do not need to trouble the Committee with any further remarks as to the effect of the introduction of a gold currency on the condition of the people, who, according to Lord Lawrence's testimony, are living on scanty subsistence, and who, according to Lord Cromer, are already "extremely poor." Our friends the Anglo-Indians have to bear in mind that they are taking already from the mouths of the poor Indian about Rs. 150,000,000 or more every year as salaries, allowances, pensions, etc., to the so much deprivation of the provision of the children of the soil. Will they never understand or consider this, and what evil that means to India?

A word about the proposal to stop free coinage of silver. Now we know that a trade, internal or external, especially internal, requires abundant currency in a country like India; the curtailment of the coinage of the rupee will dislocate and cripple the free action of the trade of the country, especially internally, and will inflict serious injury and create some new complications. Secondly, the rupee, being thus artificially raised to a fictitious value by being made scarce, will depress the price of produce, and the ryot will be obliged to part with more of his poor produce to meet the demands of Government. Will this be a benefit to him? Further, by this restriction of coinage the wretched Indian taxpayer will not be relieved on a single ounce of produce in his forced remittances for the Home Charges of £19,000,000—in gold. Whatever the exchangeable value of gold is in relation to produce will have to be paid by the poor ryot, be the forced artificial exchange or the fictitious value of the rupee what it may. By restricting the coinage of silver—the price of silver in relation to produce being artificially enhanced—the taxpayer will have to pay the salary of all the European and other officials in such higher priced rupee, with so much more produce to part with! which in short, will in effect be a far heavier burden, by increasing the *whole* salary of the officials of all the services, both Indians and Europeans, at so much the greater sacrifice of the wretched ryot.

The agitation for stopping coinage of silver or introducing gold currency, far from relieving the Indian taxpayer from the present loss by fall in exchange, which in all conscience is very heavy indeed, will actually inflict greater injury upon the helpless fellows. All attempts at artificial tampering with currency will, besides injuring the people, recoil upon the perpetrators of the mischief. They can no more raise the value of silver fictitiously than they can suspend gravitation.

The evil of the present loss from exchange does not arise from the fall in exchange, but from the unfortunate unnatural political and economic condition of British India. Were there no compulsory remittances to this country (any ordinary *free* transactions of business or loans between two countries not mattering beyond the usual risks of business), there would be no evil or embarrassing loss to Government such as we are considering. The excessive European services are the cause of all such calamity upon the Indians. Any other silver-using country—for instance, China—has no problem like that which at present embarrasses the British Indian Government.

(2) Coming to the second branch of the question, *viz.*, the effect of the fall in exchange on international trade (for it is

in such trade or business only that exchange is concerned), the best thing I can do is to give below the letter I wrote to the *Times* in September, 1886, and some other letters (I have inserted those letters, which I need not repeat here). Of the letters to the *Times* that paper was pleased to write approvingly in one of its leaders.* Further, I have made, in the statement, some remarks as to the action of the United States in endeavouring futilely to stop the silver storm, instead of allowing it to run its course. This I need not give here.

The step which the Government has now taken will, I am afraid, produce much mischief, and inflict great injury on the taxpayer, crushingly heavy loaded as he already is. The utmost that the Government might have done would have been, as I was afraid they were determined to do, to give some fixed exchange to the officials for their remittances to this country—to as much as half the salary. This would have been bad enough, but the course the Government have adopted, and for which there was no great necessity, will, I fear, prove far more injurious.

II.—STATEMENT SUBMITTED TO THE INDIAN CURRENCY COMMITTEE OF 1898.

Washington House,
72, Anerley Park, S.E.
October 20th, 1898.

DEAR SIR WILLIAM,—Since my letter of 28th July last, I have perused the Blue Book of the evidence given before the Currency Committee, and I feel it necessary to make a further statement.

---

* The *Times*, January 26th, 1889:—"We observe with pleasure that Lord Cross says nothing on the bounty alleged to be enjoyed by the Indian wheat grower through the fall in the value of silver. This piece of nonsense has been again and again exposed in the letters of our correspondents, and never more clearly and forcibly than by Mr. Dadabhai Naoroji."

"BRITISH INDIA."

2. These words are often used in a very misleading and confusing manner. I give below an extract from a statement which I have submitted to "the Royal Commission on Indian Expenditure and apportionment of charges," which I hope will place the matter in a clearer light.

3. "Before I proceed further let me clear up a strange confusion of ideas about prosperous British India and poverty-stricken British India. This confusion of ideas arises from this circumstance. My remarks are for British India only.

4. "In reality there are two Indias—one the prosperous, the other poverty-stricken.

(1) "The prosperous India is the India of the British and other foreigners. They exploit India as officials, non-officials, capitalists, in a variety of ways, and carry away enormous wealth to their own country. To them India is, of course, rich and prosperous. The more they can carry away, the richer and more prosperous India is to them. These British and other foreigners cannot understand and realise why India can be called 'extremely poor,' when they can make their life careers; they can draw so much wealth from it and enrich their own country. It seldom occurs to them, if at all, what all that means to the Indians themselves.

(2) "The second India is the India of the Indians—the poverty-stricken India. This India, 'bled' and exploited in every way of their wealth, of their services, of their land, labour, and all resources by the foreigners; helpless and voiceless, governed by the arbitrary law and argument of force, and with injustice and unrighteousness—this India of the Indians becomes the 'poorest country in the world, after one hundred and fifty years of British Rule, to the disgrace of the British name. The greater the drain, the greater the impoverishment, resulting in all the scourges of war, famine, and pestilence. Lord Salisbury's words face us at every turn: 'Injustice will bring down the mightiest to ruin.' If this distinction of the 'prosperous India' of the slave-holders, and the poverty-stricken India' of the slaves be carefully borne in mind, a great deal of the controversy on this point will be saved. Britain can, by a righteous system, make both Indias pros-

perous. The great pity is that the Indian authorities do not or would not see it. They are blinded by selfishness—to find careers for our boys.' "—

(Letter to LORD WELBY, dated 31st January, 1897.)

5. This state of affairs arises from the evil system of an un-British foreign dominion, as predicted by Sir John Shore in 1787. This evil makes the action of the British trader and capitalist an exploitation which otherwise, under ordinary circumstances, under *true* British system, would be legitimate trade and investment.

6. Almost throughout the Blue Book the thing chiefly considered is the requirements and benefits of "The Foreign Prosperous British India." "Indian's India" chiefly comes in only for the consideration as to how to tax the Indians in order to meet the requirements and benefits of the British official bleeders and non-official exploiters. Earnestly and repeatedly are questions put and answers given how additional taxation should be raised—*not how to probe the evil and to find the true remedy.*

7. The main scope and direction of the evidence is as if India were a country and property of the Anglo-Indians, and British traders and capitalists; as if, therefore, their wants and requirements, and the means of enabling them to carry away as much wealth as they possibly can to England, were the chief object; and as if to consider the land, resources, and labour of India as only the instruments for the above purpose.

"INDEBTEDNESS OF INDIA."

8. This expression is repeatedly brought out for the self-satisfaction and justification of the exploitation. Let us examine how this particular phenomenon is brought about.

9. The process is this: The total amount of "Home Charges" is £15,795,836 (Statistical Abstract for 1896-7, p. 106 c. 9,036], 1898).. Out of this I deduct fully: Railways £5,790,567, and Stores Department, £951,700. In deducting these two items I do not mean that I admit the necessity of doing so entirely, but that I want to avoid any controversy at this stage upon what are called "Public Works Loans" made by England, and Government Stores. The remainder, after

making the above deduction, is £9,053,569 = Rs. 199,178,518, at 11*d*. per rupee, about Rs. 22 per £1, about which is the present legitimate rate for the true rupee, and which, with much more, though under disguise, the Indian taxpayer is actually forced to pay. Taking, roughly, Rs. 200,000,000, every pie of it is drawn from the people of British India and becomes an addition to the capital or wealth of England, and is altogether spent in England every year.

10. Next, the European services are paid in India every year (at Rs. 1,000 and upwards per annum, not including lower salaries) about Rs. 94,679,627 (including a small amount of pensions paid to Eurasians not separately given). (Parl. Ret. 192 of 1892.) I do not know whether this amount includes the payments made for and to European soldiers in India. I think not. If so, this has to be added to the above amount. To it has also to be added, I think, the illegal exchange compensation which is allowed to Europeans, thereby out-Shylocking Shylock himself by not only taking the pound of flesh, but an ounce of blood also. Almost the whole of this amount of Rs. 94,679,627, say roughly, Rs. 95,000,000 *plus* soldiers' payments and exchange compensation, is a loss to the people of British India, excepting, in a way, a small portion which goes to the domestic servants, house-owners, etc. But these amounts, would have gone all the same to these domestic, etc., even though Indians had been in the place of the Europeans. The services rendered by such domestics, etc., being consumed by others than the children of the soil, are so far a loss to the country.

11. But I do not propose to argue this point here. I allow for the present this expenditure in British India by the European officials as not forming a part of the loss by the drain. I think it is generally claimed by the Anglo-Indians that such expenditure in India by European officials is about, on an average, half of the salaries and emoluments paid to them in India, and that the other half is about the amount which is remitted to England for families and the savings. Taking, therefore, this half of Rs. 94,679,627 = Rs. 47,339,813, and adding this amount to Rs. 200,000,000 (paragraph 9), the total is roughly, Rs. 250,000,000 every year; probably more

if the two additions mentioned above of European soldiers' payments and exchange compensations were made. This enormous amount of annual political drain causes what Sir George Wingate very properly calls a "cruel and crushing tribute." Never could India have suffered such a cruel fate in all its history or existence.

12. The first step, therefore, towards the so-called "indebtedness" is that British India is "bled" every year to the amount of about Rs. 250,000,000 clean out of the country, and this enormous wealth is year after year poured into England. Will the India Office be good enough to make a return of the enormous wealth which England has drained out of India during its whole connexion?

13. Now, the second stage is the process of the manufacture of "indebtedness" is that out of this enormous wealth drawn away from India—sufficient and far more than sufficient to build thousands of miles of railways and every possible public works, and to meet every possible requirement of good government and progress, to the highest prosperity and civilisation—out of this enormous drain a small portion is taken back to India as "British capital," when it is nothing of the kind, and by means of the so-called "British capital" all Indian resources of land and labour are further exploited by "British" (?) capitalists of every kind. All the profits made thereon are so much more wealth drawn away from India and brought to England.

14. Further, the foreign exploiters are not satisfied with the small portion of "Indian wealth" which they take back to India as their own capital, but they insist upon being further helped from the very current revenues of the country. So voracious are these exploiters that they clamour against Government for not putting its whole revenue at their disposal in the Presidency Banks, instead of keeping a portion in the Treasury. Thus there is at first a political "bleeding," which is the foundation evil, and in its train and by its help comes the so-called "commercial" or capitalistic exploitation.

15. Thus is manufactured that complacent "indebtedness" in the name of which the bleeding and exploitation are

unceasingly and ever-increasingly carried on, and which is so pleasant, so profitable, and so nice an excuse to the Anglo-Indian and "British capitalist's" heart.

16. In reality there is not a single farthing of "indebtedness" from India to England. It is England that is under a very vast material and moral debt to India. Of the latter—moral debt—I cannot speak much here, though it is no less enormous and grievous than the former.

17. Besides the sum of Rs. 400,000,000 now drained from India (paragraph 24) every year, (1) the British Indian Empire is built up at the *entire* expense of India, and mainly with Indian blood. Even now Indian blood is contributing in extending the British Empire and benefits in other parts of the world. And what a reward—a helotry! (2) Not only this, but in addition to the cost of building up the whole Indian Empire England has taken away from India an amount of wealth since its connexion with India which, with ordinary commercial compound interest, will amount to thousands and thousands of millions sterling.

18. It may be asked whether I mean that I do not want British capitalists to go and trade or employ their capital in India? I mean nothing of the kind. By all means let them do so. Under ordinary circumstances India will hail it, as any other country may do. But let it be with their own capital. Let them bring their own capital, and make upon it as much profit as they can, with India's blessing upon it. What I mean is that they should not first "plunder" India, leaving it wretched and helpless, then bring back a portion of "plundered" India's wealth as their *own*, exploit therewith India's resources of land and labour, carry away the profits, and leave the Indians mere hewers of wood and drawers of water —mere slaves, in worse plight than even that in which the slaves of the Southern States of America were.

19. If England can understand her true interests—political, moral, economic, or material—if she would hold back her hand from India's throat, and let India enjoy its *own* resources, England can make India prosperous, and, as a necessary consequence, can drive from India far, far greater benefit, with India's blessing, than what she derives at present

with India's curse of the scourges of war, and pestilence, and famine, and of an ever-increasing poverty.

20. The word "indebtedness" must be taken at its correct interpretation. It is simply "bleeding" and exploitation, or what Mr. Bright indirectly characterised "plunder."

"BALANCE OF TRADE IN INDIA'S FAVOUR," AND "EXCESS OF EXPORTS OVER IMPORTS AS A BENEFIT TO INDIA."

21. What is balance of trade in its true sense? Say a country exports £100,000,000 worth of its produce. It gets back in imports, say, £80,000,000 worth of other countries' merchandise. The remaining balance of £20,000,000 of the original exports, and, say, 10 per cent. of profits, or £10,000,000—altogether £30,000,000 has *to be received*. This £30,000,000 is called balance of trade in favour of that country. And when that country actually receives this balance of £30,000,000, either in the shape of bullion or merchandise, then its account is said to be squared or settled.

22. I have not included in this trade account any true borrowing or lending Such borrowing or lending can be considered by itself. A country's borrowing is included in its imports, and the interest it pays is a part of its exports. This loan account between any two independent countries can be estimated and allowed for. And that in no way affects the *bona fide* balance of trade. If India be allowed to and can *get* its true "balance of trade" it would be only too happy to make any legitimate borrowing or lending with any country, with benefit to both.

23. But such is *not* India's condition. What is India's actual condition? What is its so-called "balance of trade," of which much mistaken or wrong view is taken in the evidence? Be it first remembered, as I have already explained under the heading of "indebtedness," that what is called India's debt is nothing of the kind, but simply and solely a part of its own wealth taken away from it.

24. Let us see what the amount is (c. 9,036, 1898, p. 277). Taking the last five years as an illustration, the total net exports for 1892-3 to 1896-7 are Rs. 1,314,600,000. The total

exports for the same period are Rs. 5,688,000,000; taking 10 per cent. profits thereon, will be Rs. 568,800,000. Therefore the total excess of net exports, *plus* profits, would be Rs. 1,883,400,000. Then, again, the so-called "loans" from this country are included in imports, the net exports must be increased to that extent. The addition to commercial debt in this country after 1891-2 to 1896-7 is £6,479,000 (c. 9,036, 1898, p. 130), or, say, £6,500,000, which, at the average rate of exchange of the same years (p. 131), about 1*s.* 2*d.* per rupee, or nearly Rs. 17 per £1, is equal to Rs. 110,500,000. So that the total of net exports (excluding loans from imports) and profits will be Rs. 1,883,400,000 *plus* 110,500,000 equal to Rs.1,993,900,000, or about roundly Rs.2,000,000,000. During the five years the average per year will be about Rs. 400,000,000. Now to call this a "balance of trade in favour of India" is the grossest abuse of language. It is neither any "trade" nor "balance of trade." It is simply and solely the *remittances* of the official bleeding and the exploitation of the non-official capitalists. Not a *pie* of this tremendous amount—Rs. 400,000,000 every year—will India ever see back as its *own*: while in true balance of trade the whole of this amount should go back to India as its *own*.

25. No wonder Sir William Harcourt's heart rejoiced at the leaps and bounds with which the income-tax increased year after year in this country. In his speech on the occasion of his famous Budget he rejoiced at the increasing income-tax, never seeming to dream how much of it was drawn from the "bleeding" drain from India.

26. With what self-satisfied benevolence have examiners and witnesses talked of the great benefit they were conferring upon India by making every effort to increase the excess of exports in order to enable poor India to meet her "indebtedness." Such is the Indian myth! But what is the reality? To increase the net exports as much as possible means to increase the remittance of the bleeding and exploitations of ever year of which not a farthing is to return to India as its *own*. Extraordinary, how ingeniously matters can be and are represented, or rather misrepresented, and the public here entirely misled!

SURPLUSES AND SOLVENCY.

27. There never have been and never will be true surpluses or solvency of British India as long as the present evil system of government lasts. What is a surplus of the finance of any country? Suppose that in England you raise £100,000,000 of revenue. Suppose £95,000,000 are spent and £5,000,000 remain in hand at the end of the year, and this £5,000,000 is called surplus, and that the Government, if it does not impose any additional taxation or does not borrow, is solvent. Now, the essential condition of this surplus is that the whole of the £95,000,000 has returned to the tax-paying people themselves in a variety of ways, and continues to be part and parcel of the wealth of the country. And the remaining £5,000,000 will also go back to the people and remain a part of the wealth of the country.

28. But what is the case with India? It is nothing of the kind. Suppose Rs. 1,000,000,000 are raised as revenue. Suppose Rs. 950,000,000 are spent, leaving Rs. 50,000,000 in hand at the end of the year. Now, are these Rs. 50,000,000 a surplus? No. The Rs. 950,000,000 have not all returned to the people and have not remained as part of India's *own* wealth. Some Rs. 250,000,000 (see paragraph 12) are drained clean out of the country by foreigners, never to return to India. Till these Rs. 250,000,000 are returned to India as its own, which they never are, and which is a dead loss, to talk of the surplus of Rs. 50,000,000 is another gross abuse of language. Instead of Rs. 50,000,000 surplus there is a pure deficit or rather entire loss of Rs. 250,000,000. And such perpetual losses are pure bankruptcy.

29. I repeat, that there never has been and never will be any surplus in India as long as, from every year's revenue there is a clean drain, which at present is at the rate of about Rs. 250,000,000. In this country all that is raised as revenue returns to the country, just as all water evaporating from the oceans returns to the ocean. And England's ocean of wealth remains as full as ever, as far as revenue is concerned. India's ocean, on the contrary, must go on evaporating and drying every year more and more.

30. The only reason why the Indian Government does not go into bankruptcy—bankrupt though it always is—is that it can, by its despotism, squeeze out more and more from the helpless taxpayer, without mercy or without any let or hindrance. And if at any time it feels fear at the possible exasperation of the people at the enormity, it quietly borrows and adds to the permanent burden of the people without the slightest compunction or concern. Of course the Government of India can never become bankrupt till retribution comes and the whole ends in disaster.

31. I have referred in the above consideration to the official bleeding only, but when to this is added the further exploitation of the land (meaning all the resources) and labour of the country, which I have already described, the idea of surplus or solvency, or of any addition to the wealth or prosperity of the *people* (however much it may be of the Europeans) becomes supremely ridiculous and absurd.

IMPORT OF BULLION AND HOARDING.

32. Reference is frequently made to this matter. I think the best thing I can do is to give an extract from my reply to Sir Grant Duff :—

Westminster Review, November, 1887.

33. "Sir Grant Duff refers to the absorption of gold and silver and to hoarding. What are the facts about British India? In my 'Poverty of India' I have treated the subject at some length. The total amount (after deducting the exports from imports) retained by India during a period of eighty-four years (1801 to 1884), including the exceptionally large imports during the American War, is £455,761,385. This is for *all* India. The population at present is 254,000,000. I may take the average of eighty-four years roughly—say, 200,000,000. This gives 45*s*. 6d. per head for the whole eighty-four years, or 6½*d*. per head per annum. Even if I took the average population as 180,000,000, the amount per head for the eighty-four years would be 50*s*., or 7*d*. per head per annum. Of the United Kingdom I cannot get returns before 1858. The total amount of treasure returned by the

United Kingdom (after deducting exports from imports) is, for twenty-seven years from 1858 to 1884, £86,194,937. Taking an average of 31,000,000 of population for twenty-seven years, the amount retained for these twenty-seven years is 55*s.* 7*d.* per head, or very nearly 2*s.* 1*d.* per head per annum; while in India for more than three times the same period the amount is only 45*s.* 6*d.* per head, or 6½*d.* per head per annum. France has retained from 1861 to 1880 (Mulhall's Dictionary) £208,000,000, and taking the population, say 37,000,000, that gives 112*s.* per head in twenty years, or 5*s.* 7*d.* per head per annum.

34. "Sir Grant Duff ought to consider that the large amount of bullion is to be distributed over a vast country and a vast population, nearly equal to five-sixths of the population of the whole of Europe; and when the whole population is considered what a wretched amount is this of gold and silver—*viz.*, 6½*d.* per head per annum—received for all possible wants! India does not produce any gold or silver. To compare it with Europe: Europe retained in ten years, 1871-1880 (Mulhall, 'Progress of the World,' 1880), £327,000,000 for an average population of about 300,000,000 or 21*s.* 10*d.* per head, or 2*s.* 2*d.* per head per annum. India during the same ten years retained £65,774,252 for an average population of, say, 245,000,000; so that the whole amount retained for the ten years is about 5*s.* 4*d.*, or only 6½*d.* per head per annum, against 21*s.* 10*d.* and 2*s.* 2*d.* respectively of Europe. This means that India retained only one-fourth of what Europe retained per head per annum during these ten years. It must be further remembered that there is no such vast system of cheques, clearing-houses, etc., in India as plays so important a part in England and other countries of Europe. Wretched as the provision of 6½*d.* per head per annum is for *all* wants—political, social, commercial, etc.—there is something far worse behind for British India. All the gold and silver that I have shown above as retained by India is not for British India only, but for the Native States, the frontier territories, and the European population; and then the remainder is for the Native population of British India. We must have official information about these four divisions before we

can form a correct estimate of what British India retains. The Native States, as I have said before, have no foreign drain except the small amount of tribute of about £700,000. Some frontier territories receive something instead of paying any tribute. These States therefore receive back for the exports of their merchandise, and for the ordinary trade profits on such exports, full returns in imports of merchandise and treasure, and this treasure taken away by the Native States and frontier territories forms not a small portion of what is imported into India. It must also be considered how much metal is necessary every year for waste of coin and metal, and for the wants of circulating currency. When Government can give us all such information, it will be found that precious little remains for British India beyond what it is compelled to import for its absolute wants. I hope England does not mean to say that Englishmen or Englishwomen may sport as much as they like in ornaments or personal trinkets or jewellery, but that the wretch of a Native of British India, their fellow-subject, has no business or right to put a few shillings' worth of trinkets on his wife's or daughter's person—or that Natives must simply live the lives of brutes, subsist on their 'scanty subsistence,' and thank their stars that they have that much.

35. "I will now try to give some indication of what bullion British India actually retains. Mr. Harrison gave his evidence before the Parliamentary Committee of 1871-74, that about £1,000,000 of fresh coinage was more than sufficient to supply the waste of coin or metal. Is it too much to assume that in the very widespread and minute distribution, over a vast surface and a vast population, of small trinkets or ornaments of silver, and their rough use, another million may be required to supply waste and loss? If only a pennyworth per head per annum be so wanted, it would make a million sterling. Next, how much goes to the Native States and the frontier territories? Here are a few significant official figures as an indication. The 'Report of the external land trade and railway-borne trade of the Bombay Presidency for 1884-85' (p. 2) says of Rajputana and Central India :—'13. The imports from the external blocks being greater than the exports to them, the balance of trade due by the Presidency to the other provinces

amounts to Rs. 12,01,05,912, as appears from the above table and the following.' I take the Native States from the table referred to.

EXCESS OF IMPORTS IN BOMBAY PRESIDENCY.

		Rs.
From Rajputana and Central India	...	5,55,46,753
" Berar	...	1,48,91,355
" Hyderabad	...	8,67,688
Total	...	7.13.05,796

Or £7,130,579. This means that these Native States have exported so much more merchandise than they have imported. Thereupon the Report remarks thus :—'The greatest balance is in favour of Rajputana and Central India, caused by the import of opium from that block. Next to it is that of the Central Provinces. It is presumed that these balances are paid back '*mainly in cash*' (the italics are mine). This, then, is the way the treasure goes; and poor British India gets all the abuse—insult added to injury. Its candle burns not only at both ends, but at all parts."

36. Far from any important quantity or any quantity of bullion going to British India and as "balance of trade," Rs. 400,000,000 worth of British India's wealth at present goes clean out of the country every year never to return to it as its *own*.

BENEFITS DERIVED FROM CHEAP SILVER.—A LOW RUPEE AND LOW EXCHANGE PROMOTES AND DEVELOPS EXPORTS.

37. That there is some temporary advantage from low exchange to silver-using countries over gold-using countries, I have already explained in my letter to the *Daily News* of September 24th, 1886 (Appendix A. of my letter already submitted). But in British India this little advantage is of not much avail to the poor people. What becomes of it when that must perforce lose every year, never to return to them, Rs. 400,000,000 of wealth out of their miserable total produce, leaving them so much more poor and miserable? It is idle to talk of the people of British India deriving benefit from low

exchange or from anything as long as these tremendous bleedings and the exploitation go on.

PRICES AND WAGES.

38. The above remarks apply equally to prices and wages. How on earth, under such drain, can there be any healthy increase of prices or wages arising from true prosperity? Before the Royal Commission on Indian Expenditure and Apportionment, a member having asserted that there was general rise of prices, Mr. Jacob, as official witness, confirmed the statement. Thereupon I prepared some questions, took the paper to Mr. Jacob, and gave it to him to enable him to prepare the replies. And, what was my surprise when he told me that the subject was not of his department, and he would not answer the questions, though he did not hesitate to say that there was a general rise of prices! If of any use I shall produce the questions before the Committee. But, first of all, there are no reliable statistics sufficient to draw any correct conclusions; and conclusions of any value cannot be drawn about any one factor from prices or wages which are the results of many factors.

39. I would not lengthen this statement by noting several other points in the Blue Book, but conclude by repeating what Sir John Shore has said more than a hundred years ago (in 1787). His words were true then, are true to this day, and will remain true in future if the evil pointed out by him continues. He said: "Whatever allowance we may make for the increased industry of the subjects of the State, owing to the enhanced demand for the produce of it (supposing the demand to be enhanced) there is reason to conclude that the benefits are more than counterbalanced by evils inseparable from the system of a remote foreign dominion."

40. This evil system must be altered, or, as I have said before (paragraph 5), what, under natural circumstances, would in any country be legitimate trade and investments by British people become, under this evil system of an un-British rule, cruel exploitation. Unless the evil is remedied, there is no hope for British India, and disaster both for England and India is the only look out.

41. Let England pay fairly and honestly her share of expenditure incurred for her own interests, and end the bleeding by a careful consideration of the following words of the Duke of Devonshire, as Secretary of State for India, spoken in 1883: "There can, in my opinion, be very little doubt that India is insufficiently governed..............If the country is to be better governed, that can only be done by the employment of the best and most intelligent of the Natives in the Service." And the best means of attaining this object is to give honourable fulfilment to the Resolution passed by the House of Commons in June, 1893, about simultaneous examinations.

42. Unless Acts and Resolutions of Parliament and Royal Proclamations are honourably fulfilled, and a righteous Government, worthy of the English character and promises and professions is established, no currency or financial jugglery, or "political hypocrisy," or any "subterfuges," or un-British despotic ruling will avail or remedy the ever-growing and various evils that *must* constantly flow from an unrighteous system.

43. Lord Salisbury's eternal words stare us in the face: "Injustice will bring down the mightiest to ruin."

APPENDIX—C.

REPLIES TO QUESTIONS PUT

TO THE

PUBLIC SERVICE COMMISSION

THE PUBLIC SERVICE COMMISSION.

My paper on the Indian Services, dated 7th December, 1886, covers a large number of these questions, and renders some of them unnecessary to reply to. I now reply to those which need reply from me.

I would first make a few general remarks.

The only firm rock upon which a Foreign Rule, like that of the English, can be planted in a country like India, is that of equal justice to all British subjects, without any regard to any class or creed. The principles of high policy and statesmanship, which the statesmen of 1833 and 1858 laid down, are the best and the only right ones that can be adopted by a civilized and advanced nation like England. Every deviation from this "plain path of duty" cannot but lead to troubles, complications and difficulties. Like a step-mother, England can win the love and affections of her step-children by treating them with the same love and justice with her own. Children might submit to tyranny and injustice from their own mother, but would always resent the least injustice from a step-mother.

The more firmly and steadfastly England would adhere to the noble principles of 1833 and 1858, the stronger would be her hold upon the loyalty, gratitude and attachment of the

Indian people. Diverse as the races and the classes are in India, it will be the strongest self-interest of each and all to preserve the headship and rule of a just power, under which all could be equally protected and prosperous.

Under the simple principle of equal justice to all, none could reasonably ask for special favours, and a host of complications and troubles would be avoided. As in the case of every law of nature, this moral law will gradually adjust everything into natural and harmonious action and development, though, as in all transitions, some temporary difficulties may occur. It is admitted from experience that the larger the field of competition, the higher is the standard of the results. By the simultaneous first examinations in India and England, India will have the benefit of the best talent of the country. The backward provinces or classes will be stimulated by emulation and ambition to spontaneous exertions, and the best help Government can give to them will be to aid them in their education. The best service that the leaders of such classes can do to their community is to encourage them to depend upon their own exertions, to help them to prepare themselves for fair and manly struggle, and thus to win their position both in the services and in other walks of life, and not under the debasing and demoralising influence of favouritism. This manly course will keep them backward for a short time, but it would be the best for them in the end. Favouritism *cannot* last long under the British administration. It must break down and these classes will have to begin their manly course then. The sooner they set themselves to work in that way, the better for them, and the quicker will they come to the front and obtain whatever they may deserve.

One of the best results of the first simultaneous examination in India and of the general carrying out of the 4th Resolution of the National Congress of 1885, will be a great impulse to education. The New York State Commission in their report say:—"Nor does there seem to be any reason to doubt that opening of the Public Service to competition will give to education here, as it did in Great Britain, a marvellous impulse, The requirement proposed in the 4th Resolution of the National Congress of India of last December, for the successful candidates of India to finish their studies and examinations with the successful candidates of England is a very important matter. It has to be considered by us not as a condition to be imposed by Government, and as an injustice to us, but as a thing to be highly desired by ourselves in order that our native officials may, in every possible way, stand on a perfectly equal footing with their English colleagues, and there may not be left any ground to cast any slur of inferiority upon them. Moreover, without a visit to, and study in, England for sometime, our officials will never sufficiently acquire a full feeling of self-respect and equality with their English colleagues, their education will not acquire that finish which it is essential it should have to administer an English system, by studying that system in its birthplace itself. The visit of the successful India candidates to England is much to be desired for our own benefit, at least for some years to come, when experience will show the desirability or otherwise of continuing it.

The standard and tests of qualification, Mental, Moral and Physical—to be alike for all candidates. Age to be same, and all British subjects to be admitted without any disqualification for race, creed, or colour. The competitions in the different provinces of India for the Uncovenated Services to be in the same way open and similar for all.

The circumstances of qualifications being alike, there should be no difference of pay, pension, leave, etc. etc., for the same office or duties.

The remark made by Sir C. Aitchison in his minute on the age question is well applicable to the whole question of the competition for the Services. He says :—

" I think they are right in rejecting the Statutory system and resenting it as an unjust imputation upon their capacity and intellectual ability, and in demanding that the conditions of competition shall be so framed as to make it possible for them to enter the competition on a fair footing as regards their European fellow-subjects, and to win by their own exertions an honourable position in the Civil Service."

Such fair footing cannot be obtained by the Indian candidates without a simultaneous examination in India.

"I. WORKING OF THE EXISTING STATUTORY SYSTEM.
II. MODE OF SELECTION OF STATUTORY CIVILIANS."

Questions 1 to 45.

Following the lines of my first paper, it is evident that the Statutory Service should cease, if simultaneous examinations are held in England and India. Otherwise, it would be an undue favour to the natives. Any system of scholarships also to enable natives to go to England to qualify for the Civil Service, than would be unnecessary.

III. COMPETITION IN ENGLAND FOR THE INDIAN CIVIL SERVICE.

Questions 46 to 67.

No additional facilities need be given to the Native candidates to go to England. The simultaneous first examination in India puts them on an equal footing with the candidates in England.

54. From this Province, there have been Hindu, Mahomedan and Parsee candidates in England; and I think, 1 Hirdu, 1 Mahomedan and 3 Parsees have passed.

55. Expense, risk of failure and the greater risk of young lads going wrong, and the consequent unwillingness of parents to let their children go out of their own and family control and influence, are very serious objections to sending young boys to England. Out of those few who have sent, some have regretted it. Among certain classes of Hindus there is religious objection. The elderly people will for some time yet continue to feel it objectionable to go to England, but such youths of the rising educated generation as would succeed in the first competition, will not object to go. Even the general feeling is now gradually diminishing.

IV. COMPETITION IN INDIA FOR THE INDIAN CIVIL SERVICE.

Questions 68 to 92.

72. The present Educational establishments will not for some time quite adequately furnish all the requirements of the Indian candidates, but by the very fact of the demand arising, the existing institutions will develop themselves, and new ones will arise.

73-74. An open Competition will not be likely to give any decided advantages to any particular class or caste, except to those persons who are competent to pass it and who would in time form a class of their own. It could not be otherwise, where fitness should be the only pass. The Third Annual Report of the United States Civil Service Commission says:—

"The fundamental idea of this reform, that public office is a public trust, to be exercised solely for the public welfare, and that offices should be filled only by those best qualified for the service to be rendered, after their fitness have been ascertained by proper tests, is the corner-stone of popular government."

This principle applies with far greater force to a *foreign* Government.

75. Far from there being any political or administrative objections to open simultaneous competition in India, there are important reasons why it should be so. For politically, just treatment will be the greatest political strength.

On administrative grounds, this policy will be the best means of getting the fittest and best British subjects for service, and will relieve Government of a host of difficulties with which they are beginning to be assailed, and which will go on increasing as long as they keep astray from the plain path of duty and from the easiest, justest, and most natural principles of government. In taking this plain path of duty, the roots of their power will sink deeper and deeper into the hearts and affections of the people.

76. The question of getting the aristocracy into the Service is a very important one. Their influence is great and their attachment to the Rule is desirable. But the exigencies and requirements, and the whole system of civilized British administration rests upon educational, moral and physical fitness. It will be no service or kindness to put any cadet into a position for which he is not fit. He soon falls into ridicule, and leaves the service in disgust. If a cadet is well educated and competent, his own aristocratic feeling of dignity would impel him into a fair and manly contest. And he would not like to be in a position, to be looked down upon as inferior and as a creature of "mehrbany" (favour). If he is incom-

petent, Government cannot put him into a place for which he is not fit. In the old and no passing regime of Native States, a cadet may be put any where to draw his pay, and a deputy or some subordinate does his work. But in British Administration this is utterly out of the question, and will not be tolerated a single day. As Sir C. Aitchison has said:—"Manifestly it is our duty to the people of India to get the best men we can"; or as the Civil Service commissioners in England have shown the necessity of obtaining the advantage of getting "not merely competent persons, but the best of the competent."

So all attempts to draw the cadets by favour will naturally end in failure and disappointment. It will be an anachronism. The best way in which Government can do the aristocracy real and permanent good and true kindness is to induce them, by every means, to give their sons suitable education, and whether they afterwards care or not to get into the Services, their general advance in knowledge and intelligence will enable them to appreciate truly the merits of the British Rule, and will make them intelligent and willing supporters of it. The best favour, therefore, that Government can do to the aristocracy is to persevere still more earnestly in the course it has already adopted to promote education among them, and the whole problem of the true position and dignity, in the new state of circumstances, will naturally and smoothly solve itself. The more they attain their self-respect, the more able will they be to preserve their dignity, position and influence among their countrymen, and the more will they appreciate the true merits of the British Rule.

To a great many of the aristocracy, a military career would be more congenial, and it would be very desirable to adopt suitable means in this direction to draw them to become attached and devoted, in their self-interest and self-respect to British Rule.

78. For the higher service the simultaneous competition in India ought to be from the whole of India, to secure "the best of the competent" for such high service.

For the Uncovenanted Service, each Province should be left to itself for the necessary competition.

79. Under simultaneous examination in India and further study and examinations in England with the English successful candidates, the position of the Indian official will be quite equal to that of the English official.

80. Any fixed portion of the service to be allotted to natives, will violate the fundamental principle of the Act of 1833 and of the Proclamation of 1858—will not hold in itself reasonable elements of finality and will not do full justice to the claims of the natives. Should, however, Government be now not prepared "to do full justice" and to allow the chance or possibility of all successful candidates turning out to be natives, Government may, for the present, provide that, till further experience is obtained, a quarter or half of the successful candidates should be English.

With the fair field opened freely by the simultaneous examinations, the Statutory Service, as I have already said, will have no reason to exist for first appointments.

81. The age must be the same for all candidates, so that no stigma of inferiority or favour might stick to any. About what the age should be, I agree with Sir C. Aitchison, and the Resolution of the Congress of last year, that it should be 23 maximum, and 19 minimum.

82-83. The Civil Service Commissioners in England are most fitted from their experience to fix all necessary tests and qualifications that would be fair to all candidates, and such tests or qualifications should be the same for all. Lord Macaulay's Committee has said, as to some test for moral qualifications:—

"Early superiority in Science and Literature generally indicates the existence of some qualities which are securities against vice—industry, self-denial, a taste for pleasures not sensual, a laudable desire of honourable distinction, a still more laudable desire to obtain the approbation of friends and relations. We therefore believe that the intellectual test which is about to be established will be found in practice to be also the best moral test which can be devised."

In regard to physical fitness, I think that, beyond merely looking to freedom from any physical organic defects, some tests should be instituted to test certain physical accomplishments of all candidates, such as riding, swimming, shooting and military and gymnastic exercises.

At the Cooper's Hill College, in the Public Works and Telegraph Departments (and I think Forest is also now included), the following rules exist :—

"37. Every student will be required to go through a course of exercise in the gymnasium, and of Military exercises, including the use of the rifle."

"39. Every student selected for the Indian Service before proceeding to India, will be required to furnish evidence of his competency in riding."

85-6. The very essence of equal competition is that every subject, test qualification or condition should be alike in England and India for all candidates—fair enough not to handicap any unreasonably, and with an eye to secure the best fitness, the highest educational and mental training, and suitable physical capacity. This will give the best men all round.

89. With training on such thorough equality of tests, etc., there will be no difference of circumstances in the case of persons who enter through the simultaneous examinations, and there will be no reason to make the rules for pay, leave, pension, etc., different. On principle also the duties of an office should carry its own remuneration, etc., the fittest person being got for the office, and such reasonable remuneration should be fixed for the purpose as would induce superior men to seek the service.

90-92. The Covenanted Servants will be sufficiently tested, and will not, I think, need a probation, after joining service in India, beyond what is at present required. However, whatever probation may be deemed necessary, it should be the same for all—Europeans and Natives.

V. Promotion from the Uncovenanted Service.

93 to 101.

This is an important chapter. It is very desirable that some prizes should be held out for marked, meritorious and able service in the Uncovenanted Services.

Any scheme for the purpose must be such that the person promoted, being thus considered qualified, should afterwards be on a footing of equality, with regard to pay, etc., etc., with the Covenanted Servant occupying similar situation. The promotion to be open on the principles of 1833, without regard to race or creed. The recommendation of any Provincial Government with satisfactory reasons, to be subject to the confirmation of the Viceroy and the Secretary of State.

That not more than one such promotion should be made in any one year in any one Province—or some maximum must be fixed.

That in the year in which such promotions are made, the number of appointments to be competed for at the regular first competitive examination of that year, should be lessened by the number of promotions.

In such promotions, probation will not be necessary, as Government would not select anybody for such a prize, where capacity and fitness for business is not already marked and proved.

VI. Pay, Leave and Pension. 102 to 120.

Under the principles of 1833 and 1858, the Statutory Service ceasing to exist, no distinction being reserved for any class or race, and equal qualifications being fixed for all, by the simultaneous examination in England and India and future associated study and examinations in England, no distinction of Pay, Leave or Pension can be justified. The duties and responsibilities should carry their own recompense fixed on a reasonable scale. Equal furlough, I think, will induce persons to visit England, which is desirable. After all the European could only need about 5 weeks more for going to and from England.

The question of Admission from the professional classes is rather a difficult one. Those who succeed in their profession are generally not likely to seek service, and those who would seek service are generally not likely to be superior men. Then, after severe competitions and suitable qualifications are required from those who enter the service at the regular door, and who for that purpose devote themselves to the necessary preparation, it becomes unjust to them to open a side-door for others. It may be a matter for consideration, which I think it is already, whether, after the first general competition in England and India to test high culture and capacity, a division should not be made, out of the passed candidates, for Judicial and Executive services, so that their subsequent preparation, for two or three years in England, be devoted in the respective direction. The point to be borne in mind is that if a side-door is opened, the principle of competition and fairness will receive a serious blow, and nepotism, favouritism, interest, etc., will force their way into the services,—a thing most to be deplored.

Under the present system of the Uncovenanted Service, judicial appointments are, I think, made from persons called to the Bar who prefer service to practice. But when a proper system is adopted for all the Uncovenanted Services so as to secure the best men for first appointment through a regular door, this necessity will no longer exist.

VII. General.

121 to 165.

123-125. The Indian schools develop force of character and other qualities, as similar institutions in England do. In fact, the Indian schools are on the model, and follow in the footsteps of English schools.

The full development of force of character and other qualities depends upon their future exercise and opportunities. When any limb of the body or faculty of mind is not used or exercised, it gradually decays. The actual responsibilities and performances of duties develop and strengthen all necessary qualities, and in time become hereditary in classes. The British advanced system of administration, requiring intellectual, moral and physical fitness, will in turn create from the educated its own new class of administrators, and an intellectual aristocracy who would, from self-interest, right appreciation and gratitude, become and remain devotedly attached to the British Rule, and to the system in which they would have been born and bred. The present old land-marks cannot and will not continue. The world, and especially the present progression of India, cannot stand still. Circumstances are fast changing in these days, and the condition of things must change therewith.

The wisdom of the Government will be in directing these changes aright and in their own favour with grace, instead of forcing them into opposition against themselves.

The exclusion of the natives for nearly a century has much to answer for any decay of administratorship or fitness that may be now observed. The change of this policy and the adoption of the noble policy of the Act of 1833 and the Proclamation of 1858 will give new life to the nation, will redress the past wrong, benefit India, and benefit and bless England. Richly will then be realised those noble and glorious hopes of the Proclamation: "In their prosperity will be our strength; in their contentment our security; and in their gratitude our best reward."

126-131. The objection for want of sufficient means to be risked for the purpose operates to a very large extent. It is chiefly the educated and middle class that makes some attempt. The rich do not much care, even up to this time, both for education and for service, though education is forcing some progress among them. That great difficulty is the natural unwillingness of parents to cast their raw young sons, unformed in character, at the most critical period of their life, among strangers in a land far away, and full of temptations and snares for them; without the parental and family control and influences to guard and guide them. Several parents have regretted the day when they allowed their dear ones to part from them.

In a hundred ways that can hardly be described, a raw native youth has difficulties, temptations and risks.

By confining the examinations to England we get only a few of those who can afford to risk some money, but we cannot get the *best* of the talent and fitness from the *whole* country, besides it being utterly unjust to handicap the Natives so heavily. The few that go are not necessarily of the best.

By residence in England, young boys do often more or less get out of touch and sympathy with the people in India.

These remarks do not apply to those who go at a higher age, and after their character is formed and their intelligence fully developed. They derive great advantage from the visit. They are able to understand and study things intelligently, make comparisons with things in their own country, are vividly struck with striking differences, and are inspired with a desire to improve by them. They do not cast of their touch and sympathy with their own people. On the contrary, they are generally more sharpened. With the novelty and intelligent observation, they return with a sort of enthusiasm, to do some good in their country. The kind of young men who will go to England after the first examination in India, will be just the persons who will derive the greatest benefit from the visit. Every moment of their sojourn will be well and profitably spent, their great stakes and formed character keeping them straight and desirous to do their best.

132. The requirement of temporary residence in England '*precedent*' to first competition is the main grievance. This requirement '*following*' on success in India in a simultaneous examination, will remove the grievance, and will not have the effect of preventing any considerable or important section, who are prepared for competition, from competing.

133-4. Once the first competition is freely opened to all, and the Statutory Service abolished, excepting so far as it is adopted to give a reasonable opening for the most meritorious among the Uncovenanted Servants, another special service for any class cannot be justly made, and for no long time will all classes of Hindus allow the present caste-objections to continue.

135-141. It is desirable to avoid opening many doors for admission to the Services, once the regular doors are so freely opened to all. The cases of servants not knowing English will become rarer every day. Should such cases arise of very meritorious servants, they might be rewarded in some way, such as a special extra personal allowance.

There may arise sometimes a case, such as of some important political mission in which any certain individual, owing to connection, influence or position, becomes especially most fitted for the task. Power should be reserved to Government, with the sanction of the Secretary of State to make such extraordinary appointments outside the Services—

though it is desirable to avoid this as far as possible. The peculiarly special fitness becomes a special reason for the occasion.

142. No, there should be no proportion or show of any favour introduced. In a free and open competition, numbers will in time have their proportionate share. Any such departure and complication vitiates the principal of 1833. The natural ambition of each community will bring it into the field in proportion to its number and capacity, and the principle of 'the fittest' will be observed with the greatest advantage to the whole country, without trouble to Government and with best service done to every class, by having been set to help itself manfully.

143. No such classifications are needed. They will be contrary to the principles of 1833, and will be the source of much trouble and difficulty. It is undesirable to crystallize or select any class or classes to monopolise any services. In the present transition state, things should be left to develop and arrange themselves naturally, with free field and scope.

144. For the high Covenanted posts, it is not desirable to restrict the natives to their own provinces, and this cannot be done for a general competition by simultaneous examinations in England and India. We must get the advantage of the best and fittest from the whole country, and then they may be distributed as Government may think best, or the present system may be continued by which the selection of the Provinces is left to the candidates in the order of their merit in the first competition. But even then the Government has the power of making transfers.

145-157. All such schemes violate the fundamental principles of the Act of 1833. They will deprive us of what we already possess by this law. The simple machinery of a fair field for all, and the employment of the fittest can be the only best scheme founded on a just and sound principle and giving the best results.

164-5. I do not know whether there is any such system in Bombay. Any system cannot be good, if it be not based on some sound principle and fitness. Once the field is opened freely and fairly to all, every such contingency will in time naturally settle itself, and Government will be saved much trouble and complication of the vain endeavour of satisfying everybody or class separately.

VIII. Composition, Recruitment, &c., of the Subordinate Executive and Subordinate Judicial Service. 156 to 184.

167. The sections who take advantage of education—and they mainly belong to the middle classes.

168. The rich and the commercial classes do not much care for service. It is chiefly from the natives of middle class, good family and education, that most of the candidates come. And every native who is educated is desirous to confer the same blessing upon his children.

169. Some prefer an independent line or a profession and some willingly accept appointments.

172-5. After a fair field is opened for all, there will be no justification for any appointments being practically reserved for natives of pure descent or for any other class. Fitness must be the only principle—the principle of 1833—and then no just complaint can arise.

176-183. Suitable high education and fitness must be an essential qualification. It cannot be otherwise under the British system; and after educational, moral and physical fitness is decided upon as the only right basis for employment, Government are the best judges as to what the tests should be to secure the necessary qualifications.

Separate examinations may be established to test separate requirements of the different departments of the Subordinate Services, a certain extent of high general education and training being necessary for all. Open competition for all classes and fitness to be the fundamental principle, and the examinations and tests so arranged as to secure the best qualifications for the service for which the appointment is to be made.

Something like the Civil Service Commission of England may be founded here, who would be able to arrange all suitable details, and go on improving the system as experience suggested—the sole principle and aim being justice to all subjects alike and fitness for the duty.

Each Province will be better left to make its own arrangements suitable to its wants for the Subordinate Services. Probation is useful, and the length of this also will be best fixed by the authorities or the Commission as experience suggests.

Some probation will be advisable, though it is not absolutely necessary. The Civil Service Commission of the United States say in their third Report of 1885-6:—

"It could be shown statistically that those who pass highest in the examinations are likely to make the most useful public servants." . . . "A man taken from the head of a register is far more likely to be a valuable public servant than one taken from the foot and therefore the examinations do test superior capacity for the public service."

"Despite all the antecedent probability of fitness which the precautions just described create, it is beyond question true that we cannot be absolutely certain, that a well-informed man of good habits will prove a good worker. A real test of the fact by doing the public work is precisely what the merit-system provides. That test is a probationary service of six months before an absolute appointment."………

"This practical test, by actually doing the public work, is not only an integral part of the merit-system, but originated with it. If these facts were generally understood, they would doubtless be regarded as a full answer to the oft-repeated criticism, that mere information is not proof of business capacity."………

"The experience of the Commission has shown how great is the majority of those, having passed the examination, who have proved themselves to be persons of good business capacity." After giving some statistics:—"The results, indeed, go far towards showing that a probationary term is not essential, though unquestionably useful, under the new system."

184. It would be desirable, if candidates in the first examination of the Covenanted Service, who may have shown decided proficiency, but failed to secure a place among the successful candidates, and who are passed the age of competition, are allowed, if they so desire, to be placed at the head of the list of the successful candidates of the year in one of the Uncove-

nanted Services. For, a superior class of servants will thus be secured without any injustice to anybody—only that the person will have passed a much higher examination and a higher order of tests and qualifications, which will be an advantage.

It will be a good field for the recruiting of the Subordinate Service, if such persons can be secured. As such persons will have to commence at the bottom of the service, they will often prefer with their high acquirements to strike out some new lines for themselves or enter the professions. But should they desire to enter the Subordinate Service, they should be allowed.

General Remarks.

Though I have answered some of the questions relating to schemes or details, and whatever may be their suitability, all I have to urge is that the principle of 1833 and 1858 must be the foundation of the whole edifice, and every scheme be based upon, and in accordance with it. We should not, after half a century of progress, be now deprived of our great Charter in the slightest degree. Once this principle is faithfully adopted, Government can easily arrange to devise suitable schemes to secure the best results. For the Covenanted Services the machinery already exists, all that is necessary is to make the first competitive examination simultaneously in India with that of England. And for the Uncovenanted Services, Civil Service Commission may be devised, who would prepare suitable schemes in detail for every department and carry them out.

The chief point which I desire to urge is this. Let Government adopt any schéme of competition, only let every one,—European or Native—have a free and fair field, so that neither should be in any way handicapped, and all are subjected to the same tests.

No distinction of race, creed or colour being left, Government will be relieved of all the troubles and complications that must otherwise arise, and the whole machinery of Government will settle itself into smooth work under a just and sound principle, with benefit to the country and glory to the Rulers.

As I have often said, the question of the services or foreign agency, is a question of the highest importance for the economic condition of India, and the material condition of the masses. It is *the* one "evil incident to a foreign rule" which requires to be *minimised as much as possible*, if English rule is to be a true and great blessing to India. The following words of the Secretary of State for India, show what political danger also lies in this foreign "character of the Government":—

Parl. Ret. [c. 4868] 1886, page 4.

"The position of India in relation to taxation and the sources of the Public revenues is very peculiar, not merely from the habits of the people and their strong aversion to change, which is more specially exhibited to new forms of taxation, but likewise from *the character of the Government which is in the hands of foreigners, who hold all the principal administrative offices and form so large a part of the Army*. The impatience of new taxation which would have to be borne wholly as a consequence of the foreign rule imposed on the country, and virtually to meet additions to charges arising outside of the country, would constitute a political danger, the real magnitude of which, it is to be feared, is not at all appreciated by persons who have no knowledge of, or concern in, the Government of India, but which those responsible for that Government have long regarded as of the most serious order." (The italics are mine.)

APPENDIX—D.

STATEMENT TO THE SELECT COMMITTEE ON EAST INDIA FINANCE, 1871.

FINANCIAL ADMINISTRATION OF INDIA.

A considerable number of the best informed and most influential Native and English inhabitants of India, together with others of Her Majesty's subjects of all ranks who have the welfare of that portion of the British Empire at heart, asked for Parliamentary inquiry. Parliament readily granted a Select Committee of the House of Commons, though for an inquiry which was to be limited to Financial Administration. It is, I think, due to Parliament and to the Select Committee that those who prayed for inquiry should say in time what they want, for it would be both unreasonable and useless for them to complain afterwards that the Select Committee did not do this or that. As a native of India, and one who joined in a petition from the East India Association, I most respectfully submit for the consideration of the Select Committee a few remarks as to what I hope and desire from it.

The Financial Administration of any country, like all other human institutions, requires, four important elements:—

1st. Materials.

2nd. Head to design.

3rd. Hand to execute.

4th. Sound principles of design and execution. Upon the degree of perfection of each and all of these requisites depends the measure of success.

1.—MATERIALS.

This is the *most important* and fundamental question for decision. Without sufficient and suitable materials to work with, all the other requisites are of no avail whatsoever.

The question, then, is: Does India, even at the present day, produce enough to supply, without hardship or privation, both its ordinary wants as a nation, and its extraordinary and peculiar want, to remit to a foreign distant country, a portion of its produce as the natural economical result of a foreign rule? I say that India does not produce enough even for the ordinary necessary wants of its children, much less for all their social and peculiar political wants. Is this a fact or not? The Indian Government is bound to answer this question definitely. If the India Office should prove me to be wrong, no one will rejoice more than myself. If I be right, then, no ingenious device of even ten Wilsons or Temples will relieve the Financial Administration of its difficulties unless the Indian legislators and financiers possess the Divine power of creating something out of nothing. The poverty and privations of the country once admitted, the question then will be, how to remedy this fundamental evil. The subject of the remedies ultimately resolves itself into the following:—

1st. Provision of capital necessary for all public works of a permanent character, both ordinary and extraordinary, which are required to increase production and facilitate distribution, to be provided, if India is impoverished, and has it not.

2nd. A just adjustment of the financial relations between India and England, so that the political drain may be reasonably diminished.*

---

* I give this chief cause of the impoverishment of a country in the words of Sir R. Temple himself, written under the direction of Lord Lawrence. (Punjab Administration Report for 1856-8, Parliamentary Return 212 of 1859, page 16):—

"In former reports it was explained how the circumstance of so much money going out of the Punjab contributed to depress the agriculturist. The native regular army was Hindustanee; to them was a large share of the Punjab revenues disbursed, of which a part only they spent on the spot, and a part was remitted to their homes. Thus it was that, year after year, lakhs and lakhs were drained from the Punjab, and enriched Oudh. But within the last year, the native army being Punjabee, all such sums have been paid to them, and have been spent at home. Again, many thousands of Punjabee

3rd. The best way of attracting capital and enterprise to utilise the vast culturable waste lands.

4th. The best way of increasing the intelligence of the people by a comprehensive plan of national education, both high and popular.

If the fact of the poor production of India can be proved directly, any indirect test may not be considered necessary; but as questions have been already put in the Committee about such tests, and as these tests are frequently appealed to as proving the prosperity of the country, I think it necessary to say a few words regarding them. The tests I refer to more particularly are "rise" in prices and wages, and imports of bullion. I hope mere general assertions on these points will not be considered sufficient. To understand correctly the phenomena of prices and wages, it is absolutely necessary for the India Office to prepare a return of the prices and wages of all districts from, say, twenty years prior to the British acquisition, to the present day, giving also opposite to the figures for each year the causes of the rise or

---

soldiers are serving abroad. These men not only remit their savings, but also have sent quantities of prize-property and plunder, the spoils of Hindustan, to their native villages. The effect of all this is already perceptible in an increase of agricultural capital, a freer circulation of money, and a fresh impetus to cultivation." . .

"The Report has been prepared under the direction of Sir John Lawrence, K.C.B., Chief Commissioner of Punjab, by

"R. TEMPLE,

Secretary to Chief Commissioner, Punjab."

May I appeal to Sir R. Temple to ponder over this extract and in his new place of a financier of India, look this same evil for all India boldly in the face, and firmly suggest its proper remedies; so that the burden of the millions and millions that are "year after year drained" from India to England may be reasonably lightened, and the ability of the people to meet the legitimate portion of the drain increased to the necessary extent? Is it also too much for India to expect, or even to claim from Lord Lawrence to represent this evil to the Select Committee and to Parliament, and to obtain for India full redress?

fall, as the case may be. Such a return alone will show the effect of "the drain," after the British acquisition, either as to how far any rise, on the one hand, was the result of scarcity of production, or of increase of prosperity, or of local expenditure on public works; or, on the other, how far any fall was the result of abundance of produce or the poverty of the district; and, further, whether the rise or fall was general or local, permanent or temporary. The average of a collection of districts of the whole country must also be taken correctly, and not in the erroneous manner in which they are at present made up in the Administration Reports.

To show the necessity of what I ask in the above paragraph, I give a few instances. In the Madras selection from Government Records, No. XXXI., of 1856, prices are given of certain periods for several districts. I take those of Chingleput (page 23), for the years 1841-50, (Fuslee, 1251-60), during which the prices suddenly rose from Rs. 82 per garce of paddy in 1254, to Rs. 126 in the next year 1255, and to Rs. 124 in 1256, and again went down to Rs. 96 and 69 in the succeeding years. So at Rajahmundry, in the prices for the years 1236 to 1245 (1826 to 1834), there is a sudden rise from Rs. 64 in 1241 to Rs. 111 in 1242, and to Rs. 168 in 1243, going down again to Rs. 95 and 63 in the succeeding two years. Now, are these high prices in the two couples of years the result of scarcity or prosperity? If the former, how very wrong it would be to take the high averages of these ten years for comparison or as an indication of prosperity? The last two years in the Punjab have been bad seasons, and the price of wheat has risen from 1st January, '68 to 1st January, '70 at Delhi, from 26 seers (of 2 lbs,) per Re. 1 to 9 seers; at Ambala from 24 seers to 9 seers; at Lahore, from 18 seers to 9¾ (Punjab Adm. Report for 1869-70, p. 95).

Now, is it right from high averages occasioned in this manner to infer prosperity? An hon'ble member recently quoted in Parliament the high price of rice at Jubbulpore. Had his informant been a little more communicative, he would have learnt that, while at Jubbulpore, say in the average good season of 1867-8, the price was Rs. 3¾ per maund, in the adjoining division of Chutteesghur, the price at Raipore and Belaspore was only Re. 1 per maund, or nearly one-fourth; and that therefore Jubbulpore, with its local expenditure on public works, was no criterion for the rest of the country. In the North-West Provinces, the price of wheat was about the same in the years 1860 and 1868. But during that interval the province passed through a great famine, and had famine prices. Now, will the average taken with these famine prices be a proper criterion for inferences of prosperity? With regard to the erroneous mode of taking averages of a number of districts, by adding up the prices and dividing the total by the number of the districts, without reference to the quantity produced in each district, I need simply refer to the average taken in the Report of the Central Provinces for 1867-68. It is there made out for rice to be Rs. $2\frac{3}{8}$ per maund, when the actual average was only about Rs. $1\frac{1}{8}$.

These few instances will, I hope, suffice to show how carefully the test of prices, and similarly that of wages, have to be ascertained and applied. With reference to wages, two important elements must be borne in mind—the number of the labourers who earn each rate of wages, and the number of days such wages are earned during the year.

So far as my inquiries go at present, the conclusion I draw is, that wherever the East India Company acquired territory, impoverishment followed their steps, and it is only from the time that loans for irrigation and railways and other public works, and the windfall of the benefits from the American War returned back, as it were, some of the lost blood, that India has a little revived. But it will require vigorous and steady efforts to increase the production of the country, and diminish its drain to England, before it will be restored to anything like ordinary good health, and be freed from famines.

With regard to imports of bullion, there are sufficient returns for the past seventy years; but they require to be carefully examined to draw any correct inferences from them, taking into consideration the non-production of bullion in the country, the revenue being required to be paid in money, and thereby making silver a necessity in all ordinary transactions of life, the *vast* population among whom these imports are distributed, and the amount of treasure the East India Company and their servants carried away during the last century in the shape of salaries, bribes, booty, etc. Cannot the India Office make some return on this point, to show the exhaustion of the country thus caused which required to be replenished by subsequent imports? It is no use simply depending upon the re-echoing of the general exclamation, "What an enormous quantity of silver has gone to India!" I entreat most earnestly that the first element—*viz.*, the material condition of India—may be most carefully sifted, and the necessary remedies be applied. If this question be not boldly and fairly grappled with, it will be, in my humble opinion, the principal rock on which British Rule will wreck. It is impossible for any nation to go on being impoverished without its ultimate destruction, or the removal of the cause.

II. HEAD TO DESIGN.

The head which designs the Imperial financial legislation is the Supreme Legislative Council, while local legislation is designed by the local Councils. All these Councils have a controlling head in the India Office Council in London. The questions, then, to be decided, in order that the designing head may be as efficient and adapted to the end as possible, resolve themselves into these :—

1st. Can any legislation ever do its work satisfactorily in which the opinions, feelings, and thoughts of the people paying the taxes are not fairly represented? Englishmen, no matter how able and with whatever good intentions, cannot feel as the natives feel, and think as the natives think. The co-operation of a sufficient number of intelligent natives in all the Councils* is an absolute necessity to any satisfactory financial legislation. As to any fear of political mischief from taking natives more largely into confidence, I think it to be entirely groundless. But, even granting that there was any risk, I need simply refer to the Act of 1861, in which ample checks and securities are provided. With a sufficiently large number of natives, with a corresponding increase in the number of non-official English members, there will not only be no risk, but, on the contrary, every cause for satisfaction. I may just point out the checks I allude to—

"Provided always, that it shall not be lawful for any Member or Additional Member to introduce, without the previous sanction of the Governor-General, any measure affecting—

"1. The public debt or public revenues of India; or by which any charge would be imposed on such revenues.*

"2. The religion or religious rites and usages of any class of Her Majesty's subjects in India.

"3. The discipline or maintenance of any part of Her Majesty's Military or Naval Forces.

"4. The relation of the Government with Foreign Princes or States." (Clause 19.)

Moreover, the Governor-General has his power of veto; and the ultimate consent of Her Majesty's Indian Secretary is also necessary. (Clauses 20 and 21.)

Clause 22, limits even the power of the Governor-General as to what he shall not legislate upon, and Clause 43 repeats, with certain additions, as to what the local Council cannot legislate upon except with the sanction of the Governor-General. With such checks there can be nothing to fear.

2nd. Whether decentralization, such as Sir Charles Trevelyan and Sir C. Wingfield, and others who agree with them, propose, is necessary or not to solve difficulties like the following. Some provinces complain that they are taxed more to make up the deficits of others. For instance—supposing that the Zemindars of Bengal are right in claiming exemption from any additional burden on lands, under the

*Though the Indian Councils are thus prohibited from imposing charges on Indian revenues without direct legislation, and the sanction of the Governor-General first obtained to introduce the measure, the Indian Council in England is, in a very anomalous way, left to do what it likes with the revenues of India; take, for instance, the way in which certain charges connected with the Cooper Hill Civil Engineering College are put upon Indian revenues or the large sum of money spent upon the India Office, or any other charges that the Indian Council chooses to make.

Regulation of 1793, would not the scheme of decentralization enable the Bengal Government to provide in some other appropriate way for its own wants, instead of the Supreme Council being obliged to impose the same taxes upon the other parts of India also, as it cannot tax Bengal by itself.

The distant Presidencies complain that the Supreme Council is not able to understand fully their peculiar requirements. With the Governor-General having a veto upon all the legislation of the subordinate Governments, could not the Supreme Government be better able to attend to all Imperial questions without any loss of dignity or power, and yet leave fairly upon the heads of the different Presidencies their fair share of responsibility? These and similar questions with regard to the Constitution and work of the Councils in India have to be decided.

Similar questions have also to be considered with regard to the Indian Council in England. First, need there be such a large Council? Secondly, need the Council have the work of supervision of everything that is done in India; or will it act merely as an appellant power, to interfere when appealed to? Is the constitution such as could satisfactorily perform its work with the due knowledge and appreciation of the continuous change of conditions going on in India? And is it not necessary, moreover, that, as in the Councils in India, some suitable representation of native views and interests should exist in the India Office? Lastly, is it right that this Council should have the power to spend the revenues of India as it likes, without some such open legislation, discussion, and check, as is provided for the Councils in India? From this, I hope it will be sufficiently apparent that the element of "the head which design and controls" the financial administration of India requires careful consideration. The necessity of a fair expression of the views and feelings of the natives has another aspect—*viz.*, that with such co-operation Government will be very largely relieved of the odium of any dissatisfaction among the natives.

All the remarks with reference to the necessity of a fair representation of natives in the Legislative Councils apply equally to all taxation and expenditure of local funds. For, besides the Imperial revenue of some £50,000,000, there are local funds raised as follows :—

LOCAL FUNDS.

Gross Receipts for 1867-8, *according to Part I. of Finance and Revenue Accounts of India, published by the Government of India, Calcutta,* 1870, *Account No.* 34 *pages,* 116 118, 120, *and* 122

	£.
Government of India	41,028
Oudh	194,728
Central Provinces	173,410
British Burmah	105,550
Bengal	623,722
N.-W. Provinces	825,007
Punjab	326,870
Madras	459,199
Bombay	1,093,133
Berars (11 months of 1866-67, £130,148) Not given.	
Total ...	£3,842,647

III.—HAND TO EXECUTE.

This hand is formed by all the different services in the Administration. The questions are :—

1st. Can these services be fully efficient without a proper proportion of natives of talent and integrity in all grades? I consider the question here solely with reference to successful financial administration, independently of its very important, social and especially, political bearings, of the claims of right and justice, and of the great evil of no elders of wisdom or experience being prepared among the natives, as all the wisdom and experience of English officials is lost to India on their retirement, except perhaps of a few, who have conscience enough to feel the debt they owe to India, and to do what they can in England to promote its welfare.

2nd. Can the English officials, no matter however clever, manage the natives as well as natives of the same standing, ability, and integrity? A word of persuasion and assurance from a native of official position will, in the nature of things, carry more influence than that of an Englishman. A native will far more easily understand and know how to deal with the ways of natives. The assistance, therefore, of a proper proportion of natives in all departments is a necessity for successful organization and working of details. Even now it is the native in many instances who is the real soul of the work, though the credit is all taken by his English superiors.

Conscientious men, like Sir Henry Ricketts, of the Bengal Civil Service, make no secret of such a circumstance, and rightly urge to let credit be given to whom it belongs. It is only natural that the Englishman, with his frequent changes and his ignorance of the people around him, is depended upon, and at the mercy of, his subordinates. If there were in the service natives of the same position with himself, he would, by comparing notes with them, be much helped in understanding the feelings, views, and idiosyncrasies of natives, which he has no other means of learning.

Successful administration requires complete knowledge, and for such knowledge the co-operation of the natives is simply a necessity.

There is, moreover, the economical, and, therefore, the immediately financial, point of view from which this subject has to be considered. Supposing that the native official was paid as highly as his English colleague, the mere fact that all the earnings of the native official remain in the country, as he has no remittances to make to a foreign land for the education or maintenance of his children or family, or of his savings, is in itself so far an economical and, therefore, a financial advantage to the country; and it is the bounden duty of the English rulers to allow the Indian this economical saving, consistently with their political supremacy. In some of the services, such as the Public Works, Telegraph and Forest, political considerations have no place; while economy and justice, and the oft-repeated pledges of Parliament, demand that qualified natives should have free and fair admission into all the services. Unless this economical saving is allowed to India to a fair extent, all professions of administering the finances of India for the good of India cannot but be merely a mockery and a delusion. Politically considered, it is not at all improbable that before long the English rulers of India will have some troublesome questions to solve, if due foresight is not used in this matter.

IV.—Principles of Design and Execution.

As a whole the questions are :—

1. Whether, by the present principles and, modes of taxation, the burden is equitably distributed over the shoulders of all classes of people?
2. Whether the present expenditure is not capable of being largely curtailed, and much waste prevented, without impairing the efficiency or strength of the English rule?

To solve these two important questions it is necessary to work in the way in which the Committee has already commenced, to examine the principle and necessity of each item of receipt and expenditure. Now, there is no doubt that the opinion of this governor, or that revenue officer, or such a commander, may be worthy of all weight and respect; but, at the same time, in order that the Committee should arrive at an independent judgment of their own, it is necessary that they should not be satisfied with mere general opinions of the witnesses, but should require a clear statement of some satisfactory *proofs* upon which those opinions are based. I hope, therefore, that mere assertions of officials, that "all is right," will not be considered sufficient. For instance, we may take the question of the land revenue, which is the very subject the Committee has commenced with. There is a variety of land tenures, and each is based upon several principles. I take the instance of one of these principles—*viz.*, the proportion of the rate of assessment to the income of the cultivator, or the produce of the land.

There are two questions. First, Are the principle or principles of the rates sound? and, second, if so, are the rate or rates adopted, such as to encourage increase of cultivation, lead to increase of capital, and thereby to increase of production and prosperity?

First take the *principles* of the rate.

In Bombay, one and the chief principle of the last settlement seems to me to be this. It is illustrated by a table by Captain (now Sir George) Wingate and Lieut. Nash. (Bombay "Selection," No. CVII., New Series, page 14. See also pages 109 and 110.)

The soil is divided from No. 1 to No. 9. The gross produce of soil No. 1 is supposed, for illustration, to be Rs. 172-4 as. for every Rs. 100 of cultivation expenses—*i.e.*, Rs. 72-4 as. is net produce; and for soil No. 9, the gross produce is supposed to be Rs. 127-6 as. 3 p. for every Rs. 100 of cultivation expenses—*i.e.*, Rs. 27-6 as. 3 p. is net produce. The Government assessment is then adjusted as follows: Out of the net produce of Rs. 27-6 as. 3 p. of No. 9 soil, the Government rate is, for supposition, taken as Rs. 5-13 as. 4 p. leaving to the cultivator Rs. 21-8 as. 11 p.—*i.e.*, something like 75 per cent. of the net produce. But what is proposed to be left to the cultivator of No. 1, whose net produce is Rs. 72-4 as.? One would think that, like the rate of the No. 9 soil, Government would take one-forth, or say, Rs. 18, and leave to the cultivator three-forths, or Rs. 54. Such, however, is not the case. The cultivator of No. 1 soil is also to keep only Rs. 21-8 as. 11 p., and give up to Government Rs. 50-11 as. 1 p.—*i.e.*, Government takes above two-thirds and the cultivator less than one-third; the principle being that, no matter what the net produce for every Rs. 100 invested may be, every cultivator is not to have a definite proportion of his net produce, but an absolute fixed quantity. This would be something like imposing the income-tax upon the principle that if one merchant makes a profit of £50 on an investment of £100, and another of £10 on the same investment, they are not to pay some definite proportion or proportions of their profits; but if the latter is to pay £2 out of £10 and retain £8 the former should also retain £8 only, and pay £42 to Government. I wonder how British merchants and manufacturers would like this principle! However, it is not my object here to discuss the merit of this principle, but only to state it, for comparison with that of the other provinces.

Now take Madras. There the principal is, after allowing for ridges, boundaries, unproductive portions of fields, seasons.

cultivation expenses, etc., to adjust the Government Assessment at two-thirds of the net produce on wet or irrigated lands, and a sort of compromise between two-third of net produce and one-forth of gross produce on dry lands; the balance of about one-third of the net produce being left to the cultivator, ("Madras Selection," No. XIV., of 1869, pages 142—160, Settlement of Chellumbrum and Manargoody Talookas, of South Arcot). Taking Punjab, the principle of the first settlement was on the basis of two-thirds of the net produce, but by the revised settlement it is on one-half of the net produce for Government. In the N.-W. Provinces (Adm. Report, '67-'68, page 47) "the standard of assessment is now 55 per cent. of the assets, of which 5 per cent. goes for cesses; the remaining 45 per cent., after defraying the village expenses, forms the profit of the proprietors."

To sum up the whole, I give an extract from a memorandum of the India House (Return 75, of 1858): "And in all the improved systems of Revenue Administration, of which an account has been given in the preceding part of this paper, the object has not been merely to keep the Government demand *within the limits of a fair rent, but to leave a large portion of the rent to the proprietors.* In the settlement of the N.-W. Provinces, the demand was limited to two-thirds of the amount, which it appeared, from the best attainable information, that the land could afford to pay *as rent.* The principle which has been laid down for the next settlement, and acted on wherever settlement has commenced, is still more liberal; the Government demand being fixed at one-half instead of two-thirds of the *average net produce—that is, of a fair rent.* The same general standard has been adopted for guidance in the new settlement of the Madras territory. In Bombay, no fixed proportion has been kept in view, but the object has been that land should possess a saleable value." (The italics are mine.)

Now, in giving this extract I have also the object of directing attention to the use of the words "net produce" and "fair rent" as synonymous. Is it so? Is the *net produce*, of which one-half is settled as Government assessment, *rent* only in the sense in which economists use the word, and for

" leaving a large portion of which " Government claims credit of liberality?

Now to the next question. Taking the *absolute* amount of the net produce, is the portion allowed to cultivators sufficient, on an average, for their year's ordinary wants of common necessaries, and some reasonable comforts, together with a saving to face a bad season, or to increase the capital of the country for increasing production?

The test of "the satisfaction of the ryots " is often quoted as a proof of soundness. But it requires to be ascertained whether because an element like that of fixity of tenure and non-interference for a long period is felt satisfactory, it follows that the other elements or principles of the settlement are also necessarily satisfactory or just, even though, as a general result, the agriculturists may feel themselves somewhat better off than they were before? Or is the fact of such profits as the Bombay Presidency had the good fortune to make from the late American War, and the improvement of condition by railways, though a cause of satisfaction of the cultivators, a proof of the soundness or justness of each and all the principles adopted in the settlement? To come to a right conclusion, each principle requires to be examined on its own merits, without reference to general results: for if *all* the principles were sound, much more satisfactory may be the results.

The Bombay settlement, as well as that of other parts, is now under vision. It is important to ascertain the real present incidence of land revenue, and the reasonable increase that may be made, with enough left to the cultivator to subsist on, and to save for increase of capital. I am afraid, the Bombay re-settlement is not quite reasonable.

I shall take one or two more instances in connection with land revenue. Whether the Zemindars of the Permanent Settlement can be taxed for extra cesses has been the subject of much controversy and dissatisfaction, and even up to the present day the India Office is divided against itself. Now, as long as mere opinions of this official or that Indian Secretary are the sole guides, I do not see how the controversy will ever end. It is a simple question of documentary evidence—the interpretation of a regulation. Would it not be the best plan to subject this question to the decision of a judicial authority, such as the Privy Council after hearing the arguments of counsel on both sides? The decision of such a tribunal must end the matter. The same course, either on the original side of the High Court of Bombay, or in the Privy Council, might be adopted with regard to the extra anna-cess imposed upon the existing Bombay settlements. I believe it is the opinion of many that it was a breach of faith on the part of Government. A decision of a competent judicial tribunal would be satisfactory to all parties.

The *prestige* of the British name for good faith should never be in the least imperilled, if it is to exert for Government the moral influence it possesses, independently of political and other reasons.

Lastly, in reference to the principles of the land revenue, as a part of the whole design, is the burden of taxation on the cultivator of land in an equitable proportion with other classes? Government claims the rights of a landlord. Does that mean that Government *must* have a certain portion of the produce no matter even though the exaction be inequitably higher than that from other classes of people? Or is the Government demand upon-land to be adjusted on the principle that Government requiring a certain revenue, the land should pay its equitable quota with all other industries? or is it that, because richer interests can resort to agitation, and make themselves heard, while the poor labourer and cultivator cannot, it is felt easier to squeeze them than the other classes?

II. Is the machinery for the collection of the land revenue sufficiently economical? I think the evidence of a person like Dewan Kasi Shahabudin, for the Bombay side, will be valuable; for, as a native revenue official as he once was, he knows the feelings and views of the natives in a way and to an extent which it is almost impossible for an English official to acquire.

After this one instance of the land revenue, I do not think I need go into the details of the other items of the Budget further than to say that the test of Questions I and II under the fourth head has to be rigidly applied to all the items; and to ascertain whether the system of keeping accounts is such as it should be. I shall take only one more item. The salt-tax, especially, requires most anxious consideration. It is the cause of the poor, who cannot speak for or help themselves. Is it at all right to tax salt; and, even allowing the necessity, is the incidence of its burden on the poor similar to that on the other classes for the share they pay towards revenue?

The salt gross revenue for different parts is as follows for 1869-70:—

(Ret. c. 213 of 1870.)

		Population about.	Per head about. s. d.
Bengal ...	...£2,583,562	40,000,000	1 3½
Oudh	1,219	11,000,000	...
Central Provinces.	115,167	9,000,000	0 3
N.-W. Provinces...	488,728	30,000,000	0 4
Punjab	923,060	17,500,000	1 0½
Madras	1,164,736	23,000,000	1 0
Bombay	599,407	14,000,000	0 10
Total ...	5,875,879	144,500,000	0 9¾ average.

Now, taking the share of the agricultural produce which can be considered as left to the mass of the poor, agricultural, and other common labouring population, to be 20*s*. a-head, an ordinary cooly or workman pays in his salt some 4 per cent. out of his wretched pittance. But it must also be borne in mind that 4 per cent. out of 20*s*. is far more important to the poor man than 10 or 20 per cent. out of the income of the richer classes. Taking 25*s*. a-head, the rate will be 3¼ per cent.

Of the four elements I have described above, the first three are essentially questions for Parliament.

1. It is Parliament alone that can decide what the financial relations between England and India should be; how far the guarantee of England can be given for the alleviation of the burden of the public debt, which is the result of English

wars in India, or other countries of Asia; and how far the benefit of England's credit and capital can be given to help in the restoration of India's prosperity and prevention of famines.

2. It is Parliament alone that can modify the constitution of the Legislative Council and the Indian Council, or give the people of India such a fair voice in their own affairs as they are now capable of exercising, because these Councils are the creation of an Act of Parliament.

3. It is Parliament alone that can insist on the faithful fulfilment of the repeated pledges they have given by Acts of Parliament for the admission of natives into the various services, according to competence and character, and without any regard to caste, creed, colour, or race. In the Public Works Department there is a farce of a regulation to admit natives in India on proof of competence; but very good care is taken that natives do *not* get in. On the Bombay side, as far back as 1861, three natives proved their competence (and one did the same in 1866), and to my knowledge none of them had found admission into the Engineering Department up to 1868. Whether they have since been admitted I do not know, though during the interval dozens of appointments have been given every year. English interests exercise such pressure upon the Indian Governments, that unless Parliament does its duty and insists that, in accordance with its pledges, justice shall be done to the children of the soil, there is but little hope on that score.

4. The principles of the whole design of Financial Administration, or of its details, will have always, more or less, to be settled and controlled by the Indian Governments themselves, according to change of circumstances. The best service, therefore, that Parliament can do on this head—and which Parliament alone can do—is to inquire, at certain reasonable intervals—say every ten or twelve years—how the Indian Governments have discharged their trust. This simple necessary control of the great Parliament of the Empire will prevent many of those evils which freedom from a sense of responsibility induces, and infuse into the Administration all that care and forethought necessary to its success.

After I had posted the foregoing part of this pamphlet from Alexandria, I came across a speech of Lord Mayo, in the *Times of India's* summary, of 8th April last. I read one paragraph in it with feelings of mixed regret and hopefulness; regret, that one in the position of a Viceroy should have put forth what, in my humble opinion, is an erroneous and misleading statement; and hopefulness, because now that the Viceroy has directed his attention to the all-important subject of the insufficient production of the country, he will, I hope, be able to grapple with it, investigate its causes and evil consequences, and earnestly endeavour to apply suitable remedies.

I refer here to the paragraph in which His Excellency endeavours to refute the assertion that Indian taxation is "crushing." His Lordship on this point has made several assumptions, which require examination. I shall, therefore, first consider whether the conclusion drawn is legitimate, and whether all necessary elements of comparison have been taken into account.

Last year, in my paper on "The Wants and Means of India," which was read before the East India Association, a rough estimate was given of the total production of India (including opium, salt, minerals, manufactures—in short, production of every kind) as about 40*s*. a-head per annum.

Mr. Grant Duff, in his speech of 24th February last, referred to the relative incomes of England and India, and endeavoured to show that while the former was estimated at £30 a-head, the latter was "gussed" as 40*s*. a-head per annum. Now, his lordship the Viceroy quotes Mr. Duff's statement of 40*s*., and believes that Mr. Duff has good reasons for his statement. So that we have it now on the highest authority that the total production of India is only 40*s*. a-head per annum.

His Excellency the Viceroy, after admitting this fact compares the taxation of India with that of some other countries. In doing this his lordship deducts as land revenue (*whether rightly or wrongly, will be seen hereafter*) the opium, tributes, and other small receipts from Indian taxation, and then compares the balance with the taxation of other countries.

Being on board a steamer in the Red Sea, I cannot refer to returns to see whether his lordship has made any similar deductions from the taxation of the latter. The result of the comparison would appear to be that, while India pays only 1*s.* 10*d.* per head of taxation per annum, Turkey pays 7*s.* 9*d.*, Russia 12*s.* 2*d.*, Spain 18*s.* 5*d.*, Austria 19*s.* 7*d.*, and Italy 17*s.* per head per annum. The conclusion drawn is that the taxation of India is not "crushing." What idea his lordship attaches to the word "crushing" I cannot say, but his lordship seems to forget the very first premise that the total production of the country is admitted to be 40*s.* per head. Now, this amount is hardly enough for the bare necessaries of life, much less can it supply any comforts or provide any reserve for bad times; so that, living from hand to mouth, and that on "scanty subsistence" (in the words of Lord Lawrence), the very touch of famine carries away hundreds of thousands. Is not this in itself as "crushing" to any people as it can possibly be? And yet out of this wretched income they have to pay taxation as well.

His lordship has, moreover, left out a very important element from account. He is well aware that, whatever revenue is raised by the other countries, for instance, the £70,000,000 by England, the whole of it returns back to the people and remains in the country; and, therefore, the national capital, upon which the production of a country depends, does not suffer diminution; while, on account of India's being subject to a foreign rule, out of the £50,000,000 of revenue raised every year, some £12,000,000, or more, are carried clear away to England, and the national capital—or, in other words, its capability of production—is continuously diminished year after year. The pressure of taxation, therefore, if proper remedies are not adopted to counteract the above evil must, necessarily, become more and more crushing every year, even though the amount of taxation be not increased. It is quite intelligible that the English people, with an income or production of some £30 per head, aided by or including some £12,000,000, or more, annually drawn from India, may not feel the taxation of £2 10*s.* a-head as crushing: or the nations which his lordship has instanced, having no price of some £12,000,000 annually to pay for a foreign rule, and being, most probably, able to produce enough for all their wants, may not feel the 7*s.* to 19*s.* 7*d.* as crushing; but in my humble opinion, every single ounce of rice taken from the "scanty subsistence" of the masses of India is to them so much more starvation, and so much more "crushing."

I shall now consider what would have been the fairest way of making the comparison of taxation. Every nation has a certain amount of income from various sources, such as production of cultivation, minerals, farming, manufactures, profits of trade, etc. From such total income all its wants are to be supplied. A fair comparison as to the incidence of taxation will be to see the proportion of the amount which the Government of the country takes for its administration, public debts, etc., to the total income. You may call this amount taxation, revenue, or anything you like; and Government may take it in any shape or way whatsoever. It is so much taken from the income of the country for the purposes of Government. In the case of India, whether Government takes this amount as land tax, or opium revenue, or in whatever other form, does not matter, it is all the same, that out of the total income of the country Government raises so much revenue for its purposes which otherwise would have remained with the people.

Taking, therefore, this fair test of the incidence of taxation, the results will be that England raises £70,000,000 out of the national income of some £900,000,000—that is, about 8 per cent., or about £2 10*s.* per head, from an income of about £30 per head; whereas the Indian Government raises £50,000,000 out of a national income of £300,000,000—that is, about 16 per cent. or 6*s.* 8*d.* per head, out of an income of 40*s.* per head.

Had his lordship stated the total national income and population of the countries with which he has made the comparison, we would have then seen what the percentage of their revenue to their income was, and from how much income per head the people had to pay their 7*s.* to 19*s.* 7*d.* per head of taxation, as quoted by his lordship.

Further, if in consequence of a constant drain from India from its poor production, the income of the country continues to diminish, the percentage of taxation to income will be still greater even though the amount of taxation may not increase. But, as we know that the tendency of taxation in India has, during the past twelve years, been to go on increasing every year, the pressure will necessarily become more and more oppressive and crushing, unless our rulers by proper means restore India to at least a healthy, if not a wealthy condition. It must, moreover, be particularly borne in mind that, while a ton may not be any burden to an elephant, a few pounds may crush a child; that the English nation may, from its average income of £30 per head, bear with ease a burden of even £5 or £10 of taxation per head, while, to the Indian nation 5*s*. out of 40*s*. may be quite unbearable and crushing. The capacity to bear a burden with ease or to be crushed by it, is not to be measured by the percentage of taxation, but by the abundance, or otherwise, of the means or income to pay it from. From abundance you may give a large percentage with ease; from sufficiency, the same burden may be just bearable, or some diminution may make it so; but from insufficiency, any burden is so much privation.

But as matters stand, poor India has to pay not only the same percentage of taxation to its income as in England, but nearly double; *i.e.*, while England pays only about 8½ per cent. of its national income for the wants of its Government, India has to pay some 16 per cent. of its income for the same purpose; though here that income per head of population is some fifteenth part of that of England, and insufficient in itself for even its ordinary wants, leaving alone the extraordinary political necessity to pay a foreign country for its rule.

I sincerely trust, and very hopefully look forward, that when those in whose hands the destiny of India is now placed —such as Mr. Grant Duff, the members of the India Office, the Viceroy, and Sir R. Temple—understand this great evil, it will not be long before really effectual remedies shall be adopted, with the assistance of Parliament. Parliament being the fountain of all power, and as the Indian Government can only act as Parliament directs, it becomes its bounden duty to God and man to lay down the great principles of a just, efficient, and beneficent government for the administration of India, and to see from time to time to their being acted on.

In stating the Viceroy's views, I am obliged to trust to memory, but I hope I have not mis-stated them. Now that we have the testimony of the two latest Viceroys—Lord Lawrence stating that the mass of the people live on scanty subsistence, and Lord Mayo believing Mr. Grant Duff's statement of the income of India being only 43*s*. a head per annum as well founded —the Select Committee may not think it necessary to ask for any returns, but take the fact as proved. Perhaps the time thus saved to the Select Committee may be well employed in ascertaining the best remedies for such a deplorable state of affairs, and it may not seem very reasonable to request the Committee to put the India Office to the trouble of making any returns on this subject. But I hope that, though the Select Committee may not now think it necessary to ask for any returns for its own use, it will recommend—or the Indian Government will, of its own accord, require—the return of a table of total income of the country as an essential part of the Annual Administration Reports of all the different provinces, and embody it in the Return now annually published, showing the moral and material progress. The House of Parliament and the English and the Indian public will then be able to see every year clearly what the material condition of India really is, and how far measures are adopted to improve the present state of matters. To prepare Returns of the total production of the country, there are ample materials in the tables required by the Calcutta Statistical Committee in the Administration Reports. All that is necessary is simple calculation. For instance, one table gives the total acreage of cultivated land in each district; another table gives the acreage of the different crops grown; a third table gives the produce per acre of each kind of crop; a fourth table gives the prices of the produce in the markets of the districts. Now it is easy to see that, with these materials, the value of the total produce of all the districts of a province can be easily worked out.

An erroneous principle has crept into the Administration Reports. I have already once referred to it in connection with the question of prices. I point it out here again, so that it may be avoided in this important calculation. In the above tables of the Administration Report averages are taken, for instance of the prices of all the districts of the province, by adding up the prices of the different districts and dividing the total by the number of districts. This is evidently absurd, for one district may have produced a million of tons of rice, and may sell it at Re. 1 a maund, and another may have produced only a thousand tons, and the price there may be Rs. 5 a maund. It will be incorrect to make the average price as Rs. 3 per maund, when it will actually be only a little more than Re. 1. In the same manner the produce per acre may be very large in one place where probably the acreage under cultivation also is very large, while in another district the cultivated acreage may be small and the produce per acre may be small also. If the average is taken by simply adding up the produce per acre of each district, and dividing by the number of districts, the total of the produce thus obtained will be less than the actual quantity. Avoiding this mistake in the principle of taking averages, from the abovementioned tables can be calculated the total production of cultivated land. Then there are other sources of income to be added, such as stock, opium, salt, minerals, manufactures, fisheries, etc. The Reports already have the figures for most of these items, and thus the grand total of income available for human consumption and saving may be ascertained. Such a Return, with two others I shall refer to hereafter for every province, would be of great importance.

If this calculation of the total income of the country is made out every year, we shall have the most direct evidence of the actual condition of the people, instead of being obliged to draw inferences indirectly from the complicated and misleading phenomena of differences of prices or wages.

Except Bengal, all the provinces have the means of obtaining the necessary materials for the different tables required by the Statistical Committee. In Bengal, the perpetual settlement, I think, makes it unnecessary for the Revenue Department to ascertain the actual extent of the whole cultivation, and of the different crops. But for such an important purpose, I have no doubt, the Bengal Government will devise some means to procure the necessary information. In the Report for 1869-70, they have, I think, intimated their intention to do what they can.

Not commanding the time and the means necessary for minute calculations, I have made a rough estimate, and I think that if averages are worked out by the statistical staff at the India Office or at Calcutta, the result will be very nearly what Mr. Duff has stated, and which His Excellency the Viceroy adopts—*viz.*, a total income of about 40*s.* per head per annum. From this, the European residents and the richer classes of natives above the common labourer get a large proportion, and the portion remaining for the mass of the people must, therefore, be much less.

It must also be remembered that this average of 40*s.* per head is for the whole of India; but for the different Presidencies or Provinces, each of which is as large and as populous as some of the countries of Europe, the proportion of distribution of this total production is very different. For instance, in Bombay the total production, if accurately worked out, may be found to be 100*s.* per head; Punjab perhaps about 45*s.* to 50*s.* per head; consequently the other provinces will have under 40*s.* per head. Then, again, there is another drawback—*viz.*, the want of cheap communication—by which even this insufficient production of 45*s.* per head is not fully utilized, so as to allow the plenty of one Presidency to be available for the population of another. Not only does this difficulty of distribution exist between different Presidencies, but even between parts of the same province. I shall give just one instance—that of the Central Provinces. While at Raipore and Belaspore the price of rice at the end of 1867-8 was Re. 1 for a maund of 80 lbs., at Hoshungabad it was Rs. 5 per maund, at Baitool it was Rs. 4 per maund, at Jubbulpore Rs. 3-12 per maund. In this way, while in one district a part of the produce was perhaps rotting or being wasted, other districts were suffering from scarcity.

Upon the whole, I think the average income per head of the poor labouring population of all the provinces (except Bombay and Punjab) will be found hardly above 20*s.* per head per annum, or may be, from 20*s.* to 25*s.*

This can be tested directly if the Administration Reports give, in addition to the return for the total income of the province, a second return, something like the following (I believe they have all the requisite materials, or can obtain them):—The number of people living upon unskilled labour, and rates of wages, with details; the number of adults (male and female) capable of work, say between twenty-one and fifty; the number of youths, say from twelve to twenty-one years of age (male and female); the number of the old incapable of work, or, say, above fifty years of age, the number of children under twelve years of age; the average wage earned by males and females of the above different classifications (calculating the average on the correct principle of taking the *number* of labourers earning each rate into account); the number of the sick and infirm; and the number of days during the year that the different rates of wages are earned. From these materials it will be easy to ascertain the real average income of the unskilled labourer, who forms the majority of the population, and upon whose labour depends the subsistence of the nation. I hope the India Office will order such returns to be prepared for the Select Committee. It will be a direct proof of the actual condition of the mass of the people of each Presidency, and will be a great help to the Committee.

I may now give a few particulars, which are at hand, of the cost of living, for the bare necessaries of life.

The Bombay Report for 1867-68 gives Rs. 41-13-10 as the average cost for diet per prisoner, and Rs. 5-10-11 for clothing and bedding. The N.-W.-Provinces Report gives the average cost for central gaols—for diet, Rs. 18-1-8¾; for clothing and bedding, Rs. 3-5-1¼. For divisional gaols—for diet, Rs. 24-6-10¾; and clothing and bedding, Rs. 4-3-4½; and for district gaols—for diet, Rs. 15-8-11⅜; and for clothing and bedding, Rs. 3-2-6. In the Central Provinces, the cost for diet is Rs. 25½, and for clothing and bedding, Rs. 5½; and in the Punjab—for diet, Rs. 23-6; for clothing and bedding, Rs. 31-13-6.

This is what the State thinks it necessary to give to criminals as bare necessaries of life. There may be little allowance to be made for the proportion of females and the young being smaller is a prison than in the outside world. Making this allowance, can it be said that the labourer gets the necessaries of life to this extent? To this has to be added some cost for lodging, something for reasonable social wants, and something to save for a bad day or old age. Do the people get this ?

Surgeon S. B. Partridge, Government Medical Inspector of Emigrants, in a statement, dated Calcutta, 26th March, 1870,* proposes the following as a scale of diet, to supply the necessary ingredients of nourishment, for the emigrant coolies during their voyage, living in a state of quietude :—

RICE DIET FOR ONE MAN.	ozs.		FOR FLOUR DIET.	ozs.	
Rice	20	0	Flour	16	0
Dhal	6	0	Dhal	4	0
Preserved Mutton ...	2	5	Preserved Mutton ...	2	5
Vegetables	4	27	Vegetables	4	27
Ghee	1	0	Ghee	1	5
Mustard Oil	0	5	Mustard Oil	0	5
Salt	1	0	Salt	1	0
Total...	35-27		Total...	29-77	

This is absolutely necessary to supply the necessary ingredients of nitrogen and carbon; not the slightest luxury—no sugar, tea, or any little enjoyment of life—but simply animal subsistence.

From the above data, returns can be worked out, at the prices of particular districts and provinces, of the absolute necessaries of life, which will show whether a province produces enough for these, and for all its political, social, economical, and administrative wants. With these three returns—first, of the total income per head per annum; secondly, the average per head of the earnings of the mass of the labouring population; and thirdly, the average actual requirements per head for all the different absolutely necessary wants of the labouring population—the ruler of every province will be able to give a clear picture of the actual, material condition of his charge, and will get any credit he may deserve for the improvements made by him. I hope the India Office will place these three returns before the Select Committee. Complacent assertions of officials that all are

* The *Indian Economist* of 15th October, 1870 : 'Statistical Reporter," p. 45.

happy and prospering can be had in any quantity; but unless the test of actual facts is applied by such returns, these assertions are not only worth nothing, but are positively mischievous as they mislead Parliament and the English public, who, believing such statements, become indifferent to India, to be roused only by some great calamity, either physical or political.

If the facts brought to light by those returns show that the people are really suffering from insufficiency to supply their absolute wants for ordinary healthly human life, and that, therefore, having no reserve either of strength or means, or no intelligences they are easily swept away by hundreds of thousands in time of scarcity, what responsibility lies upon our British rulers to remedy this wretchedness! Remedy it *they could*, if they but chose to set about their work with a due sense of the responsibility, and with earnestness and determination. India needs the help of their capital and credit, needs reduction in expenditure, needs an efficient and economical administration of which native co-operation must form an essential, and not an incidental element, needs a wise and fair adjustment of her financial relations with England, and, finally and imperatively, a wise and rapid diffusion of the blessings of education.

THE MORAL POVERTY OF INDIA AND NATIVE THOUGHTS ON THE PRESENT BRITISH INDIAN POLICY.*

In my last paper I confined myself to meeting Mr. Danvers' line of argument on the question of the material destruction and impoverishment of India by the present British Indian policy; I endeavoured to show that this impoverishment and destruction of India was mainly caused by the unnatural treatment it received at the hands of its British Rulers, in the way of subjecting it to a large variety of expenditure upon a crushing foreign agency both in India and England, whereby the children of the country

* Submitted to the Secretary of State for India, 16th November, 1880.

were displaced and deprived of their natural rights and means of subsistence in their own country; that, by what was being taken and consumed in India itself, and by what was being continuously taken away by such agency clean out of the country, an exhaustion of the very life-blood of the country was unceasingly going on; that not till this disastrous drain was duly checked, and not till the people of India were restored to their natural rights in their own country, was there any hope for the material amelioration of India.

In this memorandum I desire to submit for the kind and generous consideration of his Lordship the Secretary of State for India that, from the same cause of the deplorable drain, besides the material exhaustion of India, the moral loss to her is no less sad and lamentable.

With the material wealth go also the wisdom and experience of the country. Europeans occupy almost all the higher places in every department of Government directly or indirectly under its control. While in India they acquire India's money, experience, and wisdom; and when they go, they carry both away with them, leaving India so much poorer in material and moral wealth. Thus India is left without, and cannot have those elders in wisdom and experience who in every country are the natural guides of the rising generations in their national and social conduct, and of the destinies of their country; and a sad, sad loss this is!

Every European is isolated from the people around him. He is not their mental, moral, or social leader or companion. For any mental or moral influence or guidance or sympathy with the people he might just as well be living in the moon, The people know not him, and he knows not, nor cares for. the people. Some honourable exceptions do, now and then, make an effort to do some good if they can, but in the very nature of things these efforts are always feeble, exotic, and of little permanent effect. These men are not always in the place, and their works die away when they go.

The Europeans are not the natural leaders of the people. They do not belong to the people; they cannot enter their thoughts and feelings; they cannot join or sympathise with their joys or griefs. On the contrary, every day the estrangement is increasing. Europeans deliberately and openly widen it more and more. There may be very few social institutions started by Europeans in which Natives, however fit and desirous to join, are not deliberately and insultingly excluded. The Europeans are, and make themselves, strangers in every way. All they effectually do is to eat the substance of India, material and moral, while living there, and when they go, they carry away all they have acquired, and their pensions and future usefulness besides.

This most deplorable moral loss to India needs most serious consideration, as much in its political as in its national aspect. Nationally disastrous as it is, it carries politically with it its own Nemesis. Without the guidance of elderly wisdom and experience of their own natural leaders, the education which the rising generations are now receiving is naturally leading them (or call it misleading them if you will) into directions which bode no good to the rulers, and which, instead of being the strength of the rulers, as it ought to be and can be, will turn out to be their great weakness. The fault will be of the rulers themselves for such a result. The power that is now being raised by the spread of education, though yet slow and small, is one that in time must, for weal or woe, exercise great influence; in fact, it has already begun to do so. However strangely the English rulers, forgetting their English manliness and moral courage, may, like the ostrich, shut their eyes, by gagging acts or otherwise, to the good or bad influences they are raising around them, this good or evil is rising nevertheless. The thousands that are being sent out by the universities every year find themselves in a most anomalous position. There is no place for them in their motherland. They may beg in the streets or break stones on the roads for ought the rulers seem to care for their natural rights, position and duties in their own country. They may perish or do what they like or can, but scores of Europeans must go from this country to take up what belongs to them, and that in spite of every profession, for years and years past and up to the present day, of English statesmen, that they must govern India for India's good, by solemn Acts and declarations of Parliament, and, above all, by the words of the august Sovereign herself. For all practical purposes all these high promises have been hitherto almost wholly the purest romance, the reality being quite different.

The educated find themselves simply so many dummies, ornamented with the tinsel of school education, and then their whole end and aim of life is ended. What must be the inevitable consequence? A wild-spirited horse, without curb or reins, will run away wild, and kill and trample upon every one that comes in its way. A miss-directed force will hit anywhere, and destroy anything. The power that the rulers are, so far to their credit, raising will, as a Nemesis, recoil against themselves, if, with this blessing of education, they do not do their whole duty to the country which trusts to their righteousness, and thus turn this good power to their own side. The Nemesis is as clear from the present violence to nature, as disease and death arise from uncleanliness and rottenness. The voice of the power of the rising education is, no doubt, feeble at present. Like the infant, the present dissatisfaction is only crying at the pains it is suffering. Its notions have not taken any form or shape or course yet, but it is growing. Heaven only knows what it will grow to! He who runs may see that if the present material and moral destruction of India continues, a great convulsion must inevitably arise, by which either India will be more and more crushed under the iron heel of despotism and destruction, or may succeed in shattering the destroying hand and power. Far, far is it from my earnest prayer and hope that such should be the result of the British Rule. In this rule there is every element to produce immeasurable good, both to India and England, and no thinking native of India would wish harm to it, with all the hopes that are yet built upon the righteousness and conscience of the British statesmen and nation.

The whole duty and responsibility of bringing about this desired consummation lies upon the head and in the hands of the Indian authorities *in England*. It is no use screening themselves behind the fiction and excuse that the Viceroys and authorities in India are difficult to be got to do what they ought, or that they would do all that may be necessary. They neither can nor will do this. They cannot go against Acts of Parliament on the one hand, and, on the other, the pressure of European interests, and of European selfishness and guidance, is so heavy in India, that the Viceroys in their first years are quite helpless, and get committed to certain courses; and if, in time, any of them, happening to have sufficient strength of character and confidence in their own judgment, are likely to take matters in their own hands, and with any moral courage, to resist interests hostile or antagonistic to the good of the people, the end of their time begins to come near, their zeal and interest, begin to flag, and soon they go away, leaving India to roll up Sisyphus's stone again with a new Viceroy. It is the highest Indian authority here, the Secretary of State for India, upon whom the responsibility wholly rests. He alone has the power, as a member of and with the weight of the British Cabinet, to guide the Parliament to acts worthy of the English character, conscience, and nation. The glory or disgrace of the British in India is in his hands. He has to make Parliament lay down, by clear legislation, how India *shall* be governed for *India's good*, or it is hopeless for us to look forward for any relief from our present material and moral destruction, and for future elevation.

Englishmen sometimes indulge the notion that England is secure in the division and disunion among the various races and nationalities of India. But even in this new forces are working their way. Those Englishmen who sleep such foolish sleep of security know very little of what is going on. The kind of education that is being received by thousands of all classes and creeds is throwing them all in a similar mould; a sympathy of sentiment, ideas, and aspirations is growing amongst them; and, more particularly, a political union and sympathy is the first fruit of the new awakening, as all feel alike their deprivation and the degradation and destruction of their country. All differences of race and religion, and rivalry, are gradually sinking before this common cause. This beginning, no doubt, is at present insignificant; but it is surely and steadily progressing. Hindus, Mahomedans, and Parsees are alike asking whether the English rule is to be a blessing or a curse. Politics now engross their attention more and more. This is no longer a secret, or a state of things not quite open to those of our rulers who would see. It may be seen that there is scarcely any union among the different nationalities and races in any shape or ways of life, except only in political associations. In these associations they go hand in hand, with all the fervour and sympathy of a common cause. I would here touch upon a few incidents, little though they are, showing how nature is working in its own quite way.

Dr. Birdwood has brought to the notice of the English public certain songs now being spread among the people of Western India against the destruction of Indian industry and arts. We may laugh at this as a futile attempt to shut out English machine-made cheaper goods against hand-made dearer ones. But little do we think what this movement is likely to grow into, and what new phases it may take in time. The songs are at present directed against English wares, but they are also a natural and effective preparation against other English things when the time comes, if the English in their blindness allow such times to come. The songs are full of loyalty, and I have not the remotest doubt in the sincerity of that loyalty. But if the present downward course of India continue, if the mass of the people at last begin to despair of any amelioration, and if educated youths, without the wisdom and experience of the world, become their leaders, it will be but a *very, very* short step from loyalty to disloyalty, to turn the course of indignation from English wares to English rule. The songs will remain the same; one word of course for the rule will supply the spark.

Here is another little incident with its own significance. The London Indian Society, a political body of many of the Native residents of London, had a dinner the other day, and they invited guests. The three guests were, one Hindu, one Mahomedan, and one Parsee. The society itself is a body representing nearly all the principal classes of India. It is small, and may be laughed at as uninfluential, and can do nothing. But it shows how a sympathy of political common cause is bringing the different classes together, and how, in time, such small seeds may grow into large trees. Every member of this little body is carrying back with him ideas which, as seeds, may produce crops, sweet or bitter, according to the cultivation they may receive at our rulers' hands.

I turn to one bright incident on the other side. True to their English nature and character, there are some Englishmen who try to turn the current of Native thought towards an appreciation of English intentions, and to direct English thought towards a better understanding of England's duty to India. The East India Association is doing this beneficent work, more especially by the fair and English character of its course of bringing about free and full discussion upon every topic and from every point of view, so that, by a sifting of the full expression of different views, truth may be elicited. Though yet little appreciated by the English public the English members of this Association are fulfilling the duty of patriotism to their own country and of benefaction towards India. How far their good efforts will succeed is yet to be seen. But they at least do one thing. The Englishmen, as well as public writers like Fawcett, Hyndman, Perry, Caird, Knight, Bell, Wilson, Wood, and others, vindicate to India the English character, and show that when Englishmen as a body will *understand* their duty and responsibility, the Natives of India may fairly expect a conduct of which theirs is a sample—a desire, indeed, to act rightly by India. The example and earnestness of these Englishmen, though yet small their number keep India's hope alive—that England will produce a statesman who will have the moral courage and firmness to face the Indian problem, and do what the world should expect from England's conscience, and from England's mission to humanity.

I have thus touched upon a few incidents only to illustrate the various influences that are at work. Whether the result of all these forces and influences will be good or bad remains, as I have said, in the hands of the Secretary of State for India.

In my last paper I said the thinking Natives were as yet staunch in their loyalty to the British Rule, as they were yet fully hopeful of the future from the general character and history of the English people. They believe that when the conscience of the English nation is awakened, it will not be long before India receives full and thorough redress for all she has been suffering. While thus hopeful of the future, it is desirable that our rulers should know and consider what, as to the past, is passing in many a thinking Native mind.

They are as grateful as any people can be for whatever real good of peace and order and education has been done for them, but they also ask what good, upon the whole, England has done to India. It is sadly poor, and increasing in poverty both material and moral. They consider and bewail the unnatural treatment India has been receiving.

They dwell upon the strange contrast between the words and deeds of the English rulers; how often deliberate and solemn promises are made and broken. I need not here instance again what I have at some length shown in my papers on the Poverty of India * under the heading of "Non-Fulfilment of Solemn Promises."†

I would refer here to one or two characteristic instances only. The conception for an Engineering College in London was no sooner formed than it became an accomplished fact; and Mr. Grant Duff, then Under-Secretay of State, in his place in Parliament, proclaimed what great boons "we" were conferring on the English people, but quite oblivious at whose sacrifices. It was an English interest, and the thing was done as quick as it was thought of. On the other hand, a clause for Native interests, proposed in 1867, took three years to pass, and in such a form as to be simply ineffectual. I asked Sir Stafford Northcote, at the time of the proposal, to make it some way imperative, but without effect. Again, after being passed after three years, it remained a dead letter for seven years more, and might have remained so till Doomsday for aught any of the Indian authorities cared. But, thanks to the persevering exertions of one of England's true sons, Sir Erskine

* In this book, pp. 90-125.

† The Duke of Argyll, as Secretary of State for India, said in his speech of 11th March, 1869, with regard to the employment of Natives in the Covenanted Service: "I must say that we have not fulfilled our duty, or the promises and engagements which we have made."

Perry, some steps were at last taken to frame the rules that were required, and it is now, in the midst of a great deal of fine writing, making some, though very slow, progress. For such, even as it is, we are thankful; but greater efforts are necessary to stem the torrent of the drain. Turning to the uncovenanted Service, Sir Stafford Northcote's despatch of 8th February, 1868, declared that Europeans should not be allowed in this service to override "the inherent rights of the Natives of the country." Now, in what spirit was this despatch treated till very lately? Was it not simply, or is it not even now, almost a dead letter?

In the matter of the load of the public debt of India, it is mainly due to the wars of the English conquests in India, and English wars abroad in the name of India. Not a farthing has been spent by England for its British Indian Empire. The burden of all England's wars in Asia has been thrown on India's shoulders. In the Abyssinian War, India narrowly and rightly escaped; and in the present Afghan War, her escape from whatever portion she may be saved is not less narrow. Though such is the character of nearly the whole of the public debt (excluding for public works), being caused by the actions by which England has become the mistress of a great Empire, and thereby the first nation in the world, she would not move her little finger to give India any such help as is within her power, without even any material sacrifice to herself—*viz.*, that of guaranteeing this public debt, so that India may derive some little relief from reduced interest.

When English interests are concerned, their accomplishment is often a foregone conclusion. But India's interests always require long and anxious thought—thought that seldom begins, and when it does begin, seldom ends in any thorough good result. It is useless to conceal that the old, pure and simple faith in the honour and word of the English rulers is much shaken, and were it not for the faith in the conscience of the statesmen and people in *this* country, any hope of good by an alteration of the present British Indian policy would be given up.

The English rulers boast, and justly so, that they have introduced education and Western civilisation into India: but, on the other hand, they act as if no such thing had taken place, and as if all this boast was pure moonshine. Either they have educated, or have not. If they deserve the boast, it is a strange self-condemnation that after half-a-century or more of such efforts, they have not yet prepared a sufficient number of men fit for the service of their own country. Take even the Educational Department itself. We are made B.A.'s and M.A.'s, M.D.'s., etc., with the strange result that we are not yet considered fit to teach our countrymen. We must yet have forced upon us even in this department, as in every other, every European that can be squeezed in. To keep up the sympathy and connection with the current of European thought, an English head may be appropriately and beneficially retained in a few of the most important institutions; but as matters are at present, all boast of education is exhibited as so much sham and delusion.

In the case of former foreign conquests, the invaders either retired with their plunder and booty or, became the rulers of the country. When they only plundered and went back, they made, no doubt, great wounds: but India, with her industry, revived and healed the wounds. When the invaders became the rulers of the country, they settled down in it, and whatever was the condition of their rule, according to the character of the sovereign of the day, there was at least no material or moral drain *in* the country.* Whatever the country produced

---

* Sir Stafford Northcote, in his speech in Parliament on 24th May, 1867, said:—"Nothing could be more wonderful than our Empire in India, but we ought to consider on what conditions we held it, and how our predecessors held it. The greatness of the Mogul Empire depended upon the liberal policy that was pursued by men like Akbar availing themselves of Hindu talent and assistance, and indentifying themselves as far as possible with the people of the country. He thought that they ought to take a lesson from such circumstance, and if they were to do their duty towards India they could only discharge that duty by obtaining the assistance and counsel of all who were great and good in that country. It would be absurd in them to say that there was not a large fund of statesmanship and ability in the Indian character." *Times*, of 25th May, 1867.

remained in the country; whatever wisdom and experience was acquired in her services remained among her own people. With the English the case is peculiar. There are the great wounds of the first wars in the burden of the public debt, and those wounds are kept perpetually open and widening, by draining away the life-blood in a continuous stream. The former rulers were like butchers hacking here and there, but the English with their scientific scalpel cut to the very heart, and yet, lo! there is no wound to be seen, and soon the plaster of the high talk of civilisation, progress, and what not, covers up the wound! The English rulers stand sentinel at the front door of India, challenging the whole world, that they do and shall protect India against all comers. and themselves carry away by a back-door the very treasure they stand sentinel to protect.

In short. had England deliberately intended to devise the best means of taking away India's wealth in a quite continuous drain, without scandalising the world, she could not have hit upon a more effectual plan than the present lines of policy. A Viceroy tells us the people of India enjoy but scanty subsistence; and this is the outcome of the British Rule.

No doubt the exertions of individual Europeans at the time of famines may be worthy of admiration; the efforts of Government and the aid of the contributions of the British people to save life, deserve every gratitude. But how strange it is that the British rulers do not see that after all they themselves are the main cause of the destruction that ensues from droughts; that is the drain of India's wealth by *them* that lays at their own door the dreadful results of misery starvation, and deaths of millions; England does not know famines, be the harvest however bad or scanty. She has the means of buying her food from the whole world. India is being unceasingly deprived of these means, and when famine comes the starving have to be taxed so much more to save the dying.

England's conduct in India is in strange contrast with her conduct with almost any other country. Owing to the false groove in which she is moving, she does violence to her own best instincts. She sympathises with and helps every nationality that struggles for a constitutional representative Government. On the one hand, she is the parent of, and maintains, the highest constitutionalism; and, on the other, she exercises a clear and, though thoughtlessly, a despoiling despotism in India, under a pseudo-constitutionalism, in the shape of the farce of the present Legislative Councils.

Of all countries in the world, if any one has the greatest claim on England's consideration, to receive the boons of a constitutional representative Government at her hands, and to have her people governed as England governs her own, that country is India, her most sacred trust and charge. But England, though she does everything she can for other countries, fights shy of, and makes some excuse or other to avoid, giving to the people of India their fair share in the legislation of their country. Now I do not mean to say that India can suddenly have a full-blown Parliament, and of such widespread representation as England enjoys. But has England made any honest efforts to gradually introduce a true representation of the people, excepting some solitary exceptions of partial Municipal representation? I need not dwell upon the present farce of the nomination system for the Legislative Council, and of the dummies that are sometimes nominated. I submit that a small beginning can be well made now. I would take the Bombay Presidency as an instance. Suppose the present Legislative Council is extended to twenty-one members, thirteen of these to be nominated from officials and non-officials by the Government, and eight to be elected by the principal towns of the Presidency. This will give Government a clear majority of five, and the representative element, the minority, cannot do any harm, or hamper Government; in England, the majority determines the Government. In India, this cannot be the case at present, and so the majority must follow the Government. It would be, when something is extremely outrageous, that the minority would, by force of argument and truth, draw towards it the Government majority; and even in any such rare instance, all that will happen will be that Government will be prevented from doing any such outrageous things. In short, in such an arrangement, Government will remain all-powerful, as it must for a long time to come; while there will be also independent persons, actually representing the people, to speak the sentiments of the people; thereby giving Government the most important help, and relieving them from much responsibility, anxiety, and mistakes. The representative element in the minority will be gradually trained in constitutional Government. They will have no inducement to run wild with prospects of power; they will have to maintain the reasons of their existence and will, therefore, be actuated by caution and good sense. They can do no harm, but a vast amount of good, both to the Government and the governed. The people will have the satisfaction that their rulers were doing their duty, and endeavouring to raise them to their own civilisation.

There are in the Bombay Presidency the following towns of more than 50,000 population. Bombay having by far the largest, and with its importance as the capital of the Presidency, may be properly allowed three representatives.

The towns are—

Bombay.	Poona.	Ahmedabad.	Surat.	Karachi.	Sholapore.
644,405 ...	118,886 ...	116,873 ...	107,149 ...	53,536 ...	53,403.

Thus, Bombay having three, the Gujerati division of the Presidency will be represented by Ahmedabad and Surat, the Maratha portion by Poona and Sholapore, and Sind by Karachi, making altogether eight members, which will be a fair, though a small, representation to begin with. Government may with advantage adopt a larger number; all I desire and insist is, that there must be a fair *representative* element in the Councils. As to the qualifications of electors and candidates for election, Government is quite competent to fix upon some, as they did in the case of the Bombay Corporation, and such qualifications may from time to time be modified as experience may suggest. With this modification in the present Legislative Council, a great step will have been taken towards one of the greatest boons which India asks and expects at England's hands. Without some such element of the people's voice in all the Legislative Councils, it is impossible for Englishmen, more and more estranged and isolated as they are becoming, to be able to

* "Statistical Abstract of British India, 1879," page 21.

legislate for India in the true spirit and feeling of her wants.

After having a glorious history of heroic struggles for constitutional Government, England is now rearing up a body of Englishmen in India, trained up and accustomed to despotism, with all the feelings of impatience, pride, and high-handedness of the despot becoming gradually ingrained in them, and with the additional training of the dissimulation of constitutionalism. Is it possible that such habits and training of despotism, with which Indian officials return from India, should not, in the course of time influence the English character and institutions? The English in India, instead of raising India, are hitherto themselves descending and degenerating to the lower level of Asiatic despotism. Is this a Nemesis that will in fullness of time show to them what fruit their conduct in India produced? It is extraordinary how nature may revenge itself for the present unnatural course of England in India if England, not yet much tainted by this demoralisation, does not, in good time, check this new leaven that is gradually fermenting among her people.

There is the opium trade. What a spectacle it is to the world! In England, no statesman dares to propose that opium may be allowed to be sold in public houses at the corners of every street, in the same way as beer or spirits. On the contrary, Parliament, as representing the whole nation, distinctly enacts that "opium and all preparations of opium or of 'poppies', as 'poison', be sold by certified chemists only, and every box, bottle, vessel, wrapper, or cover in which such poison is contained, be distinctly labelled with the name of the article and the word 'poison,' and with the name and address of the seller of the poison." And yet, at the other end of the world, this Christian, highly civilised, and humane England forces a "heathen" and "barbarous" Power to take this "poison," and tempts a vast human race to use it, and to degenerate and demoralise themselves with this "poison"! And why? Because India cannot fill up the remorseless drain; so China must be dragged in to make it up, even though it be by being "poisoned." It is wonderful how England reconciles this to her conscience. This opium trade is a sin on England's head, and a curse on India for her share in being the instrument. This may sound strange as coming from any Natives of India, as it is generally represented as if India it was that benefited by the opium trade. The fact simply is that, as Mr. Duff said, India is nearly ground down to dust, and the opium trade of China fills up England's drain. India derives not a particle of benefit. All India's profits of trade, and several millions from her very produce (scanty as it is, and becoming more and more so), and with these all the profit of opium, go the same way of the drain—to England. Only India shares the curse of the Chinese race. Had this cursed opium trade not existed, India's miseries would have much sooner come to the surface, and relief and redress would have come to her long ago; but this trade has prolonged the agonies of India.

In association with this trade is the stigma of the Salt-tax upon the British name. What a humiliating confession to say that, after the length of the British Rule, the people are in such a wretched plight that they have nothing that Government can tax, and that Government must, therefore, tax an absolute necessary of life to an inordinate extent! The slight flash of prosperity during the American War showed how the people of India would enjoy and spend when they have anything to enjoy and spend; and now, can anything be a greater condemnation of the results of British lines of policy than that the people have nothing to spend and enjoy, and pay tax on, but that they must be pinched and starved in a necessary of life?

The English are, and justly and gloriously, the greatest champions of liberty of speech. What a falling off must have taken place in their character when, after granting this boon to India, they should have even thought of withdrawing it! This act, together with that of disarming the people, is a clear confession by the rulers to the world that they have no hold as yet upon the affection and loyalty of the people, though in the same breadth they make every profession of their belief in the loyalty of the people. Now, which is the truth? And are gagging and disarming the outcome of a long benign rule?

Why do the English allow themselves to be so perpetually scared by the fears of Russian or any other foreign invasion?

If the people of India be satisfied, if their hearts and hands be with England, she may defy a dozen Russias. On the other hand, do British statesmen think that, however sharp and pointed their bayonets, and however long-flying their bullets, they may not find the two hundred millions of the people of India her political Himalaya to be pierced through, when the present political union among the different peoples is more strengthened and consolidated?

There is the stock argument of over-population. They talk, and so far truly, of the increase by British peace, but they quite forget the destruction by the British drain. They talk of the pitiless operations of economic laws, but somehow they forgot that there is no such thing in India as the natural operation of economic laws. It is not the pitiless operations of economic laws, but it is the thoughtless and pitiless action of the British policy; it is the pitiless eating of India's substance in India, and the further pitiless drain to England; in short, it is the pitiless *perversion* of economic laws by the sad bleeding to which India is subjected, that is destroying India. Why blame poor Nature when the fault lies at your own door? Let natural and economic laws have their full and fair play, and India will become another England, with manifold greater benefit to England herself than at present.

As long as the English do not allow the country to produce what it can produce, as long as the people are not allowed to enjoy what they can produce, as long as the English are the very party on their trial, they have no right, and are not competent, to give an opinion whether the country is over-populated or not. In fact, it is absurd to talk of over-population—*i.e.*, the country's incapability, by its food or other produce, to supply the means of support to its people—if the country is unceasingly and forcibly deprived of its means or capital. Let the country keep what it produces, for only then can any right judgment be formed whether it is over-populated or not. Let England first hold hands off India's wealth, and then there will be disinterestedness in, and respect for, her judgment. The present cant of the excuse of over-population is adding a distressful insult to agonising injury. To talk of over-population at present is just as reasonable as to cut off a man's hands, and then to taunt him that he was not able to maintain himself or move his hands.

When persons talk of the operation of economic laws they forget the very first and fundamental principles. Says Mr. Mill, "Industry is limited by capital." "To employ industry on the land is to apply capital to the land." "Industry cannot be employed to any greater extent than there is capital to invest." "There can be no more industry than is supplied by materials to work up, and food to eat; yet in regard to a fact so evident, it was long continued to be believed that laws and governments, without creating capital, could create industry." And while Englishmen are sweeping away this very capital, they raise up their hands and wonder why India cannot have industry.

The English are themselves the head and front of the offending, and yet they talk of over-population, and every mortal irrelevant thing but the right cause—*viz.*, their own drain of the material and moral wealth of the country.

The present form of relations between the paramount Power, and the Princes of India is un-English and iniquitous. Fancy a people, the greatest champions of fair play and justice, having a system of political agency by which, as the Princes say, they are stabbed in the dark; the Political Agents making secret reports, and the Government often acting thereon, without a fair enquiry or explanation from the Princes. The Princes, threfore, are always in a state of alarm as to what may befall them unawares. If the British authorities deliberately wished to adopt a method by which the Princes should always remain alarmed and irritated, they could not have hit upon a more effective one than what exists. If these Princes can feel assured that their treaty rights will be always honourably and faithfully observed, that there will be no constant nibbling at their powers, that it is not the ulterior policy of the British to pull them down gradually to the position of mere nobles of the country, as the Princes at present suspect and fear, and if a more just and fair mode of political agency be adopted, I have not the least hesitation in saying that, as much from self-interest alone as from any other motive, these Princes will prove the greatest bulwark and help to perpetuate British supremacy in India. It stands to reason and common sense that the Native Princes clearly understand their interest, that by a power like the British only, with all the confidence it may command by its fairness as well as strength, can they be saved from each other and even from themselves. Relieved of any fear from the paramount Power, they will the more readily listen to counsels of reform which they much need. The English can then exercise their salutary influence in advising and helping them to root out the old corrupt *regimes*, and in making them and their countries to understand that power was not self-aggrandizement, but responsibility for the good of the people. I say, from personal conversation with some of the Princes, that they thoroughly understand their interest under the protection of the present paramount Power.

It is unless for the British to compare themselves with the past Native rulers. If the British do not show themselves to be vastly superior in proportion to their superior enlightenment and civilisation, if India does not prosper and progress under them far more largely, there will be no justification for their existence in India. The thoughtless past drain we may consider as our misfortune, but a similar future will, in plain english, be deliberate plunder and destruction.

I do not repeat here several other views which I have already expressed in my last memorandum.

I have thus given a general sketch of what is passing in many Natives' minds on several subjects. It is unless and absurd to remind us constantly that once the British fiat brought order out of chaos, and to make that an everlasting excuse for subsequent shortcomings and the material and the moral impoverishment of the country. The Natives of the present day have not seen that chaos, and do not feel it; and though they understand it, and very thankful they are for the order brought, they see the present drain, distress and destruction, and they feel it and bewail it.

By all means let Englishmen be proud of the past. We accord them every credit for the order and law they brought about, and are deeply thankful to them; but let them now face the present, let them clearly realise, and manfully acknowledge, the many shortcomings of omission and commission by which, with the best of intentions, they have reduced India to material and moral wretchedness; and let them, in a way worthy of their name and history, repair the injury they have inflicted. It is fully in their power to make their rule a blessing to India, and a benefit and a glory to England, by allowing India her own administration, under their superior controlling and guiding hand; or, in their own oft-repeated professions and words, "by governing India for India's good."

May the God of all nations lead the English to a right sense of their duty to India, is my humble and earnest prayer.

DADABHAI NAOROJI.

APPENDIX—E.

MEMORANDUM ON A FEW SETTLEMENTS

IN THE

REPORT OF THE INDIAN FAMINE COMMISSION, 1880.*

Part II., Chapter I., Section VII. treats of Incidence of Taxation.

I submit that the section is fallacious, gives an erroneous notion of the true state of the matter, and is misleading.

We shall see what the reality is.

The income of a country consists of two parts—

1. The internal total annual material production of the country (Agricultural, Manufactures, Mines and Fisheries).

2. The external annual profits of Foreign Trade.

There is no other source of income beyond these two, excepting, in the case of British India, the tributes, and contributions of Native States of about £700,000.

The incidence of taxation of any country means that a certain amount or portion is taken out of this income for purposes of Government. Call this portion revenue, tax, rent, service, contributions, blessing, curse or by any name from A to Z in the English vocabulary. The fact simply is, that the country has to give a certain proportion out of its income for purposes of Government. Every farthing that the country has thus to contribute for Government, has to be produced, or earned from Foreign trade, or, in other words, has to be given from the annual income. No portion of it is rained down from heaven, or produced by some magic by the Government of the country. The £24,000,000 which the Commissioners call "other than taxation," do not come down from the heavens, nor are to be obtained from any other source than the annual income of the country, just the same as what they call taxation proper. And so also what the Commissioners call "rent," with regard to the revenue derived from land.

---

* Submitted to the Secretary of State for India, Jan. 1881.

Whatever plans, wise or unwise, a Government adopt of distributing the incidence of the revenue among different classes of people; from whatever and how-many-soever different sources, Government may obtain its revenue; by whatever hundred-and-one names may these different items of revenue be called;—the sum total of the whole matter is, that out of the annual income of the country, a certain portion is raised for the purposes of Government, and the real incidence of this revenue in any country, is the proportion it bears to the actual annual income of the country, call the different modes of raising this revenue what you like.

Now England raises at present for purposes of Government about £83,000,000. The income of the United Kingdom is well-nigh £1,000,000,000* a year. The proportion therefore of the revenue of £83,000,000 or even £84,000,000, is about 8½ per cent. out of the annual income.

Now India's income, as I have first roughly shown in 1870 in my paper on the Wants and Means of India, and subsequently in my papers on the Poverty of India, is hardly £300,000,000 per annum. This statement has not been refuted by anybody. On the contrary, Mr. Grant Duff, though cautiously, admitted in his speech in 1871, in these words:—"The income of British India has been guessed at £300,000,000 per annum." And Lord Mayo quoted Mr. Grant Duff's speech soon after, without any contradiction, but rather with approval. If the fact be otherwise, let Government give the correct fact every year. Out of this income of £300,000,000, the revenue raised in India for purposes of Government is £65,000,000 or very near 22 per cent.

Thus, then, the actual heaviness of the weight of revenue on India, is quite 2½ times as much as that on England. This is the simple fact, that out of the grand income of £1,000,000,000—of only 34,000,000 of population, England raises for the purposes of Government only 8½ per cent., while out of the poor, wretched income of £300,000,000 of a population of nearly 200,000,000—two-and-a-half times more, or nearly 22 per cent., are raised in India for the same purpose, and yet people coolly and cruelly write that India is lightly taxed. It must be further realised, what this disproportionate pressure, upon a most prosperous and wealthy community like that of England, and the most wretched, and poverty and famine-

*The *Westminster Review* of January 1876 gives the National production for 1875 of the United Kingdom as £28 per head of population. I do not know whether profits of trade are included in this amount. Mr. Grant Duff, in 1871, took £800,000,000—or roundly £30 per head of population. The population is above 34,000,000,—which, at £28, gives £952,000,000.

stricken people of India, means. To the one, it is not a flea-bite, to the other, it is starvation and death of millions, under her present unnatural treatment. For, this is not all. A far deeper and worse depth lies behind.

Let me then once more repeat that out of the grand income of £1,000,000,000 a year, England gives only 8½ per cent. for Government purposes, while out of the wretched poverty of India of an income of £300,000,000—she gives 23 per cent. for the purposes of Government. Now comes the worst evil of the whole, to which English writers, with few exceptions, always shut their eyes.

Of the £83,000,000 of revenue, which is raised in England, every farthing returns in some shape or other to the people themselves. In fact, England pays with one hand, and receives back with the other. And such is the case in every country on the face of the earth, and so it must be—but poor India is doomed otherwise. Out of the £65,000,000, taken out of her wretched income, some £30,000,000 or £40,000,000 are never returned to the people, but are eaten up in the country, and taken away out of the country, by those who are not the people of the country—by England, in short. I pass over this mournful topic here, as I have to refer to it again further on.

I may be taken to task, that I am making a very indefinite statement, when I talk of "some £30,000,000 or £40,000,000—as being eaten up and taken away by England." The fault is not mine, but that of Government. In 1873, Sir D. Wedderburn moved for a return for the number, salaries, etc., of all the services. The return was ordered in July 1873. It is now past 7 years, but has not been made. Again 1879—Mr. Bright moved for returns (salaries, etc., 19th June, '79) and Sir D. Wedderburn moved for returns (East India Services—20th and 23rd June, '79.) and (East India Services—24th June, '79). These returns have not yet been made. I hope they are being prepared. When these returns are made we shall know definitely and clearly what the amount is, that, out of the revenue of £65,000,000, does not at all return to the people of India, but is eaten up in, and carried away from, India every year, by England. Such returns ought to be made every year. Once it is made, the work of succeeding years will be only the alterations or revision for the year, or revised estimates every 2 or 3 years even will do. To Government itself, a return like this will be particularly useful. They will then act with clear light, instead of groping in darkness as at present, and though actuated with the best of intentions, still inflicting upon India untold misfortune and miseries. And it will then see, how India, of all other countries in the world, is subjected to a most unnatural and destructive treatment.

The next Sections VIII and IX on Trade and Railways, are pervaded with the same fallacies as those of Mr. Danvers' Memo. of 28th June, 1880, and to which I replied with my letter of 13th September, 1880. I, therefore, do not go over the same ground here again. I need only refer to one statement, the last sentence of para. 4 of Section VIII :—

"As to the other half of the excess, which is due to the cost of English Administration, there can hardly be room for doubt that it is to the advantage of India, to pay the sum really necessary to secure its peaceful government, without which, no progress would be possible; and so long as this condition is not violated, it does not seem material whether apart of the charge has to be met in England or not."

A statement, more wrong in its premises and conclusion, can hardly be met with. Let us see.

By "the other of the excess" is meant £8,000,000.

The Commissioners tell the public that India pays £8,000,000 for securing peaceful government. This is the fiction. What are the facts?

England, of *all* nations on the face of the earth, enjoys the utmost security of life and property of every kind, from a strong and peaceful Government. For this, England "*pays*" £83,000,000 a year.

In the same manner, India "pays" not £8,000,000, but £65,000,000 for the same purpose, and should be able and willing to "*pay*" twice or thrice £65,000,000, under natural circumstances, similar to those of England.

Thus, England "pays" £83,000,000 and India "pays" £65,000,000 for purposes of peaceful Government. But here the parallel ends, and English writers, with very few exceptions, fight of going beyond this point, and mis-state the matter as is done in the above extract. Let us see what is beyond.

Of the £83,000,000 which England "pays" for security of life and property, or peaceful Government, every farthing returns to the people themselves. It is not even a flea-bite or any bite to the people of England that they "*pay*" £83,000,000 for peaceful Government. They simply give with one hand and receive back with the other. The country and the people enjoy the *full benefit* of every farthing they either produce in the country or earn with foreign trade.

But with India, the *fact* is quite otherwise. Out of the £65,000,000 which she "*pays*" like England for peaceful government, £30,000,000 or £40,000,000 do *not* return to the people of the country. These £30,000,000 or £40 000,000 are eaten up in the country, and carried away from the country, by a foreign people. The people of India are thus deprived of this enormous amount, year after year, and are as, a natural consequence, weakened more and more every year in their capacity for production, or, in plain words, India is being simply destroyed.

The *romance* is, that there is security of life and property in India. The reality is, that there is no such thing.

There is security of life and property in one sense or way, *i.e.*, the people are secure from any violence from each other or from native despots. So far, there is real security of life and property, and for which India never denies her gratitude. But from England's own grasp, there is no security of property at all, and as a consequence no security for life. India's property is not secure. What is secure and well secure is, that England is perfectly safe and secure, and does so with perfect security, to carry away from India and to eat up in India, her property at the present rate of some £30,000,000 or £40,000,000 a year.

The reality therefore is, that the policy of English Rule as it is (not as it can and should be), is an everlasting, unceasing and every-day-increasing foreign invasion, utterly, though gradually, destroying the country. I venture to submit, that every right-minded Englishman, calmly and seriously considering the problem of the present condition and treatment of India by England, will come to this conclusion.

The old invaders came with the avowed purposes of plundering the wealth of the country. They plundered and went away, or conquered and became the natives of the country. But the great misfortune of India is that England did *not* mean, or wish, or come with the intention of plundering, and yet events have taken a course which has made English the worst foreign invader she has had the misfortune to have. India does not get a moment to breathe or revive. 'More Europeans,' 'more Europeans,' is the eternal cry, and this very report itself of the Commission is not free from it.

The present position of England in India has, moreover, produced another most deplorable evil from which the worst of old foreign invasions was free. That with the deprivation of the vital, material blood of the country, to the extent of £30,000,000 or £40,000,000 a year, the whole higher "wisdom" of the country is also carried away.

I therefore venture to submit, that India *does not* enjoy security of her property and life, and also moreover, of "knowledge" or "wisdom." To millions in India, life is simply "half feeding" or starvation, or famines and disease.

View the Indian problem from any point you like, you come back again and again to this central fact that England takes from India every year £30,000,000 or £40,000,000 worth of her property with all the lamentable consequences from such a loss, and with a continuous diminution of the capacity of India for production, together with the moral loss of all higher wisdom.

India would be quite able and willing to "pay," as every other country, or as England "pays," for peaceful Government. But no country on the face of the earth can stand the deprivation of property that India is subjected to, without being crushed to death.

Suppose England were subjected to such a condition at the hand of some foreign power; and would she not to a man clamour, that far better would they fly at each other's throat, have strifes in streets of civil wars, or fights in fields for foreign wars, with all the chances of fame of fortune on survival, than to submit to the inglorious, miserable deaths from poverty and famines, with wretchedness and disease in case of survival. I have no hesitation in appealing to any Englishman to say which of the two deaths he would prefer, and I shall not have to wait long for the reply.

What is property worth to India, which she can only call her own in name, but not in reality, and which her own children cannot enjoy? What is life worth to her that must perish by millions at the very touch of drought or distress, or can have only a half-starving existence?

The confusion and fallacy in the extract I have given above, therefore, consists in this. It is not that India pays for peaceful Government some £8,000,000. She pays for it £65,000,000, just as England pays £84,000,000. But there is one feature peculiar to India. She needs British wise and beneficent guidance and supervision. British aid of this kind can, under any circumstances, be but from outside the Indian family, *i.e.*, foreign. This aid must be reasonably paid for by India. Now, if the whole foreign agency of European men and materials, required under the direct and indirect control of Government, both in India and England, in every shape or form, be clearly laid down, to be confined within the limit of a fixed "foreign list" of say £5,000,000, or even say £8,000,000, though very much, which the Commissioners ask India should pay; India could very probably pay, without being so destroyed as at present. But the present thoughtless and merciless exhaustion of some £30,000,000, or £40,000,000, or may be even much more, is crushing, cruel, and destructive.

In fact, leaving the past alone as a misfortune, the continuance of the present drain will be, in plain English, nothing less than plunder of an unceasing foreign invasion, and not a reasonable price for a beneficent rule, as the Commissioners wrongly and thoughtlessly endeavour to persuade the public.

The great misfortune of India is that the temptation or tendency towards selfishness and self-aggrandisement of their own countrymen, is too great and blinding for Englishmen (with few exceptions) connected with India, to see that power is a sacred trust and responsibility for the good of the people. We have this profession to any amount, but unless and till the conscience of England, and of English honest thinkers and statesmen, is awakened, the performance will remain poor or nil as at present.

Lord Ripon said--India needs rest. More true words cannot be spoken. Yes—she needs rest—rest from the present unceasing and ever-increasing foreign invasion, from whose unceasing blows she has not a moment allowed to breathe.

I said before that even this Famine Report was not free from the same clamour, "more Europeans, more Europeans."

Whenever any question of reform arises, the only remedy that suggests itself to English officials' minds, is "apply more European leeches, apply more European leeches!"

The commission suggests the institution of an Agricultural Department, and a very important suggestion it is. But they soon forget that it is *for India* this is required, and that it is at India's expense it has to be done, that it is from India's wretched income, has this expenditure to be provided, and that India cannot offord to have more blood sucked out of her for more Europeans, and deprive so much her own children; in short, that native agency under a good English head or two, would be the most natural and proper agency for the purpose. No, prostrate as India is, and for which very reason, the Commission was appointed to suggest a remedy, they can only say, "more Europeans"—as if no such thing has a people existed in India.

Were any Englishman to make such a proposal for England, —that French or German youths be instructed at England's expense, and that such youths make up the different public departments, he would be at once scouted and laughed at. And yet, these Commissioners thoughtlessly and seriously suggest and recommend to aggravate the very evil for which they were expected to suggest a remedy.

I appeal most earnestly to His Lordship, the Secretary of State for India, that though the department suggested by the Commissioners is very important, His Lordship would not adopt the mode which the Commissioners have suggested with good intentions, but with thoughtlessness, about the rights and needs of India. That with the exception of some thoroughly qualified necessary Europeans at the head, the whole agency ought to be native, on the lines described by the Commissioners. There can be no lack of natives of the kind required, or it would be a very poor compliment indeed to the Educational exertions of the English rulers during the past half-a-century.

A new danger is now threatening India. Hitherto India's wealth *above* the surface of land has been draining away to England. Now the wealth *under* the surface of the land, will also be taken away, and India lies prostrate and unable to help herself. England has taken away her capital. That same capital will be brought to take away, all such mineral wealth of the country as requires application of large capital and expensive machinery. With the exception of the employment of the lower classes of bodily and mental labourers, the larger portion of the produce will, in several shapes, be eaten up and carried away by the Europeans, first as servants and next in profits and dividends, and poor India will have to thank her stars, that she will get some crumbs, in the lower employments of her children. And great will be the sounding of trumpets of the wealth found in India, and the blessing conferred on India, just as we have sickeningly dinged into our ears, day after day, about Railways, Foreign Trade, etc.

Now, this may sound very strange, that knowing full well the benefits of foreign capital to any country, I should complain of its going to India.

There is, under present circumstances, one great difference in the modes in which English capital goes to every other country and India. To every other country, English capitalists *lend*, and there is an end of their connection with the matter. The *people* of the country use and enjoy the benefit of the capital in every way, and pay to the capitalists their interest or dividend, and as some capitalists know to their cost, not even that. But, with India, the case is quite different. English capitalists do not merely lend, but with their capital, they themselves invade the country. The produce of the capital is mostly eaten up by their own countrymen, and after that, they carry away the rest in the shape of profits and dividends. The people themselves of the country *do not* derive the same benefit which is derived by every other country from English capital. The Guaranteed Railways, not only ate up everything in this manner, but compelled India to make up the guaranteed interest also from her produce. The remedy then was adopted of making State Railways. Now under the peculiar circumstances of India's present prostration, State-works would be, no doubt, the best means of securing to India the benefits of English capital. But the misfortune is that the same canker eats into the State-works also,—the same eating up of the substance by European employés. The plan by which India can be really benefited would be, that all kinds of public works, or mines, or all works, that require capital, be undertaken by the State, with English capital and *native* agency, with some thoroughly competent Europeans at the head, as may be absolutely necessary.

Supposing that there was even extravagance or loss, Government making up any deficiency of the interest of the loans from general revenue, will not matter much, though there is reason why, with proper care, a native agency cannot be found good enough for efficient and economic working. Anyhow, in such a case, the people of India will then really derive the benefit of English capital, as every other country does, with the certainty of English capitalists getting their interest from the Government, who have complete control over the revenues of India, and can without fail provide for the interest.

For some time, therefore, and till India, by a change in the present destructive policy of heavy European agency, has revived and is able to help herself in a free field, it is necessary that all great undertakings which India herself is unable to carry out for developing the resources of the country, should be undertaken by the State, but carried out chiefly by native agency, and by preparing natives for the purpose. Then will India recover her blood from every direction. India sorely needs the aid of English capital. But it is English *capital* that she needs and not the English invasion, to come also and eat up both capital and produce.

As things are taking their course at present with regard to the gold mines, if they prove successful, great will be the trumpeting of India's wealth being increased, while it will all be being carried away by England.

In the United States the people of the country enjoy all the benefits of their mines and public works with English capital, and pay to England her fair interest; and in cases of failures of the schemes, while the people have enjoyed the benefit of the capital, sometimes both capital and interest are gone. The schemes fail, and the lenders of capital may lament but the people have enjoyed the capital and the produce as far as they went.

I have no doubt that in laying my views plainly before the Secretary of State, my motives or sentiments towards the British Rule will not be misunderstood. I believe that the result of the British Rule *can be* a blessing to India and a glory to England,—a result worthy of the foremost and most humane nation on the face of the earth. I desire that this should take place, and I therefore lay my humble views before our rulers without shrinking. It is no pleasure to me to dwell incessantly on the wretched, heart-rending, blood-boiling condition of India. None will rejoice more than myself if my views are proved to be mistaken.

Printed at the Methodist Publishing House, Mount Road, Madras, 1917,
for G. A. NATESAN & Co., Publishers, Georgetown, Madras.